THE PRIEST OF LOVE

THE PRIEST
OF LOVE

A Life of D. H. Lawrence

REVISED EDITION

*

HARRY T. MOORE

*

SOUTHERN ILLINOIS UNIVERSITY PRESS
Carbondale and Edwardsville

Library of Congress Cataloging in Publication Data

Moore, Harry T.
  The priest of love.

  Reprint of the rev. ed. of The priest of love published by Farrar, Straus and Giroux,
New York, which was first published in 1954 under title: The intelligent heart.
    1. Lawrence, David Herbert, 1885–1930—Biography. 2. Authors, English—20th century
—Biography. I. Title.
[PR6023.A93Z685   1977] 823'.9'12   77-5714
ISBN 0-8093-0839-8

This edition printed by offset lithography in the United States of America

The letters in this volume are published with the kind permission of the Viking
Press, Inc., holders of the American publication rights in all letters of D. H.
Lawrence, and are contained in *The Collected Letters of D. H. Lawrence*, edited
by Harry T. Moore, Copyright © 1962 by Angelo Ravagli and C. Montague Weekley, Executors of the Estate of Frieda Lawrence Ravagli. All inquiries about
reprinting of the letters in other volumes or elsewhere should be referred to Viking.

Grateful acknowledgment is extended to Alfred A. Knopf, Inc., for persmission
to quote from *The Plumed Serpent*, by D. H. Lawrence (Copyright 1926 and
renewed 1954 by Frieda Lawrence Ravagli) and *The Later D. H. Lawrence*, edited
by William York Tindall (Copyright 1952 by Alfred A. Knopf, Inc.).

This is a revised and enlarged edition of a book originally published under the
title *The Intelligent Heart*.

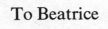
To Beatrice

PREFACE

'I shall always be a priest of love,' D. H. Lawrence said in a letter written on Christmas Day, 1912, soon after he had completed his first major novel, *Sons and Lovers*. That statement gives the present book its title. In earlier incarnations, beginning in 1954, this biography of Lawrence was called *The Intelligent Heart*. I had wanted to name the first edition *The Priest of Love*, but ran into walls of opposition and settled for *The Intelligent Heart*, a title suggested by a friend. That remained its title in the British and American reprints of 1962. But it has always embarrassed me because it doesn't seem truly Lawrencean and is really a somewhat pretentious oxymoron—at least an overextended metaphor. I had favored *The Priest of Love*, not out of any attempt at sensationalism, but because it is so appropriate and because, once again, Lawrence called himself that. So now, in this extensively revised and augmented edition—I have written what is really a new book—we have Lawrence as the 'priest of love'; and, as Lawrence added, just after using that phrase, 'I shall preach my heart out, Lord bless you.'

In the last few years the picture of Lawrence has changed significantly. A great many new facts about his life have appeared, some of them in the excellent 'composite biography' assembled by the late Edward Nehls, others in the letters Lawrence wrote to Blanche Jennings and Louisa Burrows, as well as in numerous other documents. Further, Warren Roberts's *A Bibliography of D. H. Lawrence* has greatly added to our knowledge of the man and the writer. Not least, an adjustment of critical perspectives has made him a major subject in university courses.

Lawrence critics now generally agree that his finest work is found in the pair of somewhat related novels, *The Rainbow* (1915) and *Women in Love* (1920). Two fairly recent volumes devoted to Lawrence—by Eliseo Vivas and George H. Ford—have dealt with Lawrence's post-1920 writings in earlier parts of their books and have saved the last sections for climactic discussions of *The Rainbow* and *Women in Love*, emphasizing their supremacy. But the Lawrence of the last decade of his life (1920–30) can't be dismissed, for even if he never matched those two books in their genre, he wrote at least one important novel in that period, *Lady Chatterley's Lover* (1928), our epoch's most astonishing and significant romance. (Today some of us prefer the earlier—second—draft of that book, published in 1972 as *John Thomas and Lady Jane.*) And Lawrence in that final decade produced various brilliant achievements: novellas, short stories, poems, and essays.

I can further say that the extensive revision of the present book, with its many augmentations, was exhilarating. I shall always remember the kindness shown by John Peck in suggesting this edition, as I shall always remember the kindness of Stanley Young in encouraging me to write the first version.

This volume is primarily a biography, though I have of course discussed many of Lawrence's works, which are essentially what he was and is. Even more than in the case of other intensively autobiographical authors, his life helps to illuminate his writings.

Harry T. Moore

Southern Illinois University
September 11, 1973

Contents

Illustrations follow pages   170 and 416

CORRIGENDA

Page 70, line 18: *For* Messauges *read* Messuages

Page 131, line 33: *For* Jessie Chambers's emphatic criticism of it. *read* Jessie Chambers's emphatic criticism of it. (The imprisonment of the father in Lawrence's crude early draft was based on the experience of one of his uncles who had killed his son in a quarrel and had served a term for involuntary manslaughter.

Page 143, line 17: *For* a post at the university there. *read* a post at the university there. She had been Max Weber's mistress.

Page 145, lines 31–32: *For* his lips eaten away *read* his nostrils eaten away

Page 222, line 14: *For* felt a respectul affection *read* felt a respectful affection

Page 241, line 16: *For* the Duke of Portland *read* A. Cavendish-Bentinick

Page 345, line 21: *For Mastro Don Gesnaldo read Mastro-don Gesnaldo*

Page 350, line 21: *For* both sides spit out *read* both sides spat out

Page 356, line 35: *For* Freida *read* Frieda

Between pages 416–417, drawing of Kiowa Ranch: *For* Sangro de Cristo *read* Sangre de Cristo

Page 417, lines 8–12: *For* In her record of the time, she had made it supremely clear that at the hotel cottage at Ravello each of them not only had a separate room but went to it, Lawrence turning to his quarters 'with a cheery good night', and Brett fumbling with matches and a candle to find her own 'hard, relentless bed'. *read* In *Lawrence and Brett* (1933), she said that at the hotel cottage at Ravello, each of them had a separate room and went to it. In 1974, however, she admitted, in a revision of her book, that Lawrence twice went to her room to have sex with her, but that he failed (he had been impotent since his severe illness in Mexico).

Page 426, line 33: *For* Alichtram *read* Altrincham

Page 433, line 29: *For* Mohr, though not a Jew *read* Mohr, who was Jewish

Page 507, line 22: *For* fulfilment *read* fulfillment

Page 517, lines 15–16: *For River of Dissolution: D. H. Lawrence and the Romantic* (1969) *read D. H. Lawrence and English Romanticism* (1969)

Page 517, line 32: *For* Mark Kinkaid-Weekes's *read* Mark Kinkead-Weekes's

Page 530, line 25: *For* Mr. Irwin Swerdlow *read* Dr. Irwin Swerdlow

NOTE: The endpaper map from the original hardbound edition has been placed between pages 519–23 in this edition. Page 525, "Books by D. H. Lawrence," has been amplified.

March 2, 1977   H.T.M.

THE PRIEST OF LOVE

*

PROLOGUE

*

A woman who had been a schoolteacher married a coal miner, in the borough of Nottingham, two days after Christmas of 1875. She had never seen him dressed for the pits, and she knew nothing of the colliers' lives in the outlying villages. He took her to live in one of them, and on the first night he came home from the mine she thought a Negro had burst into the house.

The man grinned through his coal-mask and insisted that he was her husband. When at last she was convinced, she told him to hurry and bathe himself, for supper was ready. He washed his hands and sat down at the table in the kitchen.

'But you're not *clean*,' she said.

'Ah, lass,' he said, 'I weshed m'hands, didn't I? This is coal dirt—that's *clean* dirt.'

She forced herself to eat.

Afterwards, her husband asked her to heat a tubful of water. When it was ready, he stripped to the waist and said, 'Come now, lass, tha's got t'wesh m'back.' When the woman hesitated, the man said, 'I canna wesh it mysen.'

With her gorge rising, she scoured the coal dust off his back. As he felt the warm cloth rub across his flesh, he sang softly. Many of the miners sang, and his voice was famous among them.

It was this man and this woman who became, nearly ten years afterwards, the parents of D. H. Lawrence.

*

PART ONE

The Nottingham Years

---

*

1 ANCESTRAL VOICES

DAVID HERBERT RICHARDS LAWRENCE was born in 1885 at Eastwood, a Nottinghamshire mining village on the hills above the Erewash valley. There the natural beauty, the remaining fragments of Sherwood Forest, comes up against the industrial ugliness, the collieries that thrust their headstocks and their smoke above the farmfields.

In the last part of the twentieth century, sections of the place look much as they did when Lawrence's young eyes first saw them. Today there are fewer black-faced miners about, and they no longer come home singing through the dusk. The buses that lurch down the Nottingham Road and the motorcars that nudge along the lanes certainly belong to a later time, but many of the houses that Lawrence saw in childhood still stand on the same thin streets. The older buildings of Eastwood wear the brick uniform of the industrial revolution, though the history of the place goes far back. In the days when the Normans made a survey of their prize-lands, they listed Eastwood (then Estewic) as a manor. There, yeomen stumbled behind their ploughs, and huntsmen rode with falcons on their leathered wrists. Estewic was less than nine miles above the stronghold of Nottingham, the shiretown that centuries later was to be of great consequence in the life of the young Lawrence.

Most of the other scenes of importance to his early youth lie in the opposite direction from Nottingham, to the north and northeast of his native town. He knew this country inch by inch: as a frail boy he stepped lightly, day after day, through the landscapes of his future work.

*

In the autobiographical early chapters of *Sons and Lovers* (1913), Lawrence dramatized the enduring battle between his parents as something more than a conflict between two individuals: it was class warfare, bourgeoisie against proletariat. Lawrence here was putting himself between classes, and in a sense he was always in such a no-man's-land, often a position of advantage to an artist; but the 'Red-Herring'

7

poem of his later life ('My father was a working man . . . My mother was a superior soul . . .') was in some respects an exaggeration. True, his father had gone into the pits in childhood, but there was no genuine, seasoned proletarian heritage, for Lawrence's father had a bourgeois background. Indeed, he came from the same family as Lawrence's 'superior' mother; at least the families had become related by marriage.

The Lawrences came from Nottingham. The John Lawrence who was D.H.'s grandfather was brought up in that town, was perhaps born there. He became a tailor and settled in Brinsley, just north of Eastwood. He had learned the trade in Nottingham from his stepfather, George Dooley, who—according to D.H.'s brother George Lawrence—had married John's mother after her husband was killed at Waterloo.

John Lawrence was a physical giant, in his youth a famous athlete. In those days aquatic sports were popular on the river Trent, particularly the four-oared races in Colwick waters, and John Lawrence was one of the great rowers of the time. He was best known, however, for his exploits in the boxing ring, where his height and weight and his huge hands gave him unusual power. Indeed, it is a Lawrence family legend that he once met Ben Caunt in an informal fight. Caunt in 1840 became 'champion of England' after winning a 101-round match, but the legend says that when he fought John Lawrence unofficially, Lawrence beat him.

John Lawrence moved to Brinsley in 1853 or 1854, and at the beginning his work there was steady, for in those days the mine owners supplied the men with the clothes they wore in the pits. D. H. Lawrence remembered from childhood his grandfather's shop with its great rolls of flannel for the vests, and the 'strange old sewing machine, like nothing else on earth, which sewed the massive pit trousers'. The recollections of Lawrence's sister Ada, however, shed more gentility on the scene, for she remembered chiefly that her grandfather had specialized 'in making gentlemen's livery'.

John Lawrence's wife, Sarah, was the daughter of Adam Parsons, a Nottingham lace and silk manufacturer. John and Sarah Lawrence became the parents of Arthur John Lawrence—D.H.'s father—on June 18, 1846. The 'superior soul' he was to marry, Lydia Beardsall, was six years younger. Lydia was a native of Nottingham, where her forebears on her father's side had settled after leaving Wirksworth, in Derbyshire. The Beardsalls had been tanners there, but some of them migrated to Nottingham when the lace industry began to thrive. According to family tradition, Lydia's grandfather prospered in the larger town, but lost his fortune in a collapse of the lace market. This was probably during the depression of 1837, when about one-tenth of the lace manufacturers had to close down, and when nearly one-twelfth of the local population had to go on the dole.

The descent to poverty of Lydia's grandfather 'bitterly galled' his son, if we can believe the statement made about the situation in *Sons and Lovers*. This 'galled' man—D. H. Lawrence's grandfather, George Beardsall—was fiercely religious. An engineer who was an admirer of St. Paul, Beardsall didn't confine his interest in theology to reading; he was a noted preacher who often took over the Wesleyan pulpit. To Lawrence's brother George, this ancestor was 'a grand old chap', and on a visit to Sheerness, in Kent, in the 1920s, George Lawrence found people who after fifty years 'still remembered him and his preaching there'. George Beardsall was, like his poet grandson, also widely known for his quarrels; the most famous of these were with the chemist Jesse Boot (later Lord Trent) over governorship of a chapel in Nottingham, and with William Booth, who Lawrence used to say was his grandfather's associate in founding the organization that became the Salvation Army.

As a young man George Beardsall worked in Nottingham for James Carver and John Mosley, bobbin and carriage makers at 3 and 5 Butcher Street. Before leaving to become dockyards foreman at Sheerness, Beardsall married Lydia Newton, the story of whose grandfather on her mother's side, John Newton, makes another important contribution to the understanding of Lawrence's background.

This great-grandfather of D. H. Lawrence's was a hymn writer, a famous one; he should not be confused with the earlier hymn writer John Newton (1725–1807), the collaborator of Cowper. The Nottingham John Newton, who lived from 1802 to 1886, was best known in his native region, but his hymns are still sung in chapels throughout England. Indeed, his 'Sovereignty' has been one of the great Nonconformist tunes.

D. H. Lawrence's brother George knew the old man; once during George's childhood, when his mother was ill, he stayed for a year with his great-grandfather in Sneinton. He remembered John Newton as 'slim and spare', physically frail in somewhat the same way D. H. Lawrence was to be. The old man, retired after his many years of work as what was then called a twisthand in the lace-making industry, 'was always at the piano' when at home, George Lawrence told the author of the present book in 1950.

A man who knew John Newton wrote of him, 'He had nine children, and in his old age thanked God for his gift, and that he could still in imagination hear the music, for it was in his soul, and he was a most religious man.' George Lawrence recalled the devotion of one of the old man's daughters who kept house for him for many years.

Lawrence knew some of these people only slightly, if he knew them at all, yet each of them must have had an influence on his childhood. He knew his father's parents well; he certainly would have seen his mother's father at least several times; and Lydia Beardsall Lawrence must have spoken frequently of her hymn-writing grandfather and played his hymns on 'the tinkling piano' in the Lawrences' parlor.

John Lawrence, the athlete who became a colliery tailor, and his son Arthur, who was a miner from childhood; George Beardsall, an evangelistic and quarrelsome engineer, and his sensitive daughter, who was on her mother's side the granddaughter of a noted hymn writer—it was these people, amid the redbrick houses and the drifting soot of Midland industrial towns, who were (to use the idiom of that region) D. H. Lawrence's 'come-from'.

*

Arthur Lawrence met Lydia Beardsall at his aunt's home, which was also the home of Lydia's uncle. This may seem a bit complicated, but Alice Parsons, the sister of Arthur Lawrence's mother, had married John Newton, Jr., brother of Lydia Beardsall's mother. Thus when Arthur Lawrence and Lydia Beardsall became husband and wife, they made an intrafamily marriage.

Arthur Lawrence had come over to Nottingham from Brinsley late in 1874, to help sink a mine shaft at nearby Clifton. Evenings he sometimes went up to visit his aunt's home in Basford, at the north end of Nottingham. This aunt's husband, according to George Lawrence, was 'a clever man on lace machines' who later emigrated to America, where he died, in New York State. His sister Lydia, another of those nine children of John Newton, had married George Beardsall, and her daughter who met Arthur Lawrence at the younger Newtons' was, as previously noted, also named Lydia.

Born on July 19, 1852, Lawrence's mother spent a good part of her early life at Sheerness, where she became a schoolmistress. And she had written verses. Her daughter Ada said years later that the account of the mother's youthful experiences in *Sons and Lovers* was substantially true; she had been jilted by a 'refined' young man who married an older woman with money. Ada Lawrence Clarke added that the story of the meeting of the parents was also taken from life. The collier was dashing and gay, a lively dancer, a type of man Lydia had never met before; he made his work in the collieries sound romantic. Ada further said that her father had never put a razor to his face, and that he had black hair and a full black beard; Lawrence says in *Sons and Lovers* that the mother had never been 'thee'd' and 'thou'd' before meeting him—and although this idiomatic usage apparently amused her then, she later tried to prevent her children from adopting it.

On December 27, 1875, Arthur and Lydia were married at St. Stephen's, the parish church at Sneinton. They didn't go immediately to Eastwood and Brinsley, but lived first in Sutton-in-Ashfield and then in Old Radford. Sutton-in-Ashfield is a town with a few mines, about eight miles north of Eastwood; Old Radford is a former village now incorporated into the western districts of the present-day city of Nottingham.

Arthur Lawrence before long returned to his old job in the pits at Brinsley. He and Lydia lived in a cottage there, in the valley below Eastwood.

Gradually she turned against him. He had taken the nondrinking pledge, but he broke it and on the way home from work began stopping at the pubs for mugs of beer with his friends. When he finally did arrive at home, his wife nagged and scolded, he flared up, and they would fight. Yet Mrs. Lawrence, through all her troubles, maintained a kind of cheerfulness, even if it was often no more than the desperate cheerfulness of one determined to be optimistic. She remained a pleasant companion to the children, always joining in their activities. She was proud of these children, and fought fiercely to give them good lives: her sons would not go into the mines, her daughters would not become servants. And through the galling poverty of those years she made intense sacrifices for them, particularly in furthering the education of David Herbert—or Bert, as the family called him.

Unfortunately, this is only part of the story. The intensity of love that was in this woman's being drove itself outwardly in two directions: she hated her husband and, just as extravagantly, she loved her children. These children became a battleground in the parents' war.

Ada Lawrence Clarke said in her memoir that her mother had

turned the children against the father; Ada felt in later life that they all should have shown him more sympathy. And Lawrence's friend Achsah Brewster reported that in Ceylon in 1922, ten years after Lawrence had completed *Sons and Lovers,* he told her and her husband that he had done his father an injustice in that book 'and felt like rewriting it'. Now he could see that his father had a relish for life and that his mother with her militant self-righteousness had damaged both father and children. 'Shaking his head at the memory of that beloved mother, he would add that the righteous woman martyred in her righteousness is a terrible thing and that all self-righteous women ought to be martyred.'

Lydia Lawrence, early in her martyrdom, had moved with her husband into Eastwood, to the small brick house on the downslope of Victoria Street which was to be D. H. Lawrence's birthplace. There Mrs. Lawrence set up a little shop in the front room, on the street level; she used the large square window of that room for display, and inside she sold linen and lace, the caps and aprons of the Victorian housewife.

As her family grew, Mrs. Lawrence relinquished the shop. Over a period of ten years, from 1877 to 1887, she gave birth to five children. Of these, D. H. Lawrence was the next-to-youngest, and the youngest of the three sons.

Bert Lawrence was a frail child who from the first drew much of his mother's attention and love, though he didn't become the center of her life until years later. He used to say, after he had grown up, that he had nearly died of bronchitis barely two weeks after he was born. William Hopkin, the Nottingham antiquarian, recalled that when Bert Lawrence was a month old, 'he looked like a skinned rabbit'. Hopkin, then a young man of twenty-three—and destined to outlive Lawrence by twenty-one years—had met Mrs. Lawrence wheeling her newest child in a pram down the Nottingham Road, Eastwood's main thoroughfare. She shook her head sadly as she told Hopkin that she didn't expect her baby to live three months. 'I'm afraid I s'll never rear him.'

But from the first, Lawrence showed the tenacious urge to live that, to the later amazement of doctors, kept him going for forty-four and a half years. People who knew him in childhood have said he was the thinnest little boy they ever saw. The older of his brothers, George, with whom he quarreled in later life, remembered him affectionately as a child: 'Oh, Bert was a grand little lad—he was always delicate

—it was a source of grief to him that he wasn't able to enter the boys' games—he used to gather the girls together to go blackberrying —he was so delicate that I've carried him on my shoulder for miles. We all petted and spoiled him from the time he was born—my mother poured her very soul into him'.

D. H. Lawrence wrote, towards the end of his life—in a sentence that emphasizes both his frailness and the frequency of the colds to which he was subject—that he had been 'a delicate pale brat with a snuffy nose, whom most people treated quite gently as just an ordinary delicate little lad'. All the reports coming from the time of his childhood speak of his gentleness and the eager friendliness that made people like him.

The family moved from the Victoria Street house when he was two, settling north of town in the lowlands known as the Breach. It was an old landmark, listed in medieval records as *le Breche.*

Some years before the Lawrences moved to the Breach, the colliery owners had constructed six tenement blocks there—two rows of three blocks of twelve houses each—for the miners' families. The Lawrences paid sixpence extra rent every week in order to live at the end of one of these blocks, and although this gave Mrs. Lawrence a house with an extra strip of garden, she hated the place. For by custom all the families spent most of their indoor time in the kitchens at the back, looking out on the ash pits and on the alley that separated the two rows of houses—a noisy circuit of the community's life, where men and women strolled and talked, and children ran and screamed.

Lawrence remembered that place well; he wrote of it most fully in *Sons and Lovers,* where the Breach is called the Bottoms. He lived there four years, until his family moved away when he was six: four years of the alleys of ash pits, with the brook beyond, its hawthorn hedges and willows, and the adjoining farmlands.

Lawrence could look over all this from the new home, which was on Walker Street at the north edge of Eastwood, at the top of the slope that led down to the Breach. 'Go to Walker Street,' he wrote to a friend many years later, '—and stand in front of the third house— and look across at Crich on the left, Underwood in front—High Park woods and Annesley on the right: I lived in that house from the age of 6 to 18, I know that view better than any in the world.'

But always when, as a boy, he went into that countryside, he was aware of the town that lay behind him as he took the roads and footpaths northward across the farmfields and towards the patches of forest. This Eastwood that for hundreds of years had been only a hamlet—with twenty-eight inhabited houses by the 1780s—was one of the villages that grew rapidly under the stimulus of the industrial revolution. The mines had been there long before the expansion: some of them dated from the sixteenth century, and a map showing 'Veins of Coal as Survey'd in Jany 1739' places Eastwood on the western edge of a vein of coal that 'ranged North.^{ly} thro'y Counties of Derby & Nottingham into Yorksh.' also includes Greasley, Brinsley, and the other nearby collieries which were still in operation in the twentieth century. Lawrence's father was a miner at Brinsley from childhood to old age.

It was in the eighteenth century that the builders of modern Eastwood, the Barbers and the Walkers, began to take control of the collieries in the district. A tomb in the Greasley churchyard, a mile from Eastwood, shows that the Barber family was burying its dead there as long ago as 1710; and at Bilborough, a few miles to the southeast, coal works had been leased by 1791 'to a Mr Walker and a Mr Barber'. By 1800 the firm of Barber, Walker and Company was officially in existence. At that time, according to William Hopkin, 'farm labourers swarmed in from Lincolnshire and other counties, attracted by the higher wages.'

The Erewash Canal, constructed in the 1770s, took the coal barges to the Trent, and into important commercial traffic. But in the early nineteenth century, Barber, Walker, and the other colliery proprietors in the region north of Nottingham began to lose the Leicestershire market because of competition from a railway in that county; they convened to discuss the matter at the Sun Inn at Eastwood. A plaque on the outside wall of this building commemorates the meeting of 1832 because it resulted in the founding of the Erewash Valley Railway, which later became the famous Midland line. The colliery owners at that meeting subscribed £32,000 towards the establishment of the railway; of this amount, Barber, Walker and Company guaranteed £10,000.

And Eastwood grew. Spreading over its hills amid a circle of collieries and small settlements, it became the market town of the area. It showed the greatest increase in population per square mile of any parish in Nottinghamshire during the nineteenth century: 63.5 percent. In 1801 Eastwood had 735 inhabitants, in 1881 (four years before Lawrence's birth) it had 3,566, and in 1901, 4,815. A translation of these statistics into human terms tells us much about the bias of Lawrence's writings, for the multiplication was chiefly at the working-class and small-shopkeeper level; additions at the level of the Barber and Walker families were slight. And what did these minority but all-powerful industrialists do, in that century when the towns were eating into the countryside? Lawrence gave part of the answer to that question in *Women in Love,* one of the themes of which was the destruction of the better part of man, of nature itself, by industrialism.

One of Lawrence's last essays, 'Nottingham and the Mining Countryside', states that 'the great crime which the moneyed classes and promoters of industry committed in the palmy Victorian days was the condemning of the workers to ugliness, ugliness, ugliness: meanness and formless and ugly surroundings, ugly ideals, ugly religion, ugly hope, ugly love, ugly clothes, ugly furniture, ugly houses, ugly relationship between workers and employers. The human soul needs actual beauty more than bread.' The town *'might* have been like the lovely hill-towns of Italy, shapely and fascinating'—but no, it was one of the myriad Eastwoods, thick soot and drab brick.

> If the company, instead of building those sordid and hideous Squares, then, when they had that lovely site to play with, there on the hill top: if they had put a tall column in the middle of the small market-place, and run three parts of a circle of arcade round the pleasant space, where people could stroll or sit, and with the handsome houses behind! If they had made big, substantial houses, in apartments of five and six rooms, and with handsome entrances. If above all, they had encouraged song and dancing—and provided handsome space for these. If only they had encouraged some form of beauty in dress, some form of beauty in interior life—furniture, decoration. If they had given prizes for the handsomest chair or table, the loveliest scarf, the most charming room that the men or women could make! If only they had done this, there would never have been an industrial problem. The industrial problem arises from the base forcing of all human energy into a competition of more acquisition.

As often as he could, the boy Lawrence turned his back on the brick-and-soot ugliness and walked into that landscape to the north and northeast famous as Robin Hood's Sherwood Forest, and which readers of English literature now know as the Lawrence Country. One of the places there that Lawrence visited from earliest childhood was Brinsley, about a mile north of Eastwood on the Mansfield Road. Here his grandparents lived, in the house where his father had been born. And it was to the nearby colliery that his father now went to work each day: his son, seeing the surface of the earth there, the wheels on the headstocks, the smoke rising from the high chimney, and the coal wagons on the little track, would know that the father was far underground, toiling in the broken darkness.

Sometimes, instead of walking north, the young Lawrence would go a mile to the east, to Greasley, where he could see the remnants of the thick walls, moat, and earthworks of a fourteenth-century castle. But there was a more impressive ruin a mile north of Greasley, where farm buildings were wedged between the jagged, shattered walls of Beauvale Priory. This was the setting of one of Lawrence's youthful stories, published in its final form as 'A Fragment of Stained Glass'. As an evocation of the violent medieval past of that little valley, this story shows how strongly Lawrence felt the magnetism of its history.

In other tales he summoned up High Park Wood, which stretched north and northwest of the priory. Here Byron as a young man had come over from Newstead Abbey when he was courting Mary Chaworth, who lived at Annesley, at the north end of High Park Wood.

A body of water on the western edge of this wood, Moorgreen Reservoir, was to be another important landmark in Lawrence's work. But the most familiar landscape in his stories lay just above Moorgreen, stretching towards Underwood: the farmfields known as Greasley Haggs, and the patch of woodland to the west of it, called Willey Spring. This is the true Lawrence Country, the setting of *Sons and Lovers* and of many of the early stories and poems.

> *This is our own still valley,*
> *Our Eden, our home.*

These places, then, may be remembered as the essential geography of Lawrence's youth and of his early writings: brick Eastwood on its hilltop, smoking Brinsley below it, Greasley with its traces of castle, Beauvale with its broken medieval walls, and High Park Wood beyond it, then the sheet of water at the western edge of the wood, and at last the little valley between High Park and Willey Spring.

Towards the end of his life, Lawrence in Italy remembered this north-of-Eastwood landscape and wrote of it, 'That's the country of my heart.'

*

The Walker Street house was never a house of peace, for the parental quarrels continued there. The children in bed at night could hear their father and mother arguing in the kitchen. Sometimes their voices rose even above the wind as it roared through the ash tree that then stood across the street; Lawrence describes all this in *Sons and Lovers* and in one of his poems, 'Discord in Childhood': the scars of these experiences are evident all through his writings.

His early childhood, however, was not all misery. He had not yet run into the cruelty of the schoolyard, where he was to meet with the traditional fate of the delicate boy who dislikes cricket and football. As noted earlier, he loved from the first the land that lay all about him, and he took a deep pleasure in it, long before he knew why. In the spirit of the nineteenth century, landscape became to him a form of worship.

The little boy who recognized the terribleness of nature in the ash tree across from the Walker Street house, and connected it with a terrible aspect of humanity, also responded to the beauty of nature as he could see it from that house, set out before him like a picture book: 'It was still the old England of the forest and the agricultural past; there were no motor-cars, the mines were, in a sense, an accident in the landscape, and Robin Hood and his merry men were not very far away.'

The part of this landscape Lawrence knew best in early childhood spread between Eastwood and Brinsley: on most Saturdays he and his sisters, Emily and Ada, walked over the fields to visit their Lawrence grandparents. Their grandfather the tailor, then in his eighties, invariably had snuff powdered over the front of his waistcoat. In apple season he always asked the children, 'Would you like some apples, my duckies?'—and at their eager nods he would go into the yard and pick Keswicks for them from his tree. The older Mrs. Lawrence had become querulous; her husband's deafness protected him from her scoldings.

At Brinsley the children also used to visit their three aunts, two of them Arthur Lawrence's sisters and the third his brother James's widow. Their Aunt Sarah (or Aunt Sally), Mrs. Jem Swain, was rarely cordial; her widowed sister, Emma Saxton, was always friendlier to the children. Her house was not so neat as Aunt Sarah Swain's, and she didn't mind if her nieces and her nephew tracked in mud; when they arrived she immediately sat them down and fed them.

The aunt by marriage was Aunt Polly, who, some years after the children's uncle, James Lawrence, had been killed in a mining accident, married James Allum. Years later Lawrence used this aunt as the leading character in his story 'Odour of Chrysanthemums' and in its dramatization as *The Widowing of Mrs Holroyd*. Her daughter by her first marriage, Alvina Lawrence—D. H. Lawrence's first cousin—was one day to marry one of his closest friends, Alan Chambers. But that was much later: Lawrence didn't really know the Chambers family until he was fifteen and used to walk north of Brinsley to their farm above Greasley Haggs, the Willey Farm of *Sons and Lovers*.

2 THE ETERNAL VILLAGE

Lawrence, having lived so deeply in one village, wrote always of a kind of universal village. Cities never figured importantly in his writing, and he never lived in them for long. The settings of his stories are occasionally suburban, but mostly they are rural. And the utopian colony he several times tried earnestly to establish was an idealized village.

The Eastwood in which he had grown up was hardly that. Of course the families of the mine owners, with their splendid estates, had overwhelming advantages in that best-of-all-times-to-be-a-squire, and the mass of people in those cheap redbrick houses found life somewhat less enjoyable. Yet, like all people at all times, they made their own pleasures.

There were, for example, the fairs (or feasts) held twice a year, for three days at a time, in September and November. The first of these, the Hill Top Wakes, took place in the east end of the town, Hill Top. The Wakes ground then was a cleared space before the Three Tuns Inn (the Moon and Stars of *Sons and Lovers*), Arthur Lawrence's favorite tavern. In the first chapter of *Sons and Lovers,* the children go excitedly to the Wakes; the father, coming home late at night, says he has been working at the Moon and Stars, though he has been paid 'nowt b'r a lousy hae'f-crown', and when the wife says he has 'made the rest up in beer', he growls, 'Eh, tha mucky little 'ussy, who's drunk, I sh'd like ter know?'

The rival of the Hill Top Wakes, the Statutes and Fair, held in November, dated from the time when farm labor came into town for hiring: the employer in the old days would engage a man by giving him a 'fasten penny' to seal a contract for a year's work. These annual gatherings survived their origin; the 'feast' aspect of them remained, and people still thronged into town for the fair that had always accompanied the hiring process. This fair was held at the west end of Eastwood, near the parish church of St. Mary's, just south of the Nottingham Road.

On his last visit to Eastwood, in September 1926, Lawrence insisted on going to the Wakes and stayed until he was weary. But he enjoyed it, the pale, red-bearded man living over the scenes of that far past; it was apparently the only part of the visit he did enjoy.

Another feature of his childhood had been the performances of the strolling theatrical troupes that occasionally visited Eastwood. The most popular among these was Teddy Rayner's company, which acted under a huge tent. Several times they found business in the Eastwood district so good that they remained for months, playing everything from Shakespeare to *Sweeney Todd, the Demon Barber of Fleet Street,* and *Maria Martin, or Murder in the Red Barn.* Lawrence once wrote of having seen *Hamlet* at 'the tuppenny travelling theatre' and having 'sat in pale transport' while the armored Ghost chanted, ''Amblet, 'Amblet, I *am* thy father's ghost' (*sic*).

One cultural activity of Lawrence's childhood has not survived: the 'penny readings'. These took place at the British School on Albert Street, where at eighteen Lawrence would begin his career as a teacher. The 'penny readings', named for their entrance fee, were well attended. Local people provided the entertainment, which was often musical, with vocal or instrumental solos. The principal feature, however, was the readings, frequently from Dickens: one of the men of the town would recite from a platform, as Dickens himself had done on his tours.

Another Eastwood custom was the invitation to the miners' children to go every year, on the day after Christmas, to the home of the mine-owning Barbers, Lamb Close. Each of the children was given an orange and a bright new penny. One of Lawrence's childhood friends, Mrs. Mabel Thurlby Collishaw, told Edward Nehls that, on one occasion, Lawrence was too shy to go forward and receive his gifts from the Barbers' butler. Mabel handed him what had been given to her and then went back for another penny and orange for herself. When the butler glared at her, she said to him, 'Please, I am not taking two pennies for myself. One was for Bertie Lawrence.' Afterwards, as she and Lawrence walked back to Eastwood, they discussed what they would do with the presents. He finally decided —and this is a comic glimpse of the later Lawrence—that he would give *his* penny to his mother, and that they would buy sweets with the girl's penny and then divide them.

When the Scots minister Robert Reid came to take over the pulpit of the Congregational chapel in 1898, he formed a literary society which met at the British School, next to the chapel. This is where the Lawrences went to church, although the mother had come from a Wesleyan Methodist family. The Reverend Mr. Reid became a good friend of hers and enjoyed having tea with his cultivated parishioner. As William Hopkin said, 'Mrs Lawrence loved to have a parson in the house.' An amusing scene in *Sons and Lovers* shows the father coming home from the pit to find a minister there in a theological discussion with the mother, who has set out the finest tablecloth and the best tea cups. The father's behavior on this occasion is probably a fair representation of what happened more than once. (' "Why, look yer 'ere," said the miner, showing the shoulders of his singlet. "It's a bit dry now, but it's wet as a clout with sweat even yet. Feel it." ')

The Reverend Mr. Reid's chapel had been constructed in 1868 of stone from nearby Bulwell; it was in an imitation-Gothic style with a high spire; Lawrence liked this chapel and remembered it as 'tall and full of light, and yet still; and colour-washed pale green and blue, with a bit of a lotus pattern. And over the organ-loft, "O worship the Lord in the beauty of holiness", in big letters.'

The young Lawrence and his brothers and sisters became well acquainted with that chapel, now destroyed. Lawrence recalled years later, in the essay he intended as an introduction to Frederick Carter's *Apocalypse,* that he had been brought up on the Bible and had it in his bones: 'From early childhood I have been familiar with Apocalyptic language and Apocalyptic image: not because I spent my time reading Revelation, but because I was sent to Sunday school and to Chapel, to Band of Hope and to Christian Endeavour, and was always having the Bible read at me or to me.' And even though he didn't often pay close attention, or couldn't always understand, the language and symbols penetrated his consciousness.

In his essay 'Hymns in a Man's Life' Lawrence said, 'I think it was good to be brought up a Protestant: and among Protestants, a Nonconformist, and among Nonconformists, a Congregationalist.' He was glad that the Congregationalists 'avoided the personal emotionalism which one found among the Methodists when I was a boy.' He was glad, too, that the Reverend Robert Reid 'on the whole avoided sentimental messes such as "Lead, Kindly Light", or even "Abide With Me". He had a healthy preference for healthy hymns.' And white-bearded Mr. Rimmington, the Sunday-school superintendent, earned Lawrence's gratitude by making the children sing the militant hymns 'Sound the Battle-Cry', 'Hold the Fort, for I Am Coming', and 'Stand Up, Stand Up for Jesus'. The martial rather than the mawkish governed Lawrence's taste in such matters:

> The ghastly sentimentalism that came like a leprosy over religion had not yet got hold of our colliery village. I remember when I was in Class II in the Sunday School, a woman teacher trying to harrow us about the Crucifixion. And she kept saying: 'And aren't you sorry for Jesus? Aren't you sorry?' And most of the children wept. I believe I shed a crocodile tear or two, but very vivid is my memory of saying to myself: 'I don't *really* care a bit.' And I could never go back on it. I never *cared* about the Crucifixion, one way or another. Yet the *wonder* of it penetrated very deep in me.

And it was the *wonder* that he felt in the hymns. He confessed, in his essay on them, that the poems which had meant the most to him, such as Wordsworth's 'Immortality' ode, Keats's odes, certain lyrics of Goethe and Verlaine, and parts of Shakespeare—'all these lovely poems which after all give the ultimate shape to one's life; all these lovely poems woven deep into a man's consciousness, are still not woven so deep in me as the rather banal Nonconformist hymns that penetrated through and through my childhood.'

For the title of one of the volumes of poetry he wrote in later life, Lawrence adapted a line—'Birds and beasts and flowers'—from 'Now the Day Is Over', a hymn which Sabine Baring-Gould had written in 1865. But among all Lawrence's works, *The Plumed Serpent* owes the greatest debt to the songs of the miners' bethel; in the plaza of a village in far-off Mexico, the dark-faced men on the streets —a projection of the singing miners of Eastwood strolling home at night—stand in the glare of ocote torches that light up the bougainvillaea and the pepper trees, to chant the Hymns of Quetzalcoatl:

> *But the Morning Star and the Evening Star*
> *Pitch tents of flame*
> *Where we foregather like gypsies, none knowing*
> *How the other came.*   [*The Plumed Serpent*]

I ask for nothing except to slip
In the tent of the Holy Ghost
And be there in the house of the cloven flame,
Guest of the Host.   [Nonconformist hymn]

There is, of course, more in the Quetzalcoatl chants and in the *Birds, Beasts and Flowers* poems than the emotional overflow of a man remembering the hymns of his childhood. In all his observations of nature and in all his portraits of animals, Lawrence wrote as one to whom close observation of his subject was an ingrained faculty, part of his 'gift'. He didn't realize, until he was about eighteen years old, precisely what his gift was, what form it would take, and how he could develop it; yet it had been with him all the while, preparing itself in darkness and silence.

Lawrence in young manhood gave up his Congregationalism, turning for a while to Unitarianism. But eventually he developed his own kind of religion, based upon the 'dark gods' he felt every man should commune with. He was always intensely religious, never more so than in his account of Etruscan civilization, which he discovered late in life. He always saw life itself as a religious manifestation, a fact that must be continually kept in mind as one reads Lawrence's writings. He was consistently one of the most religious men who ever wrote.

In childhood, when Lawrence saw people and landscapes and animals, they struck upon his sensitivity more sharply than upon the sensitivities of others, and this too was an intrinsically religious feeling; but he was then only receiving, as a quiet child, the hints of what he would one day transmit so forcefully.

His early experiences with pet animals were in many respects unfortunate. Mrs. Lawrence never wanted her children to have pets: the world of animals, like that of colliers, was an unclean area that existed beyond the range of her ideal of refinement. That she did yield at least twice to her children's craving for pets, Lawrence showed in his comic sketches 'Adolf' and 'Rex'. The first of these is the story of a rabbit the children tried to tame, the second, of a puppy they attempted to bring up. The sketches are lively portraits not only of these animals but also of the Lawrence family: the children full of love and concern for the animals, the father in each case a friendly ally, the mother an implacable opponent, barely tolerating the pets and rejoicing when they had to leave.

When Adolf the rabbit grew too wild to keep in the house, the children gravely turned him over to their father, who put him into the pocket of his miner's jacket and promised to release him in the woods. Before leaving, Arthur Lawrence had his little joke: ' "Best pop him i' the pot," said my father, who enjoyed raising the wind of indignation.' Later, Bert Lawrence often yearned after that rabbit, and thought of its whisking tail in flight as its cry of '*Merde!*' to the world, as its signal of defiance, the insolence of the meek.

As Mrs. Lawrence had disliked the rabbit, so she disliked the puppy, Rex, and apparently allowed the children to have it only because her brother Herbert requested them to keep it for a while. Herbert was a favorite of hers, despite the fact that he was the black sheep of the Beardsalls; he even kept a public house in Nottingham, the Lord Belper, on the northeast corner of Robin Hood and Lamartine streets, Sneinton, at the bottom of that Blue Bell Hill which Lawrence used for some of the important scenes in *Sons and Lovers.*

He portrayed his Uncle Herbert as Daniel Sutton in the story 'The Primrose Path'. There he tells of the man's unhappiness in marriage, of his journey to Australia with a woman he later accuses of trying to poison him, of his managing a taxi business in Nottingham, and of his working for a sporting paper there, all actual experiences of Herbert Beardsall. In 'Rex', when the uncle appears suddenly one day to take the dog back to Nottingham, he is furious: 'Why, what ha' you done wi' the dog—you've made a fool of him. He's softer than grease.' He drives away with Rex, who cries hideously, to the children's distress: 'Black tears, and a little wound which is still alive in our hearts.'

Lawrence eventually wrote poems or stories about almost every kind of animal, from whales and elephants to porcupines and bats. In his wandering later life he had three pets—in New Mexico, the cat Timsey and the dog Bibbles; in southern France, the cat Mickey. (The cow Susan, the 'mystic' friend of Lawrence at his New Mexico ranch, was perhaps too large to qualify as a pet.) This is a point sufficiently important to require comment and a little cataloguing: after all, Lawrence, more than any other writer, could bring animals forcefully to life in his prose and poetry.

Ada Lawrence Clarke has told of her brother's becoming sick at school one day when he had to cut up a frog: sick not because of a delicate stomach but because he regarded dissection as cruel. Ada had in many ways a similar temperament. One day when she and her husband were showing an American visitor through the grounds of Newstead Abbey, they saw some fish caught in a barred-iron trap in a stream. Ada bent over to release them, but her husband stopped her, pointing out that the keepers would make trouble. To the visitor, Ada Lawrence's face at that moment looked as her brother Bert's must often have looked when he saw animals impounded or cut up in biology laboratories. Thwarted on that day at Newstead, Lawrence's sister stood there suffering as she watched the fish struggle in the iron trap.

*

A studio photograph of the Lawrences has come down from the early nineties, the parents and the five children in their Sunday clothes, in a family group at a photographer's studio. It is a provincial, Victorian, melancholy souvenir, valuable for both its inward and its outward view of these seven individuals.

The father, lower right, catches the eye at once, as he sits, rather ill at ease, with watch chain, boutonniere, and gleaming shoes, his fists in his lap. His face, however, has a pleased expression above the full beard, as if he is proud of the family.

The photographer placed little Bert, standing, between his father and mother; the three of them form a dominant triangle. The mother is seated, with one hand in her lap nervously holding the other. Her face is difficult to describe, for it is so worn with fatigue that neither the lines of determination nor a suggestion of kindness in the features predominates: a woman of barely forty, she looks nearly twenty years older, with an air of malady.

Beside her mother, in the far corner of the picture, little Lettice Ada sits in a white dress bound with a light-colored sash. Ringlets come down each side of her face and below the shoulders, and she looks towards the camera in a kind of dazed surprise, her mouth hanging open. Ada was the youngest member of the family (born June 16, 1887); the closest to Bert in years, she was his closest friend among the children, and remained fiercely loyal to him.

Emily Una, five years older, stands above her, a tall girl in a white dress with a narrow dark sash. Her lips are slightly parted, and her face seems to bear a look of adolescent perplexity. Her hair, which was red like her brother Bert's, falls across her shoulders. In her childhood, the family called her Injun Top Knot and, later, Pamela, or Virtue Rewarded.

In this family portrait we see the oldest child, George, standing in the center at the rear; indeed, he is no longer a child, this 'most handsome member of the family'—the picture substantiates Ada's praise —a clear-eyed young man with a high collar and white tie. George Arthur Lawrence, born on September 26, 1876, had lived with the family only sporadically: as previously noted, he had spent a year of his childhood in the household of his great-grandfather John Newton, the hymn writer; and he had in his tenth year moved permanently to Nottingham. He had first been apprenticed to an uncle who made picture frames, work which the boy disliked; he eventually became an engineer like his grandfather.

William Ernest Lawrence, standing in the right rear of the picture, was then the pride of the family. Here he is an animal-looking young man, with flat cheekbones and strong, out-thrust jaw. Ernest—born June 22, 1878—is half a head above George in the picture. Ada described him as 'tall, well-built, with thick brown hair with reddish tints and twinkling blue eyes'. He was an excellent athlete, winner of many prizes at swimming, and he was a hurdler, too, who when he came to a gateway would usually jump over it rather than walk through it.

Ernest had gone to work when he was about twelve, after an impressive career at Beauvale Board School. He was employed first as a clerk in the colliery offices at Shipley, just across the Derbyshire border, then at the Co-operative Society at Langley Mill, the town in the lowlands west of Eastwood. He kept up his schooling at night and learned shorthand and typewriting. Later he taught himself French and German. He worked at Coventry for a time, and then went into the London business world when he was twenty-one.

It was this vigorous, swift, brilliant brother with whom Bert Lawrence, seven years younger, had to compete—as a student at a school that remembered his brother's record, and at home as a candidate for the mother's love.

All the Lawrence children attended Beauvale Board School, a series of redbrick Gothic-style buildings with turrets, high, gabled roofs, and tall, factorylike chimneys. D. H. Lawrence went to classes there for five years.

For the most part, he was unhappy at Beauvale. He would have had a more casual attitude towards schoolwork but for his mother: Ernest's scholastic efforts there had delighted her, and she was determined that the youngest son match them. George Lawrence recalled in 1950 that the enforced studying gave Bert headaches, 'and but for my mother he would have given it all up—she nursed him along'.

Bert himself looked back with envy on his father's escape from the educational process. His father's generation, Lawrence wrote in 1929, in his 'Enslaved by Civilisation' essay, 'was still wild'. Arthur Lawrence 'had never been to anything more serious than a dame's school', Mrs. Eite's—in that essay wrongly called Miss Hight's—at Brinsley. Mrs. Eite never succeeded in making his father 'a good little boy. She had barely succeeded in making him write his name.' Above all, his feelings 'had escaped her clutches entirely: as they escaped the clutches of his mother. The country was still open. He fled away from the women and rackapelted with his own gang.'

There was no such escape for Lawrence's generation, the first to be 'captured'. Most of the boys, miners' sons expecting to go into the pits, felt that school was prison and that the masters were their jailers. Lawrence himself wept with anguish the first day of school, because he felt he 'was roped in'. And he soon got into trouble with authority. He disliked the name David and refused to answer to it, though the schoolmaster raged at the stubborn child: 'David is the name of a great and good man!'

This fierce old teacher, W. W. Whitehead, eventually helped Lawrence to obtain an important scholarship. But that was several years and many thrashings later. Meanwhile, the bearded old Whitehead—whom the boys called Gaffer, the colliery idiom for boss— 'gradually got us under'. He had the backing of all the parents, so he persuaded and beat much of the savagery out of the colliers' sons during the years he had them under his influence. And when at last they got away from him and went into the pit, they found it was tame and mechanized, no longer 'the happy subterranean warren' their fathers had known.

At school these tough boys found a tender lad in their midst, the frail Bert Lawrence. His elder brothers had been able to fight their own battles, and Ernest had even been an athletic hero: but here was Bert, who didn't participate in sports, Bert, whom the small boys, with their crowlike ability to discover and pick away at a wound in one of their number, soon fixed upon. As William Hopkin said, 'I well remember the day when I was passing the school as the scholars were leaving for their dinner. He was walking between two girls, and a number of Breach boys walked behind him, monotonously chanting "Dicky Dicky Denches/Plays with the wenches." That charge branded him as effeminate—the local term is "mardarse". Bert's chin was in the air as though he cared not a jot, but his eyes were full of anger and mortification.'

Lawrence eventually learned to defend himself, in a way, by his sharpness of phrase; he began to make use of some of the talents which differentiated him from the crowd in the first place. As one of Lawrence's old schoolmates told William Hopkin years later, 'We were a bit hard on him for, after all, he couldn't help his constitution. . . . He wor a bit to blame, for he wor rayther stuck up, and when Gaffer gin him a bit o' praise we didn' like it.' But: 'When he got nigh fourteen he began hittin' back wi' his tongue an' he could get at us wheer it hurt.'

Another assault upon Lawrence's sensitivity in childhood was the jeering of the men who paid the miners' wages. As nothing else, this accented both the family humiliation and the personal humiliation of the small boy. The jeering would take place on Friday afternoons in the offices of Barber, Walker and Company, where the colliers frequently sent their wives or children to collect the pay. The offices were located on the Mansfield Road at the corner of Greenhill Road, in the lowlands directly north of the west end of Eastwood and across from Squire Walker's vast estate, Eastwood Hall. In *Sons and Lovers* Lawrence gives several pages to one of Paul Morel's painful experiences in going down to those offices to collect his father's wages, thereby earning sixpence for himself.

Paul 'suffered the tortures of the damned on these occasions' when, amid the lines of colliers in the pay room, he had to submit to the jibes of the supervising company official, Mr. Braithwaite, large and patriarchal-looking and white-bearded. Small boys were fair game to Braithwaite, who had a 'large and magisterial voice' that would humiliate the children for the sins of their fathers. Mr. Braithwaite in life was Alfred Woolston Brentnall, cashier for Barber, Walker and Company until two years before his death at the age of ninety, in February 1924, twelve years after Lawrence had put him into *Sons and Lovers*.

Brentnall's father had worked for the mining company before him, for forty years, and had also been cashier. The son, a particular favorite of Squire Walker's, had been a drunkard—as William Hopkin told the author of this book, 'the beer used to run out of his mouth' —but in his later years this Brentnall became a pillar of temperance. He was, Squire Walker felt, a good example for the miners. Bert

Lawrence's brothers, in their time collecting the father's pay, could answer him back, but little Bert went all to pieces when, amid the laughter of the colliers, the bearded old man would lean over the edge of the counter and roar, 'Ho, lad, wheer's your Pa—too drunk to come and collect the pay hissen?' To have to put up with that every Friday afternoon was not worth sixpence to Bert Lawrence.

But however Lawrence felt about Eastwood, he left his mark on it. In the 1970s, the Nottinghamshire County Council approved, according to the London *Times,* 'a proposal to rehabilitate the Erewash valley particularly as a tourist attraction associated with Lawrence'. But 'there has been a noticeable lack of warmth from certain quarters in Eastwood, where the author is still regarded in local parlance as "That mucky man" '. One of the principal growlers was an Eastwood alderman with a surname familiar in Lawrence's writings, one William Lamb, aged seventy-seven in 1973. He said Lawrence 'never came back to his home town after he left us, so how can you revere a man like that?' Lamb stated that it was only through the efforts of William Hopkin that Lawrence was 'revived'. He said further that another generation would have to pass before Lawrence could be fully appreciated: 'I suppose we were prudes, but standards were different then.' And, Lamb went on (to *Times* reporter Arthur Osman), 'after he became famous I and others would have liked him to come back to give us the benefit of his experiences, but he never did. I cannot forgive that.' It is easy to imagine the comedy of Lawrence's returning to Eastwood and one evening taking over the pulpit of the Albert Street chapel to tell Eastwood what he had learned about life and to defend *Lady Chatterley's Lover.*

Not all residents of the town were hostile to Lawrence, however, for in 1973 a former miner's house was converted into a Lawrence museum, and a room was given over to a permanent collection of materials relating to him and his work. In that same year, Miss Laura Cliffe, eighty-nine, told Roy Perrot of the *Observer* that she remembered Lawrence in school, not caring for games and spending most of his time with girls: 'Quite good at painting. I don't know what he did after that as a trade.' On being told that he had become a schoolmaster for a time, she added, 'Well, I didn't think he were clever enough for that or to write books. But he were no duffer.'

*

He was able to escape from some of the tormenting elements of Eastwood life when, at the age of twelve, he won a scholarship to Nottingham High School. This was a County Council scholarship for which the irascible old 'Gaffer' Whitehead had coached him. Lawrence's friend George Neville, whom Whitehead also trained, said he was a fine disciplinarian and a good teacher: 'That school *prepared* students.'

The institution that now invited Lawrence was very old and locally famous. Nottingham High School, which up to thirty years before had been the Grammar School, was in existence as far back as 1289; it was refounded in 1513 by a woman whose endowment still helps towards its upkeep—Dame Agnes Mellers, whose husband Richard had been a mayor of Nottingham.

The records of that ancient school show that David Herbert Lawrence of 3 Walker Street, Eastwood, enrolled on September 14, 1898, three days after his thirteenth birthday. Yet he had come near missing attendance altogether, for the scholarship paid only 12 pounds a year, and this barely provided for the tuition fees and the railway transportation between Eastwood and Nottingham. But Lawrence's mother, by holding down family expenses and making other readjustments, crushed all difficulties. She rejoiced in her sacrifices and pushed Bert to school.

The County Council scholarship was of great importance to Lawrence's future, though in later life he used to suggest that it had harmed him, seriously damaging his health. And it is true that for three years he had to go to Nottingham and back daily, in all kinds of weather, through the damp Midland autumns and springs, and the chill winters. Wearing the student's uniform—the little blue cap, the knee breeches, the high socks—he left home each morning at seven, returning at the same hour in the evening. George Neville reported that already, at that time of their daily train rides between Newthorpe and Nottingham, 'Lawrence had that little troublesome, hacking cough that used to bring his left hand so sharply to his mouth —a cough and an action that he never lost.'

The headmaster of the school, Dr. James Gow, Neville recalled as 'a wonderful chap, a great educator', though Neville and Lawrence, as out-of-town boys always hurrying for the evening train, never came to know him personally. But they were good friends of his son, their schoolmate James Gow, Jr., later to be killed in the battle of Jutland. The elder Gow in 1901 became headmaster of Westminster School at London.

George Neville believed that the Nottingham school's teaching staff had been an excellent one, and among its members he particularly recalled Samuel Corner, the senior master; the huge 'Jumbo' Ryles and his thin brother, 'Nipper' Ryles; S. A. Stanley, the arts master; S. R. Trotman, the chemistry and physics teacher; and T. B. Hardy, the classics instructor and chaplain, who was to receive the Victoria Cross in World War I.

It was good for Lawrence, disciplined in the cane-application school of Whitehead at Eastwood, to attend an institution directed by so tolerant, versatile, and talented a man as the Reverend James Gow. Lawrence between his fourteenth and seventeenth years probably received as fine a general education as he would have almost anywhere else at the time. Those who have dismissed him as 'uneducated', as T. S. Eliot and others have so facilely done, should scrutinize the facts of his schooling at Nottingham High School and at the institutions he attended later, a point F. R. Leavis forcibly made in the course of a ferocious attack on Eliot.

For what it is worth, here is the résumé of Lawrence's last years at Nottingham High School, as provided by a later headmaster, C. L. Reynolds:

> At Easter 1900 he was awarded the prize for the Upper Modern 4th form, and in the list for July 1900 he holds the 10th place out of 21 boys in the Modern 5th form and takes the Mathematical Prize for set 4. In this form he was placed 13th in English, 13th in German and 19th in French. Our last record shows that he was 15th out of 19 in the Modern 6th form in July 1901.

In extenuation of Lawrence's apparently poor showing in his last year, Mr. Reynolds has said: 'In this form he was competing with a number of able boys, most of whom were probably older than himself.' Indeed, it is a wonder that Bert Lawrence, with his incipient illness, his general fatigue, and the competition of his brother's success, didn't collapse altogether. His record in mathematics is perhaps the most surprising part of his early school career. His standing as thirteenth out of twenty-one in English can only cause smiles: the story of authors-to-be who are poor at grammar and composition in school is a familiar one.

Years later Lawrence recalled that while attending the high school he 'made a couple of bourgeois friendships, but they were odd fishes' —he 'instinctively recoiled away from the bourgeoisie, regular sort.' But Eastwood people later remembered that Lawrence once went to tea at the 'bourgeois' home of one of his Nottingham high-school friends. When the boy's parents learned that Lawrence's father was a collier, they forced their son to break off the relationship. July 1901: and that is the end of it all, or so it seemed then. As C. L. Reynolds has explained, the education of most boys in those days terminated in their seventeenth year, 'so Lawrence's career may be regarded as normal.' But what of the ambitious mother harassing the boy to do his utmost all those years, fighting to get him the money for those 7 A.M. to 7 P.M. ordeals? And what were the fruits of those efforts? There could be no more schooling, apparently; no money for that. The mother has kept the boy out of the mines, but now she sees that, after all, modern industrialism still confronts him. His fate is to become clerk in a factory.

*

During those years of his weekday trips to Nottingham High School, Lawrence didn't lose contact with his native town. One of his most valued friends at this time, one who helped him with his eternal and fatiguing lessons, was a woman to whom he paid a quiet tribute in his novel of 1920, *The Lost Girl*. There his friend Miss Wright became Miss Frost, governess of the 'lost' girl. Knowing Miss Wright and the family she worked for was an important experience for Lawrence: it gave him the background and leading characters for that book of his which, next to *Sons and Lovers,* deals most exclusively with Eastwood. *The Lost Girl* is a comedy, full of caricatures, among which Miss Wright's employer is the most prominent.

The James Houghton (pronounced Huffton) of the novel was in life George Henry Cullen, merchant, dandy, and promoter. William Hopkin remembered him as 'a man who fancied himself', an elegantly dressed gentleman with Dundreary side whiskers. He was best known for his ownership of the London House—the Manchester House ('lovely fabrics') of *The Lost Girl*—on the Nottingham Road. The once independent London House, with a new front at the pavement level, later became one of the famous 'Burtons—the leading grocers' shops, 19 Nottingham Road.

Like Cullen, Houghton fails in his attempt to bring better standards of dress and decoration to the colliers' wives. And Houghton's further speculations parallel very closely those of George Cullen. In the novel, as in life, Houghton-Cullen attempts to operate a mine in the Hill Top district of Eastwood, just below the south side of the Nottingham Road. This 'rickety, amateurish' affair serves only to arouse the scorn of the miners, who call it Throttle Ha'penny (in the book as in life) and refer to its product as dirt: 'I'm sure I shan't burn that muck, and smother myself with white ash.' After the mine fails, the entrepreneur begins to make other plans: he sets up a cinema in Langley Mill—Lumley in the novel—and for a while has another activity; then that too fails.

At the time of these events, Lawrence's friend and tutor, Miss Wright, kept the household together, with the somewhat sullen cooperation of Cullen's chief assistant at the shop, Miss Pidsley, whom Lawrence put into *The Lost Girl* as Miss Pinnegar. The Alvina Houghton of the novel, the 'lost' girl herself, was also taken from life: at least the outward circumstances of her existence were. Like Florence (Flossie) Cullen, Alvina becomes a nurse. But, Lawrence's sister Ada insisted, the *character* of Alvina was Lawrence's 'own creation'. Flossie didn't run away and later marry a young Italian strolling player from one of the companies that appeared at her father's theater. Rather, she married a local collier's son, George Hodgkinson, who was the doorman at the theater, and they went to the north of England to live.

An examination of the Cullens and their associates shows us how closely Lawrence drew upon the life about him, and it also demonstrates how well he knew his native town. In *The Lost Girl,* as in most of his other fiction, Lawrence took actual places and people and described them with physical accuracy, but in working out the stories, he would often put the people through entirely different experiences from those they had known in life. Their remarkably rendered counterparts would follow the behavior of the originals in some details, but in larger matters they would obey the laws of Lawrence's vision —as Alvina Houghton, in *The Lost Girl,* is taken to a place the real Flossie Cullen did not know, the cold Italian mountain region of the impressive Lawrencean finale of that novel, where she goes to live in the settlement which is at once so similar to and different from her native village.

An interesting clue to Lawrence's method in finding names for his characters occurs in C. N. Wright's *Directory of Parishes, Townships, and Hamlets Twelve Miles Round Nottingham Market Place* (published about 1892), which lists merchants, bankers, bootmakers, mine owners, and so on, in Eastwood, Brinsley, Greasley, and their neighboring constablewicks. Here we may find many surnames familiar to Lawrence, who borrowed them for his fiction, though he did not connect the actual names with recognizable portraits. When he was using actual people as characters, he often disguised their names thinly. Wright's *Directory* merely gives us the names used for quite different kinds of people; we find, for example, Chatterley and Mellors, Annable and Sisson. There is also the name Crich, which is identical with a nearby stony upland village in Derbyshire, which the Lawrence children could see from their hilltop house on Walker Street. The Greasley entries include an Adam Crich and Sons, joiners and wheelwrights. Gerald Crich (the *i* is pronounced as in *ice,* the *ch* as in *church*) of *Women in Love* is the friend of Rupert Birkin; a William Birkin operated the Coach and Horses. There are many other names in the *Directory* that also appear in Lawrence's fiction: Millership, Bricknell, Leivers, and others. (Several pages of this *Directory* were reproduced in *A D. H. Lawrence Miscellany* [1959].)

A further illustration of Lawrence's use of local materials may be taken from another social class. A man whose appearance and circumstances Lawrence several times used importantly in his fiction was the late Sir Thomas Philip Barber of the mine-owning family of Barber, Walker and Company. Lawrence knew T. P. Barber only distantly, yet he drew upon him for the outward physical aspects of several of his major characters.

Lawrence in his youth often saw the Barber estate, Lamb Close house, and from his seventeenth year until he left Eastwood at twenty-three, he walked or cycled past it on the trips he made to Haggs Farm on an average of several times a week. He must often have seen the young squire, the nine-years-older Thomas Philip Barber, riding on horseback about the property, perhaps—like his counterpart Gerald of *Women in Love*—'on a red Arab mare'. Indeed, Eastwood residents reported that Lawrence once saw Barber mistreating his horse when it was frightened by a train at a crossing gate, an episode introduced into *Women in Love.*

Barber and Lawrence met and spoke at least once, according to George Neville's recollection. Neville and Lawrence were crossing the Barber property when the young squire—who was already a justice of the peace and would at thirty-one become high sheriff of Nottinghamshire—rode up and ordered them off. The thin, red-headed young trespasser, instead of answering in the educated speech he had learned from his mother and his schoolmasters, replied impudently in the dialect of the colliers. Squire Barber said, 'I remind you that I am a J.P.' Lawrence muttered to Neville, 'He sounds to me like a b.f.'

Whether or not Lawrence was really familiar with the interior of Lamb Close—and we have seen that Mrs. Collishaw placed him there at least once—it frequently appears in his imaginative writings. It was a building of fairly recent addition, originally a farmhouse (parts of which still exist at the rear of the new mansion) which the owner (Matthew Lamb) turned into a shooting box in the eighteenth century, before the Barber family bought and rebuilt it. The place appears in Lawrence's first novel, *The White Peacock,* as Highclose, a 'proud house . . . on a hill beyond the farthest corner of the lake'— Moorgreen Reservoir, the Nethermere of this novel. In *Women in Love,* Lamb Close is Shortlands, 'a long, low old house, a sort of manor farm, that spread along the top of a slope just beyond the narrow little lake of Willey Water'—again Moorgreen, which is also an important part of that book. Also, in the play *Touch and Go,* which duplicates several of the characters and incidents of *Women in Love,* some of the scenes take place at Lilley Close, home of the mine-owning Barlows. Even the portrait of Wragby Hall in *Lady Chatterley's Lover,* of which at least one notable country house—the Renishaw of the literary Sitwell family—has claimed the honor of being the subject, looks and sounds strangely like Lamb Close: 'Wragby was a long, low old house in brown stone, begun about the middle of the eighteenth century, and added on to, till it was a warren of a place without much distinction.' The house 'stood on an eminence in a rather fine old park of trees,' and from there the smoke and steam of the nearest colliery could be seen—as well as 'the raw straggle of Tevershall village', or Eastwood. (Locally, Lamb Close is often spelled Lambclose.)

Most of the male members of the family that has for so long owned Lamb Close have had the Christian name Thomas, from Thomas P. F. H. Barber (1778–1857) through two other Thomas Barbers (1805–1874 and 1843–1893) and on to the Thomas Philip Barber (born 1876) whom Lawrence used to see. Thomas Philip's father, who died in 1893 at the age of fifty, carried on his father's charitable activity among the colliers' families: here we have the paternal sentimental days of the magnate-miner relationship that Lawrence so often mentioned, dramatizing it in *Women in Love.*

In his fifty years Thomas Barber knew great personal grief. His first wife died in 1870 at the age of twenty-five, and shortly before his own death he lost two of his children. His second son, Kenneth Forbes Barber, was accidentally killed in 1890, in his thirteenth year, by his brother, the Thomas Philip Barber of Lawrence's time, an incident Lawrence refers to in *Women in Love*. (The local newspaper reported that 'the jury returned a verdict of "Accidental death", and expressed their sympathy with parents and relatives of the deceased.') Finally, in 1892—in the year before the death of the father —the little girl of the family, Cecily, died in her seventh year. She drowned in Moorgreen Reservoir, just as the girl in *Women in Love* drowned in Willey Water, in the chapter called 'Water-Party'. In the novel as in life, the girl fell into the water from her father's steam houseboat; the young Dr. Brindell who in the novel dived after her in an attempt to save her was actually the young son of Dr. Bingham of Alfreton; like his prototype, he drowned when the girl in her terror seized him around the neck and pulled him under.

Lawrence's fictional account of this incident is one of his most striking pieces of narrative: the moving colors of the gay crowd in the afternoon, the descent of darkness and the lighting of the lanterns on the boats, the music over the water, all of it drawn into the story, into the developing relationship of the characters; then the scream of a child who has seen her sister slip into the black water, the utter confusion, the frantic diving, the smash of the water being let out through the sluice, later the raw clay banks emerging in the bleak dawn, and at last the two bodies, the girl still with her arms around the young man's neck. Lawrence must have seen part of this; the whole village would have gone out to Moorgreen, the six-year-old Bert Lawrence and his sister probably in the crowd.

In *Women in Love* the disaster affects the whole district: 'The colliery people felt as if this catastrophe had happened directly to themselves, indeed they were more shocked and frightened than if their own men had been killed.' They discuss it on the streets, and at their Sunday dinners, as if the angel of death were hovering over them all. 'The men had excited, startled faces, the women looked solemn, some of them had been crying. The children enjoyed the excitement at first. There was an intensity in the air, almost magical.' All this, presented with a concreteness that makes it virtually as real as something that has actually happened in the life of the reader, certainly must have come out of Lawrence's own experience. And in the novel he uses all the factual circumstances as background for some important psychological phases in the lives of his characters. The 'Water-Party' chapter also helps along the development of the central themes of love and death in *Women in Love:* Gerald, diving after his drowning sister, discovers 'a whole universe under there', in the cold—a fore-shadowing of his own icy death in the Austrian Alps.

In a hundred other ways, Lawrence used local settings and local people for his stories, always depicting them with a sharp surface reality and, as in the examples just provided, usually giving them an important imaginative heightening.

3   LAWRENCE LAUNCHES INTO LIFE

Lawrence met Jessie Chambers in the summer of 1901, at her fam-ily's farm, while he was still attending high school in Nottingham and not long before he went to work in a factory there. Jessie, more than a year younger than Lawrence (she was born on January 29, 1887), was the second daughter of the large family at Haggs Farm, about two miles north of Eastwood. The tormenting relationship of Lawrence and Jessie, which was to last for about a dozen years, be-came one of the principal themes of *Sons and Lovers,* with Lawrence as Paul Morel and Jessie as Miriam Leivers.

Jessie's grandfather, Jonathan Chambers, was a resident of Brins-ley, where he had an off-license for beer. Jessie's father, Edmund Chambers, had grown up there and had gone away to be married. He returned in the nineties with his wife and children and for three years lived in a cottage in the Breach, where he had a milk round. About three years before Lawrence met Jessie, Edmund Chambers became tenant farmer at the Haggs. He was out in all weather, in his milk-float or about the farm, despite his severe rheumatism. As his sons grew up, they began to help with the farm work.

William Hopkin had gone to school with the father of this family, some thirty years before. The mischievous Willie Hopkin and the 'quiet and earnest' Edmund Chambers became close friends in one of those schoolyard alliances of opposites. Hopkin remembered, about eighty years afterwards, that Edmund Chambers was a pains-taking student whom 'the teacher never had to call out for the cane'. In out-of-school hours, Edmund Chambers and Willie Hopkin 'but-tied' at marbles, which meant, in pit language, that if one of them gambled away all his marbles, the other 'staked him up' until he could recover them. In 1950 Hopkin spoke of his old schoolmate as 'a steady, plodding, reliable man with a particularly nice disposition'; he and his wife had been 'a quiet, admirable pair, old-fashioned, harmonious—as nice a couple as anyone could know'. The youngest member of the Chambers family, Professor J. David Chambers, stated before his death in 1970 that Hopkin made Edmund Chambers out to be more placid than he actually was: 'He certainly grew up to be a dashing, handsome, irresponsible, and quick-tempered young blood, riding his penny-farthing bicycle with reckless speed down hills.'

Jessie Chambers first clearly remembered seeing Bert Lawrence during a Sunday-school session at the Congregational chapel, but she might never have become acquainted with the boy if at about this time their mothers hadn't met. Lydia Lawrence found in Mrs. Chambers a comparative newcomer to the mining country who would listen to her twenty years' grievance against it. She promised to visit the Chamberses, but some three years passed before she went out to the farm, escorted by her son Bert. Mr. Chambers had told him how to cross the fields to reach the Haggs and how to find the short cut—a path that no longer exists—through the lower end of Willey Spring Wood.

That and similar routes to the Haggs, Lawrence came to know well in the years to follow, when the Chamberses were his second family. In *Sons and Lovers* he memorialized that first walk out there, on a summer day when 'on the fallow land the young wheat shone silkily' and one of the neighboring collieries 'waved its plumes of white steam, coughed, and rattled hoarsely'.

When mother and son arrive at the farmyard and go into the little garden beside the house, 'in the doorway suddenly appeared a girl in a dirty apron. She was about fourteen years old, had a rosy dark face, a bunch of short black curls, very fine and free, and dark eyes; shy, questioning, a little resentful of strangers, she disappeared. In a minute another figure appeared, a small, frail woman, rosy, with great dark brown eyes.' This, in the novel, is Paul Morel's first sight of Miriam and her mother. Jessie Chambers, writing of the event in her reminiscence of Lawrence, didn't show herself as disappearing in shy resentment from the doorway, but merely reported that her mother went out to greet the visitors and bring them into the parlor, where 'Mrs Lawrence, complaining of the heat, said in her crisp way' that she was glad 'you haven't got a fire in here'.

Mrs. Lawrence seems never to have gone back to the Haggs. But Bert became a regular visitor, often bringing a magazine for the family. He and the father got on well, though the brothers remained somewhat aloof at first, as if afraid that Lawrence would give himself airs. Jessie had no special recollection of him 'during that first summer except as a quiet presence coming suddenly out of the sunshine into the kitchen, warm with the fragrance of baking bread.' After his school ended and he became a clerk in Nottingham, they 'saw rather less of him' for a while.

*

Lawrence obtained work in that summer of 1901 when his brother Ernest, home for a few days from his increasingly successful business career in London, helped him compose an application. Ernest could fill the letter with the appropriate phraseology he used constantly in his position with the shipping underwriters John Holroyd and Company, of Lime Street, EC1. The district was full of historical associations, the Monument, the Tower, and London Bridge, as well as the Thames itself, with its gliding boats and the bustling life of the wharves.

The love between Ernest and his mother continued to be intense. It was so strong that, in his younger brother's view, Ernest's attempt to break it broke Ernest himself. Mrs. Lawrence kept this son in her orbit as long as he remained at home, for the provincial girls who came to the house looking for Ernest were easy to frighten away. But it was a different matter when he brought his London girl, Gypsy Dennis, to Eastwood for a visit.

Mrs. Lawrence did what she could to be polite to this dark, lively girl, but privately she condemned Gypsy's shallowness. Gypsy (the Louisa Lily Denys Western of *Sons and Lovers*) was a stenographer who lived only for parties, who thought and spoke only of waltzes, tasseled dancing cards, and silver slippers. Mrs. Lawrence was deeply disturbed: 'She lets him buy her boots!'

In her memoir of Lawrence, Jessie Chambers spoke of one of Gypsy's visits, apparently in the summer of 1901, as lasting 'a fortnight's holiday' that 'had proved something of a strain'. It was probably at this time that Ernest wrote the draft of the business letter that his younger brother copied and sent off to an employer who had advertised for a junior clerk in the *Nottinghamshire Guardian*. Soon Bert Lawrence received instructions to call at the business establishment of J. H. Haywood at 9 Castle Gate, Nottingham.

The house of Haywood, 'manufacturer of surgical appliances and wholesale dealer in druggists' sundries (Est. since 1830)', had notepaper headed by drawings of elastic stockings and wooden legs. Paul, in *Sons and Lovers,* feels 'alarmed' at the pictures he sees on the stationery used by Jordan's, as Haywood's is called in the novel: 'He had not known that elastic stockings existed. And he seemed to feel the business world, with its regulated system of values, and its impersonality, and he dreaded it. It seemed monstrous also that a business could be run on wooden legs.'

It is ironic that D. H. Lawrence, of all men, should have gone to work for dealers in artificial limbs. But he did, at a salary of thirteen shillings a week, once again taking that early train to the city, six mornings out of seven. There was no half-holiday at midweek, as in his schooldays: the factory didn't close until eight at night, even on Saturdays, though sometimes work finished about two hours earlier on Thursdays and Fridays.

From the boy's first interview with the caustic owner, the experience at Haywood's appears at great length in *Sons and Lovers:* indeed, at far greater length than in actual life. Lawrence had his hero work there for a number of years; his own stay was brief. Yet, while he was there, the sensitive boy absorbed every phase of the factory activity, which the man would use later in his writings.

Lawrence's life now centered on a different part of Nottingham than he had known before. He was nearly a mile to the south of that region of park and woodland which surrounded the high school; he was in an industrial quarter, working in a tiny dark old street whose quaintness was already being sullied by the factories and offices that were either replacing or taking over the stately Georgian houses there. Lawrence in *Sons and Lovers* gave Castle Gate the name of an actual nearby street, Spaniel Row. He describes it in rather Dickensian terms as 'gloomy and old-fashioned, having low dark shops and dark green house-doors with brass knockers, yellow-ochred doorsteps projecting on to the pavement, then another old shop whose small window looked like a cunning, half-shut eye'.

Altogether Lawrence had three careers in the city of Nottingham: schoolboy, clerk, and, several years later, college student—and of these three he chose to memorialize in his work that brief period of his employment at Haywood's. He was there only a few months, as against his three years at high school and his subsequent two years at Nottingham University College, yet in *Sons and Lovers* it is the clerkship rather than the studentship that he dramatizes. It is the young clerk rather than the student who wanders in that novel through the Castle ground at lunchtime or walks across the old squares or alongside the canal which, between the high factory walls, seemed, to an imaginative youth, 'just like Venice'. In *Sons and Lovers* Lawrence of course drew upon his student experiences, but he kept them within the range of a young man working at Haywood's.

As clerk in the spiral department, which made the elastic hose and the suspensory bandages, Lawrence sat on a high stool and read letters, some of them in French or German, both of which he had studied at the high school. He translated and copied them, with those in English, into the entry book from which the work orders were made out. And he drudged away at checking and invoicing during those twelve-hour days.

He also became acquainted with the girls in the factory, those who made the trusses and artificial limbs, and those who worked on the spiral machines. The latter were specialists who felt that they were refined and gave themselves airs. Lawrence in *Sons and Lovers* paints tender and friendly portraits of the girls, particularly of the hunchback, Fanny, with her beautiful hair and her rich singing voice. George Neville said, however, that the girls in the factory were not refined or tender, and that Lawrence had sentimentalized them in the novel.

In 1950 the director of Haywood's—which after being bombed in World War II moved to Warser Gate, near St. Mary's Church—recalled those days and said that 'in *Sons and Lovers* the surroundings are based on our warehouse, although the names mentioned are fictitious.' This director, A. E. Gill, remembered the boy Lawrence 'quite well, but did not associate with him out of business hours, as he had to travel by train home. To me at that time he was a very quiet and reserved young man. Tall and dark-haired, very little to say in conversation, both in work time and outside.' (Various people have remembered Lawrence as dark-haired in youth; his hair became redder as he grew older.)

Lawrence had been at Haywood's only a short while when his brother Ernest returned home from London for a few days, just before his death at the age of twenty-three. He came at the time of the Goose Fair held in Nottingham for the last three days of the first week in October. He stayed first at Eastwood with the family and then visited his brother George and his wife in Nottingham.

The physical cause of Ernest's death was erysipelas, later complicated by pneumonia. In the weeks before his visit to Eastwood and Nottingham, Ernest had been so obviously ill that his employer's son, Captain Thomas Holroyd, had invited him to sail aboard his ship to the Mediterranean, but Ernest had refused because he didn't want to go so far away from his mother.

On Sunday night, October 6, 1901, George Lawrence put Ernest on the train at Victoria Station, Nottingham, for his return trip to London. George realized how ill his brother was, and told him to see a doctor when he got back, and to stay in bed for a few days. Ernest's cold was worse, and his face was inflamed with what seemed to be fever. The next morning he went to his office, but he seemed so ill that his employer sent him back to his lodgings. There his landlady told him to take some Seidlitz powders and go to bed. She forgot him, George Lawrence said, for two days, until she looked into his room and saw him lying unconscious on the floor. She telegraphed his mother.

Mrs. Lawrence arrived at Ernest's lodgings after strenuous difficulties in making her way through the maze of South London. He was in a coma and died without recognizing her. Arthur Lawrence, fetched from the pit (' 'E's niver *gone,* child?'), was dazed as he set out for London for the second time in his life. 'He was no help', Mrs. Lawrence told Jessie Chambers later: the grieving mother had to deal with officials and undertakers and handle all the practical matters. The body was brought to Eastwood at the end of the week, and the huge coffin was placed across some chairs in the parlor of the Walker Street home, which the Lawrence children had long ago nicknamed Bleak House.

Ernest was buried in the cemetery at New Eastwood on Monday, October 14.

In Lawrence's 1912 synopsis of *Sons and Lovers,* written for Edward Garnett, he said the older brother 'gives his sex to a fribble, and his mother holds his soul. But the split kills him.' In Lawrence's later story 'The Lovely Lady', the elder son had fallen in love with an actress, and 'his mother had humorously despised him' because of this. 'So he had caught some ordinary disease, but the poison had gone to his brain and killed him. . . . It was clear murder: a mother murdering her sensitive sons, who were fascinated by her: the Circe!'

After Ernest's death, Mrs. Lawrence lost the gaiety that would sometimes break through her grimness; she just sat and grieved. Again, *Sons and Lovers* provides a sharply remembered picture of the time: the mother, greeted by her younger son on her return from London, 'let him kiss her, but she seemed unaware of him'; after the burial, 'she remained shut off'; and in the weeks to come, when he returns home at night from Nottingham and tries to tell her about his day, 'his mother sat blankly looking in front of her, her mouth shut tight.' And this continues: 'He was cut off and wretched through October, November, and December. His mother tried, but she could not rouse herself. She could only brood on her dead son; he had been let to die so cruelly.'

At last, as if in imitation of his brother, Bert Lawrence came down with pneumonia. He nearly died; but his mother's nursing saved his life. A member of the family is reported to have remarked that it saved Lydia's as well. Her youngest son lived: and for the remaining nine years of his mother's life, he was to be almost the only recipient of her crushing love.

*

'After leaving school I was a clerk for three months,' Lawrence wrote many years later, 'then had a very serious pneumonia illness, in my seventeenth year, that damaged my health for life.' He never went back to Haywood's.

A possible cause of this 'damaging' illness has been suggested: the neglected boy may have unconsciously engaged in a kind of mimesis of his brother's illness in an effort to attract his mother's love. George Neville, who knew Lawrence very well at the time, expressed a somewhat different theory. Neville indeed made various comments on Lawrence's experiences at Haywood's, which he always saw as crucial in Lawrence's development.

In 1931 Neville wrote that Lawrence's 'cynical attitude towards some women dates from an incident that occurred shortly after the death of his brother, "Ern". . . . This attitude was further "burnt" into him by the "blistering" his young soul received when he was working as foreign correspondent to a firm of manufacturers in Nottingham.' In an interview in 1950 with the author of this book, Neville explained that the first of these statements referred to the letter Gypsy Dennis wrote to Mrs. Lawrence soon after Ernest's death. Gypsy protested overmuch that she could never again love anyone else so much, that she would never marry—at which Mrs. Lawrence remarked bitterly, 'She's thinking of *that* already.'

At the time of his statement about the 'blistering' of Lawrence's 'young soul', Neville had amplified his statement by saying, 'The girls at the factory appear to have taken a sheer delight in searing his youthful innocence. You may be of the opinion that such a remark is a queer one to be made in respect of D. H. Lawrence. It is; but believe me, it is a true one.' Exactly what he had meant Neville explained in conversation nearly twenty years later: The girls at Haywood's were not the decent girls of *Sons and Lovers,* but a rather rough gang who continually pelted the village boy with coarse jests.

They seem indeed to have resembled the savage girl tram conductors of Lawrence's wartime story 'Tickets Please', who knock down an irritating superintendent and rip off his clothes. The girls at Haywood's once cornered young Bert Lawrence in a downstairs storeroom, pounced on him, and tried to expose his sex. He fought free of them, but was left breathless and disgusted and retching. George Neville said he believed that this shock and exertion brought on Lawrence's attack of pneumonia in that winter of 1901–1902.

Lawrence's belief that his illness 'damaged' his health for life was not shared by Dr. Andrew Morland, the tuberculosis specialist who attended him shortly before his death; at least he didn't think that this illness led to the fatal tuberculosis. In a letter of September 12, 1952, he wrote, 'It is very hard to say when his tuberculosis began. I do not think the childhood illnesses or the pneumonia at sixteen had any bearing on his tuberculosis. The onset of this probably predated his first attack of haemorrhage by at least a few months or possibly considerably longer.' And Lawrence's first hemorrhages didn't occur till the middle 1920s.

The illness may have affected his vocal cords: William Hopkin recalled that it left Lawrence with the high-pitched voice that so many of the memoirists have noted.

In any event, that illness in his seventeenth year did help to change his attitude towards life. If during his convalescence he absorbed much of his mother's love, he must also have absorbed much of her bitterness.

On mild days that winter, Lawrence sat in a chair in the back garden of the Walker Street house, wrapped in blankets and trying to drink in the thin Midland sunlight. His illness had distressed his new friends at the Haggs—he called the Chambers family the Haggites —and he began to exchange messages with them, carried by the father, whose dairyman's rounds took him to Eastwood daily. Then one day in spring Jessie's father brought him to the farm in the milkfloat. Lawrence was 'frail and eager', happy to be with them all again. The elder Chamberses welcomed him as if he were their own son, and even the boys' gruffness towards him began to wear off.

Mrs. Lawrence sent Bert to spend a month of convalescence with her sister Lettice (Mrs. Berry) at her 'select' boarding house, in flat, red-roofed Skegness on the Lincolnshire coast. It was a place of enchantment to the boy from Eastwood, who wrote frequent letters to the Chamberses about it.

When he returned to Eastwood he resumed his visits to the Chambers farm. At this time Jessie was not Lawrence's special friend among the Haggites—he gave far more attention to the parents and to the two oldest Chambers boys, Alan and Hubert—but he was aware of her. And things he said had awakened in her a desire for more education. Because this seemed impossible, she became discontented. But at last Jessie's mother, perhaps at Lawrence's instigation, permitted her to go back to school, as a pupil-teacher.

Lawrence continued to enter into the family activities, teaching the smaller children whist, cleaning the hearth for Mrs. Chambers, and peeling vegetables. He found none of the household tasks boring, and at harvest time he joined Mr. Chambers and his sons in their hayfields, four miles from the farm, opposite Greasley church: these fields were part of the setting of *Sons and Lovers,* and they supplied the background for the story 'Love Among the Haystacks'.

Jessie heard her father say, 'Work goes like fun when Bert's there.' Another time, Mrs. Chambers remarked, 'I should like to be next to Bert in heaven.'

Many years later (in 1928), Lawrence wrote Jessie's youngest brother, David, a letter flavored with memories of the place and its people, and Flower the horse and Trip the bull terrier: 'Whatever I forget, I shall never forget the Haggs—I loved it so. I loved to come to you all, it really was a new life began in me there. . . . Oh, I'd love to be nineteen again, and coming up through the Warren and catching the first glimpse of the buildings. Then I'd sit on the sofa under the window, and we'd crowd round the little table to tea, in that tiny little kitchen I was so at home in . . . whatever else I am, I am somewhere still the same Bert who rushed with such joy to the Haggs.'

4 CONGREGATIONAL YOUNG LOVE

Ada Lawrence Clarke says in her memoir that Jessie Chambers first attracted Lawrence because her seriousness, her interest in schoolwork and in books, set her apart from the thoughtless, gayer girls of the Eastwood area. Unlike the others, Jessie cared nothing about sweethearts or flashy clothes. Misunderstood by her brothers, who used all the little vulgarities of farm life to embarrass and torment her, she welcomed Lawrence as her first friend. She listened to him, shared his interests, and helped him develop his theories about life and literature.

Jessie at first refused to visit Lawrence's home. He accused her of being afraid to meet his father, and although she had from childhood a terror of drunken men, she assured Lawrence that his father had nothing to do with her reluctance. As if not fully believing her, Lawrence said, 'There's nothing for you to be afraid of. You'd never see him—he's hardly ever in.' She found this to be true. Yet there was 'a curious atmosphere' in that hilltop house in Walker Street, 'a tightness in the air'. Jessie found this both terrifying and exciting. She thought it was made up of the mother's grief over Ernest, of her antagonism towards her husband, and of her tense love for her son Bert.

At this time Mrs. Lawrence frequently organized touring parties for the young people. Escorted by Mrs. Lawrence and a friend, they would go by brake to Matlock, the popular watering place in the Peak District in Derbyshire, with its High Tor, its caves, its imitation-medieval castle, and its 'Heights of Abraham'. On such trips Lawrence would eagerly take over direction of the party, pointing out all the sights and naming the different kinds of birds and flowers. Jessie of course liked such occasions best when they were unchaperoned by the older people, for then Lawrence, although still commanding the party, could pay more attention to her.

Jessie Chambers (E.T.) in her book, *D. H. Lawrence: A Personal Record,* recalled with special sharpness an incident that occurred during one of the trips in their own county (apparently on Good Friday 1903). She 'had a sudden flash of insight which made me see Lawrence in a totally new light. . . . I turned and saw Lawrence in the middle of the road, bending over an umbrella. There was something in his attitude that arrested me. His stooping figure had a look of intensity, almost of anguish. For a moment I saw him as a symbolic figure. I was deeply moved and walked back to him.' She asked what the matter was, and he replied, 'It was Ern's umbrella, and mother will be wild if I take it home broken.' They walked on together, but she 'did not tell him what I had seen. This was perhaps the beginning of our awareness of sympathy for one another.'

This important episode also appears in *Sons and Lovers,* somewhat differently. Indeed, an examination of it as shaped by Lawrence will show not only how Lawrence and Jessie differed in outlook, but also how Lawrence adapted material from life for that novel.

Jessie's version is probably 'true' enough; like Miriam in *Sons and Lovers,* she apparently kept a journal, for by most tests her reminiscences are accurate. She had evidently written an earlier version of the umbrella incident, about eight or nine years after it happened, when she was supplying Lawrence with suggestions for *Sons and Lovers* in the early stages of its composition; regrettably, her original account of this episode has apparently not survived with her other contributions. Fortunately, however, one of the remaining fragments of Lawrence's early versions of the novel preserves that passage.

Perhaps at this point we need a statement of the relationship of the various manuscripts and notes mentioned previously. After some two years' work on *Sons and Lovers,* Lawrence completed it in Italy in 1912; it came out in 1913. For this book, Jessie Chambers had, apparently in 1911–1912, written some narrative sections which Lawrence revised and incorporated into the novel. He sent her part of one of the later manuscript versions of the book; in this she wrote comments in the margins and between the lines, and then added several pages of notes.

Like many of these fragments of *Sons and Lovers,* this one probably came almost directly from Jessie's original account of the episode. Certainly other parts of the preserved material match closely the surviving bits of her own contribution; Lawrence often took sentences from her manuscript, though he usually enlivened an incident by adding a stroke of color here and there or shifting the narrative point of view.

One of Lawrence's earlier versions of the umbrella incident is accompanied by Jessie's comment on it. In Lawrence's account, he puts the blame for the breaking of the umbrella on the girl's brother (Geoffrey, the second son in Miriam's family in *Sons and Lovers*):

... Paul was left so entirely alone on the empty road, and the sunset light showed him up so distinctly, that, suddenly, it revealed him to her. He did not see her, but continued to mend the umbrella. What there was in him at that moment made clear to her, something for which she loved him passionately, with all the strength of her nature, she did not know. But she walked down slowly, and stood still, until he looked up.

'Why,' he said, 'have you waited for me?' She treasured his grateful tone [Jessie drew a line under this sentence and wrote above: *His tone was grateful*]. They walked on together.

She was hurt that he, who never worried over trifles, or over property at all, should seem so put out because the spring of an umbrella was broken.

'It's only an old umbrella, isn't it?' she said reproachfully.

'Yes, but it was William's [Ernest's]—and Mother will be sure to know.'

Miriam was silenced. She understood. They walked on together.

Jessie's comment on this, on another sheet, was: 'The revelation over the broken umbrella was a spiritual awakening. Miriam [she originally wrote, then crossed out, *I*] had a glimpse of the inner Paul, and it set her wondering and eternally seeking.' This was probably the moment she fell in love.

The two treatments of the situation that have just been quoted are fairly pedestrian: they are statements about the experience rather than dramatizations of it. Even Lawrence's version of it is circumstantial and dull, and hobbled by unnecessary commas. But in a later draft of *Sons and Lovers,* carried on into the printed version, he presented the scene strongly. He took the 'revelation' aspect of it rather lightly, using quotation marks to make Miriam's response more of a minor subjective matter than a really transfiguring experience; and, except for the addition of the trite phrase about mountains and molehills, he sharpened, colored, and improved the passage in every way:

He remained concentrated in the middle of the road. Beyond, one rift of rich gold in that colourless grey evening made him stand out in dark relief. She saw him, slender and firm, as if the setting sun had given him to her. A deep pain took hold of her and she knew she must love him. And she had discovered him, discovered in him a rare potentiality, discovered his loneliness. Quivering as at some 'annunciation', she went slowly forward. . . .

'It's only an old umbrella, isn't it?' she asked.

She wondered why he, who did not usually trouble over trifles, made such a mountain of this molehill.

'But it was William's, an' my mother can't help but know,' he said quietly, still patiently working at the umbrella. The words went through Miriam like a blade. This, then, was the confirmation of her vision of him! She looked at him. But there was about him a certain reserve, and she dared not comfort him, not even to speak softly to him.

'Come on,' he said. 'I can't do it'; and they went in silence along the road.

Here the drama concentrates on Miriam, who has been drifting along, in a kind of *rapport* with the scenery in the late-afternoon glow; but with the appearance of Paul in the roadway, the reader is brought up sharply and taken immediately inside Miriam's consciousness. When at last the characters speak, the phrase from the earlier version about the gratefulness of Paul's tone is now neatly reduced to an adverb. Lawrence adds a few effective bits of circumstantial detail, including some conversation; then the emotional importance of the umbrella is intensified when it is described as *injured*. Not only has Miriam's brother done the damage, but Miriam feels shame because of this. And Paul's concern over what his mother will think gives Miriam a realization of irony that further increases the range of the entire experience.

It is not often in literary history that we have so full a factual background in relation to a novel. Here are Jessie's early and later comments on *Sons and Lovers,* along with a discussion of Lawrence's early work on the book as well as of his final text of 1912–1913. The reader directly enters into the situation in a way that enables him to see the story at various angles and at various stages of its development. Lawrence once said that the first half of *Sons and Lovers* reflected the truth about his early life, though in her memoir Jessie maintains that his picture of those times is substantially false. In any event, we have the excitement of seeing a novel in the process of growth, with the projected attitudes of two of the three principal characters. But we must always remember that, however closely Lawrence followed 'reality', so often a subjective matter, he was writing an imaginative work.

Another episode that appears in what have been called the 'Miriam Papers', a very brief episode, further shows the difference between the two versions of *Sons and Lovers.* In the earlier draft that Jessie corrected, the following paragraph—again, probably written

from her notes—occurs in a description of the young people's visit
to Wingfield Manor, in Derbyshire, on an Easter Monday (still 1903,
most likely):

> There was one very tall tower, out of which they believed Mary
> of Scots to have looked for help, when she was prisoner at
> Wingfield. Miriam would climb the massive stone steps of the
> ruin, as the Queen had done. She was first, Paul next. A high
> wind blowing through the loopholes filled the girl's skirts like a
> balloon, so that she was ashamed, until Paul laid hold of the
> hem of her dress, and held it down for her, chatting naturally all
> the time.

Jessie scratched out the last phrase and wrote after it: 'There was no
need to chat. It was an act of the purest intimacy. Do not degrade it.'
In his final revision, Lawrence expanded the passage somewhat,
removing awkward constructions (such as 'believed Mary of Scots to
have looked'), and livening it with a bit of dialogue in which Paul and
Miriam discuss the Queen. Then:

> They continued to mount the winding staircase. A high wind,
> blowing through the loopholes, went rushing up the shaft, and
> filled the girl's skirts like a balloon, so that she was ashamed,
> until he took the hem of her dress and held it down for her. He
> did it perfectly simply, as he would have picked up her glove.
> She remembered this always.

Jessie's *D. H. Lawrence: A Personal Record* (by 'E.T.') accused
Lawrence of having a bias (he 'handed his mother the laurels of victory'); Jessie's own bias is obvious. Lawrence was the great event of
her life: she was obsessed with him and wrote of him obsessively. Yet
Jessie was merely a part of Lawrence's life: an important part of his
early development, as he often acknowledged, but by the time of the
final writing of *Sons and Lovers* he was already growing beyond her,
as he was growing beyond the influence of his mother. In that novel,
however closely he was reflecting life, he was after all writing imaginatively, and he had no obligation to be literal. Yet he wrote with self-
critical candor and without self-pity: no matter how much he may have
illuminated his material by imaginative additions, his book ultimately
gives the effect of essential truth. Jessie's *Personal Record* is a disclo-
sure of frustration and resentment. To say this is not to deny that Law-

rence and the situation in which the girl at last found herself were both frequently cruel, or to deny the intensity of Jessie's suffering.

5 STRIFE AND SCHOLARSHIP

In 1902, after twelve years at the Walker Street house, the Lawrence family moved. They didn't go far—actually the new place was only around the corner—taking a house amid the brick regularity of Lynn Croft (sometimes Lynncroft), which ran uphill past the eastern end of Walker Street to the Hill Top district.

George Neville wrote in 1931: 'The "Little Woman" had never appeared quite comfortable in the Walker Street house after the death of "Ern", and a move was next made to the Lynn Croft house, chiefly owing to the influence of "Franky" and "Grit" of the "Pagans", whose father owned the property.'

The Pagans was a name adopted by a group of Lawrence's friends; Franky and Grit were Frances and Gertrude Cooper, who lived next door at Lynn Croft, in the house that was to serve Lawrence as a model for Aaron's residence in *Aaron's Rod*. Indeed, the girls' father, Thomas Cooper, was to be used for at least the outward aspects of Aaron in that novel. Like Aaron, Tom Cooper was a sensitive musician, a flutist and piccolo player; and like Aaron he was a checkweighman, that is, a man employed by the miners (later under government requirement) to oversee the masters' weighing. Thomas Cooper had taken up this kind of work because it paid him more than he had earned teaching at the National School. Lawrence, when he first moved to what now is 97 Lynn Croft, would at night hear Tom Cooper's flute piping away next door; twenty years later, Lawrence had Aaron Sisson take his flute and leave that plain little house for a life of adventurous wanderings such as Tom Cooper would never know.

Jessie Chambers recalled that when she first visited the Lynn Croft house, Lawrence took her around it 'with quiet pride'. She and Lawrence at this time read and studied together constantly. She used to walk into Eastwood one evening a week, to the library of the Mechanics' Institute, one of the town's little pockets of culture, open only on Thursday evenings, for two hours; Jessie and Lawrence invariably went there together, and he would select the books for each of their families to read during the following week.

Jessie would usually stop for Lawrence, though his home in Lynn

Croft was at the opposite end of Eastwood from the library. In one of the surviving narrative sections she prepared for his use years later, when he was working on *Sons and Lovers,* Jessie wrote: 'She announced to Paul one evening that she would call for him no more: if he wished to go with her to the library, he could meet her somewhere. To this Paul would not agree, so the Thursday evenings at the library were dropped.'

Lawrence drew this into his novel, taking it over from Jessie's notes, but making it sharper and crueler with terse dialogue; and the brief introduction of his mother at the end of his version of the episode adds further to its dramatic force.

Some readers unfamiliar with the richness, complexity, and variety of Lawrence's work might at this point have the idea that Jessie was a major collaborator in *Sons and Lovers.* For them an additional explanation must be made. Although Lawrence had from the feminine elements in his own nature a remarkable intuitive understanding of women, he would sometimes ask the women he knew to write down what they had felt or possibly would feel in certain situations: in this way various women provided him with some of his 'sources'. His wife, Frieda, said in her volume of memoirs (in 1935) that when *Sons and Lovers* was in its last phases, 'I wrote bits of it when he would ask me: "What do you think my mother felt like then?"' Lawrence's 1912 novel, *The Trespasser,* was based on parts of a manuscript of his friend Helen Corke, who subsequently expanded her material into the novel *Neutral Ground* (1933). In later life Lawrence attempted to collaborate on novels with Mabel Dodge Luhan and Catherine Carswell, and he rewrote the novel of a third woman, M. L. Skinner, which he published under their combined names as *The Boy in the Bush.* Women were always part of his source material, as were his experiences as a boy in the mining country, his later readings in anthropology, and his travels: if a writer used what women said and did as a basis of his knowledge of them, why not also use what they might write?

All this has taken the present story, at one level, years ahead, into a discussion of Lawrence's methods of writing fiction. It was a necessary jump, for at this point Jessie's personal revelations, written in her youth while she was still close to the experience, give us a full and authentic account of her own feelings at the time. If these revelations seem to subtract from Lawrence's originality, one must bear in mind the difference between Jessie's contribution and Lawrence's achievement, abundantly demonstrated in the consideration of the passages quoted: she as a recorder gave him a sequence of remembered facts; he as an imaginative artist dramatically intensified them and made them into literature.

But the main interest in Jessie's contribution to *Sons and Lovers* is here biographical rather than critical. These fragments of her notes in the 'Miriam Papers' give an insight into the situation which nothing else could provide.

One of Jessie's significant protests dealt with Lawrence's account of Miriam's showing Paul a wild-rose bush in the long English twilight— an episode that also appears in the 'Lad-and-Girl Love' chapter of the novel. Lawrence had written:

> He did not wish to kiss her, as she wished, almost for the first time, to be kissed. Passion was sealed in him [originally, *The doors of passion were sealed to him*] with a kind of fervour of soul. His mood was abstract, purely religious. A touch of lips would have been a spiritual agony to him. He could not kiss cool kisses.
>
> So, when Miriam had made it impossible for him to kiss her, she wanted his mouth. She had taken him to his [*God's,* apparently, blotted out] holy of holies, and wanted him there to clasp her body. That was her tragedy: she purified his love too much. For it was pain to him even to touch her, then.

Jessie wrote after this, 'Astonishing misconception. Miriam was sixteen—as pure and fierce in virginity as Paul.' In the next paragraph, in Lawrence's sentence 'Miriam wanted him, even more than he gave: and his mother, all that part of him which belonged to his mother, strained against Miriam', Jessie put a wavering underline of objection as far as the word *gave.* In one of her later notes, Jessie commented on the 'rose-tree' incident: 'At that time no instinct of sex was awake in either. To suggest it in Miriam destroys the purity of the whole incident: it was all spiritual for Miriam as well as for Paul.' And Lawrence heeded this: as the episode develops in *Sons and Lovers,* it contains no erotic suggestions. In a letter to Blanche Jennings, January 28, 1910, Lawrence refers to Jessie Chambers: 'We have fine, mad little scenes now and again, she and I—so strange, after ten years, and I had hardly kissed her all that time.' In Lawrence's later view, Jessie Chambers seems an almost classical case of frigidity.

Jessie in her book gave no hint of an eventual seduction, such as the one that occurs in *Sons and Lovers,* but after Lawrence's death she wrote to Émile Delavenay (in 1933) about the Whitsuntide holidays of 1910, when Lawrence apparently was in Eastwood: 'I could not conceal from myself a forced note in L's attitude, as if he was pushed forwards in his sensual desire—and a lack of spontaneity. The times of our coming together, under conditions both difficult and irksome, and with Lawrence's earnest injunction to me not to try to hold him, would not exhaust the fingers of one hand.' Lawrence's attitude towards these experiences is expressed in the *Sons and Lovers* chapter appropriately titled 'The Test on Miriam', and in several poems, including 'Coldness in Love', which contains such lines as, 'Is it with pain, my dear, that you shudder so?' In another poem, 'Scent of Irises', Lawrence wrote, 'You upon the dry, dead beech-leaves, once more, only once / Taken like a sacrifice in the night invisible.' Jessie told Dr. Delavenay that it was upon the 'flimsy foundation' of those early sexual encounters that Lawrence built 'the relation with Miriam; and on this slight and inadequate experience he judged and condemned me, without stopping to inquire whether his own attitude was beyond reproach.'

It was on page 220 of Lawrence's early manuscript that Jessie made one of her profoundest comments on the relationship. From behind the mask of 'Miriam', in sentences meant for Lawrence's eyes only, she spoke with far greater candor than she did in the book about him she published under disguising initials after his death. Of course, that book was written long after the events, perhaps nearly thirty years after. The note that follows was written only eight or nine years later than the incidents it refers to; and it was written at a time when Jessie Chambers must have at last realized that she would never be able to hold the volatile young man whom she had loved for so long. This increases the poignancy of what she scratched across the lovers' discussion, in the manuscript, about the reciprocity of love:

> You see, at that time the balance of strength was on the side of Miriam, so that she had great reserve strength. At this time her love for Paul had not grown beyond herself—not beyond her control. It was not until it became invested with holiness like religion and had behind it the whole force of the 'will to live' that the denial of it was terrible to her.

*

In the autumn of 1902 Lawrence began his career as a schoolmaster. The British School at Eastwood had a vacancy for a pupil-teacher, and the Reverend Robert Reid recommended him for the post after consulting with Lawrence's mother. The British School was on Albert Street, in the building where penny readings and concerts were held, adjoining the Congregational chapel.

The pupil-teacher system, which had been in operation since 1846, provided stipends for apprenticed pupil-teachers who acted as instructors in the lower forms and received tutoring themselves from the head of the school. Lawrence, during his time as a pupil-teacher, particularly at Ilkeston, Derbyshire, had to control a large class that met with other classes in the clamor of a huge room, with much battling among the groups. Lawrence long afterwards spoke of his 'three years' savage teaching of collier lads', but this was a slip of memory, as if he unconsciously wanted to minimize the ordeal. Actually, at both Eastwood and Ilkeston, he spent four school years at this 'savage teaching', from the autumn of 1902 to the summer of 1906.

William Hopkin, who first came to know Lawrence well during this period, said that the head of the British School who instructed Lawrence in that first year, George Holderness, was 'just an ordinary schoolmaster'. Lawrence was unhappy as a collier's son teaching colliers' sons. It was a mistake, Hopkin thought, for Lawrence to teach in Eastwood, where he couldn't win the respect of his students' parents. His salary when he started was five pounds annually; this was to be tripled within three years.

The Education Act of 1902 brought a change in that it centralized teacher training: Lawrence and other apprentices in the Eastwood region, including Jessie Chambers, in the fall of 1903 were drafted to the Pupil-Teacher Centre at Ilkeston. The young people usually went three days a week to this municipal borough about three miles from Eastwood, just across the Erewash Canal in Derbyshire. They took the train in the morning and often walked back across the fields in the late afternoon. George Neville, who had been teaching in the Greasley Gilt School, joined this group, which was the one known as the Pagans.

Lawrence and his friends at Ilkeston in 1903 received their training at the Wilmot Street Schoolroom. This was in a Methodist chapel just off Bath Street, the steep main thoroughfare that goes uphill from the railway station to the wide marketplace.

Jessie Chambers spoke of Lawrence's years at Ilkeston, 1903 to 1905, as 'very happy' ones, but George Neville recalled that they were not; Lawrence was merely going through the paces then. His own subsequent statements on the subject don't indicate happiness, particularly his projection of that phase of his life in *The Rainbow,* in which he gave Ursula Brangwen many of his own experiences and reactions. Now it is true that Lawrence based the character of Ursula partly upon a girl he knew at Ilkeston, Louisa Burrows, and that he gave many of her adventures to Ursula; but essentially the Ilkeston chapters of that novel reflect his own vision of the place, of the time, and of the events that took place there.

Although in *The Rainbow* Lawrence described Ilkeston as 'a black, extensive mount', and the school as 'grimy', the most unpleasant object of all may have been the headmaster, Thomas A. Beacroft. In a letter that appeared in the scholastic magazine *Teacher,* March 25, 1905, Lawrence said that at Ilkeston Centre he 'received the greatest assistance from the Principal, Mr. T. A. Beacroft.' Yet ten years later Lawrence caricatured him in *The Rainbow* as Mr. Harby, bully and tyrant. Jessie Chambers, determined to take an optimistic view of Lawrence's Ilkeston years, said that he and Beacroft 'got on extremely well together', but the evidence of *The Rainbow* is against this, as is the testimony of George Neville, who said that the teachers at Ilkeston all disliked Beacroft, who was 'not a *nice* character at all'. Lawrence, Neville said, 'was not happy with him'.

He was happier among the Pagans, as they all traveled together, back and forth, between Eastwood and Ilkeston. Besides Lawrence and Ada, Richard Pogmore, and the lively Neville (whom Ernest Lawrence had nicknamed Teufel and whom D. H. Lawrence called Diddler), and Jessie Chambers and occasionally her brother Alan, the group included the Cooper girls from Lynn Croft, Alice Hall (the Beatrice Wyld of *Sons and Lovers*), and Edith (Kitty) Holderness, daughter of Lawrence's former supervisor at the Eastwood British School. Eventually another girl became a member of the Pagans, one who was some years later to stand for a while between Lawrence and Jessie Chambers. This was the Louisa (Louie) Burrows previously mentioned, who lived at Cossall, a village just outside Ilkeston, and who later (1940) became Mrs. Frederick Heath.

Louisa Burrows, already indicated as one of the prototypes of Ursula in *The Rainbow,* was to be the subject of some of Lawrence's most intense love poems, such as the flagrantly phallic 'Snap-Dragon'. She was two and a half years younger than Lawrence, having been born in Ilkeston on February 13, 1888. By 1895 her father, Alfred Burrows, had formed a village carving-class which produced the oak reredos in St. Catherine's Church at Cossall. Alfred Burrows was the original of

Ursula's father in *The Rainbow,* the dreamy, Ruskinized young man who loves Gothic carvings. He and his family lived next to St. Catherine's, in Church Cottage, the honeymoon house in what Lawrence in *The Rainbow* called Cossethay (from another town in the region). Alfred Burrows had married Louisa Wheatley of Cossall, who as late as 1947 erected with him a thanksgiving stained-glass window in the south aisle. A later window, of 1949, is dedicated to the memory of Alfred Burrows.

The farm which in *The Rainbow* is the home of most of the Brangwens was actually Marsh Farm, about half a mile east of Ilkeston and not quite that far north of Cossall. In Lawrence's time it was tenanted by the Fritchleys, a family that had held it for two centuries; Lawrence and Louie Burrows used to visit the old stone farm, which later became derelict save for a few sheds used by an Ilkeston butcher. It has at last been demolished and replaced by a bungalow.

At the Burrows's home, where Louie's parents gave Lawrence scant welcome, he became acquainted with a quite different kind of family from his own or Jessie's. His emotional relationship with Louie didn't bloom, however, until some years later, after he had left the Pupil-Teacher Centre. In the period from 1903 to 1905, it was Jessie who primarily claimed his personal attention, along with her brother Alan. The matter may be summed up in three sentences quoted from different paragraphs of the 'Lad-and-Girl Love' chapter of *Sons and Lovers:* 'Personally, he was a long time before he realized her . . . Edgar was his very close friend . . . But the girl gradually sought him out.'

Lawrence's friend and enemy of later life, John Middleton Murry, in pointing out the similarity between Edgar in *Sons and Lovers* and the young farmer George Saxton in *The White Peacock,* said (in *Son of Woman,* 1932), discussing Lawrence's youth, that 'for the original of George and Edgar he must have felt something for which the best name is the simple one of love.'

Such an emotion at the time of adolescence is neither infrequent nor 'unnatural', as the world learned somewhere between Freud and Kinsey. Murry discussed one scene in particular from *The White Peacock* (Lawrence's first novel), the one in which the young men bathe together in the pond, in the chapter called 'A Poem of Friendship'. The incident occurred at harvest time, and Murry identified this with the 'hay-harvest which Paul and Edgar worked through together in *Sons and Lovers*'. Murry, trying to elaborate a highly debatable theory to the effect that Lawrence was a pitiable victim of the Oedipus complex, commented that 'what genuine and unhesitating passion there was in Lawrence's life before his mother's death went to a man, not a woman.' The entire working out of Lawrence's early love affairs, if not with Louie Burrows at least with Jessie Chambers and with Alice Dax, the married woman in Eastwood who introduced Lawrence to physical love, disproves Murry's contention. It is true, however, that Lawrence's strong bond with his mother made it difficult at that time for him to create a permanent relationship with a woman; and it is true that Lawrence's friendship with Jessie's brother Alan was a profound one.

Compton Mackenzie claims, in his autobiography, *My Life and Times*—'Octave 5', 1966—that Lawrence told him, 'I believe that the nearest I've ever come to perfect love was with a young coal-miner when I was about sixteen.' If this is precisely what he said, he could hardly have been referring to Alan Chambers, a farm boy, though Chambers may have gone into the pits later. Lawrence spoke of Alan Chambers in a letter to Blanche Jennings, to whom he wrote some highly important confessional letters from 1908 to 1910. On July 30, 1908, he confided to her:

> You tell me I have no male friends. The man I have been working with in the hay is the original of my George [in *The White Peacock,* then titled *Laetitia*],—lacking, alas, the other's subtlety of sympathetic discrimination which lent him his nobility. But I am very fond of my friend, and he of me. Sometimes, often, he is gentle as a woman towards me. It seems my men friends are all alike; they make themselves, on the whole, soft-mannered towards me; they defer to me also. You are right, I value the friendship of men more than that of women. . . . But better a woman vibrating with incoherent hum than a man altogether dumb, eh? So to make a Jonathan for me, it would take the natures of ten men such as I know to complete the keyboard.

Lawrence went on to say that 'most people marry with their souls vibrating to the note of sexual love—and the sex notes may run into beautiful aesthetics, poetry and pictures and romance.' But conditions were 'much finer', Lawrence thought, 'when not only the sex group of chords is attuned, but the great harmonies, and the little harmonies, of what we will call religious feeling (read it widely) and ordinary sympathetic feeling.' He went on to relate these utterances to the love-and-marriage themes of *The White Peacock*. He then spoke of mowing hay with 'three men, whom I really love, in varying degrees', perhaps two of the Chambers boys as well as Edmund Chambers, their father. He described the scene at the Greasley field, with the Reverend Rudolf von Hube's vicarage nearby, where one night when Lawrence and the Chambers boys were sleeping out under a haystack, a tramp appeared—'It's all right, young 'un, I'm only luikin' for a rough 'un, like your sen'—foreshadowing Lawrence's story 'Love Among the Haystacks'. Indeed, the entire description of the experience in the Greasley fields presages various scenes in *The White Peacock,* notably in the chapters 'A Poem of Friendship' and 'The Education of George'. In the latter, Cyril speaks of working in the fields with George: 'Day after day I told him what the professors had told me; of life, of sex and its origins; of Schopenhauer and William James.'

As mentioned earlier, Lawrence's friendship with Alan Chambers also appears in *Sons and Lovers,* where Alan is given the name Edgar. In that novel, Paul in the early stages of his relationship with Miriam 'often avoided her and went with Edgar'. She and Edgar 'were naturally antagonistic. Edgar was a rationalist, who was curious, and had a sort of scientific interest in life.' Miriam was embittered 'to see herself deserted by Paul for Edgar, who seemed so much lower'. Yet Paul and Edgar were happy in one another's company. 'The two men spent afternoons together on the land or in the loft doing carpentry, when it rained. And they talked together, or Paul taught Edgar the songs he himself had learned from Annie at the piano.'

In the fragment of one of the earlier versions of *Sons and Lovers* quoted from previously, Edgar is mentioned as liking 'his friend's wholesale, impetuous manner'. The following passage also appears there, though not in the published version of the novel:

Another day, Paul was drawing some pine trees at evening, and Edgar leaned over his shoulder in a protective, affectionate manner. Suddenly Miriam came out. All three were silent, until Paul declared, after screwing up his eyes and staring at the trees:
'A pine-trunk's not a tree-trunk, it's a bit of fire.'
'How do you make that out?' asked Edgar, amused.
'Look at the trunk—is it red?'
'Rather,' replied the young farmer.
'Does it burn—does it seem to burn?'
'No-o.'
'What an awful liar you are! I can feel it burning just as the sun

burns. Now speak the truth—just let yourself speak the truth for once—does it seem to burn?'

'Well—' the doubt, and a shade of fear, crept into Edgar's voice—'it might—you might think it did.'

'There you are,' cried Paul. 'And what 'ud make you think it did, if it didn't!'

The young farmer laughed uncomfortably, stuck his hands in his pockets, in front of his belt, and went away to work.

Jessie, in looking this over, drew a wavy line under Paul's statement calling Edgar 'an awful liar'; she wrote, 'Paul was fifteen—Edgar nineteen!' With two young men on terms of such intimacy, however, this accusation, obviously playful, wouldn't have been out of place even in that historical epoch of 'respect for one's elders'.

These friendship passages between the Lawrence hero and another male, not only in earlier but also in some of the later novels, have caused a raising of eyebrows but, despite all innuendoes, Lawrence doesn't seem to have been a homosexual; at least not a complete or continually practicing one. Frieda Lawrence used to insist that her husband was not in any way a homosexual, but towards the end of her life she changed her tune somewhat; as she wrote in 1949 to Edward Gilbert, who was studying Lawrence, 'Murry and he had no "love affair". But he did not disbelieve in homosexuality.' Not long afterwards, Frieda wrote to Murry that she was sure Lawrence had had no homosexual feeling for him, that Lawrence's homosexuality had lasted only a brief time (apparently in the World War I days of the Cornish farmer), and that she had fought with him over it, and had won.

Certainly no one spoke out on sexual matters more boldly and clearly than Lawrence, and there is no passage in his works in which he writes approvingly of *sexual* relations, that is, of sexual gratification, between men. Indeed, he writes disapprovingly of such things, though in the unused 'Prologue' to *Women in Love* (now available in *Phoenix II*), Birkin's inclinations seem definitely homosexual. Yet how much of this actually reflects Lawrence himself is problematic. (In the film made from the novel, the director erred in giving Birkin a beard, like the author's, which Lawrence hadn't done. Birkin may have been somewhat of a spokesman for the author, but he was not the author himself.) Lawrence told Henry Savage in 1914 that, even if one can get satisfaction with a man, physically it is only with a woman that one can find satisfaction of both body and soul: 'And one is kept by all tradition and instinct from loving men, or a man—for it means just extinction of all the purposive influence.'

This may seem contradictory because of passages in Lawrence's fiction such as the bathing scene in *The White Peacock* and the wrestling scene in *Women in Love*. Perhaps the matter is best explained in Catherine Carswell's *The Savage Pilgrimage,* in which she reports, 'I have heard Lawrence say that sexual perversion was for him "the sin against the Holy Ghost", the hopeless sin. But he cherished the deep longing to see revived a communion between man and man that should not lack its physical symbols. He even held that our modern denial of this communion in all but idea was the cause of our modern perversions.' He believed further that the recovery of 'true potency' and the restoration of 'health and happiness between man and woman' depended upon 'a renewal of the sacredness between man and man'.

This is imbued with the mysticism of the later Lawrence, which is difficult to simplify and bring into everyday terms. The truest understanding of it is not a matter of rational interpretation, but rather of a merging into the full reading experience Lawrence provides—towards which a book such as the present one can only point. The subject now under discussion is important, however, in any consideration of Lawrence, who was not merely writing novels and stories and poems; he was often, through them, recommending a way of life; and to understand what he was recommending is part of the necessary evaluation of his works. Émile Delavenay, in *D. H. Lawrence and Edward Carpenter: A Study in Edwardian Transition* (1971), suggests that Lawrence may have been influenced by Carpenter, who lived not too far from Eastwood, and notes that 'the intellectual and moral environment of Carpenter was for Lawrence synonymous with the circle of William E. and Sallie Hopkin and of Alice Dax', though there is no record of Lawrence's having ever met the author of *The Intermediate Sex*. Professor Delavenay points out that Jessie Chambers said in 1935 that Lawrence had undoubtedly read Mrs. Dax's 'advanced' books, a number of which were by Carpenter, who among other things was an advocate of women's rights. William Hopkin spoke to this writer (in 1950) of his friendship with Carpenter. Hopkin's daughter mentioned in a letter that Carpenter was one of the celebrated guests who used to visit the Hopkins in Eastwood. But neither she nor her father suggested that Lawrence ever met Carpenter at their house. Nevertheless, Delavenay's hypothesis as to Lawrence's possibly having read the books of the outstanding and extremely bold advocate of homoeroticism is convincingly backed by numerous somewhat parallel ideas expressed in the writings of the two men.

As previously suggested, the physical contact in the 'friendship scenes' in Lawrence's novels didn't necessarily mean a sexual contact. To Lawrence, touch was important: he was a man always quiveringly sensitive, with projecting nerves, who entered into the understanding of things by touching them, as shown, for example, in such stories as 'The Blind Man' and 'You Touched Me'. Consider Birkin in *Women in Love*. After his mistress has nearly murdered him—he escapes with a blow on the head—he goes out to a wooded hill and strips himself naked, lying on the earth amid flowers and thorns and the roots of trees: 'It was such a fine, cool, subtle touch all over him, he seemed to saturate himself with their contact.' Now most people might not want to have so tangible a communion with nature (though the popular sport of swimming is for many an equivalent of this); but because Lawrence wanted such a communion, he could express nature all the more palpably in his writings, through which it projects with such vital realness. His vision is not more keen and sharp than his tactile sense: and in the most primary meaning of the word, his writings *touch* the reader.

Lawrence dealt with another aspect of the subject of homosexuality in a letter to Bertrand Russell in 1915, a letter in which he expressed his repugnance to sodomy, of course referring to anal copulation between men. The true human relationship, Lawrence said, is one of discovery; regrettably, most modern men don't seek a woman in order to challenge the unknown and thus enter into a new creative relationship, but rather they want to repeat with her an already known sensation, a familiar reaction. This leads towards sodomy in the modern world: 'The man goes to the man to repeat this reaction upon himself. It is a near form of masterbation [*sic*]. But it still has some *object*— there are still two bodies instead of one. A man of strong soul has too much honour for the other body—man or woman—to use it as a means of masterbation. So he remains neutral, inactive. . . . Sodomy only means a man knows he is chained to the rock, so he will try to get the finest possible sensation out of himself.' Lawrence went on to say that this condition occurs 'whenever the form of any living becomes too strong for the life within it: the clothes are more important than the man: therefore the man must get his satisfaction beneath the clothes.'

Beyond moral considerations, still another part of the problem remains for discussion: what might be called its psychological aspect. The clinical view of Lawrence as a lifelong victim of the Oedipus complex, with all conventional outcroppings of that affliction, including homosexuality, is easily dismissed.

Murry, in his autobiography (*Between Two Worlds,* published five years after *Son of Woman*), explained that he was not at all trying to attribute to Lawrence 'what is generally understood by the word homosexuality'. As to the so-called Oedipus complex, the idea of its persisting with Lawrence has been convincingly repudiated by a man whose perspective was not joggled because he knew Lawrence. This critic is the Anglican priest Father Martin Jarrett-Kerr, who under the pseudonym of Father William Tiverton wrote one of the most penetrating books on Lawrence (*D. H. Lawrence and Human Existence* [1951]), in which he pointed out that 'writers on Lawrence have . . . much exaggerated his Oedipus complex'. For, after he had shaken off his mother attachment by writing *Sons and Lovers,* he grew 'into a separate existence which cannot be interpreted in terms of Mrs Lawrence'. If the attachment had survived, it would have appeared obsessionally in the later works, but they only occasionally contain a faint echo of such a relationship, as in the artificial and superficial late-period story 'The Lovely Lady'. (Richard Aldington, who disagreed with such findings as those of Father Jarrett-Kerr, stated in a letter of March 16, 1960, 'I should say D.H.L. was about 85 per cent hetero and 15 per cent homo.')

Psychologically, however, there is still another way of looking at the problem under discussion: in Lawrence's celebrations of maleness, he may have been the frail boy ('mardarse') forever seeking a wish fulfillment of strength. This was not compensation-by-identification—that is, Lawrence writing as from the point of view of physical gianthood, and by a process of introjection 'becoming' the admired strongman—no, rather Lawrence could, in this hypothesis, keep his identity intact and yet mingle as it were with the strong, taking strength from them. As Cipriano, the brilliant, small-statured general in *The Plumed Serpent,* Lawrence could dream himself into an ideal leadership-friendship with the physically powerful Don Ramón, the ritual of whose new religion included a physical—again, *not* sexual—contact between men. Also, in the wrestling scene in *Women in Love,* the spare and wiry Rupert Birkin astonishes Gerald Crich with his use of jujitsu and his general quickness and agility. Now all this is only a suggested possibility: the suggestion does not carry with it any idea

that the process was at all conscious, or was even of the type of unconscious activity motivated by a dominant obsession.

*

This discussion has seemed to swing away from Eastwood; yet it has
actually attempted to deepen the view of that setting, for it has shown
what might have grown, or might not have grown, out of Lawrence's
early background. And the most important conclusion is that most
trails to Eastwood lead to Jessie Chambers and to a married woman
with whom Lawrence had his first genuine love affair.

Lawrence shared a strong friendship with Jessie's brother, and he
eventually got on with Jessie's older sister May, as noted by her
youngest brother, J. D. Chambers: 'She knew everybody and everybody knew her', and although 'she held herself aloof from D. H.
Lawrence and his circle', he nevertheless, after she had married and
moved away, brought to her house the married German woman with
whom he was soon to elope. Professor Chambers admired May for
her 'flaming vitality' and because she was 'fearless, gay, and tempestuous', though tender to those she loved; in their early youth, she
thought that Jessie was 'sentimental and melodramatic'.

May Chambers remembered how full of knowledge, and how instructive, young Bert Lawrence was. When he was with some young
people walking through a woodland, he asked them, 'Do you know
why the earliest spring flowers are mostly yellow?' They didn't know,
so 'he explained it was because of the scarcity of insects and therefore
the need of bright colours to attract.' The young people liked his informality in such matters, and 'the bits of information Bert let fall
because there was the spice he imparted of its being a discovery.'
May's mother, however, didn't want Lawrence talking about the
Rubáiyát of Omar Khayyám in the presence of her younger children:
'I won't have their faith destroyed. You grieve me by reading such
things, but you shan't take away the children's faith.'

J. D. Chambers recalled an event that occurred after May had become engaged to a stonemason, William Holbrook: 'He was, in his
way, almost as entertaining as Lawrence himself, and I think Lawrence may have felt some jealousy that he should have to share our
affections and admiration with this untutored workman.' When Holbrook produced a pair of effigies in stone for May, the Chambers
family put them up on each side of their garden gate. They infuriated
Lawrence, who said they were 'hideous', and on one visit he smashed

them both with a large hammer. 'They lay in ruins, and we silently swept up the pieces and resolved not to have the two young men together at the house at the same time.'

Lawrence's friendship with Alan Chambers evidently didn't last, though what was between Lawrence and Jessie endured for a long time. He grew beyond her, detached himself from most of the remnants of their relationship; she was able to accomplish such a breakaway only to a limited extent. And it must be stated in Jessie's behalf that she thought she had a legitimate grievance over *Sons and Lovers*. She felt that it represented only a biased version of the story rather than what she felt was the everyday truth of the history of that painful love affair.

Indeed, commentators looking for clues to the truth of that relationship have to tread warily between the jagged edges of the conflicting assertions. Jessie in her memoir included only the parts of Lawrence's letters that fitted in with her thesis that he had mistreated her; the rest of his correspondence she wastefully and wantonly destroyed before her death. According to a letter (January 6, 1951) from John R. Wood, whom she had married in 1915, 'My late wife destroyed (burnt) the correspondence.' The commentators in quest of the truth are entitled to censure Jessie Chambers not only for destroying significant literary documents, but also for placing herself under suspicion by putting such important evidence, which may not have been favorable to her side, forever out of reach; and how terribly her action makes memories of the Aspern Papers burn at the back of one's brain.

But that was the deed of an embittered older woman. Jessie had by then passed far beyond the hopeful girl who would, in her upstairs bedroom above the stable, wait on summer afternoons to hear the click of the chain at the gate when Lawrence arrived, wheeling his bicycle into the farmyard. As she recalled the whole experience later, one of her brightest pictures of him was at Ilkeston, when she saw him one day studying at a table. She noticed at once his 'difference', his fine features, his intensity, his vitality, his sensitiveness, and a special 'quality of lightness about him, something that seemed to shine from within. He and I were beginning to be aware of this difference, and it made a common ground between us. We didn't speak of it, but it was there, a point of attraction.'

At the moment Jessie had this 'revelation', Lawrence was studying for one of the important examinations he took at Ilkeston. There were two of these, the King's Scholarship and the London Matriculation. The headmaster whom he disliked, T. A. Beacroft, coached him for them (whatever Beacroft's faults, he knew how to pick a winner). And Lawrence felt he had assured himself of a good academic future when, in the King's Scholarship examination of December 1904, he came out first in all England and Wales. After that he was, as he later recalled, 'considered clever'.

There has been some contention over the placing of Lawrence in the lists of winners in the King's Scholarship examination. The *Teacher* of March 25, 1905, mentioned him as merely among a group of winners. And, in a subsequent letter (discovered by Émile Delavenay) to the *Teacher,* Lawrence found no fault with the listing. But the records at Ilkeston note him as first in the kingdom, 'bracketed as top boy in the country'. There is further evidence, supplied by Lawrence himself. The American publisher Mitchell Kennerley brought out Lawrence's play *The Widowing of Mrs Holroyd* in 1914, prefaced by the Swedish-American writer Edwin Björkman, who presented a biographical sketch of the author adapted from a draft Lawrence had sent to him. Lawrence mentioned this to Kennerley (October 5, 1913), saying, 'Of course I take unto myself all the beautiful and laudatory things he says about me in the preface: they seem to me very just.' Björkman had written, 'At nineteen he found himself, to his own, and everybody else's astonishment, first on the list of the King's Scholarship examination, and from that time on he was, to use his own words, "considered clever." ' Certainly if Björkman had paraphrased him wrongly, Lawrence, who didn't seek unearned honors, would have mentioned any misinformation. As to the relevance of this particular point, it was cavalierly dismissed in a letter to the *Times Literary Supplement* in 1971: What did it matter whether he was first or not? But the point is that Lawrence's astoundingly good showing in the examination would have naturally affected his relations with those about him, particularly if they cast him into the position of being 'considered clever': his basic attitude to life and his relationship to others would have been somewhat altered, and this would also make his writings somewhat different than they might have been otherwise.

Before taking the matriculation examination for training college, Lawrence still had six months of his apprenticeship to finish. By this time the Pupil-Teacher Centre had moved uphill to new quarters above the library in the marketplace at the top of Bath Street. T. A.

Beacroft moved along with the institution, and again he coached the prize student.

In June 1905 Lawrence sat for the London Matriculation examination in Nottingham. George Lawrence has recalled that his mother also went over there at this time. Whether this made Bert Lawrence nervous or whether he suffered from the fatigues of the end of another school year of study and teaching, he didn't distinguish himself as he had in the previous examination. He was bracketed in the second division.

He was eligible, however, for admission to the University College of Nottingham; but he couldn't use his scholarship grant because he lacked the twenty pounds for the advance fees.

Again his mother set her teeth: her son must have his chance. He would wait a year, go on teaching and save his money, and the family would make further sacrifices. As Jessie Chambers recalled, 'For the next year Lawrence taught as an uncertificated teacher in the British School in Eastwood, saving most of his earnings towards his college expenses. It was during this year that he began the writing of what eventually became *The White Peacock*.'

6 THE ANTIQUITY OF A LANDSCAPE

Lawrence had tried drawing and painting before he took up writing. He started by copying illustrations from magazines. He apparently had a few lessons from a relative of Lord Leighton's, George Leighton Parkinson, creator of ornamental pottery at a Langley Mill factory. Lawrence later said he had been 'thoroughly drilled in "drawing", the solid-geometry sort, and the plaster-cast sort, and the pin-wire sort'. He felt that only the geometrical, 'with all the elementary laws of perspective', helped him; the other methods were harmful.

He didn't seriously begin painting until the last years of his life, though he had always daubed away in spare moments: today, in places where Lawrence stayed in England, America, and Italy, people show mild little water colors and say, 'Here's something Lawrence did while he was here.'

In his youth, he didn't find painting from nature 'very thrilling': then nature had a plaster-cast look to him. He concentrated on copying reproductions, quiet landscapes by Camille Corot, Frank Brangwyn, and Maurice Greiffenhagen. He was particularly fond of Greiffenhagen's *Idyll,* which he copied several times. In such paintings, he added nothing of his own: there is in these replicas no suggestion of the vibrant, pulsing landscapes of his later prose and painting. Yet in those early attempts he was training his eye, developing his vision; and his writing of all types has qualities of painting.

Another important early influence on his writing was, of course, literature itself. His study of that subject in school was complemented by the books he read with Jessie Chambers, in the fields near the Haggs or in the little kitchen there, or in the parlor at Walker Street or Lynn Croft when the other members of his family were out. The Lawrences had what they regarded as a literary treasure, a set of large, green volumes of the world's literature which Ernest had bought. And the Chamberses were a family interested in literature, in vocal interpretations of it; as a little girl, before Jessie knew how to make out words on the page, she used to listen to her father on Saturday afternoons reading to her mother the installments of *Tess of the D'Urbervilles* as they appeared in the *Nottinghamshire Guardian*. After Lawrence became a friend of the family, he organized play readings, over which he became 'excited' and 'domineering', though the Chamberses 'knew him too well to take offence'. But Mrs. Chambers worried over Lawrence's outbursts against Congregational ministers: J. D. Chambers recalled that Lawrence had early 'declared in favour of a sceptical materialism and carried my eldest brother [Alan] with him'.

Early in their acquaintanceship, Lawrence brought Jessie *Little Women,* the kind of novel that he would later despise as sentimental. But in those days he saw himself and Jessie as Laurie and Jo. In poetry, he read her *Hiawatha* and *Evangeline,* though she didn't share his enthusiasm for either; and *Launcelot and Elaine,* which she found 'revolting'. Later, Lawrence owned a small red-bound copy of *The Golden Treasury* which he carried in his pocket to read from when they sat together on a hillside.

They read the adventure novels of the day, *The Prisoner of Zenda* and the romances of H. Rider Haggard, and climbed to the higher level of Stevenson and Cooper. The setting of *Lorna Doone* they transplanted from Devonshire to the nearby Annesley hills, which they now saw peopled with Doones, and they rechristened part of the local woodlands Bagworthy Forest. In their early association, Jessie and Lawrence soon agreed that their favorite was Dickens—Lawrence half-humorously seemed to identify himself with David Copperfield—particularly *Bleak House* and *Dombey and Son:* 'And to say that we read the books gives no adequate idea of what really happened,' Jessie wrote. 'It was the entering into possession of a new world, a widening and enlargement of life.'

68   THE NOTTINGHAM YEARS

Certainly it was valuable training for a future novelist to read Shakespeare and the English lyric poets and novelists, especially to read them in that legendary countryside of broken forest where the old England of the agricultural past met the grimmer England of the rising industrial smoke—and in the company of an imaginative girl who could see them as living parts of the surrounding life, making the country of those books the local scene, and their people its inhabitants.

In all this, George Eliot was of special value, for she wrote of Derbyshire. Jane Austen had done so too, in parts of *Pride and Prejudice,* and Charlotte Brontë in scenes of *Jane Eyre;* but they hadn't touched the land and its people so intimately as George Eliot had in locating *Adam Bede* in Wirksworth. Even when not centering her stories in Derbyshire, George Eliot wrote of the kind of people found there, and Lawrence particularly liked *The Mill on the Floss.*

When he was a young man he of course knew that literature, valuable as it might be in the education of a novelist, could be only secondary to what he absorbed directly from life. His personal experiences, both of living and reading, have been rather closely followed here, and a good deal has been said of the life of his village and his region. Now it is time for a further exploration of these last two elements, for at the moment Lawrence became aware that writing was his destiny, he also became aware that his subject matter lay in his village and his region. It was only much later that he visited and wrote of far-off places. In his youth his only conceivable subject was Nottinghamshire.

It was fortunate for Lawrence that at this time he came to know William Hopkin well, for Hopkin was able to tell him much about the region. Actually, it was Hopkin's wife, Sallie, who was Lawrence's particular friend; he often formed close friendships, in his youth, with middle-aged women, as he had with Jessie's mother and with Miss Wright, governess of the Cullen family; and now one began with Mrs. Hopkin. He was frequently at the Hopkins' home on Devonshire Drive, a fairly new street south of the Nottingham Road and parallel to it; Lawrence had the Brangwens settle in this street in *The Rainbow* and continue living there in *Women in Love,* in which Eastwood is called Beldover and the street, Somerset Drive.

Lawrence in 1919 made Hopkin the Willie Houghton of his play, *Touch and Go.* The portrait of this lively agitator is extremely lifelike; Lawrence from long association with Hopkin knew all his thoughts and his twists of speech. (Lawrence sent a copy of the play to Hopkin inscribed, 'Here you are, Willie!') In another book, Lawrence presented still another picture of him, and of Mrs. Hopkin as well. This was in the story he wrote a year or so after the play—the unfinished novel *Mr Noon,* first published as part of the posthumous collection *A Modern Lover,* in 1934. In *Mr Noon* the Hopkins were the Lewis Goddards. Mrs. Goddard 'was a woman of about forty, stoutish, with her glossy brown hair coiled on her head.' Her husband 'was handsome, with a high forehead and a small beard; a socialist; something like Shakespeare's bust to look at, but more refined. . . . He was a pure idealist, something of a Christ, but with an intruding touch of the goat. His eyelids dropped oddly, goat-like.' Again Lawrence had wonderfully caught the man, the mixture of animal and idealist, in a living portrait.

Hopkin was a devoted hiker, who for the last fifty-three years of his life contributed weekly 'Rambling Notes' to the *Eastwood and Kimberley Advertiser.* He and the young Lawrence often went walking together. In 1949 Hopkin recalled, 'It was a delight to go rambling with him. . . . Even as a youth he seemed to see things differently from other folk, and his descriptions were often unusual but illuminating.' If Lawrence could increase Hopkin's awareness of the natural aspects of the landscapes they passed through, Hopkin could reciprocate by deepening Lawrence's understanding of the human history of the region.

Hopkin, born in 1862, had been a socialist from his youth. When he made his first speech in Eastwood marketplace, he was pelted with rotten oranges, but he later served on the Eastwood Urban District Council for forty-five years, became a magistrate and a member of the County Council and later an alderman on the Council, with membership in thirty-six committees in 1951, the year of his death.

This perky little radical, son of the local postmaster, had been a clerk at the post office and at a colliery, then a cobbler, and finally proprietor of a boot shop. He filled Lawrence's ears with local lore, not only stories of the colliers and the farmers, but also historic bits of Eastwood's past, including the famous cave-in story that the eighteenth-century antiquarian Throsby recorded in his revision of Thoroton's earlier *History of Nottinghamshire:*

A remarkable circumstance happened here [Eastwood], about eleven years since, by the sinking of an old coal-mine. A farmer, refreshing himself in a room of a public house, ordered the landlord to fill him a cup of ale; but to the surprise of the host, when he returned, he found the farmer lying on his back, with his arms extended, holding his knife and fork in his hands, and the table overthrown, both jumbled together in a sunken part of the floor, and he expecting every moment to be swallowed up by an Earthquake. At the same time some bays of buildings, in the yard, fell down, in which were some horses; but providentially none of them were hurt.

And there was much else that Hopkin knew, or that Lawrence may have read himself, in Thoroton's *Antiquities* (of 1677); the description, for example, of the terrain just north of Eastwood, the valley that lay below Haggs Farm, to the east of it. There, a fine, many-gabled 'modern' house of brick had been built amid the ruins of the twelfth-century Felley Priory, just half a mile north of that Felley Mill which Lawrence made one of the principal settings (as Strelley Mill) of *The White Peacock*. Thoroton had collected, among his *Antiquities,* the following from Tudor days:

> The House and Site of the Priory and Monastery of the blessed Mary of *Felley,* and all the Messauges, Houses, Orchards, Gardens, Lands, and Tenements, within and without the said Site in *Felley* and Annesley . . . also one Mess, one Barn, one Water-Mill called *Felley* Mill, and two parcels of Meadow, etc., Sept. 1. 30 H. 8 [i.e., September 1, 1540] were granted to *William Bolles,* and *Lucy* his wife.

Felley Mill appears in the opening pages of *The White Peacock,* whose first sentence speaks of the mill pond there. Page 3 describes the farmhouse by the mill, which also appears in *Sons and Lovers* and other stories. And Jessie's farm, the Haggs, and the fields below it that stretch out to Felley Mill—Greasley Haggs—occur in the records of the far past, where the word *Haggs* apparently meant a cutting in a woodland. Also, that wood next to the farm, Willey Spring, and Willey Lane, where Lawrence used to push his bicycle uphill on his way to the Haggs, past Willeywood Farm and the disused quarry that appears in *The White Peacock*—all these Willeys appear in the old records, too, 'Haia de Willeg' in 1212, with variant spellings through the Middle Ages, the original name apparently 'a compound of welig, wilig, and leah, "willow clearing" ' (Gover *et al., The Place-Names of Nottinghamshire* [1940]).

The Willey Hay region was the site of a previously mentioned priory, Beauvale, the last to be established in the county. A reference to it in the sixteenth century is of sufficient importance, nationally, to earn for Beauvale a paragraph or so in most English histories of any size. This little Carthusian priory figures in all accounts of British martyrdom, for in 1535 its prior and former prior were put to death for resisting Henry VIII's breaking up of the monasteries.

The prior at the time of this trouble was named Lawrence, but there is no traceable connection between him and D. H. Lawrence. That D. H. Lawrence as a youth knew that a previous Eastwood man of the same surname was noted for stubbornly independent thought is highly probable. He would not have learned it, however, from a local history by a local clergyman, published in Nottingham in 1901. *Griseleia in Snotingscire,* advertised as 'an Illustrated History from the Earliest Times and from Reliable Sources', mentioned the martyrdom incident and the name of John Houghton, but not that of Robert Lawrence.

We may assume that D. H. Lawrence read this volume 'by Rodolph von Hube, Vicar of Greasley' because he twits it in *The Rainbow,* ascribing its authorship to one of his minor characters. In speaking there of what he calls *The History of the Parish of Briswell,* 'by Rudolph, Baron Skrebensky, Vicar of Briswell', Lawrence characterizes it as 'a curious book, incoherent, full of interesting exhumations'. And that is a fine, brief review of that scramble of history, anecdote, and sycophancy to the vicar's leading parishioners. The book is useful today, however, to students of Lawrence and the Lawrence Country. Its stories of the entire region, and of people who appear as characters in Lawrence's novels, make *Griseleia in Snotingscire*— particularly because of its scarcity—an extremely interesting item for collectors.

Lawrence apparently disliked von Hube, and besides poking fun at him in *The Rainbow,* caricatured him in his play *The Merry-Go-Round* as Baron Rudolph von Ruge, Vicar of Grunstom, where von Hube is dealt with at far greater length than in the novel. Lawrence tried in *The Merry-Go-Round,* and tried without much success, to write a lively little folk comedy; the baron and his wife figure as the terrors of Lovers' Lane, who go out at night and whack the shrubbery with cane and umbrella, to discourage spooning couples.

The actual von Hube claimed to be a Polish patriot whose revolutionary activities had forced him to leave his own country. Lawrence always doubted his stories and his 'I vas a baron in *my* country!'

Hopkin remembered von Hube as 'a rum bloke who wouldn't bury anyone after four in the afternoon'. Once a body arrived late—at half past four—because of slippery roads, and von Hube refused to conduct the burial service until the next day. The men who had brought the coffin took it out of their cart and propped it against the door of the vicarage, saying loudly, 'So we'll leave the old booger 'ere till morning'—at which the baron popped out at once to attend to the burial.

Hopkin remembered another well-known story about von Hube, which he also insisted was true. The vicar, after a dinner with the Barbers at Lamb Close on a foggy night, set off across the fields for Greasley. He had been imbibing and he lost his way, wandering into Moorgreen Reservoir up to his knees. He began to cry out, 'Lost! Lost!' Two passing colliers who heard him said, 'Oh, 'e's not wanted till Sunday,' and walked on. The people at Lamb Close finally responded to the alarm, rescued von Hube, and sent the pony cart to take him home.

Lawrence, living amid all these folk anecdotes and characters, filled his mind with them, unconsciously absorbing material for use in the future. Even local names became important to him; he drew upon many of them for his Nottinghamshire novels and stories, as we have seen, and upon some of them for fiction with settings elsewhere.

Lawrence's familiarity with the Eastwood area, however, wasn't confined to antiquarian lore and close knowledge of the lives of the miners; he also knew the tradesmen of the town. Jessie Chambers recalled that in his youth he was even employed in Eastwood, that he once made out bills for a pork butcher. This was Charles Barker, whose shop was on the Nottingham Road.

All these are particulars, small facts subsidiary to the main fact of Lawrence's achievement. Different circumstances, in a different *locale,* would have changed at least the surface.of what he wrote, might even have made him different as a human being and hence as a writer. Such matters are for guesswork: perhaps Eastwood was the best crucible of all for the maturing of the vision that was exactly his.

Jessie remembered the night he came to tell her what he would do: 'It will be *poetry.*' When he said that people would think it silly for a collier's son to want to write poems, Jessie reassured him: 'What does your father's occupation matter?' Another time, Lawrence told her there could never be a new Shakespeare; he was the product of an age that was integrated: 'Things are split up now.' Lawrence had arrived independently at the concept that T. S. Eliot was later to call 'dissociation of sensibility'. On another occasion Lawrence showed Jessie that he appreciated her encouragement; he earnestly told her, 'Every great man—every man who achieves anything, I mean—is founded in some woman. Why shouldn't *you* be the woman I am founded in?'

Lawrence years later said he remembered 'the slightly self-conscious afternoon, when I was nineteen, and I "composed" my first two "poems". One was to "Guelder-roses", and one to "Campions", and most young ladies would have done better: at least I hope so. But I thought the effusions very nice, and so did Miriam.' Miriam-Jessie 'encouraged my demon. But alas, it was me, not he, whom she loved. So for her too it was a catastrophe. My demon is not easily loved: whereas the ordinary me is. So poor Miriam was let down. Yet in a sense she let down my demon, till he howled.'

Lawrence also began to write prose. In the spring of his last teaching year at Eastwood, he started a novel, and suggested that Jessie attempt one too; they could compare notes. 'The usual plan', he told her, 'is to take two couples and develop their relationships. Most of George Eliot's are on that plan. Anyhow, I don't want a plot, I should be bored with it. I shall try two couples for a start.'

At Whitsuntide 1906 he brought the first pages to Jessie. She was interested to discover that his setting was Felley Mill. And, as time passed and he gave her more and more pages—secretly—she noted how he would weave the events of their daily lives into the story. Jessie's mother showed him an old kettle she had discovered in the woods, in which a robin had made a nest, and soon Jessie found this described in the manuscript.

Once Lawrence told her he was afraid the story would be a mosaic. His day was broken up—in the morning when he wanted to write, he had to go out and teach at the British School on Albert Street. 'And when you've done the day's teaching all your brightness has gone. By the time I get back to the writing I'm another man. I don't see how there can be any continuity about it. It will have to be a mosaic, a mosaic of moods.'

It took him four years to write that book.

*

The school year of 1905–1906, when Lawrence was trying to save money for college, was a harsh year, economically, for his family.

The couch in the parlor needed upholstering, but because Mrs. Lawrence felt they could not afford to send it out, her son Bert and George Neville undertook the work. George Neville recalled that during this period Mrs. Lawrence wept one Friday when her husband brought home only fourteen shillings and fivepence halfpenny for his week's wages. He had worked hard, but 'things were bad' at the pits. Bert Lawrence had a new flannel suit and the first time he wore it his father said, 'Is it paid for?'—and Bert slammed out of the house.

Meantime, besides working on his novel, Lawrence continued to write poems. That the first two he attempted—'To Guelder-roses' and 'To Campions'—were botanical is not surprising, since he knew flowers so well and studied and taught the subject with enthusiasm.

Of the poems he later published, 'The Wild Common' is perhaps the earliest; and its opening lines are, in a sense, botanical—'The quick sparks on the gorse bushes are leaping/Little jets of sunlight-texture imitating flame'—but not in any textbook way; they already show the quality, which Lawrence would later designate as 'quickness', that enabled him to bring a landscape to life in a stroke. The early poems are often crude in form, content, and phrasing, and many of them are struggling almost fatally to free themselves from their influences and become a bold, new-patterned idiom; yet for all their faults most of these early poems have the deftness of those first two lines of 'The Wild Common'. The eye of the painter is there, and also the eye of the poet, catching not only the image but the movement of it; and Lawrence's work always had this kinetic aspect.

His poetry was ahead of his prose; and although formed somewhat after that of the Pre-Raphaelites, with Hardy and Verlaine mixed in, and Whitman strongly intruding a bit later, it nevertheless had a distinct Lawrencean intonation from the first; it was an individual voice speaking. Within a few years the leading literary magazines published some of these Eastwood poems of Lawrence's, and Ezra Pound immediately recognized their modernness; he wrote about Lawrence to Harriet Monroe, of *Poetry,* 'I think he learned the proper treatment of modern subjects before I did.'

Jessie, his constant companion and often the subject of those early poems, accompanied Lawrence and his mother on part of their seaside holiday in the summer of 1906, to Mablethorpe on the Lincolnshire coast. There one afternoon, Lawrence subjected Jessie to a cruel interview that some years later, along with a discussion held the preceding Easter, she wrote down for him as a narrative, in her suggestions for *Sons and Lovers.* It appears there with some descriptive and dramatic improvements in the 'Defeat of Miriam' chapter, the sequence in which Paul tells Miriam they had better see one another less frequently, since they are not engaged and, in any event, not truly in love.

Jessie says in her memoir that she realized at this point 'that life was completely changed'. What hurt her most was Lawrence's statement that he could never love her as a husband should love his wife. The great bond of sympathy could no longer exist between them as it had in the past. Lawrence, in a letter to her five years afterwards, said that their painful Eastertime conversation had been 'the slaughter of the foetus in the womb'.

That spring another local couple had given the gossips a palatable morsel, the girl being 'in trouble'. The boy was the Lawrences' good friend George Neville. Jessie remembered the evening that Ada Lawrence came twittering up to the farm with news of the 'deep disgrace'. The next evening, Lawrence discussed the matter gravely with Jessie. His mother had made Victorian use of the occasion to point out how terrible the consequences 'of only five minutes' self-forgetfulness' could be. Lawrence in talking to Jessie thanked God that so far he had been spared 'that'.

Lawrence referred to the matter some years afterwards in a 1912 letter to Edward Garnett, in which he sounded considerably less tortured about the matter. Indeed, that same year he put some of the characters and events into the folk comedy *The Married Man;* and he later used them again in his short novel *Mr Noon.* In his letter to Garnett, Lawrence said in retrospect, 'the girl was only nineteen, and he only twenty. Her father, a great Christian, turned her out.' Neville had refused to acknowledge the child, 'but had to pay, whether or not'. Later, when the girl wanted to marry a collier, she appeared at Neville's home to insist that his parents acknowledge their granddaughter: 'Who's the father of that?' she demanded, presenting the little girl. The old lady cried out proudly, 'Eh bless her, it's just like him', and her husband said, 'Well, Lizzie, if our George-Henry says it isn't his'n he's a liar. It's the spit and image of him.' Lawrence said that although the end of the story was 'lovely', its 'beginning was damnable'.

Although he could take an amused view of his friend's troubles years later and reflect them in little comedies, Lawrence found sexual difficulties not so amusing when he was younger. After the discussion of intentions with Jessie, he found sex more of a burden than ever. And each time he warmed to Jessie, seemed to find her attractive, his mother tried to chill that feeling. During the August 1906 holiday at Mablethorpe, when Lawrence's eyes glowed as Jessie on a windy morning used a broad silk scarf to tie her hat, she asked whether the scarf suited her, and Lawrence passed the question on to his mother, who gave Jessie 'a bitter glance, and turned away, and the light died out of Lawrence's face'.

That evening as they walked along the coast waiting for the moon to rise, Lawrence burst out against Jessie, upbraiding her incoherently. Jessie said 'he appeared to be in great distress of mind, and possibly also of body.' When she told him she was not to blame for whatever he seemed to be blaming her, he then began to scold himself. 'This scene was repeated with increasing intensity on two successive occasions when I spent my annual holiday with the Lawrences and their friends'—at Robin Hood's Bay, Yorkshire, in 1907, and at Flamborough, Yorkshire, in 1908.

Nevertheless, in many ways the holidays were pleasant. Jessie remembered gay walks across the grassy sand at Mablethorpe. Once, when Lawrence's father went with them—and had some ale at Susannah Stone's thatched cottage while the younger people drank ginger-beer—they saw a windmill at work, with the great sails swinging, and Lawrence and Jessie thought of Gerard in *The Cloister and the Hearth*. They 'found watercress growing in a brook, and Lawrence and his father gleefully gathered some to take home for tea. Words cannot convey Lawrence's brimming delight in all these simple things.'

Lawrence and his mother stayed at Mablethorpe for two weeks, but Jessie could afford only one. She returned to Eastwood with Lawrence's father, who sat in the train 'staring dimly' at the passing landscape. He 'seemed almost old and inarticulate.' At the end of the trip he helped her 'in a kindly way' with her bag. She wondered whether he knew that—as she looked back over the pain and happiness of her week's holiday, her first at the seashore—she had difficulty in holding back her tears.

7 BIAS TOWARDS HUMANISM

In September 1906, the month in which he turned twenty-one, Lawrence entered Nottingham University College.

This was not the institution that now stands in University Park, on the southwestern outskirts of the city, whose first buildings were ready in 1928 (Lawrence noted the occasion in a mean little poem), endowed by his grandfather's old enemy, Sir Jesse Boot, later Lord Trent. The old University College of Lawrence's time, on Shakespeare Street near the now-demolished Victoria Station, is an imitation-Gothic product of 1881, later the technical college of the University and the Nottingham Free Library. In *The Rainbow,* Lawrence describes it as he saw it in his youth: 'The big college built of stone, standing in the quiet street, with a rim of grass and limetrees all so peaceful,' seemed 'a remote magic land' to his protagonist Ursula, as it must have seemed to him. 'Its architecture was foolish,' an uninspired copy of another age, 'still it was different from that of all other buildings. . . . Amorphous as it might be, there was in it a reminiscence of the wondrous, cloistral origin of education.'

Like Ursula, Lawrence was soon disappointed in the school. Their careers differed in one important respect, however, for Lawrence took the teacher's-certificate course and Ursula studied for a degree. As Hedley Pickbourne, Registrar of the University, explained the difference in a letter of August 18, 1949:

> Students admitted to the Teachers' Training Department at that time fell into two categories—those who followed courses of lectures leading to an external degree examination of the University of London in Arts or Pure Science and those taking the two-year course for the Board of Education Teacher's Certificate examination. The former selected their subjects in accordance with the Degree regulations of the University of London; the latter took the usual subjects for the Teacher's Certificate and were, I believe, allowed to take one or two additional optional subjects. Lawrence came within the latter group and appears to have offered French and Botany as optional subjects. He did not read for a degree.

He had intended to do so during his first term. But he was happy, Jessie Chambers recalled, to abandon the degree course; he could take the ordinary curriculum and have more time to spend on his writing. He went on with *The White Peacock,* which he at that time intended to call *Nethermere.* As Jessie Chambers remembered the first draft of that first novel, its hero, George, was a noble young farmer who married a Lettie who was beyond him socially; she had gone through a reductive process by letting a young man of even higher social standing seduce her. Jessie thought the story thickly sentimentalized, though she found the atmosphere 'alive'. Mrs. Lawrence's comment on the manuscript at this stage was made to Jessie, 'in a pained voice', at Robin Hood's Bay during the summer holiday of 1907: 'To think that *my* son should have written such a story.' The seduction of Lettie had upset her. Lawrence was already having troubles with censorship.

As he went on writing the novel during the next few years he turned it into an idealization of his own family circumstances. The countryside around Eastwood provided the landscape, but without the mines; they appeared only occasionally and distantly. The father of the family didn't disturb his wife and his Bert-like son and Ada-like daughter: he was a derelict who made only a sad, quiet, occasional appearance; and he died conveniently early in the story. The mother (called Mrs. Beardsall) showed only the sweeter side of Mrs. Lawrence.

But in projecting his family into a happier situation, Lawrence didn't turn away altogether from the grimness he had seen in life. The portrait of George Saxton—like that of Edgar in *Sons and Lovers,* apparently modeled after Alan Chambers—is a vital one; Lawrence shows a mature skill in depicting George's slow degradation. Much of *The White Peacock* has a nice-nellyism about it, of the kind that Lawrence later despised; but the truth-speaker that was always in him required the inclusion of the incisive Annable, the gamekeeper. This man, particularly in his relation to the young couples in the story, had probably been suggested by the voluble gamekeeper Tregarva in Charles Kingsley's *Yeast;* and in Lawrence's own writing, Annable is the ancestor of the gamekeeper Mellors in Lawrence's last novel, *Lady Chatterley's Lover.* Mellors would have Lawrence's philosophy behind him, as it had developed over the years, but the bitter-speaking Annable foreshadows much of it.

As the story progressed, the central feminine figure, Lettie, grew far beyond the character of Ada, who was in life a staid and conventional person: Lettie is flirtatious and even destructive, a white peacock of vanity. The man she marries instead of George, as in the earlier version, is Leslie Tempest, who brings her to live in Highclose, which is based, of course, on Lamb Close. Leslie is the first of Lawrence's portraits of young squires; this one is thin and not so highly individualized as the later portraits. George's sister Emily foreshadows, rather pallidly, Miriam of *Sons and Lovers.*

These are the ingredients of the story, whose principal charm remains the landscape pictures of the Eastwood region, which Lawrence invests with a morning-light quality. His prose in this book is simple, with few of the 'special effects' of his later work: the essential Lawrence rhythm, the daring but invariably 'right' images, above all the element of incantation that characterizes much of Lawrence's mature prose.

While he was working on this book, which was to be accepted by the first publisher who saw it, he was also writing class exercises at college. He was extremely annoyed with one of the women, Miss Beckett, who taught English; she returned his essays heavily corrected in red. And one of the male teachers also angered him by censoring the use of the word *stallion* in one of his essays. 'My boy, that's a word we don't use', he told Lawrence, the future author of *St Mawr,* that classic of stallion worship. And the rejection of a poem he had submitted to the school magazine irritated Lawrence. He later published this poem, 'Study', in *Amores* and, in the 1928 *Collected Poems,* with very minor changes.

At Nottingham, the professor who was head of the Normal Department, Amos Henderson, presided over a students' hostel, with the help of his wife, at Mapperley Hall. His specialty was mathematics, and his hobby was music, a subject in which he helped increase Lawrence's interest. Lawrence thought him timid and ineffectual, however well-meaning, but he liked and admired the principal of the college, the Reverend John E. Symes. He had joined the staff of University College in 1881, at the age of thirty-one, ten years after taking his M.A. degree at Cambridge. He was noted for his 'advanced' views on religious and social questions; and although his specialty was literature, Principal Symes wrote a volume entitled *Political Economy,* and before that, one called *A Companion to English History,* and various others on different subjects. He was dismissed in 1911 on grounds of administrative incompetence, though he had long been in trouble in Nottingham for lecturing on the single-tax advocate Henry George and for inviting the socialist William Morris to speak.

Lawrence's attitude towards most of Symes's staff was one of cynicism, later expressed in the college episodes in *The Rainbow.* He resented the sharp observation of one instructor, 'Botany' Smith, to the effect that his student was obsessed with ideas rather than possessed by them. Yet Lawrence wrote to him in 1909 (in an unpublished letter), 'I owe you a debt. You were my first live teacher of philosophy; you showed me the way out of a torturing crude monism, past pragmatism, into a sort of crude but appeasing pluralism.'

One faculty member Lawrence apparently admired was the head of the Department of Modern Languages, Professor Ernest Weekley. So obviously a gentleman himself, Weekley was, Lawrence felt, merely sarcastic when he addressed the provincial students as 'gentlemen'. Lawrence, however, didn't become well acquainted with Professor Weekley, a man twenty years older than himself, and at this period he was not invited to tea at the professor's house.

*

During Lawrence's college years, he and Jessie continued reading together. They began French with simple stories, then read Pierre Loti, Honoré de Balzac, and Gustave Flaubert. Lawrence in his enthusiasm for Balzac's *La Peau de chagrin* described it to the Chamberses; Jessie felt the story's symbolism 'seemed to oppress him'. He had brought her a volume of Guy de Maupassant's *Tales,* in translation, but a few days afterwards wrote her a remorseful letter: 'What am I doing to you? You used to be so vigorous, so full of interest in all sorts of things. Don't take too much notice of me. You musn't allow yourself to be hurt by Maupassant or me.'

Lawrence from his youth seemed to have a rather full knowledge of *symbolisme,* but he didn't acquire this at college, for, as Ernest Weekley wrote to this author (April 10, 1952), 'He was not a degree student at Nottingham and what work he did in French was of a fairly elementary kind.'

Sometimes Lawrence and Jessie went to the Theatre Royal in Nottingham. They saw the D'Oyly Carte company do Gilbert and Sullivan, they heard *Tannhäuser,* and once they attended a performance of *Strife,* by John Galsworthy. Sarah Bernhardt's *La Dame aux camélias,* which Lawrence saw alone, terrified him and, he told Jessie Chambers, he rushed out of the theater. He was afraid, he said, that some day he might, like Armand in the play, 'become enslaved by a woman'. He also wrote to Blanche Jennings that Bernhardt was 'the incarnation of wild emotion which we share with all live things'. She was 'fascinating' and represented 'the primeval passions of woman'. Quite prophetically he added, 'I could love such a woman myself, love her to madness.'

He and Jessie continued to read the English authors. Meredith's *Love in the Valley* seemed to have special meaning for Lawrence.

After they read Mark Rutherford's *Autobiography* and *Clara Hapgood,* Lawrence told Jessie that if she ever wrote, her work would be something like Rutherford's. Lawrence, possibly thinking of *The White Peacock,* smiled as he told Jessie that, in *Lavengro,* George Borrow had so skillfully blended autobiography and fiction that no one could tell where one left off and the other began.

*

Lawrence began seriously looking into philosophy during his second year at college. He frequently discussed it with Jessie and Alan. Schopenhauer particularly impressed him, and he persuaded Alan to give Jessie the *Essays* as a birthday present in the spring of 1908. When Lawrence read aloud to them 'The Metaphysics of Love' chapter from *The World as Will and Idea,* Jessie's brother disagreed with Schopenhauer's statement that 'fair hair and blue eyes are in themselves a variation from the type, almost an abnormality, analogous to white mice, or at least to grey horses.' Lawrence answered that he thought only brown skins were beautiful. He obviously referred to Jessie's somewhat dusky skin, though he may have been thinking of Louie Burrows's, and when he read the passage to the effect that everybody prefers and eagerly desires those who are the most beautiful, he stopped to remark that he saw what was most beautiful, but didn't desire it; and Jessie felt that he was trying to justify his own 'divided attitude'.

Lawrence annotated the gift copy of Schopenhauer, a small volume in the English version of Mrs. Rudolph Dirks. In the margins, Lawrence translated the Latin quotations and wrote his own comments on some of Schopenhauer's statements. This copy and its markings were examined by Émile Delavenay in the February 1936 number of the *Revue Anglo-Américaine.* Lawrence's annotations are as often amusing as they are interesting. Schopenhauer had written, 'From this it is obvious why we so often see very intelligent, nay, distinguished men married to dragons and she-devils, and why we cannot understand how it was possible for them to make such a choice.' Lawrence asked, 'Never vice-versa?' This prompted Delavenay to ask, in turn, *'Lawrence pense-t-il à ses parents, la mère cultivée, intelligente, le père frustre et brutal?'* Lawrence himself used French for a marginal question to Jessie—*'Qu'en pensez-vous?'*—regarding Schopenhauer's: 'Because the kernel of passionate love turns on the anticipation of the child to be born and of its nature it is quite possible for friendship, without any admixture of sexual love, to exist between two young, good-looking people of different sex, if there is perfect fitness of temperament and intellectual capacity. In fact a certain aversion for each other may exist also.'

Some of the passages Lawrence marked without question or comment, such as the one asserting that it is man's nature to be inconstant while it is woman's nature to cling to one man. Lawrence doubly underlined a statement to the effect that while 'two lovers are talking about the harmony of their souls', they are really thinking of their individual souls, and their imagined harmony 'frequently turns out to be violent discord shortly after marriage'. Émile Delavenay said in his article that he believed traces of Schopenhauer's influence show themselves throughout *The White Peacock*. Indeed, Annable is a somewhat Schopenhauerian figure. But the influence of Schopenhauer almost certainly extended beyond this first book, though Lawrence never admitted it: perhaps because he didn't recognize it.

Among some of the other philosophical works Lawrence and Jessie read in their youth, they disliked Renan's *Life of Jesus,* which Lawrence felt was somewhat autobiographical. For a while he was under the spell of Huxley and Haeckel, and he also read Spencer and Mill with interest; and he admired James's *Pragmatism* and *The Varieties of Religious Experience*. Lawrence was undergoing religious doubts, and he was particularly subject to the ideational hammerings of materialism and rationalism.

At this time he believed that *Anna Karenina* was the greatest of novels. The Chamberses all thought that the episodes in which Levin and Kitty appeared were the finest in the book, but Lawrence fastened his own interest upon Anna. In later life he held the novel in contempt, and spoke of 'old Leo' as 'wetting on the flame'.

Jessie, in her further recollections of Lawrence's youthful literary activity, reports that he originally wrote his story 'A Fragment of Stained Glass' under the title 'Legend', in the autumn of 1907, during his second year at college. The *Nottinghamshire Guardian* offered three story prizes of three pounds each, at Christmas time, and Lawrence decided to try for all three prizes, for the sake of the nine pounds. 'Legend' was one of his entries, the only one of the three that was submitted under his own name; Jessie and Louie Burrows permitted him to send in two other stories under their own identities.

The story bearing Jessie's name and address and the pseudonym 'Rosalind' was the only one of the three that won a prize. It was called 'A Prelude', and after its publication in the *Guardian* on December 7, 1907, it was not printed again until issued in a limited edition in 1949. The third story, 'The White Stocking', was, like 'Legend', used again by Lawrence and, like the expanded version of 'Legend', appeared in his first collection of short stories, *The Prussian Officer,* in 1914. When these efforts were originally submitted to the *Guardian,* 'Legend' won the comment 'a tale of the escape of a serf remarkable for its vivid realism'; 'The White Stocking' was mentioned as 'lacking finish'. The prize-winning 'A Prelude', however, was judged 'a simple theme handled with freshness and simplicity altogether charming'. Its setting is the Haggs.

As Lawrence continued attending college, writing poems, and working sporadically at his novel, he became increasingly disillusioned with his studies. Jessie Chambers, who said he had begun 'in a mood of wistful anticipation', reported that he 'got nothing' from his two years at Nottingham. He was a year or two older than most of the other students and felt they were all treated too much like 'schoolkids'. He envied the engineering students, who used to swagger about the place and 'look down on' their instructors. He particularly disliked the practice teaching, although the authorities had assigned him to an 'advanced' school. He afterwards said that his two years at the University College 'had meant mere disillusion instead of the contact of living men.'

The University, however, is proud of Lawrence's association with it and, under the direction of Professor Vivian de Sola Pinto, in 1960 sponsored the largest exhibition of Lawrence's work that had ever taken place. In 1971 a Lawrence Summer School was held at the University (under the direction of Dr. Keith Sagar), with lectures, discussion sections, and films in the mornings and evenings; in the afternoons the summer-school participants went on special buses for extensive visits to the Lawrence Country. In 1972 the University, the City Library, and other regional institutions staged an unusually large and thorough exhibition of Lawrence material.

*

After obtaining his teacher's certificate in June 1908, Lawrence refused to consider any position that would pay him less than ninety pounds a year. In his unemployment during that summer of 1908, he 'was a sardonic figure', Jessie Chambers recalled. He frequently went up to the Haggs, as usual showing Jessie his manuscripts and going about with Alan as he did the farm work. Then, in October, Lawrence received an offer from a school at Croydon, South London, at an annual salary of ninety-five pounds.

His final record as a student at Nottingham University College shows his grades as follows: 'Teaching, B; Reading, A; Drawing, B; Music, B.' The observations of his supervisor on his practice teaching indicate that Lawrence, despite his years of battling the colliers' boys—certainly rougher than the tradesmen's and factory workers' sons in Nottingham—was still weak in classroom discipline. It is further interesting to note that Lawrence, the miner's son, is described as a young man 'fastidious in taste':

Well-read, scholarly, and refined, Mr Lawrence will make an excellent teacher if he gets into the right place. His work at present is uneven according to the ordinary standard owing to his lack of experience of the elementary schoolboy and his management. He would be quite unsuitable for a large class of boys in a rough district; he would not have sufficient persistence and enthusiasm but would become disgusted.

Mr Lawrence's strong bias is towards the humanistic subjects and at times boys' interest in such lessons is intense. Intelligence, however, is cultivated in lessons on all subjects by the treatment, especially the questions, the defect being a want of that persistent driving home and recapitulation which are necessary—like many intelligent teachers, Mr Lawrence tends to teach the best pupils exclusively. Though very fluent, he sometimes has an obvious difficulty in finding words suitably simple. He is emphatically a teacher of upper classes.

Mr Lawrence is fastidious in taste, and while working splendidly at anything that interests him would perhaps easily tire amid the tedium and discouragements of the average classroom. With an upper class in a good school or in a higher school he could do work quite unusually good, especially if allowed a very free hand.

*

PART TWO

The London Years

---

*

1 SUBURBAN SCHOOLMASTER

JESSIE CHAMBERS noted that when it was time for Lawrence to leave the Midlands, 'he looked like a man under sentence of exile.' His mother kept fiercely asking, What would *she* do when he was gone, and how would he have got anywhere, even to college, if she had not called him every morning and given him his porridge?

Before departing for London, Lawrence went to say good-by to the Chambers family, and afterwards Jessie walked with her friend to the outer gate. There, he looked back towards the farm and said in French, 'the last time'. Jessie began sobbing, and he took her in his arms and kissed her. They stood, silent, in the deepening October twilight. Jessie felt everything was hopeless: she would not begin the old argument again.

Finally Lawrence left, inviting her to tea the next afternoon. She dreaded going, for she felt hostility in the Lawrence household, but she took a small basket of apples as an excuse. She found no gaiety at Lynn Croft; Lawrence was pale and upset. Jessie soon left, hurt and humiliated, and aware of her 'malady'.

Lawrence had his own 'malady', his deep attachment to his home and to his mother. But it was to Jessie and not his mother that he wrote of his first reaction to London and his new position, in a letter Jessie characterized as being 'like a howl of terror'.

He was soon singing a different song, however, judging from an early (December 15, 1908) Croydon letter to Blanche Jennings. In this letter, which begins with a discussion of Balzac, and contains a reference to his *Eugénie Grandet,* Lawrence says in part:

As for the 'gush' about the kiss—it *was* a crisis in Eugénie's life. A most productive crisis. Think—if you kissed a man on the mouth—what it would mean to you. I have kissed dozens of girls—on the cheek—never on the mouth—I could not. Such a touch is the connection between the vigourous flow of two lives. Like a positive electricity, a current of creative life runs through two persons, and they are instinct with the same life force—the same vitality—the same I know not what—when they kiss on the mouth—when they kiss as lovers do. Come to think of it and [*sic*] it is exceedingly rare that two people participate in entirely the same sensation and emotion; but they do when they kiss as lovers, I am sure. Then a certain life-current passes through them which changes them forever. . . . Somehow, I think we come into knowledge (unconscious) of the most vital parts of the cosmos through touching things.

The man who was later to refer to himself as the priest of love, and who subsequently became the author of the story 'You Touched Me', was already formulating his ideas about the erotic, apparently on the basis of little experience. And it is interesting to find the young Lawrence employing the Bergsonian expression 'life force', the phrase Shaw used a few years earlier in parodying some of Nietzsche's philosophy in *Man and Superman*.

*

The Davidson Road School where Lawrence began teaching on October 12, 1908, had been built not long before and was considered one of the best-equipped academic buildings in the London area. Lawrence, when his homesickness had thinned out, adjusted himself to the place, although he was never to be truly happy there.

Croydon was already in the process of becoming a complex of brick houses and chimney pots, past which the yellow electric trains from Victoria and London Bridge stations would speed on a high embankment; eventually the former neighborhood of the Crystal Palace became a stucco suburb, with hollow slopes still showing patches of nature, and chunks of trees between the houses. The one in which Lawrence lived during his three years at Croydon still stands: 16 Colworth Road, on a street of identical houses set behind low brick walls, the ground floor encased in red brick, the story above in rough cement, the gabled roofs shingled, drainpipes and sometimes electric wires going down the outsides of the houses.

Lawrence lodged with the Jones family, first at 12 Colworth Road, just above the busy thoroughfare of Lower Addiscombe Road and close by the Bingham Road railway station; then, in September 1911, he moved with the Jones family a few houses to the north, to No. 16.

John W. Jones, from Lancashire, was attendance officer of the school. The Joneses had two children, one an infant, and Lawrence's mother remarked to Jessie Chambers that she was glad to know there was a baby in the house, for she was certain that would keep her son 'pure'.

Lawrence had a daily walk of about three-quarters of a mile to the Davidson Road, where the school stood at the next turning to the left, at the corner of the Brampton Road. Set back from the street amid wide asphalt playgrounds, it was of red brick, the central building three stories high, the top story set in the sloping roof, with dormer windows; and, on the roof, a large, pointed turret.

Lawrence was at Davidson for a little more than three years; and he mixed well with both pupils and staff. One of his former students, Frank W. Turner, who became a Fleet Street newspaperman, has set down (in a letter to the author of this book) his recollections of Lawrence the young teacher:

> In a room below the roof, a continuous blackboard runs around the upper part of the room, and even now I can picture 'D.H.' standing some feet away, with an arm outstretched, to draw on the board. His demonstrations of perspective, making lines stretch away to nothing, still live in my memory. He also taught us watercolour painting.
>
> The visionary artist in him showed itself when the school produced *Ali Baba and the Forty Thieves* in the school hall. Leaning over canvas material covering a large part of the floor, he painted with a whitewash brush, from a bucket of colour, a backcloth of an Eastern Bazaar, and another of palm trees in the desert.

Lawrence's closest friend at Davidson, his fellow teacher A. W. McLeod, has also provided a fresh picture of Lawrence at the time, and an unusually full one:

> I am sorry I cannot help you over your specific enquiries. I do not know who Agnes Holt, Jane, and Mrs Davidson were. Lawrence had a number of friends in Croydon whom I never met. Miss Mason I knew only as a colleague in school and as I left Davidson soon after D.H.L. went, I got out of touch with her. She was older than the rest of the staff, a very able, almost over-conscientious teacher. She saw that Lawrence was far from robust and rather 'mothered' him. They became very friendly and he had soon persuaded her to try her hand at little stories and sketches and at water-colour painting.
>
> In my copy of *Love Poems* Lawrence wrote: 'Remembering

the unhappy days and the happy playtimes at Davidson when I solaced myself with his appreciation of some of these miserable poems.'

Unhappy days! Well, towards the last he said more than once: 'I'll not go on. The Committee has had blood and tears out of me for a hundred a year. I'll not endure it. I'd rather work on a farm. I know a farmer at Eastwood who would take me on to-morrow. Nay, I'd rather be a tramp.' Teaching was always a strain to him: he was always at tension; nevertheless he enjoyed much of his work, notably his nature-study lessons and his drawing periods when the whole class acquired his own free, vigorous style and painted boldly and with huge enjoyment. It was almost his one regret on leaving that his successor might cramp that freedom of handling. For enlightenment on 'child art' was then only feebly dawning. He was fortunate in coming under a Headmaster so discerning, so enlightened and so kind as Mr P. F. T. Smith who recognized his quality and gave him free scope to follow his bent. Lawrence spent some of his leisure in copying pictures—there was a whole series of Swan's animal studies—and he would say it was because he liked getting into the other fellow's skin.

He read everything he could lay hands on—plays, verse and novels especially—from Ibsen, Verhaeren, and Peacock to so humble a writer as Mary Mann. He had a strange' liking for Jessie Fothergill's *The First Violin,* and Querido's *Toil of Men* impressed him.

He got on well with all his colleagues for he was always friendly, and gay and eager in discussion. One of them told me that Lawrence was uncanny: that one day he had read his inmost heart for him: had told him things about himself he had never admitted to himself: but they were, alas, all true.

He certainly enjoyed the 'happy playtimes'—the wide view from the playground over the fields and the piles of timber by the railway to the Crystal Palace in the distance on the Norwood hills—the reading of his latest poems—and the analysis of characters in books. I found out he was at work on a novel when he asked me, if I was going into Croydon, to get him a lot of sermon paper at Boots'. Sermon paper was a new term to me and I asked whether he was writing theology. Then I heard about *The White Peacock* and one day got that sermon paper back, no longer blank, with the anxious demand to let him know if it was good.

Lawrence wrote of his Croydon experiences chiefly in poetry, in the 'Schoolmaster' series. Some of these verses were reprinted, from journals, in his *Love Poems* (1913) and *Amores* (1916) and, with later revisions, in his *Collected Poems* (1928).

Just after Lawrence's death a school inspector who had known him at Croydon, Stewart A. Robertson, recalled (in the *Glasgow Herald*, March 8, 1930) that at the meeting of a literary society, Lawrence had praised Rachel Annand Taylor's lush poems. Robertson aroused Lawrence's mirth when 'I once told him that he had lost a great deal by not having been a Boy Scout.'

Another picture of Lawrence at Croydon, an unusually full one, has been provided by Philip F. T. Smith in a letter (of February 1951) to the author of this book. Mr. Smith, who was in his eighties, looked back to the time forty years earlier when he was headmaster at Croydon. His memory remained clear and sharp, and his letter gives us a fine memoir of the young Lawrence:

Teaching, to Lawrence, was then a necessity for his physical existence and not in any sense a vocation. He certainly liked boys, as boys, but not as pupils. The liking was reciprocated with similar reservations. The routine of school life was to Lawrence abhorrent. In his poem 'Evening' he writes:

I carry my anger sullenly 'cross these waste lands,
For tomorrow will call them all back, the school hours I detest.

Then again in another verse he speaks of the 'weary waiting for the bell' dismissing school.

Lawrence was intolerant of authority. While imposing his own rule rigorously upon his pupils, he rebelled against any such process as being even suggested to himself.

The Davidson School was new, having been in session for two years previous to Lawrence's inclusion in the staff in 1910 [1908]. At that time teachers were posted to schools directly from the Central Authority without reference to the wishes of the Head Master. Thus, I have no knowledge of the circumstances which influenced his appointment, nor of his complete academic qualifications.

The school was large, the rooms spacious, well lighted, and

warmed. The staff was good and the common rooms comfortable. The environment was not inspiring. It comprised patches of undeveloped building land bounded by railway marshalling yards. This outlook was particularly repellent to Lawrence. He writes:

> I pick my way over threadbare grass, which is pressed
> Into mud—the space fast shrinks in the builder's hands.

I mention these facts since Lawrence's unsought apologists have attributed much of his future instability to repressions suffered during his period of school teaching.

Lawrence complained of one professional grievance in connection with teaching. His condemnation of the large sized class was damnatory. He said, 'I can instruct a hundred; but I doubt whether I could attempt to educate a dozen.'

When Lawrence reported at the school I recall him to be tall, very thin though of large build. He had a shock of dark hair, small ginger moustache, and vivid blue eyes. Later I noticed that his hands contrasted palpably with his general appearance. They were fragile, long fingered, expressive, well controlled. Lawrence was not a robust being. He made no pretensions in the matter of dress. His expression always showed a kind of confident amusement. It was rarely serious. He did not appear to be perturbed with his new surroundings nor doubtful of his powers to succeed in his new duties. Circumstances permitted no gradual introduction to his work. A large class of boys, the regulation 60, awaited him, and he commenced at once.

The staff at Davidson at his time was composed of young men all of about Lawrence's age, and one woman, Miss Agnes Mason, who was considerably older. He was therefore not influenced by the normal professional practice of older men usually present in a school personnel, and was at liberty to work out his own salvation.

His well-known powers of concentration and untiring industry soon became apparent. He shirked none of the drudgery of the details which hamper the routine of a teacher's life. He was interested in Art, English, and Biology. I kept for some years his note book recording a year's work in biology. The water-colour drawings and details of experimental exercises were models of correctness and clarity. His caustic humour often aroused suspicions as to the value of his most genial expressions. 'Let them play now,' he says, 'The world will teach them how to work.' To a youth called Cass, whose English was 'wanting' in every sense of the word, he remarks 'Write it down with an A.' A perfectly harmless remark as it affected the particular individual [i.e., *A* for Ass].

Lawrence hated the slightest interference with his class work. On one occasion I followed a Ministerial Inspector into his room. The intrusion was unexpected and resented. A curious wailing of distressed voices issued from a far corner. The sounds were muffled by a large covering black-board. The words of a familiar song arose from the depths:

> Full fathom five thy father lies;
> Of his bones are coral made.

The class was reading *The Tempest*. The presentation expressed the usual thoroughness of Lawrence's attitude to the exercise in progress. It must not be spoiled by even official comment. Lawrence rushed with outstretched hands to the astounded visitor: 'Hush! Hush! Don't you hear? The sea chorus from *The Tempest*.' Those were the days of conventional methods of instruction, and Lawrence's excursions into dramatic expression were not likely to meet with full approval.

The same gentleman, some months later inquired, 'Where's this book-writing fellow of yours?' Lawrence's classroom was indicated. 'I shall not go into his room,' he said. 'I have no intention of being pilloried in some book.'

Lawrence's ideas on the teaching of Art were also somewhat suspect. While I was conferring with another Board of Education inspector, a boy brought a large pastel drawing, still life, for inspection. After a glance, I made an ineffectual attempt to suppress the sketch. The official eye had, however, anticipated my effort. 'Is this sent for any particular reason?' I inquired. 'Mr Lawrence thought it was rather good,' the boy replied. The artist returned to his class leaving his masterpiece with us.

'Are you by any chance an artist?' inquired the wary dictator. 'No,' I replied. 'Neither am I,' he commented. 'We had better be careful about this man. After the session, without his knowledge, collect a sample of these drawings. I will send them to the Art Department at Kensington for an expert opinion.' Later they were returned by the inspector in person. 'Good thing we took the course we did,' he reported. 'The Department highly approves. You'll have a crowd of students down to worry you about them, I expect.'

At that period, there were in circulation a number of small periodicals designed to make some appeal to boys. Lawrence hit upon the idea of setting some of his pupils to contribute short articles to several of these publications. These he amplified and edited. Several were accepted, and to the vast surprise of the authors were actually paid for by postal orders for small sums. From henceforth the despised 'composition essay exercise' assumed an unexpected value in their eyes. Lawrence assumed quite voluntarily the responsibility for many of the least desired of school routine duties. This included the constant attention bestowed on the details connected with the school library. He used to affirm 'Let them read any rubbish they like as long as they read it at all. They will very soon discard the bad.'

Later, some of the boys discovered in a London evening news sheet one of his earlier 'School Poems'. They devised a method of registering their disapproval of some lines by writing replies in verse which were affixed to his desk lid to meet his eye at morning school. They were, however, somewhat disappointed with the reactions aroused. Instead of disapproval or perhaps reproof, Lawrence was delighted and even indicated how the lines might have been improved.

Lawrence was greatly interested in a section of boys who attended the school from the English Actors' Home. Some of these pupils bore well-known names connected in the past with the English stage. For a school dramatic performance, Lawrence painted all the scenery, revised and added to the text of the drama and, after the initial rehearsals remarked, 'These actor boys know more than we do about this kind of thing. We can't teach them the beginnings of play acting. Let them run this show as they think fit.' We agreed, with beneficial results.

Lawrence's choice of verse for class study was, for the time, unorthodox. He would have none of the 'We are seven, etc.' category. Nor would he tolerate any with what he called 'a sniff of moral imposition.' I found entered in his records such selections as 'The Assyrian Came Down' (Byron), 'The Bells of Shandon' (Mahony), 'Go fetch to me a pint of wine' (Burns).

He considered that the best approach to poetry for young people was through rhythm and the ring of words rather than the evasive appeal of an unreal and abstract morality.

Later Lawrence made no secret of his intention to abandon teaching as a career. His health deteriorated. He became restless and at times, as they say here in Lancashire, 'awkward'. He once said that he would like to terminate his professional vocation after the manner of the German composer who ended a similar period of teaching with a defiance of petty authority. Unfortunately Lawrence's decision was made for him later by the failure of his health.

Living away from home, Lawrence found that the endeavour to exist on his very small salary as a junior teacher was often embarrassing. He never complained, but I know that he was often at cross purposes with his lot. Occasionally, with a complete indifference to his future as a teacher he chose to challenge the good offices of his friends.

A branch of the English Speaking Association (the title is possibly not quite correct) had been formed in the Borough and was patronized by many of the intelligentsia including members of the Education Authority, mostly ladies. The Chief Director at that time was a scholar with a profound academic record. He was a most influential and sympathetic supporter of Lawrence's literary ambitions and he suggested that on his introduction it might be useful if Lawrence would attend a meeting and provide a reading for discussion. Lawrence agreed, and apparently chose and read a medieval romance, the text of which included some embarrassing situations and erotic conversations. I was not present, having no knowledge of the event; but the next day was interviewed by the offended official. Did I know of Lawrence's intention to read to the Society? If so, did I approve of his choice of subject? Had any of my staff influenced his selection? I refused to inquire. It was not a school business: but Lawrence lost a very good friend. Lawrence never referred to the incident in my hearing; but I can imagine his grim satisfaction at the efforts of his audience of superior intellects to preserve an unconcerned interest in his performance.

Feeling that Lawrence might welcome a change from his somewhat limited circle of acquaintances I suggested that when he was at a loss for company he might occasionally like to call on me at my home. At this time I had no idea that he had written anything more than a few verses. After a long interval, about December 1910, he unexpectedly accepted my invitation and appeared quite frequently at my house, generally on Sunday evenings. We presented a very quiet household, myself and wife only. My wife, like Lawrence, was interested in French literature. They read French verse and we sang French songs. Lawrence translated some French verse into English. He also attempted some verse in French. I regret that none of these essays survives. He talked almost entirely of his home and early life, much the same story as it appears in the numerous biographies and novels. He was fond of recounting the conquests he made among his lady friends and with some of his opinions on female shortcomings my wife disagreed strongly. When he cancelled out a period of endearment at which the lady invariably wept, the outburst only provoked him to the extent of, 'My dear, how you are enjoying yourself.' He often said—or did he quote—'If a woman cannot have love, she will have consideration'? Sometimes he spoke of his life in lodgings, describing how he bathed the two small children of the house and put them to bed after suitable devotions, thus permitting the parents to take an evening off at the pictures. Lawrence never referred to his literary work nor to school affairs nor to persons known to me.

I knew little of Lawrence's private life. He lodged with an administrative officer of the Education Service and his wife, a Mr and Mrs Jones. He always spoke most highly of their services to him, especially during his periods of illness.

Very soon after his appointment Lawrence showed signs of poor health. My attention was drawn to this by Miss Mason, who quite early showed considerable interest in his physical welfare. Miss Mason kept house for an invalid father, and Lawrence soon became a constant visitor at her home. He depended very considerably on her for the direction of his personal affairs. At Miss Mason's home Lawrence met her close friend, Miss Helen Corke. Miss Corke was of Lawrence's age. She had been a member of my staff in a former school to Davidson. She was a very well favoured and extremely attractive and accomplished young lady, and Lawrence soon began to depend upon her judgement since he consulted her on the merits or otherwise of both *The White Peacock* and *The Trespasser* before publication.

Lawrence came to like Philip Smith, who over the years treated him kindly, but in his first term at the Davidson School he had a low opinion of him, as may be seen in a letter of October 23 to Louie Burrows, which says in part:

But the head is a weak kneed windy fool—he shifts every grain of responsibility off his own shoulders—he will not punish anybody; yourself, when you punish, you must send for the regulation cane and enter the minutest details of the punishment in the Pun. book—if you do. Discipline is consequently very slack and teaching is a struggle; but it's not so bad—we shall soon be comfy. At any rate one is not killed by work. I have Std. IV— 45 lads—there is much pretence of high flown work—not much done.

He added, 'I am rapidly getting over my loneliness and despair; soon I'll settle down and be quite happy here.' It was not until winter that he met the Helen Corke mentioned by Philip Smith.

*

Parts of the story of Lawrence and Helen Corke have been written by each of the participants. Helen Corke dealt with it in her dialogue, *Lawrence and Apocalypse* (1933); in her novel, *Neutral Ground* (1933); in her memoir of Jessie Chambers, *D. H. Lawrence's 'Princess'* (1951); in a group of poems, *Songs of Autumn* (1960); and in *D. H. Lawrence: The Croydon Years* (1965). Lawrence wrote of the relationship in *The Trespasser,* in several stories, and in his 'Helen' poems.

Helen Corke had grown up on the Essex coast and in the London suburbs; her father was a shopkeeper. She had taken her teacher's training at the Pupil-Teacher Centre at Croydon, where one of her fellow students was A. W. McLeod, later Lawrence's friend at the Davidson Road School. Helen Corke was never at Davidson; she taught at the Deering Place School near the Brighton Road in the southern part of Croydon.

She met Lawrence during the winter of 1908–1909, his first at Davidson, and their acquaintance began mildly enough. It intensified in the autumn of 1909, when Lawrence returned from his summer holidays on the Isle of Wight and in the Midlands to find Helen in a state of shock from a personal disaster. It was then, in his efforts to revive her, that he became her close friend.

Ellis Brooke, the heroine of Helen Corke's *Neutral Ground,* similarly suffers from shock. She has become involved with a married man, her violin teacher—a situation Lawrence made use of in *The Trespasser* in 1912. In both these novels the man persuades the girl to go away with him for a holiday, during which they make themselves miserable. After their return to the London suburbs, the man goes back to his family and then kills himself.

In *Neutral Ground,* a young teacher named Derrick Hamilton helps Ellis after the death of her music master, Angus Rane (or Domine), at a time when 'she did not want to live'. Derrick, as 'Life's ambassador', calls frequently at the girl's home in after-work hours, and often takes her out in the evening. His therapy is not one of trying to make her forget her grief, but rather of making her identify it with all grief; his 'treatment was as skilled as his intentions were subtle. He went to the Greek tragedies for the key to her tower of sorrow. And he found in Euripides an ancient music not jangled out of tune nor distorted in rhythm by Domine's death, but ready to weave his tragedy in with its own harmonies.' He is her self-appointed comrade, sharing her grief, patiently working 'to revive the zest of life in her, always hoping that, by and by, she would turn and see him, and love him with a wiser love than she had given Rane.' Derrick rouses her interests in literature and his own writings, 'but he doubted still whether he were as real to her as the lover of her retrospective dreams.' And indeed he can have no hope, as the title of *Neutral Ground* suggests, and as the closing passage of the book symbolically states. The Helena of *The Trespasser* rejects the young teacher, Cecil Byrne, as she has essentially rejected the music master, here called Siegmund (from *Die Walküre*). And Lawrence's 'Helen' poems project a similar situation.

In those Croydon years, beyond which their friendship didn't last, Lawrence and Helen Corke were avid walkers and talkers. She then lived in Selhurst, not far from Lawrence's Colworth Road residence. On their walks, sometimes accompanied by Agnes Mason, they often went across what were then the great open spaces of South London. And they would hike over Wimbledon Common or through the beechwoods of Richmond Park. They frequently took a train to Purley, at that time a village, and from there walked out on the North Downs. Occasionally they would go to a theater or opera house in London, for performances such as Strauss's *Elektra,* which was then causing great excitement in England, or they would attend band concerts in Hyde Park. This scenery, these events, and the conversations of Lawrence and Helen Corke are all stitched into their writings of this period. The most intense account of the entire experience is in the poems in which Lawrence's own attitude to the relationship is expressed; these poems are identifiable because the name Helen appears in them; some of them may, however, be included among the love poems that are not addressed to any identifiable woman. In several cases a guess may be hazarded.

In 1968, when Helen Corke was eighty-six, she was interviewed on BBC 2 television by Malcolm Muggeridge, who had been a pupil of hers. She spoke very candidly of her experiences with Lawrence. She said that he must have been attractive because she thought little of young men at the time, indeed felt a kind of contempt for them. (The Siegmund of *The Trespasser* had been thirty-nine.) Miss Corke said that Lawrence, while writing his version of the story, had identified himself with Siegmund, had 'felt personally in the same way as his character'. Asked whether Lawrence could have been her lover, Helen Corke said no, since she would not have been his. Yet she felt sympathetic to him and 'had a great affection for him'. But she felt no physical urge towards him. She stated that she wouldn't have made a wife for him or for anyone else.

There was also the complication of Jessie Chambers, whom Helen Corke had met. Jessie felt that Lawrence was 'one of the sons of God'. She had had little experience of men and, Helen Corke felt, was too obsessed with Lawrence, thinking 'they would have an ideal companionship in marriage'. When Lawrence tried to make their relationship into a sexual one, Jessie 'was not ready for any such physical relationship'. Asked about Jessie's attractiveness, Helen Corke said that Jessie 'was extremely attractive. She certainly was to me.' In fact, Helen admitted that she had been 'much more in love with her than with Lawrence'. Asked whether she thought Lawrence was in any way homosexual, she replied that she had 'no evidence whatever' of this. He was, she thought, in the middle part of the spectrum of sex, which had its extremes, with the masculine and feminine at opposite ends, with an intermediate position which was that 'of some of our finest artists', indeed 'of most of them'. Muggeridge, mentioning that Helen Corke had used 'neutral ground' as the title of her autobiographical novel, asked her if she were in the intermediate range, and she said that she was.

When Muggeridge inquired as to whether Lawrence liked clever women, Miss Corke answered that 'he preferred the type of woman who was a mother or a mistress'. They stopped seeing each other in 1912, after Lawrence had written to her from Edward Garnett's, suggesting that she visit him there, for Garnett was 'beautifully unconventional'. Thinking she knew what this meant, she wrote back to Lawrence coldly, and that was the end of their friendship. But it lives on in his often agonizing poems to her.

The 'Helen' verses occur in *Love Poems, Amores, New Poems* and, with revisions, in *Collected Poems*.

'The Appeal' in *Love Poems* sets the stage, with Lawrence as the supplicant:

> . . . *Helen, you let my kisses stream*
> *Wasteful into the night's black nostrils; drink*
> *Me up I pray; oh you who are Night's Bacchante,*
> *How can you from my bowl of kisses shrink!*

And although no name appears in 'The Return', the reference to the violin identifies it as one of the 'Helen' poems ('Ah, here I sit while you break the music beneath / Your bow; for broken it is, and hurting to hear.'); 'Repulsed' gives a fuller picture of the relationship and illustrates Lawrence's gift of fusing people and landscape, in the way that he was later to do in the novels:

The night is immense and awful, Helen, and I am insect small
In the fur of this hill, clung on to the fur of shaggy, black heather.
A palpitant speck in the fur of the night, and afraid of all,
Seeing the world and the sky like creatures hostile together.

And I in the fur of the world, and you a pale fleck from the sky,
How we hate each other tonight, hate, you and I,
As the world of activity hates the dream that goes on on high,
As a man hates the dreaming woman he loves, but who will not reply.

'Excursion' is another of the 'Helen' poems; it records a railway journey Lawrence and Helen Corke once made together. This occurred in the autumn of 1910, when Lawrence had gone to Eastwood to visit his mother for a weekend. Helen had been at Arno Vale, in the Mapperley area of Nottingham, to visit Jessie Chambers, whose family had moved to a farm there. Lawrence and Helen returned to London together on the Sunday midnight train from Nottingham; he sat apart from her, brooding, in a corner of the compartment, and later he recorded the experience in some clumsy verses:

'Your presence peering lonelily there / Oppresses me so I can hardly
bear / To share the train with you. . . .'

> *So, dear love, when another night*
> *Pours on us, lift your fingers white*
> *And strip me naked, touch me light,*
>   *Light, light all over.*
> *For I ache most earnestly for your touch,*
> *Yet I cannot move, however much*
>   *I would be your lover.*
>
> *Night after night with a blemish of day*
> *Unblown and unblossomed has withered away;*
> *Come another night, come a new night, say*
>   *Will you pluck me apart?*
> *Will you open the amorous, aching bud*
> *Of my body, and loose the burning flood*
>   *That would leap to you from my heart?*

In *Collected Poems,* the title was changed to 'Excursion Train',
and among other alterations of text, the phrase 'dear love' in the next-
to-last stanza was changed to the name Helen.

Some of the other poems in *Amores* and *Love Poems* that may
belong in the 'Helen' series are: 'Mating' (called 'Come Spring,
Come Sorrow' in *Collected Poems*), in which the poet sees ducks
and toads and horses mating, feels the 'quickening, masculine
gleam' of the fecundating sun, and asks the woman why she shrinks
from his own desire to fill her, flush her, 'rife / With increase', with
'the vivid, ah, the fiery surplus of life'; 'A Spiritual Woman' (in the
Collected edition, 'These Clever Women'), who has been taught 'to
see / Only a mean arithmetic on the face of things', is told that she
should be kissed until blind so that she will discover new life in the
darkness (in the *Collected* version, the poem ends, 'Is there no hope /
Between your thighs, far, far from your peering sight?'); 'Perfidy' (in
the later edition, 'Turned Down'), in which the poet, after knocking
at the door of a house at night and receiving no answer, wanders in
the city street until after 'a hastening car swept shameful past', he
sees the woman 'hid in the shadow', the 'step to the kerb, and fast /
Run to the silent door' and enter, 'leaving the street aghast'.

This is a good amount of poetry for a man to have written to one
woman. But we must remember that Helen Corke was no ordinary
girl: she was an 'advanced' thinker, and she was passionately interested

in writing. She was attractive, very small physically, with reddish hair. The poems continually show that she spelled only disturbance to Lawrence. As 'Lilies in the Fire' suggests, she shrank from his love ('Your radiance dims when I draw too near, and my free / Fire enters your petals like death, you wilt dead white').

Yet, with her sensibility, her own writing talent (she was destined to have a certain amount of success as an author of widely adopted textbooks and of economic histories), and her sympathetic insight into the problems of the artist, Helen Corke was an important factor in Lawrence's development. Their discussions often helped his writing, as on the day he talked with her after a visit to the Tate Gallery and then at once wrote his poems 'Corot' ('The trees rise tall and taller, lifted / On a subtle rush of cool grey flame') and 'Michelangelo' ('God shook thy roundness in his finger's cup'). And one of the best of Lawrence's early poems, 'Coldness in Love', was what we might call 'Variations on a Theme by Helen Corke', for Lawrence took it from her own poem 'Fantasy', which was an attempt to express the feeling induced in her by the atmosphere of the Sussex coast. As she described the event in a letter to this author:

It happened that on the 1st Oct. 1910 he and I walked from Brighton over the cliffs, a 9-mile walk to Newhaven, where my summer holidays had been spent in childhood with the cousin who is called Aileen in *Neutral Ground*. The place for me was a place of ghosts, for my cousin, her mother, grandmother and grandfather, in whose pleasant, peaceful house I had stayed, were all dead. L. and I continued on round the bay, and reached Seaford, a little town from which summer holiday visitors had departed, at twilight. We asked for rooms at a boarding house on the front; the landlady conducted us to opposite ends of a corridor, and left the house. I felt horribly tired and Rip Van Winklish, but slept at once and woke into an intensely silent sea fog, which swathed the house like a huge, clammy spider-web, and filled me with cold terror. My poem was an attempt to express the atmosphere of the experience—futile, as I now realize, since atmospheres can only be suggested and never conveyed. Said Lawrence, when I showed it to him: 'I always feel, when you give me an idea, how much better I could work it out myself!' So the obverse side of 'Fantasy' became 'Coldness in Love.'

'Coldness in Love' was a kind of cousin to another Georgian love poem, 'A Memory', which Rupert Brooke wrote at Waikiki in October 1913: 'Somewhile before the dawn I rose and stept / Softly along the dim way to your room . . .' Lawrence's poem is, metrically, less smooth than Brooke's, but it has a greater force of life in it. In the *Collected Poems* of 1928, Lawrence gave 'Coldness in Love' a new last line, 'That my love can dawn in warmth again, unafraid', but otherwise left the earlier version for the most part unchanged. The first verses of the poem contain some moving evocations of the gray seacoast and the chill day and evening, the poet waking when 'dawn at the window blew in like dust', then:

> . . . *I rose in fear, needing you fearfully,*
> *For I thought you were warm as a sudden jet of blood.*
> *I thought I could plunge in your spurting hotness, and be*
> *Clean of the cold and the must.—With my hand on the latch*
> *I heard you in your sleep speak strangely to me.*

> *And I dared not enter, feeling suddenly dismayed.*
> *So I went and washed my deadened flesh in the sea*
> *And came back tingling clean, but worn and frayed*
> *With cold, like the shell of the moon: and strange it seems*
> *That my love has dawned in rose again, like the love of a maid.*

'Intime', which first appeared in *New Poems* in 1918, looked back on the Lawrence-Helen relationship in a kind of valediction. In *Collected Poems* Lawrence gave it a new title, 'Passing Visit to Helen': 'Returning, I find her just the same, / At just the same old delicate game . . .' of rousing him without satisfying him. Helen was in some ways like Jessie, whose good friend she became, and indeed Helen had a good deal in common with most of Lawrence's women friends. The one he married was the exception, and although she became the central woman of Lawrence's existence, he may still have felt somewhat drawn towards those of the other type, essentially 'spiritual', because of an unconscious recognition on his part that they were— except for Jessie, who made a contest out of the relationship—the kind of women who would have won the approval of his mother.

*

Lawrence had kept up his correspondence with Louie Burrows, to whom he sent a list of 'great' men, at her request. The enumeration is particularly interesting because it foreshadows some of the thinking on the subject that later went into his *Movements in European History*, written towards the end of World War I. In that book, Lawrence was under the influence of Gibbon, notably in his description of historical personages such as Attila, who is discussed in the history volume, and about whom Lawrence wrote a poem in the late 1920s. The list was made up almost entirely of military men, with a few political figures (Robespierre and Danton among them) and a few saints (Jerome, Francis of Assisi, Catherine of Siena). The military men included Hannibal, Julius Caesar (also a political man, like Cromwell, Peter the Great, and other generals Lawrence wrote of), Charlemagne, Napoleon, and others. This listing (which occurs in full in *Lawrence in Love* [1968], the letters to Louie Burrows, edited by James T. Boulton) is a highly interesting roster in consideration of Lawrence's life and works, for it shows what men he particularly revered, a clue to the man himself and, accordingly, to various matters discussed in his writings.

Another letter to Louie Burrows (March 28, 1909) is a lively account of events two nights before a Croydon by-election that involved an antisuffragette Conservative, Sir Robert Harmon-Hodge. It was in the days of the first militant women's-liberation outbursts of the twentieth century, which were hardly less spectacular than those of their descendants were to be. The letter to Louie about the disturbances should be read against the background of the fact that Louie, Jessie Chambers, and Alice Dax—as pointed out earlier—were eager for equality and sometimes were vigorous in their expressions, occasionally as socialists.

As Lawrence told Louie, he 'was in the fun the other night', watching a crowd of men around two suffragettes in an automobile. One of them, a Miss Cameron, cried out that 'If men cannot control themselves, it is time women had some power to control them.' The howling mob of men surged around the car, as if to overturn it—a technique often used in public disputes many years later. It would have frightened Louie's 'fresh, barbarian heart'. He went on to describe the subsequent events, with various parts of the mob trying to drown out one another by chanting. It is a particularly interesting letter, for it foreshadows the episodes of violence in Lawrence's three novels dealing with leadership—*Aaron's Rod*, *Kangaroo*, and *The Plumed Serpent*—in the early and middle 1920s.

It is further interesting to note that, after relating the events occurring two days before the election, Lawrence goes on to discuss briefly the wretchedness of poor children in schoolrooms ('Louisa, my dear, life is not gentle, and amusing, and pleasant, I am afraid'), then mentions his Sunday visit to the Dulwich Art Gallery, to look at the Titians, Hobbemas, Murillos, and the work of other masters. In further letters he speaks of concerts—performances of Wagner didn't greatly impress him—and visits to theaters. Altogether, the young man from the provinces was viewing life at various levels in the great, spreading city.

2 THE MARK OF DEATH

Jessie Chambers not only encouraged Lawrence's early efforts at writing but also submitted his poems to an editor. Jessie said that Lawrence told her she might send some of his work to the *English Review,* as she had suggested, if she gave him a *nom de plume:* he had no wish to be known in Croydon as a poet. (Her pseudonym for him was Richard Greasley, based on his unused name Richards and on the name of his parish.) Lawrence's version of the incident was different; he recalled that while he was at Croydon, 'the girl who had been the chief friend of my youth, and who was herself a schoolteacher in a mining village, copied out some of my poems, and without telling me, sent them to the *English Review,* which had just had a glorious rebirth [beginning] under Ford Madox Hueffer.'

When Jessie sent Lawrence's work to Hueffer, in the summer of 1909, and Hueffer replied that he found it interesting, Lawrence was away. He and his mother were spending part of the summer holidays on the Isle of Wight. When they returned and Jessie showed Lawrence the editor's letter, he said, '*You* are my luck.' He then took the letter to his mother, and Jessie never saw it again. Since Mrs. Lawrence never referred to it, Jessie felt she was in disgrace, 'guilty of unwarrantable interference in his affairs'.

The summer of 1909 must have been a happier one than usual for Mrs. Lawrence, inasmuch as Jessie didn't go with her and her son on their holiday that year. Several of the Pagans were in the party, but Mrs. Lawrence didn't object to most of them. George Neville, among those who went, remembered that the others were Alice Hall, Frances and Gertrude Cooper, and Ada Lawrence. Alice Hall's mother helped Mrs. Lawrence chaperon the group.

They pooled their funds and engaged Rose Cottage at Shanklin, on the southeast side of the island, where they rented beach tents. Lawrence, away from Croydon and farther away from Eastwood than he had ever been, yet also in the company of his mother, was unusually happy. The younger people hiked around the island, and went up to Cowes in the first week of August to see the review of the fleet for the king and the tsar. Lawrence was merely a young schoolmaster on holiday, but the scenery of the Isle of Wight and the review of the fleet were providing him with impressions he would make abundant use of in his second novel, *The Trespasser*. He was not even planning that book at the time, since he didn't begin using Helen Corke's manuscript as his source until early in 1910; but he could then evoke his memories of the place.

This was the last summer holiday his mother was to enjoy; she had just turned fifty-seven, and although she seemed in good health, the wear and strain of the thirty-five years of her wretched marriage had taken their toll. Exactly a year later her fatal illness began.

*

It was after his return to Croydon, when school started again, that Lawrence first went to see Ford Madox Hueffer. That genial but picturesquely unreliable reporter had his own version of the story of Jessie's sending the manuscripts and of Lawrence's first visit to the editorial office, when he came in looking like a red fox. Hueffer insisted, in some reminiscences more than a quarter of a century later, that Jessie had sent him prose as well as poetry, and that the first bit of Lawrence's writing he had read was the opening passage of the story 'Odour of Chrysanthemums', which was enough to indicate to him that Lawrence was a skilled writer; he at once put it into the basket reserved for accepted manuscripts, then left to attend a literary dinner. There, according to Hueffer, he sat at a table with Maurice Baring, Hilaire Belloc, G. K. Chesterton, and H. G. Wells, who before long was saying to someone at Lady Londonderry's adjoining table, 'Hooray, Fordie's discovered another genius! Called D. H. Lawrence!' And, Hueffer added, two publishers that evening asked for first-refusal rights to Lawrence's first novel: the name of the obscure young teacher 'was already known in London before he even knew that any of his work had been submitted to an editor.'

It may well be that the description of this incident is based on indistinct recollections or is largely an invention to dramatize the force of Hueffer's early enthusiasm for Lawrence (as well as to suggest the power of Hueffer's influence), but it is also possible that the incident is correctly reported. In any event, the account gives some of the atmosphere of the metropolitan literary society into which Lawrence was before very long to be rather tentatively admitted—the society which he was to satirize, after his subsequent recoil from it, in *Women in Love* and in other stories.

In *Return to Yesterday* (1931), Hueffer (by that time Ford Madox Ford) tells of an incredible trip to Eastwood, where at the Lawrence house he saw young people gather, after their day of teaching or their work in the mines, drifting in and out 'with the sort of freedom from restraint that I have only seen elsewhere in American small towns.' But Mrs. Lawrence always protected her house from the chattering young; the number of such visitors was rigidly kept to a minimum, as Jessie Chambers and others have indicated. Working towards the bizarre, Ford describes the father, home from the pit on Saturday evening, sitting at a kitchen table with men from the mine and counting out the money they had all earned. Parts of this last episode could have been drawn from Lawrence's early writings, but as Ford goes on, he becomes extremely fantastic, as in the following (italics added): 'All the while the young people were talking about Nietzsche and Wagner and Leopardi and Flaubert and Karl Marx and Darwin and *occasionally the father would interrupt his counting to contradict them.*'

Hueffer later said he never really 'liked Lawrence much. He remained too disturbing even when I got to know him well.' And although Lawrence didn't whine, he continually needed solicitude, as well as moral support, to replace the influence of the mother he was away from, and about whose personality and opinions he talked 'in a way that is unusual in young men out to make their fortunes'.

Perhaps Hueffer—of whom Lawrence wrote to Jessie, 'he is fairish, fat, about forty, and the kindest man on earth'—had to bear the brunt of this dependence because he first published Lawrence, and did so quite impressively. The blue-covered issue of the *English Review* for November 1909 shows Lawrence at the beginning of the journal, with his poems taking up the first six pages of an issue that also featured, in order, the novelist John Galsworthy, the belletrist G. Lowes Dickinson, the adventurer R. B. Cunninghame Graham, the economist J. A. Hobson, the journalist Henry W. Nevinson, the historian G. P. Gooch, and Hueffer. No young schoolmaster up from the Midlands could have made a more auspicious debut.

This first group of poems, written after Lawrence went to Croydon,

was doubtless the set Jessie submitted to the *English Review* (their
first book publication was in 1916, in *Amores*). The beginning poem
of the set was 'Dreams Old and Nascent', divided then into two parts,
'I. Old', and 'II. Nascent'. These verses marked the beginning of
Lawrence's schoolmaster poems, of which he was to write several
more later. 'Dreams Old' is a kind of letter to Jessie that begins:

I have opened the window to warm my hands on the sill
Where the sunlight soaks in the stone: the afternoon
Is full of dreams, my love; the boys are all still
In a wistful dream of Lorna Doone.

The *English Review* in which Lawrence made his bow as a poet was
one of the last issues that came out under Hueffer's editorship. His
former associate, Violet Hunt, later called that autumn of 1909 'a
black autumn'; the magazine, 'like a fine lusty baby well started in
life, that only wanted money for its special foods and up-to-date feeding bottles, was slipping, had slipped, out of the editor's yearning
arms.' But there was no hint of trouble when Jessie Chambers visited
London in November and went to Sunday luncheon with Lawrence at
Violet Hunt's. On Jessie's first day in town, a Saturday, Lawrence
was genial and London 'a place of wonder'. In the evening they went
to a play, *The Making of a Gentleman,* and when they arrived at
Croydon the Joneses had already gone to bed. Lawrence cooked a
macaroni supper for his visitor and then showed her his newest poems
and the play *A Collier's Friday Night.*

Jessie was tired by one o'clock; she had left her home at six the
previous morning. But Lawrence asked her to give him one more hour
before she went up to her room, and they enacted a scene that was in
substance to be repeated in the last chapter of *Sons and Lovers.* There
at Croydon, Lawrence varied the pattern a little, telling how, in the
excitement and stress of the new life, he could 'easily peg out'. He
needed a woman, but couldn't afford marriage. He then wondered
whether, without forcing marriage upon him, some girl would, apparently on a regular basis, give him 'that'.

Jessie, not stumbling over the shy euphemism of the future author
of *Lady Chatterley's Lover,* returned the traditional Victorian answer: he would probably dislike 'the kind of girl who would give him
"that" '—and when he then asked her whether she herself would
think such giving to be wrong, she answered, 'Not *wrong*. But very

difficult.' And she thought of the New Testament phrase 'whoso giveth a cup of water in My name'.

Lawrence said he might ask 'her'—a teacher whom he told Jessie he had thought of marrying—to give him 'that', and Jessie replied that everything would depend on how much the girl loved him. Then she announced that she had to go up to sleep, for it was already two o'clock.

On Jessie's second day in London, Lawrence took her to see Hueffer at the *English Review*'s combination flat and office at 84 Holland Park Avenue. Hueffer treated Jessie with great courtesy, asking her at once whether she were a suffragette, and drawing from her the reply that a good friend of hers (probably William Hopkin or his wife or Alice Dax) had enthusiastically told her all about the movement. Then Hueffer asked her whether she were 'a sort of socialist' and, although she paid little attention to politics, she suddenly decided that she was indeed a sort of socialist, and this realization may have marked the beginning of such interests in her life; it has been reported that in later years she was a Soviet sympathizer and made the pilgrimage to Moscow.

On the afternoon of the *English Review* luncheon, Jessie, Hueffer, and Lawrence walked to Violet Hunt's home, not far off, at 80 Campden Hill Road. This was the famous South Lodge, a tall Victorian villa with walls and gardens; it was furnished with mementos of Christina Rossetti, Oscar Wilde, and other relatives and friends of Violet Hunt's youth.

Violet Hunt later recalled that at the luncheon Jessie 'was obviously nervous, but pulled it off all right, though there was a snag when . . . she asked my maid, who was handling the potatoes, in a speaking whisper whether she should keep her gloves on.' (Forty-six years later Lawrence's widow Frieda wrote, 'Violet Hunt about Jessie's gloves I don't believe.' Perhaps Jessie didn't sound sufficiently *aristokratische:* but Frieda wasn't present at that luncheon, whereas Violet Hunt was.) In Jessie's recollection, the amiable and caustic chatter of another of the guests, the young American poet Ezra Pound, dominated the lunch. When Violet Hunt spoke of some of the tortures of the suffragettes in prison, Pound said that the room they were all in at the moment was like a prison.

Another party typical of the ones Lawrence was being introduced to at that time has come down to us from the recollections of Ernest Rhys, first editor of Everyman's Library. Rhys and his wife used to have poets' supper parties at their home in Hermitage Lane, Hampstead, as a kind of unofficial continuation of the meetings of the Rhymers' Club. One night Hueffer brought his new discovery, the schoolmaster from the collieries who wrote verse. Rhys saw Lawrence as 'shy and countryfied' beside the urbane Hueffer. Pound was also there, and Yeats had brought along the actress Florence Farr to speak some of his poems to the accompaniment of her psaltery. While they were all at supper, Yeats began a monologue on the art of joining poetry and music. Pound, unable to break in, began to eat one of the red tulips used as table decoration; he seemed to like it, swallowed all of it, and then took another. Yeats, deep in his monologue, was blind to this, and none of the others mentioned it. Yeats went on and on with his talk, and Pound continued to munch the tulips.

Afterwards, Yeats said he was weary of 'Innisfree', and recited 'That the Night Come' and his 'translation' of Ronsard. During the evening Ernest Radford—with whose family Lawrence was to become closely associated some years later—recited one of his own poems, Pound chanted one of his, 'Ballad of the Goodly Fere', and Florence Farr chanted to the psaltery Yeats's 'The Man Who Dreamed of Fairyland'. It was after Hueffer had delivered a bright little parody of his own that Ernest Rhys asked the quiet young man with the red mustache to read some of the poems he had brought. Lawrence 'rose nervously but very deliberately, walked across to a writing desk whose lid was closed, opened it, produced a mysterious book out of his pocket, and sat down, his back to the company, and began to read in an expressive, not very audible voice.'

The older poets waited politely for him to finish. But after a while it became doubtful that he would. Still keeping his back to them, still reading in a low voice, he turned page after page of his notebook and went through poem after poem. At the end of a half-hour the room was full of murmuring: undisturbed, Lawrence went on reading in his barely audible tone. Finally, at the suggestion of one of the women, Rhys went over to Lawrence and said that he must need a little rest: why not stop for a while now and begin again at midnight?

Lawrence smiled, 'and getting up with an awkward little bow shut the book and desk and retired to his corner.' Later, when some of the others had read, Rhys turned again to Lawrence, for 'one more lyric out of his black book, and impressed it on him that only one would satisfy our ritual needs.' But Hueffer stepped up at this moment, took Lawrence by the arm, and marched him out of the house, 'wickedly' intoning, *'Nunc, nunc dimittis.'*

*

During his years in London, Lawrence kept a close connection with the Midlands and went back during school holidays and occasionally on weekends to visit his mother and sisters and see the other women he loved there: Jessie, Louie Burrows, and Mrs. Dax.

At Croydon, besides Helen Corke, there were apparently three women with whom he was involved, the ones A. W. McLeod, in the letter quoted earlier, mentioned as not known to him: Agnes Holt, Jane, and Mrs. Davidson.

Some of Lawrence's friends, as well as his widow, questioned whether he ever really planned to marry Agnes Holt, as Jessie reported. When Jessie visited London in November 1909, Lawrence took her to meet Agnes, on the day of the lunch at Violet Hunt's. She described Agnes Holt (Jessie didn't give her name) as a red-haired schoolteacher who 'talked to Lawrence rather like an elder sister, and there was about him the curious air of bravado that I always felt arose from a lack of conviction.' According to Jessie, Lawrence by Christmas 1909 had told Agnes Holt that the idea of their getting married was a mistake. Shortly after this, Agnes left Croydon; she married another teacher with whom she went to the Isle of Man, where they managed a school.

In a letter to Blanche Jennings, January 28, 1910, Lawrence mentions a 'love' whom he doesn't like. And although this girl is twenty-seven, Helen Corke's age, and like Helen Corke has red hair, it is possible she is Agnes Holt, since Lawrence in the same letter makes a distinct reference to Helen Corke that doesn't jibe with his description of the girl he is weary of. He speaks of 'a new girl—a girl who "interests" me—nothing else—next time I write—a girl here—call her Hélène—she is very interesting.' This doesn't sound like the young woman mentioned elsewhere in the letter: 'She's rather a striking girl with much auburn hair.' She at first 'seems a person of great capacity' because she is 'alert, prompt, smart with her tongue, and independent in her manner'. Men like her, and Lawrence has 'been out with her a good bit', but he is weary of her because 'she's so utterly ignorant and old fashioned, really, though she has [unlike Helen Corke] been to college and has taught in London some years.' She tends to regard men as trifling and 'still judges by mid-Victorian standards' and 'refuses to see that a man is a male, that kisses are the merest preludes and anticipations, that love is largely a physical sympathy'. In her outlook 'she is all sham and superficial . . . and I can't change her'; she wants to 'be interested in life', but 'lapses into sickly sentimentality when it is a question of naked life.'

Jane remains a mystery of Lawrence's London life. The only direct reference to her is in his letter of February 10, 1912, to Edward Garnett: 'I met Jane and kissed her farewell at Marylebone—my heart was awfully heavy.' Those who knew Lawrence at the time—William Hopkin and George Neville as well as Edward Garnett's son David, who met Lawrence shortly after—were unable to place Jane. Richard Aldington, who didn't know Lawrence in 1912, said that Lawrence was putting 'an end to another of his unsatisfactory love affairs', though it may well have been the woman who was ending the relationship. Aldington tied this in with a Lawrence letter to Sallie Hopkin, dated August 19 of the same year, in which he said, 'Mrs —— writes me—I told her I was with another woman—but no details. I am sorry for her, she is so ill.' But when the blank in that letter is filled in, the name becomes that of an Eastwood resident, Mrs. Dax, whose first name was not Jane but Alice. (Of course, 'Jane' could be Jessie.)

The third of these London women, Mrs. Davidson, is also difficult to trace. George Neville mentioned her to this author. She was at Croydon, he said, and her first name *may* have been Jane. She was a widow and, Neville said, 'friendly' to Lawrence, 'very friendly to him'. As Neville recalled, she also lodged with the Joneses. Actually, because it was the same as that of the school that employed both Lawrence and his landlord, the name Davidson may have been a code word between Lawrence and Neville to disguise the name of a woman who was perhaps not a widow, for example Mrs. Jones.

In his interview with the author in 1950, George Neville was cordially helpful, though now and then it was plain that he was not telling all he knew. One point he insisted on was that a married woman in Eastwood, whom he didn't name, initiated Lawrence into sex—and William Hopkin corroborated this. Hopkin once inadvertently heard Mrs. Dax tell Mrs. Hopkin: 'Sallie, I gave Bert sex. I had to. He was over at our house, struggling with a poem he couldn't finish, so I took him upstairs and gave him sex. He came downstairs and finished the poem.' This is at least another wry addition to the literature of creative inspiration.

Alice Dax, who had never been sexually moved before, fell in love with Lawrence. She hoped that the child she bore sometime later was his, and tried to discern Lawrencean traits in it, but her closest friends, who were in on the secret, insisted that it was plainly her husband's. When, eventually, she and Lawrence parted, she never let another man touch her, not even her husband.

She tried not to hold Lawrence; indeed, she gave him up for what she considered to be his own good. She was often in opposition to him and felt that she would never be able to keep up a kind of quarrelsome harmony with him, as his wife did later. When Alice Dax spontaneously wrote to Frieda, long afterwards (1935), she said that she felt that he had found exactly the right mate. She had herself always felt sure of Lawrence's greatness; but 'I was never *meet* for him and what he liked was not the me I *was,* but the me I might-have-been—the potential me which would never have struggled to life but for his help and influence.' After she gave him up, however, according to Enid Hopkin Hilton, one of her closest friends of those years, she 'went through a hell of the sort we can barely imagine'.

About this time Lawrence was also in the grip of his love affair with Louie Burrows, who attracted him physically. (Lawrence's friends have spoken of her as 'Junoesque'.) He seems to have used Louie frequently to torment Jessie, who remembered that, as early as the summer of 1907, Lawrence went to Louie's home for tea in order to discover the true state of his feeling towards her. A few days later, 'with a significant glance', he handed Jessie a newly written poem, 'Snap-Dragon'. This long poem contained a number of striking passages, such as

. . . I put my hand to the dint
In the flower's throat, and the flower gaped wide with woe.
She watched, she went of a sudden intensely still,
She watched my hand, to see what it would fulfil.

I pressed the wretched, throttled flower between
My fingers, till its head lay back, its fangs
Poised at her. Like a weapon my hand was white and keen,
And I held the choked flower-serpent in its pangs
Of mordant anguish, till she ceased to laugh,
Until her pride's flag, smitten, cleaved down to the staff.

Another of the poems to Louie, as mentioned by Jessie, is 'Kisses

in the Train' ('I saw the midlands / Revolve through her hair . . .'),
and still another she definitely identified with Louie Burrows, 'The
Hands of the Betrothed', not only provides a description of the situation—the passionate girl keeping her lover's hands away from her
body—but tells what Louie looked like: tawny eyes and black hair
and large hands.

These poems present much of the story of the relationship between
Lawrence and Louie Burrows. This went on for at least five years;
but, as with all the other women Lawrence knew during his mother's
lifetime, he couldn't establish a permanent relationship.

Meanwhile he was extending his social life and his range of acquaintances in the London area. A letter of February 28, 1910, gives
an interesting picture of the young man becoming known in artistic
circles at that time; it is to Mrs. Derwent Wood, wife of the sculptor,
to whom he wrote from Croydon:

Dear Mrs Wood,
    I regret very much that I must send back the tickets. It was so
jolly nice of you to send them to me: I feel a meagre sinner returning them to you. But I am just convalescent from a sickness.
I have been laid up in bed for some days, watching the tassel of
the blind swinging endlessly and mournfully across the grey wet
sky. It would have given me real pleasure to have been at the
Bechstein tomorrow evening: but I may not be out at that time,
I am very sorry. But you will have a full grand audience so I do
not matter. I shall call to see you some Saturday evening if I may
to thank you personally.
                                        Yours sincerely,
                                        D. H. Lawrence

Another interesting social contact of that time was with a young
American woman, Grace Crawford, later (1917) to become the wife
of Claud Lovat Fraser, the British costume and set designer who died
prematurely, at the peak of his career, in 1921. Grace Lovat Fraser's
father, T. C. Crawford, financial manager for Buffalo Bill's Wild West
shows, was from Michigan, her mother from Vermont. The family
lived in the fashionable Stratton Street, London, just above Piccadilly
and next to Mayfair Place.

In her autobiographical *In the Days of My Youth* (1970), Grace
Lovat Fraser says that she first heard of Lawrence when her friend
Ezra Pound spoke of him to Hueffer and Violet Hunt while they were

living at South Lodge (which was to give Douglas Goldring the title for his biography of Hueffer). The American girl later asked Pound about the coal miner's son who had become a schoolmaster and poet, and soon after that Pound brought him to the Crawfords' for tea. Grace described him as a young man 'with a small, drooping moustache, carefully brushed hair and heavy clumpy boots' who projected 'a feeling of cool detachment rather than of shyness'. Miss Crawford very soon noticed that Lawrence had a sense of humor, whereas Pound did not. He and she became good friends, but their relationship 'remained on a formal basis'; they always addressed one another as Miss Crawford and Mr. Lawrence.

Lawrence in those days saw Pound frequently and even stayed with him one night in Kensington after he had missed the last train to Croydon. Pound remembered that Lawrence slept in a 'sort of arm-chair convertible to cot'.

Lawrence sometimes went to South Lodge on days when the young people played tennis: Pound, Grace Crawford, Hueffer, and Mary Martindale (sister of Hueffer's Catholic wife, Elsie, who wouldn't let Hueffer get a divorce and marry Violet Hunt). Lawrence never joined the others at tennis, though he enjoyed being scorekeeper and ball retriever. Violet Hunt's mother, who disliked Hueffer and Pound, would hide their tennis shoes, and the men would go roaring through South Lodge trying to find where she had concealed them. Grace Crawford was spared these ordeals, for her shoes were always to be found where she had left them. Lawrence, the nonplayer, enjoyed the little comedy of the hidden tennis shoes.

In a letter to Grace Crawford, Lawrence described Pound as he had recently appeared at Hueffer's: 'At any rate Pound's David Copperfield curls—perhaps you never saw them—like bunches of hop leaves over his ears—they were cut. They used to make me quote to myself, "Good wine needs no bush." His great-grandfather's black satin stock, which would throw into relief the contour of his chin four months ago, had given way to a tie of peach-bloom tint and texture. He wore a dark cotton shirt, no vest and a Panama hat.' He appeared at the Crawfords' in such a costume, with the addition of a turquoise earring. The elder Crawford, an unusually tolerant man according to his daughter, was angry and suggested that she break her friendship with Pound, an event which occurred anyway when she went to Rome in December 1910.

Her absence on the Continent also curtailed her friendship with

Lawrence. On August 4 he had written to her from Lynn Croft, stating that his father was a coal miner, something she had known even before she first met Lawrence. As he explained the household,

My mother, who is short and grey-haired, and shuts her mouth very tight, is reading a translation of Flaubert's *Sentimental Education,* and wears a severe look of disapproval. My father is out—drinking a little beer with a little money he begged of me. My sister [Ada], who is tall and slender and twenty-three years old, has cycled to the theatre in Nottingham with her sweetheart. I have a married brother and a married sister—they do not count.

In July, after a crowded literary party at South Lodge, Lawrence said he wished 'Hueffer wouldn't introduce me as a genius'. He had completed one of the drafts of *The Trespasser,* and Hueffer apparently took the manuscript to Germany with him; William Heinemann, who was to bring out *The White Peacock* at the beginning of the following year, wanted to see *The Trespasser.* Lawrence, just after writing of the suicide of Siegmund, had told Grace Crawford, 'Be thankful you have never to hang your hero. It leaves you with an uncomfortable strangled feeling in your neck and a desolation of death—below the diaphragm.'

When Hueffer read the manuscript, he disliked it. This apparently mattered little, since Lawrence had in any event assured Helen Corke that he wouldn't let *The Trespasser* be published without her consent. As we have seen she did permit its publication, as *The Trespasser,* in 1912, when it was brought out not by Heinemann but by Duckworth.

*

It was not only in London intellectual and artistic circles that Lawrence was having a fairly intense social life; as noted earlier, he kept up his personal relationships with various people in the Midlands, and when he was at home he was a frequent participant in the Hopkins' social discussions, meeting some of the nation's leaders in social reform. As William Hopkin's daughter, Mrs. Enid Hilton, has recalled in a letter: 'Every Sunday evening was open house, when my mother served wonderful "snacks", and we had music, talk, readings, or just plain fun. Philip Snowden, Ramsay MacDonald, Charlotte Despard, Annie Kenny, Beatrice and Sydney Webb, and others of the then "forward" group visited us frequently, and these Lawrence met. He was a silent listener or an almost violent leader of the conversation.' Lawrence at this time had a mustache and habitually 'wore a rather high collar. His face was always pale and thin under a mop of blond-to-brown hair, and there were those deep, intense eyes. When talking vehemently he would, in those days, use his hands a great deal, and I remember one old trick of his of hitting the palm of the left hand violently with the doubled fist of the right hand.'

One of Lawrence's contributions to these discussions was his essay 'Art and the Individual', which he apparently read aloud to groups at both Croydon and Eastwood. This essay began by stating that those who attended such meetings wanted to discuss 'social problems with a view to advancing a more perfect social state and to our fitting ourselves to be perfect citizens—communists—what not'. But after a light remark about the benefits of socialism, Lawrence picked up his true subject, art, and began a critical analysis of Herbart's classifications, very popular in the British pedagogy of that time.

Socialism itself never really captured Lawrence. He wrote to William Hopkin on August 24, 1910, 'I seem to have lost touch altogether with the old "progressive" clique: in Croydon the socialists are stupid, and the Fabians so flat.' Yet most of the friends of his youth, outside the family, were socialists: the Hopkins were permanently so, and for a time at least, Jessie Chambers, Louie Burrows, and Helen Corke all had 'advanced' views. And there was Alice Dax, one of the models for the character of Clara Dawes—suffragette and socialist—in *Sons and Lovers*.

Mrs. Dawes, a Junoesque type, is outwardly more like Louie Burrows or Lawrence's future wife than Mrs. Dax, who was a small woman. But in spirit Clara Dawes has much in common with Alice Dax.

Alice was married to a pharmacist, Henry Dax, who settled in Eastwood and later became an oculist; in 1912 they had moved to Mansfield, also in Nottinghamshire. Henry Dax was conservative in his manner and in the conduct of his business. In his shop, he stuck to a routine line of drugs and patent medicines until his wife introduced more 'frivolous' items such as combs, brushes, and dresser sets. The children of the village found a horrible fascination in the pharmacy because of the large jar of leeches that stood on a bench near the door. In spite of protests against these wriggling creatures, Henry Dax apologetically kept them on display because so many of the miners insisted on the old method of bloodletting; but finally his wife prevailed upon him to keep the leeches out of sight.

Enid Hopkin Hilton has provided, for this book, a sketch of Alice Dax that tells a good deal about a very important woman in Lawrence's life and writings, and a good deal about the Eastwood of *Sons and Lovers:*

Alice Dax and my mother were *years* ahead of their time (which may have been one of her attractions for D.H.L.), and both were widely read, 'advanced' in dress, thought, and house decoration. Alice was almost completely uninhibited in an age when you just weren't. . . . Part of her fight against the 'clutter' of her generation showed itself in her refusal to have one unnecessary article or item in her home. There were few pictures, only one rug, no knick-knacks collected over the years, no items of beauty or arresting interest, but lots of *tidy* books. The furniture was good, modern (then) plain oak and served its purpose with-no-nonsense. There were no little mats under the clocks, or the cookie jar, no 'hangings'. The floors were linoleum-covered or of polished wood. It reflected Alice—clear, direct, uncluttered in thought and action, to the point of harshness. . . . Together she and my mother worked for the women's cause, and I remember being taken to 'meetings' in the City of Nottingham. We waved green, purple, and white flags, and the speakers, the Pankhursts, Annie Kenny and others whose names I have forgotten—came home with us and stayed at our house, and discussions went on and on far into the night, intense, but friendly and a bit gay. . . . Meetings were held in our small town and there was much enthusiasm, many fights and some really productive effort. Keir Hardy stayed with us, Ramsay MacDonald, Philip Snowden, Edward Carpenter, Margaret Bondfield—many others. Mother was an amazing hostess and our house was 'open' every Sunday evening when many village people drifted in and there was more talk, music, food, more discussion. . . . Alice Dax carried her ideas almost to extremes. Gradually she became a NAME in the district, a person to whom people turned in trouble, and who initiated all the good community enterprises, such as nursing associations, local forms of health insurance and so forth. She successfully tackled the school system too, and new modern schools arose. Alice Dax was one of the kindest persons I have ever met, but most of the men of her generation feared her. She represented a kind of ramrod, forcing the future into their present in an uncomfortable and uncomprehended manner. And she could and did contradict their statements and words of wisdom, and she *dared* to be right—too often. So my father, I feel, subconsciously feared the impact of her personality and beliefs on my mother, and on me. As with most reformers he could change the world but liked his home intact.

As Mrs. Hilton has further remarked, 'the little community was strangely alive and rich, in that time before the great strikes and the labour troubles, and after the worst of the Victorian era and the Boer War. England was almost remade by groups such as ours in that Midland town. They were spearheads into a future whose promise has not been fulfilled.'

*

Lawrence's work continued to appear in the *English Review,* which published his short story 'Goose Fair' in its February 1910 issue, and groups of poems in the April and October numbers. Austin Harrison was now the editor, assisted by a fugitive from the diplomatic service, a zoologist, wit, and amateur classicist named Norman Douglas.

For the rest of Lawrence's life Douglas was a kind of inimical friend. In his autobiography (*Looking Back*), written after Lawrence's death, Douglas remembered him as 'an inspired provincial with marked puritan leanings', who 'sometimes turned up at the *English Review* office with stories like "The Prussian Officer" written in that impeccable handwriting of his. They had to be cut down for magazine purposes; they were too redundant; and I was charged with the odious task of performing the operation.' Douglas insisted that 'the prevalent conception of Lawrence as a misanthrope is wrong. He was a man of naturally blithe disposition, full of childlike curiosity. The core of his mind was unsophisticated. He touched upon the common things of earth with tenderness and grace. . . . There was something elemental in him, something of the *Erdgeist.*'

Lawrence's first *English Review* story, 'Goose Fair', with a Nottingham setting, has many of the qualities mentioned by Douglas, and it gives evidence from the first of Lawrence's skill as a storyteller. It also shows that by this time his prose had attained a smoothness (sometimes rather flat) not found in his verse. The poetry was untamed, as it always would be. In Lawrence's early period, it presaged the tumbling, vital quality that his later prose was to have.

If these second and third groups of poems published in the *English Review* in April and October 1910 were not up to the standard of the November 1909 set, it should be remembered that Lawrence was as yet a young poet, experimenting, and that his efforts were not equally successful. He didn't, in any event, republish several of the poorest of them. In some cases this was a loss, for even his poorest verse sometimes had excellent individual phrases and lines.

The three groups of poems in the *English Review* in 1909 and 1910, 'Goose Fair' in the same journal in 1910, and the anonymous tale 'A Prelude' in the *Nottinghamshire Guardian* comprised Lawrence's total publication before his first book appeared. The *White Peacock* came out under the Heinemann imprint in January 1911, the month after his mother died.

*

Mrs. Lawrence's illness began in August 1910 when she was visiting her sister Ada in Leicester.

Lawrence, who had completed *The White Peacock* earlier in the year, had written the first draft of *The Trespasser* (then called *The Saga of Siegmund*) between Whitsuntide and midsummer. While working on the book, he had begged Jessie not to try 'to hold him'. In August he suggested a visit to the Chambers family at their new farm in Arno Vale, and they prepared a room for him. He wrote to Helen Corke that when he saw Jessie in Eastwood, she had looked 'very pretty and very wistful'. He was afraid, now, of going to visit the Chamberses; he hoped he would 'have the heart to tell' Jessie that they should 'finally and definitely part'. A few days later, when Jessie saw him again at Eastwood, he announced that he would not go to Arno Vale. She said she was weary of his changes: she wanted either 'complete union or a complete break'. Lawrence told her it must, then, be a complete break, and they made an agreement to stop sending letters to one another. But before a week had passed, he wrote advising her to look into Barrie's *Sentimental Tommy* and its sequel, *Tommy and Grizel*. If she would read these books, he said, she might understand his own predicament (a statement that seems rather sardonic in the light of subsequent revelations about Barrie). Shortly afterwards, Lawrence sent Jessie a pathetic letter telling of his mother's illness.

He wrote to William Hopkin from Leicester on August 24, saying that 'a tumour or something' had developed in his mother's abdomen, and that the doctor was looking grave and saying the situation was serious. The grinding illness that would kill her in a little more than three months had begun.

Before Lawrence found his mother ill at Leicester, he had been on a holiday trip in Lancashire, at Blackpool, at Fleetwood, and at Barrow-in-Furness, with George Neville. They had visited Neville's aunt at Blackpool and two sisters named Stewart who had been at college with Lawrence. Thus the 'Sentimental Tommy' was forgetting his troubles. But soon all other considerations were disregarded after the appalling realization that Mrs. Lawrence had cancer.

The most thorough account of her slow dying through that autumn of 1910 occurs in *Sons and Lovers*. A number of poems in *Amores* also reflect various phases of the experience. *Sons and Lovers* contains all the circumstantial details of the visits of the doctors, the mother's return home in a hired automobile, her ultimate confinement and increasing agony. The effectiveness of the narration is heightened by its restraint, even in the passages describing the son's anxiety and grief. The poems on the subject of the mother's illness and death were written as direct expressions of Lawrence's feelings, and perhaps put down at the moment of experience. Sometimes they contain material that also appears in *Sons and Lovers,* such as the passage in which Paul, smoking a cigarette by the kitchen fire, starts to brush some ash off his coat and notices 'it was one of his mother's grey hairs. It was so long! He held it up, and it drifted into the chimney. He let go. The long grey hair floated and was gone in the blackness of the chimney.' The poem 'Sorrow', which repeats this experience, ends:

> *I should find, for a reprimand*
> *To my gaiety, a few long grey hairs*
> *On the breast of my coat; and one by one*
> *I watched them float up the dark chimney.*

Another of the poems, 'Anxiety', shows Lawrence at Croydon—from which he could get away only on weekends after school reopened in September—waiting for the news of his mother's death and, when the messenger boy passes on his bicycle, the poet wonders whether it is relief he feels, 'Or a deeper bruise of knowing that still / She has no rest.'

In October, Lawrence asked Sidney Pawling, one of the Heinemann editors, to hasten the printing of *The White Peacock:* 'Not that I care much myself. But I want my mother to see it while she keeps the live consciousness. She is really horribly ill.' Fourteen years later, Lawrence remembered: 'The very first copy of *The White Peacock* that was ever sent out, I put into my mother's hands when she was dying. She looked at the outside, and then at the title-page, and then at me, with darkening eyes.' Despite her love for him, she couldn't seem to believe that he had written an important book: 'This David would never get a stone across at Goliath. And why try? Let Goliath alone! —Anyway, she was beyond reading my first immortal work. It was put aside, and I never wanted to see it again. She never saw it again.'

Jessie Chambers reported that when Lawrence came home from Croydon on alternate weekends during this period, he was under 'a terrible strain' and, although ostensibly 'interested in things', he was 'terribly alone', it was plain, 'in his grief'. He projected a 'horror of sheer hopelessness'. Jessie said that even the sincerest and most disinterested love could not reach him, though his brother George told her that Louie used to visit the house and was 'very kind when mother was ill'. It was at this time, a week or two before his mother's death, that Lawrence sent Jessie the letter informing her that he had proposed marriage to Louie.

Lawrence wrote a direct account of his experiences at the time of his mother's illness, in a letter of December 5 to McLeod:

Mother is very bad indeed. It is a continuous 'We watched her breathing through the night—', ay, and the mornings come, snowy, and gloomy, and like this 'chill with early showers', and still she is here, and it is the old slow horror. I think Tom Hood's woman looked sad but beautiful: but my mother is a sight to see and be silent about for ever. She has had a bloody hard life, and has always been bright: but now her face has fallen like a mask of bitter cruel suffering. She was, when well, incredibly bright, with more smile wrinkles than anything: you'd never know that this was the permanent structure on which the other floated. I sit hour after hour in the bedroom, for I am chief nurse, watching her— and sometimes I turn to look out of the window at the bright wet cabbages in the garden, and the horses in the field beyond, and the church-tower small as a black dice on the hill at the back a long way off, and I find myself apostrophising the landscape 'So that's what you mean, is it?'—and under the mobile shadowy change of expression, like smiles, on the countryside, there seems to be the cast of eternal suffering. Banal! . . .

Oh, there's one thing I'll tell you—if you promise not to give me away. I went to Leicester on Saturday. There I met an old girl friend of mine, with whom I've always kept up a connexion —she was 'my girl' in Coll, though there have been changes since. Well, we were coming down from Leicester to Quorn, where Louie lives. There were five women with us in a small corridor compartment. We had been talking very sympathetically, and had got to Rothley, next station to Quorn. 'And what do you think you'll do, Bert,—after Christmas?' said Louie. I said I didn't know—then added 'Why, I should like to get married.' She hung her head. 'Should *you?*' I asked. She was much embarrassed, and said *she* didn't know. 'I should like to marry you' I said suddenly, and I opened my eyes, I can tell you. She flushed scarlet. 'Should *you?*' I added. She looked out of the window and murmured huskily, 'What?'—'Like to marry me?' I said. She turned to me quickly, and her face shone like a luminous thing. 'Later,' she said. I was very glad. The brakes began to grind. 'We're at Quorn' I said, and my heart sank. She suddenly put her hand on mine and leaned to me. 'I'll go to Loughboro' she said. The five women rose. 'I can come back by the 8.10,' she said. The five women, one by one, issued forth, and we ran out among the floods and the darkness. There are such floods at Loughboro—I saw them going up.

So I have written to my other girls, and I have written to Louie's father. She is a glorious girl: about as tall as I, straight and strong as a caryatid (if that's how you spell them)—and swarthy and ruddy as a pomegranate, and bright and vital as a pitcher of wine. I'm jolly glad I asked her. What made me do it, I cannot tell. Twas an inspiration. But I can't tell mother.

I tell you because I want to tell somebody who is interested— and you will not look shocked or doubtful as would those who know my affairs more fully. But the rest can go to the devil, so I have Louie.

But I told her 'My wealth is £4 4" 2½"'—for I counted in my pocket—'and not a penny more.'—Which is true—I haven't another bodle [small Scottish coin].

'And I haven't twice as much' she confessed. Then we laughed. But I wish I had £100—I shall try for a country school and get married as soon as possible.

Now look here—you often tell Philip [Smith] things I don't want you to tell him. I shall be ever so mad if you tell him this— or anybody. But tell him all the rest, because I don't want to force myself to write to him.

I have got my copy of the Peacock—but I don't think Pawling will publish till after the election. It looks a nice book—very nice—from the outside: I haven't looked in—haven't wanted. Mother just glanced at it. 'It's yours, my dear,' my sister said to her. 'Is it?' she murmured, and she closed her eyes. Then a little later, she said, 'What does it say?'—and my sister read her the tiny inscription I had put in. Mother has said no more of it.

I have just turned her over—she cannot move. 'Bert'—she said very strange and childish and plaintive—half audible 'It's very windy.' She had just been able to make out what the noise was. The cellars and chimneys are roaring and the windows banging. You have no idea—I hope—how many degrees of death there are. My mother's face—almost all but the cheeks— is grey, as grey as the sky.

Two days earlier, Lawrence had written to Rachel Annand Taylor, whose poems he had read to a literary society. He had become a friend or at least a confidant of Mrs. Taylor—Richard Aldington said in an unpublished letter that Lawrence had had a love affair with her—and he told her about Louie and something about his home setting ('My father is a cinder'). In Lawrence's letter to Mrs. Taylor he gave another version of the history of his affections:

Nobody can have the soul of me. My mother has had it, and nobody can have it again. Nobody can come into my very self again, and breathe me like an atmosphere. Don't say I am hasty this time—I know. Louie—whom I wish I could marry the day after the funeral—she would never demand to drink me up and have me. She loves me—but it is a fine, warm, healthy natural love—not like Jane Eyre, who is Muriel [Jessie], but like—say Rhoda Fleming or Anna Karenina. She will never plunge her hands through my blood and feel for my soul, and make me set my teeth and shiver and fight away. Ugh—I have done well— and cruelly—tonight.

*

In *Sons and Lovers,* when the son's agony becomes too great as the mother's suffering increases, Paul and his sister determine on a 'mercy killing' by putting an overdose of morphine pills in her milk: 'Then they both laughed together like two conspiring children. On top of all their horror flickered this little sanity.'

In the novel, the mother dies that same night. Whether or not Lawrence actually eased his mother's death—the euthanasia may have been put into *Sons and Lovers* to heighten the dramatic effect —Paul's grief after his mother has died is certainly Lawrence's own grief.

But the question remains: Did Lawrence kill his mother?

A possible answer is found in the autobiography of Lina Waterfield, who knew Lawrence in Italy in 1913–1914. Her husband, the painter Aubrey Waterfield, described to the poet Robert Calverley Trevelyan a visit to Fiascherino, to the villa where Lawrence was living with Frieda, who was then passing for his wife. Waterfield in a letter of June 8, 1914, said, 'It gave me a shock when he told us that every incident even to the death of his mother in *Sons and Lovers* was true, because I felt in the book that they did not kill her to put her out of her misery, he particularly says she wanted to live but because he and his sister couldn't bear it. . . .'—and the printed letter breaks off at this point.

Mrs. Waterfield, who published this letter in her autobiography, *Castle in Italy* (1961), tells more definitely of a discussion with Lawrence. Its reliability may be gauged in terms of her experience as a long-time correspondent for the London *Observer* and other journals. She says that when she met Lawrence (and undoubtedly she kept a diary) she was shy about mentioning *Sons and Lovers,* but he abruptly asked her what she thought of the book. She praised it highly, then said, 'But'—and he asked her why she stopped. She told him she thought that the euthanasia episode was 'not in keeping with the son's character' or with the adoration he had for his mother. In giving her the overdose of morphine, she said, he is behaving selfishly 'because he cannot bear to see her suffer. It is not his mother who wants to die. Surely the son's action strikes a false note?'

Lawrence told Mrs. Waterfield she was 'quite wrong. You see *I* did it—I gave her the overdose of morphia and set her free.'

Mrs. Waterfield 'was too stunned and bewildered to continue the argument'. That night she asked her husband whether he thought 'Lawrence had really killed his mother'. She was 'relieved when he said that he had taken the story as a symbol of [Lawrence's] terrible grief at the loss of a mother he had loved with a fiercely possessive love.'

*

Mrs. Lawrence was buried in a windy December rainstorm, as recorded credibly in *Sons and Lovers:* 'The wet clay glistened, all the white flowers were soaked.' The son and daughter stood together by the grave, at the bottom of which a corner of their brother's coffin could be seen. Then the oak box containing their mother was steadily lowered: 'She was gone. The rain poured in the grave. The procession of black, with its umbrellas glistening, turned away. The cemetery was deserted under the drenching cold rain.'

The day before the funeral, Jessie reported, she and Lawrence 'walked once more on the familiar lanes,' and also went over the old conversational grounds. Lawrence, who had 'brutally tossed a coin' to a beggar near Moorgreen Reservoir, explained to the angry Jessie that 'a man has sunk pretty low when he can take a copper in that fashion,' and when Jessie told him he should not have entangled Louie Burrows in their own relationship, Lawrence coldly said that he had nothing to do with *should* and *ought*. Then, as they stood by the railway track near one of the collieries, Jessie said, Lawrence told her 'in a strangled voice' that he had always loved his mother 'like a lover. That's why I could never love you.'

He then gave her 'a draft of three poems he had just written', all of which later appeared in *Amores*. They tell, more directly and more movingly than any other document could tell, the story of the relationship that had dominated his life up to that time, and that would dominate it for some time longer.

These three poems—'The End', 'The Bride', 'The Virgin Mother' —are all concerned with Mrs. Lawrence, and not in the least with Jessie, whose case was as hopeless as before: at that time, Lawrence's mother dominated him even in death. He might have been able to love Jessie if she had been essentially different from his mother.

3 BROKEN ATTACHMENTS AND A NEW BEGINNING

After Heinemann (at the suggestion of Hueffer and Violet Hunt) had accepted *The White Peacock* for English publication, Duffield and Company contracted to bring it out in New York. Duffield printed the book first, then shipped the plates to London. This resulted in some first-edition confusion because the Heinemann editors had persuaded Lawrence to change two paragraphs in the British version, while they made a slight textual alteration on another page. Consequently, the first English edition had two cancel leaves, pages 227–228 and pages 229–230. The change on the first cancel leaf was trivial, the word *mucked* on page 227 having been changed to *dirtied*. The alterations on page 230 were more extensive.

The passage that required change read as follows in the American edition: 'God!—we were a passionate couple—and she would have me in her bedroom while she drew Greek statues of me—her Croton, her Hercules! . . . Then gradually she got tired—it took her three years to have a real bellyful of me.' These lines in the British edition read: 'Lord!—we were an infatuated couple—and she chose to view me in an aesthetic light. I was Greek statues for her, bless you: Croton, Hercules, I don't know what! . . . Then gradually she got tired—it took her three years to be really glutted with me.' (All the original text has been restored in a 1966 edition prepared by the American bibliographer Matthew J. Bruccoli.)

Sufficiently tamed, the book made its first appearance in January 1911, coming out in the United States a day earlier (January 19) than in England. Perhaps because of the rather namby-pamby character of Cyril, the 'I' of the story, the review of the book in the *Athenaeum* began with the statement, 'This novel is characteristic of the modern fiction which is being written by the feminine hand,' and the *Morning Post* critic, in a favorable survey of the book, also suggested that the author was a woman. The anonymous reviewer in the *Athenaeum* found that the novel used the 'cinematographic' (new word then) method, but was not selective; he admitted that there was 'cleverness in this modern study of nerves', but found it 'impossible to avoid the conclusion that the characters were spun in the author's brain'.

Friendlier reviews appeared in the *Daily Chronicle* (Violet Hunt), the *Glasgow Herald* (Catherine Jackson, later Carswell), and the London *Academy* (Henry Savage). The London *Saturday Review* attacked the book's formlessness and its presentation of characters and episodes which did 'not seem to aid the progress of the plot', though in the main the story had 'force and power'. The *English Review* spoke enthusiastically of its protégé: 'In D. H. Lawrence we have a new writer, one most certainly to be reckoned with. . . . It is not perhaps a very good novel. Mr Lawrence is somewhat prolix in his conversations; his life's orbit would seem a little limited; there are loquacious oases of rather heavy and almost suburban dullness. But there are flashes of real genius.' In America, Frederic Tabor Cooper, in the *Bookman*, found the novel 'rather puzzling to estimate', though its realistic scenes were 'written with a relentless skill' which made them painful to read. 'But the author has no special story to tell; the book . . . leaves us with a resentful feeling that we have been very much depressed in spirit to no purpose at all.'

Lawrence reported that his father, on learning that his son had received fifty pounds' advance for the book, 'looked at me with shrewd eyes, as if I were a swindler. "Fifty pounds! An' tha's niver done a day's work in thy life!" '

The White Peacock was successful enough in England to be reprinted in March, but Violet Hunt's later statement that this novel 'took the town' is as exaggerated as Lawrence's remark at the time that 'practically all America' was 'hostile'.

His mood that year was one of continued bitterness. After his mother's death, he and Ada had felt unable to face Christmas at Eastwood. On December 23, 1910, he was at Croydon, where he wrote to McLeod: 'Nice of you to remember that I wanted those Latin poems: I'd forgotten myself: which makes it all the pleasanter now', and he sent McLeod the Everyman *Aucassin and Nicolette*, with the injunction 'Be jolly'. But Croydon was only a way station on the route south, to Brighton, where Ada joined him. Philip Smith recalled that season, and Lawrence's decline in health in the following year:

> I spent the Christmas of 1910 at Brighton. Lawrence and his sister visited the town at the same period. On Christmas Day I invited them to my hotel. There was a whist party during the evening attended by the usual boarding-house company comprising many attached ladies of uncertain age. The proceedings were somewhat languid and should be accelerated. This he proceeded to do to an extent that threatened the old ladies to join in 'hunting the slipper' and other boisterous round games. I heard then, for the first time, Lawrence's peculiar laugh which was in after years quoted (see Huxley) as a characteristic exhibition of his exuberance.
>
> The following day I walked with Lawrence for a day's tramp

over the Downs. During the day he talked more freely than formerly of his literary ambitions. I was delicately assured that I might never fear an appearance as a character in any of his forthcoming books. He gave as a reason his idea that persons who had been 'spoiled' by too easy a passage through life could make no appeal to a novelist. He discussed the publication of a recent book by a well-known author. He described the work as salacious and remarked, 'If I cannot write without dipping my finger in it I will not write at all.'

During lunch at a wayside inn Lawrence disagreed over some small matter with a chance fellow traveller. I was astounded with the sudden fury of his attack on his speedily vanquished and very subdued opponent.

During 1911 his health declined. He still visited my house but was evidently becoming restless of his surroundings. The routine of his daily life bothered him, but he never failed to keep pace with the work which he felt at the moment he could not afford to relinquish.

Lawrence long afterwards spoke of 1911 as his 'sick year', when 'for me everything collapsed, save the mystery of death, and the haunting of death in life. I was twenty-five, and from the death of my mother, the world began to dissolve around me, beautiful, iridescent, but passing away substanceless. Till I almost dissolved away myself, and was very ill.' It was apparently a year of little writing, as it was a time of little publication. The only poems by Lawrence to go into print that year were 'Lightning'—the man seeing in a flash of lightning that the girl he is making love to is flinching away from him—and 'Violets', a dialect poem, both in the *Nation* (London).

In February 1911 the Hall family of Eastwood recognized their daughter Alice, one of the Pagans, as Alice Gall in *The White Peacock*. Her husband, White Holditch, threatened a lawsuit, but William Hopkin prevented this by telling Holditch that since he was a Quaker it wouldn't be proper for him to initiate such an action. The next time Lawrence put Alice Hall into a novel, he gave her the quite different name of Beatrice Wyld—in *Sons and Lovers*.

Lawrence went home for Easter in 1911, but wanted to see no one outside his own family and close friends: 'You'll not get me in the town much, I can tell you', he wrote to Ada in advance.

At this time Ada was beginning to doubt her religion. On April 9, the Sunday before Easter, Lawrence, who had already given up Congregationalism, and then Unitarianism, for an independent creed, wrote to her: 'I am sorry more than I can tell to find you going through the torment of religious unbelief.' This was hard to bear, but she must remember that Jehovah was a Jewish God, 'not ours'. Lawrence felt that 'Christ was infinitely good, but mortal as we. There still remains a God, but not a personal God: a vast, shimmering impulse which waves onwards towards some end, I don't know what.' Lawrence thought he 'would still go to chapel if it did me any good. I shall go myself, when I am married. Whatever name one gives Him in worship we all strive towards the same God, so we be generous hearted: Christians, Buddhists, Mrs Dax, me, we all stretch our hands in the same direction. What does it matter the name we cry?' His concern, he said in a later letter, was to protect Louie from realizing how tragic life could be. 'Remember, she's seen nothing whatever of the horror of life, and we've been bred up in its presence: with Father.'

Ada was having difficulty with her father since they had given up the Lynn Croft house in March. Lawrence was sorry the father was 'proving such a nuisance . . . Let him eat a bit of the bread of humility. It is astonishing how hard and bitter I feel towards him.' He was 'tired of life being so ugly and cruel'; he had been painting recently, but hadn't written much: 'I find I can't.' He went back to Eastwood in the summer, staying at his sister Emily's. In August he wrote to McLeod from Rosewood, Victoria Avenue, Prestatyn, in northern Wales, 'We are installed very happily,' the 'we' being a party—though Lawrence anticipated some 'love à la Garvice', a reference to the now forgotten best-selling romancer of that time, Charles Garvice.

A few weeks later Lawrence, who had 'been moving about', was at Quorn, Leicestershire, staying with the Burrowses. While there he received a letter from Edward Garnett, then editor for the publishing firm of Gerald Duckworth, Ltd., who wrote on behalf of an American magazine, the *Century*, for which he was seeking stories. This was the beginning of an important friendship. Lawrence's earlier mentor Hueffer had, in Lawrence's account, 'left me to paddle my own canoe', and 'I very nearly wrecked it and did for myself'; but Garnett 'rescued' him.

At this time Lawrence was trying to write the book that became *Sons and Lovers*. A letter of October 18, 1910, shows that he then had written about one-eighth of 'my third novel, *Paul Morel,* which is plotted out very interestingly (to me).' When Jessie Chambers read the first draft of the novel, in 1911, she found it stiff and artificial and suggested that Lawrence remake the story, keeping it closer to the facts. He asked her to write out what she could remember of their early life, but before she could give him her notes, she learned that he was severely ill.

Jessie may have seen the draft described by Lawrence Clark Powell in a 1937 catalogue for a Lawrence exhibition (in this version, 'the father accidentally kills Paul's brother, is jailed, and dies after his release'); but it is also possible that Jessie saw one or both of the fragments of the early *Paul Morel* now at the Humanities Research Center of the University of Texas. Various pages are missing from these manuscripts; one of these runs to about 250 pages, the other to about forty. In the latter, which is probably the earlier, Paul and Miriam appear only as children. Miriam's mother is 'a prominent Christian' whose husband is a grocer in a town called Eberwich; Paul sustains a minor injury when a sleigh he is riding in turns over, and he subsequently suffers a severe bronchial attack. In the other, probably later fragment, Paul prays, 'Lord, let my father not drink', and sometimes says, 'or let him be killed at pit'; in the final version, *Sons and Lovers,* Paul's prayer becomes, 'Let him not be killed at pit'. In what seems to be the later of the two manuscripts now at the University of Texas, Paul has a close relationship with 'a ginger boy', Alec, whose surname appears alternately as Greenhalgh and Richards. 'The two boys, the one [Alec] lusty, big-limbed, clever but unimaginative, the other delicately made and delicate of growth, wonderfully perceptive', get along well at first, with Alec as the leader, Paul always submitting. 'But gradually the balance shifted', and Alec, instead of saying, 'We are going for a swim this morning', begins to ask, 'Shall you go for a swim, Paul, or don't you want to?' While Paul is still quite young, he and his mother clash over Miriam, who believes that she will win because Mrs. Morel 'is old'. All this is so poorly stated and presented that it warrants Jessie Chambers's emphatic criticism of it.

In Lawrence's 'sick year' he suffered not only from the aftereffects of his mother's death but also from giving so much of his limited strength to the wearisome routine of teaching and the compulsive demands of his writing. Physical elements also worked against him in the chill autumn, and the beginning of his serious illness can be traced to his being rain-soaked when returning from a visit to the Garnetts in the country.

In his growing friendship with Garnett, Lawrence in the fall of

1911 often spent weekends at the Cearne, the Garnetts' big cottage-farmhouse near Edenbridge, Kent. Sometimes he went down for the evening. One night he had to wait on a station platform in the rain, and this intensified a cold he already had, which developed into pneumonia. He wrote to Garnett, on November 7, 'This last fortnight I have felt really rotten—it is the dry heat of the pipes in school, and the strain—I must leave school, really.' This was written on the day the logbook of the Davidson School shows as the last one on which Lawrence taught his classes there.

Ada received a telegram saying that her brother was ill, and she left at once for London. Helen Corke met her at Marylebone Station and rushed her to Croydon. She found Lawrence severely ill; it was not until the middle of December that he was even able to sit 'up to tea for an hour', and it was not until the twenty-ninth that he could go for his first walk, limping from neuritis in his left leg.

During the Christmas holiday he had several visitors from the Midlands: his sister Emily brought her small daughter, and Jessie Chambers and Louie Burrows also appeared. 'Christmas was all right.' Yet, Lawrence had told Garnett on December 17, 'The doctor says I mustn't go to school again or I shall be consumptive'. So he intended to ask for a long sick leave: 'Then I can go back if I get broke.' Meanwhile, 'the head-master grieves loudly over my prolonged absence. He knows he would scarcely get another man to do for him as I have done.'

*

While convalescing, Lawrence at the beginning of 1912 started rewriting the book later to be called *The Trespasser*. Lawrence told Garnett he had 'done the first chapter—heaps, heaps better. There was room for improvement, by Jove! I was so young—almost pathetically young—two years ago.' (Meanwhile, Jessie Chambers was writing a novel, *The Rathe Primrose,* later called *Eunice Temple;* she later destroyed the manuscript of this autobiographical projection, from which she took the initials E.T. for the authorship of her memoir of Lawrence in 1935.)

Lawrence continued the rewriting of his *Siegmund* (eventually *The Trespasser*) as his health improved. On January 6, 1912, he went to Bournemouth for several weeks, and from there he wrote his head-master's wife a postcard on the ninth: 'This house is jolly.—45 old folk in—a fair leaven of old permanent ladies, but nevertheless, some

solid young folk, quite gay.' On the twenty-fourth McLeod received
a fuller report from the lively convalescent, showing that his board-
ing-house existence (at Compton House, St. Peter's Road) was not
altogether dry:

> I'm writing in the billiard room where a little Finn, whose 21st
> is today, is playing billiards with an old gent from South Africa.
> I live in constant dread of a cue in my ear and a ball in my
> eye. Also Scriven and I were celebrating our acquaintance—
> with Scotch—in his room till the small hours— So I'm dull as
> cold tea.
>
> The old ladies continue to mother me—the young ones—shall
> we say, to sister me. The men are very amiable, but nearly tee-
> totallers now. There was one chap here last week, with whom I
> had fine sport. He was mad with his wife on Friday, so he went
> out with me to Poole Harbour. There he went on the razzle. I had
> a fiendish time. He kept it up when we got back here: walked
> away with a baby in a pram in Christchurch Road—tried to
> board and drive off with a private motor car—nearly had a fight
> in the Central Hotel, and got us turned out. We were four, arm
> in arm, swaying up the main street here[,] people dodging out
> of the way like hares. It was hot. In the end, I had to throw all
> the drinks they kept forcing on me on to the floor, lest I got as
> drunk as they.
>
> Then, when at last, after superhuman struggles, I got him
> home—he was a big, well-built Yorkshire man of 35—plenty of
> cash—had been in the army—*I—I* had to stand the racket
> from Mrs Jenkinson, whom I like, who is young and pretty and
> has travelled a good bit—and who sits at my table. I wished
> most heartily on Friday evening that I was over Lethe's sooth-
> ing stream.
>
> But now I am forgiven. It is raining today—the weather is
> so-so—it has never been cold. I can scarcely say when I shall be
> back in Croydon—if ever. But I'll tell you later. I don't think I
> want to return to Davidson—but we'll let that dog lie, also.

Lawrence left Bournemouth at two in the afternoon on February 3,
and by four was at Waterloo Station. He had written to Helen
Corke, telling her he would be on his way to Garnett's home and
suggesting that she meet him at Victoria Station and ride back as far
as Croydon. She met him at Victoria, where they had tea; he looked

healthy, and said he was happy not to be returning to Davidson. Helen stayed on the train past Croydon, going on with him as far as Woldingham. There had been no tension between them, and they had kept their conversation to lighter topics—but they parted in an atmosphere of farewell, with the North Downs bright in the last moments of sunset. And although Lawrence and Helen wrote a few letters to one another in the next year or so, they never met again.

But before he could publish *The Trespasser* he had to have her permission, since the novel was based on part of her manuscript. Helen and Lawrence had agreed, in 1910, that the book should not be published for five years, but now she generously permitted him to use the story for his second novel, for she knew that he needed money. Her own novel, *Neutral Ground,* deals, in Parts III and IV, with the same material. Almost all of this novel was written in 1918 (published 1934), except, as Helen Corke explained in a letter to the present author (May 20, 1951), that

> the only part of the *Neutral Ground* papers written before *The Trespasser* appears on pp. 227 to 236 of *Neutral Ground*. This brief five days' diary was L.'s inspiration for his work, and his expansion of it occupies 193 pages of the original Duckworth edition. Beyond this point he uses some unwritten factual matter and introduces imaginary characters, two of them drawn from sketches of his colleagues on the school staff. Lawrence identified himself so closely with Siegmund that in a sense he lived the experience. The book was too nearly life, and life upon that plane of superhuman perception which is charged with danger, and avoided instinctively, by the generality of mankind. Later, when the emotional stimulus had died down, and been decently covered with ash by Hueffer, Heinemann and Co., L. tried to reshape it by intellectual processes, with the sad result noted in your comment: 'the prose of *The Trespasser* is often thick and gummy.' And it should be remembered that at the time of the revision L. was a convalescent, with his energy at low ebb.

Like Dostoevsky, Lawrence was not above adapting newspaper stories for his fictional use. For Siegmund's death he borrowed some of the circumstances from that of Helen Corke's teacher, the well-known musician Herbert Baldwin MacCartney of the Carl Rosa Opera Company, whose dramatic suicide had been a journalistic sensation a few years before; and of course he incorporated Miss

Corke's version of the affair as it appeared in her *Neutral Ground* manuscript. Lawrence also tucked pictures of various friends into odd little corners of the novel. Several members of the Croydon teaching staff recognized themselves as minor characters: Violet Mary Babbage turned up as Olivia, and two of the male teachers, R. H. Aylwin and Ernest Humphreys, appeared as Allport and Holiday. In the portrait of a third, Lawrence gives us a glimpse of his closest friend at Croydon, A. W. McLeod: 'Mr McWhirter was tall, fair, and stoutish; he was very quietly spoken, was humorous and amiable, yet extraordinarily learned. He never, by any chance, gave himself away, maintaining always an absolute reserve amid all his amiability.'

Lawrence prepared his final version of *The Trespasser* in a remarkably short time, and by April 5 he already had proofs to correct, in Eastwood. The book was published in May, after Lawrence had left England. In all the haste, the novel was ironically given the 'wrong' title. Gerald Duckworth had disliked that of *The Trespasser,* and among the others Lawrence had suggested—*The Saga of Siegmund, The Man and the Dreaming Woman, Trespassers in Cytherea, A Game of Forfeits*— Duckworth had preferred the last. But Duckworth's proofreader didn't know this, and the title Lawrence had suggested earlier slid through.

Meanwhile, he worked away at his colliery-town novel. Late in February he told Edward Garnett, to whom he now reported the details of his love affairs, that he and Ada had gone one night to a dance 'at Jacksdale—mining village four miles out. . . . My sister found me kissing one of her friends good-bye—such a ripping little girl—and we were kissing like nuts—great shocks all round, and much indignation. But—life is awfully fast down here.' Lawrence needlessly added that he was 'very well'.

Early in March, he could send Garnett news about an old school friend, 'the Don Juanish fellow I told you of'—who had shocked the younger Eastwoodites five years before by spawning an illegitimate child. Now George Neville had produced another child, whom he described to Lawrence as 'Jimmy, a very fine lad', after three months of secret marriage. The local school authorities had removed him from his teaching post 'to a little headship on the Stafford-Derby border', where he was lonely; he implored Lawrence to visit him.

When Lawrence had left Croydon for Bournemouth, his landlord, J. W. ('Super') Jones, according to a letter of his printed in Émile Delavenay's biography, told Lawrence 'to pack up entirely as I was through with him'. Something of the atmosphere of 12 Colworth Road appears in Lawrence's little story 'The Old Adam', in which a young lodger feels an erotic current between the landlord's wife and himself. Severn, the roomer, injures the landlord when helping him to carry a heavy box downstairs, and Mr. Thomas bats him across the face. The next morning they seem to be more friends than acquaintances, and Mrs. Thomas feels a bit cast down. One fledgling commentator (who apparently didn't realize that one can't know Lawrence at all until one knows all of him) thought that this little story, dating from 1910–1911, was about Lawrence, Ernest Weekley, and Weekley's wife, Frieda; but it was written a year or so before Lawrence met Frieda. And there seems to be a relation between part of Lawrence's description of Thomas in the story—'his mouth was small and nervously pinched'—and what he wrote to Louie Burrows on April 29, 1911: 'Mr Jones has shaved off his moustache, and I don't like him. He's got a small, thin mouth, like a slit in a tight skin. It's quite strange. It shows up a part of his character that I detest: the mean and prudent and nervous. I feel that I really don't like him, and I rather liked him before.'

J. W. Jones, in the letter of 1936 in which he says he told Lawrence to leave the house for good after his illness, also says, 'Lawrence had 4 female friendships. One was platonic (genuinely). One gave him up because she was morally frightened of him. One derided him and led him up the garden to the back gate. It would be mean for me to describe the other one.'

Lawrence's version of his departure from Croydon was quite different from Jones's. As he wrote to Louie Burrows on December 9, 1911, when the doctor first let him sit up in bed, 'I want to leave Colworth now. I want to leave Mrs Jones, Mr Jones, and the children.' Two days later he said that he 'shaved off my red beard', probably his first. The second, which remained, he grew during an illness in 1914.

Just which of the four girls mentioned in J. W. Jones's letter would have been Louie it is difficult to guess. In letters of early 1912 Lawrence had indicated both to Jessie Chambers and Helen Corke that he was approaching a break with Louie. He told Helen Corke, 'The common, everyday, rather superficial man of me really loves Louie. ... But do you not think the open-eyed, sad, critical, deep-seeing man of me has not had to humble himself pretty sorely to accept the imposition of the masculine, stupid decree' to the effect that everyone essentially lives alone. 'We may keep real company once in our lives —after that we touch now and again, but do not repose.' This sounds like a younger version of Birkin in *Women in Love*. As Professor James Boulton has commented, 'Compared with his letters to Blanche Jennings and Rachel Annand Taylor, Lawrence's letters to Louie assume in her a much less mature, poised and dynamic personality.'

On February 4, 1912, Lawrence wrote to Louie from the Garnetts' country cottage, to say that he had been pondering what the doctors at Croydon and Bournemouth had told him: that he shouldn't marry, at least for a long time, perhaps never. And, since he couldn't make a living as a teacher any more, he couldn't support a wife. So he asked her to break the engagement. He felt that his illness had changed him, had 'broken a good many of the old bonds that held me'. He had asked his younger sister Ada for advice, and she had said the engagement should be broken. She wrote Louie to this effect on February 16.

Louie asked him to send a telegraph to her, which he couldn't do. He told her on February 7 that he now thought he hadn't 'the proper love to marry on. Have you not felt it so?'

On Saturday, February 10, he suggested that they meet at Victoria Station in Nottingham the following Tuesday, the thirteenth. 'By a cursed irony', it would be Louie's birthday, her twenty-fourth. On Wednesday, he told her, he was to be in Nottingham with Mrs. Dax.

Somehow Lawrence and Louie moved their own meeting up to the eleventh. On the fifteenth Lawrence wrote to say he was glad that they would remain 'friends'. There was to be no return of the brooch he had given her, or of other little things that had been 'sent in good spirit'. And she could keep his books.

On February 12 he wrote to Garnett: I saw Louie yesterday— she was rather ikey (adj.—to be cocky, to put on airs, to be aggressively superior). She had decided beforehand that she had made herself too cheap to me, therefore she thought she would become all at once expensive and desirable. Consequently she offended me at every verse end—thank God. If she'd been wistful, tender and passionate, I should have been a goner. I took her to the castle, where there was an exhibition from the Art School —wonderfully good stuff. She stared at the naked men till I had to go into another room—she gave me a disquisition on texture in modelling—why clay lives or does not live;—sarked me for saying a certain old fellow I met was a bore: could not remember, oh no, had not the ghost of a notion when we had last visited the castle together, though she knew perfectly: thought me a fool for saying the shadow of the town seen faintly coloured through a fog was startling—and so on. I took her to a café, and over tea and toast, told her for the fourth time. When she began to giggle, I asked her coolly for the joke: when she began to cry, I wanted a cup of tea. It's awfully funny. I had a sort of cloud over my mind—a real sensation of darkness which lifted and trembled slightly. I seemed to be a sort of impersonal creature, without heart or liver, staring out of a black cloud. It's an awfully funny phenomenon. I saw her off by the 5.8 train, perfectly calm. She was more angry and disappointed than anything, thank God.

And there was a 'sequel—which startled *me*—I will tell you personally some time. It shall not be committed to paper.' What that 'sequel' was we shall probably never know. In the February 4 letter to Louie, Lawrence seems more like a woman than a man in detaching himself from the engagement.

It was the last of Louie in his life except for a few postcards and short letters. Years later she rented the cottage in Cornwall where Lawrence and his wife had lived during World War I. And while his body remained buried in Vence in southern France (before its removal for cremation and entombment in the United States in 1935, five years after his death), Louisa Burrows twice visited the grave. One of these visits was noticed by Frieda Lawrence's daughter Barbara, the other by Sir Herbert Read, who had probably gone to Vence to see Matisse's magnificent chapel. Read felt that Louie 'obviously had never renounced her love and devotion to Lawrence', as Jessie Chambers had never quite been able to do. He found her 'a rather dispirited and sombre kind of person, and I think she felt she had been ill-treated by Lawrence.'

Lawrence had plainly cast her off, although she magnetized him physically. What she lacked was the spiritual intensity of Jessie Chambers, in whose case it was too extreme, enough to drive Lawrence away from her. But he retreated more quickly from the attachment to Louie. During and after his severe late-autumn illness in 1911, his letters to her become more gossipy, with virtually no more literary, artistic, or musical references. By the following February he sent her that note discussed earlier, in which he firmly indicated that he was breaking away. He was unconsciously preparing himself for the woman with whom his difficult temperament could establish a relationship in which they would be, as a man in one of his later novels was to say, 'two stars in balanced conjunction.'

*

As early as March 6, 1912, Lawrence was talking of possibly going to Germany. Two months later he was actually there.

Meanwhile he had to break his connection with the Davidson School, whose logbook shows that his name was carried on the faculty roster until March 9, 1912. Philip Smith had invited him back. Smith and the staff had sent Lawrence some books, for which they were subsequently thanked in a letter of April 22. But apparently not long before this, in an undated postcard to McLeod from Nottingham, Lawrence wrote: 'The books are so nice—I'm on the point of tears like anything—It's really too ridiculous in a restaurant. I should love to come back to Davidson if there were no kids—or only half a dozen or so.'

*

One day at the beginning of April, Lawrence went to Nottingham to have lunch at Professor Ernest Weekley's home. He had asked to see his former instructor in French because he wanted advice and perhaps assistance. Maybe Professor Weekley and Lawrence's uncle by marriage, Professor Fritz Krenkow, could help him obtain a post at a German university, as *Lektor,* 'foreign teacher of his mother tongue'. Lawrence had of course intended to give up teaching, but thought that perhaps a *Lektorstelle* would not devour his health as the Croydon schoolmastership had done: he would find the university routine less exhausting, and he wouldn't have to discipline small boys. At least Professor Weekley could tell him about these things, for Weekley had supplemented his Cambridge training with study at several Continental schools, and he had once been *Lektor* at Freiburg. It was there that he had married Frieda von Richthofen, a German girl fifteen years younger than himself.

Ernest Weekley's home was in the Mapperley section of Nottingham, only about a mile from the Arno Vale farm of the Chambers family. Lawrence had sometimes visited his brother George 'on the Mapperley side', but George didn't live permanently in so elegant a neighborhood as Victoria Crescent, on the Private Road.

Years later, Frieda described Lawrence's entrance into the Weekley house, 'a long, thin figure, quick, straight legs, light, sure movements. He seemed so obviously simple. Yet he arrested my attention. What kind of a bird was this?'

Frieda took the strange 'bird' into her sitting room, where they talked for half an hour before lunch. The French windows were turned back, the curtains throbbed in the spring wind, the voices of children sounded from the lawn. Lawrence, never addicted to small talk, abruptly began a denunciation of women: he was through with them, and with attempts at knowing them. By saying this he at least found a way to capture the immediate attention of his hostess, who was an altogether different kind of woman from any he had known. There was more blaze about her than about Englishwomen: she had the assured Continental manner and a throaty, strange-accented voice, and she could range in a moment from sophisticated poise to childish eagerness. Physically, she was a magnificent blonde tall animal, with high cheekbones and greenish 'Tartar' eyes flecked with brown. Lawrence, watching her closely at lunch, saw that she paid little attention to her husband. Under the spell of her exuberance, the visitor stayed on until nightfall and then walked home, more than eight miles across the dark farmlands.

He went back to see her again at Easter, on April 7 that year; he had meanwhile written to tell her that she was the most wonderful woman in all England. She countered by asking him how many women in England he knew.

Frieda was, at the time she met Lawrence, if not actually unhappy, only missing unhappiness because she had sunk into a condition of drowsiness; as she said later, she was sleepwalking through the days. She had known *Mitteleuropa,* the expanding Germany of Bismarck, and the Kaiser's court; now, at thirty-two, she was the veteran of a dozen years of marriage and residence in the English provinces. She had three children, two girls and a boy, an automobile at her disposal, and the fine house in the Mapperley district. But she was bored. Even her occasional love affairs failed to rouse her into wakefulness. Life had not always been like this: once there had been the vast meadowlands and forests of Germany, the glittering ballrooms of Berlin, the courtship of young officers, the champagne parties. Now the enchanting princess was a *Hausfrau.*

If Emma Maria Frieda Johanna Weekley-Richthofen was not exactly a princess, she was, like all daughters of titled German aristocrats, at least a baroness. (The collier's son was impressed: some time later, when Lawrence was using her stationery, he self-consciously called his correspondents' attention to the von Richthofen coat of arms.) Actually, the family was not of the ancient nobility, for its title went back only two and a half centuries; yet it was a distinguished clan whose members held prominent posts in the new empire. The family traced its descent from a commoner, Samuel Schmidt, a pastor's son from a village just north of Berlin whom a high-ranking nobleman had adopted in 1562: Samuel Schmidt's grandson became a member of the Bohemian knighthood in 1661 and assumed the name of von Richthofen. This first von Richthofen was the great-great-great-great-grandfather of Frieda. She recalled (in a letter of December 8, 1953), 'Richthofen is for *Richter* (judge) because in the [coat of] arms is a judge on a seat in black—but they were very religious, mystically so.'

One of Frieda's distant uncles was the famous geographer and explorer of Asia, Ferdinand von Richthofen (1833–1905), and a distant cousin, Manfred von Richthofen (1892–1918), was to become the greatest of all war aces. But mostly the men of the family were diplomats, such as her father's uncle, Emil von Richthofen, who was the ambassador to Sweden, and his son Oswald (1847–1906), who was state secretary of the foreign office and Prussian secretary of state. Of course various men of the family looked after their lands. Some of the von Richthofens owned estates in the Silesian Langenthal, and they were proud of their acres of grain and of their flocks of merino sheep, which had been greatly improved and increased since Frederick the Great first introduced them into the province. The von Richthofens were ardent horsemen, they fished for salmon in the Oder, and they hunted the boar and the stag in the forests that stretched down from the Carpathians and the Riesengebirge.

Most of the von Richthofens, then, were at least fairly well-to-do, but they couldn't afford the failure of the speculations that Frieda's great-grandfather Ludwig (1770–1850) and his son Ludwig (1800–1880) engaged in, especially in combination with the misfortune which then beset them. They ventured a good part of their fortune in the sugar beet, a reasonable investment at the time, when the policies of Napoleon I had inflated the price of sugar throughout Europe; the fall of Napoleon brought about a decline in sugar prices and almost completely ruined the new industry in Silesia. Hence this branch of the von Richthofens lost most of its money and property in one of the early disasters of the industrial revolution, much as the Beardsalls of Nottingham had suffered depletion. Frieda recalled in

1953, 'My father's or rather my grandfather's place, a small castle, was called Rashowa, it is still a sugar-beet centre. What I liked about the Richthofen men I met was their individuality, all unusual men.' Frieda's branch of the von Richthofens suffered a further setback when lightning killed a flock of sheep during a severe storm. Because of this, Frieda's father, an officer with a record for valor in battle, had a lifelong dread of thunderstorms, according to his daughter, Else Jaffe-Richthofen.

It has often been stated that this Friedrich von Richthofen, born in 1845, was a general, and that he was military governor of Alsace-Lorraine. He was never a general, and at Metz he was an official in the civil service. He had begun his career in the army in 1862, and had managed to retain his commission in spite of the fact that two girls, on a forbidden visit to him and another officer in their barracks quarters, had been killed by fumes from the stove. (Lawrence made this event the center of one of his early stories, 'The Mortal Coil'.)

Friedrich von Richthofen later served in the Franco-Prussian War. He was at the siege of Strasbourg during the summer and early autumn of 1870, and took part in the campaigns and skirmishes in that area. He left a diary of the events of that time, up to the end of the year, a record of being almost incessantly under fire by day, with billets at country inns by night, violent quarrels and lively parties, a full account of a life of marches in the rain, encounters with refugees, duels between officers of the same regiment, suicides, funerals, sorties, the music of bands in the *Plätze* of captured towns. Now and then, in the fashion of Bismarck's junior empire-builders, the young baron behaved somewhat like the Prussian officer of Lawrence's story: on November 10, 'A mad scene this evening at the "Horse". I whipped an artillery officer with my sabre.' On November 11, when the baron gave a whist party, with grog, at his quarters, 'Heinrich [his servant] got drunk and I beat him.' Then, more descriptions of snow, mist, marches. At the New Year, the baron was wounded and captured—and his wound, which disabled his right hand, kept him from ever again being a soldier.

Frieda had French and Polish as well as German connections: as she explained in a letter to the author of this book, 'My mother's name was Marquier, of French origin, her ancestor was supposed to have escaped from the French revolution in a hay wagon to the Black Forest—My Richthofen grandmother was a Polish countess Lashowska.'

The Friedrich von Richthofens had three children, all girls. Lawrence described them in a letter in 1912: 'The Richthofens are an astonishing family—three girls—women—the eldest a Doctor of Social Economics—a Professor too—then Frieda—then the youngest —28—very beautiful, rather splendid in her deliberate worldliness. They are a rare family—father a fierce old aristocrat—mother utterly non-moral, very kind.' The eldest daughter, Else, who played an important role in the early relationship of Lawrence and Frieda, later became his German translator (*The Rainbow* is dedicated to her). Else had been one of the first girl students at Heidelberg, after attendance at a finishing school at Freiburg and at a teachers' college, operated by nuns, at Metz. She had written her doctor's thesis on the relation of political parties to social-insurance laws, under the direction of the great economist Max Weber. Else had married one of her teachers at Heidelberg, Dr. Edgar Jaffe, a professor of political economy, and they had moved to Munich in 1910 after he accepted a post at the university there.

Although the von Richthofens were a Protestant family, Frieda and her younger sister, Johanna ('Nusch'), began their education at a Catholic convent, half French, at Metz. Frieda's exuberance—which could still impress those who knew her in her seventies—was then apparently at its highest pitch of intensity: 'I was a wild child,' she wrote later, 'and they could not tame me, those gentle nuns.' Frieda and Johanna then attended the girls' high school in Metz. Else has recalled that Frieda was not 'bookish' in those days, though she had a favorite novel that she read continuously and often wept over: *Jane Eyre*.

When Frieda was seventeen and Nusch fifteen, they were sent to a finishing school in the Black Forest, kept by Moravian brothers. Frieda didn't want to leave her home; the house she had grown up in, outside Metz, was surrounded by gardens and fruit trees and a high wall. That house and its surroundings were full of gay memories; once, on the Kaiser's birthday, the baron's old regiment had reenacted the circumstances in which he had received the Iron Cross in the war of 1870, and afterwards when the soldiers lifted Frieda's father onto their shoulders to carry him through the hall, her 'heart beat to bursting' and she thought, 'What a hero my father is.'

John Middleton Murry cast some light on Frieda's relationship with her father, of which he presumably heard from Frieda herself: Frieda 'was a completely emancipated woman. Equality of the sexes she took in her stride, which reached gaily a little further still. She also had direct experience of "male authority" in her father, not merely as head of a Prussian aristocratic household, but as the first Prussian military [sic] governor of Metz after the war of 1870. None the less, in spite of this imposing façade, her experience of "male authority" was also of "male authority" in disintegration. Domestically, it was manifested as the right to male irresponsibility—heavy gambling debts and the like—and, in compensation for the inevitable coldness between him and his wife, an irresponsibly indulgent affection towards his daughters, who knew his secrets and smiled at his pretensions.'

There at Metz, Frieda was happy with the admiration of the soldiers who were barracked nearby; they invited her and Nusch to their Christmas parties, where sausages and gingerbread and cigars hung on the tree, along with the small dolls the soldiers had carved for the girls. In her youth, Frieda has said, only boys and men provided her the kind of interest she wanted; women and girls frightened her, and 'pleasure and social stuff' didn't fulfill her. She was happiest when playing with her boy friends around the Metz fortifications, where among the constructions of Vauban the soldiers had built huts and dug trenches. (Her interest in these fortifications was later to cause Lawrence embarrassment.)

At the Moravian school in the Black Forest, where Frieda and Nusch were both confirmed, Frieda developed a schoolgirl's infatuation for one of her teachers. She was frightened when the emotion was reciprocated. She was happy to leave school, at seventeen, 'to go into society', which meant, in this case, a year in Berlin as the guest of Oswald von Richthofen, her great-uncle's son, at that time undersecretary of state, soon to be secretary. For a beautiful young girl, it was a year not to be forgotten: her uncle's spacious residence in the Tiergarten, the carriage rides along the thoroughfares of the great flat city, the cafés and wine restaurants in the Unter den Linden, the theaters with their repertories ranging from Schiller to Schnitzler, the Royal Opera House with its eternal performances of Wagner, the balls at the Royal Palace. It was at one of these balls, when Nusch too was in Berlin, that the Kaiser asked who 'those two young ladies' were, and, on being told, said, 'Ah, the Herr Undersecretary has very beautiful nieces!'

Perhaps 'pleasure and social stuff' didn't really interest Frieda, but parties and carriage rides and theater attendance were occasions for male companionship. Else remembered Frieda as being essentially innocent, believing in 'the good of men': though outwardly gay, she took them seriously and felt she had a 'mission' to help whichever of them had caught her interest and sympathy at the moment. Some of them wanted to marry her. There were, for example, Lieutenant Karl von Marbahr and her cousin Kurt, who couldn't afford to marry her because she was not an heiress: the expense of being a young officer was a great financial burden. After Lawrence's death, von Marbahr wrote to Frieda: 'After all you would have suited me very well. I would have absorbed vigour from you, and all would have been well . . . At that time we would have had to wait ten years for a captaincy. Now I know that if I had resigned my commission and started something else, together with you, I might have amounted to something as an author or a journalist.'

Frieda was twenty when she married Ernest Weekley, whom she had met at a Black Forest resort. He brought her to Nottingham, where she began her dozen years' dream.

Frieda later wrote of her efforts to become a good English *bourgeoisie* and 'do as the other women did', shopping in the morning instead of the afternoon, using that time to exchange visits with other women, and at night attending dinner parties. She was deeply unhappy, particularly in the dark, gray winters. Her first extramarital love affair was with a Nottingham lace manufacturer who used to take her into Sherwood Forest in one of the first automobiles in England. Ernest Weekley didn't know about this, any more than he was aware of a far more serious love affair of Frieda's which began on one of her visits to the Continent. The Nottingham lace manufacturer has been identified by Robert Lucas (in his biography of Frieda) as Will Dowson, while the man Frieda first became entangled with in Vienna in 1907 was Dr. Otto Gross, a disciple of Freud's. This affair lasted for several years. Frieda later believed that Otto Gross died while serving as a doctor in the First World War. The truth is that he died in 1920 with his lips eaten away by all the cocaine he had sniffed. Frieda never knew that, all along, he had been a drug addict.

When Lawrence came into her life, his directness immediately began to rouse her from her somnolence, though at first she resented him for this directness, as when he told her she was unaware of her husband. Lawrence's straightforwardness manifested itself in other ways too. On Easter Sunday, with the maids away and the children hunting for eggs in the garden, Frieda wanted to make her visitor some tea, but didn't know how to light the gas: Lawrence scolded her for her ignorance. He was a strange bird indeed: the baron's daughter, the professor's wife, was not used to having men scold her. She knew that Lawrence was piercing below the drowsy surface, to the misery underneath. It is no wonder that the leading motif in so many of his later novels and stories was to be the Sleeping Beauty theme.

As André Maurois perceptively remarks in *Prophets and Poets,* 'women discerned in Lawrence something primitive, something akin to their own nature.' He had their taste for magic. Frieda 'said that he alone could teach human beings the art of living.' With his frailty and his nearness to death, Lawrence 'had a religious awareness of moments of happiness.' Maurois points out that Frieda stated she had not lived at all before living with Lawrence.

One day when by arrangement he met her and her two little girls at a station in Derbyshire, and took them walking through the spring woods, she realized that she loved him. The knowledge came to her as she watched him playing with the children by a brook; he had made paper boats and put matches in them, and sent them sailing on the water, to the delight of the children. Frieda saw him, frail and intent, crouching by the brookside, and 'suddenly I knew I loved him. He had touched a new tenderness in me.' This recalls Jessie Chambers's up-rush of tenderness when she saw Lawrence bending over the broken umbrella, 'the beginning of our awareness and sympathy for one another'.

On one of his Sunday visits, with her husband away, Frieda asked Lawrence to spend the night with her. He told her firmly that he would not stay overnight in her husband's house while he was absent, and insisted that they go away together instead. Frieda was planning to visit Germany for the fiftieth anniversary of her father's entrance into the army, an event which the baron's old regiment was going to celebrate. Lawrence could travel with her, and in Germany they could be together secretly. Apparently the arrangement was not at first agreed upon as a permanent one, for in a letter of April 23 Lawrence mentioned to Garnett that Frieda intended to travel to Germany early in May, and that he wanted 'to go then, for we could have at least one week together'. Yet he insisted that she tell her husband about him.

Frieda was tormented. Her husband had become to her merely another cold Englishman, a scholar interested only in his books about words, but he was kind to her, and he trusted her. Besides, there were the children: Frieda knew what the organized burgher world thought of a woman who went away from her home with a lover, and feared she might never see the children again. But Lawrence compelled her. He was wretched, too; he wrote that for both of them it was 'like being ill,' and he knew how that felt: 'There's nothing to do but shut one's teeth and look at the wall and wait.'

Jessie had seen Lawrence on Easter Monday, when she unexpectedly met him at one of the railway stations near Eastwood. She was waiting for her sister when she saw Lawrence, who appeared at the barrier with Ada and their friend Eddie Clarke; Jessie watched Lawrence for a while before he noticed her, and 'the misery I saw depicted in his face was beyond anything I had ever imagined.'

Jessie saw Lawrence again a few weeks later, at Moorgreen, when he was spending the weekend with her sister May Holbrook and her husband. Not knowing Lawrence was to be there, Jessie drove over in the trap from Arno Vale with her father on Sunday morning. Lawrence looked different: the expression of despair was gone and he was in good humor; but he was unexpectedly silent. Naturally he was thinking of nothing but Frieda, and probably didn't dare open his mouth lest he mention her. Jessie offered him a ride back into Eastwood, but he said her sister was expecting him to stay; Jessie felt that in this he was 'true to his habit of letting other people make his decisions'. But he rode part of the way towards Nottingham with Jessie and her father, speaking 'with a forced brightness' of his forthcoming trip to Germany; Jessie imagined that he was uncomfortable because of her father's tone of casualness, which contrasted with the warmth of former times. Lawrence got out of the trap by Watnall Hill, below Greasley, and walked back across the fields to the Holbrooks' cottage. There, he was quiet again, pensive; later, without warning, he said to Holbrook, 'Bill, I like a *gushing* woman.'

But the parting with Jessie had been moving, as if each of them had known it was final. When Lawrence got out of the trap, he stood in the road looking after it as it drove away. Jessie remembered, 'I turned and saw him still standing where he had alighted, looking after us. I waved my hand and he raised his hat with the familiar gesture.'

Lawrence was not telling the people at Eastwood about Frieda; he didn't at that time even let his good friend Sallie Hopkin in on the secret, though he discussed Frieda with May Holbrook.

When Keith Sagar was researching Lawrence's background in the 1960s and 1970s, several of Lawrence's Eastwood contemporaries told him they were sure that Lawrence knew Frieda long before the usually accepted time of their meeting, April 1912, which Frieda wrote of in *Not I, But the Wind*. In one version of the story, Frieda used to bring her children to the Lawrences' house in Eastwood, even when his mother was still living—and apparently approving of his friendship with Frieda. Based entirely on the far-off memories of two or three older men and women, the assertion is otherwise unproved, and most serious students of Lawrence haven't believed the story. Yet an ambiguous sentence in Frieda's 'The Bigger Heart of D. H. Lawrence' (in *The Memoirs and Correspondence*) might be taken to mean that she had met Lawrence's mother: 'I remembered how a two-penny small bunch of pansies could give her so much pleasure.' Of course, Lawrence could have told her this.

Lawrence confided in Garnett from the first; he told him that Frieda was 'ripping', that she was 'the finest woman I've ever met —you must above all things meet her . . . She is the daughter of Baron von Richthofen, of the ancient and famous house of Richthofen—but she's splendid, she is really. . . . You *must* see her next week. I wonder if she'd come to the Cearne, if you asked us. Oh, but she is the woman of a lifetime.'

The geography of Lawrence's letters during those hectic weeks of April measures his restlessness; they are dated from Leicester, from Eastwood, then from Leicester, then again from Eastwood, with references to London visits. He had found the woman of his life, but he had no money—eleven pounds was all he could raise at the time— and Frieda, however bored at home, at least had her three children. Frail, barely recovered from his illness, Lawrence had yet a great deal of personal force to rely on; in Whitman's phrase, he was one of those who convince by their presence.

Frieda left her son Montague with his father, and took the two little girls, Barbara and Elsa, to their grandparents in Well Walk, Hampstead. Out on Hampstead Heath she had said good-by to the two children, and she was 'blind and blank with pain'.

Lawrence and Frieda left from Charing Cross on Friday, May 3, crossing the Channel to Ostend. Frieda remembered a gray sea and a dark sky, and the two of them 'sitting on the ropes, full of hope and agony'.

4 NEW GROUND

At Metz, in the confusion of the jubilee, the von Richthofen house was crowded with relatives of all ages, and bands were playing in the garden. Frieda and Lawrence went quietly to a small hotel, though

Frieda's mother had wanted her to stay at home. Nusch also lodged at the hotel. The parents, amid all the festivities, knew something was wrong between Frieda and her husband; importunate telegrams arrived from Nottingham. Frieda whispered into her sister Else's ear, 'I've brought a man along with me.' She told her parents, without mentioning Lawrence, that she was thinking of leaving her husband. This shocked her father, who said that he had always thought her sensible: 'I know the world,' he told her. But Frieda felt that he had never known the best, and she meant to know that.

Lawrence, alone for the first time in a strange country, was wretched at the Deutscher Hof. Although he and Frieda were having their week together, she had to be at the family home most of the time, and her meetings with Lawrence were furtive. Frieda's sisters both liked him, however outlandish he seemed in his British raincoat and cloth cap: this was a man, they told her, whom she could trust. An old friend of the von Richthofens, an ancient baroness who had come to Metz for the jubilee, was also at the Deutscher Hof and ate at the breakfast table there with Frieda and Nusch. The baroness was near-sighted and didn't see Lawrence; the sisters thought this extremely funny and kept giggling over it, while Lawrence sat with them, shy and uncomfortable.

Lawrence on lonely walks enjoyed the valley of the Mosel, with its vineyards. He loathed Metz, which was bristling with German soldiers; among the people he met in the town and the nearby villages, he preferred the French to the Germans. Sometimes, at the Deutscher Hof, he tried to write, revising *Paul Morel,* but told Frieda he didn't have much luck getting 'to work'. On Tuesday, May 7, Lawrence wrote to Frieda that he couldn't stand the situation any longer: 'For two hours I haven't moved a muscle—just sat and thought.'

He had addressed a letter to Weekley. Frieda didn't have to send it, he said; but she must tell her husband everything. Lawrence wanted 'no more dishonour, no more lies. Let them do their—silliest —but no more subterfuge, lying, dirt, fear. I feel as if it would strangle me. . . . I love you. Let us face anything, do anything, put up with anything. But this crawling under the mud I cannot bear.' Then at last the situation exploded: One day Frieda brought Lawrence to Vauban's fortifications, where a German policeman who heard them speaking English took Lawrence into custody, accusing him of being a British officer and a spy. Frieda had to ask her father to rescue her lover, and Lawrence left for Trier, fifty miles away. Before that, however, Frieda brought him to her parents' home for tea; it was the only time Lawrence was to meet the man he later spoke of as 'the fiery little baron'. Frieda described the scene and its aftermath with harrowing simplicity: 'They looked at each other fiercely—my father, the pure aristocrat, Lawrence, the miner's son. That night I dreamt that they had a fight, and that Lawrence defeated my father.'

Alone at Trier, Lawrence also had his dreams; in one of them he fought savagely with Ernest Weekley, who at last calmed down and needed comforting. If Lawrence loathed Metz ('Curse Metz'), he liked Trier, which was not full of barracks, a town where the priests outnumbered the soldiers. He wrote to Frieda of the trees and the apple blossoms. Frieda went down to Trier for a few days around the weekend of May 11–12, and they agreed to meet later in Munich, where she was going to visit her sister Else.

Lawrence's letter to Ernest Weekley was received on May 10. It was later discovered by Émile Delavenay in two London newspapers in which it had appeared at the time of the first stages of the Weekley divorce proceedings, October 1913:

> Mrs Weekley will have told you everything, but you do not suffer alone. There are three of us, although I do not compare my sufferings with what yours must be. It is really torture to be in this position. I am here as a distant friend, and you can imagine the thousand lies it all entails. Mrs Weekley hates it, but it had to be. I love your wife, and she loves me. I am not frivolous or impertinent. Mrs Weekley is afraid of being stunted and not allowed to grow, so she must live her own life. Women in their natures are like giantesses; they will break through everything and go on with their own lives . . .
>
> Don't curse my impudence in writing to you; in this hour we are only single men. However you think of me, the situation still remains. I almost burst my heart in trying to think what will be the best. At any rate we ought to be fair to ourselves. Mrs Weekley must live largely and abundantly: it is her nature. To me it means the future. I feel as if my effort to live was all for her. Cannot we all forgive something?

Meanwhile Lawrence set off to see his Krenkow relatives in the Rheinprovinz village of Waldbröl, east of Bonn. For the eighty-five-mile journey between there and Trier, Lawrence had to change trains four times; in one of the two surviving postcards he wrote to Frieda en route, he said he was on his sentimental journey. The second of these cards was from Hennef, where he was 'sitting like a sad swain beside a nice, twittering little river, waiting for the twilight to drop, and my last train to come. . . . Now for the first time during today, my detachment leaves me, and I know I only love you. The rest is nothing at all. And the promise of life with you is all richness. Now I know.'

This note is of particular interest because of the poem 'Bei Hennef' which appeared the following year in *Love Poems* and later, without alteration, in the *Collected Poems* of 1928: 'The little river twittering in the twilight, / The wan, wondering look of the pale sky, / This is almost bliss. . . .' After describing the setting and his own mood further, the poet ended:

> *You are the call and I am the answer,*
> *You are the wish and I the fulfilment,*
> *You are the night, and I the day.*
> *What else? It is perfect enough.*
> *It is perfectly complete,*
> *You and I,*
> *What more—?*

> *Strange, how we suffer in spite of this!*

Sixteen years later Lawrence said that this poem signified a new beginning for him. In the Note to *Collected Poems,* he wrote that 'Bei Hennef' begins the new cycle in his *Look! We Have Come Through!* poems (among which he was now placing it): the earlier poems in the sequence 'belong to England and the death-experience'. So, here in the Rhineland, after his three phases of experience with Frieda, in England and at Metz and at Trier, a new Lawrence appears, a somewhat more seasoned man and lover. He sees that life is good, but he is without the sentimental illusion that life and love may be enjoyed without pain—and what else is sentimentalism but that illusion? No, writing his postcard message and his poem in the dusk by the 'twittering' little River Sieg, Lawrence was beginning to shed his past. He was only beginning to do so, and the shedding would always, as with all men, be incomplete. But his involvement with Frieda, and with the book he was then writing—*Sons and Lovers*—made it possible for him to get beyond the most crippling parts of his past and to face life, to 'come through'.

*

At Waldbröl, a quaint village that still used oxen, Lawrence worked on his novel (he told Frieda it was on his conscience), wandered across the Rhineland landscapes, dashed off letters, and flirted with his 'cousin' Hannah.

He wrote to Edward Garnett about Hannah, who in the desperation of a woman nearing thirty had married a dull man; now she was falling in love with Lawrence. He reported to Garnett that he had eyes for no girl except Frieda, and he told Frieda merely that Hannah was 'getting fonder and fonder' of him, but that he could flirt only when he was tipsy. Yet Hannah and her increasing 'fondness' were apparently good for Lawrence. He at least was able to toss some unpleasant hints at Frieda when she boasted of the lovers then besieging her in Metz. More important, however, Lawrence's dallying with Hannah gave him a better perspective on love: 'It's a funny thing, to feel one's passion—sex desire—no longer a sort of wandering thing, but steady, and calm. I think, when one loves, one's very sex passion becomes calm, a steady sort of force, instead of a storm. Passion, that nearly drives one mad, is far away from real love. I am realizing things that I never thought to realize. Look at that poem I sent you—I would never write that to you.' Their next meeting must be solemn, it must have dignity; 'no shufflings and underhandedness'. Without Frieda, he was 'a carcass', but he needed to let his sick soul heal for a time before he would 'ask it to run and live with [her] again. . . . It's a marriage, not a meeting.' Frieda said later that she was at this time in such confusion of mind and emotion that she did not realize the depth of feeling in Lawrence's letters: 'All I wanted was to be with him and have peace.'

Lawrence journeyed to Munich on May 24, and after a night there he and Frieda went south twenty-three miles, where they at last had their honeymoon for a week at Beuerberg. Years later, in 1929, Lawrence wrote to his friend Max Mohr, *'Die Frieda und ich haben unser Zusammenleben in Beuerberg im Isartal angefangen—in Mai 1912 —und wie schön es war!'*

At the time, Lawrence reported to Garnett: 'The river is green glacier water. Bavarian villages are white and gay, the churches are baroque, with minarets, white with black caps. Every day it was perfect. Frieda and I went long ways. There are masses and masses of Alpine flowers, globe flowers, primulas, lilies, orchids—make you dance. . . . The lovely brooks we have paddled in, the lovely things we have done!' (*'Und wie schön es war!'*)

He told Mrs. Hopkin, now also in on the secret, that he loved Frieda so much he didn't want to talk about it; he had never known before what love was, but now the world was 'wonderful and beautiful and good beyond one's wildest imagination. Life *can* be great— quite godlike. It *can* be so. God be thanked I have proved it.' Yes— but there is almost too much protest here. For, despite the ecstasy of love and the magnificence of the scenery—'Strange, how we suffer in spite of this!'—Frieda grieved for her children, and when Lawrence remonstrated with her, she asked him what kind of an unnatural mother he expected her to be? In one of the *Look! We Have Come Through!* poems written at Beuerberg, 'She Looks Back', the man reproaches the woman for being Lot's wife; her kisses are full of salt. Amid the glamour of the Bavarian Tyrol, she stares towards England. Yet the man feels that she is essentially with him; she has never looked 'quite back'—she has looked back 'nine-tenths, ah, more', but not all the way: 'Nevertheless, the curse against you is still in my heart / Like a deep, deep burn. /The curse against all mothers.' So it was not all paddling in the brook: if sunshine and flowers and joy often filled the day, agonies thronged the night, for the past bound Lawrence too. The *Look! We Have Come Through!* sequence reflects—it would be better to say refracts—this experience of happiness battling with misery; the sequence is not a report, but a translation into poetry of what happened, of what Lawrence felt, and of what he knew Frieda felt, during the first five years of their union.

The *Look!* sequence is almost as nakedly confessional as anything could be. Yet many of the poems, for all their realism, are intrinsically *symboliste,* often making their points by suggestion rather than explicit statement. Here, however, they will be considered only as autobiographical expressions, illuminating the details of Lawrence's relationship with Frieda. Some of the titles indicate the 'dark' side of the picture: 'And Oh—, That the Man I Am Might Cease to Be'; 'Mutilation'; 'Quite Forsaken'; 'Forsaken and Forlorn'; 'Song of a Man Who Is Not Loved'; 'Misery'; 'A Bad Beginning'; 'Why Does She Weep?'; 'Loggerheads'—these titles should be balanced against some of those with implications of another kind, such as 'Roses on the Breakfast Table' and 'A Doe at Evening', or against those which have a distinctly positive ring: 'Paradise Re-Entered'; 'Song of a Man Who Has Come Through'; 'New Heaven and Earth'; 'Elysium'

—poems occurring late in the sequence. These titles alone give an idea of the ambivalence of the relationship. But, despite all the tensions and antagonisms expressed in the *Look!* poems, they do break through into a 'New Heaven and Earth'. For they are essentially a prothalamion—a great marriage poem, a celebration of conjugality, a festival of love. At the end of that first year with Frieda, Lawrence wrote to Mrs. Hopkin, 'I shall always be a priest of love': and his career and his doctrine are caught up in that phrase.

*

After the honeymoon week at Beuerberg, Lawrence and Frieda moved north a few miles to Icking, on the Isar. Professor Alfred Weber of Heidelberg, brother of Max Weber, had at the instigation of Frieda's sister Else lent them his flat on the upper story of a small chalet-like building which in those days had a shop on the lower floor. Weber's flat consisted of four small rooms and a kitchen; the tenants ate their meals on the balcony, where Lawrence also wrote. Taking breakfast on that balcony in his dressing gown, he felt respectable, but he assured Frieda that, in her nightgown, she was not. 'She's got a figure like a fine Rubens woman,' he told Garnett, 'but her face is almost Greek.'

Lawrence and Frieda stayed at Icking until August, and their experience was a repetition of Beuerberg, the pendulum of their emotions rocking between happiness and misery. Their quarrels had an almost ritualistic pattern: after a spell of happiness, Frieda would remember the children and be sad; Lawrence would tell her that he would make a better life for all of them; Frieda would feel reassured, but before she could show this, Lawrence would be railing that she didn't really care for 'those brats' anyhow. But, he said, he had 'nailed' Frieda to his wagon: the two months at Icking were that important. As those balcony days passed—bullocks pulling wagons along the road below, the wheatfields sloping down to the river, on the far bank a forested lowland backed by lifting mountains, the beginning of the Alps—the love of Lawrence and Frieda grew strong in that enormous setting.

Though Frieda was later to become an expert cook, Lawrence attended to the meals here. They lived on berries and fresh eggs, black bread and beer. Meanwhile, Lawrence's writing continued apace. The version of *Paul Morel* he had been working on at Waldbröl—only ten pages to go when he left—was sent to Heinemann soon after Lawrence arrived at Icking. He always believed that Heinemann rejected it because he thought it an unclean book. Lawrence asked Garnett to read the manuscript for Duckworth's; it came back to him on July 25, with Garnett's notes, and Lawrence promised to 'slave like a Turk' at rewriting it, beginning the next day; he estimated that the third draft would take him three months. This was a fairly accurate forecast, for in spite of the month spent in walking across the Alps, Lawrence on November 13 completed the version that Duckworth's published the following year.

In the month in which Lawrence had left London (May 1912), *The Trespasser* had come out, and Garnett sent the reviews to Germany. Most of them suggested a disappointed friendliness. 'Had it been the work of almost any other man, it would have satisfied,' the London *Saturday Review* said, 'for it is no common novel, but for some months we have been waiting for this book with the highest hopes.' The *Athenaeum* reviewed *The Trespasser* jointly with *The Brothers Karamazov*—just then translated by Mrs. Garnett—paying the young author the great compliment of discussing him along with Dostoevsky. Some of the scenes in Lawrence's novel reminded the anonymous reviewer 'of the best Russian school'; the descriptions of Siegmund's suicide and of the discovery of the body were 'poetic realism of a Dostoevskian order'. The *English Review* tried to be as kind as possible to Lawrence in its 'Books of the Month' notices: '*The Trespasser* is his second novel, and if as a story it is somewhat disappointing, as a piece of writing it is unquestionably an achievement. . . . Here is a writer with style. We have yet to wait for the author's message.'

Thus the British reviews. Lawrence wouldn't see those from America until the fall, when he was in Italy. Mitchell Kennerley published the American edition, and the *New York Times* of November 17, 1912, gave it a long and favorable review. Entitled 'The Woman Who Kills', it concentrated on the character of Helena, a new type of woman in fiction: '*The Trespasser* is not only the frankest of serious contemporary novels; it comes near to being the best. . . . The commonplace reader will, without doubt, find *The Trespasser* commonplace and hideous; but the commonplace reader ought not to read it at all.' Earlier, while Lawrence and Frieda were at Icking, the *Nottinghamshire Guardian*—as if knowing of their circumstances—had headed its review, 'A Reprehensible Jaunt', at which Frieda laughed far more heartily than Lawrence did.

He had certainly done better with this book than he had expected:

a mild success marked his transfer from the Hueffer camp to the Garnett camp. Garnett, perhaps not too happy over *The Trespasser* despite the moderately friendly reception, looked forward to *Paul Morel,* which at first promised to be somewhat in the vein of *The White Peacock.*

Besides sending Lawrence and Frieda the reviews of *The Trespasser,* Garnett sent his son David, then just turned twenty, to see them. In July, David Garnett was in Munich, lonely, when his father wrote to him and suggested a visit to Icking. Soon afterwards a note arrived from Lawrence himself, telling the younger Garnett how to get there. Descending from the train amid the costumed Bavarian peasants, Garnett saw an Englishman of a distinct type: his hair, 'bright mud-colour, with a streak of red in it', a scrubby mat growing forward from the back of the head, was not the hair of an English gentleman, for it was 'incredibly plebeian, mongrel, and underbred'. But the blue eyes above the little mustache were lively, and Lawrence's smile seemed to be that of a man who enjoyed life. His nose, Garnett felt, was 'too short and lumpy', and his as yet unbearded chin was 'too large, and round like a hairpin'. He was like a plumber's assistant, the man for whom strikes and the dole existed, the cause of violent yet impotent hatred of the upper classes for the lower—actually David Garnett was seeing Lawrence's schoolfellows, who were now colliers and pub frequenters in Eastwood.

Garnett and Lawrence walked along the river to Wolfratshausen. There Frieda waited for them at Haus Vogelnest, where her sister Else Jaffe was staying. On the way the young visitor bathed in the Isar, 'amid clouds of horseflies'.

Garnett saw Frieda, with her direct gaze from her yellow-flecked green eyes, as a lioness; her body was as sturdy and strong as that of the peasant mothers in the train, but 'her head and the whole carriage of her body was noble.' He subsequently met the Jaffes, who had moved to a house in the pinewoods at Irschenhausen, about a mile north of Icking and farther from the river. Else Jaffe remembered from that time that Frieda used to bring her washing over to Irschenhausen and shock the Jaffes' neighbors by hanging out a man's pajamas.

Frieda kept a close watch on Lawrence. Else Jaffe remembered arriving one night on the ten o'clock train from Munich and stopping in at Icking to ask Lawrence if he would walk over to Irschenhausen with her through the darkness. But before he could answer,

Frieda plangently assured her sister that poor Lawrence was too tired
—he could never walk over there and back so late at night.

On August 2, shortly before Lawrence and Frieda left Icking,
Frieda's mother suddenly appeared, and for an hour *schimpfed* Lawrence, railing at him in German, asking him how he could expect to
have a baroness cleaning his boots and emptying his slops: 'No man
with common sense of decency could expect to have a woman, the
wife of a clever professor, living with him like a barmaid, and he not
even able to keep her in shoes.' Lawrence meekly accepted this scolding and then, when the baroness was leaving, mustered all his courtesy
and charm as he escorted her to the train. In Munich she told Else
that Lawrence was lovable and reliable.

*

Like two *Wandervögel* of the time, Lawrence and Frieda left Icking
on August 5 for Lago di Garda. The Alps rose between them and
the largest of the Italian lakes. 'The imperial road to Italy', Lawrence
wrote at the beginning of his first travel book, *Twilight in Italy,* 'goes
from Munich across the Tyrol, through Innsbruck and Bozen to
Verona, over the mountains. Here the great processions passed as the
emperors went South, or came home again from rosy Italy to their
own Germany.'

The first night of their journey Lawrence and Frieda spent at 'a
wayside inn' in the Isar valley. The next night they slept in a hay hut
in the mountains, and on the following night were in a *Gasthaus* in
Glashütte. They went on to Mayrhofen, which they seem to have left
at the end of August, stopping in the Zillerthal and at Dominicu-
shütte mit Schlegeistal, on the slopes near Sterzing. From Sterzing
they went to Meran and Bozen, and to Trient, all Austrian towns
then, and by September 7 they were in Riva, at the top of Lago di
Garda.

One of the finest achievements of Lawrence's tour was his essay
'Christs in the Tirol', a description of the painted wooden figures of
the crucified Christ that rise along the Alpine roadsides. In Bavaria
and in the northern part of the Austrian Tyrol, Lawrence found them
realistic heavy peasant types, but farther south they were foppish,
Guido Reni figures. This essay has been several times reprinted; Lawrence used a revised version of it in *Twilight in Italy,* and more than
once fitted the material into his imaginative work, notably in the
scene of Gerald Crich's destruction in *Women in Love.*

'A Chapel Among the Mountains' and 'A Hay Hut Among the Mountains', essays in the *Love Among the Haystacks* volume, describe a small chapel Lawrence and Frieda discovered, and the hay hut where they slept, on the night before they reached Glashütte. One of the lesser poems in the *Look!* sequence, 'Song of a Man Who Is Not Loved', was written at Glashütte; the man in the poem feels lost in the immensity of space (. . . 'I am too / Little to count in the wind that drifts me through').

Lawrence gave Mrs. Hopkin a full report from Mayrhofen on the status of his relationship with Frieda, whose husband loved her 'madly' and would not 'let go'. But, he said, 'for ourselves, Frieda and I have struggled through some bad times into a wonderful naked intimacy, all kindled with warmth, that I know at last is love. I think I ought not to blame women, as I have done, but myself, for taking my love to the wrong woman, before now.' Every man should find, should 'keep on trying till he finds, the woman who can take him and whose love he can take, then who will grumble about men or about women. But the thing must be two-sided. At any rate, and whatever happens, I do love, and I am loved. I have given and I have taken—and that is eternal.'

David Garnett rejoined Lawrence and Frieda at Mayrhofen. He was a student of botany then, and the flowers in the Zillerthal would provide important additions to his herbarium. Lawrence wrote most of the day in the room where Frieda and Garnett sat talking; now and then he would get up to attend to the cooking, sometimes joining in the conversation, but soon returning to his manuscript. In the evenings the three of them devised charades, or Lawrence mimicked Eastwood people or Yeats and Pound at a London party, perhaps the one at which Pound ate the tulips while Yeats delivered his monologue. David Garnett has said there was something Chaplin-like in Lawrence's acting; 'but bitterer, less sentimental'. The grim part of the day, Garnett recalled, was when the letters arrived, forwarded from England or Germany, often concerned with Frieda's children. One of the difficulties in the situation was that Lawrence all this time had a deep admiration and even affection for Ernest Weekley, in the same way that Paul Morel in *Sons and Lovers* is drawn to Baxter Dawes, whose wife Paul has taken. Frieda says that Lawrence 'felt strongly' for her husband: 'Do you remember the poem "Meeting on [Among] the Mountains", where he meets a peasant with brown eyes?'

Before Lawrence and Frieda broke camp at Mayrhofen, about August 31, they were joined by a friend of David Garnett's, Harold Hobson, son of the economist J. A. Hobson. They all walked down the great 'steps' of the Pfitscherjoch towards Sterzing, where Garnett and Hobson caught the night express from Verona, and Lawrence walked part of the way to the station with them: 'It was dark,' Garnett reports, 'there was a smell of flowers, and Lawrence's light feet were noiseless in the dust of the road.'

While at Sterzing, Lawrence wrote his poem 'Misery'. It grew out of a letter from there to McLeod on September 2, in which he spoke of the cold in the mountains, the freezing water, and the difficulty of keeping one's way. 'Don't be surprised', he told McLeod, 'if I do vanish some day in some oubliette or other among these mountains.' The first line of the 'Misery' poem speaks of 'this oubliette between the mountains', and later it asks, 'Why don't I go? / Why do I crawl about this pot, this oubliette, / stupidly?'

From Sterzing, Lawrence and Frieda moved on to Meran and Bozen, which are now Merano and Bolzano. Then, in 'pure Italian ancient decrepit' Trient (now again Trento), Frieda 'had blues enough', Lawrence wrote, 'to repave the floor of heaven'. Frieda later remembered 'a very cheap hotel and the marks on the walls, the doubtful sheets, and worst of all the W.C.s'. Lawrence, who had seen her 'walk barefoot over icy stubble, laughing at wet and hunger and cold', now found her sitting under the statue of the archetype of all expatriate poets, Dante, and weeping.

In those days there was a train between Trient and Riva: Lawrence bought tickets so that he and Frieda could ride the rest of the way. But when they arrived at Riva, they were so poor that they cooked their meals in their room, illicitly, and when the Italian maid came to make the beds, they had to hide the spirit lamp and the food. At last, however, their trunks caught up with them, and Frieda could cast off her 'peasant sack' for a good blue dress; her sister Johanna had sent some fine clothes and hats, and Frieda could now parade swankily about the Austrian garrison town, among what Lawrence called the 'Chocolate Soldiers' of Franz Joseph. Lawrence still wore an old shapeless straw hat he had bought cheaply in Munich. But comparative riches fell on him when fifty pounds in notes arrived from Duckworth on September 16. Two days later Lawrence and Frieda moved to Italian territory down the lake, to Gargnano, where he completed *Sons and Lovers*.

*

It was an altogether different kind of life from that of his past, in gray-skied Nottingham, in often-rainy England. Now he was living among the dark sun-people he would later celebrate, and almost everything was bright. The young man was adjusting himself to the sometimes vivacious, sometimes gloomy German woman, and as they acted out their story, the days were intense with the sun, which seemed closer to the earth than in the north, warmly filling the days with its yellow glare.

Life in such circumstances was having its effect on the young Lawrence. He had always appreciated the landscapes of the north: *The White Peacock* and *Sons and Lovers* are full of them, presented as the writers of the Romantic movement saw them, vibrant and living and always affecting the human beings in the midst of them. But his experience with southern settings brought about a change in Lawrence, and he gradually became angered over what had been done to the landscapes of industrial regions. This is not dealt with specifically in *Sons and Lovers,* which although finished in the south bears no hint of that area; in the previous century, Ibsen had written many of his plays in Italy, and they deal with the north, although now and then a hint of the south steals in, as when Nora in *A Doll's House* dances the tarantella. There are no tarantellas in *Sons and Lovers,* or even in the novels that grew out of material written in Gargnano, *The Rainbow* and *Women in Love.*

Further, Lawrence's dislike of the industrial derived partly from various authors of the nineteenth century whom he had read: Thomas Carlyle (the young Carlyle, before the captains-of-industry phase), Matthew Arnold, John Ruskin, and William Morris, as represented in the following extract from Graham Martin's *Industrialism and Culture 1830–1914* (1970).

Men are grown mechanical in head and heart, as well as in hand. They have lost faith in individual endeavour, and in natural force, of any kind. Not for internal perfection, for external combinations and arrangements, for institutions, constitutions—for Mechanism of one sort or another, they do hope and struggle. Their whole efforts, attachments, opinions, turn on mechanism, and are of a mechanical character. (Carlyle, 1829)

It is verily this degradation of the operative into a machine, which, more than any other evil of the times, is leading the mass of the nations everywhere into vain, incoherent, destructive struggling for a freedom of which they cannot explain the nature to themselves. (Ruskin, 1853)

Faith in machinery is, I have said, our besetting danger; often in machinery most absurdly disproportioned to the end which this machinery, if it is to do any good at all, is to serve; but always in machinery, as if it had a value in and for itself. (Arnold, 1869)

It is this superstition of commerce being an end in itself, of man made for commerce, not commerce for man, of which art has sickened; not of the accidental appliances which that superstition when put into practice has brought its aid; machines and railways and the like, which do now verily control us, might have been controlled by us. (Morris, 1883)

In most of Lawrence's work after *Sons and Lovers,* a book which only incidentally suggests any evil in the mining landscapes, such statements as these stood behind him. In Gargnano, Lawrence was also crystallizing his thoughts about the power of the blood, which, as he said in the famous letter to Ernest Collings, was in effect his religion; this would in time become a philosophy in which he attempted to put the blood in balance with the mind—in Lawrence's terminology, 'blood-knowledge' and 'mind-knowledge'. But, after knowing the sunshine of Italy, and the careless happiness of its peasants, he would certainly remember, from past readings, those nineteenth-century writers who saw the dangers of mechanism and the corroding effect of mechanism's essential cause, industrialism.

In his lecture on Lawrence in 1951, which he called 'D. H. Lawrence: Prophet of the Midlands', the late Vivian de Sola Pinto put Lawrence in the 'long line' of great prophets of English literature from 'Langland in the fourteenth century, More and Latimer in the sixteenth century, Bunyan in the seventeenth, to Blake in the eighteenth, and Carlyle and Morris in the nineteenth'; Professor Pinto added, 'Lawrence is the latest, but by no means the last figure in that line.'

5 DAWN IN ITALY

Gargnano, where Lawrence and Frieda stayed until April 1913, is one of the salient chapters of his experience. The end of *Sons and*

Lovers, as previously suggested, meant the end of a good many of the difficulties of his past. And there in Gargnano he was to begin work on what became the two novels that were the achievements of the second phase of his career, *The Rainbow,* completed in 1915, and *Women in Love,* completed in late 1916 or early 1917. Also, Gargnano was a prolongation of Icking, but now, instead of merely two months of living together, Lawrence and Frieda had seven. It is notable that the *Look! We Have Come Through!* poems began to resolve themselves into expressions of more consistent happiness during this first sojourn of Lawrence and Frieda in Italy; the last of them written there, 'Spring Morning' (following one significantly called 'Paradise Re-Entered'), says: 'Among the pink and blue / Of the sky and the almond flowers / A sparrow flutters. / —We have come through . . .'

In those days, before Mussolini's engineers had carved the *Gardesana occidentale* through the stone cliffs on the western side of the lake, the only way to reach Gargnano from Riva was by boat, 'because of the steep rocky mountainy hills at the back'. Lawrence rented the bottom flat of the Villa Igéa from Pietro Paoli (a 'grey old Italian with grand manners and a jaw like a dog and a lovely wife of forty') for eighty lire a month, in those days about sixty-three shillings without exchange fees, or about fifteen and a half dollars, 'everything supplied'.

There Frieda seriously tried housekeeping for the first time. But the stove and the huge copper pans were formidable: she often had to call Lawrence away from his work—'The pigeons are burning, what shall I do?'—and he would come in good-naturedly to save everything. 'The first time I washed the sheets was a disaster,' Frieda recalled. 'They were so large and wet, their wetness was overwhelming. The kitchen floor was flooded, the table drenched, I dripped from hair to feet'—and again Lawrence rescued her, wiped the kitchen dry, and hung the sheets in the garden. 'If you hear of us murdered', he wrote to Edward Garnett, 'that also will be F.'s fault. She empties water out of the bedroom on to the high road and a fat old lady who steals along under the wall. I had to keep all the doors locked, and we sat in the spare bedroom. There are no police.'

Occasionally there was noise in the village: wounded soldiers returning from the Tripolitan war. This must have come back to Lawrence amusingly when, fourteen years later, he translated Giovanni Verga's 'Cavalleria Rusticana', with its comic opening passage that describes the return to a Sicilian village of the swaggering soldier

Turridu, 'showing himself off in his bersagliere's uniform with the red fez cap . . .' But Lawrence's life at Gargnano was not all a matter of minor domestic calamities with humorous afterthoughts, and of wry observation of returned soldiers. The writing of the final version of *Sons and Lovers* was an agony, ripping him apart as he wrote more intensely than ever before.

Edward Garnett's notes on *Paul Morel,* comments which Lawrence felt were the work of 'a Trojan of energy and conscientiousness', served as a guide to the rewriting of the story. When Lawrence finished the last draft, he wrote to his adviser, 'I tell you it has got form —*form:* haven't I made it patiently, out of sweat as well as blood'— but the sweat and blood did not come from Lawrence's struggle with 'form' so much as from his sufferings at reliving the past. For this deeper, more vital reworking of the manuscript demanded a greater intensification of the past than the earlier versions had. Authors often try to shake off burdens of the past by writing about it. Sometimes the process is conscious, sometimes not: its effectiveness usually depends upon the strength and depth of the feeling involved. In religion, confession leading to absolution requires a painful searching of the spirit; in psychoanalysis, the patient who is uprooting a neurosis must relive, in agonizing memory, the causal traumatic experience; and in literature, the process is somewhat similar. Frieda remembered that when Lawrence wrote of his mother's death it made him ill, and his grief upset her, too. He told her that if his mother had lived she would not have let him love Frieda: 'But I think he got over it; only, this fierce and overpowerful love had harmed the boy who was not strong enough to bear it.' Yet: 'I think a man is born twice: first his mother bears him, then he has to be reborn from the woman he loves.'

She was not always sympathetic, however, to Lawrence's grief over the past. At one point she was moved to write a skit entitled 'Paul Morel, or His Mother's Darling'. When Lawrence read it he said coldly, 'This kind of thing isn't called a skit.' On another occasion, possibly at Gargnano, or perhaps earlier, at Icking or Mayrhofen, Frieda scribbled some violent marginal comments in one of Lawrence's college exercise books next to a poem to his mother:

I hate it—good God!!!! I hate it! Yes, worse luck! What a poem to write! Yes, you are free, poor devil, from the heart's home life free, lonely you shall be, you have chosen it, you chose it freely! Now go your own way—Misery, a sad old woman's misery you have chosen, you poor man, and you cling to it with all your power. I have tried, I have fought, I have nearly killed myself in the battle to get you in connection with myself and other people, early I proved to myself that I can love, but never you—Now I will leave you for some days and I will see if being alone will help you to see me as I am, I will heal again by myself, you cannot help me, you are a sad thing. I know your secret and your despair, I have seen you ashamed—I love you better, that is my reward.

Just how much Lawrence knew of Freud at this time, and of Freud's theories about the Oedipus complex, is difficult to determine. Frieda told Frederick J. Hoffman in 1942 that 'Lawrence knew about Freud before he wrote the final draft of Sons and Lovers. I don't know whether he had read Freud or heard of him before we met in 1912. But I was a great Freud admirer; we had long arguments and Lawrence's conclusion was more or less that Freud looked on sex too much from the doctor's point of view, that Freud's "sex" and "libido" were too limited and mechanical, and that the root was deeper.'

Professor Hoffman, in a careful examination of all the evidence (in his *Freudianism and the Literary Mind*), decided that although the relationship between Paul and his mother was always an important element in the story that became *Sons and Lovers,* Lawrence's discussions and arguments with Frieda over Freudian doctrine 'may have increased the emphasis in the novel upon the mother-son relationship, to the neglect of other matters, and given it the striking clarity which it enjoys in the published book.' Professor Hoffman pointed out, however, that Lawrence didn't meet official Freudians until later when, in London, Dr. David Eder and Barbara Low, who became his friends in 1914, began to provide him with professional explanations of the doctrine, which from the first he opposed in several important respects, as Frieda's letter and his own subsequent writings show.

At Gargnano, although Lawrence disapproved of Frieda's 'skits' on his youth, he was trying his own hand at little comedies. He told Edward Garnett that he hoped an audience might be found for him such as the one which had responded to Chekhov—a remark not necessarily meant to suggest that his plays in themselves had a Chekhovian quality. One or two early attempts were made to produce some of them, and Lawrence once even had an interview with the actor B. Iden Payne; but nothing came of this at the time. In the spring of 1968, however, three of Lawrence's plays were produced at the Royal Court Theatre in London: *A Collier's Friday Night, The Widowing of Mrs Holroyd,* and a drama Lawrence left incomplete (it was finished by another hand), *The Daughter-in-Law.* Critics and public gave them extreme praise, rating Lawrence high as a dramatist. Perhaps these plays, because of their extensive use of dialect, wouldn't be workable in the United States, though foreign-language productions in the vernacular might be successful.

One of the comedies Lawrence wrote at Gargnano was *Fight for Barbara,* which he turned out in three days at the end of October 1912, as a relief from the tensions of his novel. This play reflects the setting and the situation in which Lawrence and Frieda found themselves that autumn. The scenic sketch for the first act describes the kitchen of the Villa Igéa, with its 'big open fire-place of stone, with a little charcoal grate—*fornello*—on either side, cupboards, table, rush-bottom chairs with high backs—many copper pans of all sizes hanging up'.

The setting for the other three acts is 'the dining-room of the same villa—a rather large room, with piano, writing-desk, and old furniture. In the big bay window, which looks over a garden on to the Lake, is a big broad couch, without side or back.' For the characters, Lawrence drew upon five easily recognizable people, making Frieda and her family English. James Wesson, twenty-six, has run off with Barbara Tressider, 'about 26, fair'. They have been at the villa for nearly six weeks, having left England some three months before. Barbara's husband, Frederick Tressider, has called Wesson, the coal miner's son, 'lout', 'miserable worm', 'clod-hopper', and similar names. The scolding that Lady Charlcote, Barbara's mother, gives Wesson in the second act resembles the Baroness von Richthofen's berating of Lawrence at Icking: 'She is the daughter of a high-born and highly cultured gentleman. Do you expect her to carry your slops and make your beds!' Lawrence transformed Baron von Richthofen into a stuffy English gentleman; he is the least lifelike of the characters, telling Wesson, 'If I were a younger man, I would thrash you, sir.'

The outraged husband turns up, and the scene in which he appears with Barbara probably exposes a good deal of the actuality of Frieda's first marriage; those who know the background have said that some of the incidents referred to in that scene really happened.

E. W. Tedlock, Jr.'s *Frieda Lawrence: The Memoirs and Correspondence* contains two different versions of the honeymoon episode, as written by Frieda, one of them taking place at Lake Como, the other at Lucerne. In both cases the young bride describes herself climbing onto the top of a cupboard. Two hours later, in one of the narratives, after losing her virginity to the rather self-conscious and timid Englishman, she stands on the hotel balcony recalling how horrible the experience had been. In a letter written later in her life, Frieda reported, 'When we first married and I slithered down those narrow stairs, he came out of his study and said, "My God! I am married to an earthquake!" '

In *Fight for Barbara,* Barbara tells Frederick—'a haggard, handsome man of forty, brown moustache, dark brown eyes, greying at the temples'—that he did not 'warm' her: 'I thought our marriage would be a jolly thing—I thought I could have lovely games with the man. Can you remember when I climbed to the top of the cupboard, in Lucerne. I thought you'd look for me, and laugh, and fetch me down. No, you were terrified. You daren't even come into the room. You stood in the doorway looking frightened to death. And I climbed down. And that's how it always was—I had to climb down. I sat up there in my camisole with my legs dangling, and you were terrified. I had to climb down. I tell you it *was* a climb down for me.' Frederick, literal-minded, asks if she really left him because he had not fetched her down from the top of a cupboard where she had childishly climbed; she finally tells him that she has never loved him, although she has felt that she 'ought to'. She promises to try being his wife again, but later reneges, and the play ends with her saying to Wesson, 'Love me a fearful lot.'

This little comedy has slight value today, except for what biographical information it gives: Lawrence said 'much of it is word for word true,' though the elder von Richthofens and Ernest Weekley didn't go to Gargnano.

When Lawrence sent the play to Edward Garnett, he gave an account of his routine during the time he was finishing his novel. He was usually up by eight and preparing breakfast. Frieda would stay in bed and he would sit talking to her until time for the midday meal. As 'a working man by instinct', he felt guilty, but would take his punishment later. He didn't feel he was really a loafer: 'We live so hard, F. and I. And I've written 400 pages of *Paul Morel,* and this drama.'

Louie Burrows had sent Lawrence a letter and a photograph, which he acknowledged on November 19 and then added:

I want to say that it grieves me that I was such a rotter to you. You always treated me really well—and I—well, I only knew towards the end we couldn't make a good thing of it. But the wrong was all on my side. I think of you with respect and gratitude, for you were good to me—and I think of myself in the matter with no pleasure, I can tell you. And now all I can do is just to say this.

I am living here with a lady whom I love, and whom I shall marry when I come to England, if it is possible. We have been together as man and wife for six months, nearly, now, and I hope we shall always remain man and wife.

I feel a beast writing this. But I do it because I think it is only fair to you. I never deceived you, whatever—or did I deceive you? I may have done even that.—I have nothing to be proud of.—

I shall get into a bigger mess if I go on writing. Don't say anything about me and this to anybody, will you? I shall be able to be married and make everything public in the spring, I hope. —if the divorce comes off.

I am ever so well in health—poor in pocket—but healthy enough. But if we go on writing, I feel I am only doing you more wrong, and it would be easier to stop altogether now—wiser perhaps.

The best thing you can do is to hate me.

I loathe signing my name to this.

Lawrence wrote to her at least once more, in the last of the surviving letters. As if he had said everything he could in his own language, he turned to the safety of the French of his own special kind. After telling her (this item is postmarked November 25) that she by now would have received *'mon autre billet'*, he added, *'Oui, l'Italie est forte belle—je m'importe bien. . . . Il fait un merveilleusement beau temps ici.'*

*

Lawrence had wondered, in a letter to Edward Garnett, whether *Sons and Lovers* would be a better title for the novel, which he had made *'heaps* better—a million times'. He estimated, on this October 30, that he would write the last hundred pages in a fortnight. Exactly on schedule, he mailed the completed manuscript on November 13.

Except for Garnett's subsequent bowdlerizing—painful to Lawrence—the novel was at last finished. It was a far different book from *The White Peacock,* which had also been extensively revised, and from *The Trespasser,* which had been put together hurriedly. As previously pointed out, *The White Peacock* was an escape from the past through an idealization of it, and *The Trespasser* was a literary-rhetorical excursion: but *Sons and Lovers* was a partial conquest of the past, because in it Lawrence faced that past and battled with it. And he felt that the book was more than just a story: he told Garnett it was 'a great tragedy . . . the tragedy of thousands of young men in England. . . . The name of the old son-lover was Oedipus. The name of the new one is legion.' Because the writing of *Sons and Lovers* had been a therapeutic experience for Lawrence, he expected that the reading of it would be therapeutic for his generation. *Sons and Lovers* was in every way deeper, more intense, than Lawrence's earlier work, and when he concluded that book he concluded his first period as a writer.

In 'the interlude between novels', Lawrence and Frieda found themselves becoming part of the village life. They swam in the lake, and they took Italian lessons from the local schoolmistress. Lawrence had begun to feel a closeness to the Italian peasants, whom he saw as proud and upright 'kings' who knew nothing of the hurry and fret of the industrialized north, of the England that he now considered 'grubby' and 'shabby'. These peasants were poor, and perhaps without 'many ideas, but they look well, and they have strong blood'. Here the later Lawrence began to speak.

He had started writing a novel about Robert Burns, with a Midland setting. The manuscript of this unfinished novel was unearthed by Edward Nehls, who wrote to the author of this book: 'I can't see that it has any connexion with Burns. . . . It is much more like an *Aaron's Rod* beginning. It has only two or three scenes—a meeting of a young man and a girl while they are picking up faggots in a forest; another meeting when the man goes to the girl's home and chats with her at the front gate; a third scene in the pub. Too little of a manuscript to see what direction Lawrence was giving it. Heroine's name changed from Mary *Burns* to Mary *Renshaw* in the manuscript.' Dr. Nehls published this fragment in the first volume of his *D. H. Lawrence: A Composite Biography.*

Lawrence in a letter to McLeod gave a description of his situation as the year 1912 drew to an end:

The *Tom Jones* came on Sunday, before any of the rest. Don't send me anything else—I feel too guilty. I haven't any book I could give you except Garnett's *Joan of Arc*. It is more or less interesting. Don't scorn it.

I am thinking so hard of my new novel, and since I am feeling hard pushed again, am in the right tune for it. It is to be a life of Robert Burns—but I shall make him live near home, as a Derbyshire man and shall fictionise the circumstances. I think I can do him almost like an autobiography. Tell Miss Mason the *Life* came all right, and give her my thanks. I am waiting for her letter before I write. If it would amuse you just peep round and see if you can spot anything interesting about Burns in the library, during the holiday. I've only got Lockhart's *Life*. I should like to know more about the Highland Mary episode. Do you think it's interesting?

I haven't done any stories or anything lately. The strain of this business with Frieda squashes little things out of me. Perhaps after all there will be a divorce. If so, the next time you see me I shall be a married man. I am now one with all the disadvantages of illicity.

Harold Hobson is here—and it's very jolly. But I'd rather you had come. I need one of my own friends rather badly just now. I've done 4 pictures—Harold will bring them to England and send them to you, and you can pick. But if you can get a copy of the Idyll, I'll do that as well.

Thanks for the Yeats. Why didn't you put my name in it? He seems awfully queer stuff to me now—as if he wouldn't bear touching. But Frieda is fond of him.

I'm going to begin again my work. One works in two bursts —Sept. to the beginning of Dec.—and Jan. till March or April. The rest are more or less trivial and barren months. I feel that I am *resisting* too hard to write poetry—*resisting* the strain of Weekley, and the tragedy there is in keeping Frieda. To write poetry one has to let oneself fuse in the current—but I daren't. The state of mind is more like a business man's, where he stands firm and keeps his eye open, than an artist's, who lets go and loses himself. But I daren't let go just now. The strain makes me tired.

Having Hobson there was 'awfully jolly' for the lovers, Lawrence told David Garnett, and doubtless the young visitor's presence kept their spirits up: it was Frieda's first Yuletide away from her children.

On Christmas Day, Lawrence wrote to Mrs. Hopkin, saying among other things, 'If the skies tumble down like a smashed saucer, it couldn't break what's between Frieda and me.' Frieda added a post-script: 'My poor husband—I daren't think of him!'

Although Lawrence told McLeod that he was 'resisting' poetry, he occasionally added to the *Look!* sequence. He also resumed his writing of fiction before long. Despite his intention to rest for a while 'between novels', he began work on what was then provisionally titled *The Insurrection of Miss Houghton,* which he completed after the war, when it became *The Lost Girl.* He had given up Burns.

Besides his writing activity at Gargnano, Lawrence continued to paint. The *Idyll* he mentioned in the letter of December 17 to McLeod is a picture by Maurice Greiffenhagen of lovers, apparently a shep-herd and shepherdess, embracing in a woodland. It was a favorite of Lawrence's; he had begun making a copy of it on the night his mother was dying, and later he had given Louie Burrows and Ada other copies that he had made. He wanted to attempt it again at Gargnano.

During the seven months there, Lawrence depended upon McLeod and the Garnetts to send him books, which he often mentioned in his letters, as some of them that have been quoted show—as in the reference to Yeats. On the day before he left Riva for Gargnano, Lawrence had asked McLeod for 'something to read. I've not read a thing in English for 5 months, except *Under Western Eyes,* which bored me.' He told Edward Garnett that he couldn't 'forgive Conrad for being so sad and for giving in'. He also said that he hated Strind-berg, who seemed 'unnatural, forced, a bit indecent—a bit wooden, like Ibsen, a bit skin-erupty,' remarks indicating that in literary judg-ments Lawrence was at times somewhat limited.

On December 2 Lawrence informed McLeod, 'I've read *The Rev-olution in Tanner's Lane,* and find myself fearfully fond of Ruther-ford. I used to think him dull, but now I see he is so just and plucky and sound'. He found little to praise in all the current literature he was reading, and was particularly critical of his fellow Midlander Arnold Bennett, one of whose novels he had read the preceding October: 'I hate Bennett's resignation', he told McLeod. 'Tragedy ought really to be a great kick at misery. But *Anna of the Five Towns* seems like an acceptance—so does all the modern stuff since Flau-bert. I hate it. I want to wash again quickly, wash off England, the oldness and grubbiness and despair,' judgments of a perhaps more satisfactory kind, further exemplified in his 1928 essay on the limita-tions of John Galsworthy, now in print in the *Phoenix* volume.

Lawrence's birthplace, Victoria Street, Eastwood: 'Down the street between the squares, Scargill Street, the Wesleyans' chapel was put up, and I was born in the little corner shop just above.'

The Lawrence family. Seated, Lettice Ada, Mrs. Lydia Lawrence, David Herbert Richards Lawrence, Arthur John Lawrence; standing, Emily Una, George Arthur, William Ernest: 'Home was home, and they loved it with a passion of love, whatever the suffering had been.'

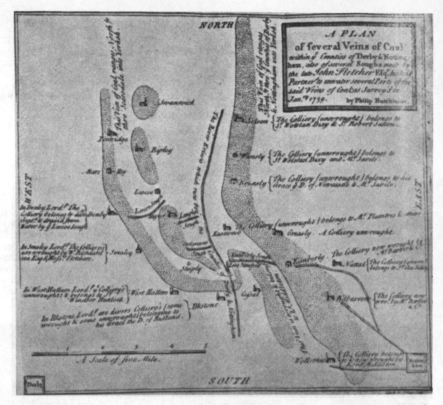

The 'Lawrence Country' in 1739, showing Eastwood and its collieries, including the one at Brinsley where Arthur John Lawrence was a miner from childhood to old age: 'At six in the morning they turned him down/and they turned him up for tea.'

Brinsley colliery: 'Look how it heaps together, like something alive almost—a big creature that you don't know.'

Moorgreen reservoir, scene of the drowning in the 'Water-Party' chapter of *Women in Love*: 'The lake was blue and fair, the meadows sloped down in sunshine on one side, the thick dark woods dropped steeply on the other.'

End house in the Breach, Eastwood (the 'Bottoms' of *Sons and Lovers*), where between the ages of two and six (1887–91?) Lawrence lived with his family: 'These mining villages *might* have been like the lovely hill-towns of Italy, shapely and fascinating. And what happened?'

Sir Thomas Philip Barber of Lambclose house (across the road from Moorgreen), whom Lawrence drew upon for part of the portrait of Gerald in *Women in Love*: '. . . fair, good-looking, healthy, with a great reserve of energy.'

The true Lawrence country. Upper left center, Haggs Farm (where Miriam lived in *Sons and Lovers*); steeple of Underwood chapel in distance; Felley Mill ('Strelley Mill' in *The White Peacock*): 'That's the country of my heart.'

Felley Mill pond: 'The whole place was gathered in the musing of old age. The thick-piled trees on the far shore were too dark and sober to dally with the sun . . . The water lay softly, intensely still.'

Haggs Farm: 'The farm and buildings, three sides of a quadrangle, embraced the sunshine towards the woods.'

Lawrence on his twenty-first birthday, 1906: A 'clean-shaven, bright young prig in a high collar like a curate, guaranteed to counteract all the dark and sinister effect of all the newspaper photographs.'

Jessie Chambers: 'Her beauty, that of a shy, wild, quiveringly sensitive thing, seemed nothing to her. Even her soul, so strong for rhapsody, was not enough. She must have something to reinforce her pride.'

Marsh Farm, home of the Brangwen family in *The Rainbow:*
'The house stood bare from the
road, approached by a straight
garden path, along which at
spring the daffodils were thick
and yellow.'

Church at Cossall, Derbyshire
('Cossethay' of *The Rainbow*):
'The old, little church, with its
small spire on a square tower,
seemed to be looking back at
the cottage windows.'

Louisa (Louie) Burrows: 'My girl is here. She's big, and swarthy, and passionate as a gipsy—but good, awfully good, churchy.'

University College, Nottingham—now the city's public library—which Lawrence attended from 1906 to 1908: 'Its rather pretty, plaything, Gothic form was almost a style, in the dirty industrial town.' *Photo: Nottingham Public Library*

NOTTINGHAM CASTLE   1890

Christmas Greetings

Nottingham Castle, where Paul Morel in *Sons and Lovers* exhibits his paintings: 'They saw the Castle on its bluff of brown, green-bushed rock, in a positive miracle of delicate sunshine.'

One of several copies the young Lawrence made of Greiffenhagen's *Idyll:* 'Now I've begun a little Idyll for Agnes Holt. She marries in early August and has asked me for this picture. I must race and get her a couple done.'

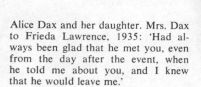

Alice Dax and her daughter. Mrs. Dax to Frieda Lawrence, 1935: 'Had always been glad that he met you, even from the day after the event, when he told me about you, and I knew that he would leave me.'

Lawrence in 1908: 'Did you like my photo? It is not bad. It represents me as gross; it has no subtlety; there is no insight in it; I like it exceedingly; I like myself bluff, rather ordinary, fat, a bit "manly".'

Lawrence's mother in her last illness: 'They used to carry her downstairs, sometimes even into the garden . . . And she watched the tangled sunflowers dying, the chrysanthemums coming out, and the dahlias.'

Helen Corke about 1912: 'I will tell you about a new girl—a girl who "interests" me—nothing else—next time I write— call her Hélène—she is very interesting.'

Lawrence about 1912: 'When in repose, he had the diffident, ironic bearing so remarkable in the educated youth of today, the very reverse of that traditional aggressiveness of youth.'

The young Frieda, in Germany: 'She is the daughter of Baron von Richthofen . . . but she's splendid, she is really.'

Frieda with her first husband, Ernest Weekley, and his parents: 'She had never met people of this stamp,' Frieda wrote of herself. 'There was a warm and cosy atmosphere about the house with big joints of meat and juicy pies on the dinner table. The great event of the week was Sunday-morning church.'

S. S. Koteliansky, painted by Mark Gertler: 'You are a great donkey, and your letters to Frieda are ridiculous.—Why the hell do you make such a palaver to her? . . . And if you're going to come and see us, why for Heaven's sake don't you come—[instead of] fidgeting and fuming and stirring and reading the portents. It is preposterous."

Catherine Carswell c. 1910: 'How exciting your letter is! . . . I only want to know people who have the courage to live.' *Photo: lent by John Carswell*

David Garnett, 1913, by Lawrence: 'You should see him swim in the Isar, that is effervescent and pale green, where the current is fearfully strong . . . F [Frieda] sits on the bank bursting with admiration, and I am green with envy.'

Drawing by Lawrence sent to Viola Meynell on March 2, 1915: 'I have finished my Rainbow.'

Lady Cynthia Asquith: 'There is something infinitely more important in you than your beauty. Why do you always ignore the realest thing in you, this hard, stoic, elemental sense of logic and truth? that is your real beauty.'

Lawrence, Katherine Mansfield, Frieda, John Middleton Murry, Kensington, 1915: 'I'm glad you and Katherine are all right . . . I know you should stick to the love you have each for the other.'

Garsington Manor, Oxfordshire, painted by
Mark Gertler: '. . . this house of the
Ottoline's—it is England—my God, it
breaks my soul—their England, these
shafted windows, the elm-trees, the blue
distance—the past, the great past, crumbling down, breaking down . . .'

Lady Ottoline Morrell: 'Why must you always use your *will* so much, why can't
you let things be, without always grasping
and trying to know and to dominate. I'm
too much like this myself.'

In January, Lawrence reported to McLeod that he had seen Enrico Persevalli and his strolling peasant troupe in plays by Ibsen and D'Annunzio, and in *Hamlet.* Persevalli was a fat, Caruso-type Italian whose Hamlet nearly made Lawrence fall out of box No. 8 trying to suppress his laughter: 'The only Englishman, and ranking here as quite a swell—they acted particularly for me.' It was amusing to hear Hamlet addressed as *Signore,* this Hamlet who went about whispering *'Essere—o non essere'* and sneaking about as if 'he had murdered some madam "*à la* Crippen" and it was *her* father's ghost chasing him'—but Lawrence put all this, and more, into *Twilight in Italy.*

The chapters of this book that originally appeared as magazine sketches—'The Spinner and the Monks', 'The Lemon Gardens', and 'The Theatre'—help us to fill in the pattern of Lawrence's life at Gargnano, for they are an exact account of many of the things he saw. And these essays are important in the development of his thought, for they contain the first of his attacks upon industrialized civilization. This theme suggested itself but lightly in the original sketches; Lawrence strengthened it when he rewrote the essays in 1915, for publication in 1916. In this rewriting he also improved the compositional style of the sketches. Here for example is the original description of his visit to the church, from the *English Review:*

... I have only been in the church once. It was very dark, and smelled powerfully of centuries of incense. It reminded me of the lair of some enormous creature, and my senses sprang awake. I expected something, I wanted something, my flesh was alive. And I hurried out again, to that wonderful table of sunshine outside. And it would cost me a great effort to go inside the church again. But its pavemented threshold is clear as a jewel.

The difference in the *Twilight in Italy* version is at once noticeable:

I went into the church. It was very dark, and impregnated with centuries of incense. It affected me like the lair of some enormous creature. My senses were roused, they sprang awake in the hot, spiced darkness. My skin was expectant, as if it expected some contact, some embrace, as if it were aware of the contiguity of the physical world, the physical contact with the darkness and the heavy, suggestive substance of the enclosure. It was a thick, fierce darkness of the senses. But my soul shrank.

I went out again. The pavemented threshold was clear as a

jewel, the marvellous clarity of sunshine that becomes blue in the height seemed to distil me into itself.

Lawrence apparently made this revision after completing *The Rainbow,* yet for the most part the passage doesn't suggest the stylistic mastery of that novel. The addition, in the later version, of Latinized words such as *impregnated* and *affected* mars the simplicity, the intrusion of the passive voice breaks the directness, and the repetitions—which Lawrence often used so skillfully—are in the main awkward. Yet the second version, for all these faults, is superior to the first, which is too abrupt in its transitions. And the first is commonplace by comparison with the second, which adds phrases and words that give a sensual immediacy to the description and project the reader into the church in a way the earlier version does not. Even the Latinate word *expectant*—a fairly simple one at that—is intensely effective in the phrase 'my skin was expectant'; and 'the hot, spiced darkness' takes the reader's senses at once into the church; the word *spiced* is perfect. (This passage is perceptively commented upon by Anaïs Nin in her book *D. H. Lawrence* [1930, reprinted 1964].)

One of the new ideas or symbols Lawrence was trying to grasp through his writing was that of darkness; it was to become an important one to him, along with that of 'the blood'. Lawrence was never a formal philosopher; nevertheless, as many formal philosophers have, he sought an ideal in equilibrium, or in the discovery of a middle way; in his own work he was later to use the term *polarity*.

Because of his emphasis on the physical and the intuitional in a world which he felt had become overintellectualized, Lawrence has often been misunderstood. In the *Twilight in Italy* essay 'The Theatre', he not only describes the acting of Persevalli—in an extension of his remarks in the letter to McLeod—but also discusses Hamlet as representing 'a kind of corruption of the flesh': in Lawrencean philosophy he is overintellectualized. Lawrence had 'always felt an aversion from Hamlet: a creeping, unclean thing he seems, on the stage, whether he is Forbes-Robertson or anybody else. . . . The character is repulsive in its conception, based on self-dislike and a spirit of disintegration.' Persevalli seemed just the right one to express 'the convulsed reaction of the mind from the flesh', for he was 'the modern Italian, suspicious, isolated, self-nauseated, labouring in a sense of physical corruption'. Lawrence was glad when the performance of *Amleto* ended, 'but I loved the theatre, I loved to look down on the peasants, who were so absorbed.'

The three sketches 'The Spinner and the Monks', 'The Lemon Gardens', and 'The Theatre' form, after 'The Crucifix', Chapters II, III, and IV of *Twilight in Italy* and deal with Gargnano. Of the remaining six chapters of the book, the last two describe one of Lawrence's later walking tours through Switzerland; the four preceding these contain pictures of the life up at San Gaudenzio, a farm in the steep mountainside above Gargnano where Lawrence and Frieda stayed for about two weeks at the end of March 1913.

They made this move about a month after a friend of Constance and Edward Garnett's, known as Mrs. Anthony, arrived at Gargnano. This Mrs. Anthony is rather a mysterious figure in Lawrence's letters; she was trying to make herself as obscure as possible, except from him and Frieda, because she was hiding in terror from her husband, a Swedish painter who was mentally unbalanced. He had followed her to England, whence the Garnetts had dispatched her to Italy. Mrs. Anthony was actually Antonia Cyriax, whom David Garnett describes most interestingly as Mrs. Anthonius in the first volume of his autobiography, *The Golden Echo* (1954).

She was an artist who painted a series of water colors of Gargnano and San Gaudenzio that inspired a qualified authority, Muirhead Bone, to praise them for their fresh and candid and 'untouristlike vision' which created 'stroke by stroke, imperceptibly almost, the *real* Italy which we in our pictures are always, somehow or other, leaving out.' Bone wrote this in his preface to *Among Italian Peasants*, by Tony Cyriax, which was published in London in 1919. The book depicts in prose and painting the life at San Gaudenzio, which the author called San Lorenzo. It was, incidentally, Tony Cyriax who first gave Lawrence the nickname Lorenzo.

Most of *Among Italian Peasants* deals with a time after Lawrence and Frieda had left, when Tony Cyriax's little daughter had joined her in the mountainside retreat. Nevertheless, it makes an interesting companion volume to *Twilight in Italy,* for it gives another view of the people Lawrence describes in the four San Gaudenzio chapters. The family there was the Capellis: they appear in *Twilight in Italy* as the Fioris and in Tony Cyriax's book as the Castellis. The Cyriax volume deals with these people and the place at greater length than the four *Twilight in Italy* chapters, but there is no comparison between the merely competent writing in *Among Italian Peasants* and Lawrence's brilliant account of these mountainside people, their 'illegal' inn, their gardens and vineyards, their dances, and their yearning for America.

It was just before Lawrence moved up to San Gaudenzio that he and Jessie finally broke off communication. He had sent her the proof sheets of *Sons and Lovers,* and had written her a letter which she had returned. The relationship was ended—though Jessie said, in a letter to Helen Corke several years after Lawrence's death, 'in essentials my feeling for him has not changed in spite of other deep affection. What he said about the indestructibility of love is quite true, on a particular plane.'

Since Lawrence's last meeting with Jessie in the spring of 1912, he had written to her several times. Soon after he had arrived in Germany he had sent her a postcard from Trier, with a picture of the cathedral, and then he wrote a letter, apparently from Waldbröl, in which he said he was going on with *Paul Morel;* Jessie would have to continue forgiving him. She felt that her forgiving or not forgiving him was immaterial. He had to discover something in himself, she thought, 'which only the inexorable logic of circumstance could show him.' She herself felt grievously injured and near collapse. A few weeks later Lawrence wrote a descriptive travel letter to the Chambers family, enclosing a note to Jessie, *'pour vous seulement'.* He wrote excitedly 'of the new attachment he had formed,' telling her to keep the information strictly secret. He told her that 'only Ada knows', though it was not much later that he was informing Mrs. Hopkin of this, and her friend Mrs. Dax as well. He reported to Mrs. Hopkin that he had 'told Jessie to leave her a chance of ridding herself of my influence'.

The news about Frieda had shocked Jessie, though it had not surprised her. Now she thought she would be free of that sense of responsibility she had always felt for Lawrence. She wrote and told him this. But she realized also that the break with Lawrence meant the extinction of her 'greater self'. The life that lay ahead looked, for all its freedom, bleak and ugly. Helen Corke pointed out that at this time Jessie, in trying to readjust herself, lacked Lawrence's advantage of the moment in that she had 'no change of personnel, scene, or circumstances to help the process'. Jessie and Helen had, however, earlier planned a Continental holiday, ironically in the Rhineland.

Both women had received letters postmarked from there, and although Jessie had told Helen that Lawrence had gone to Germany, she didn't mention Frieda. It was a gruesome holiday: Jessie was depressed, her conversation was all irony, she had lost her poise, and she seemed to move 'in an enemy world, warily'. In Germany the

August sun gleamed on ancient buildings and attractive gardens, but Jessie seemed unaware of the charm of Wiesbaden and Mainz and Heidelberg. For the most part she left Helen Corke to herself and sat reading *The Brothers Karamazov,* seeing in it 'the wreckage of my life', but at the last it was spiritually refreshing because it 'placed a distance between me and the catastrophe of life.'

Lawrence had not replied to Jessie's letter saying that she felt freed, but in the spring of 1913 he had Duckworth's send her a copy of *Love Poems.* She knew most of the contents, enjoyed seeing the pieces in print, asked her sister for Lawrence's address, and wrote him a note of thanks. He replied in March 1913 from Gargnano, in a letter that under the circumstances contained some astonishing intimacies. And it rather monstrously suggested that Jessie join him and Frieda on the Continent: 'This last year hasn't been all roses for me. I've had my ups and downs out here with Frieda. But we mean to marry as soon as the divorce is through. We shall settle down quietly somewhere, probably in Berkshire. Frieda and I discuss you endlessly. We should like you to come out to us some time, if you would care to.'

Jessie didn't know 'whether to laugh or cry'. The tone of that letter offended her in its affected lightness combined with an attempt to arouse her sympathy. She felt the letter had a 'clumsiness' and was 'priggish', yet it 'suffocated' her.

At this time Jessie's sister happened to visit her, and in her dismay Jessie for the first time showed May a letter from Lawrence. May was furious—'How dare he send a letter like this to *you!'*—and at her suggestion Jessie returned it. She felt that this was 'a brutal thing', but she also felt the time had come for a final break. That she didn't hurt Lawrence, however, is shown in the letter from Lawrence to his sister that follows below; indeed, in this note, with its mock-Dickensian signature ('Your afflicted brother, D. H. Gummidge'), Lawrence told his sister something that Jessie, over the years, never knew: He felt that in returning the letter she had taken a good line of action:

We leave here on Sunday—go to San Gaudenzio—which is a farm about 2 miles up the Lake. . . .

I have received £50 on account of *Sons and Lovers.* I send you £5 on account of all the insurances and things you have paid for me. You will see, when you have read these proofs, why

I sent them to J. The things Frieda will write you are probably untrue. I had not heard from J. for 8 months—nor written to her. I asked the publishers to send her a copy of the poems. She thanked me. I sent her the proofs and a note. The note came back. I say by mistake. Still if J. did it on purpose—all the better.

So Lawrence recognized at last that the relationship with Jessie had come to an end. Frieda twice commented on this in letters to the author of the present book. In one of them (May 27, 1950) she said, 'L. talked to me by the hour about Jessie Chambers. He owed her a lot, considering L.'s home, but the human relation between them did not work, she was a bluestocking and he had more warmth for her than she for him—she sort of wanted to run him too much in that humble bullying way—she would have wanted him to be a nice tame english little poet.'

Of the final break with Jessie, at Gargnano, and of the competition between Jessie and Lawrence's mother, Frieda wrote (January 30, 1951):

L. felt unhappy about hurting her feelings. She was the 'sacred love', you know the old split of sacred and profane. She tries to defend her position by insisting on the 'purity', which gives the show away—Humanly as a whole she wasn't the person his mother was, so the best horse won—She bored me in the end. There was some correspondence between L. and her about the book, but when she had read it, she never wrote again—In writing about her, he had to find out impersonally what was wrong in their relationship, when so much had been good—but what was insufficient in her, how could she admit or even see it? . . . L. had to have a woman as a sort of confirmation or test in his writing.

In his next letter to Ada, a few days after the move to San Gaudenzio, Lawrence mentioned that he had kept on with his imaginative writing there. The novel that he spoke of as 'rather more cheerful' than the one he had sent to her in proof sheets (*Sons and Lovers*) was evidently *The Sisters,* which was to grow into *The Rainbow* and *Women in Love.* On the same day he wrote to David Garnett that a novel he had been working on, apparently *The Insurrection of Miss Houghton,* had become 'improper'. He said he had put it aside to try what he spoke of as a pot-boiler, as he then thought of *The Sisters.*

But, he told Garnett further, it was developing 'into an earnest and painful work'.

Lawrence's letter to Ada from San Gaudenzio on April 5 mentions a possible early return to England; and there is an important addition by Frieda:

> This is a lovely place—a farm high on the mountainside. It has grounds a mile round, and vines, olive gardens. I sit in a deserted lemon garden that gets so warm with the sun. There are little grape hyacinths standing about. They are all over the mountains—and violets. Peach blossom in rosy pink among the grey olives and cherry blossom and pear are white. We love the people of the farm, such warm folks—at evening we play games in the kitchen. On Sunday there was a band of 4—cello, mandolino and 2 guitars playing in a corner queer lovely Italian music while we danced. The peasants of the mountains were in. One was a good looking wild fellow with a wooden leg. He danced like anything with Frieda and Mrs Anthony, a friend of ours who is staying here, and she danced well— so you see we have quite a life of it. Frieda was awfully pleased with your last letter. She uses it against me as a proof of what a difficult and unpleasant person I am to live with. I say you never meant it in that wise.

> _____

> [In Frieda's hand:] Yes, so shall I, your letter just came when L had made me so miserable that I began to think I was the scum of the earth, unfit for a human being—*His* misery was all *my* doing, so your letter came as a help to me from the Almighty. L looks well I think but of course it is hard our life, but now I *hope* the worst is over of misery the children, illness and all. But of course he is really good and it is hard for him as it is for me. It will be nice to see you, we shall live very quietly till we are married. We might just as well (He says I am writing a lot to you. He is already jealous of you!!) I always tell him I wish he were as nice as you—so I hope to see you soon.

6 BRIGHT NEW FRIENDS

Lawrence and Frieda stayed for a few days in the Verona of Romeo and Juliet, and on April 14 took the night train up through the Brenner to Munich. Lawrence's letter to Ada a few days later describes the Jaffes' house at Irschenhausen where they stayed, and the letter also refers to her forthcoming marriage:

First of all the village is Irschenhausen, so you draw a line under that, then München, which is Munich, has two dots on it, and then Isartal, means Isar valley, and the Isar is a tributary to the Danube, well known in English poetry as

> Eiser rolling rapidly
> And dark as winter was the flood
> Of Eiser rolling rapidly.

It is pronounced Eser, à la Anglaise, where Hohenlinden is, and when the battle was fought God knows. . . .

We are in a lovely little house in a corner of a pine or rather fir forest looking over to the Alps, which are white with snow—they are the same ten miles away. It is quite near Icking where I was last year. The house belongs to Frieda's brother in law. It is quite new, a lovely little place. Prof. Jaffé [sic] lives in Munich so the house is empty. We make a home here for a week or two —quite alone.

Don't you think it is a nice idea?

The house stands on a high meadow in an angle of the wood. The meadow has blue patches of gentian and is speckled with Alp primulas, and with cowslips. The village is a tiny place. An ox brought up our luggage in dignity from the station. I sit in the little dining room in the lamp light.

It is a room all of wood. There is a warm old stove of green tiles, and queer Bavarian pottery. Directly I am going to bed, because I have a cold. When I was up at Innsbruck coming from Italy I found the whole land under snow. I tell you it was a shock, the air was so fierce after the Garda. But my cold is fleeing with the snow, which is all gone.

Now I do not know when I shall be in England—perhaps not before your wedding. I am excited to hear of Emmie Limb being bridesmaid with Hilda Pettit, and having delicate sprigged muslin frocks. Look here, don't you go and be too grand. Don't make Eddie wear a frock coat for God's sake.

I want to wear a jacket. I will wear a white waistcoat and a white buttonhole if you insist, and I would never give you away.

Parson—'Who gives this woman in marriage?'
Me—'I'm sure I don't!'

But father will no doubt be glad of the opportunity. Don't deprive him of his paternal right. You keep discreet silence about *Sons and Lovers* though.

As for the divorce it will be a very quiet affair. Don't worry. It will be nice to stay with you in Ripley. I want to go to Pentrich. And do you remember the pub where we saw Daft?, and the Womans Guild—oh *Dio Dio!* Give my love to everybody.

Frieda is very busy and sends her love, and she is looking after me.

Give my love to Father. Has he flitted yet? Again my love to you.

Lawrence had written to Edward Garnett only two days earlier, also from Irschenhausen, expressing his disappointment and Frieda's (she was 'very cross') that *Love Poems and Others* had sold only a hundred copies. The next month (on May 13) he complained to Ernest Collings that the reviewers, even those who were friends of his, 'were so faint', fearful of praising him lest they be called immoral, or stupid, that it was all 'enough to break the heart of a granite boulder'.

Lawrence had better hopes for *Sons and Lovers.* On arriving at Irschenhausen he had told Edward Garnett that he knew he could 'write bigger stuff than any man in England. And I have to write what I can write. And I write for men like David and Harold [Hobson]—they will read me, soon. My stuff is what they want: when they know what they want.' He spoke of *The Sisters,* which had reached the length of one hundred and eighty pages—he expected it to go to three hundred—as 'a queer novel, which seems to have come by itself,' and of *The Insurrection of Miss Houghton,* now at two hundred pages, as 'very lumbering', but 'fearfully exciting. . . . It lies next my heart, for the present.' But *The Sisters,* he felt, was more important, dealing seriously with the relations between men and women, '*the* problem of today'. On April 26 he wrote to McLeod that he had arrived at page 145 and had no notion what the book was about; he hated it, though Frieda said it was good. But to Lawrence it was 'like a novel in a foreign language I don't know very well—I can only just make out what it is about.'

At Irschenhausen, Lawrence was discovering a new dislike for Germany, even for southern Germany. He kept hoping the landscape would roll back and show him Lago di Garda. He couldn't know that Germany was only fifteen months from the iron march into Belgium, but even in prewar Bavaria he could feel the shaking of the earth. On his first visit in 1912 he had sent Edward Garnett a narrative poem set in Wolfratshausen, 'The Young Soldier with Bloody Spurs', in which the soldier's cruelty to his horse is in counterpoint with his cruelty to a servant girl. Back in Bavaria in 1913, Lawrence wrote a story, with an Isartal setting, about a Prussian officer; he called it 'Honour and Arms', his best short story so far, he told Garnett. Perhaps at this time he also wrote 'Vin Ordinaire', another tale of the German army which like 'Honour and Arms' appeared the following year in the *English Review;* 'Vin Ordinaire' later became 'The Thorn in the Flesh'.

Garnett angered Lawrence in 1914 by changing the name of 'Honour and Arms' to 'The Prussian Officer' and using that for the title of Lawrence's first volume of short stories, which Duckworth published under Garnett's guidance: perhaps Lawrence resented having people think that he may have written the story to order; since his correspondence shows it was completed in the spring of 1913, it was prophetic rather than backward-looking or vogue-catching.

And it was prophetic of something more than the brutalities that manifested themselves in the war, which after all were directed against the enemy, even if he was often only a harmless civilian. 'The Prussian Officer' was more concerned with the kind of militarism that the 'Zabern Affair' brought to light in 1913–1914. Zabern, about sixty miles from Frieda's home in Metz, was the scene, in the autumn and early winter, of pronounced military harshness against Alsatians who, though 'pure' Germans might regard them as aliens, had been part of the Empire for more than forty years. In 1913, name-calling, violence, and imprisonment of civilians preceded the act that most of Germany regarded as an outrage: Leutnant von Forstner, earlier disciplined for insulting Alsatian recruits, used his saber to cut down a lame cobbler. A court ultimately freed von Forstner on the ground of 'supposed self-defense'. This decision so angered the members of the Reichstag that they voted by a large majority to censure the government. The von Forstner incident was merely a symptom of much else that was going on in an army dominated by caste and a desire for conquest. Lawrence, visiting Metz with purely romantic intentions and being arrested as a spy, had there and elsewhere in Germany an opportunity to experience Prussianism at close range.

Another element in his Prussian-officer story was the suggestion of homosexuality. In the great German scandal of that time, the guilt or innocence of the Kaiser's favorite, Count Philip zu Eulenberg—who had fallen into disgrace a few years before Lawrence first visited Germany—was debatable; but the scandal had shaken the country, particularly the court and military circles. Lawrence, who had never been herded with other men into a disciplined, all-male community, had nevertheless a fine understanding of what such enforced herding tended to produce in some, a homosexuality that often edged over into sadism. For a young man who may not yet have read Freud, Lawrence had a serviceable insight into such matters. From Gargnano the preceding autumn he had written to Edward Garnett about the latter's play, *Jeanne d'Arc,* which seemed 'a living historical document', one that was 'fearfully' interesting: 'Cruelty is a form of perverted sex. I want to dogmatise. Priests in their celibacy get their sex lustful, then perverted, then insane, hence Inquisitions—all sexual in origin. And soldiers, being herded together, men without women, never being satisfied by a woman, as a man never is from a street affair, get their surplus sex and their frustration and dissatisfaction into the blood, and *love* cruelty. It is sex lust fermented makes atrocity.'

That is the underlying impulse of the Prussian-officer story written seven months later. The Germany of the spring of 1913 provided the scenery and costumes, but the idea had been working in Lawrence's consciousness for some time. Frieda's father, in his own time in the army, like most of his fellow officers, was (as we have seen) a beater of orderlies, though not obsessively so. One of the stories of her youth which Frieda later recalled telling Lawrence was that of a young corporal who had revealed to her how he hated the bullying and injustice of military life; after that, the parades and bands had less glamour for her. Lawrence of course saw no glamour in the military, and both of his German-army stories reflect, sympathetically, the view of the conscript trapped in the lower ranks. Indeed, both tales follow the same pattern, a soldier getting into trouble for attacking his superior, though 'The Prussian Officer' is more serious and intense, and a profounder story.

In his first version of 'The Thorn in the Flesh'—as 'Vin Ordinaire' —in the *English Review* for June 1914, Lawrence didn't identify the setting, but in the version that appeared in December, in the book, he mentions Metz in the first paragraph. The story describes Frieda's home, and her father appears as one of the characters, the baron whose right hand had been shattered when he was a young man, in the Franco-Prussian War. The story as it came out in the magazine had considerably milder love scenes than the later version, and the original ending was different, with the baron as a harsher man than in the later version. Lawrence may have changed this ending, made the baron more 'human', at Frieda's importunity, but perhaps he remembered that, after all, the baron had rescued him in Metz: without his help Lawrence might have been imprisoned or deported, either contingency of greater convenience to the baron than Lawrence's freedom, under the circumstances of Frieda's elopement. In July 1914, when Lawrence sent Edward Garnett his short stories for book publication, he held out 'Vin Ordinaire', which he said needed to be written over, 'to pull it together'. Possibly, then, he merely felt it strengthened the story, as a story, to make the baron kinder.

In any event, Lawrence, as we have seen, was in a state of disliking Germany, even pleasant Bavaria, at the time he apparently wrote both his antimilitary tales. Frieda was straining to return to England, and Lawrence agreed to go with her, though he now wanted most of all to return to Italy. He even considered settling on the Isle of Man, where his one-time friend, the former Agnes Holt, was helping her husband conduct a small school. He wrote to McLeod on June 11, 'How rotten the English [the *English Review*] is. What do you think of *Sons and Lovers?* I am anxious to know. Have you seen any more reviews? The libraries refused it at first—then consented. I am leaving here in a week's time—probably for England. But don't say anything. . . .'

When he did get back, he and Frieda went to the Cearne, where they stayed with Mrs. Garnett and David. On June 21 Lawrence wrote to Edward Garnett's office in London to say he was pleased with the fifty pounds he had received that morning from Duckworth's, and with the reviews of *Sons and Lovers,* which Garnett had collected for him. These notices made his return to England timely and auspicious. Most of them were kind to the book, though it was probably beyond the imaginations of the critics to foresee that *Sons and Lovers* would be one of the few novels of its period discussed seriously in the far future, and then with the prospect of its reputation's being far greater in that future. The London *Saturday Review* did admit at the time, however, that, 'after reading most of the more "important" novels of the present year, we can say that we have seen none to excel it in interest and power,' adding that 'the sum of its defects is astonishingly large, but we only note it when they are weighed against the sum of its own qualities.'

The reviewer in the *Saturday Westminster Gazette* deplored 'the change of view (we will not call it a mistake) which has led Mr Lawrence, in common with other novelists of great repute or promise, to place more emphasis on feeling than on action'; this 'resulted in a draining of interest from the whole of his work.' The book was, however, 'charged with the beauty of atmosphere and observation, of which Mr Lawrence is so complete a master'. The *Academy* found the novel 'a very fine study of the cruelty of life, and very depressing'. The *Athenaeum* reviewer sniffed out an autobiographical element he believed weakened the book, and felt that the girl would not have been 'so abnormal a person as represented' if her story had been truly told; 'but, although we may rebel, we are held captive from the first page to the last, and certain figures will, we think, remain engraved upon the memory.' In the American reviews, Alfred Kuttner in the *New Republic* said of *Sons and Lovers* that it contained some parallels to Freud and that 'with all its power and its passion, it remains to a certain extent incomprehensible. We may, for the moment, accept it intuitively.' In the *New York Times Book Review,* the novelist Louise Maunsell Field found *Sons and Lovers* 'a novel of rare excellence.'

*

At this time Lawrence didn't expect to see many people in England; he felt that he was cut off from his past life. But he and Frieda gathered new friends, including their intimate companions of the future, John Middleton Murry and Katherine Mansfield, who had coedited *Rhythm,* a magazine to which Lawrence had contributed, and were now editing the *Blue Review,* which was about to expire.

Murry was a poor boy from the South London suburbs who had gone to Oxford on a scholarship. (Lawrence: 'I think Oxford did you harm.') He moved into London journalism and eventually made a fair living as a reviewer. In December 1911 he met Katherine Mansfield, at that time little known as a writer. When she and Murry fell in love, they couldn't marry because her curiously brief marriage to the musician George Bowden had not been dissolved: it was not until 1918 that Murry was able to marry her. Meanwhile they lived together and apart, edited little magazines, quarreled, and wrote. Murry at the time he met Lawrence and Frieda in July 1913 was almost twenty-four, handsome, wide-mouthed, with large gray eyes; he then wore his hair in a long bang coming down above his right eye. His former friend Henri Gaudier-Brzeska, who after quarreling with Murry smashed the head he had sculpted of him by throwing stones at it, described Murry at the time as 'strong in body, with refined features and magnificent head like a great god, an Apollo or Mars'. Gaudier-Brzeska, who came to hate Katherine Mansfield, described her as 'a curiously beautiful person, Slav in appearance, and very strong-minded'. She was not tall, had intense dark eyes, and spoke with tight lips; she too wore bangs, and she had bobbed hair years before it became the fashion.

In that summer of 1913, before Lawrence and Frieda went to Kingsgate, on the Kentish coast, where they spent most of July, they called on the Murrys (as they were everywhere known) in London. When Lawrence knew the Murrys only by correspondence, he had spoken of their magazine as 'a daft paper, but the folk seem rather nice'. When he and Frieda first went to see them, the Murrys had a three-room flat at 57 Chancery Lane, which also served as the office of the magazine. Lawrence's first view of Katherine Mansfield was of a young woman sitting beside a bowl of goldfish on the floor of a bare room. When Lawrence told this to Catherine Carswell, Frieda added that Katherine was very pretty, 'such lovely legs', and Lawrence snapped, 'If you *like* the legs of the principal boy in the pantomime' (who was then always a girl).

Murry remembered from their first day together that 'Lawrence was slim and even boyish,' wearing a large straw hat which became him, while 'Frieda's lovely fair hair glowed under her panama.' They all went to lunch in Soho, and Frieda loved the Murrys at once when, in the bright sunlight on the upper deck of the bus, she caught them making faces and sticking their tongues out at one another.

Frieda thought 'theirs was the only spontaneous and jolly friendship that we had,' although those aspects of the friendship were not to last. To Frieda, Katherine Mansfield was a younger sister, and Katherine immediately became the messenger to Frieda's son and daughters, going out to Hampstead to bring them greetings and letters from their mother. Frieda had one morning waited for the children on their way to school and they had danced around her joyfully: 'Mama, you are back, when are you coming home?' But the next time she met them, she discovered that they had been told not to speak to her, 'and only little white faces looked at me as if I were an evil ghost.' Meanwhile, Frieda's attempts to obtain a divorce made no progress.

At Kingsgate, Lawrence and Frieda met other new friends as a
letter of July 22 to McLeod shows:

We are quite swells. Edward Marsh came on Sunday (he is the
Georgian Poetry man and Secretary in the Admiralty to Winston
Churchill) and he took us in to tea with the Herbert Asquiths—
jolly nice folk—son of the Prime Minister. Today I am to meet
there Sir Walter Raleigh. But alas it is not he of the cloak.

I have been grubbing away among the short stories. God, I
shall be glad when it is done. I shall begin my novel again in
Germany.

We bathe and I write among the babies of the foreshore: it
is an innocent life and a dull one.

Poor Philip [Smith]. He'll soon be like Alexander, with no
more worlds to conquer. But I wouldn't like touring Europe
with no German and Italian, and yet watching the pence filter
out.

Frieda sends warm greetings—*une bonne poignée.*

Edward Marsh, who had written to Lawrence at Gargnano to ask
for the use of the poem 'Snap-Dragon' in *Georgian Poetry: 1911–
1912,* sent him his check in care of Edward Garnett, who he knew
was a friend of Lawrence's. It was forwarded to Kingsgate, and when
Lawrence delightedly wrote to thank Marsh for the three pounds, he
expressed the hope that if Marsh ever came down to the Kentish coast,
he would visit Frieda and himself. Marsh had already planned to see
the Asquiths there on Sunday, July 20, and arranged to bring Lawrence and Frieda with him. In a letter written that night to Rupert
Brooke, he reported that both of them 'were a tremendous success'
at the Asquiths': 'He looks terribly ill, which I am afraid he is—his
wife is a very jolly buxom healthy-looking German, they seem very
happy together.' Frieda hurt Marsh's feelings by saying he didn't
look like the type of man who would care for poetry. Lawrence subsequently apologized to Marsh for gaining 'a false entry' by introducing his mistress as his wife.

Soon afterwards, when Lawrence wrote to Cynthia Asquith from
Bavaria, he was uncertain whether to address her as Mrs. or Lady.
As she once explained in an interview, she was Mrs. Asquith until
the following year, when her grandfather, Earl of Wemyss and March,
died, leaving the earldom to Cynthia Asquith's father. She then at
once became Lady Cynthia (*not* Lady Asquith).

The younger Asquiths had taken a small house at Broadstairs, and Lawrence and Frieda went there for dinner several times and walked with them on the sand at the foot of the chalk cliffs, sometimes singing 'What Are the Wild Waves Saying?' The Hon. Herbert Asquith recalled Lawrence as 'a poet living on a plane far removed from the dust of politics, but more deeply in revolt against the values of the day than any political leader.' We have another portrait of Lawrence at the time, from a memoir by Henry Savage, the friend and biographer of Richard Middleton. Savage had reviewed *The White Peacock* for the *Academy,* and the letter of thanks he received from Lawrence began a friendship that lasted for several years. In 1930 Savage recalled the Lawrence of nearly twenty years before:

He was young then, but a sick man; the seeds of phthisis which he fought so long were already in him. At Kent, where I was once staying with him—he had just achieved a romantic elopement with the married lady he was afterwards himself to marry —I received a curious impression. We were lying sprawled on the cliffs. *À propos de bottes,* he suddenly struck his chest violently. 'I've something here, Savage,' he said, 'that is heavier than concrete. If I don't get it out it will kill me.' He may have been referring to his physical condition, but I am inclined to think that he meant the dark, strange forces afterwards to find expression in his various novels.

The Murrys were among other visitors to Kingsgate. The first time Lawrence invited them, they failed to appear; Marsh astonished Lawrence by suggesting that perhaps they lacked the money. He had believed that Murry and Katherine Mansfield were well off, and could far more easily earn money by writing than he could. He wrote Murry a scolding note on July 22, saying he would have lent him a pound; he invited the Murrys again for the following weekend, and they came down, bringing their friend Charles Henry Gordon Campbell, an Irishman then practicing as a barrister in London. They all had an exuberant time, with swimming and conversation. Murry said later that Katherine Mansfield could swim superbly and that he could swim well—'the only thing I could ever do better than Lawrence'—and that they ate steak and tomatoes heartily: 'For some reason those tomatoes gleam very red in my memory.'

Lawrence and Frieda, who planned to spend another winter in Italy, invited the Murrys to join them there. Murry said yes—if they could. When they were leaving Kingsgate, Lawrence handed them a copy of *Sons and Lovers* to read on the train, and the opening pages of the novel gave Murry an 'impression of warm rich darkness'.

Lawrence was glad enough, at the end of July, when it was his turn to leave Kingsgate, 'that half-crystallized nowhere of a place'. Creatively the weeks he had spent there seem to have been lost weeks; but after the rapid production of the previous year he needed to let his writing rest for a while. And although *Sons and Lovers* didn't have a big enough sale to give him a financial guarantee for the future—indeed, Duckworth's lost money on the first edition—the book established him as a serious and important author. The coal miner's son could meet the prime minister's son and daughter-in-law, and at their house charm Professor Raleigh of Oxford.

That summer, the two most important people, from a personal point of view, that Lawrence came to know were John Middleton Murry and Cynthia Asquith. Murry, who was to become the villain in Lawrence's life—as in a way Lawrence was to become the villain in Murry's—was for years the possible ideal friend Lawrence quested after. And Lady Cynthia (later, as we shall see, to be suspected by her friends and family of having a love affair with Lawrence) became an ideally worshipped dream woman. Lawrence, though he always loved Frieda, indicated again and again in his work a special kind of love for Cynthia Asquith. He most probably didn't mention this to her, and he remained a good friend to both her and her husband, but in his writing and perhaps even in his painting he seems to have made love to her indirectly.

*

PART THREE

The War Years

---

*

1 ITALIAN PRELUDE

WITH THE COMPLETION OF *Sons and Lovers,* Lawrence had entered into a new period of his writing. The *Look!* poems had presaged this almost from the first, but it took some time for the process to become active in his prose, for what he wrote at Gargnano after *Sons and Lovers* was of the same pattern as his earlier work. Even *The Sisters* in its first phases was apparently 'just another novel'.

Revisiting his native land after the publication of *Sons and Lovers* and its generally favorable reception, Lawrence found that he was becoming 'a somebody'. And Frieda's continued presence kept his confidence going. He had wrenched a woman away from her husband and security, in spite of her vigorous love of her growing children; and he had succeeded in keeping this woman. Even her Lot's-wife return to see the children didn't cause her to leave him, and as they faced southward again, they knew that they would travel together for the rest of their lives.

The book that was to become *The Rainbow* burned in Lawrence now. This was not an easy novel to write, and he had to struggle with it for a long time. He carried on this struggle in Germany, in Italy, and, finally, in England. It was a great day when at last he could draw a picture of the mystic rainbow archway over the farmfields and the mines, and could write below it, 'I have finished my Rainbow!'

But that day was nearly two years ahead. Meanwhile Lawrence and Frieda had still another long time to spend on the Continent. It began on the August day of 1913 when they arrived at Irschenhausen, again to stay at the Jaffes'. 'For the time being, at least,' Lawrence noted, Frieda was 'getting better of her trouble with the children.' He told his new correspondent, Henry Savage, 'I have a good old English habit of shutting my rages of trouble well inside my belly, so that they play havoc with my innards. . . . I am just learning, thanks to Frieda, to let go a bit.' Some later observers might think that he learned too well.

It was a restless summer for Lawrence; work on *The Sisters* went slowly during the Bavarian interlude. When the time came for him and Frieda to leave, after five and a half weeks at Irschenhausen, they went by different routes. Frieda wanted to visit her parents again in Germany; Lawrence preferred to walk through Switzerland. At first they planned to meet at Basel after a week and go south together, over the old imperial road into Italy. But they gave up this idea, and Lawrence made the trip alone, by way of the Saint Gotthard Pass. Frieda had had enough of scrambling over mountains: her imperial road would be the railway.

Lawrence spent nearly two weeks on his tour across Switzerland, a country he found to be 'too touristy' and 'banal' and 'spoilt'. He felt like an insect as he went up the snow-gleaming mountains, where the villages hung perilously 'in the flux of death'. In one valley the smoke rising from factory chimneys reminded him unpleasantly of the pollution near his home: 'It is the hideous rawness of the world of men, the horrible, desolating harshness of the advance of the industrial world upon the world of nature, that is so painful.' The peasants bringing their fruit into the towns seemed to escape the hideousness, but it would soon overwhelm them too.

Lawrence couldn't force himself to feel happy in Switzerland, and even after he crossed over into Italy he still saw 'the process of disintegration' at work. At least it had a certain vigor there, he felt, as he waited in Milan for Frieda. Sitting in the Cathedral Square and drinking a Campari, he noted that even the city men he saw about him knew a life that was 'still vivid', though it too existed under the threat of 'perfect mechanisation'. It was on this note, describing this scene and incorporating his observations, that he ended *Twilight in Italy,* published in 1916 with all those changes in chapters which had earlier appeared in magazines.

*

The small house at Fiascherino, near Lerici, which Lawrence and Frieda rented, proved to be fairly unspoiled and primitive. Their *villino* at the fishing village was a square pink building divided in two by a stone staircase with a sitting room on one side and a bedroom above it, the kitchen on the other side, and a bedroom over it also. The house (the Villa Gambrosier), set on a cliff above the sea, backed into a mountain of olive woods and lemon groves. Lawrence rented it for sixty lire a month, with twenty-five more for servants' fees. He and Frieda remained there for eight months.

Work on *The Sisters* still went haltingly. Soon after arriving at Fiascherino, Lawrence had said (October 5) that the star of *Sons and*

Lovers 'is already sinking in my sky, now I am well on into another very different novel'; but by October 27 he could add, 'I have been so much upset, what with moving and Frieda's troubling about the children . . . and what not, that I haven't been able to work.' He went on to say that it was 'no joke to have done as Frieda and I have done —and my soul feels very tired.' On December 2, work was still going too slowly: 'But here, it is too beautiful, one càn't work.' On December 21 Lawrence told Edward Garnett, 'The novel goes slowly forward. . . . In a few days' time I shall send you the first half of the MS.'

And although he completed one draft of *The Sisters*—what he thought would be the final version—by the middle of May 1914, that sojourn at Fiascherino was a fairly unproductive period for Lawrence, especially in contrast with the equivalent stay at Gargnano. At Fiascherino, Lawrence apparently didn't add a single poem to the *Look! We Have Come Through!* sequence, and he evidently didn't write short stories or articles during that time. He did, however, keep fussing over the play *The Widowing of Mrs Holroyd,* which was to be published in New York by Mitchell Kennerley, who had brought out the American edition of *Sons and Lovers.* On the advice of Edward Garnett, Duckworth planned to publish the play in London, using sheets imported from America.

The Widowing of Mrs Holroyd is an expansion of the short story 'Odour of Chrysanthemums', and in both play and story the central character is based on Lawrence's Aunt Emma of New Brinsley. Soon after he had arrived in Bavaria, Lawrence told Kennerley that the manuscript had been in Edward Garnett's possession for nearly two years and that it needed 'refining'. Now he wrote from Italy: 'It pleases me very much to think the play will be published one day. . . . I do hope also that you may find my writing a good speculation. But I think you will. My thanks for advertising *Sons and Lovers* so widely. I do like the reviews. But—*bisogna dar tempo al tempo.*'

Lawrence wrote enthusiastically to Garnett about Kennerley, who was, like Lawrence, from the English Midlands, and in many ways would seem to have been an ideal publisher for him, as in later years he was an effective promoter of Alfred Stieglitz. But Kennerley, who was only the beginning of Lawrence's publishing troubles in America, in the spring of 1914 sent a check for thirty-five pounds that had an altered date; the bank in Spezia wouldn't cash it for Frieda, to whom Lawrence had given it as her 'first pin-money'; the bank returned the check to Kennerley, who 'never made it good', Lawrence wrote ten years later, 'and never to this day made any further payment for *Sons and Lovers*. Till this year of grace 1924, America has had that, my most popular book, for nothing—as far as I am concerned.'

Kennerley meantime was living in first-class hotels, always keeping a bit ahead of the game until his melancholy suicide in 1950. The references to him in Edna St. Vincent Millay's published letters indicate that his relationship with Lawrence was typical of that with his other writers, though Van Wyck Brooks defended him: 'He made little or nothing out of his exasperated authors, and who else would have printed them, who else would have looked at their first little books, which Kennerley delightedly acclaimed and so charmingly published? . . . He should be remembered as the friend of a whole generation of writers whom, in surprising numbers, he first brought out.' These are kind thoughts, but the lovers at Fiascherino would doubtless have preferred some genuine money.

Financially, the second Italian sojourn was one of continual anxiety for Lawrence. On his arrival he asked Edward Garnett to send ten pounds 'from what I have left', and he again requested funds from time to time while at Fiascherino. That *Sons and Lovers* had lost money in its first printing distressed him: 'If a publisher is to lose by me, I would rather it were a rich commercial man like Heinemann.' He was not sure he wanted to continue with a small firm such as Duckworth's, for two leading agents, J. B. Pinker and Curtis Brown, had written with good offers for his novels from publishers who could 'believe in them commercially', which Lawrence thought Garnett couldn't: 'I must have money for my novels, to live.' Lawrence thanked Pinker: '*Sons and Lovers* does not seem to have done wonders, but I believe Duckworth and Mitchell Kennerley advertised it pretty well. As for giving you a novel—I can't in decency, in the near future. Later on I will if I can. . . . I only write one novel a year.'

Money worries were not Lawrence's sole distraction at Fiascherino. He and Frieda became socially active in a way that had been impossible in the comparative isolation of Gargnano. *Love Poems* and *Sons and Lovers,* however poorly they may have done financially, had at least made Lawrence a well-known author, and now various writers went out of their way to see him on their journeys through Italy. The Anglo colony on the Gulf of Spezia adopted Lawrence and Frieda for a while, 'so that we are always out to tea, or

having visitors.' The English consul at Spezia, Thomas Dacre Dunlop (later Sir Thomas), became their good friend, and the English
chaplain took a fancy to 'Mr and Mrs Lawrence' too ('When all our
dark history comes out', Lawrence told Garnett, 'I shall laugh').
When he and Frieda went over to Lerici they traveled by land, because Lawrence refused to ride in the rowboat with Frieda after she
nearly upset it during a quarrel they once had on the way home.
Lawrence remembered that Shelley had drowned in that sea.

Among the English residents in the Lerici area, the two whom
Lawrence and Frieda came to know best were Aubrey Waterfield and
his wife Lina. He was a painter, and she was to become Italian correspondent for the *Observer* from 1921 until World War II, and then
for an association of newspapers. The Waterfields lived at Aulla,
among the Apennines, in a castle-fortress about sixteen miles inland from Spezia. Lawrence first met Aubrey Waterfield when the
latter went to Fiascherino with some of the Georgian poets, Lascelles
Abercrombie, Wilfrid Wilson Gibson, and Robert Calverley Trevelyan. They found Lawrence and Frieda at a peasants' wedding. Lawrence liked the visitors, but told McLeod that 'it was so queer, to
leave the feast and descend into the thin atmosphere of a little
group of cultured Englishmen.'

Lawrence and Frieda went two or three times to Aulla, which he
described in contrary ways, quite typically liking and not liking it, in
letters written on the same day.

One of the visitors to Fiascherino was Ivy Low, the young novelist
who later became the wife of Ambassador Maxim Litvinov. Ivy Low
had written to Lawrence after reading with indignation what Henry
James had said of him in the course of his 1914 articles on 'The
Younger Generation' in the *Times Literary Supplement:* James had
praised such authors as Gilbert Cannan, Arnold Bennett, Hugh
Walpole, and Compton Mackenzie while slighting Lawrence. James
spoke of Bennett's having 'launched the boat' of a 'new' movement,
and commended Walpole's 'fresh play of oar'; James went on,
elaborately mixing the metaphor, to say that Lawrence 'hung in the
dusty rear'. Edith Wharton recalled that, at the time, when a friend
insistently asked James if he had ever really read Lawrence's novels,
he at last mischievously said, 'I—I have trifled with the exordia.'

Ivy Low's objections to James's articles typified the enthusiastic
response of many of the younger generation to Lawrence's work. In
that same year of 1914, for example, a future friend of Lawrence's,

Philip Heseltine, wrote to his music master, Frederick Delius, that he had just read Lawrence's three novels and found them 'simply unrivalled, in depth of insight and beauty of language, by any other contemporary writer'; and in the *New Republic* of February 27, 1915, a twenty-two-year-old writer who was to defend Lawrence several times again—Rebecca West—criticized James for granting merely 'a scornful parenthesis' to 'the only author of this young generation who has not only written but also created, and created with such power that he would be honourable in any generation.'

The somewhat contrary opinion John Galsworthy delivered to Edward Garnett in a letter of April 13, 1914, has become well known: Galsworthy liked the family scenes in *Sons and Lovers* but not what he called 'the love part. . . . It's not good enough to spend time and ink describing the penultimate sensations and physical movements of people getting into a state of rut; we all know them too well.' The book had 'genius', but not in *those* scenes. This is the kind of response Lawrence could count on, all his life, from those who spoke officially or semiofficially for 'literature'.

Ivy Low shared her enthusiasm for Lawrence with Viola Meynell, and these two young writers confronted their friends with an ultimatum: the author of *Sons and Lovers* was a genius, and those who did not believe this 'walked in darkness' and could not be their friends. Ivy Low wrote a letter to Lawrence which brought an invitation to Fiascherino; she invested her available money in a return ticket and borrowed clothes from Mrs. Catherine Jackson, who was later to meet Lawrence and Frieda.

Ivy Low's visit was, to her, bewildering and disintegrating, for Lawrence began at once to hunt out all her defects, finding them 'one by one, and quite a few that no one else ever discovered.' She left, as she remembered, after 'about six weeks', to Frieda's quite obvious relief. Ivy Low was in a trance as she returned to London; Lawrence had shaken the self-confidence of this young woman who had already published two novels, and she felt that she could never write again and that this would somehow be good.

Two expected guests who didn't appear at Fiascherino were Middleton Murry and Katherine Mansfield. Lawrence had written suggesting that since Katherine had an allowance of a hundred pounds a year, she and Murry should live on it in Italy. When Murry refused to consider this idea, Lawrence told him this showed that he didn't trust her love for him; that he must realize that he insulted Katherine by working in order to give her petty luxuries she really didn't want: 'A woman unsatisfied must have luxuries. But a woman who loves a man would sleep on a board.' Lawrence later wrote that he hoped Murry and Katherine wouldn't look upon him 'as an interfering Sunday-school superintendent sort of person'. He felt they would all make money one day, and they would 'all be jolly together'. He was 'fed up with miseries and sufferings.'

Lawrence was still—and it was another distraction from his work —having trouble with Frieda over their situation and over the children, though this broke out into his letters only occasionally, as when he told Cynthia Asquith, in November 1913, that he was feeling too disagreeable to write short stories and novels. And he said in a letter of April 3 to Murry, 'But now, thank God, Frieda and I are together'; he reported that *The Sisters* was two-thirds completed, 'and the work is of me and of her, and it is beautiful, I think.' On June 2 he told McLeod, 'I think *the* one thing to do, is for men to have the courage to draw nearer to women, expose themselves to them . . . Because the source of all life and knowledge is in man and woman, and the source of all living is in the interchange and the meeting and mingling of these two. . . .'

Perhaps, in this harassed year, Lawrence was putting more of his energy into establishing his relationship with Frieda on a permanent basis than into his work. Yet he did a great deal of theorizing at that time which may have helped his growth as an artist. He argued at length with his two mentors—Marsh, who guided him in poetry, and Garnett, who guided him in prose. Lawrence was casting off guides.

It was a friendly enough process. Marsh even came for a visit to Fiascherino in January while on a tour with his friend James Strachey Barnes, who more than twenty years later became an ardent supporter of Mussolini's fascism, to the extent of embarrassing many Italian fascists who cringed at Barnes's stentorian fervor.

The 1914 visit of Barnes and Marsh occurred after Lawrence had accused the latter of being 'a bit of a policeman in poetry'. But Marsh remained his friend in those 'earlier days' when Lawrence 'had a rich fund of gaiety and sweetness.' Marsh wrote modestly, more than a quarter of a century later, that he had tried Lawrence severely 'by carping, with what I see in retrospect to have been overweening presumption, at his use of rhyme and metre.'

Lawrence's quarrel with Edward Garnett was more than technical: it was also ideological and moral. Lawrence, after some deference and self-doubts, went his own way as stubbornly as he had with Marsh; and though Garnett's criticisms of *The Sisters* disturbed him, Lawrence wouldn't alter the book along the lines suggested. Ultimately this meant a break with Garnett. Lawrence said he would not write again in the manner of *Sons and Lovers,* 'in that hard, violent style full of sensation and presentation'. The new book was 'in another language almost'; Lawrence would be sorry if Garnett didn't like it, but he was 'prepared'.

In April 1914 Lawrence notified Garnett that he was sending him all the pages typed so far by Dunlop at Spezia; only eighty remained to be written, and Garnett should have those within three weeks. On May 8 Lawrence notified Garnett that he hoped to finish the book within two days. Actually, Dunlop's wife, Madge, seems to have done most of the typing. Asked in 1952 if he could recall some of the differences between that earlier version and *The Rainbow* as later published, the then Sir Thomas Dunlop said in a letter that he and his wife wouldn't have known of any differences, because they had 'obeyed' Lawrence's injunction not to read his books, which he told them were written only to get them 'off his chest'. They 'obeyed' Lawrence despite the fact that he later sent them a copy of *The Rainbow;* such compliance with a whimsical remark of the kind almost every author occasionally makes is perhaps possible only for diplomats.

In his letters to Garnett, Lawrence continually expressed his fears as to his mentor's possible response to the book. He was sure that the novel was important and beautiful. 'Before,' he wrote in April, 'I could not get my soul into it. That was because of the struggle and resistance between Frieda and me. Now you will find her and me in the novel, I think, and the work is both of us. . . . The first *Sisters* was flippant and often vulgar and jeering. I had to get out of that attitude, and make my subject really worthy.'

A few days before Lawrence and Frieda left Fiascherino to go north again, Garnett wrote once more about the new book, which Lawrence now called *The Wedding Ring*. Garnett disliked it. Lawrence answered him straightforwardly, telling him he was wrong. Lawrence admitted that his work was imperfect, for he was not yet expert in what he wanted to do. But Garnett had no right to say that the book was 'shaky'. Garnett expected the novel to develop along the lines of certain characters: Lawrence explained that his characters fell 'into some other rhythmic form, as when one draws a fiddle-bow directly across a fine tray delicately sanded, the sand takes lines unknown.' Garnett was wrong in his criticism of the psychology of the characters because Lawrence had taken 'a different attitude to my characters, and that necessitates a different attitude in you which you are not prepared to give.' There was more to the book, Lawrence assured him, than the cleverness he seemed to find there. The novel was 'quite unconsciously . . . a bit futuristic'.

Lawrence quoted Filippo Tommaso Marinetti to Garnett; in a letter to McLeod a few days before he had shown how thoroughly he had looked into the Futurists: 'I got a book of their poetry—a very fat book too—and a book of pictures—and I read Marinetti's and Paolo Buzzi's manifestations and essays and Scoffici's essays on cubism and futurism.' At Gargnano the preceding year, when Lawrence had found fault with the contemporary writers—Conrad, Bennett, Galsworthy—whose books Garnett had sent him, Lawrence was casting off the traditionalists, as he was still ridding himself of parts of his past; and by the end of his stay at Fiascherino, where he had been creating a nontraditional work of his own, he was ready to assess the Futurists. He thought they were right in trying to destroy the ancient forms and beliefs and sentimentalities, but they went about their destruction too mechanistically.

In the letter to Garnett, Lawrence spoke of his interest in Marinetti's ideal of an 'intuitive physiology of matter': the nonhuman element in humanity had become more interesting to him 'than the old-fashioned human element—which causes one to conceive a character in a certain moral scheme and make him consistent.' In Lawrence's novel, Garnett should not look 'for the old stable ego of the character. There is another ego, according to whose action the individual is unrecognisable, and passes through, as it were, allotropic states which it needs a deeper sense than any we've been used to exercise to discover are states of the same single radically-unchanged element.' It was like diamond and coal, which were 'the same pure single element of carbon. The ordinary novel would trace the history of the diamond—but I say, "Diamond, what! This is carbon." And my diamond might be coal or soot, and my theme is carbon.'

Here, in an important moment, a moment of culmination, Lawrence showed that he knew what he was doing, and why he was doing it. He had reached a plateau of understanding from which he could see his writing in relation to the world about him. It was a world whose thoughts had been shaped, were being shaped, by Darwin,

Marx, Einstein, and Freud, whose influence no one could really evade. Artistically it was a world that would soon belong to Stravinsky, Picasso, and Joyce. As Lawrence didn't take anything important from the Futurists, so he consciously took nothing from these artists—indeed, he cared little for their achievements—but once again, his work, like theirs, demonstrates a modernity of vision. (One aspect of the avant-garde, however, he had for some years been familiar with: primitivism, a matter discussed further on in this section.)

In 1913, as we have seen, Ezra Pound had told Harriet Monroe he thought Lawrence 'learned the proper treatment of modern subjects before I did.' Lawrence wrote his manifesto to Garnett before the publication of Joyce's *A Portrait of the Artist as a Young Man*, Dorothy Richardson's *Pointed Roofs,* and other novels now looked upon as the beginning of modernism in England; and there is no evidence that he then knew of the existence of Marcel Proust's *Du côté de chez Swann,* published in November 1913. The point is that Lawrence, in his different way, was as 'modern' as the authors of these novels.

With the book he was then writing, he was creating a new self and a new future, in literature as he had done in life. It was a cruelly difficult process, as the tracing of it here has shown. But Lawrence was never to have again a time of uncertainty: he might find life bitter and murky, but he would never again hesitate in his writing.

*

On May 28, 1914, an event of explosive importance to Lawrence and Frieda occurred in London. In the Probate, Divorce, and Admiralty Division of the High Court of Justice, Mr. Justice Bargrave Deane granted a decree *nisi* in the divorce case of 'Weekley v. Weekley and Lawrence'.

Lawrence and Frieda moved up by nearly a month their time of departure from Italy. Lawrence walked once more through the still-unloved Switzerland, and Frieda went by train to Baden-Baden, where she saw her father for the last time. The sick old baron was to die the following year; in those weeks before Sarajevo he kept muttering that he no longer understood the world.

Lawrence, walking north, was accompanied this time by an engineer named Lewis, of the Vickers-Maxim works at Spezia. They went through the Great St. Bernard Pass, then swung towards Interlaken and from there turned west to go into France. The exact date of their arrival in England isn't known, though Lawrence and Frieda were both there by June 27, as indicated by Edward Marsh's journal entry for that day: 'Saturday June 27th. Lunched at the Moulin d'Or with D. H. and Mrs Lawrence and Rupert [Brooke], all to Allied Artists at Holland Park.'

Lawrence and Frieda stayed at 9 Selwood Terrace, Kensington, with Gordon Campbell, whose wife Beatrice was in Ireland that summer with their year-old son. Campbell, the Irish barrister whom Murry had brought to Kingsgate to meet Lawrence and Frieda the preceding summer, was interested in literature and was trying his hand at a novel. A month younger than Lawrence, he had served for five years as an officer in the Royal Engineers. He amused Frieda with his constant grieving over 'Areland', to which he later returned, as Lord Glenavy, to help organize important departments of the Irish Free State.

While staying at the Campbells', Lawrence met one of his own future biographers, Catherine Carswell, at that time Mrs. Jackson. Soon after he returned to London, she gave a tea for him, attended by their friend-in-common Ivy Low and by Viola Meynell. Mrs. Jackson at once discerned in Lawrence 'a swift and flame-like quality. . . . I was sensible of a fine, rare beauty in Lawrence, with his deep-set jewel-like eyes, thick dust-coloured hair, pointed underlip of notable sweetness, fine hands, and rapid but never restless movements.' Frieda seemed 'a typical German *Frau* of the blonde, gushing type. She wore a tight coat and skirt of horse-cloth check that positively obscured her finely cut, rather angry Prussian features.' Mrs. Jackson became aware of Frieda's handsomeness later, when she saw her in overalls and in peasant costume, 'maching about a cottage'.

Mrs. Jackson, who had for some years been divorced, talked to Lawrence from the first as if she had always known him. Her abrupt plunge into friendliness was evidently not of the kind that could so easily arouse Frieda's jealousy; and although Mrs. Jackson became one of the most worshipful of the women who knew Lawrence, there was always an impersonality in her relations with him; unlike the others, she made no emotional demands upon him. Soon Lawrence was reading and criticizing Mrs. Jackson's first novel, not published until 1920—an autobiographical story of her youth in Glasgow.

The Murrys were offended because Lawrence hadn't come to see them first. In that summer of 1914 the Murrys were particularly sensitive and unhappy. They were poor and living in rooms they hated; Katherine Mansfield was unable to write; Murry was struggling to make a living as an art critic; and they had both been ill with pleurisy. Lawrence and Frieda, when they did come to supper at the Murrys' flat, seemed fairly prosperous; Lawrence had taken J. B. Pinker as his agent and expected to receive an advance of £300 from his new publisher, Methuen, and Frieda was looking forward to an assault on the dress shops. Her eagerness distressed Katherine; and she and Murry were jealous of most of the other friends Lawrence was making, in the Murrys' view, too easily—'a not unnatural jealousy,' Murry wrote, 'considering how deep an inroad Lawrence made upon one's intimacy.'

At this time the Freudians had discovered *Sons and Lovers,* and one of the pioneer psychoanalysts in England, Dr. David Eder, frequently called on Lawrence to talk with him. Murry would be lost in bewilderment because people could discuss sex so seriously. Lawrence and Frieda became good friends of the Eders—Edith Eder was the sister of Ivy Low's father—and of Mrs. Eder's sister, Barbara Low, who became a well-known psychoanalyst. As she told the author of this book, 'There is no doubt that Dr. Eder's views and knowledge made a great impression on Lawrence, though he feared to be influenced by Freudian Science—as you might expect!'

Once these new friends of Lawrence's invited the Murrys to a picnic on Hampstead Heath. As Lawrence and Frieda and Gordon Campbell and the Murrys emerged from the Hampstead tube station, a loud shriek of 'Lawrence!' startled them, and they saw and heard a young woman running downhill dressed in what looked like a kimono, her arms outspread as she screamed her enthusiasm. Campbell muttered, 'Good God!' and Katherine Mansfield said, 'I won't have *that!*' When Ivy Low reached Lawrence, he turned to introduce his friends, but they had disappeared. Next time he saw them, Katherine explained that, because of her dislike of effusiveness, she would only have sulked if she hadn't run away.

The Murrys were present when Lawrence married Frieda. The ceremony took place at the Kensington Register Office on July 13, with the Murrys and Campbell as witnesses; Marsh was unable to get away from his diplomatic entanglements. Lawrence at once sent Mrs. Hopkin news of the wedding: 'I thought it was a very decent and dignified performance. I don't feel a changed man, but I suppose I am one.' He and Frieda planned to go to Ada's home in Derbyshire, at the end of the week, he said, but he doubted that they would visit Eastwood. He said they would travel to the west of Ireland in August.

On the day after his marriage, Lawrence wrote Garnett a business letter discussing the volume of short stories Duckworth's planned to publish; for this book, the one Garnett finally titled *The Prussian Officer,* Lawrence suggested the name *Goose Fair.* At the end of the letter he tossed in a personal note: he and Frieda were now 'irrefutably' married, and he wondered whether Garnett thought this was dull and respectable. Then Lawrence added: 'The trouble about the children is very acute just now.' Frieda managed to see them at a lawyer's office: it was, as her daughter Barbara recalled it, a nervous half hour, with Frieda smiling through her tears and the children tense.

Lawrence in his letters to Marsh at this time was discussing his short stories and a book he contemplated writing about Thomas Hardy. He seems to have composed but little poetry in the year since he left Gargnano. In the *Look! We Have Come Through!* volume, only three poems—'Wedlock', 'History', and 'Song of a Man Who Has Come Through'—stand between one labeled 'San Gaudenzio' (which Lawrence last saw in April 1913) and one signed 'Kensington' (Lawrence lived there from late June to late August 1914). After a poem written at Kensington, 'One Woman to All Women', only nine more were to occur in the entire sequence; these nine were spread out over a period of at least two years, for the last was composed at Zennor, in Cornwall, where the Lawrences lived from February 1916 to October 1917.

All these later *Look!* poems are songs of fulfillment. But they don't evade the problems of conflict: they admit the existence of these problems and confront and find a solution for them in 'equilibrium'— as noted earlier. Lawrence was later to adopt the word *polarity* instead. And it was this 'balanced conjunction'—such as that sought by Birkin in *Women in Love*—which was to remain Lawrence's ideal, in the relationship of man and woman and of spirit and flesh.

Even though Lawrence was not writing much verse at this time, he was still thought of as a poet. His verses had awakened the interest of the American poet Amy Lowell, who was a member of the famous New England family, a collateral descendant of James Russell Lowell, the poet who had been minister to England in Queen Victoria's time. After Amy Lowell had arrived in London in the early summer of 1914, she invited Lawrence to dinner at the Berkeley Hotel. Her companion, Ada Russell, and Richard Aldington and his wife, the American poet H.D., were also there. Aldington recalled some dozen years later that this dinner party on the eve of war was 'inane', though he found Lawrence's 'fiery blue eyes and the pleasing malice of his talk' impressive.

Lawrence had come into Amy Lowell's suite 'with a lithe, springing step', and brought news of the war crisis. As they all sat there at the gleaming table, dusk coming down outside—the lamps had not quite yet gone out all over Europe, and Piccadilly blazed into light—Miss Lowell and her dinner guests talked only of the war that was raging in poetry. The British artists and intellectuals of the time hadn't thought much about the possibilities of a conflict between nations; that was the summer a generation of schoolboys went into military service expecting to be at their chosen universities for the autumn term.

Meanwhile, in the poetic war, Amy Lowell was taking over the *Imagiste* movement (as it was then called) which Ezra Pound had created two years before out of a few theories, and fewer poems, by T. E. Hulme. The dinner parties at the Berkeley were a strategic attempt to strengthen Amy Lowell's position. Pound, behaving like a hedgehog trying to discourage a bear, was resisting this massive, hearty, and wealthy Bostonian who had so recently broken away from traditional poetry. Pound remarked at the time that Imagism should be called Amygism.

Now she wanted to enlist Lawrence, by Pound's standards one of the foremost of the young moderns, on her side. When she asked Lawrence to become a member of her group, he replied that he was not an Imagist. For answer, she quoted the opening lines of his poem 'Wedding Morn': 'The morning breaks like a pomegranate / In a shining crack of red. . . .'

Lawrence genially submitted, and agreed to appear in the Imagists' publications, though he never gave public adherence to their credo. He also kept publishing in the volumes of Marsh's *Georgian Poetry,* though he had little in common, either, with members of that rival group; his landscapes, the most passionate post-Romantic absorption of 'nature', contrasted violently with the polite scenery of the Georgians, whose verse only occasionally had a ragged patch of nature, glimpsed beyond the tennis court.

Imagist or Georgian or not, Lawrence evidently enjoyed the talk that went back and forth across the table in Amy Lowell's suite on that warm evening of July 30, 1914. The next day he wrote to Harriet Monroe that he had dined with Amy Lowell and the Aldingtons, 'and we had some poetry'.

It had been, at least, a good way to see the old world out.

2 LET SLIP THE DOGS OF WAR

On July 31 Lawrence left for a walking tour of the Lake Country. He went with a man named Horne who worked for the Russian Law Bureau; Horne brought another friend and at the last minute induced one of his colleagues at the Russian law offices to go along too— S. S. Koteliansky, who had come to England a few years before. According to one account, he had a scholarship from the University of Kiev, for research in economics; another version of his story says that his mother paid his way to England. As a student radical, he had apparently been under suspicion by the tsarist secret police, and he stayed on in England. Swarthy, with *en brosse* hair and a fierce black glance, Samuel Solomonovich Koteliansky was a man whom Lawrence found 'a bit Jehovah-ish'. He at once liked Lawrence, whom he considered ingenuous. But Koteliansky never learned to care very much for Frieda.

The walking party—which also included a Russian lawyer, R. S. Slatowsky, and Lawrence's friend Lewis, the Vickers engineer—began as a happy one, despite the overhanging war. It was at Lewis's home in Barrow-in-Furness on August 5, amid the steelworks and the battleship factories, that the hiking party learned that England had just entered the war. Barrow-in-Furness was boiling with martial spirit, and Lawrence remembered that 'we all went mad'. But a little later he walked down the coast a few miles, and thought with horror of what had happened. Six months later he said that he was only beginning then to come out of the stupor, the living death, that had settled upon him in that first week of August.

On his return to London, Lawrence realized that he and Frieda could no longer blithely consider going back to Italy in October; now even the prospect of a trip to Ireland had become remote. He soon found a cottage called the Triangle, in Bellingdon Lane, near Chesham, Buckinghamshire, for which he paid only six shillings a month rent. He was frequently ill there and was glad enough to leave in the following January, after five months' residence.

While at Chesham the Lawrences often saw some friends of Murry and Katherine Mansfield, the Cannans, who lived in a windmill at nearby Cholesbury. Gilbert Cannan, at the time a well-known novelist, was married to James Barrie's former wife, who had been the actress Mary Ansell. A handsome woman who rolled her eyes when she talked, she was destined to flit in and out of the Lawrences' lives for years to come. Lawrence was fond of her, but in later years he found her a bore.

The Cannans had a long-term house guest in the fall of 1914, the young painter Mark Gertler, who had worn himself out with overwork and excessive sociability in London and had come to the country to recover. He too became a close friend of the Lawrences'. Through the Cannans they also met Compton Mackenzie, the successful young author of *Sinister Street* (which Lawrence privately called 'frippery', though he liked Mackenzie personally).

Mackenzie, later to be the victim of some of Lawrence's satiric shafts, wrote a good deal about him in fiction and memoir. While visiting the Cannans at their windmill, Mackenzie was taken over to meet the Lawrences at their house in Bellingdon Lane, which he later recalled as 'the ugliest cottage I had ever seen'. He found Lawrence ('We've only just got in and the place was filthy') scrubbing the floor. He had 'a small red moustache and reddish hair and the attractive pink-and-white complexion of a redhead [who] looked much younger than his twenty-nine years.'

In a letter to McLeod (January 5, 1915), Lawrence said the Cannans were their 'very good friends', and he mentioned others who had moved nearby: 'The Murrys—she is Katherine Mansfield— if you remember, they ran *Rhythm*—have a cottage at Lee, three miles off: so we are not quite isolated.' Otherwise, the Lawrences had fewer visitors from the outside than was customary. Once Amy Lowell came to Chesham in a maroon automobile driven by a chauffeur in maroon livery. Catherine Jackson, soon to marry Donald Carswell, was at Chesham only once, for the day. Frieda later recalled that Gordon Campbell also visited them, looking 'like an Irish tramp.' Koteliansky came to see the Lawrences several times.

These Chesham months—August 1914 to January 1915—Lawrence described to Cynthia Asquith (at the end of January 1915) as the time when his 'soul lay in the tomb—not dead, but with a flat stone over it, a corpse, become corpse-cold. And nobody existed, because I did not exist myself. Yet I was not dead—only passed over— trespassed—and ali the time I knew I should have to rise again.' His preserved letters of this time of 'deadness' are fewer in number than those we usually find for other five-month periods; later in the war, when he was far more bitter about it, Lawrence was also far more articulate on the subject, voluminously so. The letters from Chesham do not always seem those of a 'dead' man; Lawrence was sufficiently alive to express disgust and discouragement.

Before the war was three weeks old he wrote to Amy Lowell, 'My chief grief and misery is for Germany—so far . . . I can't help feeling it a young and adorable country—adolescent—with the faults of adolescence', which he had noted in his Prussian-officer story and elsewhere. His other available letters from Chesham do not reveal further 'grief and misery for Germany' sentiment; nor do they, on the other hand, show a flourish of pro-British spirit. Lawrence's attitude, which didn't centrally change during the four years of war or at any time afterwards, crystallized in those early months of despair: he came to hate the war itself. 'Yet,' as he later said of his character Somers in *Kangaroo,* 'he had no conscientious objection to war. It was the whole spirit of the war, the vast mob-spirit, which he could never acquiesce in'—the bullying, the servile conformity, the loss of individual 'manly isolation'. Not long after moving to Chesham, Lawrence told Pinker (on September 5, 1914) he was beginning his book on Thomas Hardy 'out of sheer rage' at the war. In October he wrote to Harriet Monroe that he thought he was 'much too valuable a creature to offer myself to a German bullet gratis and for fun,' and he told Edward Garnett that the war made him 'feel very abstract', and that what he did or did not do was of little importance. Letters that trickled through from Germany told in stout, ardent phrases of the von Richthofens' young officer friends who had fallen in the early battles. Word came through also of the continuing illness of Frieda's father.

Lawrence too was indisposed that autumn and still thought of Italy with nostalgia. Amy Lowell, who knew the conditions at Chesham, hoped that Lawrence would soon get out of Buckinghamshire. After returning to Boston, she wrote to Harriet Monroe that she thought Lawrence had 'consumption, the cottage is very damp, and must be horribly cold.' She felt that he should at least go to London, if he couldn't get to Italy, for the winter. Timid about offering him money, she told him she was sending him a typewriter. On October 16 he responded happily:

> Over the typewriter I have got quite tipsy with joy: a frightfully heady bit of news . . . I shall cherish it like a jewel. I always

say that my only bit of property in the world is a silver watch—
which is true. Now my realm is a typewriter: I am a man of
property: I feel quite scared lest I shall have incurred new
troubles and new responsibilities. . . . By the same post has come
a cheque for £50, a grant to me from the Royal Literary Fund.
But that bores me. There is no joy in their tame thin-gutted
charity. I would fillip it back at their old noses, the stodgy,
stomachy authors, if I could afford it. But I can't . . . And don't
talk about putting me in the safe with Keats and Shelley. It
scares me out of my life, like the disciples at the Transfigura-
tion. But I'd like to know Coleridge when Charon has rowed
me over.

He also thanked her for seeing Kennerley on his behalf. 'I don't
want him ever to publish me anything ever any more as long as
either of us lives. So you can say what you like to him. But I think
that really he is rather nice. Just ask him about my things, will you:
no more.' Meanwhile, he reported, 'I am having a book of stories
published shortly by Duckworth. It will be called *The Prussian Officer and Other Stories,* because it begins with that story I call
"Honour and Arms": which, by the way, is sold to the *Metropolitan
Magazine,* in America.' He added a nature note, and some news of
his own appearance: 'We have had a beautiful dim autumn, of pale
blue atmosphere and white stubble and hedges hesitating to change.
But I've been seedy and I've grown a red beard, behind which I
shall take as much cover henceforth as I can, like a creature under a
bush. My dear God, I've been miserable this autumn enough to turn
into wood, and to be a graven image of myself.' This time he kept his
beard.

A month later (November 18) Lawrence wrote to Amy Lowell
that the typewriter—which the steward of the *Laconia* had brought
across the ocean and forwarded from Liverpool—was 'bubbling like
a pot, frightfully jolly'.

He told Edward Garnett, in an October letter, that he and Frieda
'hardly quarrel any more', but this was a condition that didn't last,
according to Murry's testimony. Actually, the Lawrences' quarrels
were often therapeutic, were surface outlets for the conflicts of two
highly charged personalities. At the deepest level, the Lawrences were
inextricably bound to one another; but because the quarrels were
dramatic and violent, with curses sometimes punctuated by flung
crockery, the writers of memoirs tended to recall these excitements

rather than the longer, if sometimes duller, periods of quietness, sweetness, and gaiety. Lawrence's tenderness and gentleness should be as well known as his irritability, but as human affairs—and human reporters—go, they are not. That tenderness had surprised Frieda early in their association, when once she had bumped her head against a shutter 'and Lawrence was in such an agony of sympathy and tenderness over it.' Nobody had treated her so gently before. Frieda, who best should know, has said that 'it was a long fight for Lawrence and me to get at some truth between us; it was a hard life but a wonderful one. . . . Whatever happened on the surface of everyday life, there blossomed the certainty of the unalterable bond between us, and of the ever present wonder of all the world around us.'

At this time Lawrence and Koteliansky became responsive friends, and the Russian visited him and Frieda at Selwood Terrace and, more frequently, after they moved to Chesham. From there Lawrence wrote him a sharply personal letter early in December, which dealt with Koteliansky's obvious dislike of Frieda: 'You mustn't judge her lightly. There is another quality in woman that you do not know, so you can't estimate it. You don't know that a woman is not a man with different sex. She is a different world. You do not understand that enough. Your world is all of one hemisphere.' A few days later, in a note dealing with the manuscript of his essay on Thomas Hardy which Koteliansky was helping to type, Lawrence said, 'Frieda shakes her fist at you.' Whatever Koteliansky may have thought of Lawrence's analysis of him, he probably wouldn't accept anything Frieda said about him.

In a letter to Amy Lowell on December 18, Lawrence presented a comic little dramatization of an episode involving Frieda and Ernest Weekley:

> We have been in the Midlands seeing my people, and Frieda seeing her husband. He did it in the thorough music-hall fashion. It was a surprise visit. When we were children, and used to play at being grand, we put an old discarded hearthrug in the wheelbarrow, and my sister, perched there in state 'at home,' used to be 'Mrs Lawson' and I, visiting with a walking stick, was 'Mr Marchbanks.' We'd been laughing about it, my sister and I. So Frieda, in a burst of inspiration, announced herself to the landlady as 'Mrs Lawson.'
>
> 'You—' said the quondam husband, backing away—'I hoped never to see you again.'
>
> Frieda: 'Yes—I know.'

Quondam Husband: 'And what are you doing in *this* town[?']
Frieda: I came to see you about the children.
Quondam Husband: Aren't you ashamed to show your face where you are known! Isn't the commonest prostitute better than you?
Frieda: Oh no.
Quon. Husb.: Do you want to drive me off the face of the earth, Woman? Is there no place where I can have peace?
Frieda: You see I must speak to you about the children.
Quon. Husb.: You shall *not* have them—they don't want to see you.
Then the conversation developed into a deeper tinge of slanging—part of which was:
Q.H.: *If* you had to go away, why didn't you go away with a *gentleman?*
Frieda: He is a *great* man.
Further slanging.
Q. Husb.: Don't you know you are the vilest creature on earth?
Frieda: Oh no.
A little more of such, and a departure of Frieda. She is no further to seeing her children.
Q. Husb.: Don't you know, my solicitors have instructions to arrest you, if you attempt to interfere with the children[?]
Frieda: I don't care.
If this weren't too painful, dragging out for three years, as it does, it would be very funny I think. The Quondam Husband is a Professor of French Literature, great admirer of Maupassant, has lived in Germany and Paris, and thinks he is the tip of cosmopolitan culture. But poor Frieda can't see her children.—I really give you the conversation verbatim.

About this time, Lawrence had been reading Katherine L. Jenner's *Christian Symbolism,* and the book certainly influenced a very long letter he wrote to Gordon Campbell (the full text appears in Lawrence's *Collected Letters*). Having read the Murrys' enthusiastic reports on Campbell's novel, Lawrence told him he was disappointed to learn that its hero killed himself, which was futile:

If you are making a great book on Egotism—and I believe you may—for God's sake give us the death of Egotism, not the death of the sinner. Russia, and Germany, and Sweden, and

Italy, have done nothing but glory in the suicide of the Egoist. But the Egoist as a divine figure on the Cross, held up to tears and love and veneration, is to me a bit nauseating now, after Artzibasheff and D'Annunzio, and the Strindberg set, and the Manns in Germany.

Lawrence went on to say that 'the greatest book I know on the subject is the Book of Job. Job was a great, splendid Egoist.' Lawrence then discussed various religions, pointed out some symbols, and stated his belief in the Resurrection, a belief he kept all his life:

I understand now your passion to face the west. It is the passion for the extinction of yourself and the knowledge of the triumph of *your own will* in your body's extinction. But in the great periods, when man was great, he has faced the *East:* Christian, Mohammedan, Hindu, all.

You should try to grasp, I think—don't be angry at my tone —the *complete whole* which the Celtic symbolism made in its great time. We are such egoistic fools. We see only the *symbol* as a *subjective expression:* as an expression of ourselves. That makes us so sickly when we deal with the old symbols: like Yeats.

The old symbols were each a word in a great attempt at formulating the whole history of the soul of Man. They *are unintelligible* except in their whole context. So your Ireland of you Irishmen of today is a filthy mucking about with a part of the symbolism of a great Statement or Vision: just as the Crucifixion of Christ is a great mucking about with part of the symbolism of a great religious Vision.

The Crucifix, and Christ, are only symbols. They do not mean a man who suffered his life out as I suffer mine. They mean a moment in the history of my soul, if I must be personal. But it is a moment fixed in context and having its being only according to context. Unless I have the Father, and the hiera[r]chies of Angels, I have no Christ, no Crucifixion.

It is necessary to grasp the whole. At last I have got it, grasping something of what the mediaeval church tried to express. To me, the Latin form of expression comes very natural. To you, the Celtic I should think. I think the whole of the Celtic symbolism and great Utterance of its Conception has never been fathomed. But it must have been in accord with the Latin. . . .

But Christianity should teach us now, that after our Cruci-

fixion, and the darkness of the tomb, we shall rise again in the
flesh, you, I, as we are today, resurrected in the bodies, and
acknowledging the Father, and glorying in his power, like Job.

It is very dangerous to use these old terms lest they sound
like cant. But if only one can grasp and know again as a new
truth, true for one's own history, the great vision, the great,
satisfying conceptions of the world's greatest periods, it is
enough. Because so it is made new.

All religions I think have the same inner conception, with
different expressions. Why don't you seek out the whole of the
Celtic Vision, instead of messing about talking of Ireland. Beatrice was somewhere on the track: but she didn't know what she
was after: so she over-humanised, that is, she made subjective
the symbols she used, so spoiled them: by putting them as ema-
nations of her own Ego, instead of using them as words to convey the great whole of which her own Ego was only the Issue,
as the Son is issue of the Father.

*

At the Cannans' Christmas party Murry and Katherine announced
their forthcoming split in a kind of charade. The dinner had begun
gloomily, and the host was unusually depressing (Gilbert Cannan
was only a few years away from his crippling attacks of megalomania). Now he sat in futility before his guests, and neither he nor
they—bohemians, actors, artists, writers—could properly dismem-
ber the roast pig. But there was one thing most of them could
do, and this was to improvise and act in little plays; and they
were soon doing that, along with some heavy drinking. When Koteliansky pestered Murry to perform 'a play within a play', Murry and
Katherine realistically acted out their problems (and this was in the
days before group therapy), with the handsome and ailing young
Gertler as 'the other man'. At the end Katherine Mansfield broke
away from the scenario and refused to act out a reconciliation with
Murry: she insisted on remaining with Gertler. Lawrence came
pelting into the play and forced Murry to one side: 'Are you blind?
If not, how dare you expose yourself?' The Murry-Mansfield-Gertler
triangle in the little play was a curious foreshadowing of the fiction-
alized ending Lawrence was, about a year later, to give *Women in
Love;* there, the woman based partly on Katherine Mansfield was to
leave the man based partly on Murry for the man based partly on
Gertler.

At just this time Lawrence had been trying to enlist all three as citizens of a utopian colony he wanted to found, to be called Rananim after one of Koteliansky's Hebrew songs. Even that melancholy Christmas did not discourage him. He thought of about twenty colonists altogether. He wrote to William Hopkin about it, on January 18, 1915, as a scheme to 'sail away from this world of war and squalor and found a little colony where there shall be no money but a sort of communism as far as the necessaries of life go, and some real decency.' It would be 'a community . . . established upon the assumption of goodness in the members instead of the assumption of badness'—a description of the ideal anarchist commonwealth, though Lawrence would have balked at the word *anarchist*.

But Rananim was doomed from birth. Katherine Mansfield collected some practical information about islands and began asking Lawrence solemn questions. He knew she was jeering at him, and he fell silent.

*

On January 5, about two weeks before leaving Chesham, Lawrence wrote to McLeod to say that he was 'still revising *The Rainbow*—putting a good deal of work into it. I have done 300 pages. It'll be a new sort of me for you to get used to.' He would have liked to send McLeod a copy of *The Prussian Officer*, 'but various thieves who call themselves friends carried off copies they could well afford to buy, and I am badly off, through the war.'

Lawrence told McLeod he was 'afraid that, when Methuen gets *The Rainbow*, he'll wonder what changeling is foisted on him. For it *is* different from my other work. I am glad with it. I am coming into my full feather at last, I think.' He chided McLeod for even thinking of enlisting, since 'the war is for those who are not needed for a new life. I hate and detest the war, it is all wrong, all foolish, all a wretched mistake. Why can't it end?'

On the point of departing from Chesham, Lawrence on January 18, 1915, wrote to William Hopkin:

We are just packing up to move again—not to Italy, alas—but to a beautiful place in Sussex—Greatham, Pulborough, Sussex, is the address. It is the Meynells' place. You know Alice Meynell, Catholic poetess, rescuer of Francis Thompson. The father took a big old farmhouse at Greatham, then proceeded to give each of his children a cottage. Now Viola lends us hers. It is,

I think, a big cottage, everything nice and handy . . . on the edge of the downs—not far from Littlehampton, which is seaside.

On February 2 Lawrence wrote to Campbell from Greatham, where he and Frieda were finding their cottage beautiful and comfortable; and he spoke of a new friend to whom David Garnett had introduced him in London: 'Yesterday Ottoline Morrell came down—she is going to bring Russell, the philosophy-mathematics man.' He told Campbell to be 'decent' in his relations with Murry and Katherine Mansfield, but the admonition did no good, for Murry broke their friendship the following weekend when Campbell didn't appear at their Lee cottage although he had promised to do so. (The friendship wasn't put together again until 1949.)

Wilfrid and Alice Meynell were rarely at Greatham during the Lawrences' six months there. In a 1952 letter to this author, Viola Meynell recalled, 'My father and mother were nearly always at their London flat, so though they must have just met the Lawrences, that's about all.' David Garnett, reporting on his visit to Greatham in mid-April, described his arrival for breakfast at the elder Meynells', to which the Lawrences were also invited: 'The Patriarch was rustling the pages of the *Observer;* the room was filled with dark madonna-like girls and women; the *Poetess* was stretched upon a couch.' Frieda's memoir has a passage about 'Alice Meynell as a vision in the distance, being led by Wilfred [*sic*] Meynell across the lawn like Beatrice being led by Dante'—this was, Hugh Kingsmill commented, 'an incident about which Dante maintains a strict reserve.'

Viola Meynell further recalled, 'I think the Lawrences were happy here—if quarrelsome.' Certainly Lawrence felt, at Greatham, that he was coming back to life after the first deadening shock of the war: walking on the Downs one day, 'I opened my eyes again, and saw it was daytime.'

He helped to bring Murry out of a severe illness in February. Katherine Mansfield had gone to France, imagining herself in love with one of Murry's friends, the French writer Francis Carco. Murry accepted the Lawrences' invitation for a visit and walked across flooded and rainy marshlands, arriving soaked and full of aches from an influenza attack. Lawrence put him to bed for a few days, scolded him for having been 'stupid' about his physical condition, and cared for him as if he 'were a child'; Murry has said that Lawrence produced a 'perfect likeness' of this therapeutic side of his nature in the *Aaron's Rod* scenes in which Lilly nurses Aaron back to health.

Murry noted in his journal that the Lawrences had been kind to him: 'May I requite them!'

During Murry's convalescence, Lawrence told him that Katherine Mansfield had gone away because Murry and Campbell ignored her when they became involved in their talk. This astounded Murry, who realized that if this were true he was deficient in the Athenian virtue of self-knowledge.

Murry felt beyond his depth when Lawrence spoke of the necessity for revolution. The extracts that Murry later published from his journal show Lawrence's conversation at this time to have been remarkably similar to the letters he was then writing to Bertrand Russell. Murry found Lawrence's new doctrines baffling, particularly the one to the effect that the revolution should be a matter of an impersonal 'bond of elemental solidarity with men'. Murry, who had just lost Campbell and Katherine Mansfield, feared he might lose Lawrence also: the personal bond with Lawrence was so precious that he didn't want to 'imperil it by disagreement'.

Murry felt that Lawrence had a sense of personal doom then. He told Murry there was no use in writing anything; the conditions of present life had to be changed first; he said that he would write only one more novel after *The Rainbow,* and that he was, like John the Baptist, 'merely a forerunner' of the greater one who would succeed him. This would be Murry, whose very inertia was 'valuable', whose effort seemed 'purer'. Murry felt uncomfortable: 'It was preposterous that Lawrence should lean on me.'

A telegram relieved the situation: Katherine Mansfield, often Murry's *dea ex machina* in his entanglements with Lawrence, wired from Paris that she would arrive in London at eight the following morning. Murry left to meet her. She had returned only 'because there was nowhere else to go'; she had, after harsh trouble, succeeded in getting into a restricted military zone to meet Carco and had been disillusioned. Now she and Murry went miserably back to the cottage they shared, where she became ill; but she soon returned to Paris for another brief and hectic visit.

Lawrence continued to dream of Rananim, if not with the mocking Katherine Mansfield, then with others: on February 1 he had written to Ottoline Morrell that he wanted her 'to form the nucleus of a new community which shall start a new life amongst us—a life in which the only riches is integrity of character.' And Lady Ottoline's husband had a 500-acre estate where the scheme could be worked out: Garsington Manor in Oxfordshire. Her husband, Philip Morrell (which they pronounced Mor'l), was a member of Parliament, as a Liberal. The Morrells made their permanent home in London, and although Lady Ottoline's husband had attended an Oxford college rather than one at Cambridge, the Bloomsbury tribe welcomed him. During World War I he became their favorite pacifist M.P.

Bertrand Russell, spoken of by Lawrence as 'the philosophy-mathematics man', was heir to an earldom and grandson of Lord Russell, twice prime minister in the Victorian epoch. Bertrand Russell had written extensively on philosophy and, with Alfred North Whitehead, had produced the remarkable *Principia Mathematica* (1910–1913). He was a lecturer at Trinity College, Cambridge. He cared little for Philip Morrell, although he made speeches on Morrell's account when the latter was up for election to Parliament. But he fell in love with Morrell's wife, as he tells in his *Autobiography*.

In 1916 Lady Ottoline broke off the affair after two years: Philip Morrell had known about it but, after 1915, when she undertook the task of making Garsington into what she felt to be a center of life, she cooled towards Russell, who in Lawrence's *Women in Love* is the minor figure Sir Joshua Malleson (in some versions Mattheson). The affair was still going on when she brought Russell out to Greatham to meet Lawrence.

Russell said afterwards that she 'admired us both and made us think that we should admire each other.' Russell's growing pacifism—which would in 1916 cause his removal from Trinity College—had produced in him 'a mood of bitter rebellion,' and he found Lawrence in a similar state. Before long the two men decided to take action in the form of a series of joint lectures in London. But they began quarreling, and Russell eventually delivered his own lectures, without Lawrence. Their antagonistic friendship, which endured for about a year, was one of the most dramatic associations of Lawrence's life.

The collier's son and the heir to an earldom were both lean, spare men, intensely energetic; but Lawrence was to live only another fifteen years. Russell, forty-two when he met Lawrence (who was twenty-nine in early 1915), was lecturing in mathematics. 'Already accustomed to being accused of undue slavery to reason' at the time he met Lawrence, Russell has said of himself, he felt that his new friend could give him 'a vivifying dose of unreason'. Russell has further said he 'liked Lawrence's fire' and 'the energy and passion of his feelings'. The two men agreed on at least one point, that politics and psychology couldn't be divorced, and for a while Russell felt that Lawrence was 'a man of a certain imaginative genius' whose 'insight into human nature was deeper than' his own. Russell said he gradually 'came to feel him a positive force for evil'—exactly what Lawrence soon felt about Russell.

Lawrence's violently remarkable letters to him began on February 12, 1915, with a mildly disparaging description of another member of the Cambridge-Bloomsbury set, E. M. Forster, who had been visiting the Lawrences for three days. (Émile Delavenay has noted that Forster brought the ominous rumor that the police were planning to take action against *The Prussian Officer.*) Forster and Lawrence quarreled, yet Lawrence felt a tenderness for him. Lawrence offered Russell a short paragraph of social reform in which he said that industries, the land, and all means of communication 'must' be immediately nationalized, and that all men, whether sick or well, should receive their wages: 'Which practically solves the whole economic question for the present. All dispossessed owners shall receive a proportionate income—no capital recompense—for the space of, say fifty years.'

Lawrence, who was then finishing *The Rainbow,* turned to his *métier,* human relations; and, quite in the spirit of the last chapter of that book, he said that 'the shell, the old forms', must be broken. Men go to women now for mere sensation, as a form of masturbation, leading finally to sodomy; but 'a man of strong soul has too much honour for the other body—man or woman—to use it as a means of masterbation [*sic*]. So he remains neutral, inactive. That is Forster.'

Lawrence concluded with violent suggestions that 'we' must 'smash the frame' of the present mode of existence. He suggested that he might go to visit Russell at Cambridge early the following month, 'to meet Lowes Dickenson [*sic*]', Forster's friend, 'and the good people you are going to introduce me to'.

Later, in writing to Ottoline Morrell about Russell, Lawrence said that he felt 'a quickening of love for him'. And after Russell had agreed to the Cambridge visit, Lawrence told him it made him feel 'frightfully important'; the occasion was 'quite momentous' for him. He didn't 'want to be horribly impressed and intimidated', but he was afraid he would be. He cared only about the necessary revolution, and he wanted Russell to be his friend: 'But you are so shy and then I feel so clumsy, so clownish.' He asked Russell not to have him meet too many people at once: 'I am afraid of concourses and clans and societies and cliques—not so much of individuals.'

The next weekend, March 6–7, Lawrence went to Cambridge to

see Russell and his friends. Five weeks later Lawrence told David Garnett that his Sunday morning there, when he had met Maynard Keynes at breakfast, 'was one of the crises of my life.'

The future Lord Keynes remembered that breakfast and wrote of it long afterwards: at a party the night before, 'Lawrence had been facing Cambridge', and had apparently not enjoyed much of it. He had sat next to G. E. Moore 'in Hall that night', and the man who had just completed *The Rainbow* exchanged a cold silence with the Lecturer on Moral Science. (This picture is enlivened by the statement in the 1953 autobiography of the American mathematician Norbert Wiener, who in 1915 had been a student at Trinity, to the effect that G. E. Moore looked like Tenniel's drawing of the March Hare, and that Bertrand Russell was exactly like Tenniel's Mad Hatter.) Lawrence did, however, talk warmly and friendlily with G. H. Hardy, the Lecturer in Mathematics.

At the breakfast in Russell's rooms in Nevile's Court, Lawrence was cold again, Keynes recalled; he 'was morose from the outset and said very little, apart from indefinite expressions of irritable dissent.' Russell stood by the fireplace, and Keynes alternately rested on a sofa and stood beside Russell, the two of them talking, trying to draw Lawrence into the conversation, but he sat on the sofa 'in rather a crouching position with his head down', loathing Keynes.

Years later Lord Keynes blamed Lawrence's behavior on 'two causes of emotional disturbance'. One was Ottoline Morrell, who was living in two worlds, that of the Bloomsbury-Cambridge intellectuals and that of dwellers in the realm of art such as Lawrence and Mark Gertler and his girl friend, Dorothy Carrington. Lawrence, Keynes thought, was jealous of Lady Ottoline's 'other world' and determined to find it antagonistic; Lawrence also disliked Cambridge for its hold upon David Garnett. 'And jealousy apart,' Keynes further said, 'it is impossible to imagine moods more antagonistic than those of Lawrence and of pre-war Cambridge.' He felt that Lawrence looked at the Cantabridgians unfairly through his 'ignorant, jealous, irritable, hostile eyes', yet Keynes admitted that Lawrence was at least partly right in saying at the time that they and their way of life were 'done for'. (Keynes even seemed a little proud that in 1928 Lawrence mentioned him in a letter as 'the only member of Bloomsbury who had supported him by subscribing for *Lady Chatterley*'. Clive Bell once pointed out that he too was a subscriber, and certainly others from Bloomsbury were also.)

Keynes, with his eager interest in the arts and his vital support of them, would perhaps have helped Lawrence if Lawrence had become his friend. It was not a question of playing up, of toadying; Keynes would have wanted that least of all. It was a matter merely of friendliness, and Lawrence threw acid on Keynes's attempts at this. Later in the war, when Lawrence needed help and desperately wrote letters to the few high-placed acquaintances he had left, the friendship of Maynard Keynes might have been valuable.

But Lawrence was being strenuously independent on that spring morning in Cambridge when he sat sullenly near the fire while the other two men stood beside it, talking and trying to catch his interest. (Lawrence's new red beard was no novelty in a place where Lytton Strachey was a familiar; the other two men in that room at Trinity were thin and energetic like himself, Russell with his lively terrapin's head and Keynes with his brush mustache and the nose which in schooldays had earned him the nickname 'Snout'.) But Lawrence sat glaringly apart.

At that breakfast which, as we have seen, Lawrence called 'one of the crises of my life', he couldn't foretell that Keynes ultimately would see his old friend Russell essentially as Lawrence saw him, though without Lawrence's scornfulness.

Keynes, accepting the brilliance of Russell's accomplishment, nevertheless perceived that Russell 'sustained simultaneously a pair of opinions ludicrously incompatible. He held that in fact human affairs were carried on after a most irrational fashion, but that the remedy was quite simple and easy, since all we had to do was to carry them on rationally.' Keynes found that conversations based on such assumptions were 'really very boring', and he was, if unconsciously so, on Lawrence's side when he added that 'a discussion of the human heart which ignored so many of its deeper and blinder passions, both good and bad, was scarcely more interesting.'

Keynes and Lawrence were much closer in the deeper issues than Russell and Lawrence, yet Lawrence failed to see this and for another twelve months pursued Russell with friendship, scoldings, insults, compliments, and curses.

*

After that visit to Cambridge, Lawrence bitterly told Frieda that the men he had met there 'walked up and down the room and talked about the Balkan situation and things like that, and they know nothing about it.' And Lawrence wrote to Russell that Cambridge had made him feel 'very black and down'. He got 'a melancholic malaria' from 'its smell of rottenness, marsh-stagnancy', and he wondered 'How can so sick people rise up?' He was himself 'too sad' for further work on what, with apologies, he called his 'philosophy'. He told Russell that Ottoline Morrell was planning to have Frieda and himself take a cottage at Garsington: 'She is so generous, one shrinks a bit. One feels one would rather give things to a woman so generous.'

Meanwhile, Lawrence wrote to her frequently; his letters to her and to Cynthia Asquith increasingly became a lectureship. With his friendships for high-born women—he was, we must not forget, married to a baroness—Lawrence resembled Rilke, who was a kind of informal chaplain to a string of princesses and countesses. During the Greatham residence Lawrence occasionally saw his titled friends, when they came to Pulborough, when he and Frieda were in London, or when they visited Garsington. They saw Lady Cynthia several times when she traveled to the Sussex coast, which lay only ten miles below Greatham. They visited her at Littlehampton, and they made frequent automobile trips to other coast towns, such as Bognor, with one of the Meynell daughters, Monica Saleeby, who was suffering from a nervous breakdown after her marriage had broken up.

Another of the Meynell girls at Greatham, Madeline, was married to Perceval Drewett Lucas. The Lucases had three small daughters, the eldest of whom, Sylvia, was partly crippled as a result of a severe and almost fatal accident of two years before in which, as Viola Meynell recalled in her biography of Alice Meynell, Sylvia had cut her leg on a large knife. When Lawrence came to Greatham, the child was still undergoing operations and it was uncertain whether she would be able to keep the damaged leg. Lawrence tutored little Sylvia—in partial return, Catherine Carswell suggests, for his lodging —and at times he also tutored her cousin, Mary Saleeby, whose mother was having a nervous breakdown. Eleanor Farjeon, who had helped Viola Meynell to type *The Rainbow* before meeting Lawrence, remembered one of those rare occasions at Greatham when he was in contact with one of the elders of the community. Wilfrid Meynell 'pathetically' thanked Lawrence for helping with the children, especially Mary, whom Eleanor Farjeon remembered as 'a rough-and-tumble ragamuffin' among the Meynell grandchildren. After Wilfrid Meynell had thanked Lawrence and left, Eleanor Farjeon recalled that Lawrence 'exploded', saying that he didn't *'want* gratitude! I'm not taking Mary on because I *like* it! *But somebody has got to!'*

Mary Saleeby (by then Dr. Mary Saleeby Fisher) recalled, nearly forty years afterwards, in a memoir she wrote for Edward Nehls, that at ten she was 'passionately fond of farming' and 'ran wild nearly the whole year round on the farm and was completely uncivilised.' She added, however, that although Lawrence's tutoring took her away from her agricultural interests, she enjoyed his lessons, and apparently her cousin did also. A bit later Lawrence put Sylvia into a story about the community, in which her father, Percy Lucas, was the principal figure —a story whose repercussions will be mentioned later.

Though Percy Lucas was quiet and standoffish, most people liked and respected him; he apparently irked Lawrence. Percy was the brother of E. V. Lucas, a man of letters of the kind Lawrence disliked: the writer of genteel essays, the frequenter of London clubs, the wit at the banquets of journalists. His brother Percy, just turning forty, indulged in genealogy, an activity Lawrence scoffed at. Even Everard Meynell's memorial to Percy Lucas, mentioning all the little simplicities that endeared him to the Meynells, would have met with jeers from Lawrence. That Lucas was 'a Spartan in little things', that he was 'an able cricketer', that the innumerable bundles of his genealogical work, packages 'so practical and yet so unutterably pathetic', were neatly tied and packed away before he left for war— these little points of sympathy and admiration in Everard Meynell's memoir would have made Lawrence grind his teeth. And these activities of Percy Lucas would have given him weapons for satire, for he saw Percy Lucas as a loafer, dependent upon the bounty of Wilfrid Meynell and leaning for spiritual support upon Madeline; these things Lawrence put into the cruel portrait of Percy, as Egbert, parasitic dweller at Godfrey Marshall's family colony at Crockham in his story 'England, My England', with its quiet mockery of W. E. Henley's stentorian poem. Yet, for all its meanness, the portrait did not completely lack sympathy: the Egbert of the story was really a victim of the ostensibly benevolent paternalism that dominated the colony.

Lawrence of course had done this kind of thing before—he hadn't spared his own family in *Sons and Lovers,* though the book didn't appear until after his mother's death and his father couldn't read well enough or attentively enough to feel the sting of his son's fictional treatment of him; Lawrence's sisters, however, had to practice shutting their faces against the stares they received when they walked down the streets in their Midland towns; George Lawrence, who read only parts of the book, said to this writer in 1950 that he 'would have thrashed Bert,' if he had seen him at the time, 'for what he did to my mother and father in that book.' But the Meynells, a close-knit family group, couldn't write Lawrence off as an indiscreet kinsman; he was a stranger who had accepted kindness and hospitality from them and then treated them cruelly.

Through the years, Lawrence kept on skimpoling his friends: Ottoline Morrell, Russell, Aldington, Katherine Mansfield, and others were to feel the cut of his satire. Murry was to be the most conspicuous victim. Only a few of Lawrence's acquaintances escaped: Lady Cynthia Asquith appeared in a friendly if not glamorous light in some of the stories, probably because Lawrence felt a respectul affection, if not love, for her. Compton Mackenzie, who later was to be Lawrence's victim on at least two acid occasions, told the author of the present volume (in London in 1950) that Lawrence's fiction often gives a distorted view of his acquaintances because 'he had a trick of describing a person's setting or background vividly, and then putting into the setting an ectoplasm entirely of his own creation.' Sir Compton added that those who know these victims will never see the stories except as falsifications; but with a generous admiration for certain aspects of Lawrence's writing, Sir Compton further said that the stories have an artistic validity for other readers, who don't know the principals.

And Catherine Carswell noted that although there was 'nothing superficially' resembling herself in the female character in Lawrence's 'The Blind Man', and that there was 'nothing that could not be easily refuted', the truth of the portrait nevertheless 'smote' her as similar truths must have smitten Katherine Mansfield, Ottoline Morrell, Dorothy Brett, and others whom Lawrence had impaled. As Mrs. Carswell also said, 'Here was little of portraiture, still less of summing up. But what an incomparable reading of the pulse of life!'

It must be emphasized, however, that Lawrence didn't lampoon all his acquaintances, and that he didn't quarrel with them all. One of his new friends from the Greatham period, for example, was Eleanor Farjeon, to whom he wrote cordially over a long period of time. And she has provided a friendly description of Lawrence at Greatham, where as a friend of Viola Meynell's she spent part of her 1915 spring holiday. When she announced that she was going to walk across the Downs and into Hampshire, Lawrence said he would go part of the way with her. They left early one morning, in a Sussex mist, and kept following and losing the traces of the old Roman road to Chichester, from which Lawrence returned by train to Pulborough that evening.

They sang songs and stopped at wayside pubs. Lawrence was happy all day ('We must be springlike'), but when they had to descend to East Dean and saw the smoke rising from the cottages, the blitheness left him, and he said in a sunken voice, 'I know the people who live in homes like that, I know them as I know my own skin. I know what they think and do, I know their lives . . . I *hate* them!' Yet in the pub he spoke cordially to the men who came in from the farmfields for their shandygaff.

*

Lawrence's disgust for the artificial, a disgust that could vanish in a wave of friendliness at a touch of nature, welled up when he received a summons to the bankruptcy court. He had refused to pay £150 for divorce costs; the solicitors who were trying to squeeze the money out of him were 'beasts, bugs, leeches', and would not get a penny of his if he could help it. The publishers still owed him £190 for *The Rainbow*, which they would pay upon publication, and Lawrence felt that this was the only money he would have for two years. His hatred of the parasitic side of the law, which increases and expands with civilization, seems even more bitter and violent than that of Dickens. Lawrence wrote to Russell on April 29 that 'a very unclean creature' had served a paper on him at Greatham, and that he had to go before the registrar on May 10 and declare his debts. This 'unclean object' had given him twenty-five shillings along with the paper, 'for conduct money', and left Lawrence 'gazing blankly at the golden sovereign'. He spat on it for luck. But the experience reinforced in him his 'utter hatred of the whole establishment—the whole constitution of England as it now stands. I wish I were a criminal instead of a bankrupt. But softly—softly. I will do my best to lay a mine under their foundations.'

One of the mines he planted under the establishment was *The Rainbow*, already at the publisher's and scheduled for autumn appearance. In its last revision at Greatham, the story had been extensively changed. Lawrence dropped out some of the characters— and names—he had mentioned in his earlier correspondence with Edward Garnett. In one of his letters to Garnett, Lawrence said, 'From

this part I have sent you, follows on the original *Sisters*—the School
Inspector, and so on.' Apparently Ursula's experiences towards the end
of *The Rainbow* had occurred near the beginning of *The Sisters;* the
surviving manuscript of *The Rainbow* indicates, with its alterations of
page numbers and in order of chapters, that these experiences had been
moved back, a process which evidently pushed Birkin (the school
inspector) into the second book.

It is possible, then, that the opening sections of *The Rainbow*—
the history of the Brangwens and of the early married life of Tom
and Anna—were added later. Admittedly, the Brangwen family history, with its surface of hard realism, seems to belong rather to the
first phase of Lawrence's writing career than to the more symbolis-
tic and futuristic second phase, but we must remember that, while
he was working on the final version of *The Rainbow,* Lawrence was
writing his study of Hardy. Also, Lawrence had evidently read
Thomas Mann's *Buddenbrooks* while in Germany—he mentioned
that novel in an essay he wrote on German literature in 1913. *The
Rainbow* somewhat resembles *Buddenbrooks* in the way it ranges
across several generations, focusing on certain figures in each period.
But *Buddenbrooks* remains throughout a family-chronicle novel;
The Rainbow begins in this fashion but becomes something quite
different, a vehicle for expressing the consciousness of a single character, a character of a very special kind.

This is Ella, who becomes Ursula in the published version of the
novel. She must 'get some experience' prior to knowing Birkin; Lawrence agreed with Garnett that the Templeman affair was 'wrong' in
its attempt to provide that experience. She eventually went through
it (before Birkin) with Skrebensky, of whom Frieda Lawrence wrote
(in a 1952 letter to the present author), 'Skrebensky is a bit like a
Richthofen cousin.' Frieda further pointed out that although Louie
Burrows may have been the model for Ursula outwardly, 'the inner
relationship is Lawrence's and mine, like the ring scene in *Women in
Love,* where I throw the ring at him.' The letter of January 29, 1914,
to Edward Garnett bears this out when the blanks which appeared
in the Huxley volume of the correspondence are filled in: Lawrence
had said that the character then called Ella 'was inclined to fall into
two halves—and gradations between them. It came of trying to graft
on to the character of Louie the character, more or less, of Frieda.'
(One of the unpublished fragments of the *Women in Love* manuscript now at the University of Texas, apparently an early version of

Chapter XV, describes a lovers' quarrel between Birkin and Ella, whose last name is Brangwen; Ella's sister is already named Gudrun, but the character who will become Hermione is here called Ethel.)

On the day he completed *The Rainbow,* exactly fifteen years before the day of his death, Lawrence sent Viola Meynell a sketch he had made, with rather sexual overtones, of his rainbow arching above collieries, the farmfields, and Eastwood as seen from the Breach; and it was perhaps at this time that he gave her his crude water-color copy of Giotto's 'Joachim and the Shepherds', apparently from a halftone reproduction, for he didn't follow Giotto's color scheme; where Giotto had put pale bare rock in the background, Lawrence the vitalistic man quite typically covered this bone-colored rock with the living green of vegetation. He wrote to Viola Meynell on March 2:

> I have finished my Rainbow, bended it and set it firm. Now off and away to find the pots of gold at its feet.
>
> I don't hear from Pinker—but from Methuen asking for 70 words descriptive for his autumn announcements[.] Vile that!
>
> You will type me the MS., won't you?—and tell me the repetitions and the things I can cross out. I must cross some things out.
>
> Will you keep the MS. at your house, and send me the typed copy in batches, so I can run through it. I am *frightfully* excited over this novel now it is done.

He was 'going to write a book about Life'; it would have 'more rainbows, but in different skies'; he hoped to publish it in weekly pamphlets, 'my initiation of the great and happy revolution'. This idea was a step towards the magazine he helped to found later that year, the *Signature.*

The rest of the material which he thought of as being somewhat of a sequel to *The Rainbow* was waiting to be coordinated, revised, and extensively rewritten. People recently met and episodes recently occurring waited to be included in the book which was eventually called *Women in Love.* A letter of April 23, 1915, is a precursor of what was to happen to Ottoline Morrell in that novel. In that letter Lawrence scolded her in a way which distinctly indicates his attitude towards the *Women in Love* character Hermione Roddice. The occasion of Lawrence's prophetic chastisement of his friend was a suicide attempt by a Belgian refugee domiciled at the Morrells' country house. The girl in question was Maria Nys, later to be Mrs. Aldous Huxley. Lawrence wrote to Lady Ottoline:

We were shocked about Maria: it really is rather horrible. I'm not sure that you aren't really more wicked than I had at first thought you. I think you can't help torturing a bit.

But I think it has [shown?] something—as if you, with a strong, old-developed *will* had enveloped the girl, in this will, so that she lived under the dominance of your will: and then you want to put her away from you. And when she says it was because she couldn't bear being left, that she took the poison, and it is a great deal true. Also she feels quite bewildered and chaotic. I think she really does know nothing about herself, in her consciousness. We English, with our old-developed public selves, and the consequent powerful will, and the accompanying rudimentary private or instinctive selves, I think we are very baffling to any other nation. We are apt to assume domination, when we are not personally implicated. A young foreigner can't understand that—not a girl like Maria.

Why must you always use your *will* so much, why can't you let things be, without always grasping and trying to know and to dominate. I'm too much like this myself.

There, now I'm scolding at you, even. But *why* will you use power instead of love, good public control instead of affection. I suppose it is breeding.

Some time was to pass before Lawrence turned Lady Ottoline into Hermione. Meanwhile, there was *The Rainbow*. In the latter half of the book, even if parts of it had been written earlier than the first, there is a new Lawrence, hinted at in the *Look!* poems and in the essay on Thomas Hardy (not published until after Lawrence's death): the Lawrence who became modernistic along with Joyce and Proust, apparently not knowing their work until later. As the story progressed, its principal and terminal symbol became—in its intensification of the many references, often extremely subtle, to arches—a sign of special importance to the central figures of that book, apotheosized at the end of the story. But the symbol had a special significance for Lawrence too, for it emblemized a new way of seeing, of writing, that would be a span into his own future.

Early in *The Rainbow* (Chapter IV, 'Girlhood of Anna Brangwen'), the young lovers Will and Anna are in a moonlit grainfield where, at harvest time, they decide to put up some sheaves: 'Ever with increasing closeness he lifted the sheaves and swung striding to the centre with them, ever he drove her more nearly to the meeting, ever he did his share, and drew towards her, overtaking her.' In this place 'there was only the moving to and fro in the moonlight, engrossed, the swinging in the silence, that was marked only by the splash of sheaves, and silence, and a splash of sheaves.' The effect of incantation here and in the rest of these passages is almost hypnotic, and like other parts of the book (flood and rainbow) it suggests the Old Testament. The walking and swinging, and the splashing sound of the sheaves, are highly ceremonial, and they help to bring the parents of Ursula together.

And Ursula, a generation later, experiences a different kind of grainfield-at-night scene with the man who is to become her lover, Anton Skrebensky. Like her parents, Ursula has in her the stately, pulsing rhythms of the Bible. On first knowing Skrebensky, Ursula dreamed of him as one of 'those sons of God who saw the daughters of men, that they were fair'—a passage Lawrence adapts in several novels. Ursula also remembers the three angels who came to Abraham's house. But she is not so traditional in her own grainfield episode with Skrebensky, which seems part early Stravinsky and part later Van Gogh, yet most originally Lawrencean:

They went towards the stackyard. There he saw, with something like terror, the great new stacks of corn glistening and gleaming transfigured, silvery and pleasant under the night-blue sky, throwing dark, substantial shadows, but themselves majestic and dimly present. She, like glimmering gossamer, seemed to burn among them as they rose like cold fires to the silvery-bluish air. All was intangible, a burning of gold, glimmering, whitish-steely fires. He was afraid of the great moon-conflagration of the cornstacks rising above him. His heart grew smaller, it began to fuse like a bead. He knew he would die.

The death Skrebensky 'knows' he will undergo isn't physical as he feels the power of Ursula in her ferocious ecstasy. Ursula is of course the 'New Young Woman', like the contemporary 'emancipated' figures such as H. G. Wells's Ann Veronica or various heroines of Arnold Bennett and Bernard Shaw. But Ursula has in her much of the symbolic darkness of the *Look!* poems, and her vision is of a different kind from other female characters of the time. Much later in *The*

Rainbow, she 'kills' Skrebensky; unable to keep pace with her, he sinks back into the safety of the commonplace.

Lawrence, no longer in bright Italy, and harrowed by the war, worked, through his characters in the final version of *The Rainbow* and in *Women in Love,* towards a new kind of realization that took over his consciousness and his writing. In *River of Dissolution* (1968) —the phrase is one Birkin uses in *Women in Love*—by Colin Clarke, this process is seen to have something in common with the poets of the Romantic movement. Clarke views Lawrence as balancing corruption or decay with vitality or creativity; the culmination is found in Birkin, but the process had begun in *The Rainbow.* Clarke calls attention to Coleridge's definition of 'the secondary Imagination', given after he had dismissed fancy as a lesser element:

> The IMAGINATION then, I consider either as primary, or secondary. The primary IMAGINATION I hold to be the living Power and prime Agent of all human Perception, and as a repetition in the finite mind of the eternal act of creation in the infinite I AM. The secondary Imagination I consider as an echo of the former, co-existing with the conscious will, yet still as identical with the primary in the *kind* of its agency, and differing only in *degree,* and in the *mode* of its operation. It dissolves, diffuses, dissipates, in order to re-create; or where this process is rendered impossible, yet still at all events it struggles to idealize and to unify. It is essentially *vital,* even as all objects (*as* objects) are essentially fixed and dead.

The key thought here, in regard to Lawrence in the war years, is the statement 'It dissolves, diffuses, dissipates, in order to re-create'. Colin Clarke doesn't suggest that Lawrence borrowed ideas from this passage of Coleridge, or that he even knew it; but the reader will remember that in 1914 Lawrence wrote to Amy Lowell, 'I'd like to know Coleridge when Charon has rowed me over.' Whether he was familiar with Coleridge's work beyond a youthful reading of *Christabel* (we may assume his acquaintance with *The Ancient Mariner*), there is as yet no proof. In any event, Clarke makes out a good case to the effect that Lawrence in his attempts to achieve wholeness did so, as Coleridge had done, by incorporating decay with creation. Lawrence's completest realization of this is the motive underlying *The Rainbow* to some extent, and far more fully so in *Women in Love.* Obviously, the idea permeated him, if only in a large way in the unconscious, and we may attribute much of his behavior during the war years to this mode of apprehension.

3 THE ECSTASY OF BITTERNESS

Lawrence had planned to leave Greatham in May, but he stayed on till the end of July, tutoring the children. The project of moving to Garsington, where Lawrence saw himself building a new Jerusalem within convenient distance of Oxford and Cambridge, collapsed. But he kept in touch with the Garsington-Cambridge crowd; besides Lady Ottoline and E. M. Forster, both Russell and David Garnett visited him at Greatham. Garnett in April brought with him his future partner in the Nonesuch Press, Francis Birrell, son of the belletrist and politician Augustine Birrell. Garnett and the younger Birrell were conscientious objectors, and they depressed Lawrence. He told Garnett not to bring Birrell again, for Birrell made him dream of black beetles, as he had dreamed of them at Cambridge after meeting Garnett's friends there: 'You must leave these friends, these beetles, Birrell and Duncan Grant are done forever.' Lawrence was 'not sure' about Keynes, but he remembered his own hostility and rage at the Cambridge breakfast.

Garnett broke off his close friendship with Lawrence, but didn't become his enemy, as other members of the Bloomsbury set seem to have done. Except for the continued relationship with Russell, Lawrence had quarantined himself out of the Cambridge-Bloomsbury world. By making himself a leper to its citizens, Lawrence severely harmed himself, for this group dominated a large part of British intellectual life and maintained representatives on important journals. They kept Lawrence down for a generation, belittling him when not ignoring him. The exception to this was Forster.

To point out that Bloomsbury discredited Lawrence is not to deny that its members had honest differences of opinion with him, or to attribute direct malice to men such as Keynes—least of all to David Garnett, who went on staunchly praising Lawrence when Lawrence was an unpopular cause. But over the years those who shared the Bloomsbury state of mind were often anti-Lawrencean. The varied Bloomsbury clans—some of them famously matriarchal, some bowing to an intellectual monolith, others obviously from Plato's banquet-table Symposium—when they saw Lawrence glaring at them from outside, saw him only as an enemy totem.

That the friendship with Russell lasted as long as it did—until the spring of 1916—was miraculous. Russell went to Greatham for the weekend of June 19–20, 1915, and it was apparently then that he and Lawrence began to discuss the idea of a joint lectureship. 'For a time,' Russell wrote years later, 'it seemed possible that there might be some sort of loose collaboration between us.'

While Russell was at Greatham, Lawrence wrote enthusiastically to Lady Ottoline that Russell's lectures on Ethics and his own on Immortality would result in the establishment of 'a little society or body around a *religious belief, which leads to action.*' The geography of Rananim began to blend with that of Garsington, 'a small world' for those who wanted to escape from the temporal and 'consider the big things'. Lady Ottoline should be president of the little society, which should include Cannan 'and perhaps Campbell' and the Murrys; they were, Lawrence assured Lady Ottoline, 'genuine' and 'valuable'. Soon after, he wrote to Lady Ottoline again (apparently on July 12), saying that he had 'rather quarrelled with Russell's lectures,' but not with the man himself. Indeed, they had 'almost sworn *Blutbrüderschaft'*.

Lawrence's letters to Russell present a full, immediate statement of one side of the quarrel, a statement of greater value than Russell's angry recollections of 1952, reasserted in his *Autobiography* in 1968. Essentially what divided the men was Lawrence's not yet completely developed 'blood-knowledge' ideas; these repelled Russell, while Russell's 'mind consciousness' irritated Lawrence. Yet, by Russell's own admission, he was so completely under Lawrence's spell for a time that some of Lawrence's criticisms—for example, Russell in his self-deception didn't realize he really loved the war—nearly drove him to suicide. Instead of killing himself, however, he had lived— and hated the man who had so violently disturbed him.

Some of Lawrence's letters to Russell are ministerial. Frieda's are in most respects no less interesting. One of them, probably written at the end of May 1915, asked: 'Isn't this coalition government thrilling? Surely it's "fate" that makes the world go round, nothing could have done this except hate for the "Huns".' Frieda thanked Russell for having written to her, and told him she knew he 'must have suffered bitterly from inquisitive impertinence'; she was disappointed, however, because he had not told her anything she 'would have been the wiser for.' And: 'When I wrote that you were too much of the English Constitution (look, I write it instinctively with capitals) I did *not* mean that you were *not* human enough—but too much you represent the English *as they are,* and you want to kick them, but it is too much yourself that you must kick—I hope you don't mind my saying this—I shall be grateful if you say something critical to me!'

She wrote again, after Russell's visit to Greatham in June: 'You were a little cross with me—It seemed to you that I did not respect enough your work, which I could never [*quite* is here crossed out] understand; that particular man-made thing you call it intellect is a mystery, rather a thrilling one to me.' Russell, she felt, used his intellect to confuse people: 'It's rather jolly, it's your form of "Wille zur Macht", I should always be frightened of your intellect I feel it against women, at present anyhow.'

She added: 'I think what you represent is your national passion, it makes you unhappy, because you are too much in the old form of it which has had its day, you are in it and really it needs a wider more inclusive ring—So perhaps you believe in the war—Don't you think one might?' She believed that, 'besides the rotten Prussianism', her native land 'has got something good and a new ideal to give to itself and the world—If nations would only, only allow each other's best characteristics to come out and take and learn from each other— It's all so tight now these little nations, so unembracing—All the people are so ugly now, but the other is there, in the nations and in the individuals.'

Frieda herself might have got along with Russell. Many years later, she admitted that the young Lawrence's tone in his letters to Russell 'seems presumptuous.' She said this in a letter to *Harper's* (April 1953) after that magazine had printed the first of Russell's violent attacks on Lawrence. Speaking of Bloomsbury, Frieda said, 'There was no flow of the milk of human kindness in that group . . . not even a trickle. They were too busy being witty and clever. But Russell could be kind.' She believed that if Russell had understood and accepted some of Lawrence's ideas, 'he might have been a great philosopher as he is a great mathematician; their friendship might have been a wonderful thing . . . As for calling Lawrence an exponent of Nazism, that is pure nonsense—you might as well call St. Augustine a Nazi.' Frieda said she was 'convinced that in some secret corner of himself, Russell has another image of a young Lawrence who was his friend and not the fantastic monster he makes him out.'

Frieda's supposed pro-Germanism in World War I seems mild

enough in her letters to Russell, but Ford Madox Hueffer and Violet
Hunt remembered her, in their separate and often conflicting memoirs, as being violently pro-Prussian. Hueffer's poem 'Antwerp' was
extremely popular at the time when, in company with Mrs. H. G.
Wells and Violet Hunt, he visited Greatham.

Violet Hunt recalled that in speaking of Hueffer's poem, which had
been inspired by the sight of Belgian refugees at Charing Cross Station, Frieda exclaimed, 'Dirty Belgians! Who cares for them!' After
which, Violet Hunt continued, 'in spite of tea and cake nicely handled, it came to a regular mill between me and the Valkyric.' Although this visit apparently took place during the weekend when
Lawrence was away at Cambridge, Hueffer placed him at Greatham
and gratuitously described him as 'of course . . . a pro-German'. During Frieda's tirade, Hueffer had to retire to an outhouse, he recalled,
because of his uniform. He was, as usual, romancing, for he was not
appointed as an officer (according to British Army records) until
August 14, 1915, about a fortnight after the Lawrences had left
Greatham.

Many years later (in 1955), Frieda, in a letter to this writer, recalled, 'When they came, he and Violet Hunt, I said to him: *"Wir sind
auch Deutsch?"* That made him squirm and he hummed and hawed.
It was wartime. So I did not think much of him. I never said: "Those
dirty Belgians", I never felt like that! Lawrence was not there, there
was no outhouse Ford could have retired to, I made no tirade, he
wore no uniform, just dislike of me, which I returned, or rather despised them. That was a rotten time. All false, sentimental, the
Bloomsburies, so conceited, and not a toe on the ground. What a lot
of my-eye L. was up against! It was a load indeed!' (Arthur Mizener,
in his excellent biography of Hueffer-Ford, *The Saddest Story* [1971],
asserts that although Hueffer wasn't gazetted until August 14, he
could have had a uniform to wear before that time, and even in July.
But there is no proof of this, and the accuracy of Hueffer in such
matters—he would give Frank Harris a hard time emulating him—is
highly questionable.)

The day after the Lawrences' departure from Greatham, July 15,
1915, Lawrence wrote Viola Meynell from Littlehampton, Sussex,
where he and Frieda were staying for a few days; he used Viola
Meynell's family nickname in his salutation, 'My dear Prue':

It is a grey day with many shadowy sailing-ships on the Channel,
and greenish-luminous water, and many noisy little waves. It is

very healing, I think, to have all the land behind one, all this England with its weight of myriad amorphous houses, put back, and only the variegated pebbles, and the little waves, and the great far-off dividing line of sea and sky, with grey sailing ships like ghosts hovering motionless, suspended with thought. If one could only sweep clear this England, of all its houses and pavements, so that we could all begin again!

That last statement sounds remarkably like Birkin in *Women in Love.*

*

After Bank Holiday the Lawrences moved to 1 Byron Villas, Vale of Health, Hampstead, where Frieda could be near her children. Lawrence, telling Russell he was '*very* dislocated and unhappy in these new circumstances', felt 'delivered up to chairs and tables and doormats'. He and Frieda lived next door to the poet Anna Wickham, in the ground-floor flat of a house that backed against those ponds about whose source Mr. Pickwick had speculated. In 1954, the poet Christopher Hassall lived near 1 Byron Villas, which he described in a letter as 'an ugly little red brick building about fifty years old, with Victorian bow-windows, and frosted glass in the front door'.

As for Anna Wickham, David Garnett, in the introduction to her *Selected Poems* (1971), remembered her as 'a beautiful and powerful woman' whose voice was 'a rich musical contralto' that was 'full of caressing humor'; she had studied singing in Paris with one of the de Reszkes. Her poem 'Imperatri' dealt with one of Frieda's infidelities. Since Anna Wickham spent most of her childhood in Australia, it is possible that her stories of the place aroused the Lawrences' interest in the southern continent. And it may have been at this time that Lawrence and Frieda met James M. Barrie, with whom he had exchanged letters while he was at Fiascherino. Lady Cynthia Asquith, who became Barrie's secretary, thought 'an interesting friendship might have ensued, but unfortunately the uninhibited Frieda went straight to one particular point. She could never understand any embarrassment about money or see any reason why it should not be transferred from a well-filled to an empty pocket—had the full purse been her own, her views would have been the same. "How do you do, Sir Barrie," she said. "I hear you make an income of fifty thousand a year [interesting news for Barrie!]. Why shouldn't you give Lorenzo enough money to pay for our passage to Australia?" '

Barrie recoiled at this, for like most people he 'preferred to give unasked'. Besides, Lady Cynthia further explained, 'the discovery that Lawrence and Frieda were in close touch with Barrie's sometime wife, then Mrs Gilbert Cannan, raised yet another barrier of embarrassment.'

Whether or not it was Anna Wickham who first interested the Lawrences in Australia, she was in many ways a remarkable figure. Her husband, 'a courageous balloonist', was once president of the Royal Astronomical Society, who on one occasion when she raged at him because he didn't approve of her being a poet, put her into an insane asylum. It was after her release that she met David Garnett, through his parents. She often went with the young Garnett for walks on Hampstead Heath or to the Café Royal. As he has noted, 'she would not take me as her lover, I was too tidy-minded to like her rag-bag friends and then I became a conscientious objector and she was for the war at the beginning.' He further reports that Lawrence recommended some of her poems ('*very* good') for possible inclusion in the *Georgian Poetry* volumes. She and Lawrence used to go for walks on the Heath, with her jealous small sons following; once, after a winter storm, they pelted Lawrence with snowballs.

Although the Lawrences' furniture-hunting in the Caledonian Market and the shops on Praed Street suggested permanent residence, they stayed at Byron Villas only until Christmas, less than five months. During that time, Lawrence and the Murrys launched their short-lived magazine the *Signature; The Rainbow* was published and suppressed; and Lawrence spoke continually of going to the New World. But by the end of that year he had settled in Cornwall.

Ten years later Lawrence sneered at the *Signature,* which he said had been started because Murry said, 'Let us do something.' But Murry later insisted, 'We were all implicated.' For one shilling a week they rented an office above a shop at 12 Fisher Street, Red Lion Square, which Lawrence remembered as 'some old Dickensy part of London'. A dozen people used to attend the Thursday-night meetings, the closest Lawrence came to realizing his dream of a lecture series. The magazine came out only three times, in October and November. Katherine Mansfield, as Matilda Berry, wrote some fictional pieces for it, Murry turned out a three-part autobiographical speculation ('There Was a Little Man . . . '), and Lawrence spread his contribution, 'The Crown', over the three numbers.

This essay may have been a restatement of the 'philosophy' Lawrence referred to in letters to Russell and Lady Ottoline earlier in the year. Certainly it embodied Lawrence's deepest thought at the time, and it is a commentary on *The Rainbow,* which appeared on September 30. Lawrence later said that his 'philosophical' writings derived from his imaginative work, rather than vice versa: 'The novels and poems come unwatched out of one's pen. And then the absolute need which one has for some sort of satisfactory mental attitude towards oneself and things in general makes one try to abstract some definite conclusions from one's experience as a writer and as a man.'

In 'The Crown' Lawrence made his first important explanations of one of his symbolic uses of darkness, which here stood for the flesh, the senses, in their perennial war with the spirit. Light and dark were the lion and the unicorn fighting for the crown, symbol of the consummated true self. The iris, or rainbow, also symbolized this true self, which could be created only after the individual had fulfilled the possibilities of the warring extremes of his own nature, the suffering that came from the dark side and the joy that came from the light. None of this was new, as philosophy; the images were merely different. As philosophy, 'The Crown' is the essay of an inspired amateur philosopher, valuable chiefly as a denotative footnote to *The Rainbow.*

Bertrand Russell provided an interesting account of the *Signature* people in a July 1915 letter to Ottoline Morrell, in which he told of being taken by Lawrence 'to see a Russian Jew, Kotiliansky [*sic*], Murry and Mrs Murry—they were all sitting together in a bare office high up next door to the Holborn Restaurant, with the windows shut, smoking Russian cigarettes without a moment's intermission, idle and cynical.' Russell regarded Murry as *'beastly',* and they were all in a 'dead' and 'putrefying' atmosphere. Afterwards, they went to the zoo, where Russell found 'much cynical satisfaction' in the baboon's obvious hatred and disgust of the group, apparently not realizing that the animal's antagonism might also have extended to Russell himself.

He further reported to Lady Ottoline that he went with Lawrence up to Hampstead, where he and Frieda were staying with Dollie Radford. Russell, who was extremely tired, told Lawrence that they 'ought to be independent of each other, at any rate at first, and not try to start a school. Lawrence seemed 'wild' when he discussed politics, and told Russell that truths were more important than facts: 'His attitude is a little mad and not quite honest, or at least very muddled.'

Russell wrote to Lady Ottoline again, a few days later, after having dined with T. S. Eliot ('my Harvard pupil') and his wife. He again mentioned Lawrence to Ottoline Morrell; the day he had spent with him was 'horrid': 'Lawrence is very like Shelley—just as fine, but with a similar impatience of fact.' Lawrence's 'psychology of people is amazingly good up to a point, but at a certain point he gets misled by love of violent colouring.' Russell found that his former 'pupil', Eliot, was like a New England painter, Miss Sands, a friend of Henry James. Eliot, obviously 'ashamed of his marriage', is 'exquisite and listless.' It was certainly a bad time for Russell, when everything seemed wrong.

A few weeks before *The Rainbow* appeared, and during this time of *Signature* activity, Lawrence and Frieda witnessed the first big Zeppelin attack on London, which prefigured the end of the England which John of Gaunt had seen as a moated fortress of safety. On the night of September 8, 1915, when Commander Heinrich Mathy in his new *L-13* led the Zeppelins in, Lawrence and Frieda walked across Hampstead Heath as guns boomed below and searchlights raked the sky, and a fire burned far off, in the City. Lawrence the next day wrote to Ottoline Morrell that the raid had been a Miltonic 'war in heaven', though 'it was not angels'. He saw the Zeppelin as 'a long-ovate, gleaming central luminary, calm and drifting in a glow of light, like a new moon, with its light bursting in flashes on the earth, to burst away the earth also. So it is the end—our world is gone, and we are like dust in the air.'

This impromptu description and reaction, expressed in the hasty informality of a letter, was Lawrence's unconscious preparation for the passage he wrote in *Kangaroo* seven years later, a passage that stands above all modern writing on air raids. In that novel, Somers and his German wife see the Zeppelin 'high, high, tiny, pale, as one might imagine the Holy Ghost, far, far, above. And the crashes of the guns, and the awful hoarseness of shells bursting near the city. Then gradually, quiet. And from Parliament Hill, a great red glare below, near St Paul's.' Harriet Somers says, 'Think, some of the boys I played with when I was a child are probably in it.' Somers, looking 'up at the far, luminous thing, like a moon,' wonders whether there could be men in it, 'just men, with two vulnerable legs and warm mouths. The imagination could not go so far.'

Lawrence, whose recollections of that autumn of 1915 were embittered by the suppression of *The Rainbow,* said later that this was the season in which the trouble really began, for him and for all sensitive men who might want to resist the popular compulsions. 'In 1915 the old world ended,' and that winter 'the spirit of the old London collapsed,' to become 'a vortex of broken passions, lusts, hopes, fears, and horrors' under 'the reign of that bloated ignominy, *John Bull*'. A letter to Cynthia Asquith, written before *John Bull* screamed against *The Rainbow,* shows that Lawrence disliked that chauvinistic newspaper for its own sake and not as a matter of grudge. After the war, he said that no man who had lived with his consciousness awake during that reign of *John Bull* could 'believe again absolutely in democracy.' A people who helped that newspaper to thrive was not a people capable of governing itself.

Many of the other sensitive literary men of Europe refused, like Lawrence, to support the war effort of their own countries; authors such as Romain Rolland in France and Heinrich Mann in Germany. In England, most of the imaginative writers had at once rushed into uniform, or government bureaus, or espionage; among them, Lawrence's anti-war stand was almost unique, though never so widely known as the versified pacifism that such poets as Siegfried Sassoon were mailing back home from the trenches, a pacifism people tended to think of as merely a hysterical overflow of heroism. To officials, and to officious patriots, Lawrence soon became a man who, physically unfit for military service, was dangerous to have behind one's lines; among other perils, he had an alien wife.

In the group of English intellectuals who didn't write novels and poems—the essayists and philosophers and journalists who made up the Bloomsbury group, for example—there were many genuine conscientious objectors. But most of them were not properly registered, for they tended to be irreligious and consequently didn't belong to sects whose creeds opposed killing. John Maynard Keynes, who agreed with his friends that war was a barbaric way of settling international disputes, nevertheless worked for the government ('There is really no practicable alternative'); after his friends with pacifist convictions had been haled before unsympathetic tribunals, Keynes would try to restore their shaking nerves with dinner parties at the Café Royal. One of these friends, Lytton Strachey, used to ask, 'What difference would it make if the Germans *were* here?'

Keynes's biographer, Sir Roy Harrod, has pointed out the superficiality, the lack of historical wisdom, in such a view; for even if the differences between German and English political organizations

didn't seem worth a bloody war then, to these Bloomsbury pacifists, they blundered in not taking into consideration 'the roots and
probable development' of such systems as the German. If Strachey
had been alive during World War II, Harrod says, he would have
sounded far less plausible asking, 'What difference would it make if
Hitler *were* here?'

Harrod has suggested that much of what was wrong in the reasoning and behavior of the Cambridge-Bloomsbury group stemmed from
the teaching of their idol—whom, it will be remembered, Lawrence
particularly detested—G. E. Moore. His *Principia Ethica,* Harrod
says, was 'sadly . . . lacking in any adequate theory of moral obligation . . . It is still for the future to decide whether it was right to be a
Conscientious Objector in the First World War, but it is clear that
under Moore's guidance one might easily go wrong.' And Keynes, in
his essay 'My Early Beliefs', also projected doubts of G. E. Moore
and his teaching, and in this connection noted that Lawrence was
correct in observing that 'we lacked reverence'.

Lawrence's personal brand of antagonism to the war intensified
his desire to leave England. He and Frieda now planned to settle in
Florida, and other Rananim colonists could join them later. While
they were waiting for their passports—Cynthia Asquith's influence
apparently helped overcome Frieda's 'born in Metz' notation—the
trouble over *The Rainbow* broke out, five weeks after publication of
the book.

*

In his letter of March 2 to Viola Meynell, Lawrence had complained
because he had to prepare an announcement for Methuen's catalogue.
A later editor of Methuen and Company, John Cullen, said [in a letter
of March 4, 1953], 'We have no record of whether Lawrence wrote
the announcement himself, but it was—and still is—usual for the
author to draft the "blurb", and for the editors to make any alterations which seem necessary.' In the description of *The Rainbow* in
the Methuen announcements 'for the Second Half of the Year 1915',
a phrase at the beginning—'by one of the most remarkable of the
younger school of novelists'—was evidently not written by Lawrence,
but the rest of the description possibly was, with perhaps some
editorial interpolation. In any event, it must have had Lawrence's
approval; it has the value of a commentary on *The Rainbow* by the
author: 'A history of the Brangwen character through its developing

crises of love, religion, and social passion, from the time when Tom Brangwen, the well-to-do Derbyshire farmer, marries a Polish lady, widow of an exile in England, to the moment when Ursula, his granddaughter, the leading-shoot of the restless, fearless family, stands waiting at the advance post of our time to blaze a path into the future.'

The reviewers, however, cared nothing about paths being blazed into the future. They fell back on the standards of the Victorian past when judging the book, and most of them found it in every way bad. Gerald Gould, one of the few critics who didn't consider the book indecent ('The most improper thing about it is the punctuation'), nevertheless said, in the *New Statesman,* that it was 'just bad —dull, monotonous, pointless'. But most of the attacks were from a moral base. To the Meynells' friend Robert Lynd (in the *Daily News*), the novel was 'a monstrous wilderness of phallicism'. In the *Sphere,* Clement Shorter invoked the days when Henry Vizetelly was put in jail for publishing Émile Zola in England: 'But Zola's novels are child's food compared with the strong meat contained in an English story that I have just read—*The Rainbow,* by D. H. Lawrence.' Shorter wondered whether the firm of Methuen had actually read the book before publishing it, for it was 'an orgy of sexiness' that omitted 'no form of viciousness, of suggestiveness'. Yet, as Richard Aldington pointed out years afterwards, this novel was 'the product of a long patience' and 'of concentrated writing and rewriting'. He added that 'no man, merely wishing to write a pornographic book, would dream of wasting so much time and energy.'

Such considerations were perhaps not uppermost in the consciousness of Detective-Inspector Albert Draper of Scotland Yard when, on November 3, he arranged to have more than a thousand copies seized at the publisher's and the printer's. Arguments against the book were scheduled to be heard at Bow Street Police Court on November 13.

The publishers hadn't notified Lawrence of this; he heard of it through friends. On November 6 he wrote to Pinker, cursing the meddlers but saying he was 'not very much moved'; later in the day, however, he sent another letter to Pinker, saying that 'on second thoughts' he wanted to discuss the matter after all; on the following Monday (the eighth) he was going to Garsington, but on the way to Paddington Station would stop in at Pinker's office: 'We must do something about this suppression business. I must move a body of people, we must get it reversed.' Lawrence apparently confused seizure with suppression, as in a letter to Lady Cynthia Asquith, dated only 'Tuesday', from Garsington, and apparently written on the ninth; Lawrence again spoke of possible reversal of a decision that had not yet been made.

In that same letter, he thanked Lady Cynthia for her help with the passports, which had arrived. He dreaded leaving England with its 'falling, perishing, crumbling past, so great, so magnificent', yet: 'My life is ended here. I must go as a seed that falls into new ground.' On the eleventh, after his return to London, he wrote to tell Lady Cynthia that he and Frieda planned to sail from Liverpool on the twenty-fourth, second class, on the White Star steamer *Adriatic*. He dropped some suggestions that she might join them in America, rescuing her children from the decomposing life of England, which her husband should have left long ago—but perhaps her husband was already defeated. 'Remember you keep the choice of life, for yourself and your children, and probably your husband, always in your hands: *don't* ever relinquish it up.'

This was, perhaps unconsciously, and without unfaithfulness to Frieda, a kind of love letter. Lawrence restated the situation imaginatively in his story 'The Thimble', written at about this time and based partly on the circumstance of the younger Herbert Asquith's convalescent leave after he was slightly wounded; in another version of the story a few years afterwards, 'The Ladybird', the British husband who fails to perceive the essential reality of his wife loses her to a Lawrence-like, mystic, Czech nobleman.

In a letter of February 19, 1915, Lawrence had told Barbara Low that Lady Cynthia wearied him 'a bit'. But he later had a change of mind—or heart—and he wrote to her some of his most intense letters in the blackest time of the war. And Cynthia Asquith's friends considered a romance between her and Lawrence possible. In her diary entry for February 18, 1916, she recorded what one of her friends said: 'She told me that she had nearly asked Viola Meynell, but hearing her young man (D. H. Lawrence) was passionately in love with me she had thought better of it.' Lady Cynthia added, 'What enormous leaps to conclusions people do take!' On December 19, 1917, she noted: 'I taxed mamma with having thought I was in love with D. H. Lawrence two years ago.'

In the letter of November 11, 1915, to Cynthia Asquith, Lawrence said he hoped she would go and stay with Ottoline Morrell and bring her some cheer; Lady Ottoline was 'like an old tragic queen who knows that her life has been spent in conflict with a kingdom that was not worth her life'; she was 'something like Queen Elizabeth, at the end.' Frieda, who had not accompanied Lawrence to Garsington on this last visit, used to say to herself, when not feeling bitter over this new friendship, 'Perhaps I ought to leave Lawrence to her influence; what might they not do together for England? I am powerless, and a Hun, and a nobody.'

The collier's son who had not been welcome at Lamb Close, except on the annual charity-party basis, was now frequently an honored guest at a far more distinguished country house, where he met people of the highest intellectual and social standing in the realm; indeed, his hostess at Garsington was of greater impress even in his native region than the Barbers of Greasley. Born Ottoline Violet Anne Cavendish-Bentinck, she was the daughter of a lieutenant general, the Duke of Portland, and his second wife, the Baroness Bolsover. The name Bolsover occurs from time to time in references to the Midlands in Lawrence's writings, for Bolsover is close to Eastwood; it is the Cavendish-Bentinck family seat, a ruined castle among the collieries. Lady Ottoline was born quite near there, at Welbeck, amid the Dukeries, in 1873. At twenty-nine she had married a commoner and, kicking away the gyves of her traditional upbringing, entered the Bohemian-intellectual world of Cambridge-Bloomsbury, though without altogether giving up her birthright. In 1938 Virginia Woolf noted in her diary that Ottoline Morrell's funeral brought out not only her literary friends but also a 'vast brown mass of respectable old South Kensington ladies'.

To many people, Lady Ottoline seemed a grotesque; her closest friends excused her as an eccentric. One of them, Lord David Cecil, described her in the *Dictionary of National Biography* as 'a character of Elizabethan extravagance and force, at once mystical and possessive, quixotic, and tempestuous'. Osbert Sitwell reported that she looked like 'a rather over-size Infanta of Spain or Austria'. Lawrence, in 1929, when he and Lady Ottoline were repairing their broken friendship, wrote to her: 'Yes, I remember your coming to Sussex [Greatham]—stepping out of an old four-wheeler in all your pearls, and a purple velvet frock—and going across the meadows to the other cottages at Greatham. It is a pity something [Lawrence's lampooning portrait of her in *Women in Love!*] came across it all and prevented us keeping a nice harmony.'

George Santayana, arriving at Garsington, had discovered his hostess in yellow stockings cross-gartered like Malvolio's. Siegfried Sassoon in 1916 found Lady Ottoline heavily powdered and painted, with purple hair, and wondered why she tried to look like 'a sort of modern Messalina'. In the 1930s, Stephen Spender used to see her going through the streets of Bloomsbury carrying a shepherdess's crook with several Pekinese dogs attached to it by ribbons; and she was astonished that passers-by looked at her curiously. She told Spender, on learning he was a socialist, that she sympathized with the workers and was even willing to love them, if only they would not 'stare so'.

However satiric some of these sketches may be, they lack the cruelty of Lawrence's picture of Ottoline Morrell as Hermione Roddice in *Women in Love*. He describes her early in the novel: 'People were silent when she passed, impressed, aroused, wanting to jeer, yet for some reason silenced. Her long, pale face, that she carried lifted up, somewhat in the Rossetti fashion, seemed almost drugged, as if a strange mass of thoughts coiled in the darkness within, and she was never allowed to escape.'

And the actions she is shown performing are often unkinder than any of the descriptions of her. This was Lawrence's choice for the queen of Rananim, as he saw her in 1916, only a year after he made that choice. But in 1915 they were friendly; she and her husband gave the Lawrences thirty pounds towards the American trip and persuaded Bernard Shaw to add five more (Edward Marsh, asked for ten pounds, lent twenty, and Pinker advanced further funds). When Lawrence left Garsington on November 11, Lady Ottoline presented him with a pair of Hessian boots, tactfully adding an armful of flowers for Frieda and a promise of some embroidery for wall decoration.

Lawrence arrived in London two days before the prosecution of *The Rainbow*, but whether or not he sat in the courtroom, no one has yet recorded; he probably wasn't there. The publisher had been ordered to show cause why an order to destroy 245 bound copies and 760 unbound copies of Lawrence's novel should not be carried out. Lawrence called this 'a ridiculous affair, instigated by the National Purity League, Dr. Horton and Co., noncomformity'—apparently a reference to a conspicuous divine, Robert Forman Horton (1855–1934), who belonged not only to the Lawrence family's church, the Congregational, but also to the parish in which Lawrence was then living, Hampstead.

At Bow Street the Purity legion mounted its attack behind the solicitor Herbert G. Muskett, a literary critic without credentials who appeared 'for the Commissioner of Police'. Muskett gave himself the pleasure of reading aloud the unfavorable reviews and of adding his own opinion that the book was 'a mass of obscenity of thought, idea, and action throughout'. The publishers said that at their request Lawrence twice made deletions in the manuscript and then refused to cooperate further; they regretted that they had not examined the text more carefully, and they apologized for having published the book. The examining magistrate, Sir John Dickinson, mingled his regrets with theirs and added that the book should have been withdrawn after those notable censors, the reviewers, had attacked it. The register of the Bow Street Magistrates' Court shows that Sir John's decision against *The Rainbow* was: 'Order to be destroyed at expiration of 7 days (in the interim to be impounded) if no appeal—10 Guineas costs.'

'The real reason for the attack' on Lawrence and *The Rainbow,* Richard Aldington wrote in 1931, 'was that he denounced war. . . . They can say what they like about "obscenity".' He repeated this in his autobiography in 1941, and in a letter in 1952 he explained further: 'The statement was made by Lawrence himself and I heard it discussed in 1915 "as a fact" by such sympathizers as May Sinclair.' And Gilbert Cannan, in an article in the New York *Herald* in 1920, blamed the suppression of *The Rainbow* on 'a confusion of mind, aggravated possibly by the hysteria due to war conditions'.

That autumn of 1915 was the season not only of the first big Zeppelin raids but also of the military failure at Gallipoli, where Winston Churchill, then First Lord of the Admiralty, had tried without success to establish a second front in the east. Indeed, the news of Churchill's resignation from Asquith's cabinet broke on the day *The Rainbow* went to court, the day on which a noted literary figure, Augustine Birrell, then Chief Secretary for Ireland, said in a speech at Bristol that 'he for one would forbid the use, during the war, of poetry.'

In that day's news, 'Recruiting Problems' struck another ominous note: not enough unmarried men had volunteered, and now Lord Derby threatened conscription. It was at this time that an advertising expert, Sir Hedley le Bas, undertook the improvement of recruiting by attacks through the sense of guilt, so easy to touch in those days: posters screamed at the women, 'Is your "best boy" wearing Khaki? . . . If your young man neglects his duty to his King and Country, the time may come when he will NEGLECT YOU!' That autumn, too, as the *Official History* of the war points out, Joffre and Haig had lost the futile offensive which 'had not improved the general situation in any way and had brought nothing but useless slaughter of infantry.' It was certainly the wrong season for a novel in which an intense Ursula Brangwen made fun of her 'best boy' for taking warfare seriously: 'I hate soldiers, they are stiff and wooden.'

Commenting on the suppression of *The Rainbow,* the Commissioner of Police at New Scotland Yard stated (1953), 'The proceedings in 1915 were solely on the grounds of obscenity.' He did not, however, produce records of the entire case, though these of course might not precisely show how the prosecution slyly worked in the idea that *The Rainbow* hampered recruiting.

Journalists at the time made somewhat similar suggestions, as when the *New Statesman* on November 20 carried an article by J. C. Squire, who, as Solomon Eagle, wondered whether Lawrence were 'under the spell of German psychologists'. In the *Athenaeum* of the same date, a writer on popular-science subjects, George William de Tunzelmann, suggested that *The Rainbow* reflected German 'materialistic pseudophilosophy', the acceptance of which was responsible for 'many of the humiliating weaknesses which have so hampered our action against Germany'. The 'de' Tunzelmann who throughout his accusation connected *The Rainbow* with Teutonic absorption in the materialistic, was perhaps reacting against his own Germanic background: his actual name was Georg Wilhelm von Tunzelmann. Whether or not his statements helped the cause of British arms, they certainly helped to damage Lawrence, who, too ill for employment, was now left with little chance to make a living by his pen; for with the double stigma on him of obscenity and pro-Germanism (the latter intensified by the presence of an alien wife), he became anything but an appealing figure to most editors and publishers.

A few of Lawrence's friends and even some strangers tried to defend him from the charges against him. Catherine Carswell reviewed *The Rainbow* favorably for the *Glasgow Herald,* which thereupon dropped this contributor of ten years' standing. John Drinkwater, in a personal call at Byron Villas. and Sir Oliver Lodge, in a letter, expressed sympathy, but privately. Lawrence recalled later that Arnold Bennett and May Sinclair raised 'a kindly protest'; Rupert Hart-Davis says in his book on Hugh Walpole that Walpole 'joined in a letter of protest against the suppression'; even citizens of Bloomsbury who didn't altogether approve of Lawrence supported him now, and the Society of Authors promised to help, but ultimately did nothing.

The only attempt at positive action was by Philip Morrell, whose wife Ottoline hadn't yet been lampooned by Lawrence in *Women in Love*. On November 18 and December 1 Morrell raised questions in Parliament, but he was blandly answered each time by the Home Secretary, Sir John Simon, then rehearsing for the appeasement tactics with which he was to meet foreign aggressors in the 1930s. The police action, he said, was routine, and the publishers, who were after all 'the owners of what was seized', agreed with the judgment against the book. Sir John ended the proceedings of November 18 when, in answer to a question by an Irish member as to whether or not there was an official censor, he said there was none, and: 'I hope there never will be one in literary matters.' Certainly one wasn't needed when uncomfortable books could be so easily kicked out of the way.

Morrell's question of December 1 probed the very legality of the suppression, but Sir John Simon, who said he felt that Lawrence had not been treated unjustly, explained that 'the provisions of the law were strictly complied with.' He did, however, suggest that Lawrence could 'have another copy seized by arrangement, in order that he might defend the book.' After further hints by Liberal and Irish members that there had been a political as well as a moral censorship in the proceedings, the debate sputtered out. Sir John Simon explained that the action against the novel had been taken under Lord Campbell's Obscene Publications Act. This dated from 1857.

The researches of Émile Delavenay have brought some interesting material to light in relation to the legal background of the trouble over *The Rainbow*. He notes that all the facts haven't been made public, 'as distinct from the police-court action', although 'enough is now established to suggest that this was no ordinary obscenity police-court case and that whoever initiated it intended to bring it to the attention of the public in no uncertain fashion.' On November 15, the publishers told the secretary of the Society of Authors, 'The solicitors, in consideration of the reputation of our firm, kindly suggested that we might prefer to hand over the books rather than submit to actual search.' Professor Delavenay believes that the solicitors mentioned in that letter were not the publishers' but Scotland Yard's, Messrs. Wontner and Sons, whose senior partner was the already-mentioned Herbert G. Muskett.

Another letter from Methuen's to the Society of Authors says that the publishers turned all available copies of *The Rainbow* over to Detective-Inspector Draper, who told them that the case would not be heard in open court. Hence they didn't arrange for a legal defense and were astonished when the proceedings took place in public. The case against *The Rainbow* greatly embarrassed Methuen's, who hoped that Lawrence and his agent, Pinker, wouldn't appeal the magistrate's verdict. The publishers also dissuaded Clive Bell—as noted earlier, Bloomsbury was mostly on the side of *The Rainbow* in this matter—from writing on Lawrence's behalf.

Alexander Methuen, who was to become a baronet in 1916, was discussed by Lawrence in his 1925 foreword to the first volume of E. D. McDonald's bibliographies of Lawrence: 'Methuen published that book, and he almost wept before the magistrate when he was summoned for bringing out a piece of indecent literature. He said he did not know the dirty thing he had been handling, his reader had misadvised him—and Peccavi! Peccavi! wept the now be-knighted gentleman.' Lawrence added: 'There is no more indecency or impropriety than there is in this autumn morning . . .'

At least one of Lawrence's political friends (Philip Morrell) had tried to help him, while the literary world remained fairly quiescent, except for Clive Bell's aborted defense. Perhaps its opinion was best explained in a letter to Pinker from John Galsworthy, then the reigning Pooh-Bah of English literature and a man of supposedly liberal opinions. Galsworthy's letter, first published in Keith Sagar's *The Art of D. H. Lawrence,* is harsher in its judgments than the one he wrote to Pinker about *Sons and Lovers* (published in H. V. Marrot's biography of Galsworthy). In 1915 Galsworthy could feel that he was looking down on Lawrence from a height, and with horror. Meeting him two years later, Galsworthy condescended to note him down in his journal as 'that provincial genius. Interesting, but a type I could not get along with.' Galsworthy was original in at least one respect: he found Lawrence's eyes, so lively to everyone else, 'dead'. Lawrence recalled in 1925 that Galsworthy had told him, 'very calmly and *ex cathedra*', that *The Rainbow* was 'a failure as a work of art'. Lawrence observed, 'Impromptu opinions by elderly authors are apt to damage him who gives as much as him who takes.'

The opposition of Lawrence and Galsworthy somewhat resembles the principal plot in Galsworthy's play *The Skin Game* (1920), in which a gentleman and a *nouveau riche* character morally destroy themselves and their families as the man of high birth and the one of low birth come into conflict. The latter misbehaves in a vulgar way, but the drama suggests that all might be fairly well if the gentleman had known how to be tolerant and kind. Galsworthy's outraged and foolish letter to Pinker is a monument of nastiness. Lawrence had the last word, however, in his 1928 essay on Galsworthy. But that lies in the future.

The false hope that some other members of the literary world held out to Lawrence after the trouble over *The Rainbow* caused him to cancel his passage to America; on November 17, a week before he was to sail, Lawrence told Russell that, although he wanted to leave, he had decided to stay because the Society of Authors had told him the day before that they would fight for *The Rainbow* because he had not been given a chance to defend it. But nothing came of this. Lawrence was planning once again to go to America and asked Donald Carswell to try to find passage for him on a cargo ship. On the morning of November 29, when he was en route to Garsington, this time with Frieda, Lawrence stopped at the Carswells' and, not finding them at home, left a note—'I call to see if you know anything about the ship. Let me know at once, will you?' He inquired again from Garsington, where he and the other guests romped with the children, wrapped in colored cloths 'like an Eastern bazaar'—a *Mr. Britling*-like episode Lawrence adapted for his Breadalby (Garsington) sequence in *Women in Love*.

Russell was at Garsington during the Lawrences' visit there; the guests also included a descendant of Mahomet named Suhrawady who for a while promised to lend an Oriental touch to the next Rananim; and 'a young musician', probably Philip Heseltine, who had met Lawrence two weeks before. Heseltine, later to compose music under the name Peter Warlock, had written to his mentor, Frederick Delius, that Lawrence ('perhaps the one great literary genius of his generation') was ill and intending to go to America: could Lawrence and Frieda live on Delius's citrus plantation near Jacksonville, Florida?

Delius, answering from the Continent, poured onto this dream of Hesperides a cold northern drizzle of negation. He admired Lawrence's work but felt that California would be healthier and less expensive; Florida would be 'disastrous' for Lawrence's health, though what could have been more disastrous than the twenty-two agitated months in Cornwall that were to follow is hard to imagine. But perhaps Delius had no wish to let the priest of love take over the plantation that stood in the jungle, with warping shutters and col-

lapsing roofs, like a symbol of the broken, lost love of one's youth—
in Delius's case the quadroon girl Chloë, in search of whom, on a
later visit, he had combed the Florida swamps.

So the supreme English composer of his time did not help the
supreme English author. As friends of Heseltine's, they might have
met; two men so notably 'difficult' would perhaps have quarreled,
though Delius had shown that he could get along with artists as thorny
as August Strindberg and Paul Gauguin; but Lawrence never really
knew a 'difficult' genius of the stature of Delius, or of Strindberg, or
of Gauguin. His highest-ranking friend among the illustrious authors of his time was to be, in the late 1920s, a calm-tempered
young man named Aldous Huxley, whom Lawrence met for the first
time in that autumn of 1915, in London.

Huxley, who later described himself as having been, at twenty-
one, 'an intellectually cautious young man, not at all inclined to en-
thusiasms', had never met, even in his own famous literary family,
anyone like Lawrence, who 'startled and embarrassed' him with his
direct sincerity. Huxley agreed to accompany the Lawrences to a
Florida Rananim, though later he was glad the scheme hadn't materialized, because 'cities of God have always crumbled.'

Huxley wrote to his brother Julian in December 1915 to say that
he felt Lawrence was 'a good man', even 'a great man', who was
planning to establish a utopian colony in Florida 'with one Armenian,
one German wife and, problematically, one young woman called
Dorothy Warren.' (This was the niece of Lady Ottoline Morrell and
the goddaughter of Henry James, years later to hold an exhibition of
Lawrence's paintings in her Mayfair gallery.) Aldous Huxley was
tempted to go to Florida, if only for a visit, to see how people
awaited 'a sort of Pentecostal inspiration of new life'. But in 1920
Aldous Huxley wrote to his father to tell him the latest story about
Lawrence, 'the slightly insane novelist', whose mind was a tangle of
'dark and tufty' complexes which, discovered by a psychoanalyst,
took away not only 'his slight sexual mania' but all of his writing
talent. (The psychoanalytic reference is preposterous, but Lawrence
may have learned that such rumors were afloat, for he makes a jest-
ing allusion to such matters in relation to the autobiographical character Rawdon Lilly in his 1921 novel, *Aaron's Rod*.) Huxley made
fun of Lawrence through the character of Kingham in the title story
of *Two or Three Graces* (1926), but when he met Lawrence again
in the later 1920s, he once more liked and admired him, and wrote of
him friendlily.

In the December 1915 letter to his brother Julian, Aldous Huxley mentioned the Armenian who was one of the potential members of Lawrence's Rananim. This was Dikrān Kouyoumdjian who, as Michael Arlen, was to write the facile, best-selling novel of 1924, *The Green Hat*. A more permanent convert of this season was the Honorable Dorothy Brett, known in the Lawrencean entourage as Brett, or the Brett. Daughter of Viscount Esher and sister of the Ranee of Sarawak, Dorothy Brett was, like her friend Ottoline Morrell, an escaped aristocrat; Brett was ahead of the fashion, even in London Bohemian circles, in having bobbed hair (like Katherine Mansfield) and in wearing trousers.

A painter, deaf and shy, Brett was terrified of meeting Lawrence. When she made her first visit to Byron Villas, she had Mark Gertler as escort. She saw 'a large woman'—Frieda—'and a little man who scuttles out as we come in, Murry.' The red-bearded Lawrence, 'very upright' in a chair, spoke in a high, mischievous voice into her ear trumpet, jeering at their friend Lady Ottoline. Brett, learning that the Lawrences planned to leave England, gave a farewell party for them at her studio on the Earls Court Road, a few days after this first meeting. The party was turned into a rout by the invasion of some two dozen uninvited guests who brought bottles and mischief.

Brett remembered that strange women were carried across the polished floor, Katherine Mansfield sat on the sofa 'in some man's arms', Gertler and his girl friend Dorothy (Dora) Carrington (who preferred to be called just Carrington; she had studied art with Brett at the Slade) staged one of their quarrels, Lawrence chatted in Italian with Viola Tree, Brett played the pianola violently, and 'a very amiable, completely drunk Murry' had to be propped against the wall—indeed, it all seemed pre-war. Two nights later Brett gave another party for the same invited guests, keeping this a secret from others. In the inevitable charades, Lawrence trotted around the room pretending to be on a bicycle, his voice crying out the ting-a-ling of the bell as he ran into everyone in his way.

Farewell parties were, however, a meaningless exercise, for the Lawrences didn't leave England, although they kept their eyes for some time on Florida. On November 28 Lawrence told Cynthia Asquith that he had now decided to go to a place on the other side of that peninsula from Delius's property: Fort Myers, near the Gulf Coast, 'a little town (5,000) half negro—9 miles from the sea, on a wide river 1½ miles wide—backed by orange groves and pine forests', all on the property of American friends.

Donald Carswell arranged passage for Lawrence and Frieda on a tramp steamer leaving Glasgow on December 20 for the West Indies, and although Lawrence must have liked the name of the ship, *Crown de Leon*—for his 'Crown' essay had used the crown the lion was fighting for as a symbol of integration—again he and Frieda delayed their leaving. Lawrence told Russell, a few days after the *Crown de Leon* had sailed, that they hadn't gone because complications of money and war had held up the departure of some of the young recruits for the Fort Myers Rananim. Once more there was talk of starting 'life in a new spirit'; this time Russell was invited to 'come and be president of us.'

Murry, who had refused to be drawn into the Florida scheme, called on J. D. Beresford on December 19 and arranged for the novelist to lend the Lawrences his house in Cornwall for a few months. Murry had been in southern France with Katherine Mansfield, then grieving over the recent accidental death of her brother, Leslie, behind the lines on the Western Front; Murry, unable to compete in her affections with the dead brother, had returned to London. On the same day as his interview with Beresford, Katherine had located the Villa Pauline at Bandol, and soon her letters drew Murry there.

Lawrence, who had discovered that he could make no more plans for leaving the country unless he had a military exemption, had reported on December 11 for medical examination at Battersea Town Hall. When, after two hours of waiting in a queue, he came to the table where his name would be written down, he suddenly felt that his presence there was 'utter travesty of action': he abruptly turned 'and went across the hall away from all the underworld of this spectral submission, and after a while saw the fugitive sunshine across the river on the spectral towers at Westminster.' It was the last time he would be able to break away so easily from a military-enrollment queue.

On December 16 Lawrence wrote to Pinker, saying he was in bed with a severe cold and wondering 'why one should ever trouble to get up, into this filthy world. The war stinks worse and worse.' He was 'very anxious to see' the edition of *The Rainbow* that B. W. Huebsch was publishing in America: 'I shall hate it if they have mutilated it.' Pinker must have sent him a copy of this book at once, for Lawrence replied in a letter dated only 'Saturday', which would have to be December 18, his last Saturday at Byron Villas:

The omissions from the American *Rainbow* are not very
many. *Methuen edition*
  p. 220: lines 20–24 (3 lines)
       (He wished he were a cat . . . her flesh)
  p. 300: line 18 (let me come—let me come)
  p. 318: lines 7–10 (4 lines)
       (Ursula lay still . . . about her mistress)
  p. 425: lines 4–26 (24 lines)
       (But the air was cold . . . always laughing)
  p. 446: lines 10–40 (30 lines)
       (She let him take her . . . house felt to her)
They are not many: yet they make me sad and angry. If we
buy sheets from America to bind here, we ought to print these
pages and insert at the back, just saying: [']The following pages
from the Methuen edition are printed incomplete in the present
edition.'

We might also put a report of the process—the suppressions
—at the end of the book.

The excision on page 300 refers to a passage in which the words
Lawrence quoted in his letter are omitted after 'his soul groaning over
and over', as Skrebensky has an orgasm by frottage. The cut on page
318 took out three short paragraphs, in one of which Winifred Inger
says, 'I shall carry you into the water,' and the one which begins,
'After a while the rain came down on their flushed, hot limbs, startling, delicious.' In the Methuen version, the following material had
caused more trouble than anything else in the complaints against
the book itself:

  Ursula lay still in her mistress's arms, her forehead against
  the beloved, maddening breast.
  'I shall put you in,' said Winifred.
  But Ursula twined her body about her mistress.

The other excisions were of love scenes between Ursula and Skrebensky. At least one of them, following a sentence 'In passionate anger
she upbraided him because, not being man enough to satisfy one
woman, he hung around others', is extremely important for an understanding of the story:

  'Don't I satisfy you?' he asked of her, again going white to the
  throat.

'No,' she said. 'You've never satisfied me since the first week
in London. You never satisfy me now. What does it mean to
me, your having me—'

*

It was an embittered Lawrence who left Byron Villas at the winter
solstice. After a few days with friends in one of the northern suburbs,
he and Frieda went to Ada's, at Ripley, for Christmas. Frieda, he
noted about a week earlier, 'has seen her children once or twice, and
has almost ceased to fret.' But for him, the months in London had
been disastrous, what with the crushing of *The Rainbow,* the collapse
or at least weakening of several friendships, the prospect of continued
poverty, the ferocious patriotism of the time, and the persistence of
the war. In his letters of that period, Lawrence frequently saw London in the image of hell. The 1915 Christmas in the Midlands was
hardly more comfortable; Lawrence's older sister Emily was on hand,
too, her husband and Ada's both away at war; George Lawrence,
now an engineer in Nottingham, appeared also, to quarrel with his
brother over politics (he spoke of himself as 'a convinced Liberal')
and religion (he was what his brother called 'a radical nonconformist'). D. H. Lawrence could now see only a future of Guild Socialism
—a melancholy prospect, which to him meant a reduction of everything to the lowest terms. He looked forward to Cornwall and Florida,
where life could be aimed at the highest.

4 'A BARE, FORGOTTEN COUNTRY'

During the first part of his stay, Lawrence liked Cornwall, which he
then regarded merely as a stopping place on the way to Florida. Living in the large old farmhouse at Portcothan was 'like being at a
window and looking out of England to the beyond'—it was his 'first
move outwards, to a new life'. But soon the Cornish people, in
whom he had at first found a pleasant gentleness, began to disgust
him, particularly a local landlord named Hawken who boasted of
evicting an old woman from one of his houses. Hawken, 'mean and
stupidly cunning and base', was probably the inspiration for a portrait in *Kangaroo* some six years later: Jaz Trewhella, the sly little
Cornishman transplanted to Australia in that novel.

But on the bleak coast of Cornwall, not far from romantic Tintagel,
Lawrence felt happily removed from 'questioning and quibbling and

trying to do anything with the world. The world is gone, extinguished, like the lights of last night's Café Royal'—though alas! for his peace of mind, Lawrence brought some Café Royal lights along with him, the nervous Heseltine and the 'blatant' Kouyoumdjian-Arlen. At the end of his third week at Portcothan, Lawrence wrote Gertler (on January 20) a letter reporting, 'I've been laid up in bed again with a vile inflammatory cold. Now I am a mere rag, contemplating my latter end.' He went on:

> But it is better being in bed here, than in London. Here I can lie abed and watch the sea coming into the little cove, between the black rocks, and bursting in foam high over the yellow-brown cliffs. Which is a very great consolation.
>
> I like Cornwall, it is a bare, forgotten country that doesn't belong to England: Celtic, pre-Christian. There are very rough winds and very fine black rocks and very white bursting seas. And the house is big and silent and forsaken, looking down the lane at the bay.
>
> Kouyoumdjian is here and I don't care for him. He is going away in a few days. Heseltine is here, and I like him. At night we write a play, which is rather fun.

He was not sure how long he and Frieda would stay in Cornwall and hoped their next move would be 'out of England'. Word from the Murrys was that they were 'exceedingly happy' at Bandol: 'They have both found themselves, and each other, and the blessed sun also, at last. I am very glad.' He hoped the spring would blossom for Gertler and for Dorothy Carrington, whom Lawrence liked 'very much at the party. If you could only give yourself up in love, she would be much happier. You always want to dominate her, which is no good. One must learn to relinquish oneself, not to bother about oneself. You hold too closely to yourself, for her to be free to love you', words that suggest the struggle Birkin has with himself in *Women in Love*.

While convalescing, Lawrence corrected proofs of his travel book, *Twilight in Italy*, whose publication had been arranged (as *Italian Sketches*) by Duckworth's the preceding summer. Dr. Maitland Radford, son of Ernest and Dollie Radford—ardent Fabians—came from London to check Lawrence's health: he told his patient to keep warm, quiet, and peaceful. Lawrence had felt a numbness down his left side, and his left hand had been virtually useless. 'The stress on the nerves sets up a deferred inflammation in all the internal linings,' Lawrence reported to Cynthia Asquith on February 7, but 'all that fever and inflammation and madness' had nearly gone, and he could once again walk to the sea.

Frieda, who had been worried about his illness (which he blamed on 'soul-sickness after London and the state of things'), wrote to Russell inviting him for a visit: 'To me it would be such a help—I feel it such a responsibility—it's too much for me—He might just die because everything is too much for him—But he simply mustn't die—It's not as if [he scratched out] it concerned me alone—' She felt that Florida was 'the only solution,' and she resented the lid that had been put over 'all life.' Lawrence was full of ideas and wanted to write, but was too ill to do so.

He was, however, collecting some of his early poems in a volume, *Amores,* to be published later that year by Duckworth's. And on February 11 he wrote to Catherine Carswell about a new publishing scheme; he had thought he was dead, but was now 'beginning to feel strong again: life coming in at the unseen sources.' He and Heseltine hoped 'to publish any real thing that comes, for the truth's sake, and because a real book is a holy thing.'

They would publish by subscription, beginning with an inexpensive edition of *The Rainbow:* 'The thing is to be a crusade. . . . My dear Catherine, let us bring this off.' Mrs. Carswell could enlist the help of Ivy Low, now married to an employee of the publishing firm of Williams and Norgate—Maxim Harrison, alias of the underground Bolshevik, Maxim Litvinov.

Lawrence's new associate, Heseltine, had not yet translated himself into the hearty, bearded composer Peter Warlock; he was at this time an Eton-and-Oxford aesthete, with grandiose ideas, chewed nerves, and violent affections and antagonisms—the Halliday of *Women in Love.* He stayed in Cornwall two months, indulging in charades with the Lawrences. The play Lawrence mentioned in the letter to Gertler was a symbolic comedy 'about Heseltine and his puma'—a reference to the Soho artist's model whom Lawrence used for Halliday's mistress, the Pussum (as she appears in the early editions of *Women in Love;* her name was changed to Minette in later British editions).

Murry had originally suggested a publishing scheme to Lawrence; now Heseltine's activity along this line irritated Murry and Katherine Mansfield. Lawrence told them not 'to get into a state, you two, about nothing.' The friendship with Heseltine—now in London to make arrangements for printing—would not interfere with Lawrence's friendship with the Murrys. He begged them to be gentle with him, for he was again on the edge of collapse; they must all live together again, as 'co-believers'.

Meanwhile, Murry had written his first book, on Dostoevsky, before receiving Lawrence's violent reaction to his own rereading of the Russian novelist, whom he now saw as representing the perversion of spiritualized will. He told Lady Ottoline that he preferred the 'straight and above-board' Petronius, who was at least not guilty of foully 'mixing God and sadism'. The criticisms that Lawrence sent Murry didn't alter Murry's book; he and Katherine Mansfield were having their happiest time together, writing on opposite sides of a table; Katherine Mansfield now completed the first draft of *Prelude*. They were oblivious to the world without, although living in the country where the battle of Verdun was raging. But before long, Lawrence began to intrude on their happy isolation, urging them to join him and Frieda in Cornwall.

The Lawrences' time at Beresford's house was up at the end of February. Looking about for a new place, they decided to settle at Zennor; on February 25, writing to Catherine Carswell and assuring her once again that the world was 'foul', Lawrence said: 'The only thing to do is save oneself from it, and to build up a new world within one's soul. I felt, somehow, when we went to Zennor, that a new heaven and a new earth would take place. But to endure the cracking up of the old one is horrible.' Lawrence usually felt optimistic in new surroundings—for the first few days. In this letter to Mrs. Carswell, Rananim showed again: 'I believe, if we cannot discover a terrestrial America, there are new countries of the soul for us to land upon, virgin soil. . . . I think the Murrys will come later and live with us at Zennor. It is always my idea, that a few people by being together should bring to pass a new earth and a new heaven.' On March 4 he wrote to Gertler from the Tinners Arms at Zennor: 'We have been driven almost to Lands End, to get away from the vile people. The next step will be into the sea: or else we shall have to take wings like birds.' Frieda added a note to Gertler, implying that she approved of him as a loyal friend; the Murrys in their indignation over Heseltine's publishing scheme had accused Lawrence of treachery, and this made Frieda 'very wrathful, because they hated *The Rainbow,* and have never been loyal.'

As for Koteliansky, Gertler must tell him 'he is an old fraud, he always *pretends* he is a humble person, but in his heart he thinks he is very great.' The first real hint of trouble with another of Lawrence's friends appears here: Frieda reported that she was having 'ructions with the old Ottoline, she will say such *vile* things about me —And I think it's so mean, when she is rich and I am poor and people will take a mean advantage of one's poverty.' Still, such meanness didn't really worry Frieda, for she and Lawrence were now really happy and 'full of hope and good things, we will *not* be cheated of a good life, if we have got it in us to live one.'

On March 8 Lawrence announced to Gertler: 'We have taken a little cottage here, two good rooms, £5 a year. It is beautifully situated under the hills and above the sea. We shall furnish it and live there cheaply. . . . Our tiny cottage stands beside another, a big one, with seven rooms (it is really three cottages in one). I want Heseltine or the Murrys to take it (it is £16 a year). Think what a perfect little settlement we could be! It is all alone, just these cottages'—at Higher Tregerthen, on the St. Ives side of Zennor.

Lawrence's hopes in Heseltine were ill-founded. On that same day —when Lawrence was also writing to Murry that Heseltine 'is the only one we can all be friends with'—Heseltine wrote to the poet Robert Nichols, from London, that he had no intention of going back to Cornwall to see Lawrence, who had 'no real sympathy' and wanted only converts 'to his own reactionary creed'. Lawrence was 'a fine thinker and a consummate artist,' but personal relations with him were difficult. Heseltine told Delius, later, that 'the affair by which I found him out is too long to enter upon here'; Heseltine's biographer, Cecil Gray, writing after what he designated as Heseltine's suicide (1930), couldn't learn what the 1916 'affair' was, but surmised it concerned Lawrence's meddlesomeness.

Robert Nichols recalled that when the Lawrences were living in Hampstead in 1915, they tried at different times to get both him and Heseltine to marry a girl they knew, to the amusement of both young men and the girl. But the Heseltine-Lawrence trouble may have been caused by Ottoline Morrell's showing Heseltine a letter Lawrence wrote to her about two of Heseltine's girls.

In any event, Heseltine wrote to Lawrence accusing him of treachery, and Lawrence replied, 'I request that you do not talk about me in London.' Heseltine then sent him excerpts from imaginary reviews of a scandalous book on Lawrence by Heseltine; this, he gleefully reported to Delius, left Lawrence 'quite comically perturbed'. He might well have been: he was a serious artist already badly hurt by the public press, and these 'reviews' presaged many that were to come. But all this was comic to Heseltine, who was callow, maladjusted, and unhappy; and he had a barb of cruelty in him. He retained, however, a grudging respect for Lawrence, and within a year was back in his camp.

Another of Lawrence's friendships came to an end in the spring of 1916 and was never to be revived—that with Russell. Lawrence had written to him on February 11 asking whether his lectures were 'really a success, and really vital', and Russell had answered four days later out of deep misery: he once again contemplated suicide, and only pride and obstinacy, he told Lawrence, kept him going. He thought his lectures good, but they were having no vital effect; he was engulfed by trivialities.

Lawrence four days later wrote him another scolding letter, asking what was 'the good of living as you do, anyway?' He hoped that Russell would 'live for ever', yet when Russell made his will, would he please make Lawrence 'in some part' his heir, leave him 'enough to live on'?

About a month later, on March 19, Lawrence wrote again, hoping Russell was not 'still cross with me for being a schoolmaster and for not respecting the rights of man.' Russell must visit them at the new cottage: perhaps a 'jolly' new world was being born; he hoped soon 'to dance in the springtime'. He assured Russell, 'Nothing is born by taking thought,' which was precisely the wrong thing to tell, or try to tell, Russell.

Lawrence wrote to him once more, in the late summer, a letter which has apparently not been preserved: rather than assume the courtesy of answering it, Russell turned it over, with a note of his own, to Murry, who replied on September 3 (in a letter now in the British Museum). Murry thought Frieda was now completely triumphant, though insecure; Murry hoped that Lawrence didn't now turn on him and rend him. He regretted that Russell and Lawrence had broken off, for he thought that Russell was certainly the one man capable of giving Lawrence understanding and tolerance —an interesting misconception.

Long afterwards, Russell wrote that Lawrence at the time of their acquaintance 'could not be whole-heartedly patriotic, because his wife was German': the suggestion that if Lawrence didn't have a German wife he could have become 'whole-heartedly patriotic' reaches out to the limit of absurdity. Russell also said that 'Lawrence, though most people did not realize it, was his wife's mouthpiece. He had the eloquence, she had the ideas.' This statement shows that the noted logician Russell could indulge in wild misunderstandings.

Keynes's ideas of Russell's limitations have already been quoted; they were echoed in an article in 1952 by McEwan Lawson, who asked, 'May it be that Bertrand Russell, like other giants, has lived too much in one cave, that he has only had one eye, and consequently has missed those realms of reality which constitute the environment the human soul needs if it has to change and grow and make this world what it was meant to be?' And the posthumously published third volume of George Santayana's autobiography expresses a similar judgment (1952): Russell's information, though accurate and wide-ranging, 'was necessarily partial, and brought forward in a partisan argument; he couldn't know, he refused to consider, everything; so that his judgements, nominally based on that partial information, were really inspired by passionate prejudice, and were always unfair and sometimes mad.'

Santayana felt that although Russell was many-sided, he was 'a many-sided fanatic'. Santayana's final verdict was that, in failing to achieve his potential, 'Bertie petered out.' But he lasted long enough —after changing from pacifism to support of war measures, to belief in the efficacy of the atomic bomb, to distrust of it—to make one of his one-sided attacks on Lawrence, who had long before, and more permanently, 'caught' Russell, in the caricature of him as Sir Joshua Malleson, one of the minor figures in *Women in Love*. Sir Joshua (Mattheson, in the revised edition) is 'a learned, dry baronet of fifty, who was always making witticisms and laughing at them heartily, in a harsh horse-laugh'. His 'mental fibre was so tough as to be insentient.'

The Lawrence-Murry friendship was destined to last longer, though Lawrence's persuasiveness in uprooting the Murrys from their happiness at luminous Bandol and putting them down in stony gray Cornwall imposed a severe strain upon that friendship. Lawrence wrote coaxingly of the cottage adjoining his, which he called 'Katherine's tower'. The Murrys must come and live there; no more talk of treachery; they must learn to trust one another. 'No more quarrels and quibbles. Let it be agreed for ever. I am a *Blutbruder*; a *Blutbrüderschaft* between us all. Tell K. *not* to be so queasy.' But Katherine

Mansfield had lived in Cornwall, where she had seen a woman torturing a cat, and she knew the Cornish people; in a poem she had spoken of their eyes as 'stupid, shifty, small, and sly'. She wept when she and Murry left the sunshine of Villa Pauline. And the early April day when Lawrence met them at the St. Ives railway platform was not a day presaging confidence. The weather was cold, the sky dismal; gulls circled, crying bleakly. For Lawrence's sake the Murrys pretended to be happy, but they wanted to weep.

Lawrence, some of whose furniture had been sent on from London by Gertler, took Murry shopping for plain, cheap household equipment at Benny's salesroom in St. Ives. Lawrence had painted his own chairs and tables a bright blue, but Murry, with Katherine looking on approvingly and the Lawrences 'comically dismayed', painted his own furniture black. The Murrys, during their stay, never rose above that blackness. They found the Lawrences' violent quarrels particularly depressing, though Murry has said, in Lawrence's behalf, that in the course of time he came to understand how a woman could exasperate a man into a murderous frenzy 'really quite outside the scope of moral judgement'.

Murry's greatest difficulty, that spring, was with Lawrence's proposals of *Blutbrüderschaft*. Murry imagined a frightening ritual among the Druid stones on the dark moors. He later understood that what Lawrence was suggesting resembled the relationship between Gerald Crich and Rupert Birkin in *Women in Love,* which he had been working on during that time in Cornwall, in its final version, without telling the Murrys. He may have been reticent about the story because it dramatized the present situation of the four of them. When Murry read *Women in Love* for the first time five years later, he failed to recognize himself and Katherine Mansfield as Gerald Crich (encased in the envelope of Thomas Philip Barber, of Eastwood) and Gudrun Brangwen, though the episode of Gudrun's taking Birkin's letter from the mocking Halliday in the Pompadour Café was drawn from life: Katherine Mansfield had walked off with a copy of *Amores,* which the anti-Lawrence crew in the Café Royal were making fun of; Cecil Gray said in his biography of Heseltine that the latter wasn't there at the time of that incident, although in the novel Lawrence included him in the jeering café crowd (as Halliday). As for Murry, he didn't associate himself and Katherine with *Women in Love* until Frieda told him, years afterwards, that they were in it. Then Murry saw that the conversations between Gerald and Rupert paralleled those between Murry and Lawrence at Higher Tregerthen in 1916.

As the two men walked over the moors, Murry kept insisting he needed no sacrament: 'If I love you, and you know I love you, isn't that enough?' But Lawrence would rage at him, 'I hate your love, I *hate* it. You're an obscene bug, sucking my life away.' And one night the Murrys heard Lawrence, next door, crying out to Frieda, 'Jack is killing me.'

Certainly Lawrence, in his insistence upon the blood-brothership ceremony, seems immature, but in his life as in his writing, symbols were important to him, and everything from the smallest household task he made into a kind of religious ritual.

As for the common charge of homosexuality against Lawrence, Murry in his autobiography said (as previously quoted) that 'what is generally understood by the word homosexuality' could not be attributed to Lawrence. Frieda, in a letter of January 21, 1951, to the present writer, said that in the Lawrence-Murry relationship 'Lawrence never had any sexual feelings.' In a letter of August 6, 1953, Frieda wrote candidly to Murry, 'There was a real bond between you and L. If he had lived longer and been older, you would have been real friends, he wanted so desperately for you to understand him. I think the homosexuality in him was a short phase out of misery— I fought him and won—and that he wanted a deeper thing from you.'

Murry once observed that the wrestling episode of the two naked men in *Women in Love* perhaps suggests the kind of ritual Lawrence wanted in his *Blutbrüderschaft;* in that chapter, 'Gladiatorial', the slender Rupert shows astonishing strength and agility in throwing the muscular Gerald; Lawrence makes the point that Birkin had learned jujitsu. After their bout, Gerald and Birkin agree that the physical closeness of such activity 'makes one sane.' Similar scenes in other Lawrence novels—the towel-rubbing incident in *The White Peacock* and the ritualism-oath scene in *The Plumed Serpent*— seem to suggest a compensatory urge, an identification of a frail body with a strong, through a vicarious athleticism.

Lawrence's program was, in any event, too much for Murry in 1916; and Katherine, left alone in her cottage (she could hear Frieda moving about in the next one), wrote letters of complaint to distant friends. 'I don't know which disgusts me worse,' she told Koteliansky: 'When they are loving and playing with each other or when they are roaring at each other and he is pulling out Frieda's hair and saying

"I'll cut your bloody throat, you bitch." ' Katherine asked plaintively, 'Am I wrong in not being able to accept these people?'

At last she made Murry tell Lawrence that the northern shore of the peninsula seemed a foreign country to her, and that they must find a cottage on the south coast. Murry soon located one at Mylor, by one of the creeks of the Truro River, near Falmouth, for eighteen pounds a year. Katherine went to London for a few days, and Murry loaded their belongings onto a cart. Lawrence, helping him, would not say good-by; Frieda lightly promised to visit them. As Murry departed, he felt that he had said farewell to Lawrence forever.

5 DRUID STONES AND SURVEILLANCE

The Military Service Act of 1916 began to worry Lawrence. He wrote to Gertler (apparently on April 29), 'We are all a little bit blue, looking forward to being compelled to serve. I expect men like Murry and myself will be put into this "reserve", to do some sort of clerking. It is very disgusting, but what will be will be.' Lawrence was amused because Edward Marsh was 'beginning to rake in his debts. I had better send him a few unpublished stories' in lieu of money owed. 'It is no use praying to the Lord, because the Lord is the richest man of all. I have got something like £15 between me and complete starvation. Somehow, I don't care. One has had time to be nauseated with all care.'

The Lawrences had occasional visitors: Catherine Carswell, Dollie Radford, Barbara Low, and two American admirers, journalists Robert Mountsier and Esther Andrews (Mountsier was for a while to be Lawrence's American agent). Murry came over to Zennor once with his Oxford friend Frederic Goodyear, whom Lawrence liked. Goodyear, in love with Katherine Mansfield, was due to go to the Western Front, where he was soon killed, again reminding the little group of friends that the war was stubbornly going on across the Channel, while British generals were taking years to discover that Boer War-style cavalry charges couldn't be successfully launched against machine-gun emplacements.

Lawrence occasionally visited the Murrys, bringing little cheer to Katherine Mansfield, who fretted because her neighbors at Mylor tried to involve her in church bazaars. Once Lawrence was close to drowning: the dinghy which he was rowing nearly upset when a storm rose suddenly. But another voyage Lawrence undertook that year was far more annoying, a trip he made at the invitation of the government. The local postman chuckled as he handed Lawrence the menacing official envelope. In one of the passages taken from life in the novel *Kangaroo,* Lawrence tells of receiving his summons for conscription. The postman, an over-age Wesleyan preacher, loved the idea of hell for other men: 'He had a religious zest added to his natural Cornish zest in other people's disasters.'

On June 28, Lawrence and Frieda went to Penzance, and from there he was sent to Bodmin, sixty miles away; his German wife had to go back over the moors alone. In the chapter of *Kangaroo* called 'The Nightmare', Lawrence told of his experience at the barracks, and of his rejection: two days and a night of the military life, in the prison-like barracks, were enough for him for all eternity. The doctors' suggestions that he should perform some type of service to help his country meant no more to him than the noise of a passing cart.

Murry, also physically unfit, went to London to accept work in the War Office, but Lawrence seems to have been one of the few writers of his time who escaped such duties altogether. Ironically, later in the war, when he was low in funds and wanted employment, he could find none of any kind.

Even the Cambridge-Bloomsbury group engaged in war work. The cynical pacifist Lytton Strachey presided over a house near Pangbourne, Bucks, where exhausted war-workers could spend recuperative weekends, and a number of intellectuals put in their time at Garsington. Osbert Sitwell, a writer who was also a Grenadier Guards officer, recalled that 'some of the best brains in the country' dug and dunged in this 'arcadian colony' while Lady Ottoline Morrell sat in a green eighteenth-century drawing room 'eating bull's-eye peppermints'. Siegfried Sassoon, likewise an army officer, and one who wrote war poems, remembered from a similar visit that the laboring intellectuals would come into the manor house at night, 'to puff churchwarden pipes by the fire and talk cleverly in cultured and earnest tones about significant form in the Arts and the misdeeds of the Militarists.'

Lawrence at this time was aiming satiric shafts at Garsington. He told Catherine Carswell in a letter of November 21, 1916, that he was sending her his novel 'at last. Thank God I have got it out of the house. . . . Of course there is a last chapter, an epilogue, yet to be written: but that must wait for the wheel of time to turn.' He wanted both her and her husband to read the manuscript, 'make any corrections necessary', mark any discrepancies. '*Don't let anybody else read it.* I want to know what you both think of it. *I* think it a great book, whatever anybody else says. Ask Don if he thinks any part libellous—e.g. Halliday is Heseltine, the Pussum is a model called the Puma, and they are taken from life.' No one else was, he said, yet a few days later he wrote to Mrs. Carswell again:

I heard from Ottoline Morrell this morning, saying she hears she is the villainess of the new book. It is very strange, how rumours go round.—So I have offered to send her the MS.—So don't send it to Pinker till I let you know.

I got *Sportsman's Sketches* and have read them. No, I don't like Turgenev very much; he seems so very critical, like Katherine Mansfield and also a sort of male old maid. It amazes me that we have bowed down and worshipped these foreigners as we have. Their art is so clumsy, really, and clayey, compared with our own. I read *Deerslayer* just before the Turgenev. And I can tell you what a come-down it was, from the pure and exquisite art of Fennimore [*sic*] Cooper—whom we count nobody—to the journalistic bludgeonings of Turgenev. They are all—Turgenev, Tolstoi, Dostoyevsky, Maupassant, Flaubert—so very *obvious* and coarse, beside the lovely, mature and sensitive art of Fennimore Cooper or Hardy. It seems to me that our English art, at its best, is by far the subtlest and loveliest and most perfect in the world. But it is characteristic of a highly-developed nation to bow down to that which is more gross and raw and affected. Take even D'Annunzio and my *Trespasser*—how much cruder [and] stupider D'Annunzio is, really. No, enough of this silly worship of foreigners. The most exquisite literature in the world is written in the English language.

Don't talk much about my novel, will you? And above all don't give it to anybody to read, but Don. I feel it won't be published yet, so I would rather nobody read it. I hope Ottoline Morrell won't want the MS. And if you can prevent Aunt Barbara [Low] from knowing you have the book by you, *do*—because, having read the beginning, she is sure to claim the right to read the rest.

Why Lawrence suddenly caricatured Lady Ottoline as the monstrous Hermione is difficult to determine now, though in the previously quoted 1915 letter he scolded her for her mechanistic use of will. That he and she had a lovers' quarrel, like Birkin and Hermione, is unlikely; that part of *Women in Love* was apparently quite imaginary. Lord David Cecil told the author of this book in a letter:

> Frankly, I do not know the full story of Lawrence's quarrel with Lady Ottoline. Like yourself, I am pretty sure that the relation between them was of an 'abstract' character. Lady Ottoline was a very complex character, too complex really to be described in a brief letter in a way that I feel does her justice. The relation between patron and artist is always a difficult one, especially in a case like hers when the patron was a kind of artist herself— in the art of living, and had all the temperament that goes along with the artist. Possibly Lawrence found her too dominating and disliked being under an obligation anyway.

Lady Ottoline's daughter, Mrs. Igor Vinogradoff, said (also in a letter), 'I think what happened when L. met my mother was that they both had strong sensitive passionate sympathetic personalities and they clicked. . . . Her interest in writers of that generation *really* sprang from a genuine almost priggish-Victorian desire to help and encourage, and not from self-vanity, as so many people suppose, and imply in books written lately.' As for a possible love affair, Mrs. Vinogradoff remembered 'my father saying that Frieda told him she wouldn't have minded L. and my mother having an ordinary affair—what she couldn't stand was all this "soul-mush".' At the time, Lady Ottoline found herself deeply involved in her love affair with Bertrand Russell.

Lawrence's last letter to Ottoline Morrell—before the correspondence resumed a dozen years later—was apparently that of May 24, 1916. He told her that he had just sent back the proofs of *Amores,* to be dedicated to her, and that he had crossed out all the dedication but her name, because people were 'so jeering and shallow'. The Duckworth edition came out in July with the bare dedication 'To Ottoline Morrell'; but Lawrence apparently forgot to correct the Huebsch edition. When it appeared in New York, several months later, at the time the trouble was swelling, the dedication bloomed into: '. . . in tribute to her noble and independent sympathy and her generous understanding / these poems are gratefully dedicated.'

Augustus John recalled in his autobiography, *Chiaroscuro* (1952), that Lady Ottoline had insisted upon his reading *Sons and Lovers,* about which he was skeptical; he read it and 'hastened to announce my conversion,' which was received 'in chilly silence', for 'it turned out I was just too late.... The Master had by then offended his disciple somehow, and his name was not to be mentioned.'

Women in Love, of course, comprises a great deal more than un-flattering portraits of Lawrence's recent friends, a kind of *Point Counter Point* of pre-1920 England. In the Café Royal–Soho–coun-try-house episodes, Lawrence was doing more than merely lampoon-ing people and institutions that annoyed him: these places were the advanced outposts (however 'pacificistic' in temper) of a society which mechanized human beings, and which mechanized them into the slaughter of war. But *Women in Love* is much more than 'social': its people sometimes have (despite Lawrence's dislike of Dostoevsky) a Dostoevskian intensity. And its picture of England—its landscapes evoked for the reader as only Lawrence could evoke them, its gritty mining towns and lavish country houses, its views of 'dis-eased' parts of London, and its climax in the fierce white Tyrolean Alps for which the principal characters have left England—brings to English literature a richness of texture that for comparison must go back to the Romantics or the Elizabethans. Yet it is all in the modern mode, effectively using *symbolisme,* as in the terrible scene when Ursula agonizingly watches Birkin throw stones at the pond to shatter the female image of the moon—or in that equally terrible scene when the rabbit gashes Gudrun's arm in Gerald's presence: 'The long, shallow red rip seemed torn across his own brain, tearing the surface of his ultimate consciousness, letting through the for-ever unconscious, unthinkable red ether of the beyond, the obscene beyond'—the latter a passage incorporating the newer discoveries of psychology as well as the most effective modes of the futurism that Lawrence studied so thoroughly in Italy.

In this vein, the African statues at Halliday's Soho flat serve as an important symbol, out of which some of the leading themes of the book develop. One of these 'strange and disturbing' foetus-like carv-ings—a woman with 'transfixed, rudimentary face' who is in childbirth —shocks Gerald, though he also feels it as 'rather wonderful, convey-ing the suggestion of extreme physical sensation, beyond the limits of mental consciousness.' This last may seem to suggest Lawrencean ap-proval of the statue; but Lawrence was rarely black-and-white sim-ple; in attacking overintellectualization and the evils it had brought to modern man, he didn't recommend a return to savagery, as he showed clearly (among other places) in his first Melville essay in *Studies in Classic American Literature* (1923), in which he says that, however strongly we feel against what is called civilization, we cannot go back: 'We may have to smash things. Then let us smash. And our road may have to take a great swerve.' This might seem to be a retrogression,

> But we can't go back. Whatever the South Sea Islander is, he is centuries and centuries behind us in the life-struggle, the consciousness-struggle, the struggle of the soul into fulness. There is his woman, with her dark hair and her dark, inchoate, slightly sardonic eyes. I like her, she is nice. But I would never want to touch her. I could not go back on myself so far.

This sounds like Rupert Birkin, who in the different versions of *Women in Love* looks at and thinks about carved wooden statues from either Africa or the South Seas. Lawrence himself, in his admiration for natives and peasants, yearned after some of the freshness of the primitive spirit, but several times in his writings he said he could never haul down the flag of his 'civilized consciousness'. By the time he completed *Women in Love,* he had read Tylor and Frazer, Jane Harrison and Gilbert Murray (Frobenius apparently came to him somewhat later), and was well versed in anthropology —indeed, he was ahead of most twentieth-century authors in making use of such knowledge. As this writer first pointed out (in *The Life and Works of D. H. Lawrence,* 1951), Lawrence was a pioneer in adapting mythology for use in a modern novel. In *Women in Love,* for example, Lawrence expands his meaning by the device of giving several characters names which evoke medieval Scandinavian-Teutonic literature: Gudrun is the mate of Sigurd in the Norse *Völsunga Saga* (Gutrune is Siegfried's wife in Wagner's corresponding *Götterdämmerung*); Gerald, whose name is Germanic (spear-bearer, warrior), dies early, like Sigurd-Siegfried; and Loerke, that gnomish creature with mouse-like eyes, suggests some of the embodiments of the demon Loki in the northern myths.

As for the popularity of primitive art forms, this had first manifested itself about the time Lawrence initially went to London. Gauguin, now safely dead, was becoming fashionable; the German painter Kirchner had in 1904 begun popularizing African and Melanesian art which he discovered in the Dresden Ethnological Museum, and the advance-guard *Brücke* group drew upon this material; in Paris at the time, African sculpture influenced the *Fauves* circle and Picasso; in London, Roger Fry and others wrote essays on primitive art and, in several European capitals, ballet patrons were soon hearing about the 'barbaric' rhythms of Stravinsky's *Le Sacre du printemps.* Lawrence's introduction of the 'primitivist' motif into *Women in Love* was not merely an attempt to catch the vogue or even to satirize it, or to provide decoration or chiaroscuro—the black flesh against the white of the naked Bohemians at Halliday's flat—though all these ingredients were present. But, as with everything he touched, Lawrence adapted these elements to his own vision. (That Heseltine, the original of Halliday, told Delius in a 1916 letter that he had an African carving in his London flat provides an interesting footnote to *Women in Love.*)

Parts of the manuscript of *Women in Love* (in the University of Texas collection) add considerably to our background information about the book. An opening chapter (available in *Phoenix II*), set several years before the beginning of the one in the published novel, describes the meeting of Gerald Crich and Rupert Birkin and their trip through the Tyrolese Alps with 'a common friend, Hosken, a naval man'—the Lupton who becomes Gerald's brother-in-law in the first chapter of the final version. 'The absolute recognition' had passed between Gerald and Birkin, who 'knew [that] they loved each other, that each would die for the other.' Birkin reflected on the magnetism of both the 'ice-crystal' and the 'universal heavy darkness' types of men: 'He wanted to cast out these desires, wanted not to know them. Yet a man can no more slay a living desire in him, than he can prevent his body from feeling heat and cold.'

Yet, although Birkin was always drawn to women, 'it was for men that he felt the hot, flushing, roused attraction which a man is supposed to feel for the other sex'. And, 'although he was always terribly intimate with at least one woman, and practically never intimate with a man, yet the male physique had a fascination for him, and for the female physique he felt only a fondness, a sort of sacred love, as for a sister.'

Ursula, in a rejected fragment of epilogue, goes to Italy (apparently with Birkin) after Gerald's death in the Alpine sequence with which the book ends; in this fragment, Ursula a year later receives a letter from Gudrun, who has left Loerke and has borne Gerald a posthumous son, Ferdinand Gerald Crich: 'His hair is like the sun shining on the sea.' Still another rejected ending was a comparatively 'happy' one, with correspondences to Lawrence's later (1919) play, *Touch and Go*. In this attempt to end the novel, Lawrence didn't kill Gerald, but sent him back to England, Gudrun following. Loerke offers to marry her, though she is with child by Gerald, who himself now considers marriage—if she will pledge that 'you'll care for me more than the child,' a problem which Gudrun believes is essentially Gerald's to solve. This is a recurrent Lawrencean theme, in his life as in his work, and its introduction here repeats the motif of Will Brangwen's love for his daughter Ursula in *The Rainbow*—as the rejected epilogue plays again upon the Alpine motifs and the 'ice-crystal' quality of Gerald, related in turn to the primitive-art symbols that recur throughout *Women in Love*.

In one of the key chapters, 'Moony', Birkin recalls a statuette he used to see at Halliday's; not the one that shocked Gerald, but another female figure in which Birkin saw 'thousands of years of purely sensual, purely unspiritual knowledge'. This was a kind of 'knowledge arrested and ending in the senses, mystic knowledge in disintegration and dissolution, knowledge such as the beetles have, which live purely within the world of corruption and cold dissolution.' There was necessity in 'this awful African process'; but 'it would be done differently by the white races,' which, 'having the arctic north behind them, the vast abstraction of ice and snow, would fulfil a mystery of ice-destructive knowledge, snow-abstract annihilation.' This realization, already commented upon in relation to one of Lawrence's essays on Melville, foretells the death of Gerald in the Tyrolean Alps, a death caused not by accident but by something within Gerald himself, bringing about the 'snow-abstract annihilation'. Birkin, on the other hand, saw his own destiny in terms of the stars, and was able to realize something like 'an equilibrium' with Ursula, 'a pure balance of two single beings', like 'two equal stars balanced in conjunction'. Yet there is also Birkin's 'river of dissolution', so valuably dealt with in Colin Clarke's book, which takes its title from that phrase: to Birkin, the way to the vital is through decay and, to use his word, dissolution; and the vital does not necessarily kill the other element, but exists along with it, as in the case of the elements of the 'secondary Imagination' in the earlier-quoted passage from Coleridge.

Women in Love looked more deeply into the fundamental problems of modern man than most books of this time have done—an enormous achievement for the sick and disappointed Lawrence in war-raging, fear-haunted England; indeed, for this entire destructive century.

*

Apparently worried lest other acquaintances besides Lady Ottoline begin to identify themselves as characters in *Women in Love,* Lawrence told Gertler on December 5, 'In my novel there is a man—not you, I reassure you—who does a great granite frieze for the top of a factory, of which your whirligig, for example, is a part'—referring to a recent production of Gertler's. 'We knew a man, a German, who did these big reliefs for great, fine factories in Cologne'—the kind of disclaimer Lawrence's friends had begun to recognize as a danger signal. Not only is Gertler an easily recognizable model for Loerke (even in the sound of his name), but one of Gertler's paintings, 'The Merry-Go-Round', closely resembles, as Lawrence admitted in his December 5 letter, one of Loerke's granite friezes for the exterior of a factory near Cologne. Loerke explains it to Ursula and Gudrun as 'a representation of a fair, with peasants and artisans in an orgy of enjoyment, drunk and absurd in their modern dress, whirling ridiculously in roundabouts, gaping at shows, kissing and staggering and rolling in knots, swinging in swing-boats, and firing down shooting-galleries, a frenzy of chaotic motion.' Of course, this derives partly from the Wakes, those lively carnivals held in Eastwood, but it also borrows something from Gertler's painting, as Émile Delavenay first suggested. Gertler had sent Lawrence a picture of 'The Merry-Go-Round' in the autumn of 1916, when he was going over the last chapters of *Women in Love.* Lawrence had written to Gertler on October 9:

> If they tell you it is obscene, they will say truly. I believe there was something in Pompeian art, of this terrible and soul-tearing obscenity. But then, since obscenity is the truth of our passion today, it is the only stuff of art—or almost the only stuff. I won't say what I, as a man of words and ideas, read in the picture. But I *do* think that in this combination of blaze, and violent and mechanized rotation and complete involution, utterly mindless intensity of sensational extremity, you have made a real and ultimate revelation.

Lawrence had earlier in the year run into serious *roman à clef* trouble when he learned that Percy Lucas, the Meynell son-in-law, had died of wounds in France on July 6. Lawrence's mean little sketch of him, 'England, My England', had appeared in the *English Review* of October 1915 and in an American magazine six months later. In that story the Meynell family was held up for all to see, quite recognizably, with Godfrey Marshall setting up Crockham, a colony of cottages for his daughters, one of whom was married to Evelyn Daughtry (in later versions, Egbert), who languidly lived off the Marshall bounty.

Lawrence even blamed the little girl's accident on the son-in-law, who in the story carelessly left a scythe lying about. Yet Percy Lucas was a man who, although past the age of forty and the father of three children, had volunteered for combat service. Lawrence might have been moved by Second Lieutenant Percy Lucas's last letter to E. V. Lucas, which told of his being wounded in the pelvis and the thigh by German machine-gun bullets, and sitting for eight hours in a crater under continual shellfire, until stretcher bearers carried him two miles to a dressing station. All this he recounted to his brother in the most circumstantial manner, with no self-pity. He had been taken down the Somme for two days, in a barge, to a base hospital. He was unable to sleep, and was bilious and dyspeptic, but calmly looked forward to the return to England. The attending medical officer wrote E. V. Lucas that 'there seemed to be a fair chance of recovery till gangrene set in.' The doctors amputated his leg; he died six hours later.

Lawrence, hearing from Catherine Carswell of Percy Lucas's death, wrote, 'I wish that story at the bottom of the sea, before it had ever been printed.' But he added that it nevertheless seemed to him that 'man must find a new expression, give a new value to life, or his women will reject him, and he must die.' Lawrence regretted that he had 'gone to live at Greatham,' and he hoped the story wouldn't hurt Madeline Lucas, the widow: 'That is all that matters. If it was a true story, it shouldn't really damage.' But in a postscript he said, 'No, I *don't* wish I had never written that story. It should do good in the long run.' And in 1922 he used it as the title piece for a collection. He continued skimpoling his acquaintances, whether he liked them or not and whether they liked it or not, but 'England, My England' remains his cruelest story *à clef*.

During 1916, Lawrence didn't stir out of Cornwall. On August 14 he told Mrs. Carswell: 'I can't come to London—spiritually I *cannot*. But Frieda wants to come, to go chasing her children. . . . But I had much rather be Daniel in the lion's den, than myself in London. I am really terrified. . . . I am *much* too terrified and horrified by people—the world—nowadays.' On November 14 he told Gertler:

'It is so quiet and remote down here, there is nobody to quarrel with,' though apparently he and Frieda didn't pass up argumentative possibilities between themselves.

Catherine Carswell, who had been to Tregerthen for a brief visit in September, heard from the Lawrences the story of one of their recent quarrels. Lawrence had begun to sing, thinking their conflict was over, when Frieda stealthily came up behind him and gave him the Hermione-to-Birkin treatment, though instead of bashing him on the head with a piece of lapis lazuli, she used a stone dinner plate. He had not heard her approach because of his slight deafness: 'That was like a woman,' he said, to sneak up and deliver a blow from behind when the quarrel was apparently over—a blow which might have killed him. But, Mrs. Carswell noted, he bore no grudge. He may have interpolated that quarrel into *Women in Love,* where in the conflict scene Hermione wields the lapis lazuli with her left hand: an American scholar in London in the 1950s (Edward Nehls) noted that Ottoline Morrell's copy of the novel has at this point in the story a marginal annotation, 'Frida [*sic*] was left-handed!'

On her visit to Cornwall, Mrs. Carswell aroused her host's disapproval because, having brought no dressing gown, she got up one night for a book and appeared before the Lawrences in 'an ankle-length petticoat topped by a long-sleeved woollen vest'; Lawrence's vehement puritanism jabbed at her in the scolding he gave her. Mrs. Carswell left Cornwall earlier than she had intended, for her lonely husband telegraphed her to return to London, which she did immediately, to the chuckling tune of Lawrence's mockery.

In a letter of September 14 to Dollie Radford, Lawrence said that Frieda had been promised another interview with her children. He felt she should let them alone till they had grown up: 'Then, if there *is* a connexion, it is undeniable: if there *be* no active love, nothing can create it. It wearies me.' Frieda's daughter Barbara has recalled that Frieda took them all to an opera and gave them each ten shillings. The older girl, Elsa, said to Barbara in the ladies' room, 'You are not to *like* Mama, you know, just because we have got ten shillings.' The money was formally returned to Frieda by Ernest Weekley.

Lawrence was still thinking of leaving England. On December 7 he wrote to Amy Lowell that he would like to go to Italy if travel regulations permitted. He then referred to the British political turnover that had taken place a few days before: 'We have got Lloyd George for Prime Minister. That is a bad lookout for England. There was in Asquith the old English *decency,* and the lingering love of liberty. But Lloyd George is a clever little Welsh *rat,* absolutely dead at the core, sterile, barren, capable only of rapid and acute mechanical movements. God alone knows where he will land us: there will be a very big mess. But the country at large wanted him. . . . "Whom the Gods wish to destroy, they first make mad." '

Lawrence in his correspondence, as in his public writings, continually spoke this way of Lloyd George, even before Versailles, even before he had shown that he didn't dare dismiss Haig, whom he had distrusted—and even before the supposedly astute little Welsh lawyer had been fooled by one of Haig's staff officers when he visited Flanders at the time of the Passchendaele slaughter; the staff officer arranged for able-bodied German prisoners to be removed from the prison cages so that Lloyd George would see a 'weedy lot' of captives and would believe that Haig's attacks were demoralizing the German army. Lawrence, once the canard that he was a kind of proto-fascist is put aside, may sometimes be seen as a man of acute political insights.

On December 21 he wrote to McLeod, 'What that Welsh rarebit of a Lloyd George intends to inflict on us in the future, God above knows. He is an empty activity, and soon we shall find ourselves sheering giddily into chaos.' Two days later Lawrence wrote to Campbell, saying that he and Frieda could no longer visit London, now that the tickets between there and St. Ives were three pounds and fifteen shillings. Murry's novel (*Still Life*), which he had read in manuscript, he felt was replica rather than creation. Murry was 'utterly unwilling to take himself for what he is, a clever, but non-original, non-creative individual . . . I dislike him that he must assume himself the equal of the highest. That is the very essence of his malady, and all his twist and struggle is to make this falsehood appear a truth to himself.' It was indeed a bitter season for Lawrence, an 'ugly' and 'loathsome' Christmas. Yet always there was hope: 'The coming year will see the collapse of a great deal of us, and I hope we shall be able to begin something new.'

Despite his misery during 1916, that year was an important one for Lawrence, for it was then he completed (except for a few passages) his greatest work, his *Brangwensaga.* And he knew better than to rewrite *Women in Love* during the four years it lay awaiting publication. For, although he often wrote magnificently during the rest of his life, he never again, despite his increasing skill in the use of language, achieved the integration of art and idea that he manifested in *The Rainbow* and *Women in Love*.

With the coming of 1917, Lawrence began to think once more of the American escape. In the previous autumn, he had lamented to Koteliansky, 'Where is our Rananim? If only we had had the courage to find it and create it, two years ago. Perhaps it is not utterly too late.' On January 5, 1917, Lawrence told Catherine Carswell he felt like a cornered fox and was trying to get his passports to America renewed. On the thirteenth he wrote to her: 'I still dream of that far-off retreat, which is the future to me.' On the twenty-second he asked Campbell's help with the passports: 'I hope, in the long run, to find a place where one can live simply, apart from this civilisation, on the Pacific, and have a few other people who are also at peace and happy, and live, and understand, and be *free*.' Campbell, he knew, would understand, even though he hesitated to renounce the world: Lawrence hoped one day he would do so. On the twenty-fifth he asked again for Campbell's help, and explained that by 'the Pacific' he didn't mean California, but the Marquesas Islands, a place suggested by a recent reading of Melville; Lawrence was in the early phases of his *Studies in Classic American Literature*. He asked Campbell: 'Have you read anything lately? I have found Fennimore [*sic*] Cooper and Herman Melville such a treasure—and Dana's *Two Years Before the Mast*. They are so mature—even beyond us' (letter of January 25). The last idea became one of the leading motifs of the *Studies*. Lawrence had read Cooper with Jessie Chambers, but Melville was a new experience; and in taking him seriously and treating him as a major author, Lawrence was one of the first voices in the Melville revival.

On January 9 Lawrence had written to Pinker about his current essays on American literature: 'But I can't write for America here in England. I must transfer myself.' These essays, some of them printed in the *English Review* in 1918–1919, were intended to appear, with several others, in a book Lawrence then spoke of as *The Transcendental Element in American Literature*. But after he went to the United States in 1922, he revised them for the volume published the following year as *Studies in Classic American Literature;* the later versions are often quite different from the earlier ones, usefully put together as *The Symbolic Meaning* (1962), edited by Armin Arnold, who believes that these earlier essays are better than those in the *Studies* volume. But it was the latter which helped Lawrence so much in the eyes of his new readers after World War II, making these revised essays an important part of the restoration of interest in Lawrence.

*

In *Kangaroo,* Lawrence's autobiographical character, Somers, also requested passport validation in January 1917 from Cornwall: 'A man culminates in intense moments. This was one of Somers's white, deathlike moments, as he walked home from the tiny post-office in the hamlet, on the wintry morning, after he had posted his passports asking for visas to go to New York.' He felt as if he were walking in 'a strange, arrested land of death ... It almost frightened him. "Have I done wrong?" he asked himself. "Am I wrong, to leave my country and go to America?" '

But whatever feelings of guilt Lawrence himself may have had were soon converted to anger: 'They will not give me a passport for America,' he wrote to Mrs. Carswell on February 13. 'And only, if you please "in the interest of National Service". A new deviltry, this National Service ... I can't live in England. I can't stop any more. I shall die of foul inward poison. The vital atmosphere of the country is poisonous to an incredible degree: to me at least. I shall die in the fumes of their stench. But I *must* get out.' It was 'the country of the damned. I curse it, I curse England, I curse the English, man, woman, and child, in their nationality let them be accursed and hated and never forgiven.' Later, writing about Somers in *Kangaroo,* Lawrence spoke angrily of the refusal of the authorities to grant a passport to 'one of the most intensely English little men England ever produced, with a passion for his country, even if it were often a passion of hatred. But no, they persisted he was a foreigner. Pah!'

Not that Americans were perfect. The visiting journalist Robert Mountsier, who had returned to New York, left his friend Esther Andrews in England, feeling 'very miserable'. Yet, Lawrence said, 'there is something very nice and lovable in him. But alas, underneath is the old worldly male, that is bent on this evil destructive process, and which battens on the ugliness of the War. There is a great ugliness and vultureness underneath, quite American.' But Lawrence hoped the good would 'triumph in him also.'

He had just completed *Man and Woman*—the collection later to be published as *Look! We Have Come Through!*—the only Lawrence book to appear in 1917. The poetic experience that had begun in 1912 culminated there at Zennor: and it speaks much for Lawrence's

courage, for his persistence in hope, that he ended on a note of personal victory and gave the poems so defiantly assertive a title. His life
may have been overwhelmed by a despair reflected in parts of his
work; yet his writings had remained positive, forward-going, full of
the wonder of life-seeking. In one of the last of the *Look!* poems,
named 'Manifesto'—written at Zennor—he spoke of the 'strength
and affluence' given to him by one woman, and 'All the rocking wheat
of Canada, ripening now, /has not so much of strength as the body of
one woman'; he worked out through the poem a principle of union-
in-apartness resembling Birkin's 'balanced conjunction of two single
beings'; in such apartness and conjunction, Lawrence said in this
poem, 'we shall be free, freer than angels, ah, perfect'; and:

> *Every human being will then be like a flower,*
>   *untrammelled . . .*
> *we shall love, we shall hate,*
> *but it will be like music, sheer utterance,*
> *issuing straight out of the unknown,*
> *the lightning and the rainbow appearing in us*
>   *unbidden, unchecked,*
> *like ambassadors.*

A few days after completing the *Look!* manuscript, Lawrence told
Campbell, on February 23: 'It is spring coming here: already the
birds singing and the silveriness in the air. I wish to God it was spring
in the world of people.' About this time he wrote Catherine Carswell a
hortatory and prophetic letter, which probably referred to her unhappiness over her husband's having been called into military service:

> I don't know what to say about you and Carswell. It is misery,
> and there it is. It has got to be borne, and nothing from outside
> can help.
>   But there is this, it won't *really* hurt you, in the long run.
> Nothing bad will happen *inside* you and Don. Be sure of that.
> And only misery will hurt outside: not vital damage. One has to
> make up one's mind to endure, and not lose any faith, or even
> any triumph. Though the enemy seizes my body for a time, I
> shall subtly adjust myself so that he pinches me nowhere vitally,
> and when he is forced to release me again, I am the stronger.
>   Even, I hope Don will learn the great lesson, really to reject
> the world of man, as it now is. I hope he will learn the bitter
> lesson of repudiating his oneness with the rest. You won't be

happy with him till then. So be of good courage, and, instead of wishing to shelter him, send him forth to find out which side he really belongs to.

You see, he must not wish to be successful at the law: it is Dead Sea Fruit. So let him taste the fare of the world of which his law is part. Let him eat the crust, since he desires the crumb. Harden your heart in faith against his suffering, and love him sternly, with hope of a new life and a new world. Love the great spirit of the next even more than you love him—it is the only way.

That letter (of which only the beginning is quoted here), which was written at a period when Lawrence was not regularly exercising his imaginative faculty, had the force of a creative essay. Lawrence perhaps realized, as Rilke did, that letters could be creative; and like Rilke he might have said that 'when occasion offered,' he 'carried on a part of [his] productivity with letters.'

In Catherine Carswell's biography of Lawrence, *The Savage Pilgrimage,* she presents a level-minded view of his marriage with Frieda: 'Lawrence asserted himself on the strength of his power. And he asserted the male principle, which he believed was destined to lead. But there was no egoism in it, and it left Frieda the utmost liberty of her female assertion, so long as she did not try to "put across" mere female egoism.' Perhaps, as Mrs. Carswell noted, no other woman could have borne 'the pressure of his male probity, his "demon". Frieda was the "freest woman he had ever met". He found in her "a magnificent female probity of being, as well as of physical well-being" '.

*

Lawrence told Amy Lowell, on March 23, about a series of articles he was writing: 'Hilda Aldington is very sad and suppressed, everything is wrong. I *wish* things would get better. I have done a set of little essays called "The Reality of Peace", very important to me. I wish they would come out in America, in which case I shall send them to you.' On April 2, Lawrence told Pinker: 'Harrison wrote me about the "Reality of Peace" articles, saying he will do the last three in three consecutive months. I hoped he would have done them all . . . but he says he can't. So I suppose we shall have to swallow this. Perhaps we might place the first four elsewhere.'

Austin Harrison published three of the essays in the *English Review* in the summer of 1917, but the remaining four have apparently been lost; the three that survived were reprinted in *Phoenix;* they had never materialized into a book. In August, Lawrence told Pinker he was writing a new volume, *At the Gates,* which was 'based upon the more superficial *Reality of Peace.* But this is pure metaphysics, especially later on: and perfectly sound metaphysics, that will stand the attacks of technical philosophers.' But Pinker couldn't place this book, whose manuscript was among those he returned to Lawrence in 1920, when they parted company. It too seems to have disappeared.

In the spring of 1917, Frieda wrote to Cynthia Asquith, naïvely expressing her own disgust because Herbert Asquith had to face death in war like ordinary young men: 'What is the good of being the Prime Minister's son?'

In April 1917, Lawrence, leaving Frieda in Cornwall with Esther Andrews, went to London for about a week. He had gone, via Bristol, by way of Eastwood and Ripley. He was sorry to find Mrs. Hopkin ill at Eastwood, and his sister Emily wretched with diarrhea at Ripley. It was a time of colitis and collapsing bowels, and when he returned to Cornwall he found Frieda ill too.

Mrs. Carswell, in *The Savage Pilgrimage,* mentioned the Lawrences' visitor, Esther Andrews, who 'was unhappy, and in the strength of her unhappiness could not resist attaching herself to Lawrence and trying to match her strength against Frieda's—disastrously to herself.' Mrs. Carswell, who had 'heard the particulars from both Lawrence and Frieda,' found the report of this affair in Mabel Dodge Luhan's *Lorenzo in Taos* 'both misleading and incorrect'. Mrs. Luhan said Frieda had told her that in this affair Lawrence had been 'unfaithful' to her for the first time, adding 'with a kind of bitter triumph' that 'it was unsuccessful.' Frieda, sniffing mischief, 'showed the girl to the door', the last phrase being an *East Lynne* touch of the kind frequently used by Mrs. Luhan, who in reporting conversations was somewhat on the transalpine side of Ford Madox Ford and just barely on the cisalpine side of Frank Harris.

*

The complications in Lawrence's life in Cornwall in 1917 increased when the military authorities called him again in June. On the twenty-third he left Frieda at the doorway of the stone cottage, at seven in the morning, and as he set off across the fields he told her he would be back by nightfall. And this time his humiliation was indeed briefer. At Bodmin Barracks it took the doctors only two hours to tell him that, although he was 'unfit', the day of rejections had passed; he would be put into C₃, light nonmilitary service. But he was confident that so many men were eager to perform C₃ duties that he would not be disturbed. A two hours' ordeal was all for that day, two hours of being squeezed, auscultated, and peeped into, and then he was home, as prophesied, by nightfall.

It was about this time that Lawrence and a neighboring young farmer, William Henry Hocking, developed an intense friendship. In *Kangaroo,* Lawrence gave him the name of John Thomas Buryan, a rather facetious pun. One version of this episode, given by Mrs. Luhan, is based on what Frieda supposedly told her in New Mexico in 1922, about 'a young farmer' in Cornwall: 'Was there really a *thing* between them?' Mrs. Luhan reported herself as asking, with Frieda replying, 'I think so. I was dreadfully unhappy.' But Catherine Carswell, who at the time of the relationship discussed it with Lawrence, explained this Cornish friendship as a sacramental matter; he convinced her that 'the sin against the Holy Ghost' was not involved.

He would often go to the Hockings' farm at night to talk to William Henry and give French lessons to his younger brother, Stanley. It was like old times at the Haggs. And Lawrence worked with the men in the fields, talking of philosophy or of earthy matters, just as in the past with the Chambers family, in the hayfield at Greasley. The Hocking girls, Mabel and Mary, would bring dinner in a basket, and they would all sit together eating on the stony moorland. Mr. Chambers might almost be expected to appear and say, 'Work goes like fun when Bert's here.' Indeed, William Henry Hocking remembered, in his 1953 talk on the B.B.C., that he had once told Lawrence, 'You're getting more like us every day.' Lawrence tried to show the Hockings how to tie corn sheaves in the style of the Midlands, but they preferred the Cornish way.

Sometimes Frieda would go to tea ('croust') at the farm, but the family never felt at ease with the grand lady as they did with her husband. The Hockings were among the Lawrences' few friends in Cornwall, along with Katie Berryman of Zennor, from whom they bought bread and baked rabbit and saffron cakes; she remained their friend when even the Hockings were affected by the growing hostility to the red-bearded man and his German wife.

The Cornish people suspected them of provisioning German submarine crews on that coast, though as Frieda later pointed out, she and Lawrence couldn't have spared even a biscuit a day, in their poverty, even if they had been in touch with those crews. But they were suspected of all kinds of spying activities. (David Garnett said in 1959 that he believed Hueffer, who had been writing government propaganda, had in 1915 made a bad report about the Lawrences, which had remained in the files throughout the war.)

One day, two officers leaped out at them from behind a bush on the moors and accused Frieda of carrying a camera: 'I opened the rucksack and held the loaf of bread under their noses. I had to show my contempt, if they hanged me for it the next moment.' This was only one incident among many: the poison of suspicion began to eat into the simplest acts of their lives. Once when Frieda felt ecstatic on the seashore and began to run about gaily, her white scarf waving in the wind, Lawrence cried out, 'Stop it, stop it, you fool! Can't you see that they'll think you're signaling to the enemy!'

The sly, small Cornish eyes that Katherine Mansfield had written of were now fixed on the Lawrences at all hours; as late as the 1970s a man in Zennor was proudly displaying the spyglass through which the Lawrences' activities had been scrutinized. That the Cornish 'suspicion of foreigners was beyond belief' at this time is attested to in the autobiography (*Adventures of a Bookseller* [1937]) of Giuseppe Orioli, who first met Lawrence there in Cornwall. He remembered 'a nice old woman at Zennor' who, although she had lost no relatives in the war, said she would like to hang the Kaiser and eat his heart. (Frieda: 'I, the Hunwife in a foreign country!')

Orioli also knew in Cornwall a lecturer on Italian art who had years before married an Englishwoman and given up his native German citizenship to become an Englishman. But the Cornish people followed him when he went out on the moors and, with the immunity and the aura of heroism bestowed upon snoopers in times of hysteria, they searched his cottage whenever they pleased. His heart was too weak to permit him to walk into the nearest town, Penzance, and after the local merchants refused to deliver groceries to him, some girls Orioli knew used to bring food out to him. One day the police found a note he had left for the girls; his pathetically simple desire for a harmless confection cost him his life, for his persecutors insisted that *macaroons* was a code word for the petrol with which he was supposed to be supplying enemy submarines: 'From that day onwards he was tortured by them into such a state of depression and misery that he killed himself.'

Stories of this kind indicate that Lawrence and Frieda imagined not a single aspect of their own persecution. On August 10 he wrote to Catherine Carswell: 'Did I tell you we've got a piano—old, red silk front—five guineas—nice old musty twang with it.' But even this battered instrument became a source of trouble, for when Lawrence and Frieda pounded out Hebridean folk songs on it and sang the words, the local Celts thought these were German words—not that the Lawrences hadn't defiantly sung a few *Lieder*. But by this time the guilt-by-association technique had reached almost to the breaking point. The final episode of the Cornish troubles occurred at the home of Cecil Gray, the young man who had given Lawrence and Frieda the Hebridean music, of which he had made a professional study.

Gray was a composer and a friend of Philip Heseltine, who reappeared in Cornwall in April without bringing his bride of a few months, the former Minnie Lucie Channing. He settled in a cottage between Penzance and Zennor and once again began praising Lawrence's work: he now wrote to his friends about the greatness of the 'Peace' essays. But he became uneasy when, in the summer, the authorities began to tighten the conscription laws. In his autobiography, *Musical Chairs* (1948), Gray said that Heseltine had a 'nervous disorder' and a medical certificate that guaranteed him permanent exemption; but he fled to Ireland in August and stayed there until the war was nearly over.

In Cornwall, Gray had moved into Bosigran Castle, just above the cliffs in a wild corner of the coast. The Lawrences went there to dinner in October on a night Lawrence was to memorialize in *Kangaroo*.

Some men burst in: 'You are showing a light.' Gray later recalled that wind had disturbed one of the curtains so that a flickering light was there to convince the snoopers that Gray and the Lawrences were communicating with a submarine. Frieda rejoiced that some of the men had, while listening under the windows, fallen into mud. She remembered that when the intruders clumped in, 'Lawrence just looked at those men. What a manly job was theirs. . . . '

Gray had to pay 'a vindictively heavy fine'; the Lawrences were given a different punishment. On the morning of October 12—their cottage had been ransacked during their absence the day before—an army officer appeared with a policeman from St. Ives who had visited the Lawrences before and liked them, and with two detectives whom Lawrence described as louts and dogs. Although reminded that they had been over Lawrence's papers the day before, the 'detective louts' began prying again, finding such trophies as the meaningless word-sounds of the Hebridean 'Seal Woman's Song' and a book with suspicious diagrams, Lawrence's college botany notebook with his poems written in the blank pages. The immune investigators looked into cupboards, ruffled the bedclothes, and peeped into the clock.

Then the officer read out an order: the Lawrences must leave Cornwall within three days, must avoid living in any 'prohibited area', and must report to the police wherever they moved. Lawrence asked the officer the reason for this, and was told, 'You know better than I do.' When Frieda exploded about 'English justice', Lawrence told her to be silent. 'He was so terribly quiet, but the iron of England had stabbed his soul once more, and I knew he suffered more than I.'

Not long after, Lawrence described the experience in a letter to Montague Shearman (son of a judge of the King's Bench), a friend of Campbell and Gertler: 'We don't know in the least why this has taken place. Of course my wife was corresponding with her people in Germany, through a friend in Switzerland—but through the ordinary post.' Lawrence was perhaps too ingenuous when, on the day of the order of ejection, he wrote to Cynthia Asquith, 'I cannot even conceive how I have incurred suspicion—have not the faintest notion,' though he was entirely correct in saying, 'We are as innocent of pacifist activities, let alone spying of any sort, as the rabbits in the field outside.'

But the military officials had an order signed by Major General Sir William George Balfour Western, grizzled survivor of several African campaigns and of the current war, in which he had been wounded. To him at his desk in Salisbury, the Lawrences were bothersome names on a piece of paper necessary to sign for the sake of administrative order; the Cornish people—capable, Cecil Gray wrote, of 'the purest form of disinterested, impersonal malevolence that I have ever encountered'—had prepared their case well; there was no appeal; the Lawrences left Cornwall on October 15.

William Henry Hocking, who had been one of the candidates for *Blutbrüderschaft,* drove them to the station; he had become cautious, and some of his family avoided saying farewell to the departing exiles. In *Kangaroo,* Lawrence described graphically the trip to London on the Great Western Express, with the train full of singing soldiers and sailors from Plymouth. The wife was relieved to get out of Cornwall, but the husband 'sat there feeling he had been killed. . . . He had always *believed* so in everything—society, love, friends. This was one of his serious deaths in belief.'

Frieda said in *Not I, But the Wind*, 'When we were turned out of Cornwall, something changed in Lawrence forever.' The experience had intensified his hatred of any form of compulsion from without and had made him distrustful forever of the processes of democracy.

6 THE UNENDING WAR

Lawrence had telegraphed to Dollie Radford, asking whether he and Frieda might briefly find refuge at her home when they arrived in London. Mrs. Radford was frightened, but she welcomed them. On October 16, his second night in London, Lawrence called on Lady Cynthia Asquith at her wartime residence in Portman Mansions. She noted in her diary, 'He looks terribly ill—as though every nerve in his body were exposed.' He was railing because he had to report to the police. That experience, however, amused him later, for the police, who had never heard of the Lawrences, apparently worked 'none too smoothly with the military'. In writing of this to Gray, Lawrence again saw London in the image of hell; people were no longer people, but 'factors, really ghastly, like lemures, evil spirits of the dead. What shall we do, how shall we get out of this Inferno?'

In a letter to Catherine Carswell from 44 Mecklenburgh Square— a house famous for its literary residents, a house bombed in two world wars—Lawrence reported: 'Hilda Aldington has lent us her room here for the time—a very nice room. So far as housing goes, we are safe and sound for the moment.' As to Cornwall, 'I know nothing further about my "case" so far, but Cynthia Asquith is making enquiries, and I hope to get it settled. I want to go back to Cornwall before Christmas.'

A few days later he told Mrs. Carswell that Rananim was on again, shifted now to South America. As soon as they could break free, 'we shall sail away to our Island—at present in the Andes . . . Eder knows the country *well*.' The Rananim personnel now included Dr. and Mrs. Eder, 'William Henry [Hocking] and Gray, and probably Hilda Aldington, and maybe Kot and Dorothy Yorke.' He hoped the Carswells would go too, though Mrs. Carswell was expecting a child.

Dorothy Yorke, an interesting addition to the Lawrence group, was an American girl whom they all called Arabella. Like H.D., she was from Pennsylvania; Hilda Doolittle was a native of Bethlehem, Dorothy Yorke of nearby Reading. She was, in that year of 1917, twenty-five, six years younger than H.D. Some of the similarities and differences between the two women are perhaps implied in Aldington's novel *Death of a Hero* (1929) and H.D.'s *Bid Me to Live* (1960). The latter book suggests that Frieda tried to encourage Lawrence to make love to H.D. so that Frieda herself could have an affair with Gray, with whom, in actuality, H.D. ran away.

When the Lawrences lived in the Aldingtons' room at the front of the Mecklenburgh Square house, on the first floor, Dorothy Yorke stayed in the attic: it was all 'very jolly', Lawrence afterwards recalled. Dorothy had been brought to the place by the writer John Cournos, who had left for Petrograd with Hugh Walpole and other members of the Anglo-Russian Commission, just before the Lawrences departed from Cornwall. Cournos, a native Russian, had met Dorothy Yorke when he was trying to bring *la vie de Bohème* to Philadelphia before the war.

At nineteen, she was, he remembered in his *Autobiography*, 'tall, slender, graceful; with black copper-tinged hair; with brown eyes; with high, and as it were, carven cheekbones; her complexion was what I would call flushed, and . . . she had, I thought, a quiet restrained beauty, with an exotic flavour.' This is Lawrence's Josephine Ford, of *Aaron's Rod*, 'a cameo-like girl with neat black hair done tight and bright in the French mode. She had strangely-drawn eyebrows, and her colour was brilliant.' Lawrence described her as licking 'her rather full, dry red lips with the rapid tip of her tongue. It was an odd movement, suggesting a snake's flicker.' Her quietness 'had the dangerous impassivity of the Bohemian, Parisian or American, rather than English.'

Cournos had fallen violently in love with her, and she returned his feeling at times. Whenever he thought he had shaken himself free of her, malicious coincidence would bring them together again: unaware that she was even in Europe, he would bump into her on the street in Paris or London. After the last of these encounters, in 1917, she assured him she loved him intensely; but when he returned after the Russian Revolution had brought his mission to an end, she informed him that she was in love with one of his closest friends: Richard Aldington.

Aldington complained more than once that the people who helped

Lawrence in 1917 found themselves 'mercilessly satirized' a few years later in *Aaron's Rod*. Besides Dorothy Yorke as Josephine, Aldington is Robert Cunningham ('a fresh, stoutish Englishman in khaki . . . He drank red wine in large throatfuls'); Hilda Aldington is Robert's wife, Julia ('A tall stag of a thing' who 'sat hunched up like a witch . . . She had dragged her brown hair into straight, untidy strands. Yet she had real beauty'); Cecil Gray is Cyril Scott ('a fair, pale, fattish young fellow in pince-nez and dark clothes'); and Augustus John is the artist Struthers, who showed poor manners by talking through an opera performance—Cynthia Asquith recalled that performance, and stopping with Lawrence, on the way, at John's studio, where Lawrence chanted, 'Let the DEAD PAINT THE DEAD!'—and John in his *Chiaroscuro* remembered that, at the end of the opera, 'Lawrence announced that he would like to howl like a dog.'

Lawrence, writing *Aaron's Rod* in Berkshire the following spring (he finished it in Italy in 1921), drew heavily upon the London of late 1917, but if he caricatured acquaintances and people who befriended him, he also made fun of himself, as Rawdon Lilly, particularly in the chapter 'A Punch in the Wind', in which Jim Bricknell plants his fist in the stomach of the 'windbag' prophet.

This was an actual occurrence at the Radfords' cottage in Berkshire, where the Lawrences had moved in December after the Aldingtons wished to have their flat again. Lawrence had spent Christmas in the Midlands, and then he and Frieda stayed at Hermitage for the first quarter of 1918. It was there that they received a visit from the man who became Jim Bricknell in *Aaron's Rod,* one of Lawrence's most successful comic characters.

Lawrence introduced him first at Shottle House, another of those variants of Lamb Close. He gave Jim an Irish mother—an important touch—and for a father, a man quite different from any of the Cambridge-educated Barbers: Alfred Bricknell was Alfred Brentnall, who used to torment the boy Lawrence at the colliery pay offices. Lawrence, it will be remembered, had already portrayed him, in all his nastiness, in *Sons and Lovers;* now, in putting him into the mine owner's house, beard and Midlands accent and all, Lawrence was perhaps suggesting that lower types of people were now creeping into high places, a favorite theme of twentieth-century novelists—Proust with the vulgar *nouveaux riches* replacing the aristocrats at the top of Parisian society, Faulkner with his pushing Snopeses. Lawrence made the Bricknell son, Jim, flamboyantly crude.

In the 'Punch in the Wind' chapter of *Aaron's Rod,* Jim invited himself, by telegram, to visit Lilly and his Norwegian wife, Tanny, at their 'labourer's cottage' in the country. He was an ex-officer who had become 'a sort of socialist, and a red-hot revolutionary of a very ineffectual sort'. He felt that Lilly was the only man in England who could 'save' him, though he was unable to answer Lilly's question, 'From what?' He had visions that told him Japan and Ireland were 'the two poles of this world'; when asked what kind of visions, he could only retort that they were indescribable. He ate continually, and when not devouring a meal kept chewing pieces of bread, as if to fill his inner hollowness, and through it all kept wheezing how wonderful sacrifice could be, how splendid Christ was.

Lilly finally told him he wished he would leave. Jim's love was messiness: 'It wouldn't matter if you did no harm. But when you stagger and stumble down a road, out of sheer sloppy relaxation of your will'—and this is when Jim delivered his punch in the wind: 'I knew I should have to do it, if he said any more,' he told Tanny. In one of Lawrence's most ironical comic scenes, Lilly sat fighting to regain his breath without letting the other two know he had lost it, while Jim kept saying that he liked Lilly 'better than any man I've ever known', as Tanny kept reproving her husband and asked him what he expected.

The original of Jim Bricknell was the son of a field marshal, one of the successful British generals in the Boer War, in which his son had also fought, as a member of the Gordon Highlanders. This son, Captain James Robert White (1879–1946), helped organize the Irish Citizen Army at the time of the transport workers' strike in Dublin in 1913. Living conditions for the working class there had been so notably bad that, when the strike began, the men had the sympathy of most of the world; but they soon alienated much of this because of the hideous violence of their army, trained by Captain Jack White in the use of hurleys.

Like Jim Bricknell, Captain White was for a time not permitted to live in Ireland. Lawrence met him in London when White was conducting meetings on behalf of the strikers, and the acquaintance continued. White worked with the Red Cross in France during World War I, but in 1916 served three months' imprisonment for trying to organize a miners' strike in Wales in order to bargain with the government, thereby preventing the execution of James Connolly. White wrote several pamphlets on politics and, in 1930, an autobiography which caused one reviewer to suggest that if Captain White were trying to portray himself as a blackguard, much of the black might be burned cork. The book had the appropriately Bricknellish title, *Misfit*.

The rampant Jack White was not the only man of action Lawrence knew at this time. It is not easy to think of him working for Soviet Russia, but in a letter of February 16, 1918, Lawrence suggested to Catherine Carswell that he might assist Maxim Litvinov, recently appointed the first Soviet ambassador to the Court of St. James's.

When the British refused to oust the tsarist officials from the embassy, the Litvinovs set up a 'people's embassy' in offices at 21 Victoria Street and asked for volunteer help. Lawrence told Mrs. Carswell: 'If you see Ivy tell her from me I'm so glad Litvinov has got this office: I hope she'll become a full-blood ambassadress, I do. It pleases me immensely. I sit here and say bravo. I almost feel like asking Litvinov if I can't help—but I don't suppose I'm of much use at this point. Tell Ivy, if there is anything interesting, I do wish she'd write' —and evidently the matter ended there. (When *Women in Love* came out a few years later, Litvinov may have been surprised to find in it a minor character named Maxim Libidnikov, though this may have been partly a portrait of Koteliansky. Boris deCroustchoff, a friend of Heseltine's, has told the present writer that he was himself the model for Libidnikov.)

At this time Lawrence wrote to Gertler: 'I didn't like your last letter about women—viz. prostitution. I have an aesthetical or physical aversion from prostitutes—they smell in my inward nostrils.' He was writing his 'American' essays, but doubted that they would 'ever be published while this world stands. True, it seems cracking. But curse the old show, it will go on cracking for another century without tumbling down.' Dollie Radford—whose husband was going mad— now wanted her cottage again. 'I am at the dead end of my money, and can't raise the wind in any direction. Do you think you might know of somebody who would give us something to keep us going a bit. It makes me swear—such a damned, mean, narrow-gutted, pitiful, crawling, mongrel world that daren't have a man's work and won't even allow him to live.' He had been suffering for three weeks with a sore throat, 'which gives me a queer feeling as if I was blind.' It was an evil world: 'Nowadays one can do nothing but glance behind to see who is creeping up to do something horrible to the back of one's neck.'

At Gertler's suggestion (as a letter to him from Lawrence shows) Montague Shearman now sent Lawrence ten pounds. That Lawrence regarded this money as a gift is plain in his letter of thanks to Shearman: 'I have never been so tight put—for money and everything else —damnable. But I don't mind taking from you: no, I am glad to have the money from your hand. One man's gain is another man's loss. But, I can't help it. It is damnable people like Pinker, my agent, who dangle a prospective fish on the end of a line, with grinning patronage, and just jerk it away every letter, that make me see red.'

There is an irony here. Shearman wrote to Gertler in October 1916, 'Money is a horrible thing. I should like you to feel however that you can always have what you want from me if you like. But it must be as between friends and there must be no feeling of patronage or obligation whatever. I don't want to be a Conway or an Eddie Marsh— not that I am saying a word against Eddie Marsh, who I am sure meant to be kind.' In September 1922, Lawrence wrote to Koteliansky from New Mexico, saying: 'I am paying back at last the little bit that Eddie Marsh and Ottoline once gave me, so long ago.' In Marsh's code, apparently unlike Shearman's, Lawrence had definitely asked for a *loan,* as his letters show; and how Lawrence repaid Lady Ottoline, still enraged over *Women in Love,* is not known. In any event, it was quite a different matter with Shearman, who seemed to give rather than to lend. The matter was revived in 1928, when Shearman wrote to Lawrence, regretting the lapse of their friendship and asking whether, in payment for his ten pounds' loan, he mightn't have a free copy of the privately printed *Lady Chatterley's Lover.* In April 1928 Lawrence wrote Koteliansky to say that Shearman's letter made him feel 'rather mad', but he sent him his ten pounds at once. 'I can't remember the loan—and if he lent it, I'm sure he gave the impression of *giving* it.'

Towards the end of their stay in London, the Lawrences had known they were under continual surveillance: Aldington, Gray, and other visitors had found detectives listening in the hall. There had been parties at Mecklenburgh Square, with poets arguing, and charades such as the one of the Garden of Eden which Frieda remembered: 'Lawrence was the Lord, H.D. was the tree, Richard Aldington waving a large chrysanthemum was Adam, and I was the serpent, and a little scared at my part'—but the real serpent was the spy beyond the door.

Even in Berkshire, the Lawrences were under scrutiny, and detectives had also gone to Professor Weekley to ask whether he had any information he might lodge against Frieda. She saw her son Montague at this time, in the uniform of the Officers' Training Corps, and shocked him by saying, 'Let me hide you somewhere in a cave or in a wood, I don't want you to go and fight, I don't want you to be killed in this stupid war.'

Frieda had written to Cynthia Asquith to say that women should stop the war: 'You look like St Catherine of Siena in my picture.'

*

Lawrence loved Berkshire. He wrote of the beauty of the place in *Aaron's Rod* under the name of Hampshire, and in *Kangaroo* under the disguise of Oxfordshire. In his long story 'The Fox', he described the region under its own name, and mentioned White Horse Hill in the western distance. For his human figures in that story Lawrence took two girls he knew at Grimsbury Farms, near Hermitage. He and Frieda used to stay at Grimsbury when dislodged from the Radfords'. In 'The Fox', first written in 1918 and put into final form in Sicily in 1921, these girls—whose real names were Violet Monk and Cecily Lambert—became Nellie March and Jill Banford. Jill Banford may also be partly taken from Dollie Radford's daughter, Margaret, whom Lawrence disliked. Comically enough, the foxlike Lawrence was continually complaining in his letters that Margaret Radford wanted to drive him away from Hermitage, and this was precisely what her possible counterpart wanted to do to the young man in the story, though she failed there.

But in life, Lawrence had to leave his beloved Berkshire, of which he had written to Cecil Gray that winter: 'I no longer want the sea, the space, the abstraction. There is something living and rather splendid about trees . . . I never knew how soothing trees are—many trees, and patches of open sunlight, and tree-presences—it is almost like having another being. At the moment the thought of the sea makes me verily shudder.'

His next move was north, back to the Midlands. On April 3 he wrote to Catherine Carswell that he and Frieda were going to Ripley to visit Ada for a week; she had located a cottage for them near Wirksworth, home of his ancestors the Beardsalls, in Derbyshire. Lawrence said to Mrs. Carswell: 'Oh God, the bombs! One fell in the garden of 42, Mecklenburgh Square—all back windows smashed in 44. Thankful we weren't there.' But he also had more cheerful news, concerning his unpublished manuscript: 'Did I tell you George Moore read *Women in Love,* and says it is a great book, and that I am a better writer than himself. That is really astounding.'

Lawrence and Frieda liked the cottage at Middleton-by-Wirksworth and returned south while Ada made arrangements to rent it for them, at her expense, for a year. Back at Hermitage, Lawrence read Gibbon and was 'quite happy with those old Roman emperors'—indeed, he was happy with all of Gibbon, upon whom he drew extensively for the history textbook he was soon to write. He abandoned *Aaron's Rod* for a time and began to get two volumes of poems ready for the press: *Bay,* which didn't come out until 1919, and *New Poems,* the only book of his to be published in 1918. His single volume of the preceding year, *Look! We Have Come Through!,* had not been charitably handled by the reviewers; in December 1917 he had complained to Amy Lowell, 'As usual the critics fall on me: *The Times* says "the Muse can only turn away her face in pained distaste." Poor Muse, I feel as if I have affronted a white-haired old spinster with weak eyes.' Lawrence could not have known Bertrand Russell's comment on the volume, a copy of which Ottoline Morrell showed him one day after breakfast; Lady Ottoline's daughter, Mrs. Vinogradoff, has in a letter recalled Russell's 'saying in his nasal dry voice: "They may have come through, but I don't see why I should look." '

Lawrence's writing, indeed, met with little encouragement, public or private, in these years. When he had been in the Midlands a little more than a month, he wrote to Gertler from Mountain Cottage:

> I got your letter yesterday—bloody, things are. I have just filled in forms of application for money—help from the Royal Literary Fund—but I was not very polite and cringing, so probably shall get nothing. Curse them, that's all—curse them once more, fat fleas of literature that they are.
>
> I got military papers from Cornwall to be medically re-examined—sent them back—but expect any day to have more from Derby. Again curse them.—I will not be made to do any serving of any sort, however. Your 'commission' is another hope for roping you in. Blast it all. There is no hope on earth—not the slightest hope from the people up here, I assure you. . . .
>
> We are spending a day in the place where I was born—Eastwood. For the first time in my life I feel quite aimiably [*sic*] towards it—I have always hated it. Now I don't.

Lawrence had previously told Cynthia Asquith that he felt like Ovid in his Thracian exile, despite the beauty of the Midlands setting, the hillside cottage above the gorge known as the Via Gellia: 'It is in the darkish Midlands,' he told Mrs. Carswell, 'on the rim of a steep deep valley, looking over the darkish, folded hills—exactly the navel of England, and feels exactly that.'

Dorothy Yorke was a visitor to Mountain Cottage in June and went back to London 'in tears and grief', quite in the spirit of her counterpart in *Aaron's Rod*. At this time Lawrence asked Gertler how Ottoline Morrell was and whether 'she would like to see us again—if we went to Garsington? I feel somehow, that perhaps we might'—a complete change of tune from the complaints to Gertler, only three months before, about the 'old carrion' who was trying to prevent the publication of *Women in Love*. It would be easy to say that Lawrence was weary of cold and lonely cottages and that he longed for the warm and spacious Garsington: it would be easy indeed to say that, if so much proof of Lawrence's truculent independence were not at hand. Actually, he liked Ottoline Morrell, despite the faults he found in her. But it took him ten years to become her friend again. (And she never recovered from *Women in Love,* which as late as 1932 she described to Koteliansky as '*so horrible* . . . a wicked chaotic spiteful book' which she felt embodied Frieda's view of her.)

Recent experiences had embittered Lawrence against democracy and had increased his respect for aristocrats. He told Cecil Gray on July 3 that he was to write a history textbook for the Oxford University Press; he was 'in a historical mood' and felt that men had not changed much over the centuries; most of the species he found contemptible and in need of 'proper ruling' by a few capable individuals. But this was 'impossible, because they can only be ruled as they are willing to be ruled: and that is swinishly or hypocritically.' These ideas are implicit in the book Lawrence wrote, and they account for some of the strong objections to it, particularly his concluding passage, which says that the salvation of Europe will depend on 'one great chosen figure' who will be 'supreme over the will of the people'. And throughout, Lawrence praises the strong man, even Bismarck, whom the English were at that time blaming for so many of their troubles; Lawrence found him 'remarkably great'. Attila, to whom he wrote, years later, an admiring poem, is dramatized as 'a haughty little creature' who 'had a prancing way of walking, and he rolled his eyes fiercely, filling the onlookers with terror, enjoying the terror he inspired.' Part of Gibbon's description of Attila will indicate some of Lawrence's immense debt to his predecessor: 'The haughty step and demeanour of the king of the Huns expressed the consciousness of his superiority above the rest of mankind; and he had a custom of fiercely rolling his eyes, as if he wished to enjoy the terror which he inspired.'

Other passages reveal other close derivations, though Lawrence also put a good deal of himself into that book, which is far more vivid, plagiarism and all, than the usual school text. A publisher friend of Lawrence's, Vere H. Collins, in a letter to the present author, said he had been impressed with Lawrence's knowledge of history and 'suggested that he should not write a formal, connected textbook, but a series of vivid sketches of movements and people. He suggested *Movements in European History* for the title. I thought that good. I then induced my chief, Humphrey Milford (later Sir Humphrey Milford), Publisher to the University of Oxford, to give me leave to encourage him to do a book to be offered to the Oxford University Press.'

When the history was finished, early in 1919, 'Milford sent it to Oxford to be read by one or more of the history specialists. I believe it was approved by C. L. Fletcher [who was a Delegate of the Clarendon Press]. The only criticisms made, so far as I can remember, were of some small details of dates and names.' Lawrence, the banned writer, agreed to a pseudonym on the title page: when the book appeared in 1921, its authorship was ascribed to Lawrence H. Davison, though later editions bear Lawrence's correct name.

He even wrote an epilogue for the illustrated edition of 1925, but Oxford was too shocked to publish it, largely because Lawrence, as on several other occasions, mentioned in the same breath the recent Prime Minister, David Lloyd George, and Horatio Bottomley, the jingoistic editor of *John Bull,* then serving a sentence for fraud. It is regrettable that the Oxford people rejected that epilogue, for it would have further cleared Lawrence of the charge that he was a fascist. The epilogue was fortunately resurrected by James T. Boulton in his 1971 edition (for Oxford) of *Movements in European History*. It shows that Lawrence had written in 1924 that 'personally' he believed 'that a good form of socialism, if it could be brought about, would be the best form of government', if it weren't a form of bullying, such as Lawrence felt that socialism had become in Soviet Russia, where the Communists had been successful in their attempts at 'forcing their own will'. He noted that 'in Fiesole near Florence the Fascisti suddenly banged at the door of the mayor of the village, in the night when all were in bed. The mayor was forced to get up and open the door. The Fascisti seized him, stood him against the wall of his house, and shot him under the eyes of his wife and children, who were in their night dresses.' The mayor was killed because he was a socialist; fascism was 'only another kind of bullying'. If Lawrence had known of Hitler, he would have been even more strongly against the Nazi bullying.

While Lawrence was working on the original edition of his history book, he and Frieda escaped from Middleton for a while, in August 1918, to London (as usual 'boring and stultifying'), to Hermitage, and then to the Forest of Dean for a visit to the Carswells. Lawrence, with his only pair of trousers extensively patched, was more youthfully cheerful than the Carswells had ever seen him. He made much of their three-month-old baby, John Patrick Carswell, for whom Frieda embroidered a colored frock; Lawrence dedicated his poem 'War Baby' to the new little Carswell, and he later used the vicarage where the Carswells then lived for his story 'The Blind Man', in which Mrs. Carswell became Isabel Previn. 'There was nothing superficially like me in her', Catherine Carswell noted, 'that could not easily be refuted. Yet somewhere the truth smote me, just as I doubt not that the truth smote Katherine Mansfield when she read about Gudrun in *Women in Love,* or Ottoline Morrell when she read about Hermione, or Dorothy Brett when she read "The Princess". Here was little of portraiture, still less of summing up. But what an inescapable reading of the pulse of a life!"

Soon after his return to Middleton, Lawrence wrote to Donald Carswell, on September 11: 'Today being my 33rd birthday—sacred year—comes [*sic*] the papers calling me up for medical re-examination. I am determined to do nothing more at the bidding of these swine.' The following day he wrote to Cynthia Asquith to ask her help in obtaining some war work for him: 'I can type, rather badly —not shorthand.' This was the lowest mark of his fortunes: 'Surely I am a valuable person,' he assured Lady Cynthia. He also wrote to Arnold Bennett at the Ministry of Information; could Bennett find some work for him, since Bennett considered him a 'genius'? Frieda recalled that Bennett replied that this was no reason he should give Lawrence work, and Catherine Carswell reasonably commented that certainly Lawrence's genius would be a handicap in any position

Bennett had at his disposal. Lawrence should take up schoolmastering, Mrs. Carswell felt, but wondered 'what school would open its door to a man whose book had suffered public prosecution for obscenity?' Lawrence didn't discover until some time later that Bennett had privately given money to Pinker in his behalf. Lawrence afterwards asked Pinker who the 'E. A. Bennett' was whose loan was being refunded. And in 1930, a month after Lawrence died, Bennett wrote of him sympathetically at a time when the obituaries were unusually vicious; Bennett, however, said that he wouldn't go so far as E. M. Forster, who had just said that Lawrence was 'the greatest imaginative novelist of his generation.'

On September 26 Lawrence reported for medical examination in a big schoolroom in Derby. The account of this ordeal in *Kangaroo,* as the experience of Somers, is thorough and intense. 'He stood there with his ridiculous thin legs, in his ridiculous thin jacket, but he did not feel a fool.' Here, among his own people, he had been dealt with insolently ('his appearance had been anticipated, and they wanted to count him out'), as he had not been treated at the medical examinations in Cornwall. Now he kept his face composed, though he knew it was white, and 'the slight lifting of his nose, like a dog's disgust, the heavy unshakeable watchfulness of his eyes brought even the judgement-table to silence: even the puppy doctors.' Not until he walked out, 'with his jacket about his thin legs, and his beard in front of him', did they lift 'their heads for a final jeer'.

If Lawrence-Somers had felt a bit persecuted, he could hardly be blamed. And although the people of his own Midlands were not the sly peepers of Cornwall, even there in Nottingham and Derby they felt the war as something more than a drain on manpower and food supplies: there had been a munitions factory explosion in Nottingham in July, and in the previous year Scotland Yard had uncovered in Derby a plot among pacifists to assassinate Lloyd George. Lawrence, however much he may have ruffled the suspicions of fervent patriots of the time, knew his own essential innocence; but like many a man before and after him, he was a victim, in a time of panic, of oversimple minds driving themselves to viciousness.

In *Kangaroo,* Lawrence-Somers saw human bodies being handled as if they were furniture, and determined that he would never 'be touched again. And because they had handled his private parts, and looked into them, their eyes should burst and their hands should wither and their hearts should rot.'

When Lawrence returned home to Mountain Cottage after the medical examination, he wrote to Cynthia Asquith that 'these accursed people' would never 'paw' him again. He once more asked for her help, perhaps to find him a job at the Ministry of Education; he had had enough of being 'kicked about like an old can . . . If these military *canaille* call me up for any of their filthy jobs—I am graded for sedentary work—I shall just remove myself and be a deserter.' On the same night he wrote to Mrs. Carswell that he was 'done with society and humanity—Labour and Military alike can go to hell'; he had 'a jolly good personal life, with a few people who are friends, and the rest can do as they like.'

His bitterness was never against life itself, but against the stupid things people did with life. His anger was at the money-changers in the temple, and not at the temple; not even, indeed, at money itself. And except for his bursts of anger, he was usually, as he put it, 'jolly'. Even at this sour time, when he went to London again, the sick Katherine Mansfield reported in a letter that Lawrence, who came to her bedside day after day to cheer her, 'was just his old, merry, rich self, laughing, describing things, giving you pictures, full of enthusiasm and joy in a future where we become all "vagabonds" . . . Oh, there is something so lovable about him and his eagerness, his passionate eagerness for life—that is what one loves so.'

Katherine Mansfield, the former mocker of Rananim, now seemed almost to share in the dream of it. Murry, coming home wearily from his work at the War Office, felt 'out of it' when he heard all this gay talk of a new life in another country. A specialist had told him, but not Katherine, that with care she might live another four or five years: 'You couldn't begin a new life in a new country on such slender capital.'

Lawrence and Frieda had influenza in London, and in November went to Hermitage to recover. They had intended not to go back to Derbyshire, but now Lawrence contemplated a return, probably because their flight had annoyed the rent-paying Ada. From Hermitage, Lawrence told Amy Lowell about the play he had recently finished, *Touch and Go,* a quasi-sequel to *Women in Love,* with some of the same characters but with none of the power of the novel. 'Not wicked but too good is probably the sigil of its doom', he wrote to Amy Lowell about the play, which Katherine Mansfield found '*black* with miners'.

The Armistice overtook the Lawrences at Hermitage. In *Kanga-*

roo, Somers and Harriet 'sang German songs, in the cottage, away there in the country: and she cried—and he wondered what now.' Richard Aldington took this to mean that the Lawrences spent the night of November 11 there, but David Garnett insisted they were at Montague Shearman's party at his flat in the Adelphi, a gathering of which Sir Osbert Sitwell and others have written. Most of Bloomsbury wandered in and out, or went to their old headquarters at 46 Gordon Square. Garnett has recalled that Lawrence delivered a tirade against the war, at Shearman's. 'It was a remarkable day,' Garnett has written to the present author, 'and every event in it is clear. I had started that day by going to work as an agricultural labourer. It struck me that evening that my personal liberation was arriving fast, and naturally I was in no mood for Lawrence's jeremiad.'

Elsewhere Garnett noted that, amid the glitter and happy turbulence of the party at Shearman's, Lawrence 'held forth on the worse and more destructive war which would follow immediately,' all this declaimed 'in a spirit of hellish prophecy and hate'. Lawrence moved up World War II by some twenty years, but at least he should be given credit for seeing, through the saturnalia of Armistice night, that the big war had settled very little. It took even the brilliant and expert Keynes, who was also at that party, several months to discover this and to bring out, in 1919, *The Economic Consequences of the Peace.*

7 FAREWELL TO ENGLAND

After the Armistice, Frieda stayed on in London, while Lawrence dutifully returned to Derbyshire. From there he wrote to Katherine Mansfield a series of remarkable letters in a lyric vein, beginning with a description of his arrival, at the end of November, on a pouring black night, and of the local coachman waiting with what he called the 'Vektawry', then the dark trip 'through a rustle of waters' to the cottage, where the neighbor, Mrs. Doxey, had a fire in the grate, and tea ready. The next morning found 'the world rather Macbeth-looking—brownish little strokes of larch trees above, the bracken brown and curly, disappearing below the house into shadowy gloom' —and most of these letters to the sick girl in London continued in this vein. When writing to her, Lawrence was thinking creatively, imaginatively, and ideas he later used in stories began to spring up through his prose.

Once, for example, Lawrence told Katherine, after a heavy fall of snow, of a pheasant that had crept near their house for shelter: the description of this pheasant ('his green head and his long, pointed feathers . . . clear as he is and formal on the snow') should be matched with that of the peacock Lawrence wrote of to Cynthia Asquith, a crying peacock he dreamed of as being mauled in mid-air by two dogs until it fell to earth and 'a woman came running out of a cottage not far off, saying it would be all right'; these memories and images were, in fusion, probably the motive for his writing the story 'Wintry Peacock'.

In another of the letters to Katherine Mansfield, Lawrence told of a December train ride between Wirksworth and Ripley, when he saw the flames of the ironworks at night from Butterley reservoir, and on the railway platform 'everything was lit up red—there was a man with dark red brows, odd, not a human being. I could write a story about him. He makes me think of Ashurbanipal.' And Lawrence did write a story beginning: 'Flame-lurid his face as he turned among the throng of flame-lit and dark faces upon the platform'—the story 'Fannie and Annie', which like 'Wintry Peacock' was included in the *England, My England* collection in 1922.

In a letter written to Mrs. Carswell, apparently in early December of 1918, Lawrence mentioned another of his current efforts: 'I have written four little essays for *The Times*—"Education of the People"—good, but most revolutionary. Still, as it is Education, not politics, Freeman might print them'—but he did not. George Sydney Freeman, editor of the educational supplement of the *Times,* returned the essays to Lawrence with the suggestion that they be made into a book; Lawrence apparently reworked them in Sicily in 1920, but for publication they had to await the posthumous *Phoenix* volume. Lawrence's motive in writing the first draft of these essays, in the late autumn of 1918, was possibly that he wanted to establish himself as something of an authority on education in order to obtain an administrative position in that area.

In a letter of December 6, 1918, to Eleanor Farjeon's brother Herbert, Lawrence asked to borrow the Everyman's edition of *Legends of Charlemagne* (by Bulfinch) for his history volume, but he doesn't seem to have used it as a source.

Frieda returned from London in time for that Christmas of 1918, which she and Lawrence spent at Ripley. It was a Merrie England party, with young and old celebrating vigorously. Then, on the day

after Christmas, some of them went 'roaring off in the dark wind to
Dr Feroze's—he is a Parsee—and drank two more bottles of musca-
tel, and danced in his big empty room till we were staggered, and
quite dazed.' Lawrence, never one to let an interesting character go
to waste, used Dr. Feroze in the second chapter of *Aaron's Rod,* in
which (in Christmas season) 'the little greenish man, evidently an
Oriental'—and also a doctor—has an argument with Aaron in a pub.
Aaron feels a menace in the man's 'black, void, glistening eyes'.

After Christmas, Lawrence was 'infuriated to think of the months
ahead, when one waits paralysed for some sort of release,' he told
Katherine Mansfield. 'I feel caged somehow—and I *cannot* find out
how to earn enough to keep us—and it maddens me.' He still felt
the pull of America, as he told Amy Lowell in a letter written after
he returned home the following day:

> Christmas is over now, and we must prepare for a New Year.
> I hope it will be a real new year, and a new start altogether. The
> old has been bad enough.—I was in London in November—saw
> Richard [Aldington], who was on leave. He is very fit, looking
> forward to peace and freedom. Hilda also is in town—not so
> very well. She is going to have another child, it appears. I hope
> she will be all right. Perhaps she can get more settled, for her
> nerves are very shaken: and perhaps the child will soothe her
> and steady her. I hope it will.
>
> England is wintry and uncongenial. Towards summer time, I
> want to come to America. I feel that I want to be in a new
> country. I expect we shall go to Switzerland or Germany when
> Peace is signed. Frieda wants to see her people. Her brother-
> in-law is now Minister of Finance to the Bavarian republic, one
> of my friends is something else important, and F's cousin–Hart-
> mann von Richthofen, whom they turned out of the Reichstag
> six months ago because he wanted peace—he is now a moving
> figure in Berlin. So Germany will be quite exciting for us. But I
> want to come to America: I don't know why. But the land itself
> draws me.

*

New Poems (1918) was the first of Lawrence's books to appear under the imprint of Martin Secker, who in 1921 became Lawrence's
principal publisher in England for the rest of his life (to be suc-

ceeded in the Depression of the 1930s by his original publisher, the house of Heinemann). Secker, described by Frank Swinnerton as 'resolute in negative' but 'with a kind heart and a reluctance to give pain which have landed him in many difficulties', had made an impressive beginning with some of the newer writers such as Mackenzie, Cannan, and Walpole; in taking up the neglected Lawrence in 1918 he showed a sense of adventure, for it might be expected that the *New Poems* would have a bad press.

Typically, the anonymous reviewer in the February 1919 *Athenaeum* said that Lawrence had since the early days tortured his poetic gift 'with a kind of neurotic fury'. Nevertheless, Lawrence's 'gift was struggling into sight again,' partly because of a 'return to conventional verse form'. Ironically, most of the 'new' poems were old poems, dating from the Croydon period and earlier; some of them even show traces of the aestheticism of Wilde, Symons, and Le Gallienne: 'Embankment at Night: Outcasts' does—'Oh, the singing mansions, / Golden-lighted tall / Trams that pass, blown ruddily down the night!'

Lawrence had his set of poems that were actually new (*Bay*) ready for publication by Cyril Beaumont, who didn't bring them out until November 1919. In September 1918, Lawrence complained to Cynthia Asquith that Beaumont, who already had held the poems for at least six months, was 'waiting for some opportunity or other.' As Lawrence's only publication in book form in 1917 was poetry (*Look! We Have Come Through!*), as well as in 1918 (*New Poems*), so in 1919 *Bay* was to mark his only appearance in a volume of his own.

Bay came out in the very month that he left England. Beaumont, in *First Score* (1927), the story of the first twenty books he published, said the delays were Lawrence's fault, because he was moving around the Mediterranean. But Lawrence didn't go south until the middle of November; Beaumont was simply wrong.

For Lawrence, 1919 had been another year of continued poverty and neglect and illness. His letters, in those days of living in chill cottages, almost invariably contained health bulletins. Often he would report that Frieda had a cold; several days later he would announce that he had caught it. On January 23, 1919, for example, he told Catherine Carswell that Frieda had a severe cold. He was glad that the Carswell baby had recovered from his illness ('My God, teeth already! He'll be smoking a cigarette in our faces before we know where we are'), but not long after he was writing about his own poor health to Amy Lowell, to whom he said on February 5: 'It is very cold here. We have both been ill. I want spring and summer terribly.' Within a month he was nearly dead of influenza (he told Amy Lowell on April 5 he had 'nearly shuffled off the mortal coil'), and from this he had a slow recovery.

During that time he had a serious quarrel with Murry, who had been made editor of the *Athenaeum*. Lawrence appreciated Murry's suggestion that he become a contributor and said he would 'try to be pleasant and a bit old-fashioned.' He even offered to appear anonymously. His first contribution, under the signature Grantorto, appeared in the April 11 issue as 'The Whistling of Birds'. It was an essay signaling his return to life from the perils of illness and war: he described the fading of frost, the arrival of warm winds, and the triumphant whistling of the returning birds.

Murry liked this but rejected 'Adolf', the story of the Lawrence children's rabbit which disappeared at the end of the sketch with his white tail bobbing at the reader as if to say *'Merde!'* in his face— most unsuitable for the *Athenaeum*'s staid readership. Murry, who felt his position 'precarious', wanted to change the magazine gradually, from a 'journal of reconstruction' to a literary paper, and even under a *nom de plume* Lawrence was too violent.

Katherine Mansfield wrote to Koteliansky on April 7 of 'a rumpus' with the Lawrences: 'I see this "rumpus"—don't you? a very large prancing, imaginary animal being led by F.—as Una led the lion. It is evidently bearing down on me with F. for a Lady Godiva on its back.' Katherine wanted none of this: 'I have not the room nowadays for rumpuses. My garden is too small and they eat up all one's plants —roots and all.' Lawrence told Katherine in a 'Thursday' letter (April 10?), 'The complication of getting Jack and you and F. and me into a square seems great—especially Jack.' Lawrence had been 'sure of' Katherine 'ever since Cornwall, save for Jack—and if you must really go his way, and if he will *never* really come our way— well! But things will resolve themselves.' Resolve themselves, however, 'things' never did.

Murry braved the 'rumpus' in May, a month after the Lawrences had left Mountain Cottage, at the expiration of their year's lease, and had moved back to the Radfords' place in Berkshire. Murry had heard of a cottage near Newbury which he thought might be pleasanter for Katherine in her illness; on his way to look over the house, he stopped to see the Lawrences, who joined him in his inspection tour; and on Lawrence's recommendation he didn't rent the cottage. Lawrence, ill and tired, was still Rananiming, and hoped for a new start in a new country. Murry, who 'had no particular faith in this remedy and no chance of applying it,' was glum and unresponsive as Lawrence damned England.

Murry's sharpest memory of this meeting was 'of the sight of the bright yellow wood chips which we gathered from the coppice': Lawrence mentioned these in several letters of the time and was to recall them later in *Kangaroo,* in his passage about the hazel copses and 'the real old English hamlets, that are still like Shakespeare—and like Hardy's woodlanders.' Murry said those Berkshire wood chips were 'more golden-rich than any . . . I have seen since.'

Shortly before leaving Derbyshire, Lawrence had discussed with Dr. Eder the possibility of going to Palestine—Eder was now an executive on the Zionist Commission. But Lawrence was soon thinking of America again, as he wrote to Amy Lowell from Hermitage on May 20:

> I had a letter from [B. W.] Huebsch the other day, about the publishing of the poems etc. He seems very nice. He said he would arrange for me to lecture in America. I am not best in lecturing, but don't mind if it *must* be done. I am making every arrangement possible to come to New York in August or September. I want very badly to come—to transfer myself. Huebsch said you told him you didn't think Boston would be the place for me to lecture in. Are you shy of me?—a little doubtful of the impression I shall, or should make? I hope not. I believe you are the only person I know, actually in America, so I was hoping you'd help me a bit to find my feet when I come. Anyhow, tell me how you feel about it, won't you. Probably I shall come alone, and Frieda will follow. If you don't want to be bothered—I admit it is a bother—just tell me.—I do hope your health is good now.

In panic, Amy Lowell warned Lawrence that New England would not receive him cordially. Even Boston's renowned Athenaeum library found it necessary to conceal the 'superb' *Sons and Lovers* in its 'scruple' room. America, she went on, would only disgust Lawrence, for Americans couldn't 'see the difference between envisioning life whole and complete, physical as well as spiritual, and pure obscenities like those perpetrated by James Joyce.'

Lawrence replied that he knew America was no El Dorado; he

was not eager to lecture; he felt he could earn a fair living by his writing. 'All I want is to feel that there is somewhere I could go, if necessary, and somebody I could appeal to for help if I needed it.' Amy Lowell had fought valiantly for modern poetry and had compelled in Boston and Brookline a certain acceptance of her bohemianism and cigar-smoking—after all, she was a Lowell—but the prospect of the Lawrences' appearing there terrified her, and she wrote each of them a letter urging them not to come. The advice was accepted, for when Lawrence did leave England in the autumn, he went to Italy. Before his departure he sold Amy Lowell's typewriter to Catherine Carswell's brother for five pounds.

Despite Lawrence's having to endure near-poverty in cold cottages, his financial situation had improved slightly in 1919. On May 5 he wrote to Pinker: 'Thank you for the cheque for fifty-five pounds which came so nicely on Saturday,' and five days later he expressed gratitude to Edward Marsh for sending 'the twenty pounds' from Rupert Brooke's will: 'Queer, to receive money from the dead: as it were out of the dark sky.' He believed 'in Rupert dead' and fighting beside him, though he disliked Oliver Lodge's brand of spiritualism, with its 'hotel bills and collar studs. The passionate dead act within us and with us, not like messenger boys and hotel porters. Of the dead who really live, whose presence we hardly care to speak—we know their hush.' Ironically—as Christopher Hassall disclosed after Sir Edward Marsh's death in 1953—Brooke did not specifically leave Lawrence money; in sending it, Marsh showed an executor's discretion and a good heart.

By the first week of July—when the naval blockade had helped starve the Germans into signing the Versailles Treaty—Lawrence planned to go to London to apply for passports again. He told Cynthia Asquith, 'It was a great mistake that we did not clear out in 1915, when we had those other passports.' He felt, despite Amy Lowell's warnings, that he could 'make enough to live on in America, fairly easily.'

Later in July, Lawrence and Frieda went to Pangbourne as guests of Rosalind Baynes, whom they had met through Eleanor Farjeon. Her brother Herbert was married to Rosalind Baynes's sister. Rosalind Baynes, mother of three children, had been married since 1913 to Godwin Baynes, an analytical psychologist of the school of Jung. Her father, Sir Hamo Thornycroft, was the sculptor whose statue of Cromwell stands outside the House of Commons.

302   THE WAR YEARS

From Myrtle Cottage, Pangbourne, in August, Lawrence gave a summer report to Mrs. Carswell, in which he spoke of the farm girls he used as characters in 'The Fox':

Thos. Cook said passports would not be granted till Peace was *ratified*. God knows when that will be. Will Don please fill in the passport, and forward it to Thos. Cook. At any rate it will be ready.

We are here, I think, till the 25th—then to Hermitage, either to stay in the Cottage or with those farm girls. The wretched Margaret [Radford] is at the cottage now—she turned us out. She leaves on the 23rd, but comes back again in September for a week or fortnight—so we shall probably stay at the farm. We had my younger sister here last week—now my elder sister.

I don't quite know what is going to happen with us. I shan't go to Germany at present—nor even America, I think. When I come near to the thought of U.S.A.—New York, Prince of Wales, etc.—it sickens me. . . .

Nothing happens—except Martin Secker wants to bring out my *Collected Poems*—why, heaven knows.

'Nothing happens': as far as writing was concerned, it was a fairly uneventful summer. Lawrence's principal activity seems to have been the rewriting of 'The Fox', which Katherine Mansfield liked best among his tales. That summer Pinker returned the story 'Monkey Nuts', a little comedy about some soldiers in Berkshire who meet a land girl named Stokes, possibly based upon the farm girl named Monk whom Lawrence had also used in 'The Fox'.

At that time he also wrote the preface for his play *Touch and Go* (published 1920), in which he discussed the labor problems occurring in the play and said that Galsworthy's *Strife* was pathetic. A more important product was the preface, written at Pangbourne, to the American edition of *New Poems,* which Huebsch was to publish the following year. Lawrence felt the preface really belonged to the *Look!* volume, 'but is it not better to publish a preface long after the book it belongs to has appeared?'

This *New Poems* preface could stand as an introduction to all Lawrence's verse: 'Poetry is, as a rule, either the voice of the far future, exquisite and ethereal, or it is the voice of the past, rich, magnificent . . . The poetry of the beginning and the poetry of the end must have exquisite finality, perfection which belongs to all that is far off.' But there was another kind of poetry, that of 'the immediate present' where there was 'no perfection, no consummation, nothing finished. The strands are all flying, quivering, intermingling into the web, the waters are shaking the moon.' For 'life, the ever-present, knows no finality, no finished crystallization.'

Of such poetry, the best was that of Whitman, who 'truly looked before and after. But he did not sigh for what was not.' Most *vers libristes,* Lawrence thought, made the mistake of trying to formalize their material: after breaking 'the lovely form of metrical verse' they failed to realize 'that free verse has its own *nature, that it is neither star nor pearl, but instantaneous like plasm.'* As an explanation of the 'secret' of Lawrence's poetry, this preface stands beside 'The Novel', the essay (in *Reflections on the Death of a Porcupine*) which discusses his attitude to prose: as in the *New Poems* preface, 'The Novel' of a few years later goes to the source of Lawrence's vision, in which he discusses the 'relatedness of all things' as 'quick'.

*

At last the passports came. Lawrence refused to go to Germany with Frieda, who left England in October. Somers, parting from his wife in *Kangaroo,* 'said good-bye at the Great Eastern Station, while she sat in the Harwich–Hook of Holland express. She had a look of almost vindictive triumph, and almost malignant love, as the train drew out. So he went back to his meaninglessness at the cottage.' But Lawrence soon decided to leave, and arranged for the recently demobilized Aldington to take over the house, an action which resulted in a bit of comedy, for the subleasing Radfords kept forgetting to turn over Aldington's rent to the original owner, and Aldington eventually had to hire a lawyer to get him out of the mess. But by that time Lawrence had left England; and it is significant that in two of his early post-war novels, *The Lost Girl* and *Kangaroo,* his two leading characters, upon leaving England, see it as a coffin sliding into the sea.

England: how well Lawrence knew it, from the coal-and-forest Midlands of his childhood to the Cornish coast and the copses of the southern counties; he had lived three and a half years at the southern edge of London, and from time to time in London itself; he had made excursions to Barrow-in-Furness and to the York and Lincoln and Kent and Welsh coasts—England was in his bones, but it was not to have either Lawrence's bones or his ashes.

After 1919, his journeys to England were few and brief: in 1923, 1925, and 1926. Each time Lawrence found the place 'hateful'. His reasons for this feeling, although he didn't fully recognize them at the time, went back to his childhood, when the 'soulless' mine owners made the mass of men work underground like moles; and malignant censorship contributed to his loathing of England, and the bullying of the wartime officials and other busybodies, even though Lawrence could admit that some of the evils of those days were 'necessary' evils. 'The conscription, all the whole performance of the war was absolutely circumstantially necessary,' he wrote in *Kangaroo*. 'It was necessary even to investigate the secret parts of a man. Agreed! Agreed! *But*—' And there it was: '*But*—. He was full of a lava of rage and hate, at the bottom of his soul. And he knew it was the same with most men. He felt desecrated.'

The rage had an impersonal quality. Lawrence never sentimentalized his own predicament, never filled up with self-pity: his typical hero, Paul Morel of *Sons and Lovers*, didn't enjoy the grimness of his lot, but accepted it without crying, 'Why must this happen to *me?*' And Lawrence's later autobiographical heroes were likewise without snuffling self-pity; like Lawrence, they were often angry men, but they were angry at the perversion and abuse of the good. As noted earlier, Lawrence never cursed life itself: 'Once be disillusioned with the man-made world,' he wrote in 1926, 'and you still see the magic, the beauty, the delicate realness of all the other life.' As one of the few authors of his time with a sense of values that was both deep and consistent, Lawrence viewed everything from the sympathetic point of life itself, of growth. When he saw life being murdered, growth being stifled, his rage was not on behalf of himself, who was only a channel of rage, but on behalf of life and growth.

And in 1919, 'this England of the peace was like a corpse'; life and growth were elsewhere. In the darkness of November he turned again to the bright fields of the Mediterranean south, the fruitlands, the flowery valleys, the glowing seas. He would go to Italy, where Frieda would meet him, as before. He had heard of a farm in the mountains near Cassino, and this would be a good place to live for a while.

Shortly before he left, Lawrence walked down a crowded London street with Aldington, who noticed how the passers-by glared with quick hostility at this bearded man, even threw a few jests his way, which he ignored. Aldington felt relieved when 'the tall slim figure with the firm quick tread' disappeared down the steps to the underground—an appropriate last glimpse for Aldington, who wrongly thought he would never see Lawrence again. Aldington felt that in any event it was better for this man whose very presence aroused the jeers of strangers in his native land, to leave it.

When the Carswells saw 'the solitary pilgrim off' at the station on November 14, he 'felt the wrench of departure, but he was glad, very glad, to be going'; and he would never settle in England again. Like his hero in *Kangaroo,* he now

left England, England which he had loved so bitterly, bitterly— and now was leaving, alone, and with a feeling of expressionlessness in his soul. It was a cold day. There was snow on the Downs like a shroud. And as he looked back from the boat, when they had left Folkestone behind and only England was there, England looked like a grey, dreary-grey coffin sinking in the sea behind, with her dead grey cliffs and the white, worn-out cloth of snow above.

*

PART FOUR

The Wander Years

*

1 INTO THE SOUTH WIND

TOO POOR TO PAY for accommodations in a sleeper (if there were any), Lawrence sat up on shrilly crowded trains that dragged across Europe. He found Paris 'nasty', and the French repellent. He arrived at Turin with red eyes and stretched nerves, and spent two days wrangling with the wealthy old Englishman at whose villa he stayed. Except for a change of names and a shift of the setting to Novara, Lawrence faithfully reproduced this visit in Chapters XII and XIII of *Aaron's Rod:* this annoyed his host, who later complained that, among other crimes, Lawrence had made him seem dull. Richard Aldington, despite his own protests against Lawrence's treatment of the Aldington set in that novel, believed that the originals of Sir William and Lady Franks should have been 'honoured at sitting as models for an artist in words'.

Like Aaron in the novel, Lawrence had argued half-mockingly with the old man, who spoke for security and a plump bank balance against Lawrence's 'naked liberty'. The host, one of the best-known Englishmen in Italy, had since 1880 built a fortune as a ship owner there and in Sicily. He took a leading part in charitable activities and, during the war, in promoting the British cause locally. The original of Sir William Franks was Sir Walter Becker (1855–1927), knighted the year before he met Lawrence.

On his way farther south, Lawrence stopped nostalgically at Lerici for a day, arriving at Florence on November 19 in cold black rain. Norman Douglas had booked him at his own *pensione,* the Balestri. There Lawrence settled in a huge 'stone-comfortless room' with a view of the river. Douglas had a sycophant in tow, a European-American named Maurice Magnus, who eyed Lawrence 'in that shrewd and impertinent way of the world of actor-managers: cosmopolitan, knocking shabbily round the world.' Asked about Magnus, Douglas explained that his companion had been Isadora Duncan's manager and a journalist and, before the war, editor of the *Roman Review;* he had a back-alley knowledge of most of the European capitals. Frieda, who met Magnus later, has recalled Lawrence's horror at seeing him toadying to the lordly and imperative Doug-

309

las: 'To Lawrence's logical and puritanical mind Magnus presented a problem of human relations.' The hearty, red-faced Douglas told Lawrence, 'All the better for me, ha-ha!—if he *likes* to run around for me. My dear fellow, I wouldn't prevent him, if it amuses him.'

On meeting Magnus, Lawrence, the tailor's grandson, had at once measured him: 'He stuck out his front rather tubbily, like a bird, and his legs seemed to perch behind him, as a bird's do.' Lawrence had never met anyone like him, dapper and yet down-at-heel; he tried to convince Magnus that his own hair and beard ('Such a *lovely* colour!') were not dyed.

He was 'rather glad' when Magnus departed for Rome, though shocked at the man's traveling first-class; even Douglas seemed a bit put out at that. Lawrence had only nine pounds with him, and twelve more in the bank in London. On her way to Germany, Frieda had run into 'a nightmare of a muddle', delays and hardships, her trunks stolen in Holland. Magnus, leaving Florence on the midnight train, cooed that traveling was so beastly anyhow, why not go in style?

Frieda recovered her trunks but not their contents. When she arrived in Florence at four o'clock in the morning of December 3, Lawrence took her for a drive in an open carriage. She saw the bridges and towers in the haze of moonlight: the copy of the David and the other public statues proclaimed to her that this was a male city. When she came to know the Anglo colony, however, she thought Florence was a Cranford, a male Cranford: 'And the wickedness there seemed like an old maid's secret rejoicing in wickedness.' Lawrence emphasized this aspect of Florence in the café and party scenes of *Aaron's Rod*. In them he neatly portrayed Oscar Wilde's little hummingbird of a friend, Reggie Turner, as Algy Constable. Douglas, who appeared as Argyle, roared his protest a few years later in his anti-Lawrence pamphlet: 'Me, under the transparent disguise of Jimmie McTaggart or something equally Scotch . . . [a] high-handed old swaggerer, rather unsteady on his legs.'

While storing up all this Florentine material for later use, Lawrence stayed in the city just three weeks. On December 9, he and Frieda went south. At Rome, they appeared at the *pensione* where Catherine Carswell's Italian cousin, Ellise Santoro, had taken rooms for them, but the proprietor wouldn't admit them when he discovered that Frieda was German. Ellise Santoro took them in, and almost immediately someone in her mixed and turbulent household robbed them.

In his embarrassment Lawrence said nothing, for their hostess, who had refused to accept money for their lodgings, would have insisted on paying back the amount stolen.

After a few days Lawrence and Frieda went south, to a farmstead above the village of Picinisco, in the province of Caserta, which proved to be too cold and primitive: they couldn't recommend it to Rosalind Baynes as a home for her and her children.

The Lawrences' journey there reappeared, in circumstantial detail, in *The Lost Girl:* the railway trip to Cassino, which lies six miles below Picinisco, and then the bus ride into the ice-fanged mountains. From Picinisco—Pescocalascio in *The Lost Girl*—Lawrence and Frieda had to scramble like goats for two miles along a steep mountain pathway, to the rude home of the Cervi family. There, the former model for Mrs. Baynes's father, Thornycroft, the Italian farmer Orazio Cervi (Pancrazio in the novel), welcomed them to his farmhouse, through which hens wandered while the mule stood in the doorway to deposit his droppings.

The pilgrims soon had enough; on the Saturday before Christmas the snow fell all day; on Monday, Lawrence and Frieda got up in the pre-dawn blackness and walked several miles to find a bus to Cassino. On the jouncing ride, Lawrence saw on the craggy mountain 'the monastery crouching there above, world famous, but it was impossible to call then . . . We fled south,' to the white sunlight of Capri. As he wrote to Martin Secker. 'Picinisco was too icy-mountainous—we escaped here, and like you, we spent a night on board that rolling saucepan of a boat, off Sorrento. Now we have a little apartment here, right over Morgano's [a café], on the neck of Capri, looking to the sea and Naples on the right, the sea and space on the left, the duomo the apple of our eye, gall-apple.'

The Lawrences remained two months in Capri, that 'gossipy, villa-stricken, two-humped chunk of limestone', where the slanderous chitchat would make Suetonius blush and Tiberius 'feel he's been a fleabite'. Lawrence soon planned to move on.

Meanwhile, Katherine Mansfield, feeling miserable at the Italian Riviera town with the symptomatic name of Ospedaletti, had moved to Menton, where Lawrence early in February wrote to her, 'I loathe you. You revolt me stewing in your consumption. . . . The Italians were quite right to have nothing to do with you.' And Murry was 'a dirty little worm'. All this was passed on to Murry, then in London, who subsequently reported, 'This letter to Katherine was so monstrously, so inhumanly cruel that I wrote and told him that he had committed the unforgivable crime: that I sincerely hoped that we should never meet again, because, if we ever did meet again, I should thrash him.'

Lawrence seemed to have been more grouchy than usual on Capri, and to have missed much of the spectacular beauty of the place, with its high cliffs and steep hills with their climbing white houses, its cypresses and olive trees, and the native palms that flourished there.

Lawrence wrote to Amy Lowell on February 13:

> Today I have your letter, and cheque for thirteen hundred Lire. How very nice of you to think of us this New Year. But I wish I needn't take the money: it irks me a bit. Why can't I earn enough, I've done the work. After all, you know, it makes one angry to have to accept a sort of charity. Not from you, really, because you are an artist, and that is always a sort of partnership. But when Cannan writes and tells me he has collected a few dollars—which of course, I have not received—he wrote me to tell me he was collecting a few, but never wrote again. Cannan annoys me with his sort of penny-a-time attempt at benevolence, and the ridiculous things he says about me—and everybody else—in the American Press. I am a sort of charity-boy of literature, apparently. One is denied one's just rights, and then insulted with charity. Pfui! to them all.—But I feel you and I have a sort of odd congenital understanding, so that it hardly irks me to take these Liras from you, only a little it ties me up. However, you must keep one's trust in a few people, and rest in the Lord. . . .
>
> No, don't go to England now, it is so depressing and uneasy and unpleasant in its temper. Even Italy isn't what it was, a cheerful insouciant land. The insouciance has gone. But still, I like the Italians deeply; and the sun shines, the rocks glimmer, the sea is unfolded like fresh petals. I am better here than in England.—Things are expensive, and not too abundant. But one lives for the same amount, about, as in England: and freer to move in the air and over the water one is, all the while. Southwards the old coast glimmers its rocks, far beyond the Siren Isles. It is very Greek—Ulysses['] ship left the last track in the waves. Impossible for Dreadnoughts to tread this unchangeable morning-delicate sea. . . .

We have got two beautiful rooms here on the top of this old palace, in the very centre of Capri, with the sea on both hands. Compton Mackenzie is here—a man one can trust and like, which—as far as the first goes—is more than one can say of Cannan.— But Capri is a bit small, to live on. Perhaps I shall go to the mainland—perhaps not. Anyway this address will always find me. I have just begun a new novel.

Lawrence, who found Capri 'a stew-pot of semi-literary cats', soon moved to Sicily. But before he did that, he made two visits to the mainland. He went once with Frieda to try to find a suitable house on the Amalfi coast, and once to visit Maurice Magnus at Monte Cassino.

Norman Douglas had satirized Capri and its inhabitants in his 1917 novel, *South Wind,* and didn't live there again until after World War II when, in *Footnote to Capri* (1952), he wrote that its 'foreign residents, having more money than was good for them and nothing whatever to do, broke into cantankerous little cliques (amusingly described in two of Compton Mackenzie's books) and made the place almost uninhabitable for those who refused to take sides with one or the other of them.'

Out of the money Amy Lowell had sent him, Lawrence mailed off five pounds to Magnus. Lawrence had heard from him in Capri and had felt a between-the-lines appeal for funds. On receiving them, Magnus wrote at once to say that they had saved his life; he had fallen into an abyss; he was now on his way to Monte Cassino, and Lawrence should join him there. The hinted disasters seemed to Lawrence an American hyperbole, but Magnus had phrased his invitation nicely, for although 'he was a common little bounder' he had a 'curious delicacy and tenderness and wistfulness'. Lawrence delayed going and then received another letter, in which Magnus seemed to have his hand out for more money, 'as if he had a right to it.' This annoyed Frieda, but Lawrence wanted to see the monastery, so on one February day he got up before dawn to cross to the mainland: 'Strange dark winter morning, with the open sea beyond the roofs, seen through the side window, and the thin line of the lights of Naples twinkling, far, far off.'

At the end of the day Lawrence arrived at the monastery after a long ride from the railway station, up the twisting road. Magnus, who hastened through the gateway to greet him, 'walking with his perky, busy little stride, seemed very much at home in the place.' He was a convert, and a good friend of the guest-master, Don Martino, who appears as Don Bernardo in Lawrence's memoir of Magnus. Don Martino greeted Lawrence and assigned him a room which looked down on 'the gulf where the world's valley was', and on the far mountains where the twilight still glowed on the snowy peaks. Magnus cried out in eagerness at the view: What peace—what better than to end one's days there? And indeed, as Lawrence looked out the next morning on the valley and the mountains, he felt the anguish of being a child of the present: the monks in the garden below, the farmers and their bullocks in the fields, belonged to the splendid and terrible past of the Middle Ages, with its nonchalance and grandeur and violence. Far below, the railway trains scudded along under their white smoke, stopping at the station where trucks waited and people, tiny as flies, swarmed around the coaches: 'To see all this from the monastery, where the Middle Ages live on in a sort of agony, like Tithonus, and cannot die, this was almost a violation to my soul, made almost a wound.'

Lawrence wrote his description of Monte Cassino in the long introduction he later provided for Magnus's book, *Memoirs of the Foreign Legion*. When, twenty-four years later, bombs destroyed the monastery, Lawrence's prose evocation of it could still bring back the presence of the place as no one else's descriptions or any photographs could do. Lawrence wrote his Magnus memoir two years after his visit to Monte Cassino, but his projection of the atmosphere was as forceful and intense as if noted down at the moment— perhaps more so, for his sharp visual memory often operated best in retrospect; long afterwards, he could remember exact details of a place, remember them in poetic abundance, and could then transfigure them beyond the range of mere reporting. He did this with Monte Cassino, its long, cold arched corridors, its stupendous marble church, its colonnaded Bramante courtyard, and its exciting panoramas of the world below.

Lawrence put Magnus into all this: the plump little squeaking man trying to be sincere, but always as sycophantic in his devotion to the Church as in his subservience to Douglas. He had an estranged wife somewhere; but his mother 'was his great stunt', and he carried everywhere a rather dramatic picture of her. Magnus showed Lawrence this portrait as well as his manuscript about the French Foreign Legion, which he had joined during the war under the mistaken impression that he could in this way fight against the Germans he hated so much. After a little taste of North African barracks life, he had deserted. Lawrence found *Dregs,* which Magnus originally called his story, poorly written and lacking in focus, like everything else in the life of that man, who was 'always working, but never *properly* doing anything.' And he usually seemed to expect money from Lawrence, who for this very reason wanted to withhold it. He had deliberately left his checkbook in Capri, though he shared his pocket money with Magnus. But when Lawrence offered him twenty-five lire at departing, Magnus sadly rejected the paltry gift.

Instead of staying a week at the monastery, Lawrence left—almost as if in flight—after two days. His experience there had been an intensified vision of the Ways of Modern Man, presented in the form of temptations. The monks in the unheated stone building—Lawrence sat shivering in a borrowed overcoat—tried to recapture the past; the peasants in the sloping fields lived in the blood, in mindlessness, yet money was 'their mystery of mysteries, absolutely'. Then there was Magnus, the true modern man, split like the other types but more horribly so: the furtive little city-man imprisoning himself in monastic discomfort to play around the edges of monkhood.

So Lawrence fled like Joseph, leaving the borrowed overcoat, from that 'last foothold of the old world' to 'democracy, industrialism, socialism, the red flag of the communists and the red, white and green tricolour of the *fascisti.* That was another world . . . barren like the black cinder-track of the railway, with its two steel lines.' Yet this was the avenue of escape: 'Sitting there in the dining-car, among the fat Neapolitans eating their macaroni, with the big glass windows steamed opaque and the rain beating outside, I let myself be carried away, away from the monastery, away from Magnus, away from everything.'

And on February 26, five days after his return to Capri, Lawrence crossed to Sicily to find a place to live. He had liked only a few people on Capri. Mackenzie, of whom he wrote friendlily to Amy Lowell, he mocked at in letters to others: 'One feels the generations of actors behind him and can't be quite serious.' Merely to note that 'he seems quite rich, and does himself well, and walks a sort of aesthetic figure' was, for Lawrence, to disapprove. Yet Mackenzie treated Lawrence kindly: because of his negotiations, Mackenzie made it possible for Lawrence to have Martin Secker as his publisher, an excellent choice; and Mackenzie lent Lawrence a typewriter.

For a long while, Mackenzie had dreamed of going to the islands of the South Seas and had bought many books about them. He was planning to write one of his own and, as his wife Faith recalled, 'there was talk of taking a cinema outfit'. Mackenzie wrote to his agent, 'Lawrence is also bitten with the idea of doing half the writing', and because his expenses would have to be paid, the expedition would need to have a large financial guarantee. Lawrence didn't take the idea of the Pacific jaunt any too seriously, as he told Lady Cynthia Asquith in a January 25 letter. Mackenzie, who was 'amusing and nice', talked about 'the South Seas: and of my going: but alas, a sort of réclamé trip, written up and voiced abroad and even filmed. Alas, I could not be filmed. I should feel, like a savage, that they had stolen my "medicine".'

Mackenzie had gone so far as to insert an advertisement in the *Times* for a secretary. His wife later wrote that Secker, 'with friendly craft'—since he didn't want Mackenzie so far away—called his attention to another advertisement in the *Times* saying that some of the Channel Islands could be leased from the British Government. Mackenzie then settled on Jethou, for which he paid £1,000 a year. In doing so he made himself the target of Lawrence's later unflattering story, 'The Man Who Loved Islands'.

In his autobiography Mackenzie records himself as once saying to Lawrence, 'Except for the two people who are indulging in it the sexual act is a comic operation.' (In reporting this earlier to the present writer, Sir Compton used a stronger, more Lawrencean term than 'the sexual act'.) Lawrence turned pale and departed, returning the next day to comment, 'Perhaps you're right. And if you're right . . .' His gesture was one of despair for the human race.

Mackenzie also remembered another conversation with Lawrence. As they walked together along the Via Tragana, Lawrence abruptly proclaimed that there would not be another war and then suddenly shouted, '*I* won't have another war.' Mackenzie felt this went beyond 'the limits of egocentricity': yet Lawrence was speaking not for himself, but for all men. In his portrait of Magnus, Lawrence said he was engaged in a war against 'these foul machines and contrivances that men have conjured up . . . I, a man will conjure them down again . . . I am not one man, I am many, I am most.'

But Lawrence still strongly asserted his individuality. He could report zestfully to his Eastwood friends the Hopkins that the colored kerchief they sent him for Christmas was immediately appropriated by a Rumanian of their political faith who 'with true socialistic communism must at once carefully fold the hanky and try it round his neck, looking very much pleased with himself and cocking his black eyebrows.' Yet Lawrence found people to like, besides Mackenzie, on Capri; for example, old Charles Ellingham Brooks, the island's beachcomber, a faded scholar who translated the Classics. And the Lawrences were happy to discover Mary Cannan on Capri, 'one of the decentest people' there, 'now Gilbert-less'.

It was about this time that Gilbert Cannan was certified as insane, though Aldington, who saw him not long before that, had found nothing in his behavior to suggest insanity: 'A highly strung man agitated by grief and exasperated by treachery might easily say and do things which two complaisant or unintelligent doctors could certify.' Aldington added that Lawrence agreed with him in finding Cannan no crazier than anyone else. But Murry, who had always felt that Cannan hid megalomania just below the surface of his consciousness, had seen him after his return from America, a 'disquieting' encounter: 'He talked strangely of the magnitude of his own exploits there.' Murry, seeing Cannan as detached from all reality, 'fled, miserably, from the stare of that wild unseeing eye, with the certainty that I should never encounter it again.' Lawrence was soon to encounter it, however, for Cannan came down to the Mediterranean.

This was after Lawrence had moved to Taormina, Sicily. He had gone to that island with the popular novelist Francis Brett Young and his wife, Jessica, to look for a place to live; Magnus had said that Sicily had been waiting for Lawrence since the time of Theocritus, so he set off, without Frieda, to find a suitable villa there. At Girgenti (now Agrigento) he told the Brett Youngs that some sulfur miners they passed were hostile and 'would like to throw stones at us'. This statement has been transmitted into a legend to the effect that the men actually threw stones; they didn't, however.

When darkness came down suddenly and a fierce wind blew, Lawrence disappeared. The Brett Youngs called out to him, but there was no answer. Back at the hotel, Brett Young assured his wife that Lawrence would come back; if not, an expedition with lanterns would go out to look for him. Lawrence did return: 'Oh, I just blew away through a hole in the wall like a piece of waste paper.'

He announced that they must all leave as soon as possible, so his companions were forced to go with him on a train at four in the morning. At Siracusa he nearly rented what Mrs. Brett Young called a 'dreadful-looking' house, but she and her husband pulled him away from it. At Catania, near Mount Etna, he found the lava-encrusted soil 'too volcanic. Europe is finished. Where *can* I live?' At Taormina, however, he found a pleasant villa, and the Brett Youngs went back to Capri as Lawrence telegraphed to Frieda to come over.

Francis Brett Young wrote to Secker describing Lawrence as a 'timid, shrinking, boastful brazen creature', but added that they hadn't quarreled: 'I find him a restless and disturbing personality and yet somehow pathetically attractive.' That journey with Lawrence gave Brett Young some of the episodes in his 1921 novel, *The Red Knight*.

In Taormina, during the first week of March 1920, Lawrence rented for a year the upper floor of Fontana Vecchia, a large-roomed old farmhouse with a garden amid almond and lemon and olive trees. That upper floor had, in its salon, a cowled fireplace, beside whose blazing Sicilian pines Lawrence sat writing on chill days; and it had in all weathers a spectacular view from gothically pointed windows. When he looked in one direction he saw, across 'the sunny Ionian sea, the changing jewel of Calabria, like a fire-opal moved in the light,' and in the other direction Mount Etna, 'low, white, witch-like under heaven, slowly rolling her orange smoke and giving sometimes a breath of rose-red flame'; the Greeks, who in recognizing Etna's remoteness from the world called her the Pedestal of Heaven, 'had a sense of the magic truth of things. Thank goodness one knows enough about them to find one's kinship at last.'

Lawrence found Sicily 'peaceful and still', the earth 'sappy', and he liked 'the strong Saracen element in the people'. He and Frieda reveled in the greenness and the bright flowers: 'Sicily tall, forever rising up to her gem-like summits, all golden in the dawn, and always glamorous . . . Sicily unknown to me, and amethystine-glorious in the Mediterranean dawn: like the dawn of our day, and the wonder-morning of our epoch.' Lawrence came into this brilliance and warmth after the years of darkness and cold and mist of wartime England. His imagination ripened now in the Mediterranean sun, as it had not done amid the zealous gossip on Capri.

During the two years he lived at Fontana Vecchia—years broken by trips to Malta and Sardinia and two summers on the Continent— Lawrence completed *The Lost Girl* and *Aaron's Rod,* wrote his two books on the unconscious, and some of his finest short novels and stories as well as most of the *Birds, Beasts and Flowers* poems. These last, particularly, glow with the hot, rich colors of Sicily.

The best known of these poems, 'Snake', tells of an experience that occurred 'on the day of Sicilian July, with Etna smoking'. He had gone down to the water trough, 'in pyjamas for the heat, to drink there', and had seen the yellow-brown snake that 'sipped with his straight mouth, / Softly drank with his straight gums, into his slack long body, / Silently.' Several years before, in 'The Reality of Peace', Lawrence had written:

> If there is a serpent of secret and shameful desire in my soul, let me not beat it out of my consciousness with sticks. Let me bring it to the fire to see what it is. For a serpent is a thing created. It has its own *raison d'être*. In its own being it has beauty and reality. Even my horror is a tribute to its reality. And I must admit the genuineness of my horror, accept it, and not exclude it from my understanding. . . . Come then, brindled abhorrent one, you have your own being and your own righteousness, yes, and your own desirable beauty. . . . But keep to your own ways and your own being. Come in just proportion, there in the grass beneath the bushes where the birds are. . . . But since it is spring with me, the snake must wreathe his way secretly along the paths that belong to him, and when I see him asleep in the sunshine I shall admire him in his place.

This was one of the seeds of the poem, waiting in Lawrence's consciousness until that burning Sicilian noontime when he saw the snake he liked despite his human education, which told him that gold snakes were dangerous and should be killed. 'Was it cowardice that I dared not kill him? / Was it perversity that I longed to talk to him?' He felt honored that the snake should seek his hospitality. But as the reptile wriggled away, 'into that horrid black hole', revulsion came over the man and he threw a log at the snake, which 'writhed like lightning and was gone', leaving the man full of regret at his own meanness, thinking of the albatross. For the snake seemed 'Like a king in exile, uncrowned in the underworld, / Now due to be crowned again,' while the man felt that he had missed his 'chance with one of the lords / Of life' and that he had 'something to expiate: a pettiness'.

This division of the consciousness, here split between admiration and repulsion, again reveals Lawrence's essential polarization, of the kind found in Birkin in *Women in Love,* who sees both the flower and the mud it is rooted in. The 'Snake' poem is also reminiscent of the two opposing forces in Lawrence's 1915 essay 'The Crown';

and there is always in Lawrence the battle between darkness and light. 'Snake', one of his finest poems, is also one of the most revelatory.

Various other Sicilian poems were of this kind: vivid projections of the physical aspect of an experience, with a 'philosophic' lesson drawn from it. Hence the poems give some unforgettable images of place and thing as well as an inward picture of Lawrence. In 'Bare Fig Trees', Lawrence described the subject acutely, then presented it as an 'equality puzzle', with every twig 'the arch twig' and 'Each imperiously over-equal to each, equality overreaching itself / Like the snakes on Medusa's head.' In 'Hibiscus and Salvia Flowers', Lawrence pictured the local Bolshevists wearing hibiscus flowers as boutonnieres on Sundays, and he asked them, 'Come now, speaking of rights, what right have you to this flower?' In 'Peace', the black lava was congealed on the doorsteps of the island, but the volcanic hill above seethed with 'white-hot lava' waiting to burst forth and wither the earth again: 'Call it Peace?' And similarly, in other poems, the almond blossoms, the ironlike bare almond trees of another season, the red moon of the southern night, the anemones and cyclamens, all stood for more than their livingly rendered presences on the page.

Lawrence's prose flourished, too, at this time. He received the manuscript of his unfinished novel, *The Insurrection of Miss Houghton,* from Elsa Jaffe; it had remained in Bavaria during the war. Lawrence went at it again, making it into *The Lost Girl,* which he had once also considered calling *Mixed Marriage* as well as *The Bitter Cherry.*

The part Eastwood (as Woodhouse) played in the early life of Lawrence's heroine, Alvina Houghton, has been discussed earlier. For the last section of the book, as we have seen, Lawrence drew upon his experiences in the Italian mountains, though he didn't permit Alvina to escape, as he and Frieda had.

In the novel, Alvina's Italian lover was a native of the region. For his nickname, Lawrence took that of the proprietor of the Fontana Vecchia, Francesco Cacopardo—Ciccio (in the British edition, Cicio) —of whose 'romance' Lawrence wrote to Amy Lowell in a letter of June 26, when Ciccio Cacopardo was away on a trip to America: 'Gemma and her family, with 1,000 other refugees, were shipped down here from the Venetian province when the Austrians broke in.' Gemma, her mother, and her nine brothers and sisters had arrived barefoot, without money. 'Ciccio fell in love with her: female half of

Taormina enraged for Ciccio is rich and speaks 3 languages. One irate woman attacked Gemma and tore the blouse off her back.' Meanwhile, Gemma's family, the Mottas, 'viewed Ciccio with wild suspicion and said he was going to make poor Gemma his concubine. Still they refused to believe he was married. So this time before he left for Boston, he went up to the Veneto with his wife, and my heart, she was rigged up: silk stockings, suède shoes, georgette frock: she who had never worn a hat in her life till Ciccio bought her one: *propria contadina*.'

On June 26 Lawrence wrote to the publisher Cecil Palmer: 'The *Studies in Classic American Literature* I finished revising ten days ago. They make a book about 70–80 thousand words. Secker wants to sell the book to America and he will buy sheets for England. I had rather it were set up in England but am negotiating with America'— where Thomas Seltzer finally brought it out in August 1923, ten months before Secker published it, from new plates, in England. During the years which Lawrence spent on those essays, from the time *Women in Love* was completed until his imaginative talent flared up again in Sicily—he rewrote some passages later, in America—the *Studies* was his most impressive creative achievement. At the same time, it was authentic criticism: profound, if often informal. And although the book baffled many of the reviewers when it came out, later American critics exploring the literature of their own country (Edmund Wilson, Austin Warren, Alfred Kazin, and others) expressed pleased astonishment at its brilliance and power. Thornton Wilder, preparing for his Harvard lectures on American literature, wrote to the present author (June 22, 1950) concerning Lawrence's book, 'There are passages of nonsense in it, but there is much of electrifying insight and help.'

Critics have generally pronounced the essays on Melville and Poe the best among the *Studies:* in *Moby-Dick,* the *Pequod* was the 'ship of the American soul' and the white whale 'the deepest blood-being of the white race . . . And he is hunted, hunted, hunted by the maniacal fanaticism of our white mental consciousness'; Poe was 'doomed to seethe down his soul in a great continuous convulsion of disintegration, and doomed to register the process. And then doomed to be abused for it, when he had performed some of the bitterest tasks of human experience'—but there is much more, developed at length and in depth, about Melville and Poe as representatives of the American consciousness, Melville escaping from Home and

Mother to the South Seas, then escaping from that Purgatory to
Home and Mother again, with its repeated unhappiness, and yearning
after the South Seas—and Poe 'an adventurer into vaults and cellars
and horrible underground passages of the human soul'; and there is
much about Hawthorne and Franklin and Whitman and Dana, in a
colloquial idiom that lets through more intensity than the flat prose of
scholarship usually transmits.

2 BIRDS, BEASTS, AND SICILY

Legend, as it followed Lawrence everywhere, traced him to Sicily. And
legend swelled, as ever, with the passing of time. A Milan newspaper,
for example, the *Corriere d'Informazione,* published in December
1947 a long story about Lawrence in Taormina, a report of him as a
breakfast host—this was the only time he would see people, the story
said, and then he would give them buttered toast and ham and eggs
with cups of milk. In this way he was supposed to entertain local
magistrates as well as illustrious visitors. One morning, according to
this story, the mayor had arrived for breakfast and had just seated
himself when he looked up to see a plate of fried potatoes in mid-air,
thrown at Frieda by her husband—and the mayor left at once. Although Lawrence's former landlord, Francesco Cacopardo, also tells
the plate-throwing story, the reliability of this newspaper reporter—
who sounds as imaginative as any of the Taos group who wrote of
Lawrence—may be tested by his assertion that, at Taormina, the King
of England slipped ashore incognito to pay Lawrence a secret visit
of homage!

Several of Lawrence's Sicilian adventures, however, were almost
as fantastic as the stories fabricated about him. One of them was the
expedition in April 1920 to Siracusa with a group of new friends
who included Réné Juta (Mrs. Hansard), future author of *Concerning Corsica* and *Cannes and the Hills,* and Réné Juta's brother, Jan,
a young painter who was to illustrate his sister's travel books as well
as Lawrence's *Sea and Sardinia;* Jan and Réné were the children of
Sir Henry Juta of Cape Town, South Africa. On that Sicilian trip, the
Lawrences and Jutas were accompanied by Alan Insole, another
painter, a wealthy young Welshman. Frieda was 'much impressed by
the way Réné Hansard, with the experience of a true colonial, was
fortified with a hamper of food and a spirit lamp' and could at once
convert 'the railway car into a live little temporary home'. Lawrence

borrowed the idea of the spirit lamp in the railway car for his young travelers in *Aaron's Rod*. Of that journey, he remembered, above everything, 'lovely days, with the purple anemones blowing in the Sicilian fields, and Adonis-blood red on the little ledges, and the corn rising strong with her crown of snow.' But the most striking part of the journey Lawrence didn't write of, at least for publication.

This was the visit to Randazzo, a town of black lava on the slopes of Etna. The place fascinated Lawrence, but his sojourn at the nearby castle of Maniace irritated him. At the castle, Lawrence and the others were guests of Alexander Nelson-Hood, Duke of Bronte, a descendant of the brother of Lord Nelson, on whom the title had first been conferred. As Jan Juta has remembered it, as the Lawrences and their friends approached the castle, all of them riding mules, six or seven lackeys of the duke tottered out to greet them—aging shepherds whom Nelson-Hood had arrayed in costumes like those of the Pope's Swiss Guard. One of these collapsing retainers who knew English doffed his cap, bowed, and presented greetings from the master. The party entered the castle, whose authentic Norman façade clashed with the Victorian furnishings of the interior, though these were appropriate to the appearance of Nelson-Hood's sister, who affected the style of Queen Alexandra. The duke himself went around staring at his guests through a monocle fastened like a pince-nez to the bridge of his nose. Lawrence in his exasperation roughed out, with the Jutas, the scenario of a skit on the place, but before long his humor gave out altogether and he had to escape.

He went back to Taormina and the continuance of an even more bizarre adventure. On his first morning there, at dawn, he heard a noise on the stairway to the terrace and discovered Magnus creeping about: 'A terrible thing has happened.' Lawrence, detesting 'terrible things, and the people to whom they happen', heard then of Magnus's escaping from Monte Cassino with the police at his heels: 'I couldn't let myself be arrested up there, could I? So awful for the monastery!' The guest-master, against the rules of the place, had actually lent Magnus money from the monastery fund. Scampering down the mountainside, he had caught a train south: 'I came straight to you— Of course I was in *agony:* imagine it! I spent most of the time as far as Naples in the lavatory.' Lawrence asked him in which class he had traveled. He had gone second-class, but upon arriving ('more dead than alive') at Taormina during Lawrence's absence, had immediately put up at the most expensive hotel, in full expectation that Lawrence would pay his bills on the strength of possible income from Magnus's 'manuscripts'. Magnus strutted around the yard, admiring the villa and dropping hints to the effect that Lawrence must be affluent and that there was plenty of room there: 'Palatial. Charming! . . . *Much* the nicest house in Taormina.' Magnus didn't mention precisely what his trouble was; Lawrence, who didn't want to know, suspected rightly that it was some form of swindling. He would not take Magnus in at Fontana Vecchia, but he did settle the hotel bill. Three days there cost more money than the Lawrences used for living expenses in a week.

Frieda, who met Magnus for the first time, despised him as a leech and scolded Lawrence for encouraging him. Magnus, on the strength of his prospects, moved into a local villa, and lived there in high style until the patience of the unpaid landlord was exhausted. After being 'insulted', Magnus left for Siracusa on his way to Malta and Egypt. Although Lawrence 'breathed free now he had gone', he felt still a kind of horrible responsibility for Magnus: and while loathing the man's parasitism, he couldn't help admiring his arrogance. Lawrence, though he lived scrupulously by bourgeois standards, really hated the bourgeoisie, whom Magnus flouted in the manner of the grand rascals. Lawrence apparently didn't know until after Magnus's death that the preposterous little rogue was an offshoot of the highest aristocracy, the social group that Lawrence seldom criticized. Before leaving Taormina, Magnus had chosen Lawrence to go to Cassino to pick up his clothes and manuscripts, but Lawrence refused to do this, not only because of the fatiguing journey but particularly because he didn't want to become any more involved than he already was in Magnus's dubious activities.

Meanwhile, like most people who collided with Lawrence, Magnus had already served him as literary fodder. As a kind of preliminary sketch for the biographical introduction he was to write later for Magnus's Legion *Memoirs,* Lawrence put him into *The Lost Girl* as Mr. May, the American theatrical manager in the English town. Here he showed the worst of Magnus: the pushing, worldly man of theatrical back-alleys, oozing guile and seething with bitchiness.

Lawrence completed *The Lost Girl* in the first week of May 1920, just as Magnus was leaving Taormina. A few weeks before, Secker had finally made Lawrence the offer he wanted: publication of *Women in Love* and *The Rainbow* with royalties of a shilling per copy on the first two thousand, one shilling and sixpence to five thousand, and two shillings beyond that.

Meanwhile, the small new American publishing house of Thomas Seltzer had arranged with Lawrence and Mountsier to bring out *Women in Love,* which was first issued in a limited edition in November of that year. Lawrence had by now dropped Pinker, whose kindly efforts on his behalf during those meager years of the war were for the most part futile. The two men parted friendlily enough, and for a year or so Pinker sent Lawrence an occasional check for material which had been delayed in publication. He returned a sheaf of manuscripts, chiefly consisting of the stories soon sold to magazines by Curtis Brown, the American newspaperman who had built one of the biggest agencies in London. Most of those stories went into the *England, My England* collection of 1922; one of them, however, was the short novel 'The Fox', which Lawrence revised once again at Taormina and included in the volume of novellas published in 1923, called *The Captain's Doll* in its American edition and *The Ladybird* in its British appearance.

Only two days after completing *The Lost Girl* he had plunged into the new novel, *Mr Noon,* which was in some ways a realization of his old ambition to write a story about a Robert Burns of the Midlands. He used Eastwood as his setting, calling it Woodhouse as in *The Lost Girl* and even introducing Alvina Houghton as a minor character. His hero, the flirtatious schoolmaster Gilbert Noon, was once again his old 'Don Juanish' friend George Neville, who had already sat for the portrait of the doctor in Lawrence's play *The Married Man.* Only Part I of *Mr Noon* has so far been published, but Lawrence wrote more of it than that, and additional sections have been discovered which, at an auction in New York in 1972, brought in $17,000.

In the same month in which he began *Mr Noon,* Lawrence went to another Mediterranean island with Frieda and an old friend of theirs, as he reported to Catherine Carswell on May 28:

> Mary Cannan lured us away to Malta—we were to stay only two days—then a steam-boat strike, and we only got back to-night, after some 11 days. Oh, and it was *so* expensive, and I feel so displeased. Malta is a strange place—a dry, bath-brick island that glares and sets your teeth on edge and is *so* dry that one expects oneself to begin to crackle. Valletta harbour is wonderful: beautiful. But I get set on edge by the British régime. It is very decent, I believe, but it sort of stops life, it prevents the human reactions from taking full swing, there is always a

kind of half-measure, half-length, 'not quite' feeling about, which simply arrests my digestion.

I found your two letters and your cheque. The last, you understand, I shall not use, I shall merely keep it for you for when you want it.

Mrs. Carswell's fifty pounds represented one-fifth of a 'first-novel' prize she had just won for *Open the Door*. On May 31 Lawrence wrote to her: 'As for the cheque, I suddenly decided to burn it. I got 2,000 Lire from America. I have enough money. And why should I hold any of yours in fee. So I accept the gift all the same: and have burned the cheque.' A man so reluctant to take money from generous friends who were not rich had some right to begrudge Magnus's sponging, despite Douglas's lordly sneer at Lawrence for upholding 'the fine middle-class tradition' (Douglas) of keeping 'a few pounds between me and the world' (Lawrence).

On the Malta trip Lawrence of course met Magnus again, first in Siracusa, where he had been detained by the strike. Again he confronted Lawrence with a hotel bill, and again Lawrence paid it. On Malta, he found it impossible to dodge Magnus, who introduced him to two young Maltese, friends of the guest-master at Monte Cassino. Months afterwards, when Magnus's inevitable debts had to be settled, the two Maltese behaved as if Lawrence were responsible for their own involvement, although they already knew Magnus when they met Lawrence.

Back in Taormina, he was 'thankful to be home again', assured that Magnus 'was safely shut up in that beastly island.' But before long Lawrence left 'home' once more—as he told Catherine Carswell later in the year, in a letter as yet unpublished, 'Taormina blazes too hard after June'—but he still would not accompany Frieda to Germany. So, when they returned to the mainland on August 2, they separated for a time, to go back again in the autumn to Fontana Vecchia. Meanwhile, Lawrence went to Naples, Amalfi, Fiuggi (then called Anticoli), Rome, Florence, and various parts of northern Italy.

Lawrence later recalled that on his journeys through the country in 1920 he found it shaken by violence: 'Florence was in a state of continual socialistic riot: sudden shots, sudden stones smashing into the restaurants where one was drinking coffee, all the shops suddenly barred and closed.' When he went to Florence again, 'there was a great procession of *Fascisti* and banners: *Long Live the King.*' Lawrence was observing actions that he would in the next few years transmit into dramatic episodes in his 'leadership novels', *Aaron's Rod, Kangaroo,* and *The Plumed Serpent.*

*

Lawrence reported on September 12 to Amy Lowell from the edge of Florence: 'I have been wandering around Lake Como and Venice, and now am here for a while in an explosion-shattered villa which a friend has lent me'—the friend being Rosalind Baynes (later Mrs. A. E. Popham), who had been the Lawrences' hostess at Pangbourne the preceding summer. The windows of a villa she had rented in the hills above Florence had been blown out by an explosion at a nearby ammunition dump. She moved higher up, to Fiesole, where Lawrence used to go for tea or dinner on her terrace during the weeks he stayed in the windowless villa.

At this Villa Canovaia, San Gervasio, Lawrence wrote some of his most striking *Birds, Beasts and Flowers* poems, including 'Pomegranate', which stands at the head of the collection and begins with these now-famous lines: 'You tell me I am wrong. / Who are you, who is anybody to tell me I am wrong? / I am not wrong.' In the 'abhorrent, green, slippery city' of Venice, the pomegranates had been 'barbed with a crown . . . of spiked green metal,' but now Tuscany had 'Pomegranates to warm your hands at . . . And, if you dare, the fissure!' In the poem 'The Peach', Lawrence again found vulval suggestions: 'Why the groove? / Why the lovely, bivalve roundnesses?' This would not be found in a man-made peach, 'And because I say so, you would like to throw something at me. / Here, you can have my peach stone.' And 'Fig', another of the San Gervasio experiences:

> *The fig is a very secretive fruit.*
> *As you see it standing growing, you feel at*
> * once it is symbolic:*
> *And it seems male.*
> *But when you come to know it better, you agree*
> * with the Romans, it is female . . .*

The rest of the poem was an exploration of female secretiveness and the desire of women to break away from it at the last and 'burst into affirmation'; but 'bursten figs won't keep.' The poem 'Medlars and Sorb-Apples' praised the Orphic and Dionysiac experiences of the Underworld of love, with its exquisite farewells amid 'the winding, leaf-clogged, silent lanes of hell,' finding that 'its own isolation' was the 'Strangest of all strange companions, / And best,' in 'the intoxication of final loneliness.' The last poem of the series, 'Grapes', extolled the power of wine to take us back to 'a green, muddy, web-foot, utterly songless world' of before the Flood; but moderns, clutching at their 'vistas democratic, boulevards, tram-cars, policemen', sought the safety of soda fountains.

At San Gervasio, Lawrence also composed 'The Evangelistic Beasts', his poems on the four authors of the Gospels. And he possibly wrote his *Tortoises* poems in or around Florence at this time; when he returned to Venice to meet Frieda, he told Catherine Carswell on October 7, the day before Frieda's arrival: 'I wrote in Florence a little book of verses which I like,' perhaps the six *Tortoises,* in which Lawrence projected the sex experience of man in the image of the tortoise, at once delicate and blundering, viewed by Lawrence in a mood combining sympathy, amusement, and participation. The tortoise was a 'Poor little earthly house-inhabiting Osiris', and the cross on his shell became the crucifixion of sex.

In that letter from Venice to Mrs. Carswell, Lawrence reported himself 'still stuck in the middle of *Aaron's Rod,* my novel. But at Taormina I'll spit on my hands and lay fresh hold.' Meanwhile: 'Venice is very lovely to look at, but very stagnant as regards life. A holiday place, the only one left in Italy—but even here écœuré. Italy feels very unsure, and for the first time I feel a tiny bit frightened of what they might do, the Italians, in a sudden ugly "red" mood. However, Sicily will be moderately safe.'

During his wandering, Lawrence had written an essay, 'America, Listen to Your Own', which appeared in the *New Republic* in December: he described Americans as awed by the museum pieces of Europe, and then told them they 'must take up life where the Red Indian, the Aztec, the Maya, the Incas, left off. . . . They must catch the pulse of the life which Cortés and Columbus murdered. . . . The President should not look back towards Gladstone or Cromwell or Hildebrand, but towards Montezuma. . . . To your tents, O America. Listen to your own, don't listen to Europe.' Walter Lippmann, one of the editors of the *New Republic,* answered this (and was answered in turn by Mary Austin, later to meet Lawrence in New Mexico). Lippmann said that America was 'a nation of emigrants who took possession of an almost empty land', destroying or interning 'the natives' they found there. Lippmann had in 1920 scolded the

American people for having 'just overwhelmingly elected a President [Harding] who took pains to put himself on record against excellence,' and for their poor taste, and for letting their bureaucrats forbid Lawrence's novels to go through the mails; but, to Lippmann, Lawrence's 'Noble Savage' view of America and its traditions was 'mostly paste and paint'. Lippmann had evidently not read Lawrence's *Studies* as they appeared in the *English Review,* or perhaps had not seen in them the merits that have become discernible with time. And Lawrence perhaps didn't see Lippmann's literal answer to his half-poetic statement; apparently he never made a rejoinder, although some of his writing after he had gone to New Mexico indicates that he had changed his mind. Such stories as 'The Woman Who Rode Away' and the novel *The Plumed Serpent* celebrate ancient Indian rites, but often Lawrence felt the great difference between himself and the red men. His essay of 1923, 'Indians and an Englishman', illustrates that point, although the essay indicates some ambivalence, as in Lawrence's New Mexico poem, 'Red Wolf'. Towards the end of 'Indians and an Englishman' he says, 'I never want to deny them or break with them. But there is no going back. Always onward, still further. . . . I stand at the far edge of their firelight, and am neither denied nor accepted. My way is my own, old red father; I can't cluster at the drum any more.' These passages are, of course, a glimpse into Lawrence's future, but here they form a comment on Lawrence's *New Republic* article and Lippmann's literal riposte; and they provide a clue to Lawrence's later attitude. At the time he wrote the article he had been reading American authors for the American-literature volume and was impressed by the stories of Indians, particularly in Cooper, though he had made fun of Indians in the antics of the strolling players in *The Lost Girl.* Lippmann had, however, touched a weak place in Lawrence's thinking, that part of his nature that would in time account for the extremes of *The Plumed Serpent.*

*

Lawrence and Frieda returned to Sicily on October 20, at just about the time that Maurice Magnus's difficulties began to overwhelm him on Malta. On the twenty-third, the Maltese who had made it possible for him to remain there by standing as his surety, withdrew his guarantee when he heard that Magnus 'was outliving his income' and increasing his local debts. On November 4, two detectives invited Magnus to accompany them to the police station. They didn't mention that they had extradition papers there. Magnus locked the detectives outside his house, wrote to the guest master at Monte Cassino ('I cannot live any longer. Pray for me'), and took hydrocyanic acid. The police burst into the house in time to call in a priest, who administered extreme unction before Magnus died.

From Malta and from Monte Cassino, letters and newspapers brought the story to Lawrence: 'I knew that in my own soul I had said, "Yes, he must die if he cannot find his own way." ' In spite of this, Lawrence now 'realized what it must have meant to be the hunted, desperate man: everything seemed to stand still. I could, by giving him half my money, have saved his life. I had chosen not to save his life.' For Magnus was guilty of 'Judas treachery', of 'selling the good feeling he had tried to arouse, and had aroused, for any handful of silver he could get.' Yet there was something heroic in his arrogance, 'he was a strange, quaking little star.' And, Lawrence discovered, Magnus was even of royal stock. His hatred of the Germans was an extravagance, for German was even his native tongue, rather than English: 'But perhaps something happens to blood when once it has been taken to America.' According to Don Martino of the great monastery which knew most of the great European political secrets, Magnus was on his mother's side the illegitimate grandson of Kaiser Friedrich III, father of Wilhelm II. Norman Douglas believed that Magnus was the grandson of still another, earlier Kaiser, Wilhelm I.

Magnus had left a note saying that Norman Douglas was his literary executor, but his Maltese creditors refused to turn his manuscripts over to Douglas. They sent Lawrence the Foreign Legion *Memoirs*, and he agreed to prepare it for publication, though it didn't appear as a book until 1924. Then Douglas lashed out in a pamphlet, *D. H. Lawrence and Maurice Magnus: A Plea for Better Manners,* which complained of Lawrence's treatment of Magnus (and Douglas) in the Foreign Legion introduction and accused Lawrence of making profits belonging to Douglas, as Magnus's literary executor.

In writing this polemic Douglas was encouraged, Aldington reported, by a wealthy woman who hated Lawrence and gave Douglas a hundred pounds for attacking him. Douglas denied this in *Late Harvest* (1946); Aldington said in *Pinorman* (1954) that the denial was ineffective. (Aldington and Lawrence were both scolded by Nancy Cunard in a magazine article in 1954, shortly before the appearance of her extremely friendly biographical pastiche of Douglas, *Grand Man.*)

Lawrence had ignored Douglas's *Plea for Better Manners* until in 1925 Douglas reprinted it in his *Experiments,* and then Lawrence, 'weary of being slandered', replied in the *New Statesman* (February 20, 1926), saying that he had portrayed Magnus truthfully and had written of him only to help Magnus's creditors on Malta. Further, it had taken several years to induce the publishers, who wanted to issue the introduction only, to bring out the book, of which Lawrence's share would be only a part of what he had lent Magnus, whereas Michael Borg, the principal Maltese creditor, would be repaid in full. Lawrence used Douglas's italics in quoting a 1921 letter from him to Lawrence: 'By all means do what you like with the MS. . . . *Pocket all the cash yourself.*'

The unhappy subject of these squabbles had been buried on his forty-fourth birthday, November 7, 1920, saved from a pauper's grave by his Maltese friends, who paid the funeral expenses—later refunded by the widow. One of Magnus's last little notes, scribbled as he locked himself away from the police and took his poison, had said, 'I want to be buried first class.'

3 LOWER AND UPPER CENTRES

On the third day of January 1921, Lawrence and Frieda were up before dawn for a trip to Sardinia. From the description of that first morning ('the queen bee shivering around half dressed, fluttering her unhappy candle,' and outside, 'the ominousness of . . . that long red slit between a dark sky and a dark Ionian sea, terrible old bivalve which has held life between its lips so long') to the last pages (with the return on the steamer, when 'morning came with sunny pieces of cloud: and the Sicilian coast towering pale blue in the distance')— Lawrence's travel book *Sea and Sardinia* is a complete account of their voyage.

There is the long coastal train journey to Palermo, with 'rain, continual rain, a level wet grey sky, a level wet grey sea, a wet and misty train winding round and round the little bays, diving through tunnels' in the hills of lemon-tree forests; there is Cagliari, their first Sardinian port, 'a naked town, rising steep, steep, golden-looking . . . without trees, without cover, rising bare and proud, remote as if back in history, like a town in a monkish, illuminated missal. . . . It has that curious look, as if it could be seen but not entered'; there are the peasant women with full-petticoated costumes, dresses 'of dark-blue-and-red, stripes-and-lines, intermingled,' so that when they walk 'the red goes flash-flash-flash, like a bird showing its colours'; there is the dirty-shirted barman in the filthy little inn up among the stony mountains, a man 'with no brow at all; just flat, straight black hair slanting to his eyebrows'; there is . . . But *Sea and Sardinia,* a masterpiece of lyric and of sharply observational prose, of bright colors that fill the reading eye, of movement and feeling, cannot be summarized or paraphrased; it must be read for itself.

Lawrence and Frieda went from Cagliari, at the bottom of the island, to Terranova, near the top: a little map Lawrence made shows their route, by train and bus, up and down the mountains. In the hinterland the weather was cold, the food was bad, and most of the rooms were dirty. For the Lawrences it was a journey 'back, back, back down the old ways of time', to the finality of realization that 'it is all worked out. It is all known: *connu, connu!'* Man must move forward to be whole, Lawrence felt, must move forward to the 'unknown, unworked lands where the salt has not lost its savour.'

As Lawrence and Frieda went south by train in Italy, from Civitavecchia, where the boat from Sardinia had taken them, to Naples, he suddenly saw Monte Cassino on its hill above the world, and again he felt the magnetism of the place. 'In a wild moment' he suggested to Frieda that they get off and spend the night up there, 'and see the other friend, the monk who knows so much about the world, being out of it'. Frieda shuddered at the thought 'of the awful winter coldness of that massive stone monastery, which has no spark of heating apparatus.' So the proposal collapsed: Lawrence stepped out of the train for only a moment at Cassino station, 'to procure coffee and sweet cakes'.

After his return to Taormina, Lawrence wrote to various friends that Sardinia was not a place to live in. (This was, of course, long before the beaches became popular and modern-style hotels sprang up.) As for Tuscany, although it was more alive than Sicily, he would stay on in Taormina for a while. He had promised to visit his sisters, but couldn't cross the Channel to the 'mud-bathos' of England. He would, if he 'knew how to,' join the revolutionary socialists, for the time had 'come for a real struggle. That's the only thing I care for: the death-struggle.' He disliked politics, but he felt 'there *must* and *should* be a deadly revolution very soon'; he would take part in it if he 'knew how.'

In the English-speaking countries, meanwhile, Lawrence was being widely published again. The American edition of *New Poems* in 1920 drew mostly reviews that were caustic, chiefly devoted to the preface; Raymond M. Weaver, in the *Bookman,* said that the volume offered 'the pathetic spectacle of a shabby manikin pirouetting in caricature of the Muse.' The limited edition of *Women in Love,* ventured by Thomas Seltzer in November 1920, was not widely reviewed; one of the few discussions of it, Evelyn Scott's in the *Dial,* called it a confessional: 'Having written it, Lawrence might turn philosopher or priest.' She found his solutions unsatisfactory: 'If Mr. Lawrence were a Russian he would take the answer to life as his art gives it, in terms of otherworldliness,' but because he belonged 'to the English race of moralists', he would persist 'in a search for temporal solutions'.

Women in Love boldly appeared under the Secker imprint in London in May 1921, two months after Oxford had published the history book with its authorship ('Lawrence H. Davison') disguised; Bottomley's *John Bull,* however, didn't pass up the chance to attack the novel as 'a loathsome study of sex depravity leading youth to unspeakable disaster'. And Murry, in the *Athenaeum,* not recognizing himself in Gerald Crich, swam through 'five hundred pages of passionate vehemence, wave after wave of turgid, exasperated writing impelled toward some distant and invisible end,' one which left Murry in a state of agnosticism about the book. He did, however, find it obscene. Earlier, when Secker had brought out *The Lost Girl* (in November 1920), Murry had pronounced Lawrence to be in a state of 'decay'. It was *The Lost Girl*—along with *The Trespasser* and *The Virgin and the Gipsy,* among the lowest of Lawrence's fictional achievements—that brought him, in 1921, the only official recognition he received during his lifetime: the James Tait Black Prize of Edinburgh University, a hundred pounds. Lawrence wrote to thank Rachel Annand Taylor, a friend from his days as a teacher, for the part she played in helping to give the award to *The Lost Girl.*

Early in April 1921, Frieda left for Baden-Baden, and Lawrence went with her as far as Palermo. Else Jaffe had telegraphed that her mother was ill, and Lawrence had thought this a trick, but later correspondence showed it was not. Alone at Taormina, Lawrence felt 'the house very empty without F. Don't like it at all,' and although people continually invited him to tea and dinner, he didn't want to accept. After a month of loneliness, during which Millicent Beveridge painted his portrait ('I look quite a sweet young man'), Lawrence decided to join Frieda in Germany. But he took his time, stopping for visits en route.

On Capri he met a couple who were to remain uncritical friends to the end of his life: Earl and Achsah Brewster, two Americans who had some years before spent their honeymoon at the Fontana Vecchia. They were interested in painting and in Buddhism, these two Jamesian expatriates whom Lawrence years later satirized in his story 'Things'. Soon after meeting them at Capri, he told them in detail the plot of *Aaron's Rod* up to the point where Aaron leaves his wife, and they suggested that now Aaron must either 'go to Monte Cassino and repent, or else go through the whole cycle of experience.' Lawrence chuckled his agreement, for he had at first meant to put Aaron in the monastery, but instead determined that he 'had to go to destruction to find his way through from the lowest depths': rather than the Benedictine rule, the Lawrencean way.

Lawrence delighted the Brewsters with his mimicry. They had expected a morose man, not the cheerful companion he proved to be. Mrs. Brewster thought that with his blunted nose he looked like Socrates—and, with his beard, somewhat like Whistler's portrait of Carlyle. Before leaving Taormina he had inspected a Mediterranean sailing ship, which he would have bought if he had the money. He told the Brewsters it would be good if they all owned such a boat and could go voyaging around the world in it as they pleased. In his correspondence with them he again and again returned to this idea.

After Capri, Lawrence stayed briefly at Rome and at Florence on his way north. At Florence, Norman Douglas introduced him to Rebecca West, who was already one of his most energetic admirers. She discovered that he made friends as easily as a child, or as a wise old philosopher who at once recognized the quality of another personality and seemed to give it his blessing. Before taking her to meet Lawrence, Douglas with a heavy laugh told her that his friend had just arrived, and that it was his habit, as soon as he landed anywhere, to go straight to his room and write about the place in elaborate detail. When they went to his hotel on the Arno (probably Berchielli's, the Bertolini's of *Aaron's Rod*), they found Lawrence sitting at a typewriter. Douglas asked if he were writing an article about Florence, and he said he was, at which Douglas gave way to loud laughter; it was, Rebecca West recalled, 'malicious as a satyr's'.

Lawrence told her and Douglas and Reggie Turner of the discomforts of his travels. She later reflected, 'These were the journeys that the mystics of a certain type have always found necessary'—certainly the neatest of all explanations of Lawrence's famous restlessness. Rebecca West saw him as wandering like the Indian Fakir and the

Russian Saint, going on journeys with a spiritual rather than a geographical goal: 'Lawrence travelled, it seemed, to get a certain Apocalyptic vision of mankind that he registered again and again and again, always rising to a pitch of ecstatic agony.'

In the last week of April, Lawrence left for Germany, via Switzerland. At Baden-Baden, where he found his mother-in-law recovering, he and Frieda moved three miles out, to a rough little inn, the Hotel Krone, in the village of Ebersteinberg. Frieda had been staying with her mother at the Ludwig Wilhelmstift, a home which the Grand Duchess Louisa had founded for upper-class widows. Lawrence was polite to the old ladies there, who called him Herr Doktor as he bowed to them, grinning through his beard; but the Frau Baronin von Richthofen shuddered lest some of the ladies read his books.

On June 16 Lawrence wrote to Amy Lowell's companion, Mrs. Ada Russell: 'We came to Germany two months ago, because my mother-in-law was very ill.' But she was better and would soon join them at Ebersteinberg, which was 'very lovely really—a little black and white village, with the big woods all round, the edge of the Black Forest, and the Rhine away beyond, in the plain below, and then the Vosges dim beyond the plain.' And Germany seemed 'so big and so *still:* strange and hushed: so very different from before the war. It is nice to be in a country where people are not so disgustingly full of money as they are everywhere else.' Regrettably, he could not refrain from adding, 'Nobody has any money any more except the profiteers, chiefly Jews, with which Baden Baden is swarming.' He invariably omitted the hyphen in Baden-Baden, but he committed a worse error in equating Jews with money grubbers: historical research has shown that not many Jews were affluent in Germany during the times of the Hohenzollern Empire and the Weimar Republic. Indeed, in the year of Hitler's ascendancy, 1933, the German Jews numbered only half a million, not quite one per cent of the total population. Most of the Nazi propaganda from the 1920s into the 1940s was a lie.

As for Lawrence, he had a certain anti-Semitic strain (which had very little in common with the Nazis) that showed itself in odd moments, as when he referred to William Heinemann as 'his Jewship' in a letter, and when, in another, he spoke of one of his later publishers, Thomas Seltzer, as 'a tiny Jew, but trustworthy seems to me'—accepting him with that terrible qualifying conjunction.

Some commentators have asserted that Frieda came from a Jewish family. If this were true, it would give Lawrence's occasional anti-Semitic remarks a special piquancy; but so far no researcher has come up with proof that the von Richthofens were really Jewish. Frieda's daughter, Mrs. Barbara Barr, said in a B.B.C. broadcast in 1961 that her grandfather, Baron von Richthofen, had told his daughters that he didn't care whom they took for husbands so long as none of them married a gambler, a professor, or a Jew—which is precisely what the three young women proceeded to do.

Among Lawrence's statements along anti-Semitic lines, perhaps the least forgivable is the one he put into the consciousness of Somers-Lawrence in *Kangaroo* when, during the war, he thinks of being 'brought to heel by German militarists'. But: 'If a man is to be brought to any heel, better a spurred heel than the heel of a Jewish financier'. This statement appeared in the edition of the book which Martin Secker brought out in London in September 1923. The passage was different in the version Thomas Seltzer published in New York shortly afterwards, from new plates. Lawrence changed the sentence quoted above so that the last part of it read, 'than the heel of a smirking financier'. Perhaps he altered the text out of respect for his host; in August 1923 he corrected proofs of the American edition at the Seltzers' cottage in New Jersey. It is possible, however, that he decided to remove the offensive word simply as a matter of general decency, from a book he had written in haste. It is ironic that the only current American edition of *Kangaroo* repeats the 'Jewish financier' epithet, as the current British editions do—another example of the lack of concern for correct Lawrence texts, based on the author's final thinking on the matter.

Lawrence's anti-Semitism, however stupid it may have been, was like that of so many middle-class Englishmen of the time (and in many ways he had become one of them), not deep, vicious, or fanatic; rather, it was mild, unthinking, and careless. It certainly would not, in any form, have survived after Buchenwald, if Lawrence had lived long enough to know about the Nazis' corpse camps.

*

While he was in Ebersteinberg in 1921, Lawrence wrote most of his *Fantasia of the Unconscious,* a sequel to *Psychoanalysis and the Unconscious,* which had just been published in New York, where George Soule said, in the *Nation,* 'Beneath its terrifying exterior it seems to correspond, in a vague way, with much we are feeling nowadays.' Perhaps if Lawrence in expressing this, Soule went on, had used 'the imagery of fiction or poetry instead of the intellectual terms which he distrusts, he might have written a great novel.' Soule, who has commented with authority on both economics and psychoanalysis, was making a judgment that might be applied, still, to both of Lawrence's books on the unconscious. They are guides to a completer understanding of Lawrence—he intimated they were 'explanations' of the novels —and they contain an inevitable seasoning of good sense on such subjects as human relationships and education and the right and wrong manifestations of love. Some of the ideas and terminology derive from theosophy, with a good deal of exploring of 'upper' and 'lower centres' in the human body; and there is some nonsense about a lost Atlantis with a 'greater' society than history hints of, though Lawrence's speculations hardly deserve H. L. Mencken's hardheaded judgment on the first of the volumes, which he thought was an 'effective if unwitting *reductio ad absurdum* of the current doctrine that Lawrence is a profound thinker. His book is not merely bad; it is downright childish.' Lawrence himself didn't fight for these two books as he was to do for some of his other work; in after years he scarcely mentioned them, and as yet no letter has come to light in which he points to these volumes as important, though at one level they are an explanation of part of the figure in his carpet: certainly the last sections of *Aaron's Rod,* completed there at Ebersteinberg, have affinities with *Fantasia.*

After Lawrence's final draft of the *Fantasia,* in Sicily, he wrote an epilogue of some length. Earlier, in Germany, he had written a briefer epilogue (on which the later one was based), which has recently come to light and is published here for the first time. It shows what he was thinking, particularly about America, in June 1921:

Hail Columbia!—I wrote this book for you, whether you like it or not. I suppose Columbia means the States. I suppose, etymologically, it means a nest of turtle doves: Lat. Columba, a dove. A nice nest of turtle-doves up a tree of Stars and Stripes.

Anyhow I wrote this book for you, Columbia, and if you don't feel flattered, you ought to. I'm going to lay it quite gently at the foot of your *Libertas* statue. If the lady doesn't [*like*—deleted] approve of it, she is not to kick it into the sea. I'll pick it up again, and put it under my arm, and set off to find old Uncle Sam. I have more faith in his sagacity. He once could read, and read [*deeply*—deleted] shrewdly. So I have a vision of him perching his old spectacles on his nose.

It really is time somebody made a move. And it's no good just moving round and round. There is a pillar of cloud by day, if you really like to open your eyes to it, and a real tall pillar of fire by night. I have seen it in my own case. Let us come down off our Pisgah eminences and set out across the wilderness again. For we're stuck.

Especially you, America. Do you think your democracy is going to last you much longer? It isn't. It's almost done. It was nearly at an end to start with. You only took it, a [*little*—deleted] half grown tree, from Europe, and made it grow into a great [*big*—deleted] sprawling tree, too big to last, under your skies. Now it is hollow, and you've got to plant new [*slips*—deleted] seeds.

I reckon this book of mine is a real American book. If there had been no America I should never have written it. So now you needn't think you can get out of it.

I offer it to you. I'll let you look in its mouth, my nice gift-horse. It's [*sic*] teeth are quite sound. But because it's a pie-bald colt, you're not to hit it on the rump and put hot cinders under its tail. It'll be woe-betide you if you do.

I intended to write you another [word deleted] volume later on, about still more plexuses and things. But not for quite a time.

Addio, Columbia, dear little Columbine of the West. I wrote this book for you. And I wrote it in the woods near Eberstein-berg near Baden Baden, in Germany, in the month of June in this precious year of scanty grace, 1921. I know it isn't graceful of me, dear Columbia, to go and write a book for you in wicked Germany. But I couldn't help heaping coals of fire on your head, for once, Carissima.

Don't be spiteful, dear. Or if you do feel that way, just turn the whole thing over to Uncle Sam: if the worthy gentleman is still alive. And if he's dead, why, then, let Liberty kick the book, the pie-bald pony and all the pack of nonsense into limbo.

*

By the middle of July, Lawrence and Frieda moved across Switzerland into the Austrian mountains. At Thumersbach, near Salzburg, across the lake from Zell, the Lawrences stayed with Frieda's sister Nusch, then Frau Max Schreibershofen. Nusch was nearing the end of what she regarded as a stuffy marriage to a former army officer. He was probably the model for the Herr Regierungsrat Trepte in the short novel 'The Captain's Doll', the last half of which takes place in the Zeller region; Lawrence wrote it shortly after leaving there. Frieda and her sister were ready-made originals for the Countess Hannele and the Baroness Mitchka in the story. For the Scottish officer, Lawrence probably borrowed the surface of Donald Carswell, whom he asked about some details of the uniform, but at the end the character becomes Lawrence himself and talks Lawrence talk.

It is strange that 'The Captain's Doll' was not used by the women's-liberation author Kate Millett in *Sexual Politics* (1970), which attacked not only Lawrence but also Henry Miller, Jean Genet, and Norman Mailer, the last of whom wrote a lively, interesting, and amusing defense of these writers (including, of course, himself) in *The Prisoner of Sex* (1971). In 'The Captain's Doll', Captain Hepburn refuses to marry the Countess Hannele unless she can convince him that she will live up to the 'honor and obey' promise in the wedding service. Here indeed the women's-liberation movement could find something to whack Lawrence with. But taking the story on its own terms, it shows that Hannele has made a little doll of Captain Hepburn in his tight-fitting tartan trews. At the end of the story, after he has seen the doll reproduced in a painting, the captain tells the countess, 'And you can say what you like, but *any* woman, to-day, no matter *how* much she loves her man—she could start any minute and make a doll of him. And the doll would be her hero: and her hero would be no more than her doll.' Hence Hepburn's defensive 'male chauvinism'.

The Villa Alpensee ('brown balconies one above the other, the bright red geraniums twinkling all round, the trees of purple clematis tumbling at one corner') appears full-fleshed in 'The Captain's Doll', as well as all the bathing that went on there during that unwontedly hot summer; Nusch's children also figure playfully in the story. And Lawrence sketched in the mountains that hung above them, part of the Austrian Alps that he and Frieda had walked across nine years before, in a summer that lay almost a lifetime in the distance. There at Zell, Lawrence became, amid the gaiety that Nusch always stirred up around her, as intrusive and alien as the dark-souled Captain Hepburn of the story.

One day while at Zell, Lawrence had gone fishing and had been stricken by guilt when he caught a live thing on his hook 'And felt

him beat in my hand, with his mucous, leaping throb.' He unhooked
the 'groping, water-horny mouth' and stared at the 'horror-tilted eye'
of the fish,

> *And my heart accused itself*
> *Thinking:* I am not the measure of creation.
> This is beyond me, this fish.
> . . .
> *He was born in front of my sunrise,*
> *Before my day.*
> *He outstarts me.*
>
> *And I, a many-fingered horror of daylight to him,*
> *Have made him die.*
> . . .
> *In the beginning*
> *Jesus was called The Fish . . .*
> *And in the end.*

4 SAILING EAST AND SOUTH

Lawrence and Frieda went south late in August. At Florence they
stayed at the spacious flat of their friend Nelly Morrison, who was
away. The house at 32 Via de' Bardi, traditionally the one George
Eliot had used for Romola's, was the scene of Lawrence's poems 'Bat'
(in which the poet, looking out from the terrace, saw 'things flying . . . Swallows with spools of dark thread sewing the shadows together') and 'Man and Bat' (describing his battle with a flickering
creature in his 'crash-box' of a room over the 'great stone rattle' of
the Via de' Bardi). But in spite of bats the apartment was a fine one,
and the Lawrences remained there for three weeks. Mary Cannan,
who now appeared from France, admired the flat and arranged to
take rooms on the top floor.

The Carswells arrived; they had left their small son in England.
Lawrence tried to be friendly, but seemed detached. Some Anglo-
Italian cousins of Catherine Carswell's, who regarded Lawrence as a
nonentity, virtually insulted him, but even this didn't rouse him. Mrs.
Carswell noticed that Mary Cannan now bored him, though he
tried to be kind to her and not show how he felt. He arranged with the
Carswells to make an excursion to Siena, and went on ahead; but he
loathed the place at once and wouldn't stay. He wrote to Catherine

Carswell from Siena on September 21, 'We must leave tonight—must get to Capri to see the Brewsters who are leaving for India. Very sorry to miss you.' He apparently returned briefly to Florence, but didn't see the Carswells.

At the Brewsters' villa at Capri, Lawrence admired the book of short stories their little daughter Harwood had written and illustrated, and he amused them all by imitating Florence Farr reading Yeats's poems to the psaltery at that literary party of long ago.

In a few days the Lawrences left for Taormina, arriving there on September 28, a night of wind and rain. The next day Lawrence dispatched a conciliatory postcard to Mrs. Carswell ('it seemed only a moment we saw you—but the sympathy is there') in which he said he was 'so glad to come to rest'; he still liked 'this place' above all, 'the sea open to the east, to the heart of the east, away from Europe.' On the same day he wrote to Brewster reminding him of the Fontana Vecchia's 'great window of the eastern sky, seaward' and promising to 'go east, intending ultimately to go west', by spring. The mail that had been waiting at Taormina irritated him: it contained the *John Bull* growl at *Women in Love*, which had made Secker tremble; agents' complaints about *Aaron's Rod;* and a solicitor's letter threatening Lawrence and Secker because the portrait of Halliday in *Women in Love* had churned Heseltine into a vengeful fury. Lawrence, in his intermittent diary, noted on October 26, 'I give Halliday black hair and Pussum yellow, and send pages back.' He also wrote, 'Have a month of loathing everybody, particularly the *Canaglia* of England. *Canaille!'* And his British and American agents, Curtis Brown and Robert Mountsier, for their 'impudent' letters about *Aaron,* were put down as '*canacci'.* On November 2, Lawrence wrote to Brewster to say he had just completed a short story and was working on 'The Captain's Doll' ('a very funny long story') and 'If I hadn't my own stories to amuse myself with I should die, chiefly of spleen.'

Nearly two years away from England with its gray skies and bitter memories had mellowed Lawrence, improved his temper. But now, the protesting agents, carping critics, and quaking publishers brought back the days of *The Rainbow* and the war, and all Lawrence's rancor against his fellow countrymen. But where was there to go? Italy, he now found, had 'gone rancid', and Taormina was, after all, just a 'continental Mad Hatter's tea party'. This to Mrs. Carswell late in October: a few weeks earlier he had written to Earl Brewster that his plan was, 'ultimately, to get a little farm somewhere by my-

self, in Mexico, New Mexico, Rocky Mountains, or British Columbia.'
The mention of New Mexico could give telepathists some comfort for
less than a month after he wrote that, Lawrence received an invitation to go there, to Taos. That town was already in Lawrence's mind,
for he had not long before looked at pictures of it at Leo Stein's home
near Florence, and at Anticoli he had seen or at least heard of the
work of Maurice Sterne, who had recently lived in Taos.

It was this painter's former wife, Mabel Dodge Sterne, who abruptly
wrote to Lawrence from Taos, offering him an adobe house on her
property. She had read *Sea and Sardinia,* had determined that Lawrence's descriptive powers should be employed in word-painting her
beloved Taos, and had summoned him. Lawrence wrote to her, ad-
mitting that he wanted to leave Europe and that Taos tempted him,
and inquiring most practically about costs: Mrs. Sterne had not made
it plain whether or not she fed the lions she enticed into her lair.
Frieda wrote to her with less caution and more enthusiasm.

The correspondence kept up for months, with Lawrence now eager,
now reluctant, and Mrs. Sterne prodding him by letter and cable.
Lawrence tried to discourage her: she discussed psychoanalysis and
her treatment at the hands of A. A. Brill, and received in return Lawrence's jolting statement that he preferred to have neurotics die: 'A
real neurotic is half a devil, but a cured neurotic is a perfect devil,'
and the entire psychoanalytical process was too mechanical. In other
letters Lawrence asked whether Taos was not an art colony: he knew
'all that "arty" and "literary" crew', who were 'smoking, steaming shits'.

Mrs. Sterne was a rich woman used to having her own way, and
when riches wouldn't buy it, perhaps a little mysticism would help.
She later told how she 'willed' Lawrence to Taos: before going to sleep
each night, she sank into the core of her being and leaped across the
distance to merge with the core of Lawrence. She told Antonio Luhan,
the massive Indian-buck lover she had acquired after casting off her
most recent husband, that Lawrence would do Taos good. Tony was
a little doubtful, but she 'willed' him into submission, and then he
helped her, in the darkness, to 'call' her elusive victim thither.

Lawrence meanwhile had written the foreword for *Fantasia,*
shipped off the complete manuscript, and composed several stories.
He had also prepared the Magnus introduction and lengthened 'The
Fox', had given it a longer tail, as he said. And he had raged at Secker
for letting Heseltine frighten him into paying five pounds and ten
guineas' costs because of his threat of a libel suit. How right Lawrence

was in thinking Heseltine should have been defied is shown in Heseltine's letters to his solicitors published after his death. Heseltine was only putting up a bluff, and had no intention of taking the matter into court, because he didn't have enough money for a lawsuit.

After the turn of the year, Lawrence wrote to Jan Juta, who after painting the illustrations for Lawrence's *Sardinia* book planned to revisit his native South Africa:

Today has come *Sea and Sardinia,* so we are thinking hard of you. I expect you have your copies. What do you think? The *reds* are disappointing—and there is a certain juiciness about the colours that I don't like—but otherwise they are not bad, I think. Do tell me your impression. I'm sure the text will be a bit of a blow to you—so wintry and unidyllic. And see yourself and M. Alain! Bet you'll think you aren't *half* nice enough, both of you. Never mind, you have now made your bow before the world. The wrapper makes me scream with agony—but you can't prevent the Americans. . . .

It is awfully cold here, the snow right down Monte Venere and on Forza all sprinkled white—Etna a shrouded horror. I hate it when it's cold. Yet the first bits of almond blossom are sparking out, and the first of those magenta anemones that Alan calls Venus tears.

I keep on with the Taos trip. If I'd been well enough we'd have sailed from Bordeaux to New Orleans on the 15th of this month. Now perhaps on the 5th Feb. We'll go Fabre line from Palermo to New York, and then overland from there. Unless some casual steamer turns up. But I expect to be in Taos by March *and then you can come when you like!* After all, the Americans would *love* a book on their own country and what with Rockies and Indians and deserts—big deserts lie below Taos, which is on a plateau 6,000 ft. high—and Mexicans and Cowboys—*you ought to find something to paint and I to write.*

Today thank heaven I have sent off the last of my MSS.—three long-short stories, will make a really interesting book those three—'The Fox', 'The Ladybird', and 'The Captain's Doll': then a collected book of short stories, most of them re-written. Oh I fairly loathe the sight of manuscripts, and the *thought* of publishing. Oh I get so sick of everything: and so double-sick of Taorminity.

But we've got good dry olive wood and the *salotta* is warm and thank God the wind is still. Only tomorrow five awful people to tea.—By the way have you heard of Gilbert Cannan out in S Africa—with young Mond and Gwen, the polyandrous wife? Mary Cannan of course going off like a wick-wack about them. But I am callous.

The 'And see yourself and M. Alain!' refers to the description of Juta and Alan Insole, in the last chapter of *Sea and Sardinia,* meeting the Lawrences outside the railway station at Rome, the two young men 'vaguely descending from a carriage, the one [Insole] gazing inquiringly through his monocle across the tram-lines, the other [Juta] very tall and alert and elegant, looking as if he expected us to appear out of the air for his convenience.'

When Lawrence wrote that letter, he was in a Taos mood. But he soon began to wobble again, particularly as he learned more and more about Mabel Dodge Sterne. In late January, Frieda told her that they were going to Ceylon: 'Lawrence says he can't face America *yet*—he doesn't feel strong enough!' So Frieda proposed, and Lawrence seconded the suggestion in a letter the following day, that Mrs. Sterne meet them in Ceylon; then they could all go to America together. This made Mrs. Sterne realize that the Lawrences were 'scared': as usual, people had 'warned' them about her. So she and Tony vigorously cranked up their will machine and sent more compulsion waves towards Lawrence's 'core' as he and Frieda turned eastward.

He has possibly, however, left his impress on Fontana Vecchia which, as Jennifer Pulling pointed out in the Rome *Daily American* in 1973, has also been inhabited by a German musician and a British television producer. (And there is the American writer Truman Capote, who is supposed to have lived there for two years.) The Englishman from the B.B.C. reported that voices and footsteps woke him up at night and that an uncanny gleam appeared on the wall. He consulted a local specialist in the occult, who told him that other tenants of the villa had also experienced such manifestations and had seen a bearded man. If legend had followed Lawrence to Sicily, it remained there after he left in 1922.

The day before departure for Ceylon, Lawrence sat in the Fontana Vecchia looking at his belongings and Frieda's, four trunks (one for books), two valises, two small bags, and a hatbox. He felt 'like

Abraham going to a new land', and his heart trembled with the pain of leaving 'home' and the people of Sicily. Perhaps, as Else Jaffe had said, he and Frieda would return to Fontana Vecchia one day: but now he tried to think of peacocks and monkeys, of elephants and palm trees.

On Monday, February 20, the Lawrences left for Naples by way of Messina and Palermo. On the night of the twenty-sixth they sailed on the R.M.S. *Osterley* for the two weeks' voyage to Ceylon, via Port Said and Aden and Suez and the Red Sea. Lawrence wrote to Frieda's mother that they had gone 'through the Straits of Messina and then for hours we saw our Etna like a white queen or a white witch there standing in the sky so magic-lovely. She said to me, "You come back here", but I only said "No", but I wept inside with grief, grief of separation.' For Lawrence had really liked Taormina, and apart from occasional carping at 'Taorminity', his letters of the time are mostly cheerful, with indications of his deep love of the place.

As he and Frieda went east and south, they saw the snow-filled mountains of Crete, and all the highly colored activity of Levantine ports, and Mount Sinai, 'red like dried blood'. It was an emphatic, however temporary, farewell to Europe. Lawrence, working on his translation of Giovanni Verga's *Mastro Don Gesnaldo,* let his ink-pot fall to the deck: 'The *Osterley* shall wear my black sign forever.'

5   TEMPLES, TEMPLE BELLS, KANGAROOS, AND POLITICS

On April 17, 1922, Lawrence wrote to Amy Lowell from Ceylon: 'We have been here the last six weeks—wonderful place to look at, but too hot to live in. Now we are going to Australia—if we don't like that, then San Francisco.' From Australia, Lawrence wrote to Earl Brewster that he had never been so ill in his life as during the last part of that visit to Ceylon.

The Brewsters lived in an enormous hilltop bungalow there, with wide verandas that looked across the jungles to the Lake of Kandy and the far hills. When the Lawrences arrived, Frieda at once declared it was the loveliest place in the world, and Lawrence said, 'I shall never leave it.' Mrs. Brewster, reporting this, added: 'That was the first day.' Soon the choking heat began to make Lawrence ill each afternoon; it affected the others too. The surface of life there was charged with brilliant colors and permeated in the daytime by that smothering heat. Lawrence did little original writing; he sat on the veranda in the mornings and scratched away at his translation of the Verga novel as the sound of temple bells drifted through the trees. He resisted all impulsion to turn away from the bright outwardness and go inward; or, as he watched Brewster set off every morning to receive instruction in Buddhism and the Pāli dialect at the nearby monastery, Lawrence decided that this was a bogus inwardness. He began to suggest his disapproval of Buddhism—in later years when he and Brewster were together and would see a statue of the Buddha, Lawrence would say, 'Oh, I wish he would *stand up!*'

The East had long tempted him, as his interest in the writings of Besant, Blavatsky, Pryse, and others showed. Brewster has pointed out that in spite of Lawrence's loss of interest in Buddhism while in Ceylon, 'his sympathy for other forms of Hindu thought remained.' A Sinhalese writer, Martin Wickramasinghe, has said (in his book *Lawrence and Mysticism* [1953]) that Lawrence had affinities with the occult form of Indian mysticism know as the Tantric. And Sri Aurobindo has suggested that perhaps 'Lawrence was a Yogi who had missed his way and come into a European body to work out his difficulties.' But in Ceylon, Lawrence realized 'we make a mistake forsaking England and moving out into the periphery of life. After all, Taormina, Ceylon, Africa, America—as far as *we* go, they are only the negation of what we ourselves stand for and are: and we're rather like Jonahs running away from the place we belong.'

Lawrence had eluded Mabel Dodge Sterne's projected will to the extent that, by the end of March, he could plan to return to England in the summer. It was a crime to leave England in the hands of the Horatio Bottomleys: England was the center of vital hope for good Englishmen, who must unite there. Buddhism, Hinduism, even Catholicism—for the last of which Lawrence had some hope, religiously though not politically—were all evasions, he felt. The heavy, muddy voluptuousness of the Orient had brought out the Englishman in him. Yet at the time of his possible return to England, he was considering Australia. On April 3 he wrote to Mrs. Sterne, who was now sending necklaces and books on glands as well as letters and cables and fiats: 'Ceylon is an *experience*—but heavens, not a permanence.'

One of his few pieces of writing in Ceylon was the poem 'Elephant'. This described the Perahera at Kandy on March 23, when the 'pale, dispirited Prince' of Wales (later to be the Duke of Windsor) rode on the elephant's back high above the torch flares. Lawrence saw the weary 'fragment of a Prince', in this poem of augury, as 'drudge to the public', like the prodded elephant: 'an alien, diffident boy whose motto is *Ich Dien*'—and Lawrence in 1922 played prophetically on the irony of that 'I serve'.

While at Kandy, Lawrence completed his translation of *Mastro Don Gesnaldo,* which Seltzer published in New York the following year. This was the first full book Lawrence translated, to be followed by Verga's *Little Novels of Sicily* (published 1925) and *Cavalleria Rusticana and Other Stories* (published 1928), as well as Il Lasca's *The Story of Doctor Manente* (published 1929). Before this, he had been credited with helping Koteliansky translate Ivan Bunin's story 'The Gentleman from San Francisco', though his name does not appear on the title page of the volume, *The Gentleman from San Francisco and Other Stories,* which the Hogarth Press published in 1922. On the title page, Koteliansky appears as translator with Leonard Woolf, though a tipped-in erratum note explains that 'owing to a mistake Mr Lawrence's name has been omitted from the title-page', where he should have been credited with translating the leading story in collaboration with Koteliansky.

The London bookseller Bertram Rota discovered that the translation of Leo Shestov's *All Things Are Possible,* published by Secker, with a foreword by Lawrence, was also a collaborative effort by Lawrence and Koteliansky, though only Koteliansky was listed on the title page. Observing that the manuscript of the translation was in Lawrence's handwriting, Bertram Rota called on Koteliansky, who said that he wrote an original English version of the text which Lawrence revised extensively. Rota informed the author of the present book that 'in some cases Lawrence altered the sense, but when Koteliansky pointed this out Lawrence impatiently declared that he could not stand foolish things and had altered the original where he thought it necessary. . . . Koteliansky says that the reason Lawrence's name does not appear as a collaborator in the translation of this book, or of Dostoevsky's *The Grand Inquisitor,* or other translations which they did together, is that Lawrence felt that it would be damaging to his reputation with publishers if he should appear as a translator. Consequently there is much work of Lawrence's which is unacknowledged, though he is credited with forewords to the translations in some cases.' This is interesting information, suggesting that Lawrence may have made several translations before losing his shyness about such matters. If, however, he actually helped with Koteliansky's version of *The Grand Inquisitor,* for which he wrote a foreword, it is strange that his name didn't appear as co-translator when the book came out in August 1930, five months after his death. But this takes us far beyond Lawrence's first Verga translation, completed in 1922.

Leaving Ceylon exactly six weeks after they arrived there, Lawrence and Frieda went to West Australia and then on to Sydney. Lawrence wrote to Jan Juta on May 20, 1922, from the steamer *Malwa,* saying that 'Ceylon was lovely to look at but not to live in.' Seltzer, who had brought out Lawrence's *Sea and Sardinia* with Juta's illustrations, wanted the two men to collaborate on a book about India, but Lawrence 'didn't feel like it'. He had found that 'on these boats one can travel perfectly second class—nicer than first, simpler —now that there is hardly anybody coming out this way.' There were less than thirty second-class passengers, 'nice simple people'. He added, 'I feel that once I've rolled out of Europe I'll go on rolling. I like it so much. But F. still hankers after "a little 'ome of 'er own." I, no.—But I love straying my own way.' He and Frieda were on their way to Sydney, after two weeks in West Australia. He found that the place had 'a marvelous sky and air and blue quality, and a hoary sort of land beneath it, like a Sleeping Princess on whom the dust of ages has settled. Wonder if she'll ever get up.' He wasn't working (although before he left Australia, he wrote a novel about it, *Kangaroo*). He told Juta that he didn't know where Bettina was, or he'd write to her.

The Bettina referred to was Juta's fiancée, Elizabeth Humes, an American (Southern) girl whom Lawrence had met at Capri. His meddling in her life irritated her, and she left Capri on his account, but he seemed to bear no grudge and spoke of her pleasantly in later correspondence. The portrait of her as the American girl, Lou Carrington, in his subsequent short novel, *St Mawr,* is not a malignant one, though her mother—who became Mrs. Witt, the mother in the story, who is also partly Mabel Dodge Sterne—fared somewhat worse; but by that time Lawrence had met Mrs. Sterne and had a lower opinion than before of will-motored American women.

In West Australia the Lawrences had stayed a few days at Perth and then moved sixteen miles inland to Darlington, at the edge of the bush. They visited Perth at the instigation of a young Australian woman, Mrs. A. L. Jenkins, whom they had met on the *Os-*

terley between Naples and Colombo; she is possibly the original of Victoria Callcott in *Kangaroo*. She took the Lawrences on a picnic with her friend Mrs. May Eva Gawler, a noted gardener, who explained the Australian flora to Lawrence. He caused a bit of excitement in his few days in Perth, meeting the local intellectuals at Mrs. Zabel's Book Lovers' Library. A woman writer, Katharine Susannah Pritchard (Mrs. Throssell), living near Perth, became so excited at the prospect of meeting Lawrence that she prematurely gave birth to her child.

Lawrence met another writer, his future collaborator, the nurse Mollie Skinner, at Darlington. It was there that he had the experience he transferred to Somers in *Kangaroo,* when he walked alone into the bush one night and saw 'a huge electric moon, huge, and the tree trunks like naked pale aborigines among the dark soaked foliage, in the moonlight. And not a sign of life—not a vestige,' though the place seemed haunted, for all its emptiness. Lawrence-Somers fled in terror, ice in his spine.

The Lawrences stayed barely a day at Sydney, just long enough to view from the heights the 'many lobed harbour', and just long enough to find that 'Sydney town costs too much'. They went forty miles down the coast, to Thirroul, and took a house on a cliff above the sea, a cottage some punster had, in the Australian fashion, named 'Wyewurk'. In the first few days there Lawrence began writing *Kangaroo,* which he completed in about six weeks, except for the last chapter, 'Adieu Australia'.

That novel begins in Sydney, with two strangers in quest of lodgings: 'a smallish man, pale faced, with a dark beard', and 'a mature, handsome, fresh faced woman, who might have been Russian'. Most of *Kangaroo* is a supreme travel book, with commentary that is at times earnest philosophic point-putting and at other times journalistic chitchat. Since Lawrence and Frieda knew very few people in Sydney or Thirroul, the other characters came in from the past: Kangaroo himself, the Jewish lawer Ben Cooley, was a projection of Koteliansky, though in a letter Lawrence denied this, as he usually did; and Frieda has said that Dr. David Eder also helped compose the character.

Jaz, the transplanted 'Cornish whisper' James Trewhella, is a memory of the cunning, evil Cornishmen, particularly the Beresfords' landlord at Portcothan. But Jack and Victoria Callcott had to be Australian, Jack with his heavy kangaroo-like thighs and Victoria with her 'colonial' quality: Lawrence probably based them on people he had met at Perth and Darlington or aboard ship.

At 'Wyewurk' Lawrence for a change regularly read a newspaper, the *Sydney Bulletin,* whose serendipity reporting style gave him an entire chapter, 'Bits'. Reading there about the noted Sydney lawyer and engineer, Sir John Monash, who had led the Australian forces in the war, Lawrence probably found the outward guise of Ben Cooley: pictures of Monash, who was, like Kangaroo, Jewish, show him with the long face Lawrence described; and pictures of him would have appeared in the *Bulletin* at that time. Likewise, as the original version of the present book (1954) first pointed out, Lawrence probably found in that paper the outward model for Willie Struthers, the socialist leader, in the frequent references to the labor leader James Holman. But though the face of Willie Struthers may have been the face of Holman, the voice was often that of William Hopkin.

Politically, that year of 1922 was a quiet one for Australia, with no riots such as the one in the novel in which the Diggers fought the socialists. A national election was due, and it took place in December, four months after the Lawrences had left. As part of this political contest, Prime Minister Hughes had toured the country, and although the campaign was a colorless one, both sides spit out a good deal of acrimony. Lawrence read all this and recalled what he had seen in Italy and Sicily the last few years, the newly formed *fascisti* battling the socialists; and he created a fascist group to give Kangaroo his weapon of leadership. And, as Curtis Atkinson pointed out in the Australian magazine *Meanjin* (in 1965), there were demonstrations elsewhere in 1921, the year before Lawrence's arrival, and he certainly must have heard of them from Australian friends. The Returned Soldiers' Politic League caused most of the disturbances. At this time a hundred thousand members of the League broke up meetings throughout the Domain.

In the socio-political dialogues in *Kangaroo,* Lawrence went back to 1915–1916 and the Russell disputes and the bitterness of wartime Cornwall (a point which has been developed at length by Ralph Maud). Indeed, on his first day at Thirroul, Lawrence wrote to his mother-in-law: 'The sky is dark, and it makes me think of Cornwall.'

The old fight, the single man against conformity, Lawrence this time fought—or refought—in his imagination. And he chose, in the story substitution, not to follow the strong leader and his fascist-like Diggers, not to heed the socialist plea for him to edit 'a constructive working man's newspaper', but rather to 'stick to one's isolate being and the God in whom it is rooted'—a procedure which is easiest to follow in a democratic society. That Lawrence was so consistently antidemocratic is an irony, yet this doesn't prevent the book from being 'one of the most profound political treatises of modern times'. That was the judgment of Middleton Murry, in one of his most illuminating comments on Lawrence: he pointed out that *Kangaroo* 'shows the complete moral demand of conscious politics upon the modern man. That Lawrence refused it—"his great refusal"—does not alter the fact that he was the first modern Englishman to *feel* the sternness of the complete demand.'

The book is full of descriptions of the Australian coast—indeed, the lyric and travelogue element of this novel is as important as the central fable. So far, only Murry and Father Jarrett-Kerr and one or two other commentators have given *Kangaroo* its measure of importance among Lawrence's books. As a novel, it doesn't rank with *The Rainbow* and *Women in Love,* partly because it isn't really a novel but a special kind of production, in the category of such books as *Sartor Resartus* or *Thus Spake Zarathustra.* Purely as writing, it stands high in all twentieth-century literature: the dawns along that coast, the man wandering by the southern sea, the scattered tin-roofed villages, the four days of smashing rains that maroon Somers and his wife in the little house—scenes which in the pages of most novelists would be routine and flaccid, Lawrence with his power of language makes into experiences that are almost as real as anything that has happened to his reader.

While he was in Australia, he received copies of *Aaron's Rod,* which Seltzer had published in April and Secker in June. Lawrence warned most of his friends to whom he sent the book that they wouldn't like it. And the reviews of it seem the product either of determinations to dislike Lawrence or of failures in understanding the novel—and in some cases both. Unexpectedly, the most favorable review was Murry's in the *Nation and Athenaeum:* 'To read *Aaron's Rod* is to drink of a fountain of life . . . *Aaron's Rod* is the most important thing that has happened to English literature since the war. To my mind it is much more important than *Ulysses*' (and it may be added that Murry was a pioneer in the appreciation of Joyce's novel). But other reviewers of *Aaron's Rod* were less enamored of Lawrence's book.

In America, H. W. Boynton, in the *Independent,* arrogantly

doubted that the author was 'anything better than a sentimental per-
vert'. Joseph Wood Krutch, in the *Nation,* discovered 'vividness,
power, and freshness' in *Aaron's Rod,* but also 'an almost hysterical
overemphasis of certain interesting things'. L.M.R., in the *Freeman,*
found the book 'not one of Mr. Lawrence's notable achievements';
Dorothy Ogburn, in the Literary Review of the *New York Evening
Post,* felt the novel really belonged in a psychoanalyst's casebook
and that its author must be 'a wilfully perverse young man'. The
British were in the main less tart, though Lawrence's friendly old *English Review* thought he had an 'ache' in him and was 'still groping';
Rebecca West, usually friendly to Lawrence, called *Aaron's Rod*
'plum-silly' in the *New Statesman.* The *Times Literary Supplement*
found Lawrence grim in somewhat the manner of Strindberg, but in
every way greater.

Anyhow, despite the coolly disapproving or tepidly approving reviews, *Aaron's Rod* fared rather well. Seltzer soon had a second printing on the way, and in England Secker had to reissue it every few
years during the rest of its author's life. By 1922 Lawrence had
found his post-war audience, a literate minority that gave him just
enough support to keep him going until his black-market best seller,
Lady Chatterley's Lover, brought him his first 'tidy amount'.

In Australia in 1922, he could tell Mabel Dodge Sterne by July 18
that he had finished his novel *Kangaroo*—only about six weeks after
he had started it (though, as mentioned, he later added the chapter
'Adieu Australia'; this was after he arrived in Taos). Mrs. Sterne had
sent a cable which made even a participle sound peremptory: 'EX-
PECTING YOU.' Lawrence had written to Katharine Susannah Pritchard that Australia was an ideal place to settle in 'when one has had
enough of the world—when one doesn't want to wrestle with another
single thing, humanly. . . . No, just to drift away, and live and forget
and expire in Australia.' In another letter he told her, 'It's a dark
country, a sad country, underneath—like an abyss. Then, when the
sky turns frail and blue again, and the trees against the far-off sky
stand out, the glamour, the unget-at-able glamour! A great fascination, but also a dismal grey terror, underneath.' He was planning to
leave in six days.

And on August 10 he and Frieda sailed on the *Tahiti* for San
Francisco, touching at Wellington, New Zealand; at Avatiu, Rara-
tonga; and at Papeete, Tahiti. From Wellington he sent a postcard
to Katherine Mansfield, with a one-word message, '*Ricordi*', to break

their years of silence. Only a day earlier, Katherine Mansfield, on the point of leaving Switzerland for London, had made her will and had named Lawrence among those of her friends who were to receive small remembrances. *Aaron's Rod* had revived her admiration for the writer, so that she could forgive the man. Reading it in July, and coming across an old story of Lawrence's, 'The Shadow in the Rose Garden' (from *The Prussian Officer*), she had spoken of these in two letters to Koteliansky. Lawrence's 'Rose Garden' story was 'one of the weakest he ever wrote', yet it was 'so utterly different from all the rest' in a collection of modern fiction that she read it 'with joy. When he mentions gooseberries these are real red, ripe gooseberries that the gardener is rolling on a tray. When he bites into an apple it is a sharp, sweet, fresh apple from the growing tree.' And the faults of *Aaron's Rod,* she thought, were minor: the book lived, and it was a relief to read it after 'all these little pre-digested books written by authors who have nothing to say!" She could not agree with much of what Lawrence said, and his ideas of sex were meaningless to her, 'but I feel nearer to L. than anyone else. All these last months I have thought as he does about many things.'

Indeed, these two writers had similarities in their physical vision, as a close examination of their prose will show: in an age of flat journalese and of pallid stereotypes, they both wrote in a style that was concrete, sharp-colored, and kinetic, each of them with a distinct personal cadence. (In the July 1954 issue of *Essays in Criticism,* Robert Liddell wrote: 'Katherine Mansfield said somewhere that there were three Lawrences: the black devil, whom she hated; the prophet, in whom she did not believe; and the man and artist whom she loved and valued. Now that it is twenty-four years since he died, can we not rid ourselves of the devil and the prophet—for whom there is no future—and find the man and artist, who is immortal?')

Lawrence sent other cards on his way to America: to Ada Clarke from every port the ship stopped at, and to the Brewsters and Catherine Carswell and others from several of these places. Lawrence told Mrs. Carswell that he found Tahiti 'beautiful—but Papeete a poor, dull, modernish place'. A fortnight later he reported to her that San Francisco was 'quite pleasant, but very noisy and iron-clanking and expensive'. One of the ugly rumors about Lawrence which has flourished with particular vigor concerns those five days in San Francisco, during which he is supposed to have slipped away from Frieda for a squalid adventure. But Frieda insisted (in a letter of

January 24, 1951), 'I was there in San Francisco every minute.' She classified the story as 'one of those charming lies'.

6 HIGH UP OVER THE DESERT

Taos was a mistake, as Lawrence realized soon after he arrived. During his intermittent three years there, he rarely stayed in Taos itself—'Taos too much. Mabel Sterne and suppers and motor drives and people dropping in'—but lived in the mountain ranches twenty miles away from that center of twittering malice; and Lawrence also made several trips to Mexico and Europe during this period. From his arrival at Taos on September 11, 1922, to his departure on September 10, 1925, Lawrence spent only about eighty weeks in the Taos region, barely more than half of those three years; and, as noted, very little of this time in Taos itself. He liked New Mexico, but wanted as much as possible to avoid Mrs. Sterne-Luhan and the people who stayed on her property, which he christened Mabeltown.

Mrs. Sterne was an intensification of all that Lawrence had found to caricature in Ottoline Morrell: and the American woman had a far larger war chest for her activities. Lady Ottoline was in any event the product of an older civilization, not of a parvenu culture; she was a grand lady in the grand style and, if eccentric, quite authentically so in the tradition of her distinguished bluestocking ancestress, the Countess of Winchilsea; and Lady Ottoline's foibles had been mostly on the surface. Mrs. Sterne (who later became Mrs. Luhan and will for convenience' sake be called that here) left an exceedingly full account of herself in a book purporting to be about Lawrence which she rushed into print soon after his death: *Lorenzo in Taos* (1932).

After two months of Mrs. Luhan, he wrote to his mother-in-law about her, in German: 'You have asked about Mabel Dodge: American, rich, only child, from Buffalo on Lake Erie, bankers, forty-two years old, has had three husbands—one Evans (dead), one Dodge (divorced), and one Maurice Sterne (a Jew, Russian, painter, also divorced). Now she has an Indian, Tony, stout chap. She has lived much in Europe—Paris, Nice, Florence—is a little famous in New York and little loved, very intelligent as a woman, a "culture-carrier", likes to play the patroness, hates the white world and loves the Indian out of hate, is very "generous", wants to be "good" and is very wicked, has a terrible will-to-power, you know—she wants to be a witch and at the same time a Mary of Bethany at Jesus's feet—a big white crow, a cooing raven of ill omen, a white buffalo.'

The account of Lawrence's New Mexican experiences which follows will draw upon Mrs. Luhan's *Lorenzo in Taos* as little as possible. Some of the incidents in it probably happened and will have to be noted, though one soon turns to the reliable memoirs of the period for relief and for a stricter truth. Above all, one may turn to Lawrence's own letters for a note of sanity.

Mrs. Luhan had thoughtfully telegraphed the Lawrences their Pullman fares to Taos from San Francisco. On the evening of Lawrence's thirty-seventh birthday he and Frieda stepped off the train at Lamy, New Mexico, and into the orbit of this squat, bustling, square-faced little woman and the chauffeur who had driven her there in her expensive automobile: the massive and stolid Indian, Tony Luhan, who was hardly the type of noble savage Lawrence was looking for. Frieda, Mabel felt at once, was trying to 'see' her and Tony 'sexually'. They all drove away together over the desert, Mrs. Luhan from the first feeling hostile towards Frieda and prehensile towards Lawrence. As she ludicrously wrote of the occasion: 'The womb in me roused to reach out and take him.' Her story about the car's breaking down on the way to Santa Fe and, as Tony Luhan puttered with the engine, Lawrence's saying, "I am a failure as a man in the world of men,' should be weighed against the probabilities. Lawrence, with his hatred of machines, thought that Indians who knew how to fix them were corrupt.

Before he had been long in Taos, he began to direct his hatred of machines in general to automobiles in particular. This was new, in spite of his ancient loathing of mechanization of almost any kind: even the idealized Birkin, in *Women in Love,* drove a car without incurring severe spiritual penalties. But now Lawrence's correspondence began to complain of 'Mabel and motor-cars'; and, as he told Mrs. Bessie Freeman in an October letter, he didn't 'like a motor-car'. This dislike persisted: in Italy several years later, Aldous Huxley tried to persuade Lawrence to take over his old automobile, but Lawrence refused: 'Why rush from place to place?' He seemed, after his first American experience, to identify Mabel Luhan and her motorized Indian with cars and rushing about and the mechanized will. After describing Mrs. Luhan to his mother-in-law, Lawrence said, 'The people in America all want power, but a small, personal, base power: bullying. They are all bullies.'

On Lawrence's first night in New Mexico it was too late, by the time the international party had reached Santa Fe, for Tony Luhan to attempt the seventy-five miles to Taos. Mabel Luhan arranged for the

Lawrences to stay at the tiny adobe house of Witter Bynner, a local poet and translator who was to wait until the 1950s, when everyone had thought the last malicious memoir of Lawrence had been published, to launch his *Journey with Genius.*

That book was ill timed in that it turned the clock back to the period twenty years before, when the hectic memoirs of Lawrence's camp followers were driving people away from his writing. By the 1950s, Lawrence's work was at last being read for its own sake, and then Bynner revived Lawrence the embittered thrower of crockery and insults. In *John O' London's Weekly,* Richard Church wrote, 'The reader may ask whether or not Mr Bynner is justified, after so many years, in reviving the record of his own irritations at the social morbidity of a man of genius.' Reviewing Bynner's memoir in the *New York Times,* Mark Schorer said the decade of the 1950s would not see another book 'so drenched in malice', with Lawrence's 'bad manners' reported 'as if by a cross between Emily Post and Hedda Hopper'; and, indeed, successive decades haven't matched this 'journey'. Bynner's delayed sting would not have surprised Lawrence, who in 1926 wrote to Mrs. Luhan that Bynner was 'a sort of belated mosquito'.

Bynner's book, however, wasn't merely an attack on Lawrence, but also a series of self-glorifications. Bynner repeatedly projected scenes in which he overcame Lawrence by speaking up to him, making him seem, time after time, 'a deflated prophet'.

Bynner's 'venom', as Mark Schorer has characterized it, was apparent from his first glimpse of the man Mrs. Luhan brought to his house: 'Lawrence's appearance struck me from the outset as that of a bad baby masquerading as a good Mephistopheles.' This was Bynner the man's first reaction—never to be modified by that third-rate poet Bynner—to Lawrence, who had long since been a first-rate author.

On that first night of the Lawrences in New Mexico, Willard (Spud) Johnson, who had been in Bynner's verse-writing class at the University of California and was then staying with him in Santa Fe, returned from a Tom Mix movie to find himself and Bynner moved into the 'studio' while the Lawrences were installed in the bedroom. Freida, according to Mabel Luhan, said, *'Un ménage, hein?* The young thin one seems rather nice.' (Frieda later reported that she never used the word *hein.*)

Before retiring, they all had supper in the kitchen, with some acquaintances joining them; when Bynner arose early the next morning to wash the dishes before breakfast, he found that Lawrence had already performed the task. Perhaps this was a breach of good manners.

Lawrence had his first glimpse of New Mexico that day: 'The moment I saw the brilliant, proud morning sun shine high up over the deserts of Santa Fe, something stood still in my soul, and I started to attend.' He had found the place, New Mexico, that was to become 'the greatest experience from the outside world that I have ever had.' He was always careful to distinguish, when he made such statements, between New Mexico itself, with its magnificent high skies and 'the fierce, proud silence of the Rockies,' and the New Mexico which was already 'the picturesque reservation and playground of the eastern states,' the New Mexico that wealthy amateurs 'wrapped in the absolutely hygienic and shiny mucous paper of our trite civilisation.'

This aspect he found at Mabel Luhan's: the bohemian, arty, dude-ranch attempt to be primitive. At her house that first night, as he and Frieda sat down to dine with her in Greenwich Village-like candle-light that glimmered on decorative bronzes, Lawrence giggled: 'It's like one of those nasty little temples in India.' The next day Mrs. Luhan helped the Lawrences move into 'their' house, which Lawrence about a week later described to Brewster as not merely an adobe cottage but 'a very smart' one. 'The drawback is, of course, the "padrona." ' She tried to be 'nice', but Lawrence told Brewster that he did not know how long he could stand her: 'Probably, as a sort of lesson to myself, until the spring.'

Earlier, on the day he arrived at Taos, Lawrence had written a hasty card to the Brewsters saying he was 'still dazed and vague'. But before he could quite catch his breath, Mrs. Luhan had Tony whisk him away in her car to the Apache fiesta, which he 'must' see. 'Tony,' Mrs. Luhan reported, 'didn't want to take Lawrence, but I made him!'

Mrs. Luhan had wanted to go to the fiesta, but stayed behind because there was not space in the car for her and her house guest, Mrs. Freeman, and Frieda. So Bessie Wilkerson Freeman accompanied Lawrence and Tony. Both Frieda and Mrs. Luhan thought this little white-haired widow, a girlhood friend of Mrs. Luhan's from Buffalo, was 'safe' enough to be a companion for their men. Lawrence formed a strange relationship with her: after she left Taos he wrote her letters far more full of gossip than was usual in his correspondence.

At Taos, during those five days when Lawrence was at the fiesta, Frieda spent the time with her hostess, whose energy she admired, and with another guest, Alice Corbin Henderson. Mrs. Henderson, the wife of a painter, was the author of several books of poetry. Before Lawrence had left, Frieda had written her hostess a note saying, 'I have suffered tortures when Lawrence talked to people, when they drew him out just to "see his goods" and then jeered at him.' But after Lawrence had gone, Frieda gave away an even better share of 'goods', candidly telling Mrs. Luhan—or so Mrs. Luhan claimed—'about the two times Lawrence had evaded her' in Cornwall. Frieda wrote later, somewhat ruefully, that Mrs. Luhan and Mrs. Henderson 'asked me many questions, which I answered truthfully, giving the show away as usual.'

Lawrence left his impressions of the Apache fiesta in his essay 'Indians and an Englishman'. He found the event at some levels impressive, but much of it must have seemed like the Indian nonsense he had mocked in *The Lost Girl,* in which the strolling players put on a melodrama about Red Indians. Lawrence wrote of the Apache fiesta, 'It is all rather like a comic opera played with solemn intensity.' Later, in both New Mexico and Arizona, the Indian dances stirred him; now he resisted. The ancient drums awoke something in his blood, yes, but 'my way is my own, old red father; I can't cluster at the drum any more.'

On the other hand, modern American life didn't allure him either, though he had seen little enough of it. But even in the comparative remoteness of Taos, the influence of the cities projected itself. Lawrence told Brewster he could understand why Brewster didn't want to live in America: 'It is just the life outside, and the outside of life. Not *really* life, in my opinion.' The sun was good, and 'the free desert, and the absence of Europe's stiflingness. . . . But this absurd will-pressure and the sense of a host of people who must all have an inferiority complex somewhere, striving to make good over everybody else, this is ignominious, it seems to me.' In that same letter to Brewster (September 22), Lawrence crowed happily that 'the "Vice" people tried to suppress *Women in Love* and other books: Seltzer won completely.' He referred to the recent decision of Magistrate George W. Simpson in the West Side Court in New York City, to which the crusading John W. Sumner had brought three Seltzer books for prosecution: Lawrence's, a novel by Schnitzler, and a volume with an introduction by Freud. In his decision, Magistrate Simpson declared, 'I do not find anything in these books which may be considered obscene, lewd, lascivious, filthy, indecent, or disgusting. On the contrary, I find that each of them is a distinct contribution to the literature of the present day.'

This was a good augury for Lawrence's immediate publishing future. On returning to Taos, he discussed with Mabel Luhan the possibility of their collaborating on a book about her life. Frieda, recalling the plan, said in her memoir, 'I did not want this'. She began to intrude on the collaborators' little meetings. Mrs. Luhan reported that Lawrence complained to her of his terror of 'the heavy, German hand of the flesh', and whether or not he ever said this, it must at least have been fun to imagine that he had. Mrs. Luhan was not attracted to Lawrence physically, she said, but felt that she must have a physical relationship with him because the body is the gateway to the soul. 'One day,' Frieda recalled, 'Mabel came over and told me she didn't think I was the right woman for Lawrence.' Frieda roared back at her, 'Try it then yourself, living with a genius, see what it is like and how easy it is, take him if you can.'

Mrs. Luhan could not, though she kept trying. Even after his death, she attempted to steal his ashes from Frieda. But someone told Frieda about this, and Frieda cemented the ashes into an altar that even Mrs. Luhan's will power and money power were not able to smash. Those very powers, of both will and money, had frightened Lawrence away from her in life. He soon saw how she was trying to be empress of the Indians. Her activities became in time as much of a bother to the townspeople and the Indians themselves as they had been to Lawrence. Eventually the county commissioners rezoned Taos in order to put her residence outside the voting district. And a young Indian, representing his generation rather than merely himself, wrote an open letter to her in the *Taos Star*. This was in answer to some of her public pronouncements to the effect that the young Indians did not really want 'progress', and 'a dismal accretion of cars, stoves, sinks, *et al.,*' for 'the blood of their forerunners is still truly stronger in them than new needs for THINGS'—a series of semi-Lawrencean ideas sounding rather hollow without Lawrence's magic of expression. In any case, the young Indian, J. R. Martinez, in his letter asked Mrs. Luhan, who had just moved into a new house with soundproof bedrooms, a magnificent kitchen, and several fine bathrooms, whether she would not like to change places with him: 'You can have all the horse and buggies you want and I'll have your nice new cars. You drink muddy water from the mountains and I and my five children will drink nice clean water from your faucets. . . . You have to understand that we want to live like humans and not like animals.' Mrs. Luhan and her arty friends had treated him and his people like monkeys by feeding them peanuts: 'Mrs. Luhan, take your peanuts somewhere else.'

This letter appeared long after Lawrence had left Taos, but he would have chuckled at it, as he probably would have chuckled—with some exasperation—at the parody of his doctrines. Lawrence had himself become involved in one of the controversies over the Indians soon after he arrived in Taos: the Bursum Bill. He mentioned this in a letter written at the end of October to Mrs. Freeman, in which he also referred to a good many other local activities, including those of another friend of Mrs. Luhan's from Buffalo who had married a one-armed former sheriff named Lee Witt; of Mrs. Luhan's son, John Ganson Evans; of Juan Concha, a friend of Tony Luhan's; and of the sociologist John Collier:

> This is just a line to say how do you do, and where are you, and what are you up to. We are here as usual thick in things: even too thick. It has been the Bursum Bill till we're sick of it. I've done an article, Alice Corbin's done one, John Collier's done one. The last named is still trotting on his reforming mission somewhere Zuñi way, we are supposed to go and meet him at San Domingo on Nov. 5th, Sunday, where all the elders from all the *pueblos* are to meet and have a Bursum Bill pow-wow. M.S. [Mabel Sterne] is very keen on going. Your old friend of the Apache trip is *not* keen. He doesn't love a motor-car. Besides, it has snowed these two days, and been so cold I have almost cried. I shall *not* be trailed to Santo Domingo if it's like this.
>
> Tony is home: had to abandon John Colly—as John Concha invariably says, in Santa Fe, because he, Tony, had such a toothache. Fortunately it was better when he got home.— Put $2 + 2$ together.
>
> John Evans got back from Wyoming last night, having motored 1,000,000 miles since Wednesday—in his new car. He now wants to marry young Alice [Henderson] in 4 weeks['] time, and take her to the Buffalo grandmother's for January 4th, when my young gentleman comes of age. Whether this speed will be allowed him, remains to be seen.—Alice Corbin here, and leaves tomorrow, full of admiration etc for Mabel, but a little worried in her maternal self, the young Alice being not yet 16.— Lee Witt didn't go home to Nina for a fortnight: went instead to his Mexican woman and had influenza with her. Nina infuriated, pondered a divorce. He growing tenderer, said if Mrs Berry

went, he'd come home. Mrs Berry went, he came home, cried, Nina's heart melted in her, the divorce is postponed.
No no, no more gossip. We still ride: on Sunday through the snow up Glorietta: very lovely too. My little pony quite likes me: and Gran'fer is wedded to Frieda, and nearly hangs himself upon the barbed wire when she won't ride, and we trot off alone. I always think of you as my first riding companion: and my first Indian mate. You'll see yourself in my 'Pueblos and an Englishman' article if ever anybody publishes it.

Lawrence's essays on the Indians had no difficulty in finding a home: 'Certain Indians and an Englishman' appeared in the *New York Times Magazine* for December 24, 1922, while 'Indians and an Englishman' was in the *Dial* for February 1923 and in the *Adelphi* for November 1923. Lawrence's rather sardonic description of John Collier, 'trotting on his reforming mission somewhere Zuñi way,' was probably the result of his having met Collier under the wrong circumstances. Actually, Collier had a kind of Lawrencean sympathy for the Indians; eventually, as Commissioner of Indian Affairs, Collier established a program of protection for them, under an administration (F. D. Roosevelt's) more interested in human rights than in landgrabbing or the benefits of a reckless 'free enterprise'. In Lawrence's time, Senator Bursum of New Mexico and the man he had succeeded, Albert B. Fall, who had left his senatorial post to become Harding's Secretary of the Interior before going to a federal penitentiary, had joined forces in an attempt to deprive the Indians of their land. Oil, which at the last was to cause Fall's public disgrace, had been discovered on some of the Navaho lands.

Collier helped to make the Indians aware of the threatened land seizure, and even Lawrence took enough interest in the matter to write against the Bursum Bill in his previously mentioned article in the *New York Times Magazine*. Indian delegations went East to appeal for protection against the depredations of the Indian Bureau, whose attitude was not changed even by the removal of Fall (March 4, 1923). His former associates then branded the Indians as Reds— that is, 'agents of Moscow'. The Indians had, however, kicked up enough dust to prevent the wholesale seizure of their hereditary lands, although they had to wait some years until Roosevelt and Ickes and Collier could set up what Collier has called 'the Indian New Deal'.

Lawrence could not foresee this, and perhaps would have found some faults with it if he had foreseen it. 'Somewhere,' he wrote to Mabel Luhan from Mexico in November 1923, 'the Indians know that you and Collier would, with your salvationist but poisonous white consciousness, destroy them.' But Lawrence's vision of John Collier was hampered by Collier's association with the woman who would make at least part of Lawrence's judgment a true one, the woman whose tactics would inspire resentful Indians of a later generation to demand plumbing fixtures. And it wasn't until 1971 that the Indians were given ownership of their sacred blue lake on Taos mountain.

About a month after his arrival in New Mexico, Lawrence in a horseback-ride interview with a young writer, Maurice Lesemann, said he found the Americans 'dangerous as a race. Far more dangerous than most of the races in Europe.' But already he had again begun to think of America as the locale of Rananim: 'I should like to see the young people gather,' he told Lesemann, 'somewhere away from the city, somewhere where living is cheap—in a place like this, for instance; and let them have a farm or a ranch, with horses and a cow, and *not* try to make it pay. Don't let them try to make it pay, like Brook Farm. But let them support themselves by their writing, or their painting, or whatever it is.' Then 'they could be themselves'; they would create a nucleus, and 'they would be able gradually to spread their influence and combat the other thing a little. At least they would know they existed.'

That was the early-New Mexico Lawrence, who daily went riding on an Indian pony, the Lawrence of cowboy boots, white riding-breeches, blue shirt, bandana tie, and wide-brimmed hat. His new idea of Rananim he mentioned in his October 31 letter to Mrs. Freeman, an important letter because of this and because it contains the first mention of the ranch he later visualized as headquarters for Rananim:

I wrote you yesterday, not knowing Mabel had telegraphed to you. Today we have been up to John's [John Evans, Mabel's son] ranch—about 20 miles from here. It was so lonely: and rather free, far more so than here. Frieda wants to go and live there. We'll try it first for a week, because it will be colder. But I think we shall do it—and try to make a *real* life there. It is much more splendid, more *real,* there, than here. You must come and see how you'd like it.

Mabel says you want to sell your Los Angeles home. Sell it. Sell it before you come here, if you can: or put it in an agent's hands. Then come, and let us plan a new life. I was thinking you might want to take up the next 'homestead' lot to us, and have your house and Mabel would take up another lot adjoining. And the rule would be, no *servants:* we'd all work our own work. No highbrows and weariness of stunts. We might make a central farm. Make it all real. This is too unreal for me.

There's the idea, anyhow—if it attracts you, we can talk more about it.

Lawrence soon discovered that obstacles stood in the way of his move to the mountains: on November 14 he wrote to Mrs. Freeman: 'We can't go to the ranch this winter. The house is broken in, and too late to repair it. So we stay in this house.'

He at least had the fun of annoying Mabel Luhan by inviting members of the local art-colony to parties at his house near 'Mabeltown'. The house belonged to Tony Luhan, and Lawrence insisted on paying rent for it.

His expressed disgust for the 'arty' crowd had given Mrs. Luhan a gloating chance to keep to herself the visiting lion and lioness-baroness; but now he had willfully broken his own privacy. Sometimes he and Frieda would quarrel before others, as on the night Mabel Luhan was present when Lawrence reportedly shouted to Frieda, 'Take that dirty cigarette out of your mouth! And stop sticking out that fat belly of yours!'—to which Frieda is said to have retorted, 'You'd better stop that talk or I'll tell about *your* things.' Those present didn't know the Lawrences' technique of cauterizing annoyances at once rather than letting them gangrene into grudges. They were astonished to see Lawrence and Frieda, a few minutes later, walking along together arm and arm in the moonlight, 'in a silent world of their own'.

Lawrence and Frieda felt that their best chance of preserving their 'silent world' was to go up to the Rockies. After two weeks, Lawrence on December 15 wrote Bessie Freeman an account of the life there:

You see we have moved: Mabel was too near a neighbour. We have come to the Hawks' ranch—next to John Evans' ranch—about 17 miles from Taos: have an old brown log cabin, and are very comfortable. We plan to stay till April, so perhaps you'll be through with your house selling by then. Perhaps it is true, you shouldn't part with your own chippendale: if it's a comfort for you to have it. Perhaps we shall see you.

We have no particular news: are going down to Taos on the

24th, and staying a day or two with Mrs Harwood—you remember, from whose house I turned back one morning. Thomas Seltzer and his wife are due to arrive in Taos on the 25th—my publisher—then we shall come on here. Mabel will be full with a wedding and Christmas lot; not my line at all. John Evans marries the young Alice Henderson on the 20th of this month. She is fifteen years old. And he will be 21 in January. But I don't care for him: a very untrustworthy youth, seems to me. I'm glad to be out of it all. The young couple will live in our (Tony's) house—and proceed east to the grandmother's for his coming of age. At least, such is the programme. All the same to me.—Dear Bessie Freeman, I must tell you I don't like Mabel very much. *Elle me paraît fausse. La strega.*

We have quite a good time here: cut down a big tree and with great exertions sawed it and split it up. Ah oh, it burns away so fast in all the fires. I think grudgingly when I see the red embers: all my labour gone into smoke! But it was a sweet balsam pine tree, very bright in the burning. We struggle with pack-rats and pigs and cats. We've got one of Lorraine's little black pups that is now growing up into a young termagant. We go riding: I on a high sorrel thoroughbred that nearly splits me as I split my logs with wedges.—In a 3-room cabin are two young Danes, painters, nice: good neighbours. And Mountsier is coming next week. Snow is quite deep round us: but no snow on the desert below. The coyotes howl by the gate. . . . We say we are going to *Greenland* in the summer. Are we?

'We are still "friends" with Mabel,' Lawrence had told his mother-in-law, 'but do not take this snake to our bosom.' The Lawrences established pleasant relations with their new landlord, A. D. Hawk, and became particularly good friends of the younger Hawks, William and his wife Rachel. The two Danes who took the other cabin at Del Monte for that icy winter were Knud Merrild and Kai Götzsche. Lawrence's disappearance into the mountains with them galled Mabel Luhan, who in Taos had snubbed the Danes and sneered at them.

Merrild eventually wrote a book about Lawrence, *A Poet and Two Painters* (1939), which dealt principally with that winter. It was a memoir remarkable only for its self-conscious efforts at detachment; most of it comprised reconstructed conversations with Lawrence, taken from parts of his work, a method of authorship at once too easy and too confusing. And Merrild sometimes applied the method wrongly, as when he lifted a passage from Stephen Potter's book on Lawrence and mistakenly attributed the words in that passage to Lawrence. They were words attempting to deny homosexual tendencies in Lawrence. The value of the reference, however, resided in the Danes' own assertions, from their close acquaintance with Lawrence during that mountaintop winter and during some later intimate travel experiences, that Lawrence was positively not homosexual.

One or two other interesting points came out in Merrild's book—incidents of that eventful winter. One of these was the visit of a girl, Meta Lehmann, who had hiked up from Taos to visit the Danes. Because the walk back on the same day would have been too much, the Danes put her up for the night in one of the rooms in their cabin, thereby enraging the puritan Lawrence. The other episode concerned Lawrence's dog Bibbles, heroine of the poem of that name in *Birds, Beasts and Flowers:* 'First live thing I've "owned" since the lop-eared rabbits when I was a lad, / And those over-prolific white mice, and Adolf, and Rex, whom I didn't own.' The portrait of Bibbles, with her little black wrinkled face and her eagerness and her indiscriminate way of making friends ('All humanity is jam to you'), is one of Lawrence's liveliest and funniest. The 'little Walt-Whitmanesque bitch' became a symbol of various American traits Lawrence despised. Merrild said that once in a rage Lawrence kicked Bibbles, though when Merrild in the 1930s published in a Santa Fe newspaper the section of his book describing this, a number of people who knew Lawrence wrote in to deny it fiercely. Merrild, who says he nearly hit Lawrence at the time, reported further that the next day Lawrence, as if in appeasement, brought him and Götzsche a cake he had baked.

By January 24 Lawrence was writing to Mrs. Freeman, 'I'm a bit tired now of *winter:* the earth frozen for so long. I am not used to it.' As for Mrs. Freeman's old friend from Buffalo—well, she was 'a liar —and false as hell'. Reports came up from Taos to the effect that she was saying around town, 'I had to get rid of the Lawrences'. Her son, too, was reported as telling people, 'Mother had to turn the Lawrences out'. Yet she was at the same time 'writing such friendly letters, pressing us to come down, to take a trip with them to Old Mexico etc. etc. What is that but false? But *basta!* I will never see her again.' And once when Mrs. Luhan's car appeared on the road near the ranch, Lawrence and the Danes ran into the woods to hide, leaving Frieda alone to entertain her former hostess.

Lawrence told Mrs. Freeman, in that January letter, that he was 'afraid whoever sits in Taos and isn't a scoundrel sits in a losing game'. He had been getting his manuscripts in order, preparing 'to take flight again. I don't know which way to go—whether to go east, and via Greenland to Russia—or else south, and perhaps via Palm Springs to Old Mexico, and so to Europe.'

Taos buzzed with things Lawrence was supposed to have said about Mabel Luhan: she had tried to make him fall in love with her (as she admitted asking, in despair, 'How *can* I give up my *will?*'), and so on and on and on. One day as she was lacing her shoes, she gave up, let her consciousness lapse, and passed out for twenty-four hours with a smile on her face. Doctors plied her with white-man's medicine, and Tony Luhan sat on her bedroom floor praying to the dark gods. After her recovery she learned that Lawrence's diagnosis, from his remote mountain, was that she had collapsed because her will had met its first defeat: 'It must have been a grand day for Lawrence when he thought that!'

At the beginning of February, Lawrence heard, from Murry and Koteliansky, of the death of Katherine Mansfield. She had left Murry for a time to live at the Gurdjieff Institute at Fontainebleau; Lawrence and E. M. Forster, she felt, were 'the two men who *could* understand [the place] . . . if they would. But I think Lawrence's pride would keep him back. No one person is more important than another.' She had died in January, on the day of Murry's first visit to the institute. On learning of her death, Lawrence wrote to Murry, 'It has been a savage enough pilgrimage these last four years,' and: 'The dead don't die. They look on and help.'

Lawrence at this time still planned to go to Mexico. He had completed *Birds, Beasts and Flowers,* including several poems written since his arrival in America, such as 'Bibbles', 'Eagle in New Mexico' ('Does the sun need steam of blood, do you think / In America, still, / Old eagle?'), 'Men in New Mexico' ('Mountains blanket-wrapped / Round a white hearth of desert'), 'Autumn at Taos' ('. . . the yellow, pointed aspen-trees laid on one another like feathers'), and several others that show once again Lawrence's ability to observe sharply and to penetrate at once 'the spirit of place'; most of these poems are symbolic and some imply social criticism, as 'The American Eagle' ('Will you feed for ever on the cold meat of prosperity?'); one, 'Spirits Summoned West', apparently written soon after the death of Sallie Hopkin, is nostalgic: 'England seems covered with graves to me, / Women's graves.'

In February, Lawrence wrote to Curtis Brown about these poems, and about other writing, publishing, and traveling activities and plans. In making out his tax returns that month, he discovered that the preceding year had, financially, been his best so far; his gross income for 1922 was $5,439.67; with deductions, he owed seventy dollars in taxes. As he told Brown, 'I am coming into my own over here'.

7 MEXICAN MORNINGS

On March 24, 1923, Lawrence wrote to Bessie Freeman from the Hotel Monte Carlo in Mexico City (the Hotel San Remo in *The Plumed Serpent*):

> Got here last night—quite a journey—tried a big American hotel and didn't like it: this is a nice little place. It is warm—not hot—rains a little—the city pleasant—much more like S. Italy than America—haven't done much yet but wander round. I think we are going to like it.

He and Frieda had slipped down through Taos on the nineteenth, dodging their former hostess; they were not to return to that region for a year and three days. They arrived at Mexico City after brief stops at Santa Fe and El Paso. Witter Bynner and Willard Johnson joined them when they had been in Mexico about a week; Johnson's little magazine, the *Laughing Horse,* had recently been driven off the campus of the University of California for printing Lawrence's letter-review of Ben Hecht's *Fantazius Mallare,* whose hero, Lawrence said, was 'a frightened masturbator' with a mental-mechanical form of sex whose results Lawrence graphically described.

The Lawrences were offered a house in the suburb of Coyoacán by the archaeologist Zelia Nuttall. In 1901 she had published a book, *Fundamental Principles of Old and New World Civilizations,* which Frieda has recalled that Lawrence read. She told this to William York Tindall, who in his book on Lawrence showed that Mrs. Nuttall's volume was one of the sources of *The Plumed Serpent,* which Lawrence began to write after settling in Chapala in May. Frieda Lawrence pointed out that Tindall was wrong in saying that Lawrence had stayed at Mrs. Nuttall's; she says he went there for lunch three times. Tindall was correct, however, in identifying Mrs. Nuttall as the original of Mrs. Norris, the suburban hostess in *The Plumed Serpent.* (Mrs. Nuttall's house, incidentally, was just across the street from the one in which, years later, Leon Trotsky was assassinated.)

At the time of the Lawrences' first visit to Mexico, they and Bynner and Johnson made various trips beyond Mexico City, visiting such places as Teotihuacán, Xochimlico (as Bynner recalled, 'the ruined monastery'), Puebla, and Orizaba, seeing Mexican villages and Aztec remains. At Teotihuacán, Lawrence wandered among the stone pyramids, standing for a long while before the outthrust heads of Quetzalcoatl, and Bynner was probably correct in assuming that these images of the pre-Aztec plumed-serpent god helped to inspire the novel Lawrence was to write about Mexico.

Lawrence told Amy Lowell in a letter of April 23 that he would like to write another novel, but that in Mexico he found it 'hard to break through the wall of the atmosphere'. The country itself was interesting, but he had not 'got the right hang of it yet'. In Mexico City he spent most of his time with English-speaking people, not always happily: at least two memoirists (Carleton Beals and Witter Bynner) have recorded that Lawrence expressed with insulting loudness his disgust at some American journalists who attempted to associate with him at his hotel. The same two chroniclers also have reported that on occasion Lawrence would shout at Frieda not to sit with her legs apart 'like a slut'. Lawrence later irritated Bynner by putting him into *The Plumed Serpent* as Owen Rhys, who attended a bullfight with his young friend Villiers (Willard Johnson), the two of them sickened by the spectacle, as they had been in life, but hysterically sticking it out because they were Americans and had to 'see' everything, even if it made them sick. Frieda wrote to Merrild that she and Lawrence 'ran away after ten minutes'. But Bynner and his companion who remained were scored in Lawrence's novel: 'How could one be like these Americans, picking over the garbage of sensations, and gobbling it up like carrion birds!'

Lawrence before long had his fill of Mexico, as he told A. D. Hawk on a postcard (from Orizaba on April 2) showing a picture of a bullfight:

> Have had about enough of Mexico—sail for New York next week—address care Thomas Seltzer. 5 West 50th St. This country is interesting for a short time, then one is through with it.—I do hope Mrs Hawk is better, and that the weather is warmer.— We saw this bullfighting—pretty disgusting.

But Lawrence didn't go to New York then: his letters of the time, to various people, indicate confusion; sometimes he would tell one person that he was leaving Mexico, and another, on the same day, that he was looking for a place to live there.

After returning to Mexico City from Orizaba, he expected to have lunch with the Secretary of Public Education, José Vasconcelos, on April 26. This noted philosopher, who called himself the 'Creole Ulysses', was popularly known as the Secretary on Horseback because he was a cultural missionary who went out personally to superintend the spread of education among the Indian tribes. In 1923 he was helping native artists such as Rivera and Orozco, by commissioning them to paint murals in government buildings. Lawrence—quite wrongly, as time has shown—carped at these paintings, both in his conversations at the time and later in *The Plumed Serpent,* in which he said that the murals were poor because the artists painted under an impulse of hatred and propaganda: 'Those flat Indians were symbols . . . in the weary script of socialism and anarchy.'

But Lawrence wrote to Murry that the members of the Obregón government were 'good idealists and sensible', though he felt himself 'as usual outside the scheme of such things'. He put himself even more emphatically out of such things one day when he and Frieda and several journalists went to meet Vasconcelos for lunch. After they arrived at his office, Vasconcelos because of a last-minute crisis had to send one of his assistants to ask the party whether the luncheon could not be postponed till next day. Frieda and the others agreed, but Lawrence hotly refused. Bynner, whose book charitably suggested that Lawrence's rages were induced by wine, couldn't in reporting this episode fall back upon such a magnanimous hypothesis because the party had not yet gone to a café. Bynner had to state, without generously excusing him on the grounds of alcoholism, that on this occasion Lawrence simply got mad. Years afterwards, Vasconcelos wrote about the long-dead Lawrence. As noted in *Dark Night of the Body,* L. D. Clark's book about *The Plumed Serpent,* Vasconcelos in 1951–1952 published in the Mexican journal *Novedades* a three-part review of that novel, which stated that it was 'one of the best books of fantasy ever written about Mexico,' but that its author had been unreasonable about the canceled luncheon: Lawrence was 'a second-rate idiot'.

The night after that broken lunch engagement, Lawrence left for Guadalajara to look for a place to live. He wrote to his mother-in-law that he now had no wish to return to Europe, where she must be weary of the 'German tragedy' and the materialism. Mexico also had 'Bolshevism and Fascism and revolutions and all the rest of it'; he stood apart, however, like the Indians, who remained the same through all revolutions and changes. 'They haven't the machinery of our consciousness, they are like black water, over which go our dirty motorboats, with stink and noise—the water gets a little dirty but does not really change.'

Lawrence found a place to live, in the village of Chapala, in the state of Jalisco. Frieda joined him a few days later; then Bynner and Johnson came too. Lawrence wrote to Mrs. Freeman, who had apparently compared Taos to the Rome of the decline:

> Your letter about Mabel. No, it is worse than Gibbon. The submerged Continent of Atlantis.
>
> I suppose you'll pay next time you go.
>
> We've got a house here—very nice—green trees—a Mexican Isabel to look after us—a big lake of Chapala outside—a little village Chapala—but at the same side a little lake-side resort for Guadalajara, which is about 35 miles away.
>
> It isn't too hot. If you feel like coming down, come down. I won't offer you this house, because Isabel would by no means come up to your standards, even if *you* did. But there is a pleasant hotel, 4 pesos a day for a short time, 3 pesos a day if you stay a month. And a peso is about 49 cents American. Cheap enough.
>
> Don't know how long we shall stay—a month or two.

A bit of Taos excitement that projected itself into the quiet of Chapala was news of the sudden marriage of Mabel Sterne, who at last officially became Mrs. Luhan. Having received a hint that Tony Luhan was, after all, a ward of the government, she foresaw that bureaucratic irritation at some of her activities might take the form of removing her Indian-buck lover, so she hastily married him. Lawrence infuriated her by sending Nina Witt, whom he had 'reviled' (Mrs. Luhan's word) while in Taos, a postcard saying, 'I hear Mabel married Tony. Why?' The new Mrs. Luhan snapped, 'None of his business why. Don't you tell him!' She admitted: 'I stole the postcard from her.'

Frieda wrote to Mrs. Luhan's other Buffalo-girlhood friend, Bessie Freeman, on May 30: 'Your world must have come tumbling about your ears, when you heard that Mabel had married Tony—In my *head* I say: Why not, but somewhere else it's *so* impossible—Merrild writes: the Indians don't like the marriage and the Taos people don't, but they have something to talk about and *that* they do like.' Frieda still felt friendly towards Mrs. Luhan, she said: 'She has failed somehow in her life, but then it is so easy to fail.' Lawrence, Frieda reported, was writing a novel and already had completed two hundred and fifty pages of it. 'At night a *mozo* sleeps outside our bedrooms with a loaded revolver! because there was a scare of bandits!'—exactly as the *mozo* had to sleep outside Kate's room in the novel.

Lawrence went down every day to the shores of the chalk-white lake that gleams through *The Plumed Serpent* and, sitting under the willow or pepper trees he wrote, as Johnson recalled, 'in tiny, fast words in a thick, blue-bound blank book, the tale which he called *Quetzalcoatl*'. This was the title he then intended to give his novel, the name of the Osiris of the pre-Columbian past.

At the lakeside, Johnson also remembered, when Lawrence was not writing or watching the fishermen, the washwomen, or 'the little boys who sold idols from the lake', he studied Mexican folklore and history. In Mexico City he had read *The Mexican People: Their Struggle for Freedom*, by de Lara and Pinchon. In *D. H. Lawrence and Susan His Cow*, William York Tindall mentions some of Lawrence's other sources besides Mrs. Nuttall's book, referred to earlier: 'Lawrence shows acquaintance with the Aztec myths, which he improved in the light of his understanding' and of his knowledge of Frazer, Tylor, and Harrison. 'I found from allusions in his works,' Tindall goes on, 'and from correspondence with Mrs. Luhan, Witter Bynner, and Mrs. Lawrence that, while or before he was in New Mexico and Mexico, Lawrence read Prescott's *Conquest of Mexico*, Thomas Belt's *Naturalist in Nicaragua*, Adolph Bandelier's *The Gilded Man*, Bernal Diáz's *Conquest of Mexico*, Humboldt's *Vues des Cordillères*, and several volumes of the *Anales del Museo Nacional de Méjico*.'

Tindall further suggests that Lawrence also may have read Lewis Spence's *The Gods of Mexico*, and that its Aztec hymns may have given him ideas for the similar hymns in his novel. This would probably have been later than Chapala, for Spence's book was published in that year of 1923 and may not have been accessible before Lawrence's departure early in July; but he may have read Spence's 1921 volume, *The Mythologies of Ancient Mexico and Peru*.

And Lawrence was thinking of the hymns in his own life, the songs of the miners' chapel. There was, for example, 'Someone Will Enter the Pearly Gate', a hymn which, Roger Dataller has suggested,

closely parallels parts of the hymns sung by the Quetzalcoatl men in
The Plumed Serpent, as:

('Pearly Gate')
Someone will knock when the door is shut,
By-and-by, by-and-by,
Hear a voice saying: I know you not.
Shall you? Shall I?
Shall you? Shall I?

(*The Plumed Serpent*)
Someone will knock when the door is shut.
Shall you? Shall I?
Hear a voice saying: I know you not.
Shall you? Shall I?

The red-bearded man sitting under the tree in the blazing day of a
Mexican village, amid the activities of boatmen and romping children
and passing goatherds, was letting his consciousness slide back to the
times of dusk in the colliery village, the men with coal-blackened faces
singing in groups as they walked homeward from the mines and
pubs. Writing by that lake, Lawrence caught the bright surface of
Mexican life—'Westwards, down the glare, rose the broken-looking
villas and the white twin towers of the church, holding up its two
fingers in mockery above the scarlet flame-trees and the dark mangoes'
—but underneath everything he saw always the darkness; the sun itself had a dark core. And the people of the town, and those coming
in from the country, became in his story the worshippers of Quetzalcoatl, singing the hymns in the plaza at night, the drumbeats accent-
ing the chant of resurrection, 'Who slee-eeps sha-ll wake! Who
slee-eeps sha-ll wake!'

The day after Frieda reported that Lawrence had, in about a month,
written two hundred and fifty pages, he told his mother-in-law that he
had completed ten chapters. A week later (June 7) he wrote to Mrs.
Carswell, 'I felt I had a novel simmering in me, so came here, to this
big lake, to see if I could write it. It goes fairly well. I shall be glad if
I can finish the first rough draft by the end of this month.' But he didn't
complete it during that last month of arguments with Bynner (Frieda
storming into these but Johnson remaining aloof), of excursions to
Guadalajara, of a boat trip up the ninety-mile-long lake. Towards the
end of June, Lawrence wrote to Merrild, now in Los Angeles, that

Mexico allured him but was 'risky', another revolution expected: why should one settle in when destruction threatened? 'So for the present I give it up.' On that same day, June 27, Lawrence wrote to Mrs. Freeman: 'The novel is *nearly* finished—near enough to leave. I must come to New York—and go to England.'

*

After a railway trip north through heavy Mexican rains, Lawrence and Frieda went along the southern part of Texas to New Orleans, 'a dead, steaming sort of place, a bit like Martin Chuzzlewit'. The prospect of traveling to New York was 'dreary', but he and Frieda made the journey, and after their arrival Lawrence wrote to Mrs. Freeman from New York City, using Thomas Seltzer's stationery, on 'Friday' (July 20, 1923):

> We got in yesterday—Today are going out to New Jersey to stay in a cottage, where I can get proof corrected. Not quite sure of the address. But it's only 50 minutes out, so either you will come and see us, or we you, as soon as you are here. I find town *wearing*.
> We'll talk Mexico and the future.
> [P.S.] Seltzer can give you exact address—it's his cottage.

The cottage was near Morris Plains, on the Lackawanna line, and 'behind the millionaire Coffin's house'. Lawrence wrote to Bynner that it was 'pleasant' there: 'The trees and hills and stillness. But it is dim to me. Doesn't materialize.' Neither did New York, which was 'like a house of cards set up'. There, the Battery appealed most to Lawrence, 'where the rag-tag lie on the grass'. He reported that he had 'met practically no one', though unpublished letters show that he had had lunch with the *Nation* editors (on August 3), and that the Seltzers gave dinner parties for him at their apartment and at that least Lawrencean of places, the Algonquin.

People in Morris Plains who remembered Lawrence's visit there have said that he used to go on long afternoon walks with Thomas A. Edison. Strange as it may seem, it is highly possible that Lawrence— in spite of his mistrust of science—may have liked the famous inventor. In any event, the idea of the two men strolling together down country roads in the midsummer heat is entrancing: because of Edison's deafness, Lawrence probably had to raise his voice, with his words of prophecy ringing out over the New Jersey meadows.

Lawrence had been intending to sail with Frieda, who was aching for her children, but as the time drew near he became reluctant. On August 7 he wrote to Amy Lowell: 'I doubt if I shall get myself as far as England. Feel I don't want to go. But Frieda will sail on the 18th— and I shall sail somewhen or other.' He told his mother-in-law on August 7, 'I find my soul doesn't want to come to Europe, it is like Balaam's ass and can't come any further.'

When Frieda left, he accompanied her to the ship. She appealed to him to remain aboard, just as he was, with no luggage, and go back to Europe with her. He refused, and they had what their friend Catherine Carswell noted as 'perhaps the very worst' quarrel of their lives; and they parted in anger, feeling that the separation would be a final one. But as the ship made its way across the Atlantic, Frieda's usual good cheer revived, and upon arriving in England 'she sent Lawrence a wifely cable', asking him to join her because she needed him. But he stayed in the Western Hemisphere.

Lawrence, planning to go to California, wrote to Bessie Freeman on August 20, two days after Frieda had sailed on the *Orbita:* 'I expect, either she'll be here again by October, or I shall be going to meet *her* somewhere.' On the way west, 'I should like to stay a night in your Buffalo—the Buffalo also of Mabel and Nina.' A week later he thanked Mrs. Freeman for having been his hostess there. He wrote from the Los Angeles Limited on August 28:

> Thank you so much for the four full days in Buffalo. I feel I had there a fuller glimpse into the real old U.S. than ever before. I was really interested, and the real Buffalos at home were much nicer than I had expected, knowing only those other two Buffalos in Taos. Only Sarah M. depressed me: the dead weight of her: and now, I also feel a bit sorry for her.—Why doesn't somebody write your *Cranford?* Buffalo is a sort of *Cranford.*
>
> It rained and fogged in Chicago, and muddy-flowing people oozed thick in the canyon-beds of the streets. Yet it seemed to me more alive and more real than New York.
>
> You were very kind to me and I am very grateful. It's another little page in my history.

Lawrence spent a month in Los Angeles, with short visits to Santa Monica, Santa Barbara, and Palm Springs. Once he, Merrild, and Götzsche went to the town of Lompoc to witness the total eclipse of the sun; an avant-garde woman poet who was in the same party, watching for the eclipse from a rough hilltop, later remembered almost nothing about Lawrence, who also seems to have been eclipsed. Merrild has reported that Lawrence was lonely and restless without Frieda. Los Angeles he found 'silly—much motoring, me rather tired and vague with it'. At last he proposed that the Danes accompany him to Mexico. Merrild, one of those types that by utterance and gesture need frequent assurances of their own integrity, balked; the simpler Gótzsche said he would go. Shortly before departing, Lawrence wrote to Mrs. Freeman: 'No, I don't trust Mabel's idea of paying her debts. I have *my* idea of what she owes me. As for a vendetta, I'm ready. To hell with her, anyhow. I'm through with her now.'

It was a rough, gritty, hot, and nerve-shredding journey, that month from Los Angeles to Guadalajara, on trains that dragged and stopped, in Fords that wobbled over mountain roads, and on horseback and muleback. Part of the way a circus followed Lawrence and Gótzsche down the coast, lions roaring all night. But with all the hazards and fatigue of travel, Lawrence worked on a novel during that trip.

He was rewriting a manuscript recently sent to him by the nurse he and Frieda had met in Australia, M. L. (Mollie) Skinner. She had written a story of the Australian frontier, *The House of Ellis,* and Lawrence had sent her a letter about this from California, saying that she had a gift for writing, but that the book needed to be recast. He offered to undertake this: their names could appear as collaborators or they could invent a pseudonym.

She cabled him to rewrite the book as he saw fit. Three months after his first letter, he wrote to her that he had been working on the manuscript as he traveled. He had followed her story closely but had given it 'a unity, a rhythm, and a little more psychic development'. But the ending would have to be considerably changed. 'You may disapprove,' he told her. 'I did,' she recalled: 'I wept.' For Lawrence increased the number of Jack Grant's women towards the end of the book. Mollie Skinner liked the title, however; Lawrence told her, 'There have been so many houses in print'. Apparently neither of them knew that an Australian novel of 1869, reprinted in 1885, was called *The Boy in the Bush.*

As this Lawrence-Skinner novel turned out, it is a fine adventure story, with the rough background of the Australian frontier, which Miss Skinner supplied, touched up with Lawrencean gusto. Indeed, some of his own recent experiences such as horseback riding, at Del Monte ranch and during the Mexican trip with Gótzsche, undoubtedly helped Lawrence in his rewriting of Miss Skinner's story. It was a strange production for Lawrence, yet, with the excellent scenario his collaborator provided, a satisfactory one.

Just how much of the book is Lawrence's remains in doubt. He spoke of rewriting it completely, but some of Mollie Skinner's friends have declared that Lawrence's contribution wasn't so extensive as he claimed. Certainly Miss Skinner provided the substance of the plot, as well as the principal characters (including the protagonist, her brother Jack) and the entire picture of Australian life in the 1880s. While on a visit to London in 1924, Miss Skinner met Edward Garnett and marked up his copy of the book (now at the University of Texas) to indicate which parts of it she remembered as being entirely her own. She credited Lawrence with the last two chapters and most of the one preceding them, as well as other parts of the novel, a book which Lawrencean critics have either ignored or passed over with little comment. (For a further discussion of these matters, see the long preface by the present writer in the 1971 and 1972 American and British editions of the book.)

The revising of the Skinner manuscript was not the only writing Lawrence worked on during that autumn of 1923. It was at this time (as noted by E. W. Tedlock, Jr.) that Lawrence wrote some fragments of essays in a composition book. One of these was 'On Being Religious', merely the seed of the article of that name which appeared in the *Adelphi* in 1924. The original version, never before published in full, is an extremely important statement about his religious beliefs:

> There is no real battle between me and Christianity. Perhaps there is a certain battle between me and nonconformity, because, at the depth, my nature is catholic. But I believe in the all-over-shadowing God. I believe that Jesus is one of the sons of God: [*only*—deleted] not, however, the only son of God. I think that the men who believe in the all-overshadowing God will naturally form a Church of God. That is, I believe in a Church. And I believe in secret doctrine, as against the vulgarity of nonconformity. I believe in an initiated priesthood, and in cycles of esoteric knowledge. I believe in the authority of the Church, and in the power of the priest to grant absolution.
>
> So that on the religious fundamentals, there is no breach between me and the Catholic Church.
>
> But I cannot believe in a Church of Christ. Jesus is only one of

the sons of Almighty God. There are many saviours—there is only one God. There will be more saviours: but God is one God.

So that the great Church of the future will know other saviours: men are saved variously, in various climes, in various centuries. A Church established on the Almighty God, but having temples to the various saviours, is the true [Church?] of man.

The great disaster of religion is that each religion tends to assert one exclusive saviour. One hates Christianity because it declares there is only one way to God. A true Church would know that there are [*various*—deleted] a few great roads to God, and many, many small tracks.

'I am the Way'.—Not even Jesus can declare this to *all* men. To very many men, Jesus is no longer the way. He is no longer the way for me. But what does it matter? He is one of the Sons of God. And I will gladly light a candle to him also.

Yet I must seek another way. God, the great God, is always God. But we have always to find our way to him. The way was Jesus. And the way is no longer Jesus.

So, for the moment, we have no way. God is God—but he has not yet sent us a prophet.

That does not mean we leave off seeking, or trying, or adventuring.

On the journey south Lawrence and Gótzsche stopped for a couple of days to visit a Swiss who owned a silver mine near Navajoa; planting Mrs. Luhan in this setting, Lawrence wrote 'The Woman Who Rode Away'.

While at Guadalajara, Lawrence and Gótzsche went one day in a car to Chapala. Gótzsche, whose reports to Merrild at the time have a moment-to-moment wryly observational quality, said that in spite of Lawrence's scorn of sentimentality he appeared 'deeply moved' at Chapala, which he found unreal and changed. And indeed he missed Frieda, who now refused to return.

She later said that this was a mistake on her part. But at the time she insisted that Lawrence meet her in England. Gótzsche, who now thought that Lawrence was intermittently insane, believed that he was 'working himself up to *will* to go to England'. Murry had joined Frieda in urging Lawrence to return: moved by *Aaron's Rod* and *Fantasia,* he had founded the *Adelphi* magazine, to give Lawrence a voice, and wrote to Lawrence saying that he himself was merely a lieutenant, literally a place-holder, waiting for Lawrence to come back and take over.

Frieda's loneliness after making her solitary voyage had been intensified in London, where she found that her children had grown up and no longer felt a primary need for her.

It was not only Frieda's disappointment over her children that made her eager for a reunion with Lawrence; she had been rebuffed by Murry, who accompanied her on a trip to Germany in September. He revived memories of this in a posthumously published 1955 entry in his diary. Frieda was going to Baden-Baden, and Murry to nearby Freiburg, to consult a specialist about the mental problems of T. S. Eliot's wife, Vivienne. On the train that September of 1923, Murry and Frieda discovered that they were in love. But Murry withheld himself: 'No, my darling, I mustn't let Lorenzo down—I can't.' But at times he regretted this 'great renunciation'.

Lawrence, however, had felt that he and Frieda would be permanently separated, as a startling communication of November 10 from Guadalajara indicates. It is a note lacking Lawrence's customary verve; one part of this unusually perfunctory letter shows how serious the separation was:

We [Lawrence and Gótzsche] keep trying for ships, but nothing so far. We should like to sail from Manzanillo through the Panama Canal: it still may be possible to find a tramp steamer. If not, we shall go to Mexico City and get the first regular boat that goes out of Vera Cruz, if that infernal port is open: if not, Tampico. I'm not keen on going to Tampico, because of the fever. And I feel I can't look at the U.S.A. again, just yet.—The quickest steamers are the Dutch—and the Hamburg Amerika—they take three weeks to Southampton or Plymouth.

Mexico is still very attractive and a very good place to live in: it is not tame. Sometimes here in Guadalajara one sees the wild Quichelote Indians, with their bows and arrows and hardly any clothing. They look so queer, like animals from another world, in the Plaza listening to the band.—We've had several thunder showers, but the sky is blue and bright again. I like the plain around Guadalajara, with the mountains here and there around. I like it better than the lake. The lake is too shut in.—The *barranca* is also very impressive—you never saw that.—I still wish

I was staying the winter on a ranch somewhere not far from this
city. I still don't believe in Europe, England, efforts, restfulness,
adelphis [*sic*] or any of that. The egg is addled. But I'll come
back and say how do you do! to it all. I am glad if you have a
good time with your flat and your children. Don't bother about
money—When I come we'll make a regular arrangement for you
to have an income if you wish. I told you the bank was to transfer
£ 100 to you.—I wonder if Seltzer is in England. I haven't heard
a word from him or Adele for three weeks, so know no news.—
The Australian novel [*The Boy in the Bush*] is very nearly done.
—*Tanti saluti.*

[P.S.] Enclose note from Mabel Luhan—she says she still
has hopes we might live in contact. *Quién sabe! Mañana es otro
día.*

Whether Frieda simply ignored the unpleasant side of this letter
(which after all announced Lawrence's return to England), or
whether Lawrence wrote more friendlily in the twelve days he had still
to remain in Mexico booking passage, Frieda in any event accepted
his trip back with jubilation. Mark Gertler used to amuse his friends
with his imitation of Frieda's storming into his studio and shouting,
'Prepare yourself—Lorenzo's coming!'

Lawrence went to Mexico City to book passage for himself to England, for Gótzsche to Denmark. From there he wrote to Bessie Freeman: 'Mabel and I have buried the hatchet. She wrote me a *Peccavi, peccavi, c'est ma faute!* letter.' In his reply to Mrs. Luhan,
Lawrence as usual advised her to stop trying to compel life.

He sailed on the S.S. *Toledo* on November 22. The ship, after a
two-day stop at Havana, went on to Plymouth. From there Lawrence
took the train to London, traveling the same route as when he had
been put out of Cornwall exactly six years before. This time Frieda
wasn't with him, but she met him at Paddington, with Murry and
Koteliansky. Catherine Carswell, to whose brother's house in Hampstead the Lawrences now went to live, has said that Lawrence immediately resented Frieda's 'chumminess' with Murry. When Lawrence
alighted from the train he had, Murry remembered, 'a greenish pallor',
and his first glimpse of London drew from him the words 'I can't bear
it'.

Later he gave Murry an essay, 'On Coming Home', which Murry
would not print in the *Adelphi*. This essay describes Lawrence's re-

turn from the sea: 'It is four years since I saw, under a little winter snow, the death-grey coast of Kent go out'; now he wrote of 'the infinitesimal sparkling of the Lands End light, so absolutely remote, as one approaches from over the sea, from the Gulf of Mexico, after sunset.' Ashore, he found England wrapped in an 'almost deathly sense of stillness . . . Landing in San Francisco gave me the feeling of intolerable crackling noise. But London gives me a muffled sense of stillness, as if nothing had any resonance. Everything is muffled or muted, and no sharp contact, no sharp reaction anywhere.' And although he considered his fellow-countrymen 'the nicest and most civilized people in the world', he saw each of them as 'enclosed first and foremost within the box, or bubble, of his own self-contained ego, and afterwards in all the other boxes he has made for himself, for his own safety.' Nothing was left of 'the old brave, reckless, manly England. . . . Look at us now. Not a man left inside all the millions of pairs of trousers. . . . One could shout with laughter at the figures inside these endless safety boxes. Except that one is still English, and therefore flabbergasted. My own, my native land just leaves me flabbergasted.'

8 THE LAST OF THE NEW WORLD

Lawrence's three months in Europe were wretched. Soon after his arrival he wrote to Bynner (December 7), 'poor D.H.L. perfectly miserable, as if he was in his tomb'. And five days before he left he wrote to the painter and mystic Frederick Carter (February 29, 1924) that he was sailing the following Wednesday on the *Aquitania,* for New York: 'I feel very weary of Europe and its fidgettiness [*sic*] and complications.'

In London he argued with Murry and tried to enlist recruits for a New Mexican Rananim. He urged Murry to use the *Adelphi* to 'attack everything', and to go to America with him. 'If I did return with him,' Murry said later, 'I should do it out of purely personal affection for him; and I told him so. No! there must be nothing personal about it, he insisted; the motive must be impersonal.' To Murry, however, a voyage to America then could be only a personal matter: and he thought that if the new life depended on people with sufficient income to go to New Mexico, it was not worth considering. Murry felt there was a dichotomy in Lawrence, and once told him, 'You always deny what you actually are. You refuse to acknowledge the Lawrence who really exists.' Murry reported that Lawrence answered, 'I'm sorry . . . I'm sorry'.

What Lawrence didn't know was that Murry and Frieda had fallen in love, though he may have had a bit of suspicion about the matter, as some of his subsequent stories, such as 'The Border Line', suggest. But Murry had made what he called his 'great renunciation'.

After Lawrence's arrival in London, the famous 'Last Supper' took place at the Café Royal. Even the most sympathetic account by an eyewitness, Catherine Carswell, cannot diminish the repulsiveness of this party which took place at the café Lawrence had treated sardonically, in *Women in Love,* as the Pompadour. It was almost as bad as similar occasions in Taos, and Mrs. Luhan's rehash of it at second or third hand seems to make this London grotesquery a part of the febrile Taos legend. At the Café Royal the Lawrences were hosts, and for guests they had the Carswells, Murry, Koteliansky, Dorothy Brett, Mary Cannan, and Gertler. Lawrence invited them all to join him in founding a colony on the slopes of the Rockies, and most of the answers he received were insincere and evasive, except for Dorothy Brett's—and she went to New Mexico with the Lawrences.

Koteliansky jumped up and began smashing wineglasses and shouting, 'No woman here or anywhere else can possibly understand the greatness of Lawrence!' It would have been ironic if Lawrence remembered what he had written to Koteliansky about Frieda some years earlier: 'You mustn't judge her lightly', adding: 'There is another quality in woman, so you can't estimate it. You don't know that a woman is not a man with different sex. She is a different world. You do not understand that enough. Your world is all of one hemisphere.'

On that lurid night at the Café Royal, before Koteliansky broke all the glasses, the communicants had drunk a good deal of the sacramental wine—at one point Murry said, 'I love you, Lorenzo, but I won't promise not to betray you'—and finally the 'habitually temperate' Lawrence collapsed, sick and vomiting.

Murry and Koteliansky conveyed him to a taxi in which they took him to Hampstead. At the Carswells', Lawrence's two friends carried him, still unconscious, upstairs. On the upper floors their stumbling sounds awoke Catherine Carswell's brother, who added to the legend by telling his sister afterwards that when he got up and looked down the stairway, 'he saw clearly before him St John and St Peter (or maybe St Thomas) bearing between them the limp figure of their master.'

The common wisdom and sense of humor of the miner's son returned the next morning when Lawrence, in quick recovery from his hangover, told Mrs. Carswell he had made a fool of himself. 'We must all of us fall at times. It does not harm so long as we first admit and then forget it.'

During this visit to England, Lawrence and Frieda—through Murry —met the South African author Sarah Gertrude Millin. She and her husband invited the three of them, as well as Koteliansky, to dinner, and Murry asked whether he could bring 'the most charming girl in the world', who proved to be Dorothy Brett, carrying the case which held her hearing apparatus; Murry privately told Mrs. Millin that Dorothy Brett had deliberately become deaf so that she wouldn't have to listen to the conversations of her aristocratic family.

The Lawrences were very late in arriving, and Koteliansky didn't come with them because he and Lawrence had quarreled over Tolstoy. The dinner, with Lawrence telling anecdotes, was termed 'a failure' by Mrs. Millin.

*

During that London visit, Lawrence heard from Mrs. Carswell that she wanted to write a novel (based on something she had read) about a primitive tribe that kept in isolation a young girl they wished to bring up to become a goddess. Lawrence said that he and Mrs. Carswell should collaborate on the novel. He promptly composed a synopsis and told her to write the opening chapters. But she was overcome at the idea and wasn't able to comply. Only Lawrence's synopsis remains:

> A woman of about thirty-five, beautiful, a little overwrought, goes into a shipping office in Glasgow to ask about a ship to Canada. She gives her name Olivia Maclure. The clerk asks her if she is not going to accept the Maclure invitation to the feast in the ancestral castle. She laughs—but the days of loneliness in the Glasgow hotel before the ship can sail are too much for her, and she sets off for the Maclure island.
>
> The Maclure who claims to be chief of the clan and has bought the ancestral castle on his native isle, is a man of about forty-five, rather small, dark-eyed, full of energy, but has been a good deal knocked about. He has spent ten years in the U.S.A. and twenty years in the silver mines of Mexico, is somewhat grizzled, has a scar on the right temple which tilts up his right eye a little. Chief characteristic his quick, alert brown eyes which seem to sense danger, and the tense energy in his slightly work-twisted body.

He has lived entirely apart from civilised women, merely frequented an occasional Indian woman in the hills. Is a bit cranky about his chieftainship.

Olivia arrives a day too soon for the festival, at the patched-up castle. Maclure, in a shapeless worksuit, is running round attending to his house and preparations. He looks like a Cornish miner, always goes at a run, sees everything, has a certain almost womanly quickness of perception, and frequently takes a whiskey. He eyes Olivia with the quick Mexican suspicion. She, so distraught, is hardly embarrassed at all. Something weighs on her so much, she doesn't realise she is a day too soon, and when she realises, she doesn't care.

As soon as he has sensed her, he is cordial, generous, but watchful: always on the watch for danger. Soon he is fascinated by her. She, made indifferent to everything by an inward distress, talks to him charmingly, but vaguely: doesn't realise him. He, a man of forty-five, falls for the first time insanely in love. But she is always only half conscious of him.

She spends the night in the mended castle—he most scrupulously sleeps in the cottage below. The next day, she is mistress of the absurd feast. And at evening he begs her not to go away. His frantic, slightly absurd passion penetrates her consciousness. She consents to stay.

After two days of anguished fear lest she go away, he proposes to her. She looks at him very strangely—he is just strange to her. But she consents. Something in her is always remote, far off —the weight of some previous distress. He feels the distance, but cannot understand. After being in an agony of love with her for six months, he comes home to find her dead, leaving a little baby girl.

Then it seems to him the mother was not mortal. She was a mysterious woman from the faëry, and the child, he secretly believes, is one of the Tuatha De Danaan. This idea he gradually inculcates into the people round him, and into the child herself. It steals over them all gradually, almost unawares.

The girl accepts from the start a difference between herself and the rest of people. She does not feel quite mortal. Men are only men to her: she is of another race, the Tuatha De Danaan. She doesn't talk about it: nobody talks about it. But there it is, tacit, accepted.

Her father hires a poor scholar to be her tutor, and she has an ordinary education. But she has no real friends. There is no one of her race. Sometimes she goes to Glasgow, to Edinburgh, to London with her father. The world interests her, but she doesn't belong to it. She is a little afraid of it. It is not of her race.

When she is seventeen her father is suddenly killed, and she is alone, save for her tutor. She has an income of about three hundred a year. She decides to go to London. The war has broken out—she becomes a nurse. She nurses men, and knows their wounds and their necessities. But she tends them as if they were lambs or other delicate and lovable animals. Their blood is not her blood, their needs are not the needs of her race.

Men fall in love with her, and that is terrible to her. She is waiting for one of her own race. Her tutor supports her in the myth. Wait, he says, wait for the Tuatha De Danaan to send you your mate. You can't mate with a man. Wait till you see a demon between his brows.

At last she saw him in the street. She knew him at once, knew the demon between his brows. And she was afraid. For the first time in her life, she was afraid of her own nature, the mystery of herself. Because it seemed to her that her race, the Tuatha, had come back to destroy the race of men. She had come back to destroy the race of men. She was terrified of her own destiny. She wanted never again to see the man with the demon between his brows.

So for a long time she did not see him again. And then her fear that she would never see him any more was deeper than anything else. Whatever she wanted, she wanted her own destiny with him, let happen what might.

*

Outside the circle of Lawrence's immediate friends, his work was that autumn and winter of 1923–1924 receiving the usual public comments, about equally divided between praise and disparagement. Reviewing *Kangaroo* in the *London Mercury,* J. B. Priestley intimated that Lawrence's admirers were for the most part adolescents and that Lawrence would have done better if (as Priestley himself was preparing to do) he had imitated nineteenth-century novels; Priestley had 'come to the conclusion that it is more dangerous and difficult these days to abide by the rules than it is to challenge them.' *Kangaroo* also proved too much for Gerald Gould in the London *Saturday Review;* he found it a 'fantasia of the self-conscious' by a man who 'no longer seems even to try to write clever rubbish'. But Martin Armstrong spoke up for the book—'permeated with the strangely subtle and beautiful atmosphere which Mr Lawrence names Australia'—in the *Spectator;* and J. C. Squire, who was to admire the 'curious intensity' of *Birds, Beasts and Flowers* in the *London Mercury* the following January, was less enthusiastic about *Kangaroo* in the *Observer* in September, with the usual 'genius but confused' statement about Lawrence, 'utterly honest, however bewildered, and endowed with a power of compact expression, of making things live on the page, which would hold the attention whatever he wrote.'

In the *Nation and Athenaeum,* J. D. Beresford, dismissing *Kangaroo*'s flaws as minor, had 'to acknowledge without any qualification whatever that this is the work of genius, a thing separate in kind'; while the *New York Times* discovered 'much full rich beauty in *Kangaroo* . . . There is not a paragraph that is not luminously provocative.'

By this time Lawrence was beyond the point where he paid much heed to reviews; in Mexico he had told Bynner he no longer read them, and his letters of this time and later contain few references to them. As noted earlier, he had consolidated his own public—and this didn't entirely consist of adolescents and cultists; the income from this minority writer's uncompromising books and articles permitted him, if not to live in opulence, to travel as he pleased, second class.

*

Lawrence went to the Midlands to spend the Yuletide with his sisters, leaving Frieda in London. In the first week of 1924, he traveled to Pontesbury, in Shropshire, to visit the Frederick Carters for a few days. Lawrence had become acquainted with Carter after the latter sent him the manuscript of his book *The Dragon of the Alchemists.* It pleased Lawrence, who on June 18, 1923, wrote Carter a very long letter (printed in *Collected Letters*) discussing astrology and mysticism in general, based partly on his reading of Mme Blavatsky and her associates. 'The subtle thing', he wrote, 'is the relation between the microcosm and the macrocosm. Get that relation—the Zodiac man to me—and you've got a straight clue to apocalipsis.—The ancients thought in images.' Somewhat echoing his books on the unconscious, Lawrence spoke of 'the four great centres of inspiration', which he connected with the stars. He also said, 'You'd never get an ordinary publisher to publish this text. It is *absolutely* unintelligible to the ordinary reader. And yet there *is* something great and liberating behind it all: makes life seem noble again.' He also wrote, 'If I come to England we'll talk about it.'

Carter mentioned in a letter (May 7, 1952) Lawrence's 'short visit to Pontesbury and discussion of Apocalyptic symbols there'. His experiences in Shropshire provided the background of *St Mawr* and even the red horse. The duplicate symbolism of woman and dragon became a motif of *The Plumed Serpent*.

Not long after the visit to the Carters, Lawrence and Frieda crossed to the Continent. From the Hôtel de Versailles, Paris, on January 25 (or 24), he wrote to Catherine Carswell: 'We had an easy journey—Paris looking rather lovely in sunshine and frost—rather quiet, but really a beautiful city. We're both tired—almost stupefied from London.' The next day he wrote to her more fully: 'Today it is dark and raining, and very like London. There really isn't much point in coming here. . . . I'm just going to sleep a good bit, and let the days go by: and probably next week go to Baden Baden to get *that* over. I somehow *can't* answer to Europe any more. Paris has a great beauty—but all like a museum. And when one looks out of the Louvre windows one wonders whether the museum is more inside or outside—whether all Paris, with its rue de la Paix and its Champs-Élysées isn't also all just a museum'—and apparently at this time, in this mood, he wrote his 'Paris Letter' that first saw print in the April 1926 *Laughing Horse*. Here Lawrence, disliking the crowds amid the museum pieces, spoke again his distrust of democracy and said further, 'But I can't believe in the old sort of aristocracy, either, nor can I wish it back, splendid as it was. What I believe in is the old Homeric aristocracy, when the grandeur was inside the man, and he lived in a simple wooden house.' Lawrence concluded that 'monuments, museums, permanencies, and ponderosities are all anathema. But brave men are for ever born, and nothing else is worth having.'

Leaving Paris on February 5, Lawrence was soon at Baden-Baden, once again beaming among the aristocratic old ladies of the Ludwig-Wilhelmstift. The story he wrote during his fortnight there, 'The Border Line', had a 'brave man' for its hero, 'Alan Anstruther, that red-haired fighting Celt'. The woman he had married, 'daughter of a German Baron', was undisguisedly Frieda, journeying to Strasbourg, away from Paris 'with its Louvre and its Luxembourg and its Cathedral', and the trip was the Lawrences' journey east. The day before he left Baden-Baden to go back, February 19, Lawrence wrote 'A Letter from Germany' (not published in his lifetime), which has resemblances to descriptions in the story, as Anthony West has shown by quoting several parallel passages in his book on Lawrence.

'A Letter from Germany' was deeply prophetic, as many readers saw when it was published ten years later, in 1934, by which time the Nazis had taken over the country. But in February 1924, they were little known, and Hitler was still in prison because of the so-called 'Beer Hall Putsch' of the preceding November. Lawrence, who apparently never mentioned Hitler in any of his writings, possibly knew little about him: he hadn't yet published *Mein Kampf,* and it wasn't until November 1924 that the Nazis captured seats in the Reichstag. Lawrence in early 1924 felt the restlessness of the country which, he discovered, was going 'back to the savage polarity of Tartary, and away from the polarity of civilised Christian Europe. . . . These queer gangs of *Young Socialists* [did he mean young Nazis?], youths and girls, with their non-materialistic professions, their half-mystic assertions, they strike one as strange. Something primitive, like loose, roving gangs of broken, scattered tribes, so they affect one . . . within the last three years, the very constituency of the blood has changed, in European veins.' Lawrence felt that the Germans were whirling swiftly backwards to a kind of death, 'whirling to the ghost of the old Middle Ages of Germany, then to the Roman days, then to the days of the silent forest and the dangerous, lurking barbarians.'

'The Border Line' is the first of Lawrence's sexual ghost stories and evidently the first of the short stories containing a portrait of Murry, who appears as the journalist whom the powerful Anstruther reaches from beyond the grave to defeat. 'The Border Line', with its supernatural element and its supreme invocation of Strasbourg Cathedral— 'reddish stone, that had a flush in the night, like dark flesh' amid 'the ashy pallor and sulphur of our civilisation'—has a dream atmosphere that helps make it a kind of dream-restatement of all that had happened to Lawrence since his return to Europe.

He had written to Mrs. Carswell from Baden-Baden on February 12: 'We stay one more week here—then back to Paris to pick up our bags. Ought to be in London by the 26th. That hateful Seltzer writes never a word—looks as if he was up to tricks. I shall have to go quick to New York.' He would stay in London for only a week: 'Do you know a quiet hotel somewhere in town?' But: 'Don't tell anybody I'm coming. I don't want to see people.' The Continent had been 'very wearying—and no point in travelling, at least in winter. Far better to save one's energy at home.'

Three weeks later, after further visits to Paris and London, the Lawrences left England for New York on the *Aquitania*. In several of his letters at the time Lawrence repeated that excuse about Seltzer: the necessity to see him provided the reason for returning to America, though Lawrence told Bessie Freeman on March 1: 'Thank goodness we are getting out of Europe. It is a weariness to me.' And Frieda in an accompanying note said, 'I am glad to be going to America again— except for seeing my children and mother here, it's cold and weary and sad.'

Dorothy Brett went with the Lawrences to America, the only colonist for Rananim. In a shipboard letter of March 10 to Gertler, Lawrence mentioned a blue stone that, expanded in size to a ball of lapis lazuli, had probably seen service in *Women in Love* as the weapon with which Hermione banged Birkin on the head:

> We come to New York tomorrow morning—a very quick run. It was quite warm till yesterday—we were in the Gulf Stream. Now we are off America there is a strong north wind, the sea smoking its spray, and dark grey waves, and this big ship rolling. But it doesn't upset us, except Frieda a bit. The unending motion irritates her. I rather like it. Brett of course is very happy and pleased with herself. Suddenly I saw her wearing a little blue brooch I recognised as having given to Ottoline years ago—a chalcedony stone. She says Ottoline flung it at her at the time of the row. I always liked that soft blue stone. Queer how things come back to you. . . .
>
> Tuesday afternoon—Here we are in New York, in half a blizzard, snow and rain on a wild wind. Seltzer with us—not very reassuring—his business in low water. Brett only bewildered now.

*

On March 22, Lawrence and Frieda were back in Taos. In a March 1 letter from London, Lawrence had told Mrs. Freeman that he and Frieda expected to be in New York 'a week or ten days: then probably to Taos, as a jumping-off place. Of course I want to go back to Mexico: if it is quiet enough I have a novel I want to finish down there. I don't know how long we shall stay in Taos—a week or two, nothing permanent.' But he stayed in the Taos area seven months. His Taos experience this time was a retrogression, a degradation, modified somewhat by the acquisition of the Lobo Mountain ranch that formed a barrier to Taos itself.

He needed one. Mrs. Luhan's ménage had acquired some new exhibits, notably Clarence and Jaime. Clarence Thompson, described by Mrs. Luhan as 'gentle and effeminate' but given to rages because 'he was an inner ruin; he had been demolished in his childhood', was one of the minor citizens so inevitable to an art colony, a perennial camp follower. Jaime de Angulo was, on the other hand, a serious student of Jung and of the Indians. Before his death in 1950, he accomplished some excellent scholarship on the redman's myths. But in Mrs. Luhan's projection of him at Taos in 1924 he becomes a grotesque figure. So, of course, do all the other characters in her book, which suggests Matthew Arnold's remark about the comparatively milder-mannered Shelley circle: 'What a set! What a world!'

Richard Aldington's fairly detailed biography of Lawrence omits all mention of Clarence and Jaime, perhaps out of disgust. Aldington gets Lawrence up to the mountains as soon as possible. Actually it was five weeks before he went to Lobo Mountain, to John Evans's ranch, eventually renamed by Lawrence as Kiowa (pronounced KYE-o-wa). Mrs. Luhan had presented this ranch to Frieda, who in reciprocation gave her the final holograph manuscript of *Sons and Lovers*. But this gesture only offended Mrs. Luhan, who later used the manuscript as part payment of a psychoanalyst's bill. The manuscript came to light years later and is now at the University of California, Berkeley. It shows how severe Edward Garnett was in making excisions from it for the published version.

That the manuscript was given to Dr. A. A. Brill was rather appropriate, for Mrs. Luhan's account of the doings after Lawrence's re-entry into Taos belongs to the literature of psychoanalysis rather than elsewhere. Mrs. Luhan immediately resented 'the holy Russian idiot' Brett, who followed Lawrence around and protruded her ear trumpet, Toby, into every conversation. Toby was, Mrs. Luhan felt, 'a spy'. When she complained about it to the Lawrences, Frieda laughed heartily. She was not, herself, too fond of the ubiquitous Brett and Toby, but as always her Clausewitzisch strategy was to wait for a propitious moment and then smash the enemy with a single decisive stroke.

Meanwhile the upset Mrs. Luhan tried her usual game of moving people around like chess pieces. The result was some bizarre gambits and combinations. Even Tony finally walked out one night ('I think we done enough for those Lawrences'), Clarence purported to expose a plot of Lawrence's 'to kill Mabel', and Jaime left Taos in a huff. The chaos as described in Mrs. Luhan's book sounds like that of an asylum; the reader who wants reassurance at this point may turn to Lawrence's letters of the time, which ring in a counter-effect of sanity.

In a letter to Frederick Carter on June 3, a month after the move to the ranch, whose name Lawrence had changed from Flying Heart Ranch to Lobo (or wolf), he described the new home, later to be called Kiowa:

> Your letter this evening. I was glad to hear the *Beacon* news— never heard of the periodical. The *Adelphi* does one no good.
>
> I got an agent in New York to tackle my publisher, and the thing will be straightened out—but will take about a year. It wasn't nice.
>
> My wife has got a little ranch up here—about 150 acres, in the mountain foot-slopes, mostly pine trees, but two clearings—not much water, though. We are about two miles up from Del Monte Ranch, get our mail there. It's a lonely spot here—beautiful scenery—altitude 8,500 ft. We have two little log houses and a tiny cabin. We have been a month working like niggers, building up the one house, which was falling down, and shingling the others. We had four Indians working on the job, and a Mexican carpenter. The last Indians went down to Taos—17 miles— today, and we are alone, save for a friend, Dorothy Brett, who paints—and is a daughter of Viscount Esher.—We have five horses—ride down to Del Monte for milk and butter. I've just been having a struggle with three of the horses—they've gone wild, demons. With them was another man here to help, these times. It's a pity you haven't some money, to come and try the life here. You could have one of the houses, and Mrs Carter could start a little farm. Everything is all right, except the ditch to bring the water here from the canyon. But the winter is long and cold and lonely—we were at Del Monte last winter.—We have a spring, but it doesn't give enough water to irrigate.—I should rather like to see Mrs Carter tackle the place.—As for myself, I am a wandering soul. I want to go down to Old Mexico at the end of September, and my wife will go with me. It means abandoning this place, which is a pity. We should probably come back next April.

I haven't been doing much work since last autumn. The winter, and the visit to Europe, was curiously disheartening. Takes one some time to get over it.

As for the war, it changed me for ever. And after the war pushed the change further.

Lawrence didn't tell Carter that the 'Mexican carpenter' who had been working at the ranch was a drunkard whom he sacked for calling Frieda 'Chiquita'. The Lawrences eventually had good luck with two faithful young Indians, the pigtailed Trinidad and his wife Rufina. The ranch became the setting for the last part of the *novella* Lawrence wrote there that summer, *St Mawr* (which the English Lawrence scholar Keith Sagar says must be rhymed with *hour*). Carter's identification of the English setting of the first part of the story (Pontesbury, Shropshire) has already been quoted. Lawrence used several of the people at Pontesbury as minor characters, including Carter himself, who appears as Cartwright, with 'the tilted eyebrows, the twinkling goaty look, and the pointed ears of a goat-Pan'.

For the two principal characters, however, Lawrence (as we have seen) dipped into his Capri past—for Elizabeth Humes (Lou Carrington) and her mother (the mother in the story, Mrs. Witt). Having seen Americans in their own setting, Lawrence could now project these women against both European and American backgrounds: the picture in *St Mawr* of the will-powered Magna Mater (who is also Mrs. Luhan) on her daily ride through Hyde Park is one of Lawrence's best comic moments.

But above all the human characters—the restless American women; their Red Indian lackey and their proud little Welsh groom; their Mayfair and country-house friends; the rigid-minded West Country curate and his village parishioners—the figure of the red-gold stallion, St Mawr, stands out as the dominant character, image, and symbol of the story. The germ of that story may be found in a letter Lawrence wrote to Willard Johnson while he was in England in January 1924; playing with the name of Johnson's *Laughing Horse* magazine, Lawrence spoke out for horses, centaurs, Houyhnhnms, even hobby horses. 'And over here the horse is dead . . . Oh, London is awful: so dark, so damp, so yellow-grey, so mouldering piece-meal . . . Horse, horse, be as hobby as you like, but let me get on your back and ride away again to New Mexico'—which is, in capsule, the 'plot' of *St Mawr*.

Lawrence had used horses as symbols before, and in a passage in *Apocalypse,* which he wrote in 1929, he spoke once again of that animal: 'He is a dominant symbol: he gives us lordship: he links us, the first palpable and throbbing link with ruddy-glowing Almighty of potence: he is the beginning even of our god-heads in the flesh. . . . The horse! the symbol of surging potency and power of movement, of action, in man.'

This masterful horse, embodied as the powerful stallion St Mawr, was in 1924 the reversal of the situation of Gerald and his red Arab mare, which Lawrence wrote of in *Women in Love* in 1916: there the young man of the upper classes (in the years between the Boer War and World War I) could abuse the horse and let the locomotive (symbol both of Gerald's own mechanization and of his instrumental mastery over living things) frighten her; but the post-war St Mawr is masterless and able to injure the upper-class Rico, who tries to control him. And St Mawr teaches the two American women their lesson: they leave Rico and his Mayfair and country-house friends, and take St Mawr to the American Southwest and the freedom he deserves; while the two women seek to win their own freedom in another part of the Southwest, Kiowa Ranch (which Lawrence in the story calls Las Chivas, the she-goats).

The world of the mountainside ranch, then, becomes the possible last stage in the Lawrencization of Mrs. Witt and Lou; but the process is not overtly or didactically indicated; the whole force of the last part of the book is the magnetic projection of the landscape, the best possible contrast to the decadent society of the earlier section of this short novel of such astounding range. In the fullest study of *St Mawr* yet published, F. R. Leavis calls the book a 'dramatic poem' which 'seems to me to present a creative and technical originality not less remarkable than that of *The Waste Land,* and to be, more unquestionably than that poem, completely achieved, a full and self-sufficient creation. It can hardly strike the admirer as anything but major.' This statement is ideally read in its context: Leavis's essay, which works towards its conclusion through very careful reasoning, occurs in *D. H. Lawrence: Novelist* (1955), whose appendix is the reprint of a 're-view' of *D. H. Lawrence and Human Existence,* by Father Tiverton (Father Martin Jarrett-Kerr): Leavis's 'review' is nothing but an attack on T. S. Eliot, who wrote the preface to the book, whose essential content Leavis (quite typically) ignores.

Lawrence completed *St Mawr* before September 30, when he sent the manuscript to his agent; eight days later he noted in his journal, '8 Oct. 24. Packing up to leave ranch—snowy day. Finished *The*

Princess.' This was the story whose leading character was first identified by Catherine Carswell as Dorothy Brett. Again we have the New Mexico setting, the dude-ranch tourist (a middle-aged virgin) going with a guide, Domingo Romero, up into the hard masculine scenery of the higher forests of the Rockies. The sheltered 'Princess', who knows of life only at a remove, through Maupassant and Zola, wants to 'try' sex—with catastrophic results.

When she dislikes the experience, Romero, ruined survivor of a once-great landowning family, keeps her prisoner, treating her coarsely till her 'rescuers' shoot him; after which the violated princess goes away, 'slightly crazy', and subsequently marries a man who is safely old. Like the Mexican story 'None of That', this is a reversal of Lawrence's frequent use of the Sleeping Beauty or Little Briar Rose theme, in which the enchanted princess is awakened to life by the prince who breaks through the thorns surrounding her. In these two stories, the women who *will* the experience—such as Dollie Urquhart in 'The Princess' and Ethel Cane in 'None of That'—are the failures, in contrast to the women whose awakening has the true magic quality, such as the girls in 'The Horse Dealer's Daughter' and *The Virgin and the Gipsy,* and Connie Chatterley in *Lady Chatterley's Lover.*

A type of male character Lawrence disliked, based on Murry, was also slated in some of the stories of this time. Murry is Jimmy ('the face of the laughing faun in one of the faun's unlaughing, moody moments'), the editor of a highbrow magazine who becomes comically entangled with a collier's wife in 'Jimmy and the Desperate Woman'; and he is Marchbanks in 'The Last Laugh', as Dorothy Brett is. Miss James, hearing-device and all. This is another ghost story, with Marchbanks receiving a terrible punishment for denying life: he seeks mechanical sex, and in his artificial vision, the snow that falls on the city seems like whitewash. Demons thump into London by night, and the winter air is full of the smell of almond blossoms: a sexual symbol in Frazer's *The Golden Bough.* The story was somewhat in the manner of 'The Border Line', and it presaged the later sexual-supernatural story 'Glad Ghosts'. When Lawrence sent *St Mawr,* 'The Last Laugh', and 'Jimmy' to his agent on September 30, he also mailed 'The Woman Who Rode Away', the story of an American woman in Mexico who, after a dozen years of marriage to the Dutch owner of a mine, symbol of mechanistic oppression, rides out to a lost tribe of Aztec-like Indians who accept her as a sacrifice—a kind of dress rehearsal for *The Plumed Serpent.* For the setting of 'The Woman Who

Rode Away', Lawrence apparently had two sources, one of them a silver mine which had a Swiss owner; as we have seen, Lawrence and Gótzsche had visited the place, near Navajoa, on their Mexican journey. The other parts of the background seem to have been the mountains above Taos, also used in 'The Princess'.

*

During the summer of 1924, Mrs. Luhan and Tony and Clarence went up once to stay at the ranch—but only once. Mrs. Luhan invited Lawrence over to see her alone and, as she wept, asked him why he treated her 'like that'? Lawrence had offended her by scolding Tony for shooting a porcupine—probably the germ of his essay 'Reflections on the Death of a Porcupine'—and Tony's wife took this scolding as a personal injury. Lawrence told the weeping woman, 'Well, I can't stand a certain way you walk. As you went by my window this morning . . .' —at which point her howls increased. So the Lawrences and Brett were allowed privacy at the ranch.

But before long, Lawrence and Frieda went with Mrs. Luhan and Tony to the Hopi snake dances in Arizona, in August. Mrs. Luhan felt dead, like a mummy, on that trip, with Tony singing as he drove along, and the Lawrences arguing or else exclaiming over the scenery. Mrs. Luhan felt that Lawrence's first account of the dances was prosaic, though she liked the essays on them that later appeared in *Mornings in Mexico*. After the trip, Mrs. Luhan hurried east to see Dr. Brill. Lawrence wrote to her that this was good, yes, she needed a doctor, and that she must learn to curb her will. They met but briefly after her return, shortly before the Lawrences left for Mexico, with Brett, in October. ('My chest had got very raw up at the ranch: that very high altitude.') They all seemed friendly enough, but after the Lawrence party left, Mrs. Luhan wrote to Lawrence to say he was evil and treacherous. They never met again, even when he went back to the ranch the following year, though after his return to Europe they corresponded.

On October 3, 1924, while he was preparing to leave Kiowa, Lawrence told Murry that on September 10, the day before his own thirty-ninth birthday, his father had died: 'I want to go south, where there is no autumn, where the cold doesn't crouch over one like a snow-leopard waiting to pounce. The heart of the North is cold, and the fingers of cold are corpse fingers.'

Three days before leaving the ranch, Lawrence noted (October 8) in a diary, 'English bank balance, £303. Balance in Chase National Bank, Metropolitan Branch at 4th Avenue at 23rd St $2,285.21.' Then, on the eleventh, he was off, with Brett and Frieda, bound for Mexico City. He and Frieda 'had terrible colds'. Lawrence met W. Somerset Maugham and wrote him down as 'a narrow-gutted "artist" with a stutter . . . disagreeable, and no fun left in him . . . a bit rancid.' Maugham explained in a letter to the present writer that Lawrence thought he was being snubbed because Maugham's secretary dealt with him on the telephone rather than Maugham, who stammered more than usual over the telephone and hence avoided it.

During his two weeks in Mexico City, Lawrence went to a P.E.N. Club dinner, at which he was called upon to speak. After he and the two women moved to Oaxaca, he described it in a November 14 note to William Hawk:

> Your letter came today. Thank you so much for riding round and looking after the place. When I think of it, I wish I was back.
>
> We got down here on Sunday night: it takes two days from Mexico City, though it's not so very far. Oaxaca is a little town, about 30,000, alone in the south, with a perfect climate. The market is full of roses and violets, the gardens are all flowers. Every day is perfectly sunny, a bit hot at midday. The natives are mostly Zapotec Indians, small, but very straight and alert and alive: really very nice. There is a big market humming like a bee-hive, where one can buy anything, from roses to horse-shoes. I wish we could send you some of the pottery, such beautiful colours, and costs nothing. But the last lot I sent got smashed. This is where they make the serapes like the one with the eagle that hung on the wall: and the little men stalk about in them, looking very showy.—The governor is an Indian from the hills. I called on him in the palace!!!—But everywhere the government is very Labour—and somehow one doesn't feel very solid. There are so many wild Indians who don't know anything about any-thing, except that they are told that every 'rich' man is an en-emy.—There may be a bad bust-up in Mexico City: and again, everything may go off quietly. But I don't like the feeling. If only it wasn't winter, we'd come back to the ranch tomorrow. I feel so weary of *people*—people, people, people, and all such bunk, somehow, with politics and self-assertiveness.—As it is, we shall

probably take a house here for a month or two. Thank goodness my chest and throat are better, since we are here in this soft warm air. I want to get them sound this winter, and next year stay on much later at the ranch. . . .

Brett lost Toby, and has had the tin-smith make her a substitute, shaped like a funnel: much excitement among the natives when she uses it. Her machine also works very fitfully, so that her ears are out of luck.—Frieda of course pines for her ranch, and the freedom. So really do I.

Four days later the Lawrences moved from the Hotel Francia (where Brett remained) into a house belonging to an English priest, Father Rickards, brother of the British Vice-Consul at Mexico City. His house at 43 Avenida Piño Suárez was the one described in the early essays of *Mornings in Mexico,* with 'the yellow flowers that rise above the *patio* wall, and the swaying, glowing magenta of the bougainvillea, and the fierce red outbursts of the poinsettia'. Brett reported that Lawrence said Oaxaca was far more primitive than Chapala, which had been 'too touristy'. But the Indians at Oaxaca annoyed him when they pointed at him and hoarsely whispered, '*Cristo! Cristo!*'

Lawrence began to rewrite *The Plumed Serpent.* Brett helped him by typing it. Frieda became increasingly hostile to Brett, who although she lived at the hotel managed to spend a good deal of time with Lawrence. The two of them several times went out to the desert and sat under bushes, writing or sketching. One evening when Lawrence came home late after having some drinks with Brett and members of the local Anglo colony, Frieda blew into a rage. She told Lawrence she didn't want 'the Brett' in their lives any more, and he was first cross, then relieved. He wrote Brett a letter she felt was cruel, telling her to pack and be off. She delayed, and then Frieda came down to the hotel and raged at her, shouting that Lawrence and Brett had a curate-and-spinster relationship. Brett left for Mexico City, bound for Taos and the ranch.

Lawrence had meanwhile been writing violent letters to Murry, mocking the *Adelphi* and all it stood for. 'Either you go on wheeling a wheelbarrow and lecturing at Cambridge and going softer and softer inside, or you make a hard fight with yourself, pull yourself up, harden yourself, throw your feelings down the drain and face the world as a fighter.—You won't, though.'

Lawrence was trying at this time to make his own 'hard fight', completing *The Plumed Serpent* in February 1925. The third and last of the leadership stories, after *Kangaroo* and *Aaron's Rod, The Plumed Serpent* is the most ambitious failure among all his novels. In Mexico he had found no true 'leader', and for his Don Ramón he apparently had to borrow aspects of the career and personality of José Vasconcelos, whom he disliked. Don Ramón is of course partly Lawrence himself, as General Cipriano is, too. Within three years Lawrence repudiated the main theme of his novel when, in writing to Bynner about the book on March 13, 1928, he said, 'The leader of men is a back number'.

Yet even readers who dislike its theme admit that *The Plumed Serpent* contains some of Lawrence's finest prose. The hot rich deep colors of Mexico are in it; he caught the terrible surface violence of the country, from the bullfight in the first chapter—the commercialized degradation of an ancient religious rite—to the attack on Don Ramón's *hacienda* towards the end of the book. The latter episode, incidentally, was inspired by similar attacks made on the great estates by radical 'Agrarians' who felt that private property was not being nationalized quickly enough. In Mexico City just before Lawrence began writing the final version of *The Plumed Serpent,* he learned from Mrs. Nuttall the details of the death of her friend Rosalie Evans a few months before. Mrs. Evans, an Englishwoman whose *hacienda* had been several times under siege, was finally ambushed and killed near the town of Puebla, where Lawrence had been ill the preceding year.

The Plumed Serpent landscape, gray-dry and dotted with red hibiscus, and here and there softened by the green of willow trees, cries out violence and death, but how supremely that landscape comes up through the pages of the book, taking the reader physically to Mexico: 'Near at hand, a ragged shifting of banana trees, bare hills with immobile cactus, and to the left, a *hacienda* with peons' square mud boxes of houses.' Or: 'The morning was clear and hot, the pale brown lake quite still, like a phantom. People were moving on the beach, in the distance tiny, like dots of white: white dots of men following the faint dust of donkeys.' Or: 'The lake was quite black, like a great pit. The wind suddenly blew with violence, with a strange ripping sound in the mango-trees, as if some membrane in the air were being ripped.' Or: 'She could see Sayula; white-fluted twin towers of the church, obelisk shaped above the pepper-trees; beyond, a mound of hill standing alone, dotted with dry bushes, distinct and Japanese looking; beyond this, the corrugated, blue-ribbed, flat-flanked mountains of Mexico.' Or—but the novel is like this throughout, with the heat, the smell, the color of Mexico; yet there is the 'other Mexico', too, the renaissance of the sacred Aztec gods, simulated by Don Ramón and Cipriano, with the European woman Kate as their hesitant recruit.

The final effect is one of superb music with a foolish libretto. Perhaps the shrewdest comment yet made on *The Plumed Serpent* is Aldous Huxley's, at the conclusion of his *Beyond the Mexique Bay* (1934). Three years after the death of his friend Lawrence, Huxley made a tour of Central America and of parts of Mexico (Oaxaca, Puebla, Mexico City) where Lawrence had lived. The book, like all Huxley's travel volumes, is full of sharp observations and of praise for what is beautiful; this one also records disillusion (expressed fictionally in *Eyeless in Gaza* in 1936). Huxley saved his final disillusion for the last pages of *Mexique Bay,* where we find him rereading *The Plumed Serpent* on the ship taking him away from Mexico. He recognizes the force of 'passage after passage of wonderfully realised incident', but after the artistic perfection of the first two-thirds of the book he finds the rest of it falling apart because of Lawrence's lack of belief in it. Doubt had crowded in on Lawrence and 'had to be shouted down. But the louder he shouted, the less was he able to convince his hearers.'

Further, *The Plumed Serpent* is full of manifest contradictions. Soon after Kate meets Don Ramón he tells her, 'There is no liberty for a man, apart from the God of his manhood. . . . When a man has nothing but his *will* to assert—even his goodwill—it is always bullying. Bolshevism is one sort of bullying, capitalism another: and liberty is a change of chains.' Much of this sounds like the reasoning of R. L. Somers in *Kangaroo,* when in Australia he reaches a culmination in his thinking about political ideas. And Don Ramón goes on: 'I have realised that *my will,* no matter how intelligent I am, is only another nuisance on the face of the earth, once I start exerting it, and other people's *wills* are even worse.' These statements occur in Chapter IV, 'To Stay or Not to Stay', a title referring to Kate's indecision.

But she does stay, largely because the flashing little Cipriano attracts her. Yet by Chapter XXIV (called 'Malintzi' after the name she takes in the Aztec wedding ceremony with Cipriano), Kate sees that the activity of Ramón and Cipriano in restoring the old gods is chiefly an exhibition of will, after all: 'And deep in her soul came a revulsion against this manifestation of pure will. . . . Always will, will, will, without remorse or relenting. This was America to her: all the Americas. Sheer will.' She stays, but is reluctant; the last line of the book gives us another of Lawrence's deliberately inconclusive conclusions: 'You won't let me go!'

There were aspects of the Quetzalcoatl revival that Kate didn't know about, though most of the action in the book comes through her consciousness. She is of course not present at the mystic *Blutbrüderschaft* rite of Ramón and Cipriano. What is perhaps more important is that she doesn't really know about Cipriano's behavior when he is out in the country with his soldiers:

He pursued the bandits with swift movements. He stripped his captives and tied them up. But if it seemed a brave man, he would swear him in. If it seemed a knave, a treacherous cur, he stabbed him to the heart, saying, 'I am the red Huitzilopochtli, of the knife.'

Perhaps there was nothing particularly wrong in Cipriano's assumption of a god's name, but what gave him the right to render godlike life-and-death verdicts? Here indeed Lawrence came close to fascism, which he disliked (the charge that he was fascistic is answered elsewhere in this book), as well as close to downright foolishness. And when the men of Quetzalcoatl, led by Don Ramón and Cipriano, are carrying the Catholic emblems out of a church, the screamed hysteria of Ramón's protesting wife seems clumsy melodrama. Yet, as noted earlier, *The Plumed Serpent* has a kind of magic in its projection of the actual Mexico. There is, however, too much of the white-clothed people chanting the Quetzalcoatl hymns in the plazas at night, with afterwards the muttering of drums through the towns.

But the book has its advocates. Two stars in the Lawrencean firmament who were otherwise far apart, Catherine Carswell and Mabel Dodge Luhan, considered *The Plumed Serpent* Lawrence's masterpiece. A notable critic, William York Tindall, who made fun of Lawrence's 'mystic relatedness' with a cow in New Mexico, in *D. H. Lawrence and Susan His Cow* (1939), asserted that *The Plumed Serpent* was Lawrence's finest novel; Professor Tindall praised that volume again in his preface to the 1950 paperback edition, in which he found that '*The Plumed Serpent* is a great metaphor for a feeling about reality. Conditioned by place and contemporary politics (of which on one level the book is a nightmare vision), that feeling is the wonder of all things—even of such politics. Kate is always calling for the return of magic and wonder. Her story brings them back.' In *A D. H. Lawrence Miscellany* (1959), Jascha Kessler praised *The Plumed Serpent* for its mythical-anthropological elements, and L. D. Clark's *The Dark Night of the Body* (1964) devotes a whole book to it (which is incidentally an interesting and highly informative travelogue, full of photographs of Mexican places connected with Lawrence), and Keith Sagar provides a moderate defense of it in *The Art of D. H. Lawrence* (1966). There is also *Conflict in the Novels of D. H. Lawrence* (1969), a book developed out of a Ph.D. thesis at Leeds by someone identified only as Yudishtar, who sees Lawrence as the Holy Man incapable of doing any wrong and to whom literary criticism should not be applied, least of all to *The Plumed Serpent,* 'extraordinary and important'. But a great many other critics of Lawrence dislike his Mexican novel; his most vehement apologist, F. R. Leavis, finds that 'in its sustained earnest intentness *The Plumed Serpent* as a whole rings false'.

Teachers of Lawrence courses in American universities in the 1970s find that their students like *The Plumed Serpent,* perhaps in the way that so many of their generation favor Carlos Castaneda's books (featuring a Don Juan rather than a Don Ramón) and such gurus as Maharajah Ji.

*

Lawrence had become severely ill as he drew near the end of *The Plumed Serpent.* Just as he finished it, he told William Hawk on February 7, 'I have been steadily out of luck this trip down here: don't think I shall ever come to Mexico again while I live. I wondered why I wasn't well down here—thought it was the remains of the old flu—and so it was, with malaria. I've had the doctor, and heavy quinine injections, and feel like a rag: but much better.'

Then he had a relapse into the most serious illness he had ever known. He told Frieda she would have to bury him in the local cemetery, but she laughed through her misery and said, 'No, no, it's such an ugly cemetery, don't you think of it.' At this time an earthquake nearly destroyed the house. Lawrence and Frieda moved to a local hotel, and Frieda became ill too.

Finally, at the end of February they rode on a hot train to Mexico City, planning to go on to England. Dr. Uhlfelder bluntly told Frieda, in Lawrence's presence, 'Mr. Lawrence has tuberculosis.' Lawrence, mentioning his illness in his letters, didn't designate his disease, as usual. But he took the doctor's advice, which was to the effect that a sea voyage at the time might be fatal. So Lawrence and Frieda prepared to go back to Kiowa.

It was during his terrible Mexican illness that Lawrence began his unfinished narrative, 'The Flying Fish', whose first pages he dictated to Frieda. When he read the incomplete manuscript version to Earl and Achsah Brewster in Switzerland in 1928, they wanted him to finish the story, but he said it had been 'written so near the borderline of death, that I have never been able to carry it through in the cold light of day'—and later he told them in a letter that the story remained 'where it was'.

As it stands, it is one of Lawrence's finest prose creations, the story of an Englishman named Gethin Day, critically ill in Mexico, summoned home: 'No Day in Daybrook. For the Vale a bad outlook.' One of the themes of the story contrasts 'the fatal Greater Day of the Indians' with 'the fussy, busy, lesser day of the white people'. Lawrence told the Brewsters, 'The last part will be regenerate man, a real life in this Garden of Eden,' but the story remains a magnificent fragment.

*

Members of the Anglo colony at Oaxaca had been kind and helpful during Lawrence's illness; so had others at Mexico City, where the convalescent Lawrences had several pleasant visits with new English friends, the George R. G. Conways. An engineer who specialized in electric railways, Conway was director and president of the Mexican Light and Power Company. He was also an author, an expert on Mexico and the Conquistadores. It was Mrs. Conway to whom Lawrence on April 2, 1925, wrote his first letter after returning to the United States, where he was staying first at Questa, New Mexico:

> We got here yesterday—mountains snowy, wind wild and cold, but bright sun. I'm not altogether here yet: bits of me still on the way, like luggage following. We're staying with our neighbours for a while.
>
> The Emigration people in El Paso—the Americans—were most insulting and hateful. Before you grumble at the Mexicans, as the worst ever, try this sort of American. *Canaille* of the most bottom-doggy order, and filthy with insolence.
>
> The basket of food was a great consolation on the journey, es-

pecially the fruit. We ate *all* the pie: not at all like invalids. The people in the Pullman dreary: and in the drawing-room a Mexican family with seven children.—Never come via El Paso, if you can help it.

I still have a lurking hankering for Europe. I think at the end of the summer, we shall both sail.

Thank you so much for being so kind to us. Tell Conway I hope his troubles are smoothing out.—Really, Mexico City is not so bad, you know: when one finds one's own countrymen still sterling. (Even the 'bad old woman', don't you think?)

Lawrence's troubles at El Paso were more thoroughly described in a letter to Amy Lowell from Questa a few days later:

I have so often wondered if you are sitting in London, in the Berkeley, maybe: and see where we are. I got malaria in Oaxaca: then grippe: then a typhoid inside: was so sick, I wearied of the day. Struggled to Mexico City, was put to bed again for three weeks—then packed off up here. We had booked our passages to England, but the doctor said I *must* stay in the sun, he wouldn't be answerable for me if I went on the sea, and to England. So we came here. The Emigration Authorities at El Paso treated us as Emigrants, and nearly killed me a second time: this after the Consul and the Embassy people in Mexico—the American— had been most kind, doing things to make it easier for us. They only made it harder. The Emigration Dept is Dept of Labour, and you taste the Bolshevist method in its conduct.

However—after two days' fight we got through—and yesterday got to our little ranch. There is snow behind the house and sky threatening snow. But usually it's brilliantly sunny. And the log fire is warm. And the Indian Trinidad is chopping wood under the pine tree, and his wife Rufina, in her wide white boots, is struggling carrying water. I begin to feel better: though still feel I don't care whether it's day or night.

I saw notices of your Keats book. Pity after all I didn't ask you to send the promised copy here: I could have wandered in it now. But I'll write to Curtis Brown. And I'll send you a copy of my little novel *St Mawr*.

I managed to finish my Mexican novel *Quetzalcoatl* in Mexico: the very day I went down, as if shot in the intestines. But I daren't even look at the outside of the MS. It cost one so much, and I wish I could eat all the lotus that ever budded, and drink up Lethe to the source. Talk about dull opiates—one wants something that'll go into the very soul.

When Frieda refused to have Brett at the ranch, she took a cabin nearby on the Hawks' property. Lawrence, who had written her a scolding letter from Oaxaca on the subject of friendship between men and women, now sent her a curt note saying it was futile for her and him to try to get along together: he had lost all desire for intimacy with people. 'Acquaintance is enough. It will be best when we go our separate ways. A life in common is an illusion, when the instinct is always to divide, to separate individuals and set them one against the other.' *Il n'y a pas de Rananim.*

In May, when the warm weather set in, Lawrence felt better. It was at this time he completed his Biblical play, *David,* which he devised for Ida Rauh (Mrs. Max Eastman, later Mrs. Andrew Dasburg), whom he had first met at the Luhans'. Lawrence wrote the part of Michal for her, but when he read *David* to her, Ida Rauh declared she was too old to play Michal. In a letter of May 21, he reported to Eduardo Rendón, a friend of the Conways': 'The summer has come on the ranch—hot days. I go about with a hoe, irrigating—and for the time being am rancherito and *nada más.*' The publishers had sent him the manuscript of *The Plumed Serpent,* whose anglicized title he disliked—'sounds to me rather like millinery'—and: 'They urge me to go over the MS., but I feel still that I can't look at it. It smells too much of Oaxaca, which I hated so much because I was so ill.—Altogether I think of Mexico with a sort of nausea: not the friends, but the country itself. It gave me a turn that time: doubt if I shall ever come again.' He was considerably better, 'but don't quite forget my shakiness. We have an Indian and his wife on the ranch to work for us—but really I feel I never want to see an Indian or an "aboriginee" or anything in the savage line again.' Frieda's nephew, Friedrich Jaffe, was staying with them, 'and my head is full of German for a change. What a bore other languages are!'

The summer passed, with Lawrence writing little, completely avoiding Mabel Luhan, and slowly recuperating as he worked at his drainage project. And, as autumn drew on, Lawrence and Frieda prepared to leave for England.

Then, one last letter of this period, written to Mr. and Mrs. Hawk aboard the S.S. *Resolute* on September 27, when Lawrence was leaving America for the last time—a letter full of the American twenties and of his own experiences, and one of the brightest of all his letters:

Here it is Sunday afternoon—everybody very bored—nothing happening, except a rather fresh wind, the sea a bit choppy, outdoors just a bit too cold. We get in to Southampton on Wednesday morning, and glad shall I be to see land. There are very few people on board, and most of those are Germans or people from somewhere Russia way, speaking a language never heard before. We've had pretty good weather—went on board last Monday night, and sailed at 1 a.m. Queer to be slipping down the Hudson at midnight, past all the pier lights. It seems now such a long while ago. Though the weather has been pretty good, I had one awful day, blind with a headache. It was when we ran into a warm fog, so suppose it was the old malaria popping up.

I didn't care for New York—it was steamy hot. I had to run about and see people: the two little Seltzers dangling by a single thread, over the verge of bankruptcy, and nobody a bit sorry for them. The new publishers, the Knopfs, are set up in great style, in their offices on Fifth Avenue—deep carpets, and sylphs in a shred of black satin and a shred of brilliant undergarment darting by. But the Knopfs seem really sound and reliable: am afraid the Seltzers had too many 'feelings'. Adele said dramatically to Frieda: 'All I want is to pay OUR debts and DIE.' Death is a debt we all pay: the dollars are another matter.

Nina [Witt] is as busy as ever re-integrating other people— It was a pleasant house near Washington Square, but of course they were building a huge new 15-storey place next door, so all day long the noise of battle rolled.—The child, Marion Bull, is a handsome girl of eighteen and very nice indeed; trying to go on the stage, and the stagey people being very catty to her. I rather hope she won't go on the stage, it might spoil her.—The Boy Harry wasn't yet back in New York.—That woman Mrs Hare sent a car and fetched us to their place on Long Island: beautiful place. But in proudly showing me her bees, she went and got stung just under the eye, and a more extraordinary hostess in an elegant house I never saw, as the afternoon wore on and the swelling swelled and swelled. It was too bad: she was very kind to us.—The nicest thing was when some people motored us out at night to the shore on Long Island, and we made a huge fire of driftwood, and toasted mutton chops, with nothing in sight but sand and the foam in the dark[.]

I lie and think of the ranch; it seems so far far away:—these beastly journeys, how I hate them! I'm going to stop it, though, this continual shifting.

How is Miss Wemyss: not still fighting her mother, I hope— like Brett at forty? Send me a line with news of you all:

c/o Curtis Brown. 6 Henrietta St
London, WC 2

I do feel, I don't know what I'm doing on board this ship.

*

PART FIVE

The Last Years

---

*

1 THE ROAD TO THE VILLA MIRENDA

THE LAWRENCES ARRIVED at Southampton on the last day of September 1925 and went on to London, to Garland's Hotel, Pall Mall. Lawrence saw few of his old friends at the time: 'The Carswells and the Eders, but no more of the old crowd, not Kot.' Catherine Carswell, glad to find Lawrence not an invalid, thought his face seemed small and pinched under his sombrero. He wrote to the elder Hawks on October 9:

> I've been in my native land eight days now, and it's not very cheering: rather foggy, with very feeble attempts at sun: and the people very depressed. There's a million and a quarter unemployed, receiving that wretched dole: and you can't get a man to do an odd job, anywhere. My publisher, down in the country, has 16 acres of good thick hay still standing, because he can't get it cut. He told the farmer he could have it for the cutting: the farmer said that, although there were eight unemployed men in the tiny village, he couldn't get a man anywhere to do a week[']s work. If the unemployed work for a week, they go off the list of the dole, and they find it so hard to get on again, it's safer not to work. So there's a terrible feeling everywhere: and London is more expensive than New York, and the spending is enormous. They look for a revolution of some sort: I don't quite see anything violent, but added to the fog, it's horribly depressing.

> We are going today up to the Midlands, to stay with my sisters. I don't suppose we shall be in England more than another fortnight—then we go to Germany, to my wife's mother, and on to Italy.

> It's a pity, really, to leave the peaceful ranch, and the horses, and the sun. But there, one's native land has a sort of hopeless attraction, when one is away.

Lawrence again found his native region unpleasant, as he told Mrs. Carswell in a letter probably written on October 13: 'The weather's awful, and we simply hate it up here,' and in another, apparently of October 17: 'Comparative opulence here—*comparative,* of course—judging by old home standards. I liked the old better *then:* but don't want it back.' He also told Mrs. Carswell that he loathed more than ever 'past things like one's home regions'.

Lawrence and Frieda saw Barbara Weekley in London and met her fiancé. Lawrence was polite to this young man, whom Barbara, in the end, didn't marry, but with his tendency to interfere in the lives of others, he told Frieda that they must laugh her daughter out of the situation: where was her instinct? They saw Barbara again during their visit to Nottingham, when Lawrence was down with a cold. He sat up in bed to talk with her. The fiancé, he said, had no life; even her father, who had his writing activity, was more vital; but Barbara's fiancé was a man who shirked the difficulties of existence; she must shake him off, as a dog shakes off its fleas.

After their return to London, Lawrence and Frieda stayed in the rooms of Gordon Macfarlane, Catherine Carswell's brother, on Gower Street, that long thoroughfare whose boxlike houses differ only in the numbers they bear. Lawrence invited a few people to 73 Gower, including William Gerhardi (now Gerhardie), the young author of a current book, *The Polyglots,* who was surprised to see the competent-looking *Hausfrau* sit placidly by while her husband, with 'a beam on his face that was like a halo', cooked and served the dinner.

Later, when Frieda spoke vehemently of Lord Beaverbrook, who was then a patron of Gerhardi, Lawrence said, 'Not so much intensity, Frieda,' and she cried out, 'If I want to be intense I'll be intense, and you go to hell!' But the climax of the evening came when Gerhardi told of a remark that Bertrand Russell had made to him: 'Lawrence has no mind.' Lawrence 'sniffed' and said, 'Have you seen him in a bathing-dress? Poor Bertie Russell! He is all Disembodied Mind!'

That was Lawrence's epitaph on the long-dead friendship with Russell. But the relationship with Murry persisted. Murry, disappointed because Lawrence wouldn't visit him in Dorset, accepted his friend's invitation to London, though he disliked leaving his wife for even one night, because she was in poor health and expecting their second child. Murry silently took offense at Lawrence's lack of interest in the *Adelphi* contributor whom he had married—Violet le Maistre—and in their baby daughter whom he felt Lawrence would love.

In London, Lawrence rejected Murry's idea that he and Frieda should take a cottage near him and his wife, but he pleased Murry by inviting the family to Italy, a sign that he had 'accepted' the new Mrs. Murry. The two men argued about Judas, who in Murry's view 'was the broken-hearted lover', the only disciple who understood Jesus.

When Lawrence answered, Murry felt that his 'vehemence against Jesus was the measure of his identification with him'.

But the two old friends parted amicably: Lawrence insisted on going to a neighborhood shop to buy a bag of fruit for Murry to take back to Dorset with him, on the last train, which was due to leave soon; if Lawrence was late in getting back to Gower Street, Murry was to take a taxi to the shop and meet him on the way back. Time passed, Murry hailed a taxi, and it took the wrong route. At the shop, yes, 'a thin gentleman with a beard' had just left. But it was too late. Murry never again saw the thin gentleman with the beard.

Five days later (November 2), Lawrence wrote to Mrs. Carswell from Baden-Baden: 'Had a quick journey here—but no trains across the Rhine from Strasbourg, so had to come by motor. . . . My mother-in-law looking older, slower, but still very lively, walks uphill to us in our hotel.' Baden-Baden was 'unbelievably quiet and deserted—really deserted. Nobody comes any more: it's nothing but ghosts, from the Turgenev period.'

After the glare of Mexico, Baden-Baden was no more of a success than England had been. Lawrence, who could never again live in the gray north, considered spending the winter at Ragusa, in Dalmatia, or in the Isles of Greece, but at last he decided upon that same Mediterranean coast he had known a dozen years before when he lived at Fiascherino. This time, however, he went west of Genoa, to Spotorno, where Martin Secker assured him he would find few tourists. From there he wrote to his friend Vere Collins, of Oxford University Press, which was expurgating Lawrence's history book for the Irish school market:

I'm sending the mauled history by this mail. When I went through it, I was half infuriated and half amused. But if I'd had to go through it, personally, and make the decision merely from myself, I'd have sent those Irish b's seven times to hell, before I'd have moved a single iota at their pencil stroke. But do me a favour. Please keep this particular marked copy for me, will you, when you are through with it. Send it me back here, if you can. It will always serve to stimulate my bile and to remind me of the glory of the human race.

Here it's sunny. We're in hotel for a bit—probably shall look for a house for the winter here, though the village doesn't amount to much. But if the sun shines on the Mediterranean, that's a lot.

I read the volume of essays—rather soft meat—sort of

chopped up eggy mess you feed young gaping goslings on. My God, where are the *men* in England now? The place is one howling nursery.

Murry's *Keats* was quite good—many thanks—but oh heaven, so dieaway—the text might be: Oh lap up Shakespeare till you've cleaned the dish, and you may hope to swoon into raptures and die an early but beautiful death at 25.

I'm sick to death of this maudlin twaddle and England's rotten with it. Why doesn't somebody finally and loudly say Shit! to it all!

The Lawrences rented the Villa Bernarda from an officer in the *bersaglieri*. When he came to the Hotel Ligure to discuss terms, Lawrence called Frieda to meet the little military man, who looked 'so smart'; he was wearing his dress uniform because it was the queen's birthday. Frieda found a perky figure with gay plumes and blue sash— her first sight of Angelo Ravagli, whom a quarter of a century later she was to marry.

In a letter of December 18, Lawrence described the villa to William Hawk:

It's on the sea, on the Riviera, about three miles [actually many more] from Monte Carlo. The village is just a quiet Italian village, but we have friends here [Martin Secker's family]. The house is nice, just under the Castle, in a big vineyard garden, with terrace over the roofs of the village, the sea beyond. We do the housework ourselves: Frieda obstinately refused a maid. But there's a gardener lives downstairs, he does all the fetching and carrying, goes shopping every morning at 7:30, pumps the water, and is there when we want him. We've got three floors; we live mostly on the top floor, high up, where there's a kitchen and bedroom and sitting-room, and a big terrace from the sitting-room; we sleep on the middle floor: the bottom floor we store things in. It's real Italian country style—a pleasant sort of life, easier than America. The weather is on the whole sunny and dry, but we've had bitter cold winds. We go for walks in the hills—there are snow mountains behind—and do bits of things. Yesterday we got oranges from the trees and made marmelade, which I burnt a bit. But it's good. Frieda's youngest daughter Barbara is in Alassio, about 25 miles away. She comes over and stays a day or two with us. There are no horses to ride, no spring to fetch water from. The pine-trees are those puffs of umbrella pines all scattered separate on the stony slopes to the sea.

*

At the Villa Bernarda, Lawrence began what developed into the fourth and last phase of his writing career. In some of the stories of this phase and in parts of his novel *Lady Chatterley's Lover,* in a few of the poems such as 'Bavarian Gentians', and now and then in an essay, Lawrence wrote in his accustomed style, colorful and rich. But as his life span neared its end (and it is remarkable that he lived through another four and a quarter years) his work thinned out—not necessarily in interest of content; but it was different, at least in quality. The element that became dominant was one that had appeared only now and then in the earlier writings, an acid intellectual element that didn't always drop smoothly into the abundant flow of those writings. In the later work, that tartness often appeared in an almost pure state, in some of the satiric stories, in the journalistic essays, and in the *Pansies* poems. All these are often merely astringent glosses on the earlier work.

The vividness of the earlier Lawrence came through in one of the first stories he wrote at the Villa Bernarda, 'Sun'. This embodies much of his essential doctrine, dramatized through symbolism, and like many of his stories—such as 'The Ladybird' or novels such as *Lady Chatterley's Lover*—'Sun' is again a variation of the Sleeping Beauty motif of folklore. Here the hedges of thorn that surround the sleeping (sexually unawakened) woman are cacti; the kiss that brings her to life is the kiss of the sun. And the sun, as Elizabeth Goldsmith has pointed out (in *Ancient Pagan Symbols*), is 'the universal metamorphist . . . the Great Lover who rescues imprisoned maidens. . . . The Prince Charming who releases the ice maiden.' Lawrence himself, so long without the sun in that early autumn of northern Europe, from the rains of Derbyshire to the snows of Switzerland, made the sun the 'hero' of his story, and there on the sun-touched Bernarda terrace he transmuted the beneficent warmth into the body of his heroine as she lay ripely naked under the cypress tree with its swaying phallic crest: 'She remembered what the Greeks had said, a white, unsunned body was fishy and unhealthy'.

For the essential setting of the story, Lawrence drew upon his memories of Sicily, but its opening passage is a thematic expansion of the few lines he wrote about the midnight departure of his ship from

New York, in the letter of September 27 to the young Hawks, which has the effect of making 'Sun' a voyage between the third and fourth phases of his writing career and between the eighth and ninth lusters of his life.

At this time, the Lawrence-Murry relationship virtually came to an end. Murry had promised to bring his family for a visit to the Lawrences in Italy, but the doctor said that Mrs. Murry was too ill to travel safely; indeed, after the birth of the child she was then expecting, she fell into her last illness.

On learning that Murry had once again called off a visit, Lawrence sent him 'a furious letter', Murry recalled (Murry didn't save the letter). Lawrence wrote to him only a few times after that, and in January 1926 told him, 'Don't bother any more about Jesus, or mankind, or yourself. . . . Let the *Adelphi* die. . . . I don't want any man for an *adelphos,* and *adelphoi* are sure to drown one another, strangling round each other's necks. Let loose, let loose!'

But Murry didn't let loose yet. When he received Lawrence's *Reflections on the Death of a Porcupine,* he asked if he could reprint the title essay, without payment. On January 19, Lawrence said he would prefer not to have Murry publish him in the magazine. Murry must realize how incompatible the 'say' of each of them was with the other's: 'Say your say, *caro!*—and let me say mine. But, for heaven's sake, don't let us pretend to mix them.' Murry answered that he agreed it was better that they have no further association.

Lawrence apparently didn't reply to this, though in several letters that spring he spoke nastily of Murry to Brett, who was in Capri pining for Lawrence but not daring to go north and approach the Frieda-bristling Villa Bernarda. Murry, Lawrence said, was rich, very rich—this by implication was bad—and was sloppy with self-pity: 'I should have thought, after a dose of that fellow, you'd have too much desire to be different from him, to follow his sloppy self-indulgent melancholics, absolutely despicable.'

It was probably at this time that Lawrence wrote the last of the mean little anti-Murry stories, 'Smile', obviously based on the death of Katherine Mansfield (with Murry and Katherine as Matthew and Ophelia), but evidently set on that Ligurian coast where the story was written. Murry told the author of the present volume, in a letter of July 16, 1953, 'The *truth* about the Lawrence-Murry situation in 1923–1924–1925 is very remote from anything that has appeared, or is likely to appear in my lifetime; though in my considered judgement,

I don't come out of it (i.e. the true story) any better.' Regarding the lampoons, he saïd, 'I see you say, in your letter of October 2, 1952, you were perhaps influenced [in *The Life and Works of D. H. Lawrence*] by Lawrence's satiric stories about me. These, at the time, seemed to me just an outrage. And I still think they sprang from the worst and most *dishonest* part of L. Considering what the real situation had been, they strike me still as a very shabby sort of revenge.' The 'real situation' was, of course, the attitude of Frieda and Murry to one another, and Murry's renunciation, his refusal to have a love affair with her—obviously unknown to Lawrence.

While at Spotorno, Lawrence also wrote, or at least finished, his story 'Glad Ghosts'. He originally intended this for Cynthia Asquith's *The Ghost Book,* which instead carried his tale 'The Rocking-Horse Winner' when it came out in October 1926. Lawrence told his agents he had written 'Glad Ghosts' for Lady Cynthia's collection, 'but am not sure if it's suitable'—perhaps because the character of Carlotta Fell, who began as Dorothy Brett, came to resemble Lady Cynthia herself.

Carlotta as a married woman, and her husband, Lord Lathkill, are later versions of the aristocratic couples in the earlier stories 'The Thimble' and 'The Ladybird'. The identification of the Lathkills as the Asquiths was first publicly made by Lawrence Clark Powell in a bibliographical note in 1937; Richard Aldington commented that if Powell was correct in this, 'the finale of the story was a piece of reckless impudence'. In that finale, plum blossom took the place of the almond blossom of 'The Last Laugh' when the woman-or-ghost came to the Lawrence-like Mark Morier in the guest bedroom at the Lathkills' country house. Plum blossom was appropriate because the Lathkills later had a child: in oriental symbolism, the plum blossom stands for immortality, the perpetuation of life, and it also represents the new year (Lawrence completed the story just as 1925 ended).

At that time he also wrote his short novel *The Virgin and the Gipsy,* which reflected his recent visit to the stony landscapes of Derbyshire. And his present acquaintance with the now-grown Weekley girls— Barbara, it will be recalled, was at nearby Alassio, and Elsa came down from London for a visit—probably suggested the young girls in the story, whose mother had run off with a lover when they were young.

Martin Secker ('quiet little man . . . nice, but not sparkling') was at Spotorno to approve the story, though it was not published until after

Lawrence's death, and then with a note to the effect that it lacked his final revision. The story, with its water symbol as sex-giving and life-giving, with the man rubbing the half-drowned girl back to conscious-ness, evokes the earlier tale 'The Horse Dealer's Daughter'; and it was another variation on the Sleeping Beauty motif, with the 'dark' gipsy as the awakener. It looked to the future, too, in that it was also a prelude to *Lady Chatterley's Lover*.

Elsa and Barbara Weekley came to Spotorno during the time when Ada Lawrence Clarke and her Eastwood friend Mrs. Booth were also visiting at Villa Bernarda. They had arrived to find Lawrence ill with influenza.

Frieda believed that Ada was trying to draw him back into the past. One night Ada persuaded him to lock his door against Frieda, which she later said was the only act of Lawrence's that ever hurt her deeply. One morning Ada told her, 'I hate you from the bottom of my heart.' Lawrence was glad to get out of this divided camp of armed females. When he left for a trip to Monte Carlo with Ada, Frieda would give him no kind word.

*

Lawrence went from Monte Carlo to the Brewsters' villa, Quattro Venti, at Capri, just before they left for India. He helped them wrap and stow away the bric-à-brac which later became the central symbol of his rather delicately nasty story about the Brewsters, 'Things'; he sang rounds with them and told them tales of the past which recent talks with his sister had reminded him of, and he imitated his mother reproaching him: 'You used to be such a good boy, Bertie.'

There at Quattro Venti, reporters interviewed him and photograph-ers snapped pictures of him. He went for walks with the delighted Brett, telling her that he was tired after his influenza and that as soon as he had recovered even partially, he 'crawled away with' Ada to Monte Carlo and was by now 'tired to death of the whole business'. He rested on the sand, called at the villa of Faith Mackenzie, who told him her husband was away on the Channel island he had rented—about which Lawrence soon wrote 'The Man Who Loved Islands'—and he visited the Capri intellectual beachcomber, Charles Ellingham Brooks. But Lawrence was never again to be so vital as he had been, and his temper had become milder, though now and then his tongue could give a flick of sharpness.

He was well enough, when he left Capri in mid-March, to consider

Bertrand Russell, 1916: 'What's the good of sticking in the damned ship and haranguing the merchant-pilgrims in their own language? Why don't you drop overboard? Why don't you clear out of the whole show?'

Revelry at Garsington, about 1916 (Mark Gertler, Aldous Huxley, Dorothy Brett): 'Garsington must be the retreat where we all come together and knit ourselves together. Garsington is wonderful for that. It is like that Boccaccio place where they told all the *Decameron*.'

At Mountain Cottage, Derbyshire, about 1918. Left to right, Ada Lawrence Clarke, William Hopkin, W. Edward Clarke, Frieda, Mrs. Sallie Hopkin, Gertrude Cooper, Dr. Feroze ("a Parsee"), Lawrence: 'We are here in Derbyshire, just near my native place—come home, in these last wretched days—not to die, I hope. Life is very wretched, really, in the outer world. But no doubt the world will sail out again, out of the maelstrom.'

Fontana Vecchia, Taormina: 'We've got a nice big house, with fine rooms and a handy kitchen, set in a big garden, mostly vegetables, green with almond trees, on a steep slope at some distance above the sea.'

Richard Aldington, 1917: 'Richard sent me a line to say he was off to France. I believe he was glad to go. It is harder to bear the pressure of the vacuum over here than the stress of congestion over there.' *Photo: courtesy of Lt. Col. H. F. L. Castle*

Maurice Magnus: 'Spruce and young-ish in his deportment, very pink-faced and very clean, very natty, very alert, like a sparrow painted to resemble a tom-tit.'

Lawrence's map for *Sea and Sardinia:* 'We went to Sardinia—it was an exciting little trip—but one couldn't live there—one would be weary—dreary. I was very disappointed.'

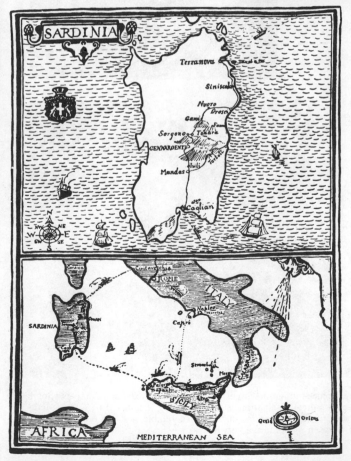

Portrait of Lawrence by Jan Juta, 1920: 'He [Somers-Lawrence in *Kangaroo*] said in his heart, the day his beard was shaven he was beaten, lost. He identified it with his isolate manhood.'

The Lawrences and some immigrant English friends on an excursion in New South Wales, 1922: 'There is a great fascination in Australia . . . If I stayed here six months I should have to stay forever—there is something so remote and far off and utterly indifferent to our European world, in the very air.'

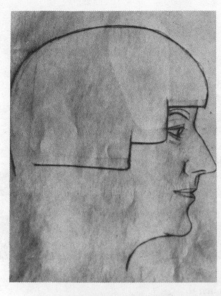

Mabel Dodge Luhan (drawing attributed to Witter Bynner): '. . . very "generous," wants to be "good" and is very wicked, has a terrible will-to-power, you know—she wants to be a witch and at the same time a Mary of Bethany at Jesus's feet—a big, white crow, a cooing raven of ill-omen.'

D.H.L., November 4, 1924: 'A man, Edward Weston, just took a good picture of me in Mexico City.'

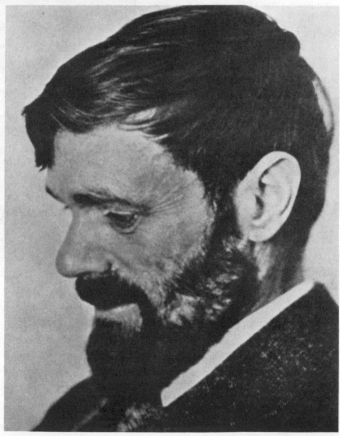

Villa Bernarda, Spotorno, Italy, November 1925–April 1926: 'The village is not much to brag about—but the hills are fine and wild and the villa is above the houses and has a big vineyard garden.'

Lawrence in 1923: 'Pan keeps on being re-born, in all kinds of strange shapes . . . The Pan relationship, which the world of man once had with all the world, was better than anything man has now.' *Photo: courtesy of Professor Majl Ewing*

Kiowa Ranch in the Sangro de Cristo range: '. . . the two cabins inside the rickety fence, the rather broken corral beyond, and behind all, tall, blue balsam pines, the round hills, the solid up-rise of the mountain flank.'

Lawrence and Frieda in Mexico City, March 1925: 'We both got malaria so badly in Oaxaca, we can hardly crawl . . . Frieda . . . now hates Mexico: and I no longer like it.'

Mrs. C. R. G. Conway, Lawrence, and Frieda, Mexico City, March 1925: 'Really Mexico City is not so bad, you know: when one finds one's own countrymen still sterling.'

Angelo Ravagli, owner of Villa Bernarda: 'The *tenente* still writes occasionally from Porto Maurizio, where he is transferred; rather lachrymose and forlorn.'

A map drawn by Lawrence showing how to get from Vingone (southwest of Florence) to his most famous residence, the Villa Mirenda, where he wrote *Lady Chatterley's Lover*. As Lawrence directed a friend to Villa Mirenda, in a letter which accompanied this map: 'Tram No. 16 from the Cathedral to Vingone—go to the very terminus [1]. From there, walk ahead about ¾ mile, keeping on the high road, but the left branch at the pagoda [2]; then on to where two cypresses stand [3], touching one another at the corner of the lane to the left. Turn there, and dip down into the valley. The Mirenda [4] is a big square box of a house on the hill in front of you, with the little church of San Paolo [5] behind.' The photo inserts show that these landmarks have not changed in more than forty years, though buses have now replaced the tram cars.

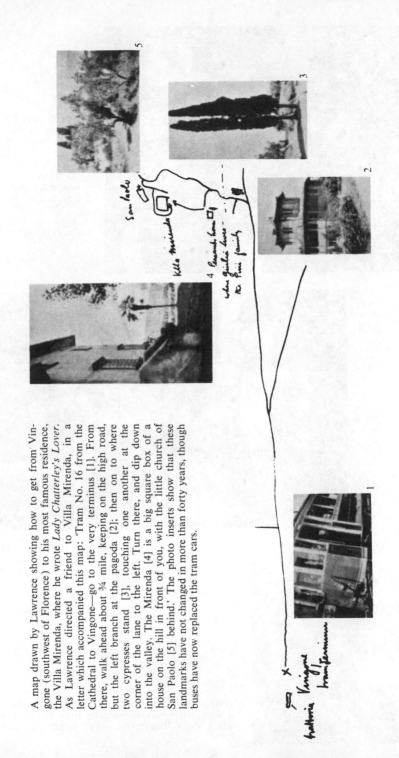

Harwood Brewster, wearing a hairband given by 'Uncle David,' with Achsah and Earl Brewster in Capri: 'I would like you and Achsah Brewster and the child to settle somewhere near. I would rather dig a little, and tend a few fruit-trees with you, than meditate with you. I would rather we did a bit of quiet manual work together—and spent our days in our own solitude and labour.' *Photo: courtesy of Mrs. Harwood Picard*

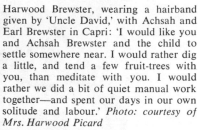

Letter from Lawrence to Robert Atkins, long associated with the Old Vic as actor and director, who was staging Lawrence's play *David* in London: '. . . If only one can get that feeling of primitive religious passion across to a London audience . . .'

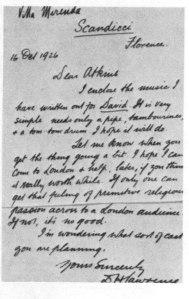

Villa Mirenda, c. 1927. Oil painting by Lawrence: 'To me, a picture has delight in it, or it isn't a picture. The saddest pictures of Piero della Francesca, or Sodoma or Goya, have still that indescribable delight that goes with the real picture . . . No artist, even the gloomiest, ever painted a picture without the curious delight in image-making.' *Collection: Humanities Research Center, University of Texas*

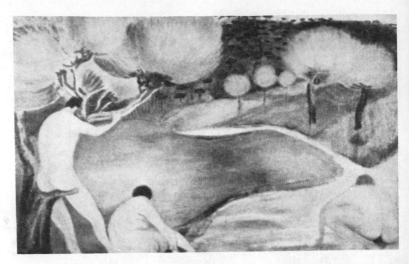

Red Willow Trees. Oil painting by Lawrence (inscribed Lorenzo), 1927: 'I've been quite happy painting my pictures, and doing my novel [*Lady Chatterley's Lover*] . . . and "Red Willow Trees" is nearly done.' *Collection: Saki Karavas*

North Sea. Oil painting by Lawrence, 1928, once in collection of Aldous Huxley, probably destroyed in the fire which devastated Huxley's California home: 'I think I get a certain phallic beauty in my pictures . . . I know they're rolling with faults, Sladeily considered. But there's something *there*.'

The Lawrences with Giuseppe
Orioli, Florence, about 1926·
'Why are you so silly? Why do
you think you want to razzle
and drink like [Norman] Douglas? . . . You'll merely kill yourself if you try to live up to
Douglas's festive standards.
You're not made that way.'

Norman Douglas and Giuseppe
Orioli on a walking tour, 1932:
'Douglas tall and portly . . .
[Orioli] the broad and thick-set
Italian in whom I can trust.'

Lawrence with his sister Mrs. Emily King, Gsteig bei Gstaad, Switzerland, 1928: 'Though I am glad to see them [family], it worries and depresses me rather. I am not "our Bert." Come to that, I never was. And the gulf between their outlook and mine is always yawning, horribly obvious to me.'

Lawrence and Frieda at Le Moulin du Soleil, near Paris, 1929: 'I shall [in coming to Paris] bloom out in my new grey suit and even a pair of Toulon gloves, most fetching—and let's hope the weather will be decent and my cough in *abeyance*—and I do hope those daffodils will come out and we can go and see them.'

From a self-portrait, 1929: 'I like . . . the big head in red chalk, done by myself—I think it is *basically* like me.'

Painting by Collingwood Gee of Lawrence reading *Lady Chatterley's Lover* to Reginald Turner, Norman Douglas, and Giuseppe Orioli: 'Ours is essentially a tragic age, so we refuse to take it tragically . . .'

Villa Beau Soleil, Bandol, where Lawrence spent the winter of 1929–30: 'It is on the sea—rather lovely—a smallish bungalow, six rooms, terrace—bath, central-heating—some neglected garden . . . It is ordinary, but poky—and wonderfully in the air and light.'

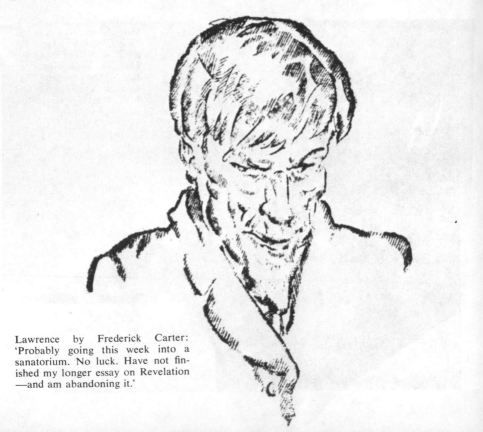

Lawrence by Frederick Carter: 'Probably going this week into a sanatorium. No luck. Have not finished my longer essay on Revelation —and am abandoning it.'

Ad Astra sanatorium, Vence, to which Lawrence went in February 1930: '. . . I have a balcony and see the coast-line and Cannes five miles off.'

Lawrence's grave (1930–5) at Vence, France, before his remains were cremated and taken to New Mexico: 'The phoenix renews her youth / only when she is burnt, burnt alive, burnt down / to hot and flocculent ash.'

Mabel Dodge Luhan, Frieda Lawrence, and the Hon. Dorothy Brett, New Mexico, early 1930s: 'You who were wives / and mothers / And always virgins / Overlooked.'

Lawrence's tomb above Kiowa ranch, Frieda's grave in foreground: 'A fine wind is blowing the new direction of Time . . .'

a tour of the Etruscan cities with his old friend Millicent Beveridge, who had painted his portrait at Taormina five years before. He crossed to the mainland to meet her and her friend Mabel Harrison at Amalfi, the faithful Brett tagging along. On Capri, she had found the fading Mary Cannan boring and had tried to edge her out of the Lawrence circle; but over on the mainland Lawrence showed that he now wearied of Brett herself.

In her record of the time, she has made it supremely clear that at the hotel cottage at Ravello each of them not only had a separate room but went to it, Lawrence turning towards his quarters 'with a cheery good night', and Brett fumbling with matches and a candle to find her own 'hard, relentless bed'. When Brett was notified that her quota papers for readmission to the United States were at the British Consulate at Naples, she tried to postpone going for them, but Lawrence ruthlessly commanded her to leave. As her little boat pulled away towards Naples, she saw him on the shore waving the blue-and-green silk scarf she had given him; and this was the last time she ever saw him.

Meanwhile, Frieda was happy with her daughters amid the fig trees and almond blooms and other emotion-ravaging Italian-spring luxuriances at Spotorno. Mabel Luhan had found an excuse to write to Lawrence again—would he advise her about the publication of her memoirs?—and during his absence from the Villa Bernarda her manuscript peremptorily arrived there. Frieda told her, 'I hope Lawrence is taking a new lease of [*sic*] life, that *Plumed Serpent* took it out of him, it almost went too far.' She confidently added, 'Lawrence will soon be back, so I keep the manuscript here.'

Frieda was not amused at a picture Lawrence sent her of Jonah confronting the whale with the question 'Who is going to swallow whom?' But in those days his whale's belly was the Etruscan tombs, as he went from Rome to Assisi, which he disliked, to Perugia, Pisa, and Florence, then to Ravenna, where he was ill and had to stay in bed a day or so.

There Peter Quennell saw him, as he has told the author of the present book; Quennell regretted that he had never known Lawrence, but provided a bright glimpse of him at Ravenna: 'He was with two solid-looking, middle-aged Englishwomen; and I did my best to overhear his conversation at the hotel dinner-table.' But all Quennell could remember of that occasion was a criticism of the local mosaics: Lawrence disliked 'the figures that have both eyes on one side of the

head—"like a flat fish" ' '. Peter Quennell was otherwise 'impressed
by the rather provincial twang of [Lawrence's] voice—the odd loofah-
ish consistency of his beard—and a look of fragility and a kind of tearing schoolboyish slyness in his attitude towards his two large and
motherly companions.'

Lawrence arrived back at Spotorno, from Milan, on the day before
Easter. Frieda had remained angry, but when his return was imminent,
her daughters said, 'Now, Mrs. L., be reasonable, you have married
him, you must stick to him.' So, 'dressed up festively', as he told his
mother-in-law, 'the three women' met his train. 'For the moment I am
the Easter lamb.'

*

On April 20 the three women accompanied him to Florence. The two
girls returned to London, and the Lawrences located a *villino* in the
country southwest of Florence, at San Polo (or San Paolo) Mosciano,
Scandicci. This was the Villa Mirenda, which became the Lawrences'
home, intermittently, for two years. It is Lawrence's most famous
residence, the place where he wrote *Lady Chatterley's Lover.*

They moved in on May 6, and a week later Lawrence sent his story
'Two Blue Birds' to his agents in London, prophetically saying that it
would probably be 'another tribulation' to them; indeed, this little satire on a successful author and his relations with his wife and his girl
secretary didn't please the Compton Mackenzies any more than 'The
Man Who Loved Islands' pleased them.

Lawrence spoke of the Mirenda in a letter to Catherine Carswell on
the eighteenth: 'We've taken the top half of this old villa, seven miles
out of Florence, for a year: only £25 a year.' He thought they 'could
keep it as a pied-à-terre, and perhaps come and go, and lend it when
we are away. The country is awfully nice round about, and no other
forestieri except one family, the Gair-Wilkinsons, Gloster Village-
arty who used to have a puppet show: they are quite nice. He's the
King of all the "beavers", with *his* red beard.'

The Mirenda was in 'the opposite direction from Fiesole', and was
'a sort of farm villa, really, and the *padroni,* quite nice people, only
come out—a man of 35 and his wife, he *capitano de Cavalleria,* but
working in the *office,* most uncavalry-like man you ever saw—
just for the week-end, or one odd day, to see the peasants. But of
course the house, though rather big, is bare and comfortless.' It was
not easy to reach, as a letter of April 25, 1928, to Enid Hilton shows:

'. . . Tram No. 16 from the Cathedral to Vingone—go to the very terminus.' From there, 'walk ahead about ¾ mile, keeping on the highroad, but the left branch at the pagoda,' on to where two cypresses stood 'touching one another at the corner of the land to the left. Turn there, and dip down into the valley. The Mirenda is the big square box of a house on the hill in front of you, with the little church of San Paolo behind. If we are away . . . go to the peasants' house and ask for Giulia, our girl—she'll have the key.' (A bus has replaced the Florence-to-Vingone tram.)

That first spring at the Mirenda, Lawrence did little writing. Early in the year, Secker had brought out *The Plumed Serpent,* and Lawrence's new American publisher, Alfred A. Knopf, issued it in New York. The reviews were as usual: the *Times Literary Supplement* pronounced the book 'rather feeble'; P. C. Kennedy in the *New Statesman* found that Lawrence had 'arrived at a negation, a barrenness, an abstraction, a repetitiveness, an emptiness'; Katherine Anne Porter in the New York *Herald Tribune* admired the vivid pictures of Mexico, but found that a 'catastrophe . . . has overtaken Lawrence'; L. P. Hartley in the London *Saturday Review* said Lawrence was 'no longer interested in the ordinary workaday relations between people'; the *Spectator* felt that in this 'bewilderingly romantic, lush, and verbose' story, Lawrence was unable 'to create characters; his heroes and heroines are phantoms projected out of his own fancy which is sterile'.

The passing of time has shown that, even if *The Plumed Serpent* is a failure among Lawrence's books, it is a magnificent failure, actually a triumph of grand fragments, a greater achievement than the smoother work of the lesser authors celebrated at that time. Its first six chapters are almost incomparably wonderful prose; but after these, the silliness sets in, though the matchless descriptions continue. Again it is helpful to recall T. S. Eliot's statement, in his essay on Dante, to the effect that a reader doesn't have to agree with the beliefs of a poet in order to appreciate what he has written.

Not all the first reviewers were hostile: Edwin Muir, despite a recent public scolding from Lawrence, discussed the good as well as the bad points of the book in the *Nation and Athenaeum.* Murry's anonymous review in his *Adelphi*—ending, 'Need we say the book contains lovely and memorable things?'—spent too much time lamenting, 'alas, now that the miracle is here, we cannot grasp it, either with our minds or solar plexuses, or our tails'.

In spite of its bad press, however, *The Plumed Serpent* sold fairly well. Knopf soon reprinted it, and during Lawrence's lifetime, Secker reissued it in 1926, 1927, and 1928, as well as in the year of Lawrence's death, 1930. Both Knopf and Heinemann have kept it in print, and Penguin Books has also published it. But back in that spring of 1926, Lawrence felt little encouragement and did little writing. His letters of the time picture him on the Mirenda terrace on lazy days of sunlight, all about him the grainfields and the slopes covered with the silvering olive trees and the green vines.

The mood lasted into summer. On July 18, five days after arriving at Baden-Baden, Lawrence wrote to Catherine Carswell: 'As for literature and publishing, I loathe the thought of it all, and wish I could afford never to appear in print again. Anyhow, I am doing nothing at all now, and have no idea of beginning again.' He also told her, 'I rather dread the thought of England,' though within two weeks he was there, for his last visit.

In London, he and Frieda stayed at the Rossetti Garden Mansions, Chelsea, a high, old, chocolate-colored building. There, Frieda's son and her husband became friends for the first time. 'Monty and Lawrence met on the stairs,' Frieda told Mrs. Luhan, 'and were all "loving kindness" to each other "all of a heap!" ' Montague Weekley, now twenty-five, who had not seen Lawrence since childhood, immediately noticed his broad Midlands accent: 'Sargent, sooch a bahd peÿnter'.

Frieda reported to Mrs. Luhan a visit to Richard Aldington and 'Arabella' Yorke: 'Arabella comes in *Aaron's Rod*. She is so like a mixture of Trinidad and Rufina, so black-haired and Richard is so fair and blue eyed and Germanic!' Aldington, who had invited the Lawrences to his Malthouse Cottage at Padworth, Berkshire, recalled in his autobiography that 'the visit began a little inauspiciously, as Lawrence declared that the cottage was sinister'.

But they all had some pleasant times, at night singing French and German songs, and in the afternoons wandering across the fields. When Lawrence told Aldington that he planned to write a book on the Etruscans, his friend arranged for the London Library to send out half a dozen volumes on the subject. He promised that he and Dorothy Yorke would go to the Mirenda for the autumn wine-harvest.

After a visit to Scotland and the Isle of Skye ('like the very beginning of Europe: though, of course, in August there are many tourists and motorcars'), Lawrence went with his sisters to the Lincolnshire coast. From Sutton-on-Sea he wrote on August 29 to the bookseller

Giuseppe (Pino) Orioli, whom he had met in Cornwall and with whom he had renewed acquaintance in Florence: 'We are here by the seaside, in my native Midlands. It is rather nice, a big flat coast with a big sky above, and a low sea rumbling. I like it much better than London.' Thirteen days later, September 11, his forty-first birthday, he again wrote to Orioli, mentioning another renewal of acquaintance that was to prove important: 'Aldous Huxley came to see me in London—he has gone off to Cortina, in the Dolomites, to take a house there. He seemed no brisker than ever.'

Renewing his acquaintance with the colliery region after leaving Sutton-on-Sea was for Lawrence a depressing experience, for although the General Strike was for the most part over, the miners were still out: 'I was at my sister's in September,' Lawrence afterwards told Rolf Gardiner, 'and we drove around—I saw the miners—and pickets —and policemen—it was like a spear through one's heart.' His last visit to Eastwood was described in a letter to the present author (October 16, 1949) from William Hopkin: 'He and I went over the old ground. When we reached Felley Dam he stood looking over at the Haggs. I sat down by the pool and when I turned to look at him he had a terrible look of pain on his face. When we got back I asked him when he would come again, and he said "Never! I hate the damned place." He never glanced once at the house in the Breach as we passed.'

In London on the way back to the Continent, Lawrence met Amy Lowell's friend Louis Untermeyer, of whom he remarked: 'Extraordinary, the *ewige* Jew, by virtue of not having a real core in him, he is eternal. . . . That is the whole history of the Jew, from Moses to Untermeyer.' Years later, in his autobiography, Untermeyer said in an amusing reply that Lawrence was the real Wandering Jew.

There in London in 1926, Mrs. Carswell boasted that her little boy had become a good traveler: Lawrence shook his head and told her, 'Nay, Catherine, but I want to hear of good stayers at home!' Mrs. Carswell, who was seeing Lawrence for the last time, worried over him when she learned he had been having bronchial hemorrhages, but he assured her they were not serious: 'Not lungs, you know, only bronchials—tiresome enough, but nothing to worry about, except I *must* try not to catch colds.'

At a farewell party the Carswells gave for the Lawrences, they all discussed money, and Koteliansky declared that unearned income of any size alienated its beneficiary from the rest of mankind. Lawrence

THE LAST YEARS

said that riches had 'a really magical touch to make a man insensitive and so to make him wicked'—a kind of restatement of the theme of 'The Rocking-Horse Winner', the story which Cynthia Asquith published later that year in her collection *The Ghost Book*. That tale again indicates Lawrence's modernness of method, for the ritualistic aspects of 'The Rocking-Horse Winner' show once more that he was among the first authors of his time who drew upon anthropology. Although parts of the story reflect his memories of his 'sporting' Uncle Herbert, Lawrence also—as Frank Amon was the first to suggest—probably borrowed from memories of the hobby dances at Padstow, Cornwall, and the New Mexican pueblo ceremonies called *maiyanyi*. 'The Rocking-Horse Winner' was one of Lawrence's few productions in a barren period, which threatened to continue after his return to Italy in early October. From there on October 18 he told Else Jaffe, 'I think I'll never write another novel'. Yet only eleven days later he had written forty-one pages of one of the major efforts of his career—*Lady Chatterley's Lover*.

2 THE ROAD TO LADY CHATTERLEY

What made Lawrence, after so many protests that he never wanted to produce another novel, suddenly begin *Lady Chatterley's Lover* a few weeks after his return to the Villa Mirenda in that autumn of 1926? Richard Aldington, who kept his promise to visit the Mirenda during the grape harvest, in early October, didn't recall that Lawrence mentioned the projected novel to him at the time, but across the years he guessed that Lawrence's inspiration for the book was his visit to the Midlands in the preceding year—that is, in the summer of 1925, when the Clarkes took him motoring through Derby and Notts.

This is only a conjecture: Lawrence had also visited that country again in 1926. But it is certainly true that, when writing once more of the modern world's mechanization of humanity, Lawrence again had in his mind one of his enduring symbols, the industrial Midlands. Discussing the origin of the book in a letter to David Garnett in 1928, Lawrence told him, 'In my early days your father said to me, "I should welcome a description of the whole act"—which has stayed in my mind till I wrote this book.' But why look for a single 'inspiration' for such a novel? Lawrence, a man who thought in terms of fable and symbol, a man disgusted with the mechanisms of civilization, produced out of his consciousness a story of a certain kind.

As he said in his essay *À Propos of Lady Chatterley's Lover,* 'When I created Clifford and Connie, I had no idea what they were, or why they were. They just came, pretty much as they are.'

Lawrence sometimes wrote in the Villa Mirenda's tower, which looked out on orchards and olive trees towards the distant scrawl of Florence, and sometimes on the sunny terrace of the villa, but most often behind the small church of San Polo, where, on days when the weather was gentle, he sat in a little wood of umbrella pines as he created his story of the lady of an English manor house who fell in love with her husband's gamekeeper.

As the red-bearded, pale man scratched away at his manuscript, life flourished around him. The steep little hills were rich with southern flowers (which he was to write of in the essay 'Springtime in Flowery Tuscany'), and nightingales sang in the trees, 'a most intensely and most indubitably male sound'. Hunters fired away in the woods, and occasionally Lawrence saw one of them pass by 'in velvet corduroys, bandolier, cartridges, game-bag over his shoulder, and gun in his hand'—arrayed very much like the gamekeeper who became Lady Chatterley's lover.

Lawrence once said that he had rewritten the story, 'from start to finish, three times'. He worked at the book intermittently from October 1926 to January 1928. Some readers, including Frieda, have preferred *The First Lady Chatterley* (published in 1944 despite the efforts of some busybodies in New York to suppress it). The second draft came out at last in 1972, in English (it had been published years earlier in Italian), as *John Thomas and Lady Jane,* an amusingly licentious little folklore title which Lawrence had once considered.

When he finished the third version, Lawrence was at first reluctant to publish it—Frieda has told how he realized that it would unleash more hatred against him—but once he decided to put the book into print, he fought for it zealously. His London and New York agents and publishers irritated him by their lack of enthusiasm; what he finally did he explained in a letter to G. R. G. Conway from the Mirenda on March 15, 1928—a letter which also contains a statement of intention:

> Now I'm busy here printing my new novel for a private edition here in Florence. You've been through it, so you'll sympathize with me.—I expect the publishers will publish an expurgated edition in the autumn. But I *must* bring out the book complete.

It is—in the latter half at least—a phallic novel, but tender and delicate. You know I believe in the phallic reality, and the phallic consciousness: as distinct from our irritable cerebral consciousness of today. That's why I do the book—and it's not just *sex*. Sex alas is one of the worst phenomena of today: all cerebral re-action, the whole thing worked from mental processes and itch, and not a bit of the real phallic insouciance and spontaneity. But in my novel there is.

This explanation is typical of many that Lawrence made during those last years of his life, in letters and in essays such as *Pornography and Obscenity*. As for the expurgated edition he spoke of in the letter to Conway, Lawrence later said that he couldn't cut the vital passages out of the book: 'I might as well try to clip my own nose into shape with scissors. The book bleeds.'

Two years after his death, however, his English and American publishers brought out a bowdlerized version, and didn't undertake the battle for the real *Lady Chatterley's Lover,* the battle which was soon to be fought on behalf of *Ulysses,* which to Lawrence's puritan mind was a 'dirty' book, a mechanization of sex. But at last, in 1959, Grove Press published an unexpurgated edition of *Lady Chatterley* in New York which was soon banned in the mails by that distinguished literary critic, Postmaster General Arthur Summerfield. Soon afterwards, however, an enlightened legal opinion by Judge Frederick van Pelt Bryan declared the ban illegal. In 1960 Penguin Books published *Lady Chatterley,* unexpurgated, in England. When the case was brought to court, the publishers were victorious.

Lady Chatterley's Lover has, despite controversy and purely on its own merits, become one of the notable books of this century. Lawrence's most startling variation of the Sleeping Beauty theme deals with an archetypal modern woman whose husband practices two professions Lawrence despised: industrialism and intellectualism. Regrettably for the story, Sir Clifford Chatterley is also a cripple, paralyzed and impotent from a war injury. Lawrence said in *À Propos of Lady Chatterley's Lover* that he couldn't tell 'whether the "symbolism" is intentional. . . . Certainly not in the beginning, when Clifford was created.' Lawrence later recognized that Clifford's lameness 'was symbolic of the paralysis, the deeper emotional or passional paralysis, of most men of his sort and class today. I realised that it was perhaps taking an unfair advantage of Connie, to paralyse him technically. It made it so much more vulgar of her to leave him. Yet the story came as it did, by itself, so I left it alone. Whether we call it symbolism or not, it is, in the sense of its happening, inevitable.'

That it was a war wound which paralyzed Clifford deepens the symbol, yet in itself it is a poor one, for Lawrence's fable. It would have been a stronger story if Lawrence had made Clifford's lack of sex the result of overintellectualization: there was a suggestion of this early in the book, in the character of Michaelis, with whom Connie had a love affair before she met the gamekeeper. Since Lawrence's drive was against the milieu of such people as Michaelis—the milieu into which Clifford drifted—rather than against cripples, he could have kept the opposition in that direction rather than drawing upon physical accident. His healing gamekeeper, another portrait of Lawrence's enduring 'natural' man, descends from Annable in *The White Peacock,* but there is also something in him of the George Saxton of that story, and in a sense *Lady Chatterley's Lover* is a restatement of parts of *The White Peacock,* after twenty years' additional writing practice and experience of suffering.

It is important to note that the author of *Lady Chatterley's Lover* criticized Flaubert and Tolstoy, on several occasions, for sending their heroines—Emma Bovary and Anna Karenina—to death. These women had merely violated a man-made social code: they were not tragic figures broken in a conflict with the forces of nature, like the men and women in the great tragedies. Lawrence set his own heroine on the road towards life. At the end of the novel, Connie and Mellors are apart—Lawrence rarely supplied tidy endings—but the reader knows they will soon be together again.

As for Lawrence's use of the four-letter words: he employed them differently than James Joyce, whom he regarded as a mechanical writer. The deliberateness evident in Joyce's prose prevented Lawrence from recognizing the merit of a contemporary whose greatness was of another kind. Lawrence's intention in writing *Lady Chatterley* was not merely naturalistic ('this is the way life is'), but therapeutic, a burning out of shame. And he was weary of British prudery.

The prose of *Lady Chatterley* is not yet the thinned, satiric writing most characteristic of that last period, but on the other hand it is not the full-bodied prose of the novels from *Sons and Lovers* to *The Plumed Serpent;* it has only occasional echoes of the old resonance. It is a weary prose, only mildly chromatic—most of Lawrence's vibrant colors in those days appeared in his pictures, when he began to paint seriously for the first time in his life, in that same autumn of 1926 in which he started writing *Lady Chatterley*.

*

The Huxleys were, somewhat accidentally, the cause of Lawrence's renewing his interest in painting. They drove to the Mirenda one day in their new car and suggested that Lawrence take their old one, but he dreaded 'learning to drive, and struggling with a machine', and (as noted earlier) he had 'no desire to scud about the face of the country'. Maria Huxley had brought along four old canvases, one of them 'busted', which had been left in their house, and she gave these to Lawrence. They tempted him to fill them with some of the paint he and Frieda had on hand for decorating the doors and window frames of the Mirenda. His first picture, 'A Holy Family', was one of the most troublemaking of all his paintings at the later exhibition, perhaps because, as Lawrence explained to the Huxleys at a time when he called the picture 'Unholy Family', 'the *bambino*—with a *nimbus*—is just watching anxiously to see the young man give the semi-nude young woman *un gros baiser*.' Lawrence didn't feel he was being profane or irreverent; his ideas of the religion of life were merely different from those of his former fellow Congregationalists. And the paintings didn't offend the peasants at the Mirenda, who loved them, though when Lawrence had his exhibit in 1929, he complained of 'people who called themselves my dear friends' who 'were not only shocked but mortally offended by them'.

Trouble over the paintings, however, lay three years in the distance: in the fall of 1926 he felt only enjoyment in the activity of producing them. His *Assorted Articles* essay 'Making Pictures' (1929) spoke of the quality of delight in all paintings, even sad ones: 'No artist, even the gloomiest, ever painted a picture without the curious delight in image-making.'

In December 1926, Lawrence wanted to go to London to see the Stage Society's production of *The Widowing of Mrs Holroyd*, but he didn't feel well enough to leave Italy. Mrs. Carswell, who had seen the 1920 staging of the play at Alichtram, reported that Esmé Percy's later presentation, with a cast which included Colin Keith-Johnston and James Whale, was a better one, but she felt, as she had earlier, that the onstage corpse-washing couldn't be dramatically effective. Lawrence told the Huxleys that people had 'hated' the play, found it 'gloomy'. The *Times* critic liked the first two acts—'I thought I was in the presence of a potentially great dramatist'—then, 'alas! the novelist got Mr Lawrence down in the third act, and the dramatist had to take the count.' As noted earlier, the response was quite different when *Mrs Holroyd* and two other plays by Lawrence were produced at the Royal Court Theatre, London, in 1968. Then the critics hailed him as a major dramatist, and Lawrence was seen in a new perspective. The critics even complained because no one had earlier discovered that his plays were so good.

*

Lawrence as usual kept up his correspondence in the late 1920s. He wrote occasionally to Gertrude Cooper of the Pagans, now staying part of the time with the Clarkes and part of the time in tuberculosis sanatoria. Typically, Lawrence never mentioned tuberculosis by name— Catherine Carswell has pointed out that he resembled the Christian Scientists at least in the way in which he refused to categorize his own affliction—and he told Gertrude Cooper not to 'weaken or fret—while we live we must be game. And when we come to die, we'll die game too.'

In other letters of that winter of 1926–1927, he worried about Brett alone at the ranch, and instructed the young Hawks to look after her, to keep her out of all kinds of troubles, including financial ones. Mabel Luhan couldn't let him go to waste: she wrote asking him to visit her old Florentine villa, the Curonia, and arrange to have her books shipped to America. He wrote saying he would have to wait until the weather was warmer before he could enter the chill tomb of the closed-up place. But he did go there that winter, with Orioli, whose subsequent reward was to have one of Mrs. Luhan's friends call him a thief.

It must have been during this season, too, that Lawrence made peace with Norman Douglas. According to Aldington, one day when Lawrence and Frieda were talking with Orioli in his shop, Douglas strode in. After a moment of tight silence, Douglas, in a gesture that for him was one of friendship, stretched out his snuffbox and said, 'Have a pinch of snuff, dearie.' Lawrence took it, saying, 'Isn't it curious'—*sniff*—'only Norman and my father'—*sniff*—'ever give me snuff?' And, Aldington has reported, the friendship was on again.

*

At this time Lawrence was remembering another acquaintance—never a friend—John Galsworthy. By the end of February 1927, Lawrence had completed his critique of the 'Saga' man for Edgell Rickword's volume of *Scrutinies* (1928). Here Lawrence attacked Galsworthy from the point of view he was himself writing from at the time: most modern men in making love were, he said in *Lady Chatterley,* 'like dogs, that trot and sniff and copulate'; in the study of Galsworthy, who was to Lawrence a denier of life, he said the Forsyte love affairs were 'doggy'; with the characters, it was 'trot, trot away, if you're not tangled. Trot off, looking shamefacedly over your shoulder.' This suggests an interesting connection between Clifford Chatterley's set and Galsworthy's men of property.

Lawrence was ill with influenza during part of that February of 1927. By March 22 he had recovered sufficiently to leave for Ravello, by way of Rome, to visit the Brewsters. Frieda went north to see her mother. Lawrence and Earl Brewster planned a walking tour of the Etruscan cities. The ballet composer Lord Berners had offered to go with them, complete with car and chauffeur and special permits, but Lawrence said, 'I simply *can't* stand people at close quarters. Better tramp it our two selves.'

He pointed out that he and Brewster were now 'at the *âge dangereux* for men: when the whole rhythm of the psyche changes. . . . It is well to know the thing is physiological: though that doesn't nullify the psychological reality.' Too many people resented the sex swindle of modern life, which was not completely the fault of the individual but was to a great extent a product of the age. One had to go through the process of change, without too much exasperation.

'I try,' Lawrence told his Buddhistic friend, 'to keep the *Middle* of me harmonious to the *Middle* of the universe. Outwardly I know I'm in a bad temper, and let it go at that.' But he stuck to his beliefs 'and put a phallus, a lingam you call it, in each one of my pictures somewhere. And I paint no picture that won't shock people's castrated social spirituality.' But this man's motive was never obscenity: 'I do this out of positive belief, that the phallus is a great sacred image: it represents a deep, deep life which has been denied in us, and still is denied. Women deny it horribly, with a grinning travesty of sex. But *pazienza! pazienza!* One can still believe. And with the lingam, and the mystery behind it, goes beauty.'

That was a good preparatory mood for a visit to the Etruscan tombs. He stayed first a few days with the Brewsters at Lord Grimstead's estate above Amalfi; the weather was cold, and Lawrence and the two adult Brewsters and chubby little Harwood huddled around the hearth, where huge logs burned. Lawrence again told them stories of Eastwood and led the family in songs. Laughing and absorbed, he started to paint the Crucifixion, with Pan and some nymphs in the foreground, but he ended by omitting the Crucifixion though keeping the 'pagan' figures.

For about a week in early April, he and Brewster wandered through the settings and the experiences of Lawrence's posthumous volume *Etruscan Places*, the fourth and the last and the most profound of his travel books, whose interpretations have sometimes been praised by archaeologists.

After inspecting the Villa di Papa Giulia, the museum in Rome which contains many important Etruscan relics, the two men went to the Maremma Romana, the swampy coastland to the northwest, where they at last visited the broken cities and their buried tombs.

Brewster, as a man sympathetic to Lawrence, was an ideal companion for this journey: that sympathy was to Lawrence both a stimulus and a check, for he was free to let himself go, imaginatively, about the Etruscan tumuli, and at the same time he was just suspicious enough of Brewster, a confirmed mystic, not to let himself go too far. A skeptic would have been unbearable: the gentle, sometimes agreeing, sometimes disagreeing, New England Brewster was precisely the right fellow voyager. They went to Cerveteri, Civitavecchia, Tarquinia, Vulci, Grosseto, and Volterra, enduring bad hotels, 'spying' *fascisti,* and malaria-eaten coachmen. Day after day the travelers visited the amazing tombs.

There was an ancestral symbolism in the descent of the collier's son into these underground places, led by a guide with a lamp or a candle that cast a glare onto the stuccoed walls which were painted, at Tarquinia, in reds and blacks and yellows that showed dancers and hunters and bulls and lions. Lawrence loved the Etruscans, who were both a 'dark' people and a sun people. They had no false literary culture and lived in the phallic consciousness, knowing 'the everlasting *wonder* of things'. But the Romans, with their money-lust and their worship of great sewers, had ruined the Etruscans, turning them into 'fat and inert Romans'. Before that time, the Etruscans had been the true exemplars of Romanism, and they met destruction at the hands of the later Romans, who were to Lawrence so much like the modern Americans.

Etruscan Places is an incomplete book; Lawrence would have added more chapters if he had lived longer. But the essays he did write, put together in the posthumous volume, show him at his finest as a philosophical writer. He drew upon George Dennis's *Cities and Cemeteries of Etruria,* dating from the 1840s and published in Everyman's Library in 1907, but he also manifested an abundant imagination in his descriptions as he examined the relics of the vanished people in whose instinct he found 'a real desire to preserve the natural humour of life' and who lived 'by delicate sensitiveness'.

Since Lawrence's time, professional scholars have made significant progress in the area of Etruscology, including a breakthrough into an understanding of the Etruscans' language, for so long a mystery. But Lawrence's contribution is a remarkable if strongly individualized achievement, as those who have visited the tombs, particularly the painted ones at Tarquinia, can see. And his book is both informative and stirring to read.

Lawrence's imagination worked energetically on his visits to the ancient burying places: on Palm Sunday when he saw a toy in a shop-window, a little white rooster coming out of an egg, he told Brewster this suggested a title, 'The Escaped Cock—a Story of the Resurrection'. Three weeks later he wrote to Brewster from the Villa Mirenda to announce that he had finished 'a story of the Resurrection, where Jesus gets up and feels very sick about everything, and can't stand the old crowd any more—so cuts out.' Later, 'as he heals up, he begins to find what an astonishing place the phenomenal world is, far more marvellous than any salvation or heaven—and thanks his stars he needn't have a "mission" any more.' Lawrence said he was calling the story 'The Escaped Cock', remembering 'that toy in Volterra'.

The day after seeing that toy, Lawrence took the bus for Florence, a rattling five hours' ride, and reached the Mirenda late at night. Frieda, with a heavy cold brought back from Germany, was well enough the next day to go into Florence and meet her daughter Barbara, who arrived with an English friend, Mrs. Seaman, 'as duenna'. Barbara was planning to marry her son. The Lawrences navigated Mrs. Seaman to the inn at Vingone, but brought Barbara to the Mirenda. She seemed less beautiful this year to Lawrence, who felt that London was deadening her. He of course had managed to catch Frieda's cold, though without serious results.

The Tuscan spring set in, and Lawrence wrote the *Etruscan Places* essays which appeared as magazine articles during his lifetime, he worked on the second draft of *Lady Chatterley's Lover,* and he painted his 'Finding of Moses' with its tall, purple Negresses. But he had plenty of distractions from the outside, including telegrams from Mabel Luhan commanding his return to New Mexico.

From London, the officials of the Stage Society sent word that they would produce his play *David* late in May and invited him to go north and help stage it, but an attack of malaria prevented his journeying to 'antipathetic' London and 'fuddling with theatrical people'. Then the 'impudent' reviews of *David* traveled down from London; Lawrence wrote to Brewster that the critics were eunuchs, and: 'I want subtly, but tremendously, to kick the backsides of the ball-less.'

The greatest distraction from the outside was the arrival of two American women Lawrence had known in New Mexico, a mother and a daughter. He had seen them again in England the preceding year, and at the time of his Etruscan tour had stayed at their flat in Rome; now, in June, he had to show them around Florence, to his horror. They spoke of 'Bo'acelli', Michelangelo's 'David' was a 'nut', every man was 'that guy', every woman 'that skirt'. They had 'the American cataract' over their vision: 'They simply *can't see* anything: you might as well ask a dog to look at a picture or a statue.' Yet 'there's the elements of a nice woman in each of them,' though they were 'stone blind, culturally', and represented 'pure atavism. They've negated and negated and negated till there's *nothing*—and they themselves are empty vessels with a squirming mass of nerves.'

Perhaps recalling Mabel Luhan's imperious summons back to Taos, Lawrence realized, 'I'd rather go and live in a hyena house than go live in America'. These comments, in his letter of June 9, 1927, to Brewster, are among the most acidulous he ever made about Americans. The two women whose visit to Florence occasioned the remarks are long since dead: Christine Hughes and her daughter, Mary Christine, on whom Lawrence was to base a journalistic sketch the following year, 'Laura Philippine' (reprinted in *Assorted Articles*). The girl in this sketch he observed with somewhat affectionate horror as an attractive young nihilist who rose at noon to have gin and bitters before lunch. Lawrence's avuncular warning that she would wear herself out by forty proved to be a melancholy truth: his abhorrence of the gin was more practical than merely puritan.

A few years later, Lawrence mentioned her in a November 1929 letter to Bynner: 'Tell Christine Hughes I will write to her, and Mary Christine I will give a wedding present if she is still married and not minding. I never give wedding presents till two years after. Wait and see, is my English motto, with regard to young marriages.'

In June 1927 the Huxleys took Lawrence up to Forte dei Marmi, on that Ligurian coast he knew so well, near Spezia. He disliked Forte dei Marmi—'beastly as a place; flat, dead sea, jellyfishy, and millions of villas'—and after the Huxleys drove him back to Florence he had a violent hemorrhage that laid him low for weeks, with Frieda and the peasant women nursing him. When he was at last well enough to travel, he wrote to Mark Gertler on July 31:

> I am up and creeping around—feeling limp—but better. I had the best doctor in Florence—Prof. Giglioli—head of the Medical Profession for Tuscany. It's chronic bronchial congestion—and it brought on a series of bronchial hemorrhages this time. I've had little ones before. It would be serious if they didn't stop, he says: but they do stop: so it's nothing to worry about—only one must lie in bed when they come on—and always be a bit careful—not take sea-baths, as I did at Forte. I think he's about right. He says now we're to go to the mountains so we're leaving for Austria—D.V.—Thursday night. I can get into a sleeper in Florence, and stay in till Villach, so I should be all right. I'll send the addresses there, as I'm not sure. These hemorrhages are rather shattering—but perhaps they take some bad blood out of the system. The doctor says no good going to a sanatorium, if I will only lie down when I don't feel well—and not work. Which I shall really try to do.—I don't really feel bad.
> So tell Kot to get a doctor himself, and not bother about me.
> We saw J. W. N. Sullivan—he came with the Huxleys—and he was nice, but sad—I thought he would be rather bouncing—not a bit. He's coming back to England directly.

Writing to Else Jaffe a few days earlier, Lawrence had said he knew his illnesses came 'from chagrin—chagrin that goes deep in and comes out afterward in *haemorrhage* or what not,' an idea he repeated in a letter of August 3 (the day before he left for Austria) to a new American correspondent, the psychologist Dr. Trigant Burrow. Not long before, Lawrence had told Burrow, 'What ails me is the absolute frustration of my primeval societal instinct,' which he thought was 'much deeper than sex instinct—and societal repression much more devastating'.

In a letter from Austria a week later, to Dorothy Yorke, Lawrence mentioned Frieda's sister Nusch, who was now Frau Krug:

> We usually get out of the heat earlier, but this year I was in bed with bronchials and bronchial *haemorrhage* all July, and felt a poor specimen. Also it was terribly hot—no rain for three

months. But I crawled into a *wagon-lit* and we got here Friday. It is cool, among the mountains, and I feel a good deal better. But I am afflicted with these bronchials of mine.

Frieda's junger sister is here with her husband, staying on the Ossiachersee about six miles away. F. has just gone there swimming—it's her birthday—I shall go out to lunch. I can't swim, or bathe—or even walk very far. Makes me so cross. But it is pleasant here, in this big *Gasthaus* in the little town—all the Tyroler mountain people going through—and the food is really good. Also, I like Villach—little old German place—and the nice full river—the Drav—that goes so quick and silent.

I think we shall stay till the 24th [August]—then move north —we're supposed to spend September in Bavaria.

Near the end of the month the Lawrences visited Frieda's other sister at Irschenhausen again ('just the same, the little wooden house in the corner of the forest, so still and pleasant'), where Lawrence walked through the pinewoods, played patience, and occasionally turned to his translation of Verga's *Cavalleria Rusticana:* 'I am glad when I don't work—I have worked too much.'

As usual, there were frequent visitors, this time including Max Mohr, a man in his middle thirties who was both a doctor and a dramatist and, as a former prisoner of war in England, fluent in English. Lawrence's first impression was that Mohr, although 'good and interesting', was a last man who had come to the last end of the road and could therefore no longer plunge ahead into the unknown. Yet as time passed, Lawrence came to value Mohr highly, perhaps because he eventually saw that his first judgment was wrong.

Mohr was indeed a man not afraid to step into the unknown: several years after Lawrence's death, Mohr, though not a Jew, left Nazi Germany to begin a new career in Shanghai, only to die there a few years later of one of the diseases he was helping to combat. He had written a magnificent letter to Thomas Mann, in which he said, 'When I arrived here last year with ten dollars in my pocket, I possessed my instruments, my medical training, a few photos of the family I had left behind in Germany, the letters of D. H. Lawrence, and the glorious feeling that I have finished with Germany.'

It is complimentary to Mohr's memory that he was one of the few doctors Lawrence would permit to look him over. Another was, once again, a literary man, whom he met in that same season: Hans Carossa, the Bavarian poet who was a tuberculosis expert. He came to Irschenhausen with Franz Schoenberner, editor of the magazines *Jugend* and *Simplicissimus*.

Schoenberner, in his *Confessions of a European Intellectual* (1946), presented a lively account of Carossa's visit and of his own friendship with Lawrence. Schoenberner, subsequently another non-Jewish voluntary exile from the Nazi state—to his disgust, Carossa remained behind—has expressed his belief that Lawrence's books should become school texts. This is interestingly different from the views of those who have seen Lawrence as a fascist, but Schoenberner was able to distinguish between an antirational outlook and a belief in fascism. As one of Germany's leading editors, Schoenberner had a close view of the entire development of fascism in Germany, and an intimate involvement with the Nazis' penetration and final dominance of the German press; he had also a close acquaintance with Lawrence and his writings, and his testimony in the matter is therefore that of an expert.

When Schoenberner asked Lawrence if he might bring Carossa to examine him, Lawrence said that if a poet who was also a doctor couldn't cure him, who could? Large-faced, soft-eyed Carossa, whom Lawrence found 'mild like mashed potatoes', appeared at Else Jaffe's and 'listened to my lung passages, he could not hear my lungs, thinks they must be healed, only the bronchi, and doctors are not interested in bronchi. But he says not to take more inhalations with hot air: it might bring the haemorrhage back.' Lawrence wrote this to Else Jaffe on October 7 from Baden-Baden, where he and Frieda had arrived three days before.

How seriously he took Carossa's advice may be seen in his report of October 12 to Orioli: 'I'm doing an inhalation cure—sit in a white mantle and hood in a cloud of vapour, with other ghostly figures, for an hour every morning! But it does my bronchials good.'

After Carossa examined Lawrence at the Jaffes', and he and Schoenberner had walked through the woods and fields to the little station at Icking, Schoenberner asked his doctor friend what he thought of Lawrence's health. Carossa said Lawrence's lungs would have long before killed an average man; but with an artist, other forces than the purely physical were involved, making normal prognosis impossible. He gave Lawrence two or three years more of life: 'No medical treatment can really save him.' This was, as Schoenberner has noted, 'cruelly right'.

A week before leaving Irschenhausen, Lawrence told Orioli, 'I've liked it here very much, the stillness and loneliness, but now it's getting a bit wintry and damp. Sometimes it pours with rain, and then we feel like two lonely pale fishes at the bottom of a dark sea.' Frieda was pining for Italy, 'but I, for some reason, rather like it: it makes me sleep a lot, and I think that's about the best thing one can do in this world.' But by October 14 he could write to Orioli from Baden-Baden, 'It begins to be foggy and wintry here, though not very cold— only the wintry darkness. We shall both be glad to be back at the Mirenda awhile, to pick up the real sunshine again.' He wanted to return in order to paint a picture he had in mind, perhaps the one he mentioned to Brewster in a letter of October 21, the day after he arrived back at the Mirenda: 'I might begin a painting of Adam and Eve pelting the old Lord-God with apples and driving him out of paradise' —another blow at the violent Old Testament Jehovah. This idea later materialized into the water color 'Throwing Back the Apple'.

But, as soon as he had returned to the Mirenda, Lawrence was restless again, and abruptly wrote to his old friends of years before, the Campbells (Gordon Campbell had become Lord Glenavy and now lived on the outskirts of Dublin):

> Here's a voice from the past! But Kot. said Beatrice was in London: and somehow I've been thinking about Ireland lately (does Gordon still say 'Ahrland', with gallons of tears in his voice?).
>
> We've just got back here from Germany—and I've a suspicion that I'm really rather bored by Italy and the Italians; and I have an idea that next year I should like to try the Wild Irish. Should I, do you think? Do you think F. and I would like to spend a year in Ireland—rent a little furnished house somewhere romantic, roaring billows and brown bogs sort of thing? Do you think we should? And is it feasible, practical, and all that? Somewhere where the rain leaves off occasionally. Of course Ireland is to my mind something like the bottom of an aquarium, with little people in crannies like prawns. But I've got a sort of hunch about it, that it might mean something to me, more than this Tuscany.

The Campbells' reply was, Lawrence thought, 'cautious but encouraging'. Campbell had become a man of prominence, a government official and a bank director, and the Lawrences' proposal of descending on him was probably as terrifying as a similar suggestion to visit Russia was to the Litvinovs. But before Lawrence could make further plans for Ireland, he found something in Florence to detain him: the project of publishing *Lady Chatterley* there. He went into town on November 17 for the first time since his return to the Mirenda, and in Florence met a one-time potential disciple, who had become Michael Arlen of Mayfair ('He too has been sick, and was looking diminished, in spite of all the money he has made: quite a sad dog, trying to be rakish'), whom he invited out to the Mirenda. But a few days later he wrote to Orioli, asking him to have his boy, Carlo Zanotti, warn Arlen not to come out—and at the same time opening negotiations for publication of *Lady Chatterley's Lover:*

> Would you mind sending Carletto over to Michael Arlen with this note—I don't know his address—Borgo San Giorgio—and please ask Carletto to wait for an answer. He—Michael Arlen—was coming out on Wednesday—But Frieda's got a cold, in bed today, and Michael A. is terrified of getting a cold. So I must warn him. The Wilkinsons are staying the night in Florence, will bring out the note tomorrow.
>
> I am seriously thinking of publishing my novel in Florence: have already written my agent about it: but you'd have to help me.
>
> Would you? I'll come and talk about it soon.
>
> Did Arlen come in and see you? I believe he's lonely—and so sad.

Orioli was lured into becoming Lawrence's publisher—not quite a publisher, however, but a kind of superior clerk for the project. In his *Adventures of a Bookseller,* seven years after Lawrence's death, Orioli seemed to gush forth resentment at having been Lawrence's errand boy and quasi-publisher, with frequent trips out to the Mirenda: which, despite 'golden moments' with Lawrence, meant the loss of half a day for Orioli each time he went there. And Lawrence, who had driven a shrewd peasant's bargain with Orioli, took ninety per cent of the book's profits. (Aldington said in his book on Douglas and Orioli —*Pinorman* [1954]—that these statements don't reflect Orioli's true attitude to Lawrence, which was one of admiring affection, and that they were written into Orioli's book by Douglas.)

Lawrence completed his final version of *Lady Chatterley's Lover* soon after Christmas. The Carswells had invited him and Frieda to join them for Yuletide in the Harz Mountains, where their host was a lung specialist who admired Lawrence's work, but Lawrence felt that Germany was 'too far, too'. At the Mirenda, 'seventeen peasants in to the tree, all happy singing'. Frieda arranged for one of the *contadini* children, Dino Bandelli, to have a rupture operation at a Florentine hospital; and after his return, the little boy was overheard by St. Frieda —as Lawrence now called her—telling his sisters about the plumbing there: 'There is a thing, and you pull, you must pull, see?'

On January 6, Lawrence told Brett he had only one more chapter to rewrite; by the tenth he could report to Mrs. Carswell that he had completed the novel:

> I wonder where you are—if in the Harzeberge. I want a little help. I wrote a novel last winter, and rewrote it for the third time this—and it's very verbally improper—the last word, in all its meaning!—but very truly moral. A woman in Florence said she'd type it—and she's done 5 chapters—now turned me down. Says she can't go any further, too indecent. Dirty bitch! But will you find some decent person who'll type it for me at the usual rates? You'd do it, I know, if you were a person of leisure. But you're *not*. So turn over in your mind some decent being, male or female, who I could trust not to let me down in any way, and who'd do the thing for the proper pay. And write me soon. But not here. I think we shall go, either on Sat, or Monday, to Switzerland, to the snow. It's so damp here. You might send me a line c/o Aldous Huxley, Chalet des Aroles. Diablerets. (Vaud) Suisse. We intend to join them there and take a little flat they have in view: stay perhaps till end of February. I want really to try and get myself better—cough still troublesome—and I want to lay hold of life again properly. Have been down and out this last six months.
>
> Then I think I shall publish my novel privately here in Florence, in March—April—1,000 copies, 2 gns each: and so, D.V., earn myself a thousand pounds, which I can do very well with—rather low water. I'll call it *Tenderness*—the novel.
>
> But please don't talk about it to anybody—I don't want a scandal advertisement.

Lawrence, as noted earlier, had let himself go in *Lady Chatterley's Lover,* with its therapy of 'shock' words. In two later statements (the introduction to the unexpurgated edition of *Pansies,* and the essay

À Propos of Lady Chatterley's Lover), Lawrence referred to Swift's poem, 'To a Lady's Dressing-Room', which had become for him a symbol of the mind's 'old grovelling fear of the body and the body's potencies. . . . The insanity of a great mind like Swift's is at least partly traceable to this cause. In the poem to his mistress Celia, which has the maddened refrain "But—Celia, Celia, Celia s***s," (the word rhymes with spits), we see what can happen to a great mind when it falls into panic. . . . Of course Celia s***s! Who doesn't? And how much worse if she didn't'—Lawrence wrote in À Propos.

But this puritan who loathed 'smoking-room stories' made it plain that he was not advocating promiscuity of speech, the fescennine for its own sake; and in another later statement, in Pornography and Obscenity, Lawrence drew a careful distinction between 'the sex functions and the excretory functions in the human body': the former represented the creative flow, the latter the 'flow towards dissolution'. And: 'In the really healthy human being the distinction between the two is instant. . . . But in the degraded human being the deep instincts have gone dead, and then the two flows become identical.' Lawrence didn't evade the fact of dissolution, but faced it, and then went on, in most of his writing, to celebrate the other 'flow', the creative, the warm phallic song of life.

This may seem to contradict the passage in Lady Chatterley's Lover in which the lover speaks in celebration of the beloved because she functions naturally, but Lawrence there was in effect answering Swift; further, he was again expressing the ideas of dissolution given in Women in Love—'the two flows' should not 'become identical,' even though they coexist, for one flow must, out of the contradiction, become creative.

Lawrence was at his most specific in the third version of Lady Chatterley's Lover. And here we need a bit of history. In 1944, fourteen years after Lawrence's death, The First Lady Chatterley was published in the United States and won its court battles against the censors. It didn't win many admirers among seasoned Lawrenceans, though some of them found the little gamekeeper, Parkin, an amusing and likable figure. In 1972, thirteen years after the final version had been published in America and England and was also victorious in its court battles, Lawrence's London and New York publishers brought out the second version, which they called John Thomas and Lady Jane, and this time met with no opposition. The gamekeeper is still called Parkin, but he is more humanized than Parkin I, and the Constance

Chatterley of this version is warmer and more tender than her two counterparts. These points, as well as the often superb writing, have led some of us who have followed Lawrence's fortunes to the conclusion that *John Thomas and Lady Jane* is the finest part of the Chatterley saga.

In one notable passage, Lawrence gave a different version of a nautical symbol for marriage from the one he had used in *Kangaroo,* in which he had shown the man and the woman as steering two hostile ships. In *John Thomas and Lady Jane,* when Connie thinks of marriage and of herself and Parkin, she sees marriage as two ships. If we grapple them together, lashed side by side, 'the first storm will smash them to pieces. That is marriage, in the bad weather of modern civilisation. But leave the two vessels apart, to make their voyage to the same port, each according to its own skill and power, and an unseen life connects them. And that is marriage as it will be...'

*

While Lawrence was still in the afterglow of completing the final version of *Lady Chatterley's Lover,* at Les Diablerets, Switzerland, where he and Frieda had gone with the Huxleys, he sent a letter on February 3 to Lady Glenavy in Dublin in which the use of his shock words was perhaps not so shocking as his threats to visit Dublin, with his suggestions of the uproar he might create there:

Your letter came on here—where we came a fortnight ago, for my wretched chest—bronchials really to wreck a ship. They said —people, even doctors—altitude and snow. But snow's no good for bronchials, makes 'em worse: though the altitude is tonicky after Tuscany, which is relaxing. Well, that's my wail: I cough and pant, but sound worse than I am, maybe. I expect we'll stick it out here till about end of this month—then back to the Villa Mirenda, to wind up there.—There's deep snow here—a certain amount of winter-sport—none for me—and now it's snowing again—tinkle of sledge bells—me sitting on my bed, with a German feather-bolster over my feet—Frieda lying on her bed reading André Gide's *Corydon,* which is a damp little production: and no sound in the white and crumbling world. We've got a flat in this chalet....

I'd really like to come to Ireland, and see you all, and Liam

O'Flaherty—and Dublin—and go to the west. I hope it wouldn't always rain, and I wouldn't have a political aspect, and be shot or arrested. But I'd like to come, and I think we will once the Mirenda is wound up—in April—and that novel more or less off my hands. Somehow I can form no picture at all of Ireland— much more easily of Ecuador or Manchuria. But I think a country which doesn't really exist and doesn't assert its non-existence violently any more—as Italy does—must be rather a relief. Geographically nowhere, as you say. Suppose one painted nudes in Ireland—not tough stucco [Augustus] John ones—would we be thrown in the Castle dungeons? Do the policemen wear orange trousers and goose feathers: no, orange is Belfast: green: green and pink policemen, and money made of glass, and all motor-cars pale pink by law? And a state harpist at every street corner —and runes all over the house-fronts—and the pavements with poems let in in little white pebbles—and lordly gentlemen in bright collars of gold, like Malachi, and two-edged swords, forcing every civilian to pronounce six words in Erse before he passes on. That's how I imagine it, so don't disappoint me. And in some streets no walking allowed, forced to dance a jig from end to end. And ladies at night walking with their white bosoms lit up with a necklace of tiny electric lights. And nuns in scarlet, and priests in lemon colour. Oh Ireland! And Gordon in a leopard-skin!

Several days later, on February 6, Lawrence reported to Orioli from Diablerets, mentioning, among others, Mrs. Huxley's younger sister, Rose Nys (who a few years later was to marry the Belgian poet, Eric de Haulleville):

> I think this place is really doing me good, I do feel stronger. I don't love snow, exactly—it's so beastly white, and makes one's feet so cold. But sometimes it's beautiful. Yesterday we drove in a sledge to the top of the pass, and picnicked there, with Aldous and Maria and Rose, and Julian Huxley, Aldous' brother, and his wife Juliette. It was brilliantly sunny, and everything sparkling bright. I really liked it. It does put life into one.
> I am just getting the typescript of my novel in from London: and Maria is typing the second half. So in a fortnight I think I shall have it all ready to send to you. I am going to make expur-

gated copies for Secker and Alfred Knopf, then we can go ahead with our Florence edition, for I am determined to do it. I hope you are still willing to help me. I think in about a fortnight's time I can send you the MS. to give to the printer.

Earlier, Lawrence had told Orioli that 'Maria will do the "worst" bits of the novel!' But her Swiss sister-in-law, Juliette, 'was *very* cross, morally so', over the book and 'suggested rather savagely' that Lawrence call it *John Thomas and Lady Jane,* and for a while he did, in the case of that third version. 'John Thomas', he wrote to Mabel Luhan, 'is one of the names for the penis, as you probably know.'

Lawrence was at this time gathering and revising his poems for the collected edition to be published in the fall of 1928. He had begun assembling them before leaving the Mirenda: 'I do bits of things—dry my underclothes and try to type out poems—old ones,' he told Huxley in November, and he worked further on the revisions in Switzerland in January.

Max Mohr and Rolf Gardiner were visitors to Les Diablerets in February. Lawrence discussed reform with Gardiner, with whom he had been corresponding for several years, and Gardiner made Gore Farm, in Dorset, where he and his youthful associates were hiking and camping, sound attractive—and Mohr said that everyone should have roots. 'Perhaps I'm due to go back to the Old England,' Lawrence told Gardiner, a cheerfully vital and friendly blond young man of Anglo-Saxon appearance and force.

Meanwhile, back in that Old England, Mrs. Carswell was sitting up nights, despite an influenza attack, to finish typing her sections of *Lady Chatterley,* worried by letters such as the one Lawrence sent to her on February 28: 'Tomorrow is the last day of the month, and the MS. isn't here: and people cabling and fussing about it. . . .' To Frieda, who had left a few days before for Baden-Baden, he wrote saying ungratefully that he was 'still waiting for the final two chapters from *that* woman'. But they arrived, giving Lawrence a complete manuscript, on March 2, anniversary of the day on which he had finished *The Rainbow*—and exactly two years before his death.

On March 3 he wrote to Orioli that he would meet Frieda in Milan on the following Tuesday, and that they expected to arrive in Florence the next evening: '*At last* I have got the complete typescript of my novel: and I shall either post it to you on Monday, or bring it with me. All is ready! We can begin. . . .'

3 THE BATTLE WITH THE
'CENSOR-MORONS'

Two days before leaving Les Diablerets, Lawrence wrote to Rolf Gardiner, 'Yes one can ignore Fascism in Italy for a time. But after a while, the sense of false power forced against life is very depressing. And one can't escape, except by a trick of abstraction, which is no good.' He went back to Florence because he wanted to publish his novel there, and because Frieda ached to return.

A few days after his arrival at the Mirenda, Lawrence painted the first water color of his later phase, 'Fire Dance': 'Two naked men—rather nice I think—not particularly "natural".' Several weeks later, 'I painted a charming picture of a man pissing,' he wrote to Huxley. 'I'm sure it is the one Maria will choose: called "Dandelions" for short. Now I'm doing a small thing in oil, called "The Rape of the Sabine Women" or "A Study in Arses".' He mentioned several other recent productions—'Yawning', 'The Lizard', and 'Under the Haystacks'—all of them included in his exhibit the following year, though 'Dandelions' was not.

As for some time past, he wrote little except letters. The preceding year, 1927, had been a thin one as far as his writing went, with only one book published: *Mornings in Mexico*. The launching of *Lady Chatterley* now took most of his interest, and a new Lawrence appeared: for a good part of the rest of his life, he was Lawrence the businessman.

This suggests a kind of conflict, for if a man hated the mechanized commercial civilization as much as he did, he must also have hated its symbols of wealth. Yet he had in him that frugal, religion-and-the-rise-of-capitalism strain of the Protestant bourgeoisie. Once in that year of 1928 he shouted at Brewster, 'It's your duty to be rich', and in the same year he wrote to Dorothy Brett, 'Be economical and get your debts paid off. It's a great bore.' Brewster has revealed—it seems incredible—that Lawrence even invested in American stocks. But perhaps, as in the passage in the Scriptures, it was the love of money, rather than money itself, that was to him the root of all evil.

This businessman side of Lawrence supervised most of the commercial details of the publication of his novel. Certainly Ernest Lawrence, who had written his brother Bert's first business letter, the application to Haywood's, never turned out anything more professionally mercantile, in his own business career, than the receipt an older Bert prepared (a copy of which still exists, in his handwriting):

Mr Orioli begs to thank you for your order for *Lady Chatter-ley's Lover,* with enclosed cheque for ——, and will forward the book by registered post immediately it is ready.

6 Lungarno Corsini
Florence.

Orioli had this printed. By the third week in April, enough orders had come in to meet the expenses of the first edition. With all this activity, it was a busy spring for Lawrence: the Mirenda had numer-ous visitors, and he kept a lively correspondence going with old and new friends, among the latter the Harry Crosbys. Lawrence had not met Harry Crosby, the emancipated young Bostonian, and his wife, the brilliant and lively Caresse, but he liked Crosby's poems—which his wife had taught him how to write when he was clerking at the Place Vendôme offices of the bank which belonged to his uncle by marriage, J. P. Morgan. And Lawrence liked the name of the avant-garde publishing house the Crosbys operated in Paris, the Black Sun Press: had not Count Dionys in 'The Ladybird' said that the sun was really dark inside its jacket of gleaming dust?

The Crosbys began buying Lawrence's manuscripts and, when they heard that his story 'Sun', privately printed in London in 1926 and about to appear in his *The Woman Who Rode Away* collection, also existed in an unexpurgated version, they arranged to issue that; and they later published *The Escaped Cock,* which after Lawrence's death his English and American publishers brought out under the detumescent title *The Man Who Died.*

In paying Lawrence, the Crosbys sent him gold pieces, along with a snuffbox that had belonged to the Queen of Naples. They had ob-tained the gold pieces with the help of Edward Weeks, who in his pre-*Atlantic Monthly* days was their American representative: the coins came into France hidden in the shoes of a friend of young Weeks's named Sykes, whom the Crosbys' maid dramatically announced as 'Monsieur Sex'. Harry Crosby wanted to rush the gold pieces to Law-rence, so he dashed with them to the Gare de l'Est, arriving just be-fore a train left for Italy; he thrust the box of gold-eagle coins at an honest-looking traveler ('Not a bomb, but gold for a poet'), asking him to have it delivered in Florence, and as the train pulled out the stranger barely had time to introduce himself as the Duke of Argyll. In Florence, a railway 'knave' who made the final delivery to Orioli charged an exorbitant fee, but Lawrence appreciated the 'treasure':

however un-Lawrencean and 1920-ish all this was, at least the golden eagle suggested his type of symbolism. But he worried because he thought the Crosbys were 'not Crœsuses to that extent'.

At this time, Lawrence was trying to conciliate an old friend who had picked up some unfavorable remarks which he was supposed to have made about her. These had been passed on to her, Catherine Carswell, via Maria Huxley and the Huxleys' friend Yvonne Franchetti, who were then in London; Lawrence explained to Mrs. Carswell that, although Mrs. Huxley was 'really very nice', London made her nervous.

In a letter of April 22, Lawrence protested he had 'never said anything more than expletives: That damned Catherine hadn't sent me any typing etc. But nothing malicious, why should I?' And: 'One feels one should have no "friends"—they do one so much harm; not really wanting to, but they can't help it.'

That spring Lawrence also wrote to appease Witter Bynner, apparently offended because Lawrence had held the mirror up to him, as Owen Rhys, in *The Plumed Serpent*. Lawrence told him he had now come to believe 'the hero is obsolete, and the leader of men is a back number. After all, at the back of the hero is the militant ideal . . . also a cold egg'; he agreed with Bynner, 'the leader-cum-follower relationship is a bore. And the new relationship will be some sort of tenderness, sensitive, between men and men and men and women, and not the one up one down, lead on I follow, *ich dien* sort of business. So you see I'm becoming a lamb at last.'

He was not becoming exactly a lamb, but he had given up the leadership ideal which had characterized his third writing phase. What he told Bynner in that letter he put fictionally into *The Escaped Cock,* when he made the man who has risen from the dead give up prophecy.

That spring of 1928, the young American publisher Bennett Cerf was among the visitors to the Mirenda. He came out from Florence with Douglas, who carped en route at the world's 'imbecile attitude' towards homosexuality; at American tourists who bought 'fake antiques' rather than privately printed Douglas items; and at Lawrence and Frieda. But at the Mirenda he hailed the Lawrences enthusiastically, and they greeted him cheerfully, although when Cerf was left alone with Lawrence for a moment, Lawrence severely asked him how he could dare bring such a man as Douglas there.

Another visitor was Rolf Gardiner's sister Margaret, who recalled that two aging spinsters (perhaps the Misses Beveridge and Harrison) joined her and Lawrence at tea. The spinsters, whom Lawrence privately called the Virgins, obviously disapproved of his paintings. They seemed to like the nuns and the soft trees in the illustration for Boccaccio's *Decameron* (Day III, Story I), though they shrank back when they saw the sleeping gardener with his sex organ lying on his naked belly: 'But why did you put *him* in?' The grinning Lawrence then displayed 'Le Pisseur' ('Dandelions'), and though the young Gardiner girl missed the point, the older women didn't: 'Really, Lawrence, you go too far.'

Margaret Gardiner further recalled (in an article, 'Meeting the Master') that after the Virgins left, Lawrence showed her the correspondence section of the American magazine *Forum,* whose readers' feathers had been ruffled by the appearance of the first part of *The Escaped Cock* in that journal: 'Not fit to read! My lovely story! Oh, their dirty, mean, poky little minds!'

*

When the Brewsters came to Florence in May, they were shocked to see that Lawrence was 'much weaker' than thirteen months before. 'We suddenly realized that he was very ill,' Mrs. Brewster remembered, 'and knew that we must not postpone to the future our time with him, but seize each passing day.' Instead of accepting the Lawrences' offer of the Mirenda, the Brewsters decided to accompany them to Switzerland in June.

Three days before departing, Lawrence wrote to Orioli, on June 7: 'Here are all the sheets signed and numbered, up to 1,000: then ten extra ones signed but not numbered, in case anything goes wrong—keep them apart—and ten blank ones. So glad that's all over.'

Now he could leave; *Lady Chatterley* was in the final stages. The Brewsters remembered a happy train journey north, with all of them alone in a compartment singing Moody and Sankey revival hymns, then a day at Turin and a few days in France, where their stay at St. Nizier was spoiled because the landlord told the Brewsters that the law forbade him to house the *monsieur* who coughed all night. The Brewsters and Frieda were furious, but their belief that Lawrence didn't know why they all suddenly left was unfounded, as we may see in this letter he wrote on the day of the summer equinox to Orioli after they had all settled in Switzerland, at the Grand Hôtel in Chexbres:

We are in this biggish hotel, with the Brewsters—well looked

after, 9 francs a day including tea—and about 2,000 ft. above
Lac Leman. So we're all right for a bit—*and if you come to England this way, stop off at Lausanne and see us.* It's above Vevey,
quite near Lausanne.—That St Nizier place was very rough—
and the insolent French people actually asked us to go away because I coughed. They said they didn't have anybody who
coughed. I felt very mad. But it's better here—dull, but comfortable. And it's no good shivering with cold and being uncomfortable. The Brewsters are here—Frieda has gone to Baden
Baden for a week, Aldous has telegraphed that he and Maria
will join us next Tuesday or Wednesday—from Paris. So we are
not likely to be lonesome, as the Brewsters say.—They are very
nice, the Brewsters, look after me so well: I ought to get quickly
fat, fatter than you or Frieda.—By the way, be sure and give
Maria a copy of *Lady C.* when she turns up. And if a man Charles
Wilson from Willington, Durham, wrote for a copy, send him one,
I know him. I'm so anxious to know what milady is doing, and
what you are doing about her. People pelting me with letters
now, to know when they'll get her.—Somehow I feel it will be
safe to post to England, day by day: start about a week after the
American copies have gone off. But once you start sending out,
go straight ahead, until something stops you. I am very anxious
to hear from you, what is happening. Wish I could have stayed
on till the thing is out, and posted.

A week later, Lawrence rejoiced when the first copies of his novel
arrived, and he wrote to Orioli: '*Lady Chatterley* came this morning,
to our great excitement, and everybody thinks she looks beautiful, outwardly.' Lawrence felt it was 'a handsome and dignified volume—a
fine shape and proportion, and I like the terra cotta very much, and I
think my phoenix is just the right bird for the cover. Now let us hope
she will find her way safely and quickly to all her destinations.'

Lawrence kept writing to Orioli about the book: in three weeks at
Chexbres, he sent him more than twenty letters and cards, discussing
not only *Lady Chatterley* but also his paintings, which the Warren
Gallery planned to exhibit in London. After a recent visit to Florence,
Enid Hilton had taken some of the pictures to England with her; now
Lawrence discussed with Orioli the problem of packing and shipping
the rest of them.

And he wrote more than letters at Chexbres: one of his *Assorted*

Articles, 'Insouciance', gives a bright vignette of the life there and of the chirpy little Englishwoman who 'cared' about things and shattered his peace of mind as he sat on the hotel balcony in the afternoon, looking down on 'the uncanny glassiness of the lake' and at the men mowing on the hill below. But his 'little over-earnest' neighbor who shared the balcony with him spoiled Lawrence's mood by chattering away in her 'busy caring about Fascism or League of Nations or whether France is right or whether marriage is threatened.' Like his resurrected prophet in *The Escaped Cock,* he wanted to give up prophecy ('my mission is over, and my teaching is ended'): now he needed insouciance.

Lawrence felt more free when he moved higher into the Alps at Gsteig bei Gstaad, where he and Frieda rented a chalet, Kesselmatte. He invited the Brewsters to come, though he realized that Achsah might find such accommodations 'too peasanty and primitive': she was 'hardly a chalet person'. Nevertheless, his statement that the region had 'a bit of the Greater Day' atmosphere drew the Brewsters, who went to a nearby hotel. This was before Gsteig had been taken over by the ski-and-martini set and had become, in the argot of a later guidebook by a language-loose American, 'the spiffiest resort in the Bernese Oberland', its name 'a weird handle that has appeared often in the newspapers, principally because of the hijinks committed by its celebrated clientèle.'

Lawrence wrote to Enid Hilton on July 20:

> I was glad to hear from you and so happy with your removal. Did I tell you I believe that is the very house we lived in, in 1917 in the Aldingtons' rooms on the first floor, on the front and Arabella had an attic at the top—it was very jolly, I liked it very much. I hope you can stay there in peace.
>
> I was a bit sorry you yielded up the pictures so easily to Dorothy Warren's messenger. I don't altogether trust her—I knew her of old, she is Lady Ottoline's niece—and she hasn't answered my letter. And now the Mirenda pictures, the big ones, have gone off to her.—If I don't hear from her satisfactorily, I will give you a letter to her and you can go and demand the small pictures back from her. Then we shall have some hold over her. I've told her I may do this.

Nine days later, Lawrence wrote to Enid Hilton again, saying he was 'in more trouble' and needed her help: 'A beastly firm of book-exporters ordered eighty copies of *Lady Chatterley's Lover*—now it turns out they have a Wesleyan connexion—they've read the book— and cancelled the order hastily—after Orioli had already posted them *seventy-two* copies from Florence. Now unless we're quick they'll send the things back to Florence—may even refuse to accept them from the post-man.' Warning Mrs. Hilton that the book was 'dangerous', Lawrence asked her, with her husband's approval, to call at the William Jackson Company for the books.

He requested her to take them to her Mecklenburgh Square flat and from there mail them to the people who had sent paid orders to Orioli in Florence. Later, other friends of Lawrence, such as Koteliansky (nervous over the ordeal), Aldington, and Derek Patmore, son of Brigit Patmore (the Clariss Browning of *Aaron's Rod*), helped him in this way, receiving the books at their city quarters or country cottages and shipping them out according to instructions from Florence. Thus *Lady Chatterley,* in view of the modest number of copies printed for its first edition, had a fairly wide and effective distribution in England.

Frieda wrote to Aldington from Gsteig on a Tuesday, perhaps July 31, to say, 'Your appreciative letter of *Lady C* came at the right moment. Lawrence was lying on his bed looking furiouser and furiouser every minute—People seem so *horrified at it!* But I feel pleased!' She told a bit about their present life ('Lawrence is really getting better') and said, 'Yours was the first pleased letter and only about 4 more,' to which Lawrence added, 'The rest a few pellets of icy disapproval, and the most, frost bound silence. Oh I am so glad to lose the fag end of my friends! especially the old maidy sort.' It is interesting to note that Lady Ottoline Morrell now stood with him again: their friendship had been renewed earlier that year, and Lawrence had written to Gertler to say that, after all, Lady Ottoline was 'a queen, among the mass of women'.

Perhaps in undertaking to work so hard for *Lady Chatterley* (from July to September, Lawrence wrote some twenty letters to Orioli alone), he was damaging his health, though all this activity recalls the *spes phthisica* of the ancients, the energy of the tuberculous that so impressed the old Greek physicians. Frieda told Orioli, in a letter from Gsteig, that she believed Lawrence was 'getting stronger, the fighting does his soul good!' An American tuberculosis expert, Dr. Edmund R. Clarke, Jr., has helpfully given an account of some fairly recent developments in the field, as they might apply to Lawrence. In a letter to this writer, Dr. Clarke pointed out that his necessarily brief comments should be read in connection with the Duboses' *The White Plague* (1952):

> From our studies of a large number of tuberculosis patients, we have become aware of the fact that almost all of them follow one pattern of human behavior which might characterize the individual who has tuberculosis or who may get it. The people that we have studied are usually individuals whose early life was one which did not provide the individual with the necessary amount of love, affection, and security. As a consequence of this early formative period, the individual develops an intense need for the satisfaction that comes of accomplishment, recognition and achievement. It is then this background of personality development which accounts for the way of life that people with tuberculosis must follow. All of the patients we have studied to date demonstrate a life performance which might be described as one of intense striving toward their goal in life, which is usually selected as one which will satisfy these basic needs. This striving increases in intensity as the life of the individual rolls by and finally reaches the point where it is no longer tolerable or it becomes obvious that the goal can never be achieved. At this point, the individual either falls flat from exhaustion or gives up in despair, and, shortly thereafter, is found to have tuberculosis. This process might better be illustrated by the man who carries a heavily loaded packsack on his back at too fast a rate for too long a time without stopping to rest.
>
> As this period of striving increases in intensity, the individual becomes less and less interested in a variety of activities outside those which contribute to the pursuit of his goal and undergoes a process of social isolation. This isolation may manifest itself by the abandonment of friends, the failure to take a vacation or by a more complete break with social stability such as is seen in the skidrow bum who leaves his home and begins to wander from place to place and job to job.
>
> From your comments about Lawrence, I suspect that he was a very restless gentleman who was always on the go and who found much satisfaction in action and I suspect that sanatorium life, with its premium on rest and its many obstructions to activity, was frustrating. If this guess is correct, I should suspect Lawrence was the type of individual who had very chronic, very indolent, so-called 'fibroid' tuberculosis, which, with or without

treatment, underwent little or no change for better or worse, with the exception of periods when he might have become discouraged and depressed, at which time he probably demonstrated some worsening of disease. He sounds like the type of fellow we see frequently in our research patients who seldom die of tuberculosis, but who likewise seldom get well and who have a high level of adrenal activity.

The suggestion of Lawrence's possibly having 'a high level of adrenal activity' is a particularly interesting one in the light of the theories which Dr. Clarke and his colleagues at Firland Sanatorium worked out. They tested the activity of the adrenal glands of tuberculous patients for secretions of steroid hormones, and discovered that, generally, low steroid levels accompanied the most active form of tuberculosis; near-normal levels went with the more common but less extensive type of the disease; and high levels were associated with infections that were localized though stubborn.

As Dr. Clarke explained at a meeting of the National Tuberculosis Association, patients in the first category were apathetic, low in spirit, and retiring. The almost-normal steroid level seemed to produce patients who were alert and better adjusted socially, while those with the high rate of steroid secretion were subject to anxieties, conflicts, and rapid alterations of blood pressure. In times of tension and anger, the glands produce extra steroid hormones. One patient who showed no improvement and was kept alive only by streptomycin injections became angered at the repeated punchings of the needle, and brought his adrenal secretions up to normal, thereby making his recovery likely. The emotion of fear, also stimulating the adrenal output, has helped other patients.

Now how does all this apply to Lawrence? Excessive adrenal secretions often make for a continually angry man: the Firland doctors believe that such patients can have their stresses, and their adrenal overactivity, reduced by sympathetic treatment. Since Lawrence apparently had 'a high level of adrenal activity', it is possible that sympathetic treatment would have helped him, if he would have submitted to it—would have helped him in every way.

On the other hand, it is possible that Lawrence's frequent spells of irascibility, and the excitement of the publishing activity in the case of *Lady Chatterley's Lover,* were unconscious attempts to protect himself. This is a layman's independent suggestion, but it is certainly not out of the range of modern psychology or of psychosomatic medicine. Lawrence's anger, which so often shocked strangers and frayed the patience of his friends, may have prolonged his life.

There is another aspect of Lawrence's eruptions of temper, a socio-psychological one, as noted by Richard Aldington in his 1932 letter to Frieda, which served as the introduction to *Apocalypse:*

> In working-class homes people let off steam much more freely than in bourgeois homes, where a sort of rancour often lurks under the superficial good manners. Very likely Lawrence was only doing what he had seen his father do a thousand times—work off his annoyance by shouting and apparently unnecessary violence. But with these people, once the scene is over, there is no ill-will at all. Everybody has worked off his or her annoyance, and is quite prepared to be affectionate again. People like ourselves are brought up to conceal our feelings; he always expressed his. Once I had worked that out for myself, I didn't at all mind his occasional crossnesses; but I did mind that sharp girding at so many people and things. Yet I believe it was not inherent in his nature. It was created in him by the spirit of persecution and hostility which met nearly everything he wrote. A little genuine effort to understand what he was trying to say, a slight gleam of intelligence in wooden-headed officials, would have spared him much humiliation and suffering. It was the humiliation he could not forgive. But I am indeed glad that he never wasted time in replying to literary 'attacks', that he made the only reply an artist need make—writing another fine book.

*

That summer at Gsteig, Lawrence rarely descended from the chalet on the heights. Almost daily the Brewsters puffed up the hill, and they would usually find Lawrence sitting under a pear tree writing his assorted articles in a child's exercise book. As Frieda reported to Orioli, 'The Brewsters come to tea, Achsah always in white and her soul is so white too, like a white of egg, and they call Lawr "David", and she paints him as a blue-eyed Eunich!' The Brewsters would sit beside him in the grass and sing folksongs. Once they acted out a song, 'Goddesses Three', on the green hill slope, with Lawrence directing. Earl Brewster, as Paris, lacking an apple, handed a round stone to Frieda, as Venus, with Mrs. Brewster standing by as Juno and little Harwood as Minerva.

Lawrence enjoyed two Hindus who visited the Brewsters: Boshi

Shen, who gave him massages, and Dhan Ghopal Mukerji, to whom Lawrence said, 'You don't really believe in God. You can't in this age. No, no, it's a conception mankind has exhausted: the word no longer has meaning.' But Lawrence found meaning in some of the Indian books he read at the time, and when he heard of Gandhi's colony and of his spinning and weaving, he said, 'He is right. We might start such a place with a few people: only I ought to do it in my own country: southern England perhaps.'

Altogether, Lawrence spent a good deal of time in Switzerland in 1928, four months (at Les Diablerets, Chexbres-sur-Vevey, and Gsteig), leaving Gsteig only when winter threatened to close in. His attitude towards that country had changed since the times when, as a young man, he used to walk across it, disliking every foot of it. But perhaps his change of heart typified the political neutrality of his last years, the neutrality of the deracinated.

And, there in Switzerland, despite his fretting over *Lady Chatterley* and producing all that handwritten correspondence which would have exhausted many apparently stronger men, Lawrence also painted several pictures and wrote some articles and stories. He painted 'Accident in a Mine' that summer at Gsteig, and finished 'Contadini', whose central figure is mustached, reminiscent of the younger Lawrence, though with the dark hair of an Italianate bronze-skinned model, Piero Pini, of the Villa Mirenda. A similar type appears in another of the Gsteig paintings, 'North Sea', perhaps a reflection of Heine's *Die Nordsee,* whose echo of Genesis 6:4 in the lines *'Und ich komme, und er mit mir kommt / Die alte Zeit, wo die Götter des Himmels, / Niederstiegen zu Töchtern der Menschen'* recalls Lawrence's own use of this passage when he has the sons of heaven coming down to the daughters of men—in *The Rainbow,* in *Women in Love,* and again in *Lady Chatterley's Lover.* The naked woman in this picture, whom the naked stranger from the sea is approaching for love, is not, for a change, Frieda: she resembles Cynthia Asquith, to whom he was possibly now making Barmecide love through the flesh of paint.

As for his writing at this time, he scratched out at Gsteig some of the bright, slangy little articles for which the journals now paid him well. One afternoon as he and the Brewsters sat among the harebells on the hillside, he read from his notebook the story 'The Blue Moccasins', and before he reached the end, he asked the Brewsters how they would close it. They wanted a conclusion which would permit the little elderly wife, in her effort to keep her young husband, to win out against her attractive competitor. Lawrence admitted he had at first ended the story in this way, but he found that he must put the domineering, motherlike little woman down in defeat: as in most of Lawrence's stories, the invader of a dual relationship usually wins, particularly when one of the partners in the relationship is a domineering type from whom the other escapes. 'The Blue Moccasins', with its sharp cruelties, was one of the typical satirical pieces of Lawrence's last period, containing no strong feeling, no color, no glow, no music. Yet at Gsteig he did write one imaginative piece that had the richness of his best prose; this was the second part of *The Escaped Cock,* with its magnificent pictures of the Lebanese coast and its story of the love of the resurrected prophet for the priestess of Isis.

Just as Lawrence finished this tale, his sister Emily and her daughter Margaret, now nineteen, arrived from England. On August 31 he told Enid Hilton: 'Though I am glad to see them, it worries and depresses me rather. I am really not "our Bert". Come to that, I never was. And the gulf between their outlook and mine is always yawning, horribly obvious to me.' They took several of his paintings to London, and Lawrence thanked Enid Hilton for meeting them at the station and added:

> Imagine those booksellers making money like that on *Lady C!* I hear in America the price is $50. Oh Lord, one is always swindled. But we are going to put up the price now on the remaining copies.
>
> I suppose you saw Kot, and heard all his alarms. He is like that. He thinks because Gertler and a few like that will say nasty things about my pictures, it means all the world. It doesn't. . . .
>
> Wonder what Alice Dax thought of *Lady C.!*
>
> Mountains are beginning to be misty and a bit damp and silent and autumny—time now to go. Thanks so much for looking after things so well. Remember me to L. [Laurence, her husband].

'Time now to go'—it always was, although this time Lawrence left Gsteig not so much from inward compulsion. His letters of late summer mentioned the cold that was creeping into the chalet. On September 18 he and Frieda at last descended to the lowlands, to the ting-a-ling of bells on the cattle coming down from the higher Alps.

*

In that autumn of 1928, Lawrence and Frieda went to Baden-Baden after Gsteig. It was another time of strolling in the Lichtenthalallee, drinking the waters at the stork fountains, and sipping the concerts in the Kursaal. 'The Brewsters are here, *of course,*' Lawrence wrote to Orioli. Before leaving Gsteig, whence the Brewsters had departed earlier, Lawrence had written to them about 'a most amusing story of mine in the American *Bookman*—called *"Things"*—you'll think it's you, but it isn't'—one of the most barefaced of all such disclaimers.

For the Brewsters to have put up with that accurately cruel story measures their devotion to Lawrence. The rootless, wandering Americans in this little tale who loved their bric-à-brac—which Lawrence had become familiar with when he helped the Brewsters pack their 'things' in Capri in 1926—'both painted, but not desperately. Art had not taken them by the throat. . . . They painted: that's all.'

The meanest and funniest thrust at them is the sentence ' "Indian thought" had let them down.' But it was good that the Brewsters didn't let Lawrence down in those last years. For although Frieda with her warmth and vigor remained the strong center of his life, he also needed some calm men-friends to talk to, and found them in Aldous Huxley and Earl Brewster. They were not subservient—Huxley was going his own way towards renown, and Brewster clung firmly to his 'Indian thought'—they had minds of their own, yet they respected Lawrence and provided him with pleasant association. 'During the last years of Lawrence's life,' Brewster has said, 'I do not recall his once being enraged with me, as had happened in the first years of our friendship. Perhaps he felt it futile to attempt my reform.'

Lawrence wrote to Orioli from the Hotel Löwen, Baden-Baden:

> We want to give up the Mirenda. I am sure it is bad for my health, because in these other places I am better than I am there. Then the *maggiore*—or the Zaira—is sending away the Pini family—Giulia, Pietro, all of them—and there is sure to be a great emotional stew. I can't stand it. So Frieda will come and pack up the few things—they are really all packed—and give up the house.—*But please don't tell anybody*—so nobody need fuss around her. I shall go to S. of France—the Aldingtons [Richard Aldington and Dorothy ('Arabella') Yorke] are having an old fortress [*vigie*] on the island of Port-Cros, about 19 chilometri from off Hyères near Toulon. It is very warm there, and no people, only 14 families of fishermen. So if we like it we shall stay the winter, and if you can, you must come. Perhaps they will give you a passport for there.

Achsah Brewster recalled that, upon leaving Baden-Baden, she and her husband went down to the French Riviera with Lawrence, while Frieda traveled to Italy to move out of the Villa Mirenda. On the way south Lawrence stopped at Strasbourg with the Brewsters; he felt that the cathedral there, combining French and German elements, was the finest Gothic exterior he had seen. Later, in the cold twilight, they all went to a motion-picture house until it was time to catch their train; they saw Ramón Navarro and Francis X. Bushman in *Ben-Hur*. Mrs. Brewster reported that such 'falsity nauseated' Lawrence; it was inhuman. He had to leave or he would be sick. Later, in the *Pansies* poems, he attacked the films as being false to humanity. But that day in Strasbourg had at least one positive value: he had once again seen the cathedral which plays so important a symbolic role in his story 'The Border Line'.

*

Lawrence didn't arrive at Port-Cros until the middle of October. He spent the intervening time on the French coast waiting for Frieda, with the Huxleys, Frieda's sister Else, and Alfred Weber. Frieda brought a cold from Italy which Lawrence soon caught. She had possibly stopped for a love affair; as she used to tell her intimates, 'Lawrence has been impotent since 1926!' Richard Aldington in his last years used to give wry imitations of Lawrence's emphasis on Frieda's '*Italian* cold'. Aldington hinted, in his autobiography, *Life for Life's Sake,* at what had happened before Frieda arrived at Port-Cros: moving out of the Villa Mirenda was 'a complicated process, since it involved a journey to Trieste'. Angelo Ravagli, in a memoir written for Nehls's *Composite Biography* of Lawrence, states that after a visit to them at the Mirenda in 1927, he 'lost track of the Lawrences' until, in March 1930, he read in *Il Corriere della Sera* that Lawrence had died; Ravagli then telegraphed his sympathies to Frieda and invited her to visit him and his wife at Spotorno. But Robert Lucas's biography of Frieda states baldly that she made a visit to the town near Trieste where Ravagli was stationed in 1928, before she went on to Port-Cros.

Altogether Lawrence's month on the island was an unpleasant one. In conversations with Aldington he carped at Huxley's successful *Point Counter Point*—he wrote to Huxley about his points of disagreement—and at the war novel Aldington was writing. Copies of the newspaper attacks on *Lady Chatterley* that arrived while he was at Port-Cros didn't improve Lawrence's disposition.

In the summer, the reviews of *The Woman Who Rode Away* had been lukewarm or patronizing, though Arnold Bennett had in the *Evening Standard* generously called Lawrence 'the strongest novelist writing today' and said that the ten stories in the collection (the British edition omitted 'The Man Who Loved Islands', which the American included) were 'characterized by superb creative power. . . . There are whole pages together where every sentence gives new light on human nature and, reading them, you know you are face to face with a rough demonic giant.'

But no one had spoken out that way for *Lady Chatterley*—Edmund Wilson's favorable *New Republic* review didn't appear until July 1929—except Lawrence's American friend Herbert J. Seligmann, who had (in 1924) written the first book about him. Seligmann praised *Lady Chatterley* in a review in the *New York Sun* of September 1, 1928, but, as he revealed to the author of this volume, 'it was deleted from later editions. Henry Hazlitt, the literary editor, told me he had never seen a piece of reading matter in the paper so blue- and red-pencilled by the editors. The *Sun* went to the unheard-of length of remaking the literary page to get rid of my contaminating essay. . . . It ended my reviewing for the *Sun*'—as Catherine Carswell's praise of *The Rainbow* had terminated her reviewing career with the *Glasgow Herald* thirteen years before.

At Port-Cros, the worst of the British attacks on *Lady Chatterley* which Lawrence read was that of his ancient enemy, *John Bull,* whose headlines called the novel 'A Landmark in Evil'. A photograph of the 'bearded satyr' who wrote the book accompanied an article calling it 'the most evil outpouring that has ever besmirched the literature of our country. The sewers of French pornography would be dragged in vain to find a parallel in beastliness.'

At this time, in a letter dated only 'Sunday' (October 21, 1928), Lawrence gave Orioli another publishing idea, but suggested caution:

I think if I were you I would prepare a series of *Italian Renaissance Novelists, text in Italian and English, with notes*—small books of about 80 or 100 pp; the same format, more or less, as the Fortini books—but not replica—not identical.

I have begun with the *Terza Cena* of Lasca. It is a very interesting story, Lorenzo de' Medici—and about 60 pp. and quite proper. Get your old professor to write you a brief life of Lasca, and to make notes on the story—I will mention what I think should have a note, as I go on.—The story of Lorenzo de' Medici and Maestro Manente.—

It is important to start the series with an interesting and *not* indecent story. We can come on with the indecent ones later. I thought we would do Lasca in 3 vols.—three *Cene*—starting with the Terza. This one won't take me very long. Let me know what you think.

There is great work going on for the *international suppression of indecent literature.* I enclose a cutting from the Evening Standard.—Also—an incident. An Englishwoman saw a copy of *Lady C.* in a bookshop in Milan—went in to buy—man demanded to see her passport and *permesso di soggiorno*—the latter had only three days to run—woman said she was just going back to England—bookseller refused to sell her the copy—I expect he was afraid Customs might hold up the book and he might be cited as having sold it—and the League of Nations be after him!

Without waiting for Orioli's approval, Lawrence went on with the translation that was published the following March as *The Story of Doctor Manente.* His businessman side prepared another advertisement:

PINO ORIOLI

will publish a series of Italian Renaissance stories, English (and Italian) text, the series to be translated by D. H. Lawrence, Norman Douglas, Aldous Huxley and other well-known writers, with introductions by the translators and with notes and maps. The first number of this series will be ready December X.—*The Third Supper,* by Lasca. Translated with introduction by D. H. Lawrence. Limited edition of 1,000. Post free 12/6 or $3.00

Lawrence further advised, 'If you print your Italian text too, you must charge 15/- and $4.' And, in the same letter, apparently October 25, he also said: 'If you like to do this, I suggest you make it your enterprise and give me 10%,' a suggestion Orioli felt it was safe to accept. But he was to lose money on this translation by Lawrence, who in the flush of success after *Lady Chatterley* induced him to print too large an edition, though the Lungarno Series itself went to eleven titles before the fall of the pound sterling made publication too painfully unprofitable for Orioli.

While at Port-Cros, Lawrence wrote his remarkable letter to the American lawyer Morris Ernst, who had sent him a copy of his book on censorship. Lawrence, telling him he could print the letter if he wished, used the occasion to attack 'the censor-moron', who hates 'the living and growing consciousness. It is our developing and extending consciousness that he threatens—and our consciousness in its newest, most sensitive activity, its vital growth.' But Lawrence in those days was arousing, once again, the suspicions of more than censors, for as Aldington remembered the Port-Cros interlude in his autobiography, 'The only people who bothered us were some French staff officers who came to investigate the suspicious alien character, Lawrence, and weren't allowed by me to see him'—Lawrence, arrested by the Germans in Metz as a British spy; pitched out of Cornwall by the British, who thought he was helping the Germans; and at last the French investigating this man to whom the very thought of espionage was nauseating.

On November 14, three days before leaving Port-Cros, he wrote to William Gerhardi about Mark Rampion, the character modeled after Lawrence in *Point Counter Point:* 'I refuse to be Rampioned. Aldous' admiration for me is only skin-deep, and out of a Mary Mary quite contrary impulse'—the Mary of course being Maria Huxley. But, despite Lawrence's occasional angers, his friendship with Huxley remained a staunch one.

In one of his less acid moods at Port-Cros, Lawrence wrote to Ada, 'It's quite good fun here. . . . Richard and Arabella are very nice—so is Brigit Patmore, a woman about my age whom we knew in the old days. They are all busy doing literary work—and they go off to swim. But it's an hour's climb from the sea and the other isles, and the mainland ten miles off. It's quite nice, somehow doesn't move me very much.'

Gales and chill winds which came later, and a deterioration of the local human situation, did move him; he went back to the mainland on November 17, in a launch whose engine broke down in the mistral. The boat began to drift out to sea in the heavy swells, but the man working on the engine was able to start it again, and the boat got to the coast safely. Lawrence, away from the storms of all kinds that had raged at Port-Cros, said farewell to Aldington for the last time in the salon of a hotel in Toulon. Aldington didn't understand why Lawrence, in leaving him, said, 'Possess your soul in patience'. Just a year later, Lawrence informed Orioli that he had disliked '*intensely*' the first part of Aldington's novel, *Death of a Hero,* which he had read while staying with him at the *vigie* on Port-Cros. 'But since the *vigie* I don't write to him—that's a long story'—apparently relating to the fact that Aldington was in the process of casting off Dorothy Yorke for

Brigit Patmore. Lawrence didn't break off with Mrs. Patmore, however; in one of Aldington's subsequent (unpublished) love letters to
Brigit Patmore he wondered whether at Port-Cros the Lawrences had
heard him stealing into her bedroom during the nights. Lawrence
seemed to be again showing his ferocious sense of puritanism, as he
had done years before when H.D. had left Aldington, to have an affair with Cecil Gray. But at Port-Cros, Aldington was the culprit, instructed, at the last farewell, to possess his soul in patience.

*

On the mainland the Lawrences went to Bandol, to the Hôtel Beau
Rivage that Katherine Mansfield had liked, where they stayed until
the following March. There they came to know, through the London
bookseller Charles Lahr, the young Welsh writer Rhys Davies, then in
Nice, to whom Lawrence wrote on a 'Monday' (November 28,
1928?):

> Mr Lahr sent me your address. Would you care to come here and
> be my guest in this small and inexpensive hotel for a few
> days? Bandol is about 20 minutes on the Marseille side of Tou-
> lon: 20 mins. from Toulon.—My wife and I would both be
> pleased if you came. I'm not quite sure how long we shall stay
> here—but anyhow ten days.

Rhys Davies went to Bandol for his first meeting with the 'bright-
plumaged' Frieda and the Lawrence whose 'features suggested a delicacy that at last had been finely tempered from ages of male and plebeian strength.' Lawrence scoffed at Davies's tributes to the younger
writers; he insisted that they could only hate him. But they were not so
bad as their elders who with their moneybags and tricks had tried
to catch him: 'I know I'm a monkey in a cage. But if anyone puts a
finger in my cage, I bite—and bite hard.'

Since Lawrence was often too weary to walk, Davies sat conversing
with him on the beach. The weather was warm that autumn, and Lawrence had come to love the southern coast; he wrote Maria Huxley a
description of Bandol 'swimming with milky gold light at sunset, and
white boats half melted on the white twilight sea, and palm trees friz-
zing their tops in the rosy west, and their thick dark columns down in
the dark where we are, with shadowy boys running and calling, and
tiny orange lamps under foliage, in the under dusk.'

This was a lyrical flare-up: the following winter, when Lawrence returned to Bandol, he wrote some magnificent poems about that coast. But while there in 1928, he concentrated on the 2,000-word articles for which the London papers were now giving him twenty-five pounds apiece: these colloquial productions took only an hour and a half to write and permitted him to say easily many of the things he had agonized to say in the dramatized terms of fiction; and though his publishers 'nagged' at him for another novel or for completion of his Etruscan studies, he felt books were not worth the effort when the government took twenty per cent of his royalties and his agent ten per cent.

At Bandol that autumn his writing energy went chiefly into little verses, about which he told the Huxleys in a letter: 'I've been doing a book of *Pensées,* which I call pansies, a sort of loose little poem form: Frieda says with joy: real doggerel—But meant for *Pensées,* not poetry, especially not lyrical poetry.' He wrote these *Pansies* sitting up in bed in the mornings, wearing a small African straw cap ('to keep my brain warm'), and between chuckles he would read them to visitors.

Meanwhile in London, plans for the exhibition of his paintings went forward, as well as a new project he mentioned in a letter to Davies:

> Orioli wrote me that the Fanfrolico [Press] people would do a portfolio of reproductions of my paintings, which hang in Dorothy Warren's gallery waiting to be exhibited. That would be rather fun. But I've heard nothing direct. If you write to the London Aphrodite people, you might mention it—if they are Fanfrolico. Because if the thing were going to come off, we'd have to hurry and get the pictures photographed before Dorothy W. shows them, in the New Year. But the idea of a portfolio amuses me very much.
>
> My wife is rather sad, with inflammation in her eye. I expect it's a chill, with the winds, but she never has anything wrong, so when she *does,* she minds.

On December 23, Lawrence wrote what was apparently his last letter to Rolf Gardiner, who with his friends was working at 'rural restoration' at Gore Farm. Lawrence, now 'chirpy and more like myself', wished Gardiner well and defended *Lady Chatterley* from Gardiner's criticisms. He ended by saying, 'This silly White Fox blarney about pure constructive activity is all poppycock—nine-tenths at least must be smash-smash!—or else *all* your constructivity turns out feebly destructive.' The 'silly White Fox blarney' refers to the name adopted by Gardiner's friend John Hargrave, head of 'Kibbo Kif, the Wood-craft Movements', which both attracted and repelled Lawrence. (Interestingly, Hargrave a bit later caught the favorable attention of a young American named John Steinbeck, who was soon to sentimentalize the political novel.)

Gardiner went on with his activity, in England and Africa, feeling always inspired by Lawrence's teaching rather than by his personal example, and broke with Hargrave when the latter became too obviously fascistic. Even in Germany, while that country was 'still unimprisoned by the paranoia of Hitlerism', Gardiner and his associates 'in the expeditions, work-camps, festivals, and centres of the German *Bunde* . . . sought flesh-and-blood validity of the Lawrencean vision.' That was what Gardiner wrote in his book *England Herself,* in 1943. In a letter to the author of the present volume, on September 11, 1952, Gardiner made a late, full statement about Lawrence and their relationship, a statement not out of place as this entire discussion of Lawrence's career nears its end:

Thinking of him today I wonder again if the weakness of his case was not due to the essentially explorative method of his pilgrimage? He often confused his values and allowed passionate petulance to cloud his sense of balance. How far did Lawrence, after his early days, seek for inner direction? I fancy that there was some confusion, some chaos here. At some point in his desire to wrest himself away from the influence of Platonic idealism and the rationalism of the *Aufklärung* he may have floundered in a sea of 'impulses'. He swung further away than any of the Romantics . . . And yet it was to balance, the doctrine of the Holy Ghost, that he returned both critically and theologically in his unembittered moments. That is why I always loved *Twilight in Italy:* a significant book that contained all the germ of his thought.

In any case, when I was a boy, it was not against puritanical repression of sex that Lawrence offered the clues of liberation, but against tyranny of intellectual abstractions, and the dead view of the universe projected by analytic science. Lawrence's quotation of D'Annunzio, '*L'anatomia presuppone il cadavere*', was very impressive. And then, above all, there was his revelation of the sources of strength in darkness, the darkness of a midwinter period closing in on our civilisation, the darkness of renewal, the darkness of the English Midlands and the north.

'Dark and true and tender is the north', Tennyson had written; but Lawrence purveyed it with his splendid writing, making it symbolic of the unexplored, inscrutable sources of the invisible world, the sources of past magic in the places and landscapes of pre-historic peoples. It was a nourishment of the mind by the senses that he effected, clothing the spirit with pulsing flesh and blood, where all other writers described 'social beings' bled white by manners and conventional feelings. Without saying so, except in his own curious 'polarity' terminology, Lawrence rediscovered for us the etheric body and the etheric forces beyond crude chemical sex. And his interest extended beyond the human individual, beyond social groups, to the landscape itself. As you so rightly say, 'his landscapes were always charged'.

What an experience it was, for someone like myself, with the urge of creative action in him, to have this brave life-explorer and life-interpreter forging ahead in the world of our time. As his books came molten from his hand, one shared in his life, projected imaginatively and continuously by his novelist's imagination and made exciting, revealing, significant, year by year. It was a great performance.

That is one of the most important statements about Lawrence's contemporary influence, made from the perspective of many years' consideration (by a man who in the 1960s became High Sheriff of Dorset). In 1929 the younger generation could do little to help Lawrence, whom most of their elders were attempting to throttle. On January 7, he mailed two copies of the *Pansies* manuscript to his agents in London, registering them as *papiers d'affaires,* and a week later he also sent, registered, the introductory essay for the volume of reproductions of his paintings. By the twenty-fourth he had begun to worry about these documents, for they hadn't arrived at Curtis Brown's.

The manuscripts had been seized in the post at the instigation of the Home Secretary, Sir William Joynson-Hicks, widely known as Jix, a religious zealot who had furiously begun to beat the bushes in England for hidden copies of *Lady Chatterley*. Lawrence's agents and publishers complained that detectives had called upon them, and policemen also went to the houses of some of his friends. The underground circulation had been all too successful: by the end of 1928, Lawrence notified Orioli that *Lady Chatterley*'s gross profits so far were £1,024.

When Lawrence wrote Brigit Patmore a friendly letter from Bandol on January 11, with a glancing reference to the difficulties at Port-Cros, he didn't yet know that her home was among those subjected to an official visit:

> Not heard from you for ages—have you evanesced? Not a Christmas word, not a New Year's note was heard from you! Perhaps you were too busy festivating. Anyhow I hope that's it. . . .
> Orioli said he'd started sending you copies of *Lady C.* I hope they've arrived safely. I told him not to send more than a dozen. Now a book-seller wants to take them over—Charles Lahr of 68 Red Lion Street, Holborn. If I tell him to fetch them from you next week, will you give them [to] him. I think he's a nice man.
> No news here—except my pictures are probably going to be reproduced in a book at ten guineas a time. I hear you whistle!
> It was a very sunny day, and we went out this afternoon on the sea in a motor-boat! When we were getting way out beyond the lighthouse, I made the man turn round, because I knew we should see the spectre of Port-Cros in the distance.
> Brigit, where art thou?

'Brigit, where art thou?'—she was in Italy with Richard Aldington, and the copies of the book sent to her in England had been confiscated. As Lawrence told Orioli on January 24, 1929: 'Her son [Derek] wrote me a detective sort of fellow called there too.—Kot. wrote—rather in a funk—perhaps fearing they may call on him.—The really annoying part is that Scotland Yard are apparently holding up two of my manuscripts, sent to Curtis Brown—these we must recover.'

That seizure again brought Lawrence's name into Parliament. This time the Labour Party, soon to win the national elections, raised the question of suppression, perhaps at the instigation of William Hopkin. On February 28, F. W. Pethick-Lawrence, who represented West Leicester, put the question on behalf of Ellen Wilkinson, absent because of illness. He asked whether the Home Secretary would tell who had acted, 'before any question of publication arose', to seize Lawrence's manuscript in the post, and: 'if he will give the names and official positions of the persons on whose advice he causes books and manuscripts to be seized and banned; what are the qualifications of such persons for literary censorship; and whether, to assist authors and publishers, he will state what are the rules and regulations, the contravention of which causes a book to be seized and banned by his Department?'

Joynson-Hicks was as deft as John Simon had been at the time *The Rainbow* was suppressed, fifteen years before. Like Simon, Jix dodged behind the ancient Obscene Publications Act, under which, he explained, any Metropolitan Police Magistrate or any two Justices of the Peace could, 'on sworn information', issue a search warrant and seize any 'obscene' book or picture. At this point James Ramsay MacDonald, whom the young Lawrence had met so long ago in Eastwood, rose to ask, 'Will the right hon. Gentleman make it quite clear whose responsibility it is to put the law into operation?'

Jix said that it was the police who had the authority, though he didn't want to deny his own responsibility; the Post Office Act of 1908 decreed that the Postmaster-General must 'refuse to take part in the conveyance of any indecent matter'—and the 1924 Postal Union Convention of Stockholm decreed likewise. Jix said that the discovery of the manuscripts occurred during a routine check of packages by inspectors looking for concealed letters sent through at the lower postal rates. Jix added that when Lawrence's manuscripts were discovered they 'were sent to the Home Office and by my directions were then forwarded to the Director of Public Prosecutions. I am advised that there is no possible doubt whatever that these contain indecent matter and, as such, are liable to seizure. I have, however, given two months to enable the author to establish the contrary if he desires to do so.'

Pethick-Lawrence still wanted to know who had decided that the matter was obscene. Jix replied, 'In the first place, in this case the Postmaster-General makes the first determination that this is *prima facie* a case of indecency. He then sends it to me, and, if I agree, I send it on to the Director of Public Prosecutions. It is not a question of literary merit at all, and, if the hon. Member has any doubt, I will show him the book in question. It contains grossly indecent matter.'

Again like Simon, Jix insisted that there was no literary censorship, and like the parliamentary debates over *The Rainbow* at that time, this one faded away, ending on a note of inquiry as to the right of the Postmaster-General to open packets.

Jix, however, like most censors, had made what he was trying to suppress seem attractive. Secker brought out a bowdlerized edition of *Pansies* in July 1929, in London, which Knopf published in New York in September: fourteen poems which had upset Jix were omitted from these volumes. Lawrence arranged for an Australian friend, P. R.

Stephensen (apparently in association with the bookseller Charles Lahr), to print an unexpurgated edition, though without Stephensen's Fanfrolico Press identifying mark; they dated this issue June 1929 but didn't release it until August; it comprised five hundred 'regular' copies, plus fifty on Japanese vellum. Later, the same plates served for a popular edition on the Continent. Lawrence could thank the 'censor-morons' for the astonishing achievement of making poetry pay well: he cleared more than five hundred pounds out of the *Pansies* uproar.

Before he left Bandol, he saw Rhys Davies several times again, and received other visitors, including the Julian Huxleys. In February, a visit from Ada depressed Lawrence: he could 'feel all those Midlands behind her, with their sort of despair'. She had passed forty and 'more or less turned against all she has lived for till now: business, house, family, garden even—doesn't want them any more.' This was of course 'something organic in women' that could not be argued with, largely 'the result of having been too "pure" and unphysical, unsensual'.

After Ada left Bandol, never to see her brother again, he, the prophet who had so often told the world what to do, couldn't find the right words of comfort for his sister; he wrote to her that he too had suffered in those miserable last years, but felt he was 'coming through, to some other kind of happiness', of a different sort that could be reached only after torture: 'This is the slow winding up of an old way of life. Patience—we'll begin another, somewhere in the sun.'

And he was hungry for the sun: the Bandol area was suffering an unwonted chill that froze the palms and the eucalyptus trees. Lawrence wanted to go to Spain, but the Italy-hungry Frieda opposed that. Finally they went north, to separate destinations, Frieda once again visiting her mother at Baden-Baden. Two days before leaving, Lawrence wrote to Earl Brewster, 'The only thing I *really* wish is that I didn't always cough and have either a sore chest or a sore throat as well as a sore spirit. Why should the gods keep me always sore inside?'

About a week earlier he had told Murry, 'I like being older—if only my chest did not scratch so much.' Murry had written for the first time since 1926, to ask Lawrence to lend a copy of *The Rainbow* to a friend of his in Switzerland who planned to write a book on Lawrence; Murry didn't want to risk sending his presentation copy. Lawrence said his own first edition had been stolen, but he told Murry that the American reprint of the book could be bought in Europe. Murry, 'ominously impressed' by the Beau Rivage address—Katherine Mansfield had suffered her first hemorrhage there—thought the letter 'friendly, but sad and tired'. In it, Lawrence told Murry he was thinking of going to Majorca, though 'I haven't any great hunch where I want to live—only, for the moment, not Italy.'

The winter at Bandol had, as we have seen, been fairly productive, at least as far as shorter pieces went. Lawrence, as the quotation from the letter to the Huxleys shows, had no pretensions about the *Pansies,* but they were an outlet for what he had so long thought and felt. In the assorted journalistic articles, he consistently had to observe a certain length, but the *Pansies* could be as long or as short as he wished: they could crystallize a single mood or thought. The epigrammatic quality of his later prose could be given even fuller play in these little verses ('For God's sake, let us be men, / Not monkeys minding machines . . .'). His earlier novels, up through *Women in Love,* didn't usually contain generalizations about life and society; what Lawrence wanted to say he either presented dramatically or stated through characters such as Birkin, who were an organic part of the story. But with *Kangaroo,* Lawrence had begun to weigh down the narrative with sententiousness; even *Lady Chatterley's Lover* begins: 'Ours is essentially a tragic age, so we refuse to take it tragically'. And in this final period Lawrence's most characteristic, most frequent, though not his best, expression in verse was in the form of these rough-edged maxims the writing of which so diverted him.

The introduction to the paintings volume was far more important than those assorted articles he also wrote at Bandol. In that introduction he discussed chiefly the work of modern French and English painters, the latter hampered by puritanism, by a fear of the body which came to Europe with syphilis. This seems almost history *à la* Huxley, though Lawrence had expressed such ideas as long before as *Twilight in Italy.*

He now found that the fear of the body drove the English painters, except Blake, to landscape, and rather astonishingly said he was himself 'not . . . profoundly interested in landscape'. True, in his own paintings the human figures predominate, though there is often beautiful scenery in the distance; but it is surprising to find the author of some of the finest prose landscapes saying that 'Van Gogh's surging earth'—so much a Lawrencean quality—worried him.

He thought the French painters' approach to sex too hygienic, though that was saner than the Anglo-Saxon 'terror-horror' of the whole subject. And although Lawrence considered Renoir 'a trifle banal', he admired him: 'What do you paint with, *Maître?*—With my penis, and be damned! Renoir didn't try to get away from the body.'

The excellence of Cézanne, to whom Lawrence devoted most of the essay, lay chiefly in technique: he felt that Cézanne failed, in his portraits of people and apples, 'to rise in the flesh' as he wanted to. He could never break 'through the horrible glass screen of the mental concepts, to the actual *touch* of life'.

If Lawrence criticized the English and French in that essay, he turned a terrible glare on the Americans in another introduction he wrote at Bandol, for the novel *Bottom Dogs* (1929), by Edward Dahlberg, which he dismissed as 'the last word in repulsive consciousness'. But the book was valuable because it showed that 'the flow from the heart, the warmth of fellow-feeling which has animated Europe and been the best of her humanity, individual, spontaneous, flowing in thousands of passionate little currents often conflicting . . . seems unable to persist on American soil. . . . Once the heart is broken, people become repulsive to one another secretly, and they develop social benevolence.'

The terror of the body was at its most intense in America: 'The secret physical repulsion between people is responsible for the perfection of American "plumbing", American sanitation, and American kitchens, white-enamelled and antiseptic. It is revealed in the awful advertisements, such as those about "halitosis", or bad breath.' Now the American repulsion was going backwards to Europe, polluting the democracies there. 'The old flow broken, men could enlarge themselves for a while in transcendentalism, Whitmanish "adhesiveness" of the social creature, noble supermen, lifted above the baser functions. . . . People rose superior to their bodies, and soared along, till they had exhausted their energy in this performance. The energy once exhausted, they fell with a struggling, not down into their bodies again, but into the cess-pools of the body.'

When Lawrence went north from Bandol, it was to carry on the war against the fear of the flesh, this time by arranging for a Paris edition of *Lady Chatterley*. On March 10 he wrote to Orioli:

We leave in the morning. The address in Paris is:
Hôtel de Versailles
Bvd Montparnasse
PARIS

Send me a line there.

Of course I've got a sore throat, to travel with.

Mr Groves, of Groves and Michaux, Librairie du Palais-Royal, says he will collaborate with me in any way, in getting out an edition [of *Lady Chatterley's Lover*]. I think I shall print it myself, and let them do the publishing and distributing—and so keep the thing in my own hands. The idea now is to bring out a little fat book that will go in a man's pocket, and sell it about 60 frs. Then people could easily carry them. What do you think? I shall try to get everything done as quick as possible.

Seems a long time since I heard from you—how are you? . . .

Wish I weren't suddenly feeling rather seedy. Frieda is going to Baden Baden direct, for a fortnight.

[P.S.] They say there's now a German pirated edition.

4 PAINTINGS AND PENSÉES AND GENTIANS

Lawrence was in Paris for nearly a month, arranging for the publication of the 'popular' edition of *Lady Chatterley* at sixty francs per copy. He called at Sylvia Beach's Shakespeare and Company bookshop and found her uninterested: after all, she published the other famous banned book, *Ulysses,* and that was 'a rival show'. At last Edward Titus, an American married to the cosmetician Helena Rubenstein, undertook to bring out the popular *Lady Chatterley,* with an introduction by Lawrence, 'My Skirmish with Jolly Roger'. This edition came out in May, the month after Lawrence left Paris.

While there, he visited the Huxleys at nearby Suresnes, of which he wrote to Orioli, March 18: 'It is very quiet and sunny—Suresnes a quiet nice little place, nice by the river, but nothing otherwise.' As for the future, 'I am not sure if we shall go to Spain—I want to, but Frieda doesn't want to very much. So perhaps we shall have to compromise, and come back to Italy.'

At the Huxleys', and at the Hôtel de Versailles in Paris, Lawrence was ill. Rhys Davies, in the next room at the hotel, would hear him strangling with coughs in the night, and once when Davies went through the communicating door he found Lawrence thrashing in torment on the bed, 'like some stormy El Greco figure'. When Davies suggested a doctor, Lawrence raged at him and then was calmer, as if he had cast out an evil spirit.

After Frieda arrived, he was well enough to go out to Ermenon-
ville, at last meeting the almost-mythical Crosbys, who lived there at
the edge of the forest in the Moulin du Soleil where Rousseau had
lodged and where Cagliostro had performed his rituals. In Caresse
Crosby's lively autobiography, *The Passionate Years* (1953), her
sharp eye and sharp pen remembered 'Lawrence, fugitive, strung taut
and full of wisdom—Frieda, upholstered, petulant and full of pride'.

In that season of daffodils, Caresse and Lawrence went botanizing
in the donkey cart, Lawrence 'with a shawl tucked round his knees,
his collar up and his soft hat pulled over his scorching eyes'. Inside the
Mill, as Harry Crosby sat writing and Frieda played the gramophone,
'Lawrence in a fit of exasperation broke record after record over her
head'. (In an unpublished, undated letter to Caresse Crosby—soon
after Lawrence's death in 1930—Frieda recalled, 'It was about this
time last year that we spent the time with you at the Mill—It's all so
vivid to me, that weekend—They were both such vivid creatures, Lorenzo and Harry, and I see you in the sailor suit and the bracelet
Harry gave you—.')

Perhaps the Lawrences were quarreling over where to move. If so,
Lawrence must have won, for on April 6 he wrote to Orioli: 'I have
settled up with Titus, and we leave tomorrow morning for Spain. I am
longing to get away from Paris, so noisy, dirty and nervous—not a bit
gay any more.' He wrote to Orioli from the Hotel Príncipe Alfonso,
Palma de Majorca, after a trip that took him and Frieda to Lyon,
Avignon, Perpignan, and Barcelona:

> This island—Majorca—is rather like Sicily, but not so beauti-
> ful, and much more asleep. But it has that southern sea quality,
> out of the world, in another world. I like that—and the sleep is
> good for me. Perhaps we shall stay a month or two—and come to
> Italy and find a house for the winter. Frieda will never take to
> Spain, and she won't even try to speak Spanish. So I expect
> we'll be back in Italy in autumn. But I like this sleep there is here
> —so still, and the people don't have any nerves at all—not nerv-
> ous, anybody.
>
> I do hope you kept the price of your last sale of Our Lady, to
> pay the postage. I should like us to be quite square now, on each
> side.

It didn't take Lawrence long to weary of Majorca: by April 24 the
people whose nervelessness he had admired had become 'dead and

staring', he told Davies: he couldn't bear 'their Spanishy faces, dead unpleasant masks, a bit like city English'. But he had been ill again: 'My teeth chattered like castanets—and that's the only Spanish thing I've done.' He admitted that, 'all in all, Italy is best when it comes to living, and France next. *Triumphat Frieda!*' In the mood of accepting Italy again, he wrote to Orioli from Majorca:

> We are still here—quite pleasant, and cool rather than hot. But I have no desire at all to live on this island, the people are all sort of dead, and it has a rather dead atmosphere. I much prefer Italy—and of course, so does Frieda. I think we shall stay here till about the end of the month, then make a little tour in Spain— to Alicante and Granada and Sevilla and Madrid—and then, I think, come to Italy to see about a house. Frieda suggests Lago di Garda, and that might be good. But I feel I'd like to be in sight of the sea. Maria and Aldous wanted us to look for a house be- hind Massa-Carrara on the mountain looking to the sea. I think I should like that, so we might go to Forte and motor from there, to see if there was a house. If you hear of anything, make a note of it. I should like a *house*—not just half a house, as at the Mirenda—not too big, and with a garden. If I found a place I liked, I would take it for some years, and furnish it, and perhaps put in central heating. If you happen to go to Forte, do take a motor and look around for me, and I will pay the expenses.—Or, if you hear of a nice place in the hills round Florence, let me know. I want to find a place, if possible, which we can keep. There are plenty of suitable houses here—but I don't want them.
>
> The only news of Our Lady is that I got a cheque for $68 from Lawrence Gomme, for eight copies. So cross him out. Now if we could make Miller and Gill pay up—and [bookseller] Davies—we shouldn't have done so badly. Titus has got the plates made, in Paris, and I think this week they start printing. So that should not take long. He sent me a specimen page, re- duced—and it looked quite well. A man in London talks of doing an edition of 500 there—printing it himself in London, right un- der Jix's nose. Don't know if this will come off.—Secker is doing the *Pansies,* omitting about a dozen poems.—Stephensen has sent me proofs of nine of the pictures. Some of them are not bad, but some very smudgy and thin.

The Lawrences lingered in Majorca. On May 26, Lawrence wrote to Rhys Davies, 'This letter is my most serious contribution to literature in six weeks', though at Majorca he wrote some of the 'More Pansies' which Aldington and Orioli gathered into the *Last Poems* volume after his death. In one of these, he suggests that riding the local tramcars could be adventuresome for tourists: he tells of a sulky-looking woman with a 'wisp of modern black mantilla' that 'made her half Madonna, half Astarte', whose yellow-brown eyes suddenly flared and looked into his, as if to say that he and she could sin together: 'She can keep her sin / She can sin with some thick-set Spaniard. / Sin doesn't interest me.'

Frieda also had strange adventures on the tramcars, as a passage in Lawrence's letter of May 26 to Rhys Davies indicates: 'A man pinched Frieda's bottom on the tram—I wasn't there—don't tell her I told you—so she despises every letter in the word Majorca, and is rampant to sail to Italy—to Marseille anyhow—on June 4th, where her squeamish rear has never been pinched.'

But Frieda had a more unpleasant accident in June: she broke her ankle. Bathing in the sea one steaming day, she looked ashore and was astonished to see a mounted officer, resplendent in his uniform, staring at her. She became nervous, scrambled over some rocks, one of her feet sank into a hole covered by seaweed, and her ankle snapped. She fell, sick with pain. The officer rode up and gallantly offered his horse, but Lawrence appeared and arranged for some men to take her in a car to the hotel. The ankle gave Frieda trouble for a long time.

She went to London to see the exhibition of Lawrence's paintings and to have a Park Lane specialist attend to her injury. Lawrence, leaving Majorca on June 18, went to stay with the Huxleys at Forte dei Marmi. But before departing from Majorca, he had to deny to several people the reports then current in England to the effect that he was dying. He told Laurence Pollinger, then of Curtis Brown's agency, that he had no intention of dying 'just yet', and he reassured Ada that the 'fool newspapers' were 'pining to announce one's death. But they're too "previous".'

His most significant letter of this group was to Murry: the last of all letters he was to write to his former friend. Having heard that Lawrence was critically ill, Murry offered to visit him in Majorca, but Lawrence answered, 'The me that you say you love is not me, but an idol of your own imagination. Believe me, you don't love me. The animal that I am you instinctively dislike—just as all the Lynds and

Squires and Eliots and Goulds dislike it.' Lawrence insisted that he
and Murry didn't know one another; they had shared 'some jolly
times, in the past' because they all pretended 'a bit', but ultimately
Lawrence and Murry belonged 'to different worlds, to different ways
of consciousness'. Lawrence said his health was 'a great nuisance',
though he had no intention of dying. Murry must accept the fact that
no good would come of their meeting again: 'Even when we are immortal spirits, we shall dwell in different Hades.'

In one of the rattling little 'More Pansies' poems of that time, 'Correspondence in After Years', Lawrence said:

> *A man wrote to me: We missed it, you and I.*
> *We were meant to mean a great deal to one another;*
> *but we missed it.*
> *And I could only reply:*
> *A miss is as good as a mile,*
> *mister!*

*

Because the Huxleys' small house at Forte dei Marmi was full, Lawrence went to a *pensione,* the Giuliani, which he described to Orioli on
June 23 as 'nice and cool, we eat out of doors under a big plane-tree.
Forte is not at all hot. Aldous and Maria are very well indeed, very
healthy—and I'm a lot better, though still coughing. . . . I hear the
show is a success, but the critics horrible—some pictures sold, I don't
know yet how many.' Lawrence had a sigh for 'Poor Reggie [Tur-
ner], burying his friends! Did you hear that [Charles Ellingham]
Brooks died in Capri?—did you know him? Douglas did.'

A few days later, Lawrence told Orioli about a Lawrence worship-
per from America: 'I have written Maria Cristina Chambers—perhaps she will come here.' Mrs. Chambers, a Mexican woman then living on Long Island, wife of the editor of the *Literary Digest,* had
wound her way in and out of his letters to Orioli for about a year: she
had communicated with Lawrence about the American customs' seizure of *Lady Chatterley,* and on August 30, 1928, Lawrence had written
to Orioli of 'Mrs Chambers, whom I have never seen, save a *large*
photograph, looks quite handsome—poor thing.'

Her name awakened echoes: the Maria Cristina was immediately
reminiscent of the American girl, Mary Christine Hughes, whom
Lawrence had recently sketched in 'Laura Philippine', and of course
the surname Chambers stirred old memories. But her visit to Forte

was hardly a happy one. As Frieda has said in a letter of May 26, 1953: 'the Maria Cristina Chambers was not of long duration, I don't remember much about her.' At the time, Frieda had written to Mabel Luhan that Lawrence dreaded seeing Mrs. Chambers: 'He is so frail and anything emotional is more than he can stand.' And at Forte, Lawrence was in a bitter mood as he watched others bathe in the sea, which he didn't dare to do after his terrifying hemorrhages of two summers before, apparently brought on by his swimming there.

He wrote some of his caustic 'More Pansies' as he looked on: 'Forte dei Marmi', with its sneer at 'the blatant bathers', and 'Sea-Bathers' ('Oh the handsome bluey-brown bodies, they might just as well be gutta percha'), which ends: 'They call it health, it looks like nullity. / Only here and there a pair of eyes, haunted, looks out as if asking: where then is life?' Some of this astringency got into one of the letters to Orioli, which also contained an account of Mrs. Chambers's visit and of Lawrence's future plans:

> Maria Cristina wears me out rather—so she is going to Pisa tomorrow, to stay the night there, and come on to Florence on Friday. She will arrive at 13.15, but I don't think there is any need for you to meet her, if you will just engage her a room at the *Moderno* for Friday at 1.15, she can drive in a *vettura*.
>
> I expect I shall come on Saturday, by the same train. Shall I really stay with you in your flat? I should like to. But don't meet me either at the station, it is so easy to drive to you.
>
> Sorry the dinner was dull. Here Maria and Yvonne Franchetti were very *cattive* with M.C.—but suddenly Maria changed, and became patronizingly sweet. They are still wondering when you are going to Montecatini with Aldous. A few more people on the beach—all so terribly aware of *themselves* and their beastly bodies. Well I shall be glad to escape an atmosphere of women, women, women, and see you again.

On Saturday, July 6, Maria Huxley drove Lawrence to Pisa, where he boarded the train for Florence. He was unaware of what had happened in London the day before at his exhibition, which twelve or thirteen thousand people had visited since its opening exactly three weeks earlier. Some of them complained to the Home Secretary. This was no longer Jix (who had become Lord Brentford), but rather John R. Clynes, who had taken over the office that spring for the new Labour Government. Clynes was a man who prided himself on his liberal opinions but, as so often happens in such cases, the position rather than the man operated, and on July 5 Detective-Inspector Gordon Hester and Detective-Sergeant Thomas brought six policemen with them to raid the gallery. They took away thirteen of the paintings, which caused Rebecca West to remark that this 'loathsome incident' had 'an infuriating lack of symmetry about it. Six shocked policemen ought to take twelve pictures; the odd one is an offence!'

The policemen also removed four copies of the volume which reproduced the paintings as well as a copy of George Grosz's *Ecce Homo* (thereby antedating Hitler as an art critic) but, after persuasion by Dorothy Warren (who had become Mrs. Philip Trotter), they didn't confiscate Louis Aragon's translation of *The Hunting of the Snark:* she explained it was a children's book, even though printed in the immoral French language. Some Blake reproductions the police also allowed to remain when they learned that Blake had been dead for a century and a year. But the thirteen Lawrence paintings and the offensive books were hustled into the cellar of the Marlborough Street police court, and rumor belled through London that they would be burned. Meanwhile the Warren Gallery kept the exhibition open, with the pictures that were left and a few 'inoffensive' paintings that Ada Clarke brought from the Midlands.

In Italy, Lawrence had repeated his Forte dei Marmi experience of 1927. When he arrived at Florence he was ill, and within a few days Orioli thought he might die and so telegraphed in panic to Frieda. Lawrence, confined to Orioli's flat and disturbed by the rattle of traffic on the Lungarno, wrote to Maria Huxley on July 10 that he knew of the suppression of the pictures: 'Had a telegram, nothing else,' to inform him that the paintings had been imprisoned 'and threatened to be burned—*auto-da-fé*;' he blamed his illness on 'sitting too late on the beach on Friday'.

Lawrence thought of returning to Bavaria, to which Max Mohr had invited him, as soon as he was well enough, but on the thirteenth he wrote to Mohr that Frieda had arrived 'suddenly' and wanted 'to go *first* to Baden Baden to her mother, and come later on to Bavaria, perhaps September'. He had rallied when he heard Frieda was en route, and as soon as she arrived, vital and exuberant in spite of her still aching and wobbly ankle, he recovered. Frieda, notwithstanding her worries lest the dampness of the cellar ruin the imprisoned pictures, or lest the police burn them, had enjoyed London, where she had felt 'like the Queen of Sheba'. The Aga Khan had given a dinner for her and suggested that he might exhibit the pictures in Paris. And she had felt that, for the first time, her three children were 'entirely' with her. 'My son Monty came up to the scratch, enjoyed the fight with the police—said: *de l'audace et encore de l'audace!'*

On July 14, Lawrence wrote to Dorothy Warren Trotter, telling her to compromise with the police rather than permit his pictures to be burned: 'There is something sacred to me about my pictures, and I will not have them burnt, for all the liberty of England. I am an Englishman, and I do my bit for the liberty of England. But I am most of all a man, and my first creed is that my manhood and my sincere utterance shall be inviolate and beyond nationality or any other limitation. To admit that my pictures should be burned, in order to change an English law, would be to admit that sacrifice of life to circumstance which I most strongly disbelieve in.' And: 'No more crucifixions, no more martyrdoms, no more *autos da fé* as long as time lasts, if I can prevent it. Every crucifixion starts a most deadly chain of karma, every martyr is a Laocoön snake to tangle up the human family. Away with such things.'

Lawrence was well enough to leave for Germany on July 16. This is probably the departure Douglas remembered wryly in *Looking Back:* Lawrence invited Orioli and Douglas to a farewell luncheon, ordered expensive food and wine, and then, when they had barely finished eating, suddenly cried out that he and Frieda would miss the train. Douglas should have been prepared for a trick—he had recently induced Lawrence to pay for some drinks for him and Orioli ('the surest way to win his respect was to make him suffer small losses of this kind')—but in the scramble at the luncheon Douglas picked up the bill. Lawrence didn't mention it again at the station, Douglas recalled, 'and as the train moved out I thought to detect—it may have been imagination on my part—the phantom of a smile creeping over his wan face.'

*

From Baden-Baden, Lawrence wrote to Orioli on July 22 that perhaps the first draft of *Lady Chatterley* could be published by Secker and Knopf: 'I believe it has hardly any fucks or shits, and no address to the penis, in fact hardly any root of the matter at all.' Orioli had the manuscript: 'I wish you would glance at the so-called hot parts and see how hot they are. I'm sure they're hardly warm. And I'm sure I could expurgate the few flies out of that virgin ointment—whereas

our Lady C. I cannot, absolutely cannot even begin to expurgate.'
A week later he wrote from a place higher in the mountains, the
Kurhaus Plättig (bei Bühl), to which Frieda and her mother had
hauled him:

> I have corrected the [Lasca] proofs and am sending them back
> at once. Will you just glance through them.
>
> Yes, I had Dorothy's [Dorothy Warren Trotter's] long and
> senseless letter: but only one card, from Aldous, none from
> you.—I can't be bothered with the Victor Cunard nonsense of
> telephones. The case of the pictures is postponed until August
> 8th, so nothing to do till then. Fancy, Secker could not supply all
> his orders for that swindling 250 edition [of *Pansies*, expur-
> gated]—over-subscribed. He is now selling the third thousand of
> the ordinary 10/6 edit.—good for poetry.
>
> Don't bother to send on the *Dials*. By the way, those are the
> last numbers, it is now dead.
>
> I shall send you Jonathan Cape's *Collected Poems* of mine, for
> you to keep for me with my books.—Heinemann is doing 'The
> Man Who Loved Islands' in an expensive edition, and giving me
> £300 down.—The Random Press [Random House] doing that
> Introduction to the Paris *Lady C* at $4. a copy: swindle, such
> a little thing!—Lahr will have his *Pansies* [unexpurgated]
> ready this week, but I ask him not to let them out till after Au-
> gust 8th when the pictures will be tried—they are still in prison.
> Dorothy continues the show—foolishly—
>
> It rains and rains here, and is bitter cold. I have to lie under
> the great feather bolster on my bed, to be warm. I have got a
> cold, and I simply hate it here. We shall go down in a day or
> two—and perhaps to Bavaria—or perhaps to Como. I wish I was
> in Florence, it is so cold and awful here.
>
> Titus doesn't want me to do an expurgated Lady C.—every-
> body else does.

Compton Mackenzie, having recognized himself as the central figure in the story, blocked the proposed Heinemann edition of 'The
Man Who Loved Islands', with the three hundred pounds' advance for
Lawrence—the loss of which hardly improved his temper. The
Collected Poems volume seems, however, to have given him some
satisfaction, for although the British reviews of the preceding autumn
had been rather cool, the American critics were that summer praising
the book and treating Lawrence as an important poet.

In London, Humbert Wolfe in the *Observer* wrote one of the typically antithetical ('genius, but') reviews that characterized the attitude towards Lawrence of his fellow writers in England: he was volcanic, Wolfe said, and although he could write lines unmatched 'elsewhere in English verse for naked force and untamed essence', the expression was nevertheless 'lava and not the fertilizing ray of light. The countryside, after it has passed, is blank and blasted.' Murry, too, was antagonistic in the *Adelphi,* finding fault with many of the poems, particularly the later ones, though also finding the total achievement 'prodigiously impressive'.

In the American reviews of the time, John Gould Fletcher in the New York *Herald Tribune,* Percy Hutchinson in the *New York Times,* Louis Untermeyer in the *Saturday Review of Literature,* and Harriet Monroe in *Poetry* responded more friendlily to the *Collected Poems,* though occasionally the antithetical tone sounded in the American reviews too. Fletcher's praise was warm: 'Of all the poets who in the present day have written about love, none have written better than D. H. Lawrence.' It was his old friend Harriet Monroe who was the coolest among the American reviewers: he was 'capable of sheer beauty', though a very careless technician. If Amy Lowell had been alive, she would have pumped up more enthusiasm than this. But Harriet Monroe felt that in revising his earlier poems, many of which had first appeared in *Poetry,* Lawrence damaged them—a point which has been persuasively argued against by Phyllis Bartlett in *Poetry in Process* (1951) and by Richard Ellmann in his essay on Lawrence's poetry in *The Achievement of D. H. Lawrence* (1953).

While the American reviews were appearing in that summer of 1929, the chilled Lawrence on his mountain height had begun a new series of poems, in the same style as *Pansies* but named after a thorny plant, as he told Orioli in a bitter letter from Bühl, Baden:

The MS. of *Lady C* came yesterday—many thanks for sending it. Of course I still don't want to make a castrato public edition, and doubt if I shall bring myself to do it. If the dirty public haven't the guts to get hold of the existing edition, let them do without. Why should I trim myself down to make it easy for the swine! I loathe the gobbling public anyhow.—I shall not in any case send this MS. to England—shall send it back to you. Now I am sending the Amer. *Collected Poems* for you to keep for me.

It has rained and been bitter cold all the time we have been up here on this beastly mountain, and I have hated it, and only

stayed because my mother-in-law got into a frenzy at the thought
of going down, because she says it does her so much good here
and gives her so much strength—*es gibt mir Kraft, Kraft!*—She
is 78, and is in a mad terror for fear she might die; and she
would see me or anyone else die ten times over, to give her a bit
more strength to drag on a few more meaningless years. It is so
ugly and so awful, I nearly faint. I have never felt so down, so
depressed and ill, as I have here, these ten days: awful! What
with that terrible old woman, the icy wind, the beastly black
forest, and all the depressing and fat guests—really, one wonders
that anyone should be so keen to live, under such circumstances.
I know I'm not.

But tomorrow we are going down, and it will be better. We
shall stay a week or so in the

Hotel Löwen, Lichtenthal bei Baden Baden[.]

It is better there—I can sit in the *Gaststube* where the men come
in from the village to drink their beer and smoke their pipes, and
I can escape a bit this awful atmosphere of old women who devour the life of everything around them. Truly old and elderly
women are ghastly, ghastly, eating up all life with hoggish greed,
to keep themselves alive. They don't mind who else dies. I know
my mother-in-law would secretly gloat, if I died at 43 and she
lived on at 78. She would feel an ugly triumph. It is that kind of
thing which does kill one. . . .

Don't sent [*sic*] me Lorenzo di Medici till I get somewhere
where I am more at ease and cheerful. At present I can do *nothing:* except write a few stinging Pansies which this time are *Nettles.* I shall call them nettles.

Lawrence usually got on better than that with his mother-in-law,
whom he was really fond of. But Frieda, in her candid biography,
admits: 'Only the last time, when my mother was so frail and old herself, being with Lawrence who was so very ill, they got on each other's
nerves.' The old Baronin outlived Lawrence, but she grieved over him
and all he had meant to Frieda, who further wrote: 'I think after
Lawrence's death her desire to live left her'. Lawrence had less than
seven months of existence remaining after that mountaintop ordeal,
and he seems never again, in that time, to have written to the
'Schwiegermutter': a few days after the return to Baden-Baden, he
complained to Else of '*Weisheit der Alten!*—nineteenth-century lies.'

He had come down from the heights on August 3, just five days before the 'trial' of his pictures before Magistrate Frederick Mead, aged eighty-two. Herbert G. Muskett, the expert-without-credentials who had helped crush *The Rainbow,* reappeared in the guise of an art critic to brand the pictures as 'gross, coarse, hideous, unlovely, and obscene'. With this on record, the magistrate felt justified in barring the accredited experts for the defense, three noted artists: Augustus John, Glyn Philpot, and William Rothenstein.

But the defense counsel, St. John Hutchinson, was at least permitted to lament, 'We have to wait until 1929, with a so-called advanced government in power, to see this new form of censorship set up in this country.' When Hutchinson referred to the 'Venus' in the Dulwich Gallery, Magistrate Mead cut in to say, 'It is a serious thing to compare these pictures with the Dulwich "Venus".' He granted that Hutchinson had argued most convincingly, but to no avail, for 'the most splendidly painted picture in the universe might be obscene'. He somehow didn't get around to pronouncing Lawrence's pictures legally obscene, for Hutchinson offered to withdraw them, with the assurance they wouldn't be shown again; the gallery owners would ship them back to Lawrence. So the police didn't burn the paintings after all.

But the newspapers continued to suggest that Lawrence was an obscene monster, and he complained, as usual, and with justification, that he had no redress. He turned his anger loose in the *Nettles* verses and in some of the poems which later appeared in the 'More Pansies' section of *Last Poems.* One of these attacked the art critic T. W. Earp, who had spoken condescendingly of the paintings in the *New Statesman,* drawing from Lawrence the riposte that began, 'I heard a little chicken chirp: / My name is Thomas, Thomas Earp!'—who couldn't paint or write, but could tell everyone else what to do.

Other victims of these verses were 'Mr Mead, that old, old lily', the *London Mercury* and its editor J. C. Squire, and even (in '13,000 People') the visitors to the gallery, whose gigglings and whose staring 'at the spot where the fig-leaf just was not' prompted Lawrence to write, 'But why, I ask you? Oh tell me why? / Aren't they made quite the same, then, as you and I?'

In such poems, Lawrence shot out anger for anger's sake as he rarely did in the great range of his work. Before this he had occasionally expressed a kind of *representative* anger, as when he spoke for all sensitive men in the war chapters of *Kangaroo;* but it was only in the

Nettles and a few of the *Pansies* that he gave way to petulance and exasperation. But by the end of his life he had had years of being sorely provoked.

And sometimes he was made out to seem far worse than he was, as a letter to Charles Lahr from Florence on July 9, 1929, shows; Lahr had sent him the review of *Pansies* by Sylvia Lynd, the Meynells' friend, whose husband had years before helped destroy *The Rainbow;* now Lawrence wrote to Lahr: 'You might get somebody to write to *Daily News* and ask if Sylvia Lynd made the misquotation on purpose—

> *Don't make it in ghastly seriousness,*
> *(Don't) do it because you hate people*

—the *Don't* omitted from her quot.—which gives an ugly face to the thing. That's the way they do me harm all the time.'

Again and again in the poems and letters of this period, Lawrence was bitter and furious. The bitterness and fury were certainly justified—and intensified by his illness. Yet he still kept his relish for the vital, as so many of the *Last Poems* show.

He had written in 1926, in a review of H. M. Tomlinson's *Gifts of Fortune* (a review not published at the time): 'Once be disillusioned with the man-made world, and you can still see the magic, the beauty, the delicate realness of all the other life.' This is a key to the enduring and of course to the later Lawrence, the author of the *Last Poems.*

His former friend Richard Aldington later showed (in his introduction to *Apocalypse*) that he sympathetically understood much of what Lawrence had expressed:

> Before Lawrence, the primacy of the intellect had been doubted by Bergson, the psychology of the unconscious had been formulated by Freud, and the whole system of values of European civilisation had been rejected in their different ways by Tolstoy and Nietzsche, and even Dostoevsky. Lawrence differs from them, partly because he was English, but chiefly because he was essentially a poet—a poet who for various reasons found his more effective medium was prose. But, being an Englishman of his class and time, he could scarcely avoid being a preacher as well as a poet. It was the preacher who brought the house down on his own head. From the point of view of the intellectuals (and this is the

reason why they treated him either with coldness or hostility)
Lawrence's fundamental heresy was simply that he placed quality
of feelings, intensity of sensations and passion before intellect . . .
what Lawrence had to give and wanted to give was a new or different way of feeling, living, and loving, and not a new way of
thinking. You cannot put him into formulas. Of course, he had to
think too—how else could he be a writer? But his problem as a
writer was to put into words these feelings and perceptions which
he believed to be independent of the conscious intellect. This was
difficult enough for Lawrence, who was dealing with his own experience; it is almost impossible for anyone else, who may entirely
misinterpret what he wrote. What did he mean when he spoke of
the Indian singing as 'mindless'? What exactly are the 'physical
life' and the 'tenderness' he used to talk to us about? I can feel,
you can feel what he meant, but they are not things which can be
pinned down with neat defining sentences. These things cannot be
expressed except through images and symbols and the evocative
descriptions at which Lawrence excelled.

*

On August 10, 1929, Lawrence wrote to H.D., who had asked him
for some recent poems for the *Imagist Anthology* she was editing with
her estranged husband, Aldington. She had apparently suggested a
meeting with the Lawrences, but the man whom she once wrote of as
looking like Van Gogh rejected the idea of an encounter, though he did
enclose some verse:

Your note this morning—here are a few bits—the typed
poems crossed out in red are omitted from Secker's *Pansies*—
these bits I have written out from some oddments. I have
changed a word or two in the typed poems, to make them possible. Now do as you like—take or leave what you like.—You
won't really like any of them, but you can't get blood out of a
stone.
We're here for another ten days or so, I expect, then really I
must go south. My cough is a great nuisance, and it is very damp
and steamy here in Baden—not good weather.
Where we shall be in the autumn I don't know—but probably
somewhere in Italy.—But now it's more than ten years since we
met, and what should we have to say? God knows! Nothing,

really. It's no use saying anything. That's my last conviction. Least said, soonest mended: which assumes that the breakage has already happened.

Douglas is in Australia, not very well and not happy. Arabella I hear is in Paris—she's not in a good way at all, poor Arabella.

'Poor Arabella': in Lawrence's letters and in his fiction he always shows her as grieving, in opposition to the cheerful Brigit Patmore. As for H.D., 'it's no use saying anything'—though in spite of Lawrence's rebuff she included six of his poems in the imagist anthology she was editing with Aldington. Lawrence sometimes turned coldly away from people because of their past actions; it was not often he cut so cruelly into possibilities, using folk proverbs in the process and assuming that 'the break has already happened'. Actually, Lawrence mistrusted H.D.'s loyalty: although he usually didn't hold grudges, he couldn't forget that, in a quarrel with some American friends of theirs a few years before, H.D. had taken the opposite side. Moreover, as noted earlier, Lawrence had disapproved of H.D.'s leaving Aldington for Cecil Gray.

At Baden-Baden that summer, Lawrence took treatments for asthma, and Frieda had her ankle massaged daily. On August 12, Lawrence told Orioli: 'Last night Frieda celebrated her 50th birthday—a party of nine, and Bowle, Trout, Duck—very good.' On August 24: 'We leave in the morning for Bavaria. I don't know why I've been so sore and miserable here. I think too many large German women of heavy years sitting on my chest.'

He had heard from Maria Cristina Chambers, who had 'had a terrible time landing in New York—sent to Ellis Island like a criminal, and all that. But now she's buzzing around.' On the same day he wrote to Charles Lahr: 'Why don't we start a little fortnightly magazine, about ten pages and about as big as this sheet of paper—called the *Squib*—and just fire off squibs in it. Do let's do that. Get Davies to help, and a few spunky people, and let us put crackers under their chairs, and a few bent pins under their bottoms. It could be done quite cheap, and without any pretensions—and we can have *noms de plume*—a bit of fun!'

*

In Bavaria the Lawrences settled into a little house beside the inn at Rottach-am-Tegernsee, near Max Mohr's farm-home, Wulfsgrube.

On August 30, Lawrence told Orioli: 'Here we are up among the mountains again. It is quite beautiful, and very peaceful, cows and haymaking and apples on tall old appletrees, dropping so suddenly. We eat in the little inn—such a smell of cows—and it's quite nice.' But he still thought of returning to Italy. And he mentioned Frederick Carter: 'I am writing to a man I used to know in the past, about a book of his, *The Dragon of the Apocalypse*[,] in my opinion very interesting. I think you might publish it one day.' Carter wrote back to explain that the 'Dragon' book Lawrence had heard of was not the study of the Apocalypse whose manuscript Lawrence had read, but *The Dragon of the Alchemists* (1926), a collection of designs originally made for the other book, with some notes.

Lawrence replied to Carter on August 30: 'Mistrustful of your second version, coming a few steps down the ladder, to more comprehensible levels,' though he believed 'we could put the Dragon across—500 or even 1,000 copies at two guineas'; they would 'make Stephensen or Random House print it—if not, we'd do it with Orioli in Florence'; and there was a hint of collaboration: 'If you like, I'll add what I can to the notes—or even take yours over and write them up.' He hoped that Carter's designs would not be 'too gnashingly baroque. You are more sincere when writing than when drawing, I believe.'

The resumption of that correspondence was important, for it led to Lawrence's writing his own last book, *Apocalypse,* on the southern French coast the next winter. Meanwhile, at Rottach, he wrote one of his most important polemics, *Pornography and Obscenity,* and returned to lyrical poetry. He also tried a health cure, about which he wrote to Orioli on September 13:

I have been doing my cure—first taking arsenic and phosphorus twice a day. This made me feel I was *really* being poisoned, so I gave it up. Now I am only doing the diet—no salt, and much raw fruit and vegetables, and porridge in place of bread. I must say I don't feel much better—in fact I have been rather worse these last two weeks. Perhaps it is the altitude doesn't suit me. The place itself is very nice, and everybody charming, but I feel rather rotten. I know I shall be better when we come lower down. But that would be foolish while the heat wave lasts. I hear there is a heat wave everywhere—and even here it is close and rather heavy, but not hot. Today has come cloudy, so I ex-

pect the weather will soon break. And then no doubt it will turn
cold, so we shall want to come down. But we can take a motor-
car to Jenbach, which is near Innsbruck, so we shall soon be
down in Verona. . . .

I suppose Frieda told you her foot is better—she limps a little
out of habit, nothing else. The bone-setter came from a neigh-
bouring village—just a well-to-do *contadino*. He felt with his
thumb, said: Yes, it's out!—gave a shove, and it was done, in
less than a minute. The bone was resting on the side of the
socket, and couldn't slip back into place. And the socket was filling in, in a couple of months she would have been lame for life.
And I paid 12 guineas to the specialist in Park Lane, and there is
a bill in Baden Baden. So much for doctors! a great fraud.

Well, dear Pino, I shall be glad to come south and to see you.
Let's hope I shall revive a bit, for there's not much use for me
here.

[P.S.] Remember me to Douglas—and Reggie.

That arsenic-vegetation 'cure' had been prescribed by a doctor
Mohr brought out from Munich. One day at Rottach, Lawrence had
been so ill that Frieda feared he was dying. But the sudden appearance of Mohr, at her behest, brought him out of bed. That evening at
Wulfsgrube, when Lawrence was playing with the Mohrs' child,
Frieda quietly asked the parents whether they weren't worried lest
Lawrence infect the little girl. But Mohr denied the possibility, for
how could anyone 'believe that any harm can come from Lorenzo? . . .
from his person, from his work, from his sickness, from his troubles,
from his sharp criticism of our times. Behind everything there stood
and stands forever the powerful and saving magic of his life.'

But Lawrence did consent to try the treatment of Mohr's friend, a
former priest who now conducted a clinic in Munich and believed in
the special diet. Anthony West was probably right in his book on
Lawrence when he said that Lawrence fell into the clutches of 'a
Bavarian dietetic quack', who with his assistant 'might as well have
beaten him and had done with it; when he went south for the winter
to Bandol, he was near death'.

Before leaving Rottach, Lawrence wrote 'Glory of Darkness', the
first of his death poems and one of the finest of all his poems; it later
became 'Bavarian Gentians': 'Not every man has gentians in his
house / in soft September, at slow, sad Michaelmas'—the gentians

that darkened 'the day-time torch-like with the smoking blueness of Pluto's gloom' and were 'black lamps from the hall of Dis'. The mine-haunted poet invoked the resurrection-vegetation myth:

> *Reach me a gentian, give me a torch*
> *let me guide myself with the blue, forked torch of*
>   *this flower*
> *down the darker and darker stairs, where blue is*
>   *darkened on blueness.*
> *Even where Persephone goes, just now, from the*
>   *frosted September*
> *To the sightless realm where darkness is awake upon*
>   *the dark*
> *and Persephone herself is but a voice*
> *or a darkness invisible enfolded in the deeper dark*
> *of the arms Plutonic, and pierced with the passion*
>   *of dense gloom,*
> *among the splendour of torches of darkness, shedding*
>   *darkness on the lost bride and her groom.*

5 TO THE END OF THE JOURNEY

Lawrence had planned to meet the Trotters in Venice, but the trip didn't materialize. As he wrote to Orioli from Rottach: 'There was a telegram from the Trotters last night—they are in Würzburg, about five hours from here, and are on their way to that place in Hungary [actually Austria] where they buy that beastly jade—and they say they are writing and sending a cheque. Which means of course that they don't want to see me, because they don't want to answer my questions. So they are slipping past.'

The doctors had warned him not to go to Florence at that time, but he felt he and Frieda must return there to get the trunks she had left behind on her last visit. By September 23 the Lawrences were at Bandol again, at the Beau Rivage, and within a week they had taken the six-room Beau Soleil, about which Lawrence wrote to Enid Hilton on October 5: 'We are here in this bungalow villa—not bad, right on the sea—and a nice woman to cook. . . . It has been sunny as usual here, but this morning heavy rain. . . . Now the sea is blue again, and the terrace full of light, so I'll get up—having written a newspaper article—and it's nearly noon.'

Lawrence told Enid Hilton, the Brewsters, and Else Jaffe, in letters at this time, that he had not been able to breathe in Germany:
the 'north was full of death'. On October 4 he wrote to Else, 'Now it
has killed Stresemann—whom will it not kill?—everybody except the
Hindenburgs and the old women in the Stifts.' The south was better:
'I still love the Mediterranean, it still seems as young as Odysseus, in
the morning.' Under the spell of that sea, he was writing the verses
of *Last Poems:*

('The Greeks Are Coming!')
Little islands out at sea, on the horizon
keep suddenly showing a whiteness, a flash and a furl, a hail
of something coming, ships a-sail from over the rim of the
   sea . . .

('The Argonauts')
Now the sea is the Argonauts' sea, and in the dawn
Odysseus calls the commands, as he steers past the foamy
   islands
wait, wait don't bring the coffee yet, nor the pain grillé.
The dawn is not off the sea, and Odysseus' ships
have not yet passed the islands. I must watch them still.

In a letter to Maria Huxley, Lawrence described that coast and
said, 'Here, to me, it is something like Sicily, Greek, or pre-Roman'.
And the mythology of his poems of the time is Greek. One of the most
striking of them, 'Middle of the World', is partly a return to the *symboliste* mode, and without being didactic it conveys much of the
Lawrencean philosophy:

This sea will never die, neither will it ever grow old
nor cease to be blue, nor in the dawn
cease to lift up its hills
and let the slim black ship of Dionysus come sailing in
with grape-vines up the mast, and dolphins leaping.
What do I care if the smoking ships
of the P. & O. and the Orient Line and all the other stinkers
cross like clock-work the Minoan distance!
They only cross, the distance never changes.

And now that the moon who gives men glistening bodies
is in her exaltation, and can look down on the sun

I see descending from the ships at dawn
slim naked men from Cnossos, smiling the archaic smile
of those that will without fail come back again,
and kindling little fires upon the shores
and crouching, and speaking the music of lost languages.

And the Minoan Gods, and the Gods of Tiryns
are heard softly laughing and chatting, as ever;
and Dionysus, young, and a stranger
leans listening at the gate, in all respect.

*

Max Mohr came to visit the Lawrences and stayed at the Goëlands Hôtel from late in September until the third week in October. Lawrence told Maria Huxley on September 29 that Mohr was 'like a bewildered seal rolling around'. The Brewsters, whose daughter was now at school in England, arrived before Mohr left, and began looking for a house in Bandol. They puzzled Mme Douillet of the Beau Rivage, who asked Lawrence: '*Pourquoi, Monsieur, pourquoi mangent-ils comme ça? Pourquoi? C'est manger sans vouloir manger, n'est-ce pas?*' Lawrence told her solemnly, '*Voyez-vous, ils sont Bouddhistes, les dévots du dieu Bouddha, de l'Inde.*'

The Brewsters eventually rented a villa, the Château Brun, about five miles away from the Lawrences' place. They met Carter at the train when he came down for a visit—Lawrence was not well enough to go to the station—and took him to the Beau Soleil, where Carter saw, after six years, how 'the sharp-shouldered figure was exaggerated now to the extreme of fragility'. The bright color had gone from his hair and beard, whose redness had darkened, and the voice had become weary; but the eyes remained bright.

That autumn, Lawrence was happy over the success of *Pornography and Obscenity* in England. Published by T. S. Eliot's firm, Faber and Faber, in the same pamphlet series as Lord Brentford's (Jix's) apologia for censorship, Lawrence's essay was in far greater demand; by December 9 he could report to Orioli that it was going at the rate of 12,000 copies a week.

In *Pornography and Obscenity*, Lawrence mocked Jix's pronouncements, though for the most part the essay is a discussion of the 'shock' words Lawrence thought preferable to the 'rubbing of the dirty little secret' by smoking-room stories and the 'half-way' literature that Lawrence the puritan disliked. Ultimately, he hoped, 'even the general public will desire to look the thing in the face, and see for itself the difference between the sneaking masturbation pornography of the Press, the film, and present-day popular literature, and then the creative portrayals of the sexual impulse that we have in Boccaccio or the Greek vase-paintings or some Pompeiian art, and which are necessary for the fulfilment of our consciousness.'

It was perhaps the popular success of this pamphlet that encouraged Lawrence to expand his 'Jolly Roger' introduction to the Paris *Lady Chatterley* by five times its original length. The result, *A Propos of Lady Chatterley's Lover,* which the Mandrake Press published in June 1930, was the finest of all his pronouncements on the subject of sex, literature, and censorship, striking once again the great Lawrencean chord: 'Life is only bearable when the mind and the body are in harmony, and there is a natural balance between them, and each has a natural respect for the other.'

These essays—*Pornography and Obscenity* and *A Propos of Lady Chatterley's Lover*—are grand statements on a grandly important subject. The meaner side of Lawrence kept trying to express itself in his proposed *Squib,* about which he continued to write to Lahr: 'K. [Koteliansky] thinks the *Squib* is a bad idea—perhaps it is. Perhaps one would collect only a little bunch of not very nice people' (from Rottach, September 16, 1929). And: 'No, I don't want to fill a *Squib* all with myself. I *don't* want to figure prominently' (from Bandol, October 7). And: 'I feel the *Squib* is not going to go off. There *must* be more than me to it' (from Bandol, October 11).

As with *Pansies,* which Lawrence used in the double sense of the flowers and of thoughts (with a suggestion, as Richard Ellmann noted, of wounds), he regarded his *Squib* as being such not only in the sense of firecracker but also in the sense of lampoon. As Lawrence told Lahr, 'I mentioned the subject to Aldous Huxley, but he is both cautious and timid.' Yet in *Vanity Fair* for November, Huxley made an uncautious and untimid defense of Lawrence's paintings and other work (Rebecca West had similarly spoken out for him in another American magazine, the *Bookman,* two months earlier); Huxley saw Lawrence as the 'crusader of . . . the reuniting of animal and thinker'; since 'our reflexes have been wrongly conditioned', Huxley said, we should 'get used to being shocked, until the conditioning is undone'.

Public voices raised in Lawrence's behalf were extremely scarce then, yet in his letter of December 18 to Orioli, Lawrence complained of Huxley: 'I shall never ask him for anything, neither for myself nor anybody else, any more. He takes not the slightest notice. He annoys me.—I doubt if you will ever get anything out of him.' But this was only a temporary lapse into petulance, for within five days Lawrence wrote to thank Huxley for a volume of reproductions by Aristide Maillol, who had 'a certain tender charm'. And Huxley and Lawrence remained good friends, to the last, though they sometimes complained about each other in letters. On February 5, 1929, Lawrence had written to Lady Ottoline, '. . . the Aldous that writes those novels is only one little Aldous amongst others—probably much nicer— that don't write novels. . . . No, I don't like his books: even if I admire a sort of desperate courage of repulsion and repudiation in them. But, again, I feel only half a man writes the books—a sort of precocious adolescent. There is surely much more of a man in the actual Aldous.'

Huxley, in a July 1929 letter to his father, spoke of Lawrence as extraordinary, a man he liked and admired, 'but difficult to get on with, passionate, queer, violent'. But age was improving Lawrence, 'and now his illness has cured him of his violence and left him touchingly gentle'. Huxley in a July 13, 1929, letter to his brother Julian spoke with annoyance of Lawrence's obstinacy in refusing medical treatment; Frieda encouraged this attitude, thereby irritating Huxley and his wife Maria. They knew how ill Lawrence really was, but unless he could be handcuffed and taken 'to a sanatorium by force, there's nothing to be done'.

As for the *Squib,* its only explosion was a tiny one, in a four-page pamphlet Lahr printed in a private, limited edition in 1930, containing Lawrence's mocking 'biography' of Murry (born 1889), with reference to his book on Jesus: 'John Middleton was born in the year of the Lord 1891? It happened also to be the most lying year of the most lying century since time began, but what is that to an innocent babe!' Or, one might sadly ask, to a dying man?

In his letter of December 18 to Orioli, Lawrence had inquired whether Orioli had heard of the suicide the week before, in a New York hotel, of Harry Crosby, who had shot a young woman companion before killing himself: 'Very horrible—the last sort of cocktail excitement. The wife is on her way back to Paris already with the ashes (his only) in a silver jar.—He had always been *too* rich and spoilt: nothing to do but commit suicide. It depressed me very much.'

The letter Lawrence wrote to Caresse Crosby the following month

was full of tenderness ('Don't you try to recover yourself too soon—
it is much better to be stunned and blind for a little time longer'); he
said Harry Crosby 'had a real poetic gift—if only he hadn't tried to
disintegrate himself so! This disintegrating spirit, and the tangled
sound of it, makes my soul weary to death.' He said his own chest had
let him down, but that his nerves were 'so healthy', whereas Harry
Crosby, with his healthy body, had sick nerves: 'So there we are. Life
and death in all of us!'

In October he had written to Mabel Luhan that when people became angry at one another, it was not their true selves functioning,
but a mysterious imposition from the outside: 'I think these violent
antipathies between people are in themselves a sign of nervous imbal-
ance.' In January he told Mrs. Luhan, 'For my own part, though I
am perhaps *more* irascible, being more easily irritable, not being
well, still, I think I am more inwardly tolerant and companionable.
Anyhow, people's little oddities don't frighten me any more: even
their badnesses.' Earl Brewster, who, in those last months of Lawrence's life, used to massage him with coconut oil, has said that 'during this time he gained a great tranquillity'. And his poem 'The Ship
of Death', written on that bright Mediterranean coast in those months,
reflects that tranquillity in symbols deriving from Egyptian and Etruscan tombs:

> . . . *The grim frost is at hand, when the apples will fall*
> *thick, almost thunderous, on the hardened earth.*
> *And death is on the air like a smell of ashes!*
> *Oh build your ship of death. Oh build it!*
> *for you will need it.*
> *For the voyage of oblivion awaits you.*

*

There was one more book to be written: *Apocalypse,* Lawrence's last
hymn to the sun. It is a vital book—though it seemed a miracle, to
those who had seen Lawrence in those last years, that he was able to
write at all. But, despite pain and the definite signs that his disease
was consuming him, he spoke and wrote, to the last day of his life, as
if he would go on living.

His interest in the Apocalypse went far back, to the days of his
childhood in the miners' bethel. The theosophy he had learned from
reading James Pryse and Mme Blavatsky provided him with materials
for a re-examination of Christianity, and the correspondence with

Carter, begun in New Mexico in 1922, increased his interest in Apocalyptic symbols. After Lawrence revived this correspondence in the summer of 1929, he wrote a number of letters which, published in full along with the earlier ones to the same correspondent, would make an excellent preface to a reprint of *Apocalypse*. Excerpts from some of these 1929 letters to Carter will show how thorough Lawrence's interest in the subject was:

[October 1] We will make a joint book. I want very much to put into the world again the big old pagan vision, before the *idea* and the concept of personality made everything so small and tight as it is now. . . . [October 10] Let the damned dead fuddled scholars be scholastic—what we want is the magic of the deep world. . . . I do hate John's Jewish nasal sort of style—so uglily moral, condemning other people—prefer the way Osiris rises, or Adonis or Dionysus—not as Messiahs giving 'heaven' to the 'good'—but life-bringers for the good and bad alike—like the falling rain—on the just and unjust—who gives a damn—like the sun. . . . [October 29] Personally, I don't care much about the bloody Revelations, and whether they have any order or not. But they are a very useful start for other excursions. I love the pre-Christian heavens—the planets that became such a prison of the consciousness—and the usual year of the zodiac. But I like the heavens best *pre-Orphic, before* there was any 'fall' of the soul. . . . [November 7] I rather wish you would do a bit of purely astronomical and astrological explanation—the planets, their signs, metals, qualities etc.—the zodiac, and its signs: the meaning of the Houses—and the exaltation and fall—and the ecliptic, and the inclination of the ecliptic to the horizon: those simple things which ordinary people *don't know,* even the people who are going to read this book . . .

Near the end of the year, Lawrence reported progress on the introduction to Carter's book, and provided Carter with current news of Bandol:

I have roughly finished my introduction, and am going over it, working it a bit into shape. I'm hoping I can get Brewster's daughter to type it—she comes this week.—God knows what anybody will think of it. When you have done your chapter, send me a copy.—I'll send *Enoch* back.

We've had the most beautiful weather lately—brilliant sunny days, and warm. This morning is another calm and lovely morning.—The Brewsters are still in the hotel—had no money to go to their house with—not a sou even to pay the hotel: but thank goodness, some has come at last—or almost come—so are a little nearer. Today the grand piano is being sent up from Toulon, and they are going to welcome it. It will be the first piece of furniture in the *château!*—all alone.—We are quite a party—Mr and Mrs di Chiara, from Capri, are in the hotel—also Mrs Eastman [Ida Rauh], from New Mexico. They all troop along to tea, so the Beau Soleil resounds with voices, and the cat goes away in disgust.

In the week before Christmas, the villa had a tempest in a fishbowl. The yellow 'marmalade' cat who had adopted Lawrence ('I never knew a French cat before—*sang-froid,* will of his own, *aimable,* but wasting no emotion') extracted from their bowl the two goldfish Mme Douillet of the Beau Rivage had presented *'pour amuser Monsieur'*. The cat, Mickey Beausoleil, killed one fish and wounded the other. Lawrence's report to Max Mohr on December 19 once again showed how he could still touch animals to life with a penstroke: 'I spanked M. Beausoleil well, and he twisted round at me like a Chinese dragon, so I spanked him some more. Now he wants to *kosen,* but I refuse. He is in disgrace!'

Harwood Brewster, now seventeen, arrived from England on that same day with hampers of food from Lawrence's sisters. She typed out his introduction to Carter's 'Dragon' book, but it proved to be too long, and Lawrence put it aside. He then wrote a shorter one, which, however, didn't appear in Carter's *Dragon of the Apocalypse.* But this 'introduction' did turn up in the *London Mercury* a few months after Lawrence's death (issue of July 1930). This is a fine essay on the Apocalypse, with some important remarks on symbols, whose power, Lawrence felt, 'is to arouse the deep emotional self, and the dynamic self, beyond comprehension. Many ages of accumulated experience still throb within a symbol. And we throb in response.'

Lawrence apparently never turned again to the 'abandoned' introduction, which Orioli was the first to publish as *Apocalypse* (1931). In it Lawrence found Christianity to be a religion for 'aristocrats of the spirit', with a dualistic conflict between its strong commands and its counsels of meekness. To him, Revelation was the great cry of the weak against the strong, and consequently was still popular among the lowly: he remembered the colliers and their wives in chapel seeing whorish Babylon as the wicked modern cities they wanted to devastate in terms of the grandiloquent images of destruction provided by Revelation—then the destroyers, the 'saved', could from a splendid heaven gloat over the fallen. This attitude disgusted Lawrence, for it had helped to make the gospel of love into the gospel of hate. His conclusion was that man cannot exist in separateness, for he is part of nature and of the human community.

At the point where he stopped writing *Apocalypse,* he turned out one of the most important passages in all his work, showing how everything he had ever written came from a deep sense of the unity of all life—the passage which begins, 'What man wants most passionately is his living wholeness and his living unison, not his own isolate salvation of his "soul",' and which ends, 'What we want to destory is our false, inorganic connexions, especially those related to money, and re-establish the living organic connexions, with the cosmos, the sun and earth, with mankind and nation and family. Start with the sun, and the rest will slowly, slowly happen.'

*

Lawrence wrote to Carter for the last time on February 4, 1930, just before he left Bandol. On a postcard that had on its front side the snarling picture of a tiger's head, Lawrence said that he was returning Carter's manuscript; he was in bed and 'probably going this week into a sanatorium. No luck. Have not finished my longer essay on Revelation—and am abandoning it. Perhaps you'd do better if you offered a shorter MS. Best of luck.' Achsah Brewster had reported that Lawrence enjoyed himself at a New Year's luncheon given by his old friends the di Chiaras (like Nan del Torre in *Aaron's Rod,* Anna di Chiara was American). Lawrence, at their luncheon at Bandol, 'lingered overlong, and walked to the village to sit down in a cutting wind. From that time on he steadily lost flesh.'

At the end of January, Lawrence wrote to Orioli: 'The Huxleys are in England, as *Point Counter Point* is being made into a play—first night tomorrow—and Aldous seems to be enjoying himself, figuring among the actors and actresses, and being *It.*'

Lawrence dreaded a proposed visit by his sisters, with again the reminders of the Midlands and all the provincial shackles. Even the faithful Ada by herself—Catherine Carswell noted that Lawrence 'did not truly want to see Ada then'—without Emily, would be too much; Ada had to be put off, in a letter of February 3 announcing that he was planning to go into a sanatorium at Vence: 'But you won't want to come here when I'm in Vence, and they will let me have visitors only twice a week. So wait a bit, till I'm walking about, and then come to Vence—they say it's nice there.'

The sanatorium had been recommended by Dr. Andrew Morland. Before Dr. Morland went to the Côte d'Azur on a vacation trip with his wife, he had received warnings from Gertler and other friends of Lawrence's in England who had arranged the meeting, that Lawrence was hostile to the idea of medical treatment and that he might brusquely refuse even to discuss it; in any event, prescriptions must be precise and simple. Lawrence, his friends explained, often ignored the accompanying directions, accepting only the parts that appealed to him and neglecting the rest.

But Dr. Morland found Lawrence pleasant and friendly as they took tea together at the Beau Soleil. 'He lost no time in making us warmly welcome,' Dr. Morland recalled. 'While his wife prepared tea he made the toast himself, treating the operation as though it were a serious matter and at the same time great fun.' Lawrence and the doctor sat talking, and although Lawrence was 'altogether charming and gently witty', the doctor soon realized that his host was tiring. The Morlands left, and the doctor arranged to return the next morning for a professional visit. Dr. Morland, in a letter to this writer, recorded the result:

> I found that although Lawrence had obviously been suffering from pulmonary tuberculosis for a very long time—probably ten or fifteen years—he had either never been properly advised about treatment or, much more likely, he had chosen to ignore most of the advice given while remembering a few unimportant details. I found him extremely emaciated, obviously very ill and needing bed rest of many months if he were to have a chance to arrest the disease. All he seemed to know about the treatment of tuberculosis was what he had learned from his friend Mark Gertler who had fully regained his health after some months in a sanatorium; the only lesson he could remember was that he should walk three or four miles every morning and that he should drink a lot of milk. Lawrence had tried with pathetic determination to do these walks but recently they had been be-

yond his strength and he had taken to driving instead. He admitted to getting tired very quickly particularly when visited by admiring strangers from across the Atlantic.

Although the severity of his illness was clear I did not feel altogether hopeless as he had never given proper treatment a chance and his resistance to the disease must have been remarkable to enable him to survive so long while doing all the wrong things. My difficulty was how to arrange for him to have the medical supervision and surroundings he needed. His own idea was to get back to New Mexico but, quite apart from the immigration difficulties, he was so ill that I did not think he could survive the journey. He was strongly averse to treatment in either Switzerland or England and the only possibility seemed to lie in finding some reasonably suitable place not too far away. The Mediterranean coast itself has a bad reputation for this type of case and the exposed situation of Bandol aggravated his bronchitis. I therefore recommended that he should move to a small sanatorium at Vence which is a well situated resort about 1,000 feet above sea level and some miles inland. Lawrence would have never tolerated a strict sanatorium but this one was more like a private hotel but with medical and nursing facilities available.

Dr. Morland had gone up to Vence and had written from there about the Ad Astra sanatorium. Lawrence, in his answer to this letter on January 30, 1930, still tried to evade the treatment and still spoke of his affliction as bronchitis:

Had your letter from Vence—many thanks—I don't much want to go *ad astra*. I lie still in bed—I don't do any work—see no one, for there is no one to see, except my wife's daughter, who is staying with us; and by yesterday the bronchitis had subsided a lot—but it's come back a bit today again, probably the North Wind. If I make good progress as I am, I shan't go to Vence: if I don't I shall.

We are both very grateful to you for your advice, which I can see is sound. I should like to give you a signed copy of the first edition of *Lady Chatterley*—if you'd care for it. I can get a copy from Florence. But where shall I send it? to Mrs Morland? What is her address in Mentone?

Shall report progress again next week.

But there was no progress to report. Brewster—who recalled that towards the end of his life Lawrence no longer objected to the word *God* and said, 'I intend to find God: I wish to realize my relation with Him'—remembered that in one of their last conversations, Lawrence told him, 'The hatred which my books have aroused comes back at me and gets me here'—tapping his chest. 'It seems there is an evil spirit in my body; if I get the better of it in one place it goes to another.'

*

Lawrence left Bandol on February 6, 1930, to surrender to the sanatorium.

Frieda wrote that 'Lawrence always thought with horror of a sanatorium, we both thought with loathing of it. Freedom that he cherished so much!' She had never let him feel like an invalid. 'Never should he feel like a poor sick thing as long as I was there and his spirit! Now we had to give in.'

As they prepared to leave, Lawrence, 'with a set face', told Frieda to bring him all his papers; she carried them to his bed, and he tore up most of them, then 'made everything tidy and neat and helped to pack his own trunks, and I never cried'. On the morning before he left, Lawrence sat up in bed correcting the proofs of *Nettles* while Mickey the cat scratched unhappily outside the closed door. Lawrence looked up when Achsah Brewster came in; he said he would soon be back to visit their pine grove, and she believed him.

The Lawrences left Beau Soleil in a car with Earl Brewster. Achsah remained in Bandol. She had taken Mickey, and she saw the party off on that morning of February 6, loading their car with almond blossoms.

It was a hard five hours' journey to Vence. They had to go by rail between Toulon and Antibes, and Frieda recalled that, at the station in Toulon, Lawrence 'had to walk up and down stairs, wasting strength he could ill afford to waste'. The train was so crowded that she had to arrange for a private compartment to Antibes, and in it she and Brewster stayed quietly with the pale sick man in the jolting train. Brewster recalled that, in spite of depression and fatigue, Lawrence tried to keep the conversation lively on that day of intermittent sunlight. At Antibes they were met by a friend of Barbara Weekley's —Blair Hughes-Stanton—who took Lawrence and his party the rest of the way in a car.

On the drive up to Vence, 'he talked and seemed very much himself', Brewster remembered. At last they came, high in the jagged mountains, to the flat little stone-and-plaster town among the vineyards, its one square tower rising above the red-tile roofs.

A poet of eight centuries before, Peire Vidal of Toulouse, had written, in praise of the land which Lawrence had gone over on that day:

> *Qu'om no sap ton dous repaire*
> *Com de Rozer tro qu'a Vensa. . . .*
> *(No journey is more beautiful*
> *Than from the Rhône to Vence. . . .)*

Lawrence went to the Ad Astra sanatorium—To the Stars. But it was more like a hotel, Lawrence wrote to Maria Huxley, 'an hotel where a nurse takes your temperature and two doctors look at you once a week'. The X-ray showed, he said, that 'the lung has moved very little since Mexico, in five years'. He still blamed everything on 'the broncs', which were 'awful': they had 'inflamed my lower man, the *ventre* and the liver'.

Dr. Morland, now back in London, received X-rays and reports. The change at first 'seemed to do a little good; in any case Lawrence wrote to me that he found the air better and that Frieda, his wife, was relieved at having him under proper care.'

Lawrence's room was painted in what Brewster called 'a deep overpowering blue', and Lawrence was grateful when Brewster 'brought masses of orange-coloured flowers to his room, counteracting those awful blue walls and making them recede somewhat'. Lawrence liked the view, however, from his little balcony: he could see Cagnes in the distance, and the gleaming coastline, and the Mediterranean.

Frieda stayed at the Nouvel Hôtel in Vence and came up to the Ad Astra daily; but in the middle of February she returned to the Beau Soleil at Bandol, where Barbara had been staying, to pack everything and turn in the key of the villa. She and Barbara moved to the house the di Chiaras had just given up at Cagnes, less than half an hour by bus from Vence.

Lawrence had begun to feel 'more chirpy' and hoped to get on his feet soon, though he found the sanatorium itself dull, 'only French people convalescing and nothing in my line'. He went down to lunch every day, two steep flights of stairs, but otherwise had to lie in bed, hoping he could soon 'practise walking again'. The French physicians, in opposition to Dr. Morland, believed that Lawrence should move about somewhat, not rest all the time; and Lawrence agreed with his new doctors: 'A certain amount of movement is better.' He sent a postcard to Orioli, telling him: 'Glad to hear you are better—*take care,* don't get really knocked up, like me.—The doctors think they can make me better fairly soon—I hope so, am so tired of this.'

Yet he could still enjoy the colors of the end of winter in that southern place, and the smell of the flowering plants. He told Maria Huxley, 'The mimosa is all out, in clouds, like Australia, and the almond blossom very lovely.' On good days he could sit in the garden, and he wrote Maria Huxley, 'Perhaps we might have a few jolly days, if you come down—just jolly, like Diabelerets.'

The Huxleys were in London for the opening of *This Way to Paradise,* as Campbell Dixon, who dramatized it, called *Point Counter Point.* Lawrence hoped the play would be a money-making success, but it was not. Rebecca West, in her *Elegy* on Lawrence, has explained why the characters, so living in the novel, didn't spring into life on the stage, though she felt that Mark Rampion did, and she reflected, 'Even Aldous Huxley, who is so far above the rest of us, feels that he has to look up to Lawrence'. After the fall of the curtain she suggested this to her companion, who said, 'You know, Lawrence is dangerously ill': Rebecca West answered at once, 'Oh, I don't believe that, it's quite impossible'—for the world without Lawrence would be like Huxley's play without Rampion: 'The best thing would then be gone'.

While confined to bed, Lawrence read many books. Brewster, who was surprised that Lawrence hadn't brought any with him, looked for readable items in the sanatorium library and found some French translations of Scott. Lawrence wrote to thank Laurence Pollinger for '*Mamba* and the Chinese book', on which he made no comment. *Mamba* is of course *Mamba's Daughters* (1929), by Du Bose Heyward. Lawrence's statement 'the girl at sea is a feeble fake' suggests that he at once saw through one of the literary hoaxes of the time, Joan Lowell's purported sea adventures in *Cradle of the Deep.* And could his comment on a book by a man—'I'm sick of self-conscious young Americans posing before their own cameras'—refer to Thomas Wolfe's *Look Homeward, Angel* (1929)?

Lawrence also thanked Maria Huxley for other volumes sent from London: *Coréine,* on which he did not comment, and for 'the Browning book', probably Osbert Burdett's *The Brownings* (1929), which he found 'somewhat humiliating—bourgeois. The bourgeois at its highest level makes one squirm a bit.'

At this time Brewster left Vence to return to Bandol; he went away reluctantly, expecting to return for another sojourn before going again to India. But Lawrence continued to have visitors during those last weeks. Ida Rauh Eastman had come on from Bandol to stay with Frieda and Barbara, and on February 27 the Aga Khan appeared, with his wife: 'I liked him,' Lawrence wrote Brewster, '—a bit of real religion.' The Aga Khan again spoke of displaying Lawrence's paintings at a private gallery in Paris; Lawrence telegraphed to Dorothy Warren to hold the pictures, which the police had returned to her, rather than ship them to Vence.

H. G. Wells, living at nearby Grasse, had visited Lawrence on February 24 and told him that he had enjoyed sitting for the American sculptor Jo Davidson, and that Lawrence should let Davidson 'do' his head. Wells, entertaining Davidson at his villa, suggested that he go to Vence immediately to sculpture Lawrence: 'I am not doing this for you but for him. You will surely do him good. I am sure he is not as ill as they think he is. You can cheer him up.'

The hearty, bearded Davidson—a minor Augustus John—went with his wife the next morning to Vence instead of carrying out his original plan of leaving for Paris. Frieda welcomed them and sent Jo Davidson upstairs, where he found Lawrence having lunch on a sunny balcony. Lawrence chatted with Davidson, who at last reached for his clay and began to work. He asked Lawrence if he had ever modeled, and Lawrence said that he had tried plasticine, but that he had hated the touch and smell of the material. Davidson handed him some of the clay he was using, and Lawrence sat holding it, liking its coolness and cleanness. Davidson promised to send him some, for Lawrence said he would like to model little animals.

After an hour, Lawrence sent Davidson down to get some lunch while he took a nap. Later, the sculptor finished the work, with Lawrence sitting up in bed in his blue dressing gown. A few days later, in Paris, Davidson told Mrs. Harry Payne Whitney of the severity of Lawrence's illness, and the wealthy American woman said, 'Can't you call up Mrs. Lawrence or someone and tell them not to spare any expense?'—she would attend to that. Davidson telephoned Wells, at Grasse, but by that time not even the money of a kind-hearted admirer could help Lawrence. For it was the end of life for the man who had often found fault with the stupidity of mankind, but not with life itself; the man without self-pity who wrote of life and its grandeur and its sorrows, and who wrote of it with matchless vitality.

He had, after seeming to be better, sunk into illness again. He had come to dislike the sanatorium, and by February 20 felt he had 'been rather worse here—think I have a bit of "flu"—pain too. There's nothing in this place—I was better in Beau Soleil.' And the next day he said, 'I am rather worse here—such bad nights, and cough, and heart, and pain decidedly worse here—and miserable. Seems to me like grippe, but they say not. It's not a good place—shan't stay long— I'm better in a house—I'm miserable.' Apparently on the same day, 'Friday' (February 21), he wrote to Orioli for the last time:

> Glad to hear you are better. I am not—rather worse. This place doesn't suit me—shan't stay long, perhaps another week. Feel wretched. Perhaps we shall take a house here for a short while.
>
> Will you send me a copy of the first edition of *Lady C*—I want to give it to my English doctor—he won't take a fee.
>
> Weather bad—I am all the time in bed again—and feel miserable.

By February 27 Lawrence could write to both Ada Clarke and Earl Brewster that he was 'about the same', in any event 'no worse', and that he was moving into a house in Vence on March 1 and would have an English nurse come out from Nice: 'I shall be better looked after.' Brewster, suddenly leaving for India with Mukerji, received his letter at the moment of departure from Bandol. He expected to return within two months, and expected to see Lawrence then.

Lawrence's final effort to write as an author was made there in the sanatorium, shortly before he left. Sitting up in bed, he scratched away at a review of a book which had come in, Eric Gill's *Art Nonsense and Other Essays*. Frieda has said, 'Lawrence wrote this unfinished review a few days before he died. The book interested him, and he agreed with much in it. Then he got tired of writing and I persuaded him not to go on. It is the last thing he wrote.'

Therefore, it can tell us a good deal of what Lawrence thought and felt in the closing days of his life.

As Lawrence Clark Powell has remarked, 'though [Lawrence] was mortally ill when he wrote this piece, one would never know it from reading it. Unfaltering in thought, the writing is as fine, regular, and flowing as ever.' Indeed, it has a humor and a liveliness one would think of as beyond the power of a dying man—not a dying man in the sense of an apparently healthy human being who was soon to die unexpectedly of a heart attack, but rather a dying man in the sense of one wasting away after a long illness. Here we find him saying, in order to get 'the bad things' out of the way first, that Gill was not a born thinker or a born writer, but rather 'a crude and crass amateur: crass is the only word: maddening, like a tiresome uneducated workman arguing in a pub—*argefying* would describe it better—and banging his fist.'

Gill was not even an artist, Lawrence said, but just a craftsman. Yet Lawrence felt Gill had a great deal to say that was valuable: his assertions, for example, that man existed in slavery when he did what he liked in his spare time and what was required of him in his working time, while man existed in freedom when he did what he liked to do in his working time and in his spare time what was required of him. These observations seemed to Lawrence to contain more wisdom than he had found 'in all Karl Marx or Whitehead or a dozen other philosophers rolled together'. Gill flung his truths 'in the teeth of modern industrialism', even though it was useless to utter such truths —this was why 'the clever blighters' never uttered them. 'But it is only the truth which is useless which really matters.'

Lawrence jibbed at Gill's Catholicism, particularly since he was a convert and therefore willing to 'swallow all the old absolutes whole, swallow the pill without looking at it, and call that Faith. The big pill being God, and little pills being terms like Charity and Chastity and Obedience and Humility. Swallow them whole, and you are a good Catholic; lick at them and see what they taste like, and you are a queasy Protestant.'

The final paragraph of this piece is so important as an illumination of what was in Lawrence's mind in those days just before his death that it must be quoted in full:

> Mr Gill has two main themes: 'work done well', and 'beauty'— or rather 'Beauty'. He is almost always good, simple and profound, truly a prophet, when he is speaking of work done well. And he is nearly always tiresome about Beauty. Why, oh, why, will people keep on trying to define words like Art and Beauty and God, words which represent deep emotional states in us, and are therefore incapable of definition? Why bother about it? 'Beauty is absolute, loveliness is relative,' says Mr Gill. Yes, yes, but really, what does it matter? Beauty is beauty, loveliness is loveliness, and if Mr Gill thinks that Beauty ought really to

have a subtly moral character, while loveliness is merely casual, or equivalent for prettiness—well, why not? But other people don't care.

As far as Lawrence was concerned, however, 'other people' did care. The Huxleys, as soon as they could get away from London, came down to Cannes; the play was in its final week. They arrived on February 25 and immediately called to see Lawrence. Huxley, who has said that for those last two years Lawrence had been like a flame that miraculously burned on although it had no fuel to feed it, saw at once that now 'the miracle was at an end, the flame guttering to extinction'. He and his wife stayed on at Cannes to be with Lawrence to the last.

Dr. Morland, in a February 25 letter to Gertler, reported what a physician at the sanatorium had noted about Lawrence: 'Both lungs appear to be affected with moderate severity, but it is his general condition which is causing the greatest amount of anxiety; his appetite is poor and he does not respond to treatment.'

Frieda, who has noted that Lawrence in all his illness 'never lost his dignity', didn't like to leave him at night. When she was going, he would say, 'Now I shall have to fight several battles of Waterloo before morning.' Once he told Barbara, 'Your mother does not care for me any more; the death in me is repellent to her.'

One night Frieda knew that he wanted her to stay; with his eyes 'grateful and bright', he turned to Barbara and said, 'It isn't often I want your mother, but I do want her tonight to stay.' Frieda tried to sleep on a long cane chair, now and then looking up to the dark sky for one comforting star, but there was no moon and there were no stars.

Frieda remained there several nights, hearing coughs from up and down the building through the hours of darkness, 'old coughing and young coughing'; it was like the hacking chorus in Thomas Mann's *The Magic Mountain,* which Frieda had probably not read. When the little girl in the next room cried out, *'Mama, Mama, je souffre tant!'* Frieda was glad Lawrence was somewhat deaf.

Sometimes he was irritable, and once he told her, 'Your sleeping here does me no good.' She went away and wept, but when she returned he said tenderly, 'Don't mind, you know I want nothing but you, but sometimes something is stronger in me.' A few weeks later, Frieda could write to Bynner (on March 13), 'Right up to the last he was *alive* and we both made the best of our days, then he faced the end so splendidly, so like a *man* and I could help him through, thank God.'

At the very end he had to get out of the sanatorium, as if he didn't want to die there. Dr. Morland, as always regretting Lawrence's inability to rest, said that 'those very qualities which gave Lawrence such keen perception and such passionate feeling made it quite impossible for him to submit for any length of time to a restricted sanatorium existence.'

Lawrence called his illness at Ad Astra 'flu or grippe'. Dr. Morland had noted the complication of pleurisy; after speaking of Lawrence's improvement upon first arriving at Ad Astra, Dr. Morland said, 'Unfortunately within a few weeks an attack of pleurisy precipitated a relapse which his emaciated frame could not withstand. Characteristically he turned against the sanatorium and insisted, within a few days of his death, on being moved to a villa in the village.' Dr. Morland wrote to Koteliansky on March 4: 'How terrible it is that Lawrence is dead. . . . I wish now that I had not urged him to go to Vence as I am afraid my efforts only made his last weeks more unhappy.'

There can be no substitute for Frieda's account of the move, on March 1 (St. David's Day), to the Villa Robermond (later the Villa Aurella), and of the events that took place there:

We prepared to take him out of the nursing home and rented a villa where we took him. . . . It was the only time he allowed me to put on his shoes, everything else he always did for himself. He went in the shaking taxi and he was taken into the house and lay down on the bed on which he was to die, exhausted. I slept on the couch where he could see me. He still ate. The next day was a Sunday. 'Don't leave me,' he said, 'don't go away.' So I sat by his bed and read. He was reading the life of Columbus. After lunch he began to suffer very much and about tea-time he said: 'I must have a temperature. I am delirious. Give me the thermometer.' This is the only time, seeing his tortured face, that I cried, and he said: 'Don't cry,' in a quick, compelling voice. So I ceased to cry any more. He called Aldous and Maria Huxley who were there, and for the first time he cried out to them in his agony. 'I ought to have morphine now,' he told me and my daughter, so Aldous went off to find a doctor to give him some. . . . Then he said: 'Hold me, hold me, I don't know where I am, I don't know where my hands are . . . where am I?'

Then the doctor came and gave him a morphine injection. After a little while he said: 'I am better now, if only I could sweat I would be better . . .' and then again: 'I am better now.' The minutes went by, Maria Huxley was in the room with me. I held his ankle from time to time, it felt so full of life, all my days I shall hold his ankle in my hand.

And then, at ten o'clock on the night of March 2, 1930, Lawrence died. 'He was breathing more peacefully, and then suddenly there were gaps in the breathing. The moment came when the thread of life tore in his heaving chest, his cheeks and jaw sank, and death had taken hold of him.'

Let me guide myself with the blue, forked torch of this flower
down the darker and darker stairs, where blue is darkened on blueness.

*

EPILOGUE

From the Ashes of Legend

---

*

ON MARCH 4, 1930, a small group of friends stood by the wall of the little cemetery at Vence as Lawrence's plain oak coffin was lowered into a grave: Frieda and her daughter Barbara were there, and the Huxleys, the di Chiaras, Ida Rauh, Achsah Brewster, Robert Nichols. There was no service. Frieda recalled, 'We buried him very simply, like a bird. . . . We put flowers into his grave and all I said was: "Good-bye, Lorenzo," as his friends and I put lots and lots of mimosa on his coffin.'

Frieda stayed on at the Villa Robermond, taking care of her daughter, who collapsed soon after the funeral. Frieda wrote to Caresse Crosby, in an undated letter of this time, 'How I miss Lorenzo, in spite of his illness and all, [miss] his generosity and the life he gave me.' Because Lawrence had left no will, Frieda under English law could receive only the interest on the £4,000 ($20,000) he had left; she doubted that she could even claim the remaining manuscripts and paintings. As she told Bessie Freeman in another undated letter from Vence, 'I have suffered the tortures of the damned and then some.'

Soon after Lawrence's death, Murry went to visit his grave in Vence, and Murry and Frieda at last became lovers. As he reflected in his diary twenty-three years later, 'With her, and with her for the first time in my life, I knew what fulfilment in love really meant.'

It was not until November 3, 1932, that the conflict over Lawrence's estate came into the Probate Court in London. Frieda asked the court to revoke the letters of administration earlier granted to George Lawrence. Her other principal opponent was Emily Lawrence King; Lawrence's younger sister Ada gave her support to George and Emily, though she had at first been neutral; but pressure from Frieda's solicitors and agents had irritated Ada, and Frieda's 'blackening' remarks about the Lawrence family had annoyed her further. Frieda won the case because of the testimony of Murry, who had published the first Lawrence biography (*Son of Woman*) the year before. Frieda had burned a copy of the book and sent him the ashes in a cardboard box; but he bore no grudge. He testified that some months after the

outbreak of war in 1914 he had made a will in favor of Katherine
Mansfield, and that Lawrence had drawn up an identical will in behalf of Frieda, who now explained that she and Lawrence had lost
this document on their travels.

Frieda wrote to a friend, 'I wasn't sure of winning[,] not until the
case came on: a severe old judge Lord Merrivale, but I pulled all my
forces together in the witness-box, just went ahead, felt I could convince crocodiles that Lawrence wanted me to have his inheritance—
They say I was convincing—But the triumph was Lorenzo's—And
the way Lawrence is pervading this England now is just surprising, I
am full of the deepest satisfaction for *his* sake—I have not lived in
vain—So there's a song of triumph for you.'

In the same letter Frieda noted, 'Ada is furious, naturally.' Ada
Lawrence Clarke's letters to the same friend bear this out: indeed, this
series of communications from both these women to a neutral friend
is a fascinating by-product of the Lawrence experience, and if there is
anger in the letters, it is partly an intensification of the different kinds
of love the two women felt for Lawrence. Ada remained bitter, and
when Murry unexpectedly called on her on Good Friday 1933, on a
peace-making mission, Ada's husband used 'lurid language' to explain
his attitude towards Frieda, while Ada made it clear that she wanted
to have no more dealings of any kind with her former sister-in-law.

Frieda's childlike nature made her more likely to forgive and certainly to forget: life continued to be full and rich, for although as Lawrence's widow she had vexations and miseries, she also had a certain
amount of fame and glory (dining with the Bernard Shaws, lecturing
at Oxford); and she was deeply in love again, as she felt Lawrence
would have wished her to be. Ada worried chronically over the health
of her elder son, Jack, who was frail and red-haired and, to her, remarkably like his uncle Bert in his own youth. Ada lived on through
World War II, during which Jack died in a German prison camp. But
in her last years Ada refused to believe that he was dead: at the end
of each afternoon she used to insist, at her home in Ripley, that she
could hear him coming down the lane on his bicycle and opening the
gate.

Many others who were closely involved with Lawrence have also
followed him into death. One of them is Ernest Weekley, who after
Lawrence's death invited Frieda to become his wife again; he died in
May 1954, in his ninetieth year. William Hopkin also lived on until
the 1950s and into his own nineties: staunch supporter of Lawrence to

the last, the sprightly little old man was fatally stricken in a town near Eastwood where he had gone to lecture on his lifelong friend. William Hopkin's widow (his second wife, Olive) continued to live in Eastwood; his daughter Mrs. Enid Hilton and her son settled in California.

William Hopkin had outlived even Jessie Chambers, whose epitaph he wrote as a poem—'Miriam'—for the Eastwood paper after her death on April 3, 1944. Jessie had written to Helen Corke in 1933 that after she returned Lawrence's last letter, twenty years earlier, 'no word ever passed between us, and I never heard news of him'. She hadn't known of his last illness, and on what later proved to be the day of his death she thought she heard him suddenly say, 'Can you remember only the pain and none of the joy?' And the next day, still not knowing he was dead, she thought she saw him for a moment, 'just as I had known him in the early days, with the little cap on the back of his head'. For about eighteen months before Lawrence's death, Jessie had, she told Helen Corke, 'felt acutely drawn to him at times, and wondered intensely how some kind of communication that seemed so urgently needed, was to be established'—a curious speculation on the part of one who, in the same letter, could speak of Lawrence as 'a man in bondage' whose 'theorisings and philosophisings only bear witness to his agony'. But this was another example of the outwardly projected self-reproach that characterized the attitude of the later Jessie towards Lawrence.

After not seeing Jessie for seven years, Helen Corke had a last visit with her in a Nottingham teashop in 1940, an occasion forcefully described in her biography of Jessie, *D. H. Lawrence's 'Princess'* (1951). Jessie, 'a bent, heavy figure', dragged herself about wearily in the aftermath of a nervous breakdown, 'as she talked, with smouldering resentment, of the war, of her illness, of the shabby treatment of her book' about Lawrence. When she felt that Helen was pitying her, she trained the resentment against her old friend, turned her face away from her, and left. 'We parted,' Helen Corke writes, 'knowing all was said.' Miss Corke survived Lawrence by many years, and in 1970 attended the Lawrence Conference at Taos, where she met the other major survivor, Dorothy Brett, at a cocktail party. Brett had refused to take part in the conference, whose sponsors would not pay the exorbitant fee she demanded. The tiny Helen Corke, who had made the transoceanic crossing when nearing the age of ninety, was, with her liveliness and charm, the star of the conference.

Catherine Carswell died soon after World War II; her husband

Donald had been killed in an accident in London during one of the early blackouts. A few other friends of Lawrence also met violent deaths, three of them by suicide. Depressed and in bad health, Mark Gertler killed himself in London in the summer before the war broke out. The Brewsters' friend Dhan Ghopal Mukerji, whom Lawrence liked, hanged himself in New York in 1936, after a nervous breakdown. The death of the unstable Philip Heseltine was more spectacular and more predictable: in December 1930, the same year as the death of the Lawrence whom he had not seen for so long, Heseltine (according to his friend and biographer, Cecil Gray) escaped from some amatory difficulties by turning on the gas in his London flat.

But some of the old Lawrenceans flourished until their deaths. Lawrence's schoolmate George Neville was a government official in Birmingham in the 1950s and looked many years younger than his age. Michael Arlen, after making a fortune from his flashy little novels of the 1920s, retired like a stockbroker to a Park Avenue apartment. Like Arlen, Aldous Huxley died of cancer, but after a writing career both profitable and distinguished, more for such 'pre-created' histories as *Grey Eminence* and *The Devils of Loudon,* and for his travelogues, than for his frail attempts at fiction. One of the few to speak out boldly for Lawrence during his lifetime, Huxley continued to do so across the years. In 1932 he edited, with Enid Hilton's help, the huge collection of letters that has been a landmark among Lawrence's books, just as Huxley's introduction to that volume of letters has been a landmark in critical appreciation of Lawrence. Richard Aldington, who died in 1962, managed to keep in the public eye with a variety of books, some of them about Lawrence. In 1954 Aldington ventured *Pinorman,* an informal biography of the late Pino Orioli and the late Norman Douglas, a book which the Douglas clique considered a disparagement; and Aldington was unfairly scorched after his biography of 'Lawrence of Arabia' in 1956, which treated a 'national hero' with something less than reverence. D. H. Lawrence's gentle friend, Earl Brewster, stayed on in India after the death of his wife; their 1934 volume of *Reminiscences and Correspondence* is one of the best books on Lawrence, largely because of the authors' sympathetic attitude and their lack of egoism.

Lady Cynthia Asquith dealt with Lawrence candidly but gracefully in her *Remember and Be Glad* (1952), and in 1969 the posthumous publication of the first volume of her diaries revealed a tolerant and friendly appreciation of Lawrence; she recorded her amusement at her friends and family for thinking she and Lawrence were having a love affair.

One of Lawrence's former friends, Bertrand Russell, a Nobel Prize winner who died in his nineties, celebrated his delayed revenge against a plain-speaking man by making a violent assertion, in a memoir published in British and American magazines, delivered over the B.B.C., and recurring in his autobiography, that Lawrence was a fascist—an oversimplification of the kind that hardly does credit to a noted philosopher.

Another Lawrence-hater, the man Lawrence had called 'a belated sort of mosquito', Witter Bynner, saved his sting for *Journey with Genius* (1951), a book that evoked the feverish atmosphere of the early memoirs at a time when a newer generation of readers was discovering Lawrence the writer.

But if Lawrence still had detractors, 'them it was their poison hurt': Lawrence has long been beyond earthly agitation. For five years his body lay in the Vence cemetery, in a grave visited by occasional pilgrims and, twice, by Louie Burrows. According to legend, Lawrence's personal symbol, the phoenix, was patterned in colored pebbles on his gravestone by a peasant who was devoted to him: the story both annoyed and amused the designer, Dominique Matteucci, who considered himself not a peasant, but a capitalist.

The stone was finally removed in 1935 when, at Frieda's behest, Angelo Ravagli went to Vence and arranged to have Lawrence's body disinterred and (in Marseille on March 13) cremated. After painful technical difficulties, Ravagli brought the urn of ashes aboard the *Conte de Savoia* at Villefranche on April 4. He faced further troubles at the port of New York, where the persistence of Dorothy Brett's friend Alfred Stieglitz helped get the urn ashore in a cruel comedy of errors. Angelo Ravagli then took the ashes west, and when Frieda met him at the station at Lamy, New Mexico, the urn was forgotten in the confusion and left on the platform. Frieda didn't discover the loss until she was twenty miles away from Lamy and had to return. As Frieda said later, Lawrence would have appreciated the humor of the situation.

The ashes at last arrived at the mountain ranch, where Frieda and Angie had built a chapel for them. Mrs. Luhan, however, decided that the ashes didn't belong to Frieda but to the world, as represented by its self-appointed spokeswoman, Mrs. Luhan. She was not then on good terms with Frieda, who had made a helpful suggestion about

Mrs. Luhan's 1932 memoir: 'I implored Mabel, write that book again, it's not doing Lawrence justice, it's small beer!' In addition, Mrs. Luhan was trying to force Taos social circles to ostracize Angelo Ravagli: she would give spite parties to which Frieda but not Angie would be invited. Frieda, famous for her loyalty—which was not always operational—would go to these affairs. But other party-givers invited Angie, who was at last permitted to enter even the sacred precincts of Mrs. Luhan's estate. At the time the ashes arrived, Mrs. Luhan decided to steal them, but someone warned Frieda. One version of the story is that Brett, whose *Lawrence and Brett* (1933) had proved to be one of the milder reminiscences, was the informer. Whoever it was, Frieda at once embedded the ashes in a cement altar. Sometime later, when Brett was coolly invited to give up her residence in one of Mrs. Luhan's houses, she struck a Bartelby-the-Scrivener attitude ('I would prefer not to') until Mrs. Luhan had the police pitch her out. Brett moved to a *hacienda* uphill from Frieda's at El Prado, where she could see through a spyglass whether Frieda and Angelo were having visitors interesting enough to go over and meet.

Mrs. Luhan died in 1962, six years before Bynner; in her last days she had a wandering mind. She had some 'secret' papers dealing with Lawrence, which were not to be published until twenty years after her death. Possibly she felt that she would have the last word, although there is certainly enough material available now to help us see the essential Lawrence. Perhaps Mrs. Luhan's papers relating to him will be about as exciting as those long buried in the quite different cases of Abraham Lincoln and Oscar Wilde: like the papers connected with those men, made public in 1950, Mrs. Luhan's 'secret' Lawrence revelations may turn out to be no more than a dud.

Still another phase of the legend of Lawrence's ashes appeared in *John O'London's Weekly* for July 21, 1950, in which the journalist S. K. Ratcliffe reported that a friend of his who had been in Taos told him that when Frieda tried to organize an interment ceremony at the chapel, with some of the Indians taking part, Tony Luhan, apparently as the instrument of his wife, 'spread among the local Indians a story about the grave's being that of a great man who must never be disturbed. If they took part in the affair they and their families would be damned forever. Frieda, said my friend, had to set a guard round the cairn, and get other Indians from a distance.'

The story of D. H. Lawrence really comes to an end with the death of Frieda at El Prado, near Taos, on August 11, 1956, her seventy-seventh birthday. She is buried in front of his tomb (sometimes ridiculously referred to as a shrine) on Lobo Mountain.

As for Villa Aurella, the house in which Lawrence died in Vence, the Japanese scholar Takanori Irie tried to locate it in 1972 and 'found nothing but a large pond filled with dirty water. A lady in the neighborhood told me that Villa Aurella was demolished in 1968. For a while I stood where the Villa was supposed to be and looked at the drizzling rain dancing on the yellow pond. Then I found two trees. I directly remembered that they were the same trees I had seen in the photograph in your [and Warren Roberts's] *D. H. Lawrence and His World* (p. 126). Taking pictures of them I was filled with deep emotion.'

*

In the case of D. H. Lawrence, biography is more important for an understanding of his work than for the majority of authors, even the most obviously autobiographical of them, if only because he lived more intensely than most human beings and projected his experience more directly. Some biographies of Lawrence have tended to be either too adulatory or too hostile to give a clear picture of the man; some others have fallen into the overbalanced 'genius, but—' category which Aldington condemned.

At this point Lawrence needs no apology, if he ever did; but he still needs to be defended because he has been largely condemned without evidence, by half-truths, plain lies, and guilt by association ('How could a sane man have put up with the people who wrote those memoirs?'). His own best defense is his work, which has a health that has outlived all the sick attempts to destroy it.

As for his biography, if it is necessary at all, all of it is necessary. The present effort makes no attempt to 'excuse' Lawrence when he was mean or ill-tempered, as he often was; on the other hand, there has been no attempt to inflate him into a monster because of this. As a man he was often cheerful, radiant as they say, but sometimes he threw crockery—and one gesture of petulance stands out more dramatically, for a memoirist and his reader, than long periods of sweetness and light. Some of us would in truth prefer a more consistently peaceful existence; but Frieda, the person most intimately concerned, felt that Lawrence was greater than his outbursts: she accepted them, often clearing the air by fighting back. When in 1932 Frieda was in court for the contest over her husband's will, her attorney rose to sentimentalize the Lawrences' life together, through their years of poverty, as a model of concord—at which point Frieda is reported to have leaped up and cried, 'But that's not true—we fought like hell!' The people in the courtroom are said to have roared with laughter, while the old justice, Lord Merrivale, grinned.

But even if Lawrence and Frieda did have their quarrels, they rose above them to maintain a fundamentally good relationship. Lawrence wrote an essay late in his life that summed up this relationship in its very title: 'We Need One Another'. Frieda's testimony to their life together is found in her reminiscences of Lawrence, notably in *Not I, But the Wind* . . . Lawrence's rather experimental spokesman in *Women in Love*—Rupert Birkin—had the urge to dominate, as Lawrence often did, but both he and Birkin more strongly wanted to have a balanced relationship. Among other statements he made along these lines, we may consider the earlier-quoted nautical metaphor in *John Thomas and Lady Jane,* in which marriage is seen as two ships steered separately but meeting at the same destination. In the face of such ideas, the quarrels of Lawrence and Frieda may be seen not only as therapeutic but as sometimes a bit comic. Thornton Wilder has said that too many of those who have written about Lawrence have done so without humor, have failed to see him as an *enfant terrible.* At the hearing over the settlement of Lawrence's property, when Frieda interrupted her lawyer in the midst of his idyllic raptures about the concord of the Lawrences' marriage, she not only injected some candor into the proceedings, but also some healthy and helpful humor.

She later exulted when Lord Merrivale spoke of Lawrence as 'this great man'. Lawrence's reputation had improved since his death: his friends had substantially won the 1930 battle of the obituaries with their vigorous public protests against the disparaging death notices that had appeared in various journals. In the *Nation and Athenaeum,* E. M. Forster made a statement that was challenged at the time, though its judgment is now widely accepted: he pronounced Lawrence 'the greatest imaginative novelist of his generation'. And the words of Rebecca West, Catherine Carswell, Murry, Ottoline Morrell, and others proved effective.

But that year of the battle over the will, 1932, marked the beginning of the downward swing of Lawrence's reputation, for that was the time when, with Mabel Luhan's *Lorenzo in Taos,* the war of the memoirs succeeded the battle of the obituaries. Many of the latter were without grace, but none of them equaled that of Genêt in *The*

New Yorker which, with the man just dead, said that he was fond of stripping himself naked and climbing mulberry trees, and that he had a paranoid belief to the effect that his theories about psychoanalysis had been stolen by C. G. Jung. Genêt (Janet Flanner) reprinted these ridiculous charges in a book in 1972 which brings back that ungraceful obituary notice. But Lawrence is out of her reach, though not up a mulberry tree, worrying about Jung. The greatness of his writings puts him beyond all malicious *canards*. Those who wrote the malignant obituaries on Lawrence couldn't write so well as Rebecca West in her memorial essay on Lawrence. And they could learn some manners from her.

In 1931, Murry's *Son of Woman,* which Aldous Huxley called 'a curious essay in destructive hagiography', had helped to begin the long damaging of Lawrence; but at least Murry did Lawrence the honor of taking him seriously; one must admit this, whatever disagreements one may have with Murry's ideas. And this first book of Murry's on Lawrence (reprinted with a new introduction in 1954) was for the most part a form of literary criticism; the disciples' memoirs which followed hardly pretended to be that. Lawrence's biographers might paint in his faults, but to include nothing else, as the Luhans and Bynners did, is to present a distorted picture and reduce Lawrence to a pigmy. Murry did not do *that:* however wrong he may have been about Lawrence as man or author, Murry at least saw him as a figure on the grand scale.

Of all the articles and books of reminiscence about Lawrence which appeared up to the 1970s, the one that stands out most clearly is Frieda Lawrence's *Not I, But the Wind* . . . (1934), a statement made with directness and candor. (Later, Frieda tried to present a somewhat different picture, in her attempts to sanctify Lawrence.) Catherine Carswell's *The Savage Pilgrimage* (1932) is staunchly built and is sound in its major judgments. As noted earlier, *D. H. Lawrence: Reminiscences and Correspondence* (1934) by Earl and Achsah Brewster, is notable for its detached observation and its selflessness. But such an attitude was rare among the memoirists.

The phoenix has nevertheless risen from his own ashes, which for a time had become the ashes of legend. And then, for a while, they had been the ashes of oblivion. Readers began to forget Lawrence as the Depression deepened, and they almost completely neglected him during World War II, though Lawrence's values were then needed more than ever; but the reminiscing camp-followers had made him seem a hysteric fool. Now, with the passing of time, the true Lawrence has at last emerged. His works are now being read all over the world, and the critical response to him is encouraging. There were always a few critics who spoke in his behalf: Huxley, Horace Gregory (author of *Pilgrim of the Apocalypse* [1933]), F. R. Leavis, and a few others. Leavis, bitterly attacking anyone who disagrees with him only slightly, has been a consistent exponent of Lawrence across the years, and fortunately his often insightful essays from *Scrutiny*, on Lawrence's novels as dramatic poems, were published in 1955 as *D. H. Lawrence: Novelist*. Father William Tiverton's *D. H. Lawrence and Human Existence* (1951) is an expert critical study looking towards excellent future criticism of the subject. 'Father Tiverton' became, in later editions, Father Martin Jarrett-Kerr, the author's actual name. Mark Spilka's *The Love Ethic of D. H. Lawrence* (1955) traces its theme throughout the major novels. Also in 1955, Leone Vivante's *The Theory of Potentiality* provided an illuminating philosophical study of Lawrence's vitalism. William York Tindall's essays and introductions to reprints indicate his change of mind towards the Lawrence whom he had earlier poked fun at (though even his negative criticisms have been valuable). Excellent articles by Mark Schorer were the auguries of his brilliant biographical and critical study of Lawrence in the long introduction to his fine anthology of this author, while the essays of younger critics, appearing beside those of somewhat older writers in *A D. H. Lawrence Miscellany* (1959), indicated that a generation of developing writers had not only come to understand Lawrence deeply but could be impressively articulate about his importance for the future. And other writers, many of them of a still younger group, have contributed valuably to the *D. H. Lawrence Review*, a highly important literary journal published at the University of Arkansas and excellently edited by James C. Cowan. In addition to many valuable articles, the *D. H. Lawrence Review* has printed numerous significant bibliographical notations and such useful features as David E. Gerard's 'Glossary of Eastwood Dialect Words Used by D. H. Lawrence in His Poems, Plays and Fiction' (Autumn 1968) and Rose Marie Burwell's 'Catalogue of D. H. Lawrence's Reading from Early Childhood' (Autumn 1970). The first issue (January 1973) of *Literature/Film Quarterly*, expertly edited by Thomas L. Erskine, contained eight articles on films taken from Lawrence's fiction.

Lawrence studies have continued apace, with such notable additions as Warren Roberts's *Bibliography*. The Collected Letters have been accused of incompleteness (there was much extra material which couldn't be used because the letters had to be compressed into two medium-sized volumes), but now a group of Lawrence scholars will edit, for Cambridge University Press, the 5,000 letters listed by Gerald Lacy. A few reasonably good editions of Lawrence's fictional, poetic, and other writings exist, but some of the books of fiction have corrupt texts, notably the copies of *Sons and Lovers* now sold in England and America, which contain (to give one example) an egregious error in a moment of climax at the end of the story, when Paul Morel 'whispered' the word *mother*. It is provable that Lawrence at this point wrote *whimpered,* as the manuscript that went to the printer (which is now at the Library of the University of California, Berkeley) and also the earliest printed editions, will show.

As for criticism, books such as Colin Clarke's *River of Dissolution: D. H. Lawrence and the Romantic* (1969) are milestones in Lawrence interpretation (but see Mark Spilka's rebuttal of Clarke's theses in the Spring 1971 issue of *Novel: A Forum or Fiction*), along with George H. Ford's *Double Measure: A Study of the Novels and Stories of D. H. Lawrence* (1965), Keith Sagar's *The Art of D. H. Lawrence* (1966), and James C. Cowan's *D. H. Lawrence's American Journey* (1970), and Scott Sanders's *D. H. Lawrence: The World of the Major Novels* (1973); and there have been other excellent books, such as those of Keith Aldritt, Armin Arnold, Anthony Beal, Ileana Čura-Sazdanic, H. M. Daleski, Émile Delavenay, R. P. Draper, Sandra M. Gilbert, David J. Gordon, Frank Kermode, Tom Marshall, Stephen J. Miko, Julian Moynahan, Chaman Nahal, George A. Panichas, Tony Slade, John E. Stoll, E. W. Tedlock, Jr., Kingsley Widmer. Many articles which help towards a fuller understanding of Lawrence continue to appear in professional journals or critical collections; in one of the latter, *Imagined Worlds* (1968), Louis L. Martz's fine analysis of *Sons and Lovers* deserves mention, along with Mark Kinkaid-Weekes's reconstruction of the composition of *The Rainbow* and *Women in Love,* an essay which can only be called invaluable.

*

One of the main points that the future will have to determine is whether the 'prophetic' aspect of Lawrence will survive along with the 'purely creative'. Perhaps we at this time will be more sympathetic to the prophetic side of Lawrence if we see that it is tripartite, with the most important phases integrating with the more widely accepted 'creative' Lawrence. The first of the three prophetic divisions may be regarded as a mixture of Mme Blavatsky, Frobenius, James Pryse, and others of similar persuasions, with a belief in such matters as a lost Atlantis and its irretrievable cultural priesthood; perhaps some highly imaginative modern poets need a border-world of mysticism and nonsense of this kind to excite their poetic talent; if so, this needs to be understood and 'placed', as most of us are willing to do in the somewhat similar case of Yeats and *A Vision*. With Lawrence, this particular aspect of his mysticism is the most difficult and sometimes the most exasperating part of his nature; it is not persistently intrusive, though at times it becomes annoying.

The second aspect of Lawrence's prophetic side is the simplest and most readily accessible: the common-sense part. This is Lawrence the practical prophet, who recommends more sunlight, condemns machines and pollution, in all ways attacking materialist values. Sometimes rhapsodic but oftener epigrammatic, conversational, and satirical, this is frequently the 'human', vulgar, journalistic reduction of the prophetic, in the writings characteristic of such volumes as *Pansies* and *Assorted Articles,* though apt suddenly to appear anywhere in his work.

The remaining phase of the prophetic in Lawrence is the most authentic and best integrated of all. It comprehends the values of our world, not in an abstruse mystical way nor yet in the easy rationalism of newspaper articles, but rather in the larger integration with imaginative values—the dramatization, the full embodiment, the fictional orchestration, of a long-familiar, deeply felt theme. With Lawrence, this was his opposition to the mechanical forces threatening the natural: 'blood-knowledge' would bring about that balance which life needs, which philosophers in their various ways strive after. And it is this Lawrence, celebrating the whole man—not the man fragmented by industrialism or money quests or mechanized love—who is the true prophetic Lawrence, bringing all his forces into play, who wrote his finest works.

One of Lawrence's essays, 'The Novel', in *Reflections on the Death of a Porcupine* (now in *Phoenix II*), is as close a description of his special gifts as any he ever provided. He believed that the novel should be 'honourable' in facing life, that it should be 'interrelated in all its parts, vitally, organically', and that it should be 'quick'. This 'quickness' is a feeling 'for the God-flame in everything', opposed to deadness; quickness 'seems to consist in an odd sort of fluid, changing, grotesque or beautiful relatedness'. A table in his room is dead: 'It doesn't even weakly exist. And there is a ridiculous little iron stove, which for some unknown reason is quick . . . and there is a sleeping cat, very quick. And a glass lamp that, alas, is dead.' Lawrence believed that the man in the novel 'must have a quick relatedness to all the other things in the novel: snow, bed-bugs, sunshine, the phallus, trains, silk-hats, cats, sorrow, food, people, diphtheria, fuchsias, stars, ideas, God, tooth-paste, lightning, and toilet-paper. He must be in a quick relation to all these things.' And, 'you can't fool the novel', though 'you can fool pretty nearly every other medium.' Even pietistic poems survive as poems, but Hamlet in a novel would 'be half comic, or a trifle suspicious . . . somehow, you sweep the ground a bit too clear in the poem or the drama, and you let the human word fly a bit too freely. Now in a novel there's always a tom-cat, a black tom-cat that pounces on the white dove of the word, if the dove doesn't watch it; and there is a banana-skin to trip on; and you know there is a water-closet on the premises. All these things help to keep the balance.'

In another essay, 'Why the Novel Matters', Lawrence spoke of the novel as 'the one bright book of life'. It alone deals with the whole of the living man. 'And being a novelist, I consider myself superior to the saint, the scientist, the philosopher, and the poet'; although they can be 'great masters of different bits of man alive', they never reach the whole man. Always Lawrence went far beyond the idea of the novel as entertainment: 'At its best, the novel, and the novel supremely, can help you. It can help you not to be a dead man in life.' For 'only in the novel are *all* things given full play, or at least, they may be given full play, when we realize that life itself, and not inert safety, is the reason for living. For out of the full play of all these things emerges the only thing that is anything, the wholeness of man, the wholeness of woman, man alive, and live woman.'

What other author of our time has, in so enormous and varied a collection of writings, left us so few unrewarding lines or so many that are so full of life, so authentically poetic, so 'quick'?

And no other writer has given us such forceful assurance

That beauty is a thing beyond the grave,
That perfect, bright experience never falls
To nothingness, and time will dim the moon
Sooner than our full consummation here
In this odd life will tarnish or pass away.

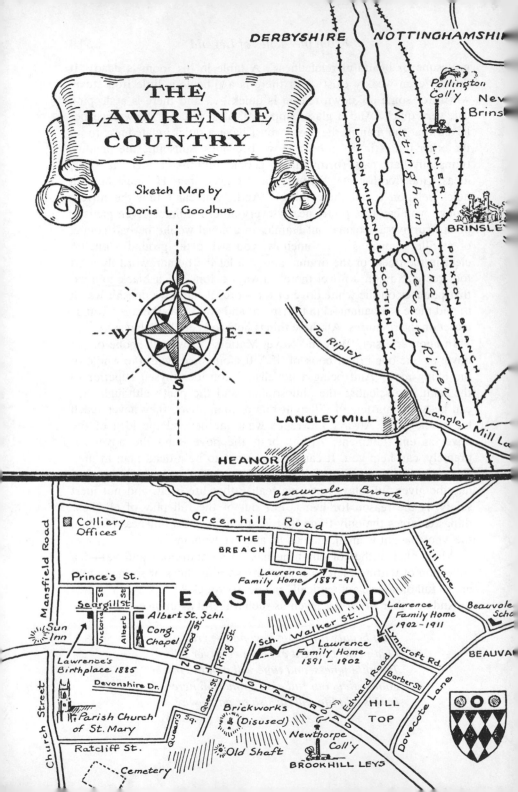

THE LAWRENCE COUNTRY

Sketch Map by
Doris L. Goodhue

DERBYSHIRE   NOTTINGHAMSHIRE

Pollington Coll'y

New Brins

L.N.E.R.

BRINSLE

LONDON MIDLAND & SCOTTISH R'Y.

Nottingham Canal

PINXTON BRANCH

Erewash River

To Ripley

LANGLEY MILL

Langley Mill La

HEANOR

W — E
S

Beauvale Brook

Greenhill Road

Colliery Offices

THE BREACH

Mansfield Road

Prince's St.

Scargill St.

Lawrence Family Home 1887-91

EASTWOOD

Albert St. Schl.

Victoria St.

Albert St.

Cong. Chapel

Wood St.

Sch.

King St.

Walker St.

Lawrence Family Home 1902-1911

Mill Lane

Beauvale Sch

BEAUVA

Sun Inn

Lawrence's Birthplace 1885

Devonshire Dr.

NOTTINGHAM ROAD

Queen St.

Queen's Sq.

Lawrence Family Home 1891-1902

Lynncroft Rd.

Edward Road

Barber St.

HILL TOP

Dovecote Lane

Church Street

Parish Church of St. Mary

Ratcliff St.

Cemetery

Brickworks (Disused)

Old Shaft

Newthorpe Coll'y

BROOKHILL LEYS

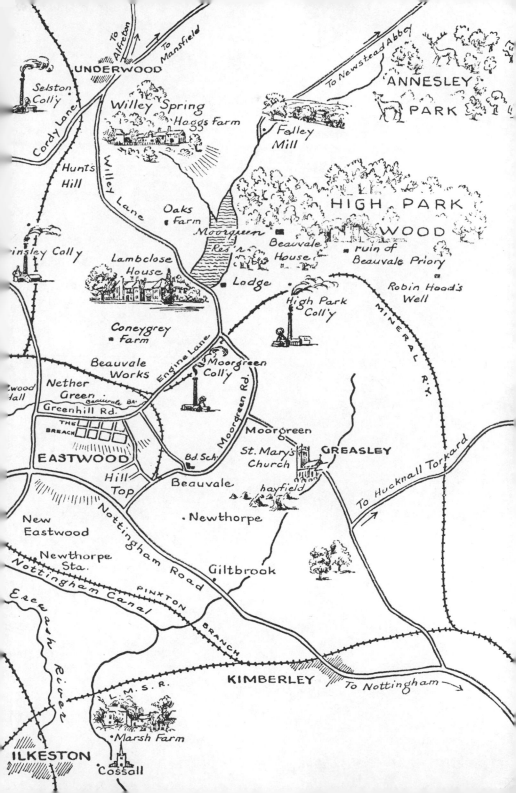

I

Books by D. H. Lawrence

*

1911   The White Peacock, novel
1912   The Trespasser, novel
1913   Love Poems and Others
        Sons and Lovers, novel
1914   The Widowing of Mrs Holroyd, play
        The Prussian Officer and Other Stories
1915   The Rainbow, novel
1916   Twilight in Italy, travel
        Amores, poems
1917   Look! We Have Come Through!, poems
1918   New Poems
1919   Bay, poems
1920   Touch and Go, play
        Women in Love, novel
        The Lost Girl, novel
1921   Movements in European History (by 'Lawrence H. Davison')
        Psychoanalysis and the Unconscious, essays
        Tortoises, poems
        Sea and Sardinia, travel
1922   Aaron's Rod, novel
        Fantasia of the Unconscious, essays
        England, My England, stories
1923   The Ladybird, tales (in America, The Captain's Doll)
        Studies in Classic American Literature
        Kangaroo, novel
        Birds, Beasts and Flowers, poems
1924   The Boy in the Bush, novel (with M. L. Skinner)
1925   St Mawr: together with The Princess, stories
        Reflections on the Death of a Porcupine, essays
1926   The Plumed Serpent, novel
        David, play
        Sun, story
        Glad Ghosts, story

1927 *Mornings in Mexico*, travel
1928 [*Selected Poems*], Augustan Books of Poetry series
    Rawdon's Roof, story
    The Woman Who Rode Away, stories
    Lady Chatterley's Lover, novel
    The Collected Poems of D. H. Lawrence
    Sun (unexpurgated edition)
1929 *Sex Looked Out*, essay
    The Paintings of D. H. Lawrence (introduction by Lawrence)
    Pansies, poems
    My Skirmish with Jolly Roger, essay
    The Escaped Cock, short novel (later called *The Man Who Died*)
    Pornography and Obscenity, essay (expansion of *Jolly Roger*)
1930 *Nettles*, poems
    Assorted Articles
    À Propos of Lady Chatterley's Lover, essay
    The Virgin and the Gipsy, novel
    Love among the Haystacks, stories
1931 *Apocalypse*, essay
    The Triumph of the Machine, poem
1932 *Lady Chatterley's Lover* (abridged edition)
    Etruscan Places, essays
    The Letters of D. H. Lawrence (ed., Aldous Huxley)
    Last Poems
1933 *The Lovely Lady and Other Stories*
    We Need One Another, essay
    The Plays
    The Tales
1934 *A Collier's Friday Night*, play
    A Modern Lover, stories
1935 *The Spirit of Place*, prose anthology (ed., R. Aldington)
1936 Foreword to *Women in Love*
    Phoenix, essays (ed., E. D. McDonald)
1940 *Fire and Other Poems*
1944 *The First Lady Chatterley*
1948 *Letters to Bertrand Russell* (ed., H. T. Moore)
1949 *A Prelude*, story
1956 *Eight Letters to Rachel Annand Taylor*
1957 *The Complete Poems*
1962 *The Collected Letters* (ed., H. T. Moore)
    The Symbolic Meaning (early versions of the *American Literature* essays)
1964 *The Complete Poems* (ed., V. de Sola Pinto and W. Roberts)
    Paintings of D. H. Lawrence (ed., Mervyn Levy)

1965 *The Complete Plays* (first professionally edited edition)
1968 *Lawrence in Love* (letters to Louie Burrows, ed., J. T. Boulton)
      Phoenix II, essays (ed., W. Roberts and H. T. Moore)
1970 *The Quest for Rananim* (letters to S. S. Koteliansky, ed., G. J. Zytaruk)
1972 *John Thomas and Lady Jane* (second draft of *Lady Chatterley's Lover*)
1973 *The Escaped Cock* (authentic edition, new material, ed., G. M. Lacy)
1976 *Letters to Thomas and Adele Seltzer* (ed., G. M. Lacy)

Reprints and pamphlets of only a few pages are usually not listed. Cambridge University Press is preparing an eight-volume edition of Lawrence's letters, ed., J. T. Boulton and W. Roberts.

NOTE: In addition to numerous stage productions of Lawrence's work, six of his stories and novels have been made into films: *The Rocking-Horse Winner* (1950), *Lady Chatterley's Lover* (1956), *Sons and Lovers* (1960), *The Fox* (1967), *Women in Love* (1968), and *The Virgin and the Gipsy* (1970); the last two are the best. On television, the British Granada company has dramatized a number of the stories, and in America the Public Broadcasting Service has presented an excellent version of Lawrence's play, *The Widowing of Mrs. Holroyd.* Several films about Lawrence have been made for television, including the 1962 Columbia Broadcasting System's *Accent* program, made at Taos, New Mexico, by the American poet John Ciardi. Lawrence studies are popular at universities all over the world, and Lawrence's own University of Nottingham has devoted two summer schools to studies of his work, under the direction of Dr. Keith Sagar of the University of Manchester. There is a Lawrence Society in Lawrence's home town of Eastwood, and another in Japan; Dr. James C. Cowan, editor of the *D. H. Lawrence Review,* has organized one in the United States.

II

A Note on the Map

*

Doris L. Goodhue's map of the Lawrence Country shows the salient features of that area and the geographical points important in D. H. Lawrence's early life and in his Nottinghamshire stories, novels, and poems. The region is a mixed one, the old splendor of Sherwood Forest broken up into collieries and farms, with here and there a redbrick town or village. Lawrence's father was born at Brinsley and from childhood worked in the mine there. Lawrence himself was born, in 1885, on down-sloping Victoria Street in Eastwood (the Bestwood of *Sons and Lovers,* the Woodhouse of *The Lost Girl,* the Tevershall of *Lady Chatterley's Lover,* and the setting of a number of Lawrence's short stories). When Lawrence was about two years old, his family moved down to the Breach, the Bottoms of *Sons and Lovers.* About 1891, when Lawrence was six, they took a house on Walker Street that looked down the rough fields to the Breach, to the rising colliery smoke and the farmfields beyond, and over to the Derbyshire hills. In 1902 the family moved to a house in Lynn Croft, where Mrs. Lawrence died in 1910. After this, the family broke up: one son had already moved away, another had died, and the youngest—D. H. Lawrence —lived at home only on holidays away from his teaching position in South London; and the elder daughter had married and left. For a short while after, Lawrence occasionally stayed with one of his sisters in Queen's Square, near the Devonshire Drive which became Somerset Drive, home of the Brangwens, in the last sections of *The Rainbow* and in *Women in Love.*

As a boy, Lawrence had attended the Beauvale Board School, just east of the town. He subsequently went to high school in Nottingham, where he also worked for a brief time as a factory clerk; later he obtained a teacher's certificate at Nottingham University College. He had his first teaching experience in Eastwood, at the school on Albert Street adjoining his family's chapel, the Congregational. He was also a pupil-teacher in the borough of Ilkeston, which with its neighboring village Cossall appears in *The Rainbow,* with Cossall as Cossethay.

The heart of the Lawrence Country, however, is north of Eastwood. In his youth Lawrence frequently walked or cycled to Haggs Farm, the Willey Farm of *Sons and Lovers,* home of the Miriam of that novel. On the way there, Lawrence would pass High Park Wood, the setting of parts of *The White Peacock* and of various stories—the lower edge of the region associated with Lord Byron as well as with Robin Hood. For his story 'A Fragment of Stained Glass', Lawrence reconstructed the past of the ruined priory of Beauvale, just south of High Park Wood. Nearby Moorgreen Reservoir became the Nethermere so important in *The White Peacock,* and the Willey Water in which Gerald Crich's sister drowned in *Women in Love.* Gerald's own home, Shortlands, was an adaptation of Lamb Close, the mansion southwest of the reservoir; Lamb Close often served as a country house, under various names, in Lawrence's novels and stories. Haggs Farm lies directly north of this, as the map shows: Lawrence often walked across the fields to it, though when on his bicycle he went up Hunt's Hill, mentioned in *Sons and Lovers.* In the valley below, to the east, a little stream connects Moorgreen Reservoir with Felley Mill, the Strelley Mill of *The White Peacock.* Lawrence once wrote of this area, in a sentence whose last five words gave Bridget Pugh the title for her valuable guidebook (1972) to the Lawrence landscapes: 'That's the country of my heart.'

III

Acknowledgments

*

Tracing D. H. Lawrence across the world, I have gone to many places he lived in and have spoken with many people he knew: the geography of these voyages and the words of these men and women have contributed importantly to the present volume. I am particularly indebted to the late Frieda Lawrence Ravagli; to Lawrence's sister, the late Ada Lawrence Clarke; and to his lifelong friend, the late William E. Hopkin. Forty years ago, Ada and Mr. Hopkin made it possible for me to have a direct acquaintance with the Lawrence Country, with some of its people, and with documents not elsewhere available. The kindness and help of Mrs. Clarke and her husband, and of Mr. and Mrs. Hopkin, gave me most of what I know of English village culture, particularly that of the industrial community of the late Victorian age whose portrait I have rather fully attempted here. This volume is not one of literary criticism, though critical values inevitably play some part in it, since without his writings, Lawrence would be now unknown. But this book is essentially a biography.

My fullest thanks go also to several librarians who have shown great kindness in helping me with this book. The late William E. Jackson, Director of the Houghton Library, Harvard University, permitted me to study and make use of the Houghton's collection of copies of Lawrence's letters to Witter Bynner, Frederick Carter, Mark Gertler, Lord and Lady Glenavy, Mr. and Mrs. A. D. Hawk, Mr. and Mrs. William Hawk, Mrs. Enid Hilton, Amy Lowell, and Giuseppe Orioli (the letters to Bertrand Russell I already knew). Likewise, Mr. Gene Magner, formerly of the Lockwood Memorial Library of the University of Buffalo, has permitted me to study and make use of copies of the Lockwood's collection of Lawrence's letters to Hilda Doolittle, Mrs. Bessie Freeman, Charles Lahr, and J. B. Pinker. Miss Ruth Bailey, former Librarian at Babson College, and her assistant, Mrs. Laurette Foster, were diligent beyond the call of duty in helping me obtain material for this book, and Miss Margaret Boyce, Research Librarian of Wellesley College, also deserves my fullest thanks for her kindness and assistance. All my later work on Lawrence has been greatly helped by the Southern Illinois University Libraries, especially by

Dean Ralph E. McCoy and Messrs. Alan Cohn, David Koch, and Ferris Randall. A number of other friends, some of whom I know only through correspondence, have also helped me with this project. A friend of long standing, the late Ben Abramson of the Argus Book Shop, Chicago, was most kind in lending manuscripts he owned (particularly the 'Miriam Papers'). John E. Baker, Jr., kindly allowed me to include in the present book one of the Lawrence manuscripts he owns, the previously unpublished early draft of the Epilogue ('Hail Columbia!') to Lawrence's *Fantasia of the Unconscious*. Professors Seymour and Sarah Betsky for years provided exciting and instructive conversation about Lawrence. Mr. John Carswell was exceedingly kind in lending me copies of unpublished letters to his mother, Catherine Carswell, from Lawrence; himself a biographer, Mr. Carswell was also kind enough to answer many questions about Lawrence. My indebtedness also extends to my friend the late Rolf Gardiner, who showed a fine sense of sportsmanship in overlooking a misstatement I regrettably made about him in a previous volume and kindly contributed an interesting recollection of Lawrence to the present book. Doris L. (Mrs. Philip E.) Goodhue deserves my special thanks for her maps which have added so much to this volume in the way of information as well as of appearance. Mr. Albert F. Green was of the greatest help in carrying on researches for me in Nottinghamshire; and I am also grateful for similar assistance by members of the 'Lawrence Circle' of Ilkeston, Derbys.: Messrs. J. T. Needham, G. R. S. Stevenson, and G. Bowley. I am greatly indebted, too, to the Rev. Fr. Martin Jarrett-Kerr, a Lawrence expert of the highest standing, for much information and assistance. Mr. George L. Lazarus kindly gave me copies of unpublished letters by Lawrence and others, and the noted collector Mr. Charles Feinberg also lent me Lawrence letters to copy; indeed he even purchased a number of them for use in this book. Lawrence's former colleague at Croydon, the late A. W. McLeod, not only sent copies of unpublished letters from Lawrence but also generously contributed a reminiscence of the young schoolmaster fresh from the Midlands. The late John Middleton Murry was also most helpful despite the onslaught against him in my earlier critical biography of Lawrence; I tried, across differences of opinion, to be fair to Murry in the present volume and hope I have succeeded. Mrs. Joyce Stevens neatly and expertly typed the manuscript of this new edition. The late Jewell F. Stevens, who divided his admiration between Lawrence and Lincoln, was a good friend who sent me copies of unpublished letters. The late Edward Nehls, himself collecting materials for his invaluable 'Composite Biography' of Lawrence, was most generous in sharing information. The Rev. Mr. A. Whigham-Price has helpfully provided information on nonconformist religion and on its hymns. For almost a quarter-century Mr. Geoffrey Woolley of the *Times* has sent me material about Lawrence which has appeared in various periodicals. Like all students of Lawrence, I am deeply indebted to Professor Warren Roberts, with whom I have had the pleasure of collaborating on two books. Also to his colleague, Dr. David Farmer.

Others who also kindly helped me in connection with this book include: the late Richard Aldington, Mr. Theodore S. Amussen, Mr. Claude Anderson, Mr. Anthony Beal, Professor Angelo Bertocci, Professor James T. Boulton, Professor and Mrs. T. E. Boyle, Lord David Cecil, the late J. D. Chambers, Mr. John Ciardi, Professor and Mrs. L. D. Clark, Dr. Edmund R. Clarke, Jr., Mr. Vere H. Collins, Miss Helen Corke, Mr. W. Coulson-Bonner, Professor James C. Cowan, the late Mrs. Caresse Crosby, Mrs. Gordon Crotch, Mr. John Cullen, the late Mrs. John Dallyn (Viola Meynell), Professor Émile Delavenay, Miss Lucy I. Edwards, Professor George H. Ford, Mr. David Garnett, Mr. David Gerard, Mr. A. E. Gill, the late Lord Glenavy, Dr. Leonard T. M. Gray, the late Christopher Hassall, the late Frederick J. Hoffman, Mr. Takanori Irie, the late Frau Else Jaffe-Richthofen, Mr. Jan Juta, Dr. Gerald Lacy, the late George Lawrence, Mr. Ralph Lewis, Mrs. Grace Lovat Fraser, the late Henry P. Macomber, Mr. Graham Martin, Dr. E. D. McDonald, the late Dr. Andrew Morland, Mr. Percy Muir, Professor Peter A. Munch, the late George H. Neville, Dr. William H. Ober, Professor John Olmsted, Mr. Hedley Pickbourne, Mlle Colette Pirenet, Dr. Lawrence Clark Powell, Mr. Peter Quennell, the late Sir Richard Rees, Lieutenant Colonel Angelo Ravagli, Mr. C. L. Reynolds, Mr. Robert Roeffler, the late Bertram Rota, Dr. Keith Sagar, Professor Mark Schorer, Professor William Simeone, Mr. Philip F. T. Smith, the late Stevie Smith, Mr. Irwin Swerdlow, Professor E. W. Tedlock, Jr., Professor William York Tindall, Mrs. Diana Trilling, Professor Lionel Trilling, Mr. Frank E. Turner, Mrs. Ivor Vinogradoff, Professor Howard W. Webb, Mr. George Weller, Dame Rebecca West, Dr. William White, Mr. Ernest Wilson, Mrs. Francis Brett Young, and Professor George Zytaruk. Also, Professor Armin Arnold, Professor Keith Cushman, Professor Richard Ellmann, Ms. Carmen Gomezplata, Ms. Linda Lee, Mrs. Lynn Warshow, Ms. Lynn C. Goldberg, Mrs. Olive Hopkin, Mrs. Margaret Needham, Mrs. Bridget Pugh, Mr. Paul Sykes, and Mr. William J. Weatherby.

Acknowledgment to William Heinemann Ltd., The Viking Press, Inc., for use of Lawrence letters has been made elsewhere in this volume; I am indebted to them also for permission to quote from various Lawrence works of which they own the copyright, and I am likewise indebted to Alfred A. Knopf, Inc., for quotations from Lawrence books whose copyright they own, specifically *The Plumed Serpent* and *The Later D. H. Lawrence* (edited by W. Y. Tindall); Viking owns copyright to virtually all other American titles.

Every student of Lawrence is profoundly indebted to three volumes of bibliography: Dr. Edward D. McDonald's *A Bibliography of the Writings* of *D. H. Lawrence* and his *The Writings of D. H. Lawrence, 1925–1930: A Bibliographical Supplement* (1925 and 1931), and William White's *D. H. Lawrence: A Checklist, 1931–1950*. A fourth, the bibliography by Warren Roberts (1960), is expert, superior, and indispensable.

My debt to one of my oldest friends, Mr. Stanley Young, is great indeed, for without his original interest and encouragement, the first version of this book would never have been written and published. Other publishing people should also be thanked for their help: Mr. Roger W. Straus, Jr., Mr. John Peck, Mr. A. S. Frere, Mr. Roland Gant, Miss Janice Robertson, Mr. Marshall Best, and Mr. Denis Halliwell. My gratitude to Mr. Laurence Pollinger, a friend of Lawrence's who has done so much over the years in the 'Lawrence revival,' is unlimited. I must also thank the John Simon Guggenheim Foundation (and its presidents, Henry Allen Moe and Gordon N. Ray) for two fellowships which greatly helped me in gathering material for this book.

*

The continuing dedication of this book to my wife, Beatrice R. Moore, is a sign of my continuing gratitude for her encouragement across more than a quarter-century. We have gone together to redbrick Eastwood; to an expanding Nottingham in which Lawrence would have been surprised to see all the black schoolchildren as well as the Pakistani bus drivers with some Japanese and Chinese passengers; we have gone to the magic little ranch that looks down to the wide Taos Valley; and we have visited other sites known to Lawrence, including those tombs on which he cast so much light in one of the last books he wrote, to which he had hoped to add before his death: *Etruscan Places*.

*

What he said in those Etruscan essays, at once informal and brilliant, may often be applied to himself, as when he discusses his first acquaintance with the Etruscans: 'Myself, the first time I saw Etruscan things, in the museum at Perugia, I was instinctively attracted to them. And it seems to be the way. Either there is instant sympathy, or instant contempt and indifference.' Again he set himself in perspective, perhaps altogether unconsciously, when speaking of the symbolic element of the tomb paintings, 'which rouses the deeper emotion, and gives the peculiarly satisfying quality to the dancing figures and creatures. A painter like Sargent, for example, is so clever. But in the end he is uninteresting, a bore. He never has an inkling of his own triviality and silliness. One Etruscan leopard, even one little quail, is worth all the miles of him.' As always, Lawrence was on the side of the 'quick'. One of his remarkable statements about his beliefs occurs in the essay 'Death of a Porcupine':

Man, as yet, is less than half grown. Even his flower system has not
appeared yet. He is all leaves and roots, without any clue put forth.
. . . Either he will have to start budding, or he will be forsaken of the
Holy Ghost. . . . Vitality depends upon a clue of the Holy Ghost inside a creature, a man, a nation, a race. When the clue goes, the vitality goes. And the Holy Ghost seeks for ever a new incarnation, and
subordinates the old to the new. . . . No man, no creature, or race can
have vivid vitality unless it be moving towards a blossoming; and the
most powerful is that which moves towards the as-yet-unknown blossom. Blossoming means the establishing of a pure relationship with
all the cosmos. This is the state of heaven. And it is the state of a
flower, a cobra, a jenny-wren in spring, a man when he knows himself royal and crowned with the sun, with his feet gripping the core
of the earth.

Index

Includes persons, places, and literary references of special significance to Lawrence's life and writings. An index of works by Lawrence follows on page 547.

534

538 INDEX

WORKS BY D. H. LAWRENCE